Lecture Notes in Computer Science   12764

More information about this subseries at http://www.springer.com/series/7409

Masaaki Kurosu (Ed.)

Human-Computer Interaction

Design and User Experience Case Studies

Thematic Area, HCI 2021
Held as Part of the 23rd HCI International Conference, HCII 2021
Virtual Event, July 24–29, 2021
Proceedings, Part III

 Springer

Editor
Masaaki Kurosu
The Open University of Japan
Chiba, Japan

ISSN 0302-9743   ISSN 1611-3349 (electronic)
Lecture Notes in Computer Science
ISBN 978-3-030-78467-6   ISBN 978-3-030-78468-3 (eBook)
https://doi.org/10.1007/978-3-030-78468-3

LNCS Sublibrary: SL3 – Information Systems and Applications, incl. Internet/Web, and HCI

This Springer imprint is published by the registered company Springer Nature Switzerland AG
The registered company address is: Gewerbestrasse 11, 6330 Cham, Switzerland

Foreword

Human-Computer Interaction (HCI) is acquiring an ever-increasing scientific and industrial importance, and having more impact on people's everyday life, as an ever-growing number of human activities are progressively moving from the physical to the digital world. This process, which has been ongoing for some time now, has been dramatically accelerated by the COVID-19 pandemic. The HCI International (HCII) conference series, held yearly, aims to respond to the compelling need to advance the exchange of knowledge and research and development efforts on the human aspects of design and use of computing systems.

The 23rd International Conference on Human-Computer Interaction, HCI International 2021 (HCII 2021), was planned to be held at the Washington Hilton Hotel, Washington DC, USA, during July 24–29, 2021. Due to the COVID-19 pandemic and with everyone's health and safety in mind, HCII 2021 was organized and run as a virtual conference. It incorporated the 21 thematic areas and affiliated conferences listed on the following page.

A total of 5222 individuals from academia, research institutes, industry, and governmental agencies from 81 countries submitted contributions, and 1276 papers and 241 posters were included in the proceedings to appear just before the start of the conference. The contributions thoroughly cover the entire field of HCI, addressing major advances in knowledge and effective use of computers in a variety of application areas. These papers provide academics, researchers, engineers, scientists, practitioners, and students with state-of-the-art information on the most recent advances in HCI. The volumes constituting the set of proceedings to appear before the start of the conference are listed in the following pages.

The HCI International (HCII) conference also offers the option of 'Late Breaking Work' which applies both for papers and posters, and the corresponding volume(s) of the proceedings will appear after the conference. Full papers will be included in the 'HCII 2021 - Late Breaking Papers' volumes of the proceedings to be published in the Springer LNCS series, while 'Poster Extended Abstracts' will be included as short research papers in the 'HCII 2021 - Late Breaking Posters' volumes to be published in the Springer CCIS series.

The present volume contains papers submitted and presented in the context of the Human-Computer Interaction (HCI 2021) thematic area of HCII 2021. I would like to thank the Chair, Masaaki Kurosu, for his invaluable contribution to its organization and the preparation of the proceedings, as well as the members of the Program Board for their contributions and support. This year, the HCI thematic area has focused on topics related to theoretical and methodological approaches to HCI, UX evaluation methods and techniques, emotional and persuasive design, psychological and cognitive aspects of interaction, novel interaction techniques, human-robot interaction, UX and technology acceptance studies, and digital wellbeing, as well as the impact of the COVID-19 pandemic and social distancing on interaction, communication, and work.

I would also like to thank the Program Board Chairs and the members of the Program Boards of all thematic areas and affiliated conferences for their contribution towards the highest scientific quality and overall success of the HCI International 2021 conference.

This conference would not have been possible without the continuous and unwavering support and advice of Gavriel Salvendy, founder, General Chair Emeritus, and Scientific Advisor. For his outstanding efforts, I would like to express my appreciation to Abbas Moallem, Communications Chair and Editor of HCI International News.

July 2021   Constantine Stephanidis

HCI International 2021 Thematic Areas and Affiliated Conferences

Thematic Areas

- HCI: Human-Computer Interaction
- HIMI: Human Interface and the Management of Information

Affiliated Conferences

- EPCE: 18th International Conference on Engineering Psychology and Cognitive Ergonomics
- UAHCI: 15th International Conference on Universal Access in Human-Computer Interaction
- VAMR: 13th International Conference on Virtual, Augmented and Mixed Reality
- CCD: 13th International Conference on Cross-Cultural Design
- SCSM: 13th International Conference on Social Computing and Social Media
- AC: 15th International Conference on Augmented Cognition
- DHM: 12th International Conference on Digital Human Modeling and Applications in Health, Safety, Ergonomics and Risk Management
- DUXU: 10th International Conference on Design, User Experience, and Usability
- DAPI: 9th International Conference on Distributed, Ambient and Pervasive Interactions
- HCIBGO: 8th International Conference on HCI in Business, Government and Organizations
- LCT: 8th International Conference on Learning and Collaboration Technologies
- ITAP: 7th International Conference on Human Aspects of IT for the Aged Population
- HCI-CPT: 3rd International Conference on HCI for Cybersecurity, Privacy and Trust
- HCI-Games: 3rd International Conference on HCI in Games
- MobiTAS: 3rd International Conference on HCI in Mobility, Transport and Automotive Systems
- AIS: 3rd International Conference on Adaptive Instructional Systems
- C&C: 9th International Conference on Culture and Computing
- MOBILE: 2nd International Conference on Design, Operation and Evaluation of Mobile Communications
- AI-HCI: 2nd International Conference on Artificial Intelligence in HCI

List of Conference Proceedings Volumes Appearing Before the Conference

1. LNCS 12762, Human-Computer Interaction: Theory, Methods and Tools (Part I), edited by Masaaki Kurosu
2. LNCS 12763, Human-Computer Interaction: Interaction Techniques and Novel Applications (Part II), edited by Masaaki Kurosu
3. LNCS 12764, Human-Computer Interaction: Design and User Experience Case Studies (Part III), edited by Masaaki Kurosu
4. LNCS 12765, Human Interface and the Management of Information: Information Presentation and Visualization (Part I), edited by Sakae Yamamoto and Hirohiko Mori
5. LNCS 12766, Human Interface and the Management of Information: Information-rich and Intelligent Environments (Part II), edited by Sakae Yamamoto and Hirohiko Mori
6. LNAI 12767, Engineering Psychology and Cognitive Ergonomics, edited by Don Harris and Wen-Chin Li
7. LNCS 12768, Universal Access in Human-Computer Interaction: Design Methods and User Experience (Part I), edited by Margherita Antona and Constantine Stephanidis
8. LNCS 12769, Universal Access in Human-Computer Interaction: Access to Media, Learning and Assistive Environments (Part II), edited by Margherita Antona and Constantine Stephanidis
9. LNCS 12770, Virtual, Augmented and Mixed Reality, edited by Jessie Y. C. Chen and Gino Fragomeni
10. LNCS 12771, Cross-Cultural Design: Experience and Product Design Across Cultures (Part I), edited by P. L. Patrick Rau
11. LNCS 12772, Cross-Cultural Design: Applications in Arts, Learning, Well-being, and Social Development (Part II), edited by P. L. Patrick Rau
12. LNCS 12773, Cross-Cultural Design: Applications in Cultural Heritage, Tourism, Autonomous Vehicles, and Intelligent Agents (Part III), edited by P. L. Patrick Rau
13. LNCS 12774, Social Computing and Social Media: Experience Design and Social Network Analysis (Part I), edited by Gabriele Meiselwitz
14. LNCS 12775, Social Computing and Social Media: Applications in Marketing, Learning, and Health (Part II), edited by Gabriele Meiselwitz
15. LNAI 12776, Augmented Cognition, edited by Dylan D. Schmorrow and Cali M. Fidopiastis
16. LNCS 12777, Digital Human Modeling and Applications in Health, Safety, Ergonomics and Risk Management: Human Body, Motion and Behavior (Part I), edited by Vincent G. Duffy
17. LNCS 12778, Digital Human Modeling and Applications in Health, Safety, Ergonomics and Risk Management: AI, Product and Service (Part II), edited by Vincent G. Duffy

http://2021.hci.international/proceedings

Human-Computer Interaction Thematic Area (HCI 2021)

Program Board Chair: **Masaaki Kurosu,** *The Open University of Japan, Japan*

- Salah Ahmed, Norway
- Valdecir Becker, Brazil
- Nimish Biloria, Australia
- Maurizio Caon, Switzerland
- Zhigang Chen, China
- Yu-Hsiu Hung, Taiwan
- Yi Ji, China
- Alexandros Liapis, Greece
- Hiroshi Noborio, Japan
- Vinícius Segura, Brazil

The full list with the Program Board Chairs and the members of the Program Boards of all thematic areas and affiliated conferences is available online at:

http://www.hci.international/board-members-2021.php

HCI International 2022

The 24th International Conference on Human-Computer Interaction, HCI International 2022, will be held jointly with the affiliated conferences at the Gothia Towers Hotel and Swedish Exhibition & Congress Centre, Gothenburg, Sweden, June 26 – July 1, 2022. It will cover a broad spectrum of themes related to Human-Computer Interaction, including theoretical issues, methods, tools, processes, and case studies in HCI design, as well as novel interaction techniques, interfaces, and applications. The proceedings will be published by Springer. More information will be available on the conference website: http://2022.hci.international/:

General Chair
Prof. Constantine Stephanidis
University of Crete and ICS-FORTH
Heraklion, Crete, Greece
Email: general_chair@hcii2022.org

http://2022.hci.international/

Contents – Part III

HCI, Social Distancing, Information, Communication and Work

Design Case Studies

Graphic Representations of Spoken Interactions from Journalistic Data: Persuasion and Negotiations

Christina Alexandris[1,2]([⊠]), Vasilios Floros[1,2], and Dimitrios Mourouzidis[1,2]

[1] National and Kapodistrian University of Athens, Athens, Greece
calexandris@gs.uoa.gr
[2] European Communication Institute (ECI), Danube University Krems and National Technical University of Athens, Athens, Greece

Abstract. Generated graphic representations for interactions involving persuasion and negotiations are intended to assist evaluation, training and decision-making processes and for the construction of respective models. As described in previous research, discourse and dialog structure are evaluated by the y level value around which the graphic representation is developed. Special emphasis is placed on emotion used as a tool for persuasion with the respective expressions, pragmatic elements and the depiction of information not uttered and their subsequent use in the collection of empirical and statistical data.

Keywords: Spoken journalistic texts · Spoken interaction · Persuasion · Negotiations · Graphic representations · Cognitive bias

1 Registration of Spoken Interaction: Previous Research

With the increase in the variety and complexity of spoken Human Computer Interaction (HCI) (and Human Robot Interaction - HRI) applications, the correct perception and evaluation of information not uttered is an essential requirement in systems with emotion recognition, virtual negotiation, psychological support or decision-making. Pragmatic features in spoken interaction and information conveyed but not uttered by Speakers can pose challenges to applications processing spoken texts that are not domain-specific, as in the case of spoken political and journalistic texts, including cases where the elements of persuasion and negotiations are involved.

Although usually underrepresented both in linguistic data for translational and analysis purposes and in Natural Language Processing (NLP) applications, spoken political and journalistic texts may be considered to be a remarkable source of empirical data both for human behavior and for linguistic phenomena, especially for spoken language. However, these text types are often linked to challenges for their evaluation, processing and translation, not only due to their characteristic richness in socio-linguistic and socio-cultural elements and to discussions and interactions beyond a defined agenda, but also in regard to the possibility of different types of targeted audiences - including non-native speakers and the international community [1]. Additionally, in spoken

© Springer Nature Switzerland AG 2021
M. Kurosu (Ed.): HCII 2021, LNCS 12764, pp. 3–17, 2021.
https://doi.org/10.1007/978-3-030-78468-3_1

political and journalistic texts there is also the possibility of essential information, presented either in a subtle form or in an indirect way, being often undetected, especially by the international public. In this case, spoken political and journalistic texts also contain information that is not uttered but can be derived from the overall behavior of speakers and participants in a discussion or interview. These characteristics, including the feature of spontaneous turn-taking [31, 39] in many spoken political and journalistic texts, are linked to the implementation of strategies concerning the analysis and processing of discourse structure and rhetorical relations (in addition to previous research) [10, 22, 35, 41].

In our previous research [2, 6, 23], a processing and evaluation framework was proposed for the generation of graphic representations and tags corresponding to values and benchmarks depicting the degree of information not uttered and non-neutral elements in Speaker behavior in spoken text segments. The implemented processing and evaluation framework allows the graphic representation to be presented in conjunction with the parallel depiction of speech signals and transcribed texts. Specifically, the alignment of the generated graphic representation with the respective segments of the spoken text enables a possible integration in existing transcription tools.

In particular, strategies typically employed in the construction of most Spoken Dialog Systems, such as keyword processing in the form of topic detection [13, 19, 24, 25] (from which approaches involving neural networks are developed [38]), were adapted in the functions of the designed and constructed interactive annotation tool [2, 6, 23], designed to operate with most commercial transcription tools. The output provides the User-Journalist with (a) the tracked indications of the topics handled in the interview or discussion and (b) the graphic pattern of the discourse structure of the interview or discussion. The output (a) and (b) also included functions and respective values reflecting the degree in which the speakers-participants address or avoid the topics in the dialog structure ("RELEVANCE" Module) as well as the degree of tension in their interaction ("TENSION" Module).

The implemented "RELEVANCE" Module [23], intended for the evaluation of short speech segments, generates a visual representation from the user's interaction, tracking the corresponding sequence of topics (topic-keywords) chosen by the user and the perceived relations between them in the dialog flow. The generated visual representations depict topics avoided, introduced or repeatedly referred to by each Speaker-Participant, and in specific types of cases may indicate the existence of additional, "hidden"[23] Illocutionary Acts [9, 14, 15, 32] other than "Obtaining Information Asked" or "Providing Information Asked" in a discussion or interview.

Thus, the evaluation of Speaker-Participant behavior targets to by-pass Cognitive Bias, specifically, Confidence Bias [18] of the user-evaluator, especially if multiple users-evaluators may produce different forms of generated visual representations for the same conversation and interaction. The generated visual representations for the same conversation and interaction may be compared to each other and be integrated in a database currently under development. In this case, chosen relations between topics may describe Lexical Bias [36] and may differ according to political, socio-cultural and linguistic characteristics of the user-evaluator, especially if international users are concerned [21, 26, 27, 40] due to lack of world knowledge of the language community involved [7, 16, 37]. In the "RELEVANCE" Module [23], a high frequency of Repetitions (value 1), Generalizations (value 3) and Topic Switches (value -1) in comparison to the duration of the spoken interaction is connected to the "(Topic) Relevance" benchmarks with a value of "Relevance (X)" [3, 5] (Fig. 1).

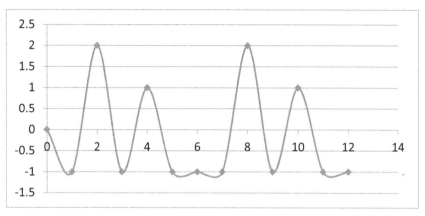

Fig. 1. Generated graphic representation with multiple "Topic Switch" relations (Mourouzidis et al., 2019).

The development of the interactive, user-friendly annotation tool is based on data and observations provided by professional journalists (European Communication Institute (ECI), Program M.A in Quality Journalism and Digital Technologies, Danube University at Krems, Austria, the Athena- Research and Innovation Center in Information, Communication and Knowledge Technologies, Athens, the Institution of Promotion of Journalism Ath.Vas. Botsi, Athens and the National and Technical University of Athens, Greece).

2 Association Relations and (Training) Data for Negotiation Models

However, in the above-presented previous research, the "Association" relation is not included in the evaluations concerned. Furthermore, the "Association" relation is of crucial importance in dialogues constituting persuasion and types of negotiation based on persuasion [34], especially if emotion is used as a tool for persuasion [30], establishing a link between persuasion, emotion and language [30]. Emotion as a tool for persuasion may be used in diverse types of negotiation skills, apart from persuasion tactics [12, 30, 34], including "value creating"/ "value claiming" tactics and "defensive" tactics [34].

"Association" relations between words and their related topics are often used to direct the Speaker into addressing the topic of interest and/or to produce the desired answers. In some cases, the "Generalization" may also be used for the same purpose, as a means of introducing a (not directly related) topic of interest via "Generalization".

For negotiation applications, the identification of words and their related topics contributes to strategies targeting to directing the Speaker-Participant to the desired goal and the avoidance of unwanted "Association" types as well as unwanted other types of relations -"Repetitions", "Topic Switch" and "Generalizations" (Fig. 2).

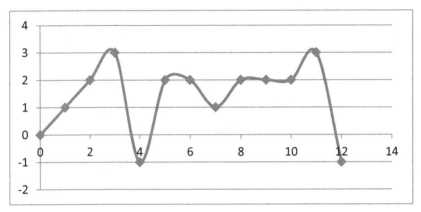

Fig. 2. Generated graphic representation with multiple "Association" relations. (Mourouzidis et al., 2019).

The "Association" relations between words and their related topics contribute to the analysis and development of negotiation procedures. In this case, Cognitive Bias and socio-cultural factors play a crucial role in regard to the perception of the perceived relations-distances between word-topics. For example, the word-topics "Country X" (name withheld) –"defense spending" or "military confrontation" – "chemical weapons" may generate an "Association" (ASOC) or "Topic Switch" (SWITCH) reactions and choices from users, depending on whether they are perceived as related or different topics in the spoken interaction. Diverse reactions may also apply in the case of the "Association" and "Generalization" relations, where "treaties" and "international commitment" may generate "Association" (ASOC) or "Generalization" (GEN) reactions and choices from users: "treaties" is associated with "international commitment" or "treaties" are linked to "international commitment" with a "Generalization" relation.

Differences concerning the perception of the "Association" (ASOC) relations between word-topics are measured in the form of triple tuples as perceived relations-distances between word-topics [3], related to Lexical Bias (Cognitive Bias) concerning semantic perception [36]. Examples of segments in (interactively) generated patterns from user-specific choices between topics are the following, where the distances between topics in the generated patterns are registered as triple tuples (triplets): (military confrontation, chemical weapons, 2) ("Association"), (treaties, international commitment, 3) ("Generalization"). These triplets and the sequences they form may be converted into vectors (or other forms and models), used as training data for creating negotiation models and their variations.

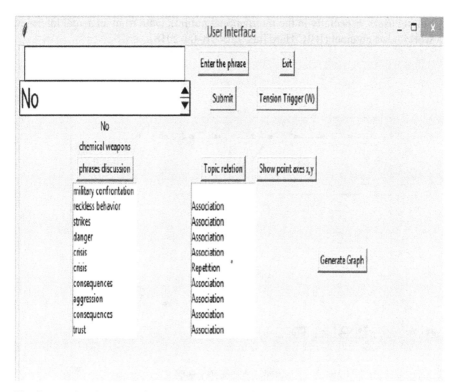

Fig. 3. Interface for generating graphic representation with multiple "Association" relations.

Possible differences in the perceived relations with the Lexical Bias concerned may play an essential role both in the employment of negotiation tactics (based on cross-cultural analysis) and in training applications. The number of registered "Association" relations in the processed wav.file or video file may be used to evaluate persuasion tactics employed in spoken interaction involving negotiations (a) and their possible employment in the construction of training data and negotiation models (b). Since the generated graphic representations are based on perceived relations, they may also be used for evaluating trainees performance (c).

We note that, independently from interactive and user-specific choices, topics may be also pre-defined and/or automatically detected with word relations based on existing (ontological and semantic) databases. However, this commonly used strategy and practice is proposed to be employed in cases where persuasion and negotiation tactics are monitored and checked against a pre-defined model, either as a form to control spoken interaction or as means to evaluate the pre-defined model.

The following examples in Figs. 3 and 4 depict the user interface and the generated graphic representations containing multiple "Association" relations: Chosen word-topics and their relations in dialog segment with two speakers-participants (resulting to a "No" answer): "military confrontation", "reckless behavior", "strikes", "danger", "crisis", "crisis", "consequences", "aggression", "consequences", "trust". (choices may vary among users, especially in the international public), Data from an actual interview on a world news channel (BBC HardTalk 720- 16–04-2018).

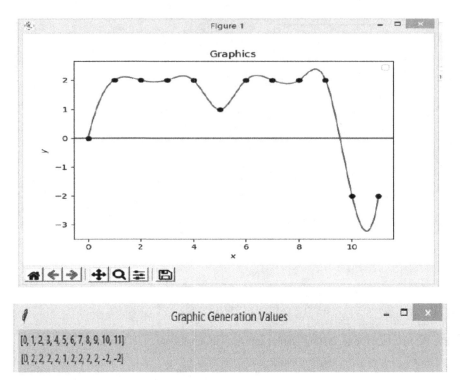

Fig. 4. Generated graphic representation with multiple "Association" relations and respective values (including one "No" Answer (−2) – presented in Sect. 3).

3 Affirmative and Negative Answers in Negotiations

In spoken interaction concerning persuasion and types of negotiation based on persuasion [12, 30, 34], perceived affirmative ("Yes") and negative ("No") answers are integrated in the present framework with the respective "0" (zero) and "−2" values.

Specifically, an affirmative answer is assigned a "0" value, similar to the initial "0" (zero) value starting the entire interactive processing of the wav.file. An example of a generated graphic representation with multiple "Yes" answers is depicted in Fig. 5. In this case, the spoken interaction (concerning persuasion or negotiation based on persuasion) contains multiple positive answers and the respective multiple "0" (zero) values (Fig. 5).

A negative answer is assigned a "−2" value, lower than the "−1" Topic Switch value (Fig. 6). Thus, a negotiation with a sequence of negative answers and several attempts to change a topic or to approach a (seemly) different topic will generate a graphic representation below the "0" (zero) value.

An example of generated graphic representations below the "0" (zero) value depicting spoken interactions (persuasion –negotiations) is shown in Fig. 6. In this case, the spoken interaction contains multiple negative answers and/or multiple attempts to switch to a different topic (Fig. 6).

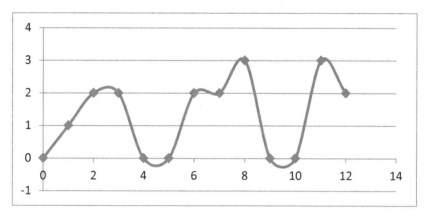

Fig. 5. Generated graphic representation with multiple "Yes" answers.

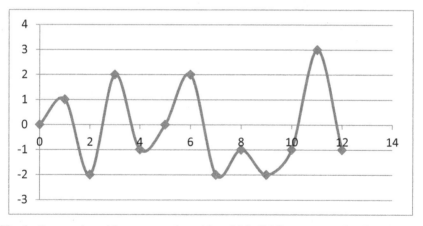

Fig. 6. Generated graphic representation with multiple "No" answers (and topic switches).

As in the above-described case of "Association" and "Generalization" relations, for affirmative and negative answers, the distances between topics in the generated patterns are registered and may be be used as training data for creating negotiation models and their variations. However, in the case of affirmative and negative answers, the topic and the respective answer is not registered as a triplet but is registered as a tuple: (stability, 0) ("Affirmative Answer"), (sanctions, −2) ("Negative Answer").

Similarly to the registered "Association" relations, the number of perceived affirmative ("Yes") and negative ("No") answers in the processed wav.file or video file may be used to evaluate persuasion tactics employed in spoken interaction involving negotiations (a), for the construction of training data and negotiation models (b) or for evaluating a trainees performance (c).

4 Registering Word-Topics and Their Impact in Persuasion and Negotiations

4.1 Word-Topics and Persuasion Tactics

The type of word-topics concerned in the registered "Association" relations and the "Yes" or "No" answers in the processed wav.file or video file may also be used to evaluate persuasion tactics employed in spoken interaction involving negotiations. Word-topics and the registered relations and answers may be linked to positive responses and/or collaborative speaker behavior or negative responses, tension and conflict. Detecting and registering points of tension or other types of behavior and their impact in the dialogue structure facilitates the evaluation of persuasion tactics and types of negotiation based on persuasion [30, 34], especially "value creating"/ "value claiming" tactics and "defensive" tactics [30, 34] and in other cases where a link between persuasion, emotion and language is used [12, 30].

4.2 Word-Topics and Word-Types as Reaction Triggers

For negotiation applications, words and their related topics can be identified as triggers for different types of reactions (positive, collaborative behavior or tension). The words and their related topics may concern the following two types of information: (1) "Association" (or other) relations that are context-specific, connected to current events and state-of-affairs, (2) "Association" (or other) relations that concern words with inherent socio-culturally determined linguistic features and are usually independent from current events and state-of-affairs.

In the second case (2) it is often observed that the semantic equivalent of the same word on one language sometimes may appear more formal or with more "gravity" than in another language, either emphasizing the role of the word in an utterance or being related to word play and subtle suggested information. The presence of such "gravity words" [1, 4] may contribute to the degree of formality or intensity of conveyed information in a spoken utterance. It is observed that these differences between languages in regard to the "gravity" of words are often related to polysemy, where the possible meanings and uses of a word seem to "cast a shadow" over its most commonly used meaning. Similarly to the above-described category, words with an "evocative" element concern their "deeper" meanings related to their use in tradition, in music and in literature and may sometimes be related to emotional impact in discussions and speeches. In contrast to "gravity" words, "evocative" words usually contribute to a descriptive or emotional tone in an utterance [1, 4]. Here, it is noted that, according to Rockledge et al., 2018, "the more extremely positive the word, the greater the probability individuals were to associate that word with persuasion" [30].

In the generated graphic representations, perceived "Gravity" and "Evocative" words are signalized (for example, as "W") in the curve connecting the word-topics. This signalization indicates the points of "Gravity" and "Evocative" words as "Word-Topic" triggers in respect to the areas of perceived tension or other types of reactions in the processed dialog segment with two (or more) speakers-participants. In Figs. 7 and 8 the perceived "Gravity" and "Evocative" words also constitute word-topics (Figs. 7 and 8).

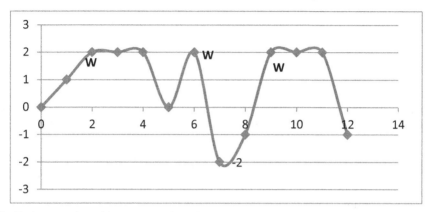

Fig. 7. Generated graphic representation with multiple "Association" relations and Word-Topic triggers ("W").

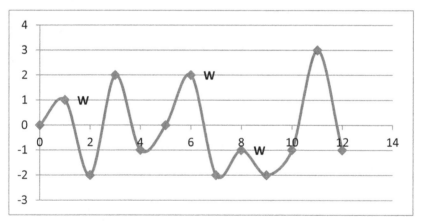

Fig. 8. Generated graphic representation with multiple "No" answers and Word-Topic triggers ("W").

The detected word types may be used as training data for creating negotiation models and their variations, as in the above-described cases. The signalized Word-Topic triggers may be appended as marked values (for example, with "&") in the respective tuples or triple tuples, depending on the context in which they occur: (sanctions, −2, &dignity) ("Negative Answer"), (military confrontation, chemical weapons, 2, &justice) ("Association"). If the Word-Topic triggers constitute topics, they are repeated in the tuple or triple tuple, where they receive the respective mark: (country, people, 2, &people) ("Association").

Signalized "Gravity" and "Evocative" words can be identified either from databases constructed from collected empirical data or from existing resources such as Wordnets.

In spoken utterances "Gravity" words and especially "Evocative" words are observed to often have their prosodic and even their phonetic-phonological features intensified [1, 4]. The commonly occurring observed connection to intensified prosodic phonetic-phonological features constitutes an additional pointer to detecting and signalizing "Gravity" and "Evocative" words [1, 4].

4.3 Word-Topics as Tension Triggers

Previous research depicted points of tension in two-party discussions and interviews containing longer speech segments. These points are detected and signalized by the implemented "TENSION" Module in the form of graphic representations [2], enabling the evaluation of the behavior of speakers-participants.

In spoken interaction concerning persuasion and types of negotiation based on persuasion, detected points of tension in the generated graphic representations enable the registration of word-topics and sequences of word-topics preceding tension and the registration of word-topics and sequences of word-topics following tension. The evaluation of such data contributes both to the construction and training of models for the avoidance of tension (i) and for the purposeful creation of tension (ii).

Multiple points of tension (referred to as "hot spots") [2] indicate a more argumentative than a collaborative interaction, even if speakers-participants display a calm and composed behavior. Points of possible tension and/or conflict between speakers-participants ("hot-spots") are signalized in generated graphic representations of registered negotiations (or other type of spoken interaction concerning persuasion), with special emphasis on words and topics triggering tension and non-collaborative speaker-participant behavior.

As presented in previous research [2], a point of tension or "hot spot" consists of the pair of utterances of both speakers, namely a question-answer pair or a statement-response pair or any other type of relation between speaker turns. In longer utterances, a defined word count and/or sentence length from the first words/segment of the second speaker's (Speaker 2) and from the words/segment of the first speaker's (Speaker 1) the utterance are processed [2, 11]. The automatically signalized "hot spots" (and the complete utterances consisting of both speaker turns) are extracted to a separate template for further processing. For a segment of speaker turns to be automatically identified as a "hot spot", a set of (at least two of the proposed three (3) conditions must apply [2] to one or to both of the speaker's utterances. The three (3) conditions are directly or indirectly related to flouting of Maxims of the Gricean Cooperative Principle [14, 15] (additional, modifying features (1), reference to the interaction itself and to its participants with negation (2) and (3) prosodic emphasis and/or exclamations). With the exception of prosodic emphasis, these conditions concern features detectable with a POS Tagger (for example, the Stanford POS Tagger, http://nlp.stanford.edu/software/tagger.shtml) or they may constitute a small set of entries in a specially created lexicon or may be retrieved from existing databases or Wordnets. The "hot spots" are connected to the "Tension" benchmark with a value of "Y" or "Tension (Y)" [2] and the "Collaboration" benchmark with a value of "Z" or "Collaboration (Z)", described in previous research [2, 3].

In the generated graphic representations, word-topics as tension triggers are signalized (for example, as "W") in the curve connecting the word-topics (Fig. 9). This signalization indicates the points of word-topics as tension triggers in respect to the areas of perceived tension in the processed dialog segment with two (or more) speakers-participants. The detected word types may be used as training data for creating negotiation models and their variations, as in the above-described cases.

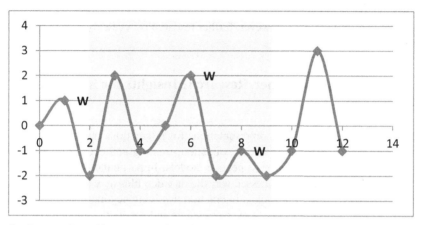

Fig. 9. Generated graphic representation with multiple "No" answers and Word-Topic triggers ("W") and Tension (shaded area between topics) in generated graphic representation and "tension trigger" ("W").

4.4   Tension Triggers and Paralinguistic Information

Furthermore, in previous research [2] "hot spots" signalizing tension may include an interactive annotation of paralinguistic features with the corresponding tags. Words classified as "tension triggers" may, in some cases, be easily detected with the aid of registered and annotated paralinguistic features, where the paralinguistic element may complement or intensify the information content of the word related to perceived tension in the spoken interaction. In some instances, the paralinguistic element may contradict the information content of the "tension trigger", for example, a smile when a word of negative content is uttered. In this case, the speaker's behavior may be related to irony or a less intense negative emotion such as annoyance or contempt. With paralinguistic features concerning information that is not uttered, the Gricean Cooperative Principle is violated if the information conveyed is perceived as not complete (Violation of Quantity or Manner) or even contradicted by paralinguistic features (Violation of Quality).

Depending on the type of specifications used, for paralinguistic features depicting contradictory information to the information content of the spoken utterance, the additional signalization of "!" is proposed, for example, "[! facial-expr: eye-roll]" and "[! gesture: clenched-fist]".

According to the type of linguistic and paralinguistic features signalized, features of more subtle emotions can be detected. Less intense emotions are classified in the middle and outer zones of the Plutchik Wheel of Emotions [28] and are usually too subtle to be easily extracted by sensor and/or speech signal data. In this case, linguistic information with or without a link to paralinguistic features demonstrates a more reliable source of a speaker's attitude, behavior and intentions, especially for subtle negative reactions in the Plutchik Wheel of Emotions, namely "Apprehension", "Annoyance", "Disapproval", "Contempt", "Aggressiveness" [28]. These subtle emotions are of importance in spoken interactions involving persuasion and negotiations.

Data from the interactive annotation of paralinguistic features may also be integrated into models and training data, however, further research is necessary for the respective approaches and strategies.

5 Conclusions and Further Research: Insights for Sentiment Analysis Applications

The presented generated graphic representations for interactions involving persuasion and negotiations are intended to assist evaluation, training and decision-making processes and for the construction of respective models. In particular, the graphic representations generated from the processed wav.file or video files may be used to evaluate persuasion tactics employed in spoken interaction involving negotiations (a), their possible employment in the construction of training data and negotiation models (b) and for evaluating a trainee's performance (c).

New insights are expected to be obtained by the further analysis and research in the persuasion-negotiation data processed. Further research is also expected to contribute to the overall improvement of the graphical user interface (GUI), as one of the basic envisioned upgrades of the application.

The presented generated graphic representations enable the visibility of information not uttered, in particular, tension and the overall behavior of speakers-participants. The visibility of all information content, including information not uttered, contributes to the collection and compilation of empirical and statistical data for research and/or for the development of HCI- HRI Sentiment Analysis and Opinion Mining applications, as (initial) training and test sets or for Speaker (User) behavior and expectations. This is of particular interest in cases where an international public is concerned and where a variety of linguistic and socio-cultural factors is included.

Information that is not uttered is problematic in Data Mining and Sentiment Analysis-Opinion Mining applications, since they mostly rely on word groups, word sequences and/or sentiment lexica [20], including recent approaches with the use of neural networks [8, 17, 33], especially if Sentiment Analysis from videos (text, audio and video) is concerned. In this case, even if context dependent multimodal utterance features are extracted, as proposed in recent research [29], the semantic content of a spoken utterance may be either complemented or contradicted by a gesture, facial expression or movement. The words and word-topics triggering non-collaborative behavior and tension ("hot spots") and the content of the extracted segments where tension is detected provide insights for word types and the reaction of speakers, as well as insights of Opinion Mining and Sentiment Analysis.

The above-observed additional dimensions of words in spoken interaction, especially in political and journalistic texts, may also contribute to the enrichment of "Bag-of-Words" approaches in Sentiment Analysis and their subsequent integration in training data for statistical models and neural networks.

References

1. Alexandris, C.: Issues in Multilingual Information Processing of Spoken Political and Journalistic Texts in the Media and Broadcast News, Cambridge Scholars, Newcastle upon Tyne, UK (2020)
2. Alexandris, C., Mourouzidis, D., Floros, V.: Generating graphic representations of spoken interactions revisited: the tension factor and information not uttered in journalistic data. In: Kurosu, M. (ed.) HCII 2020. LNCS, vol. 12181, pp. 523–537. Springer, Cham (2020). https://doi.org/10.1007/978-3-030-49059-1_39
3. Alexandris, C.: Evaluating cognitive bias in two-party and multi-party spoken interactions. In: Proceedings from the AAAI Spring Symposium, Stanford University (2019)
4. Alexandris, C.: Visualizing Pragmatic Features in Spoken Interaction: Intentions, Behavior and Evaluation. In: Proceedings of the 1st International Conference on Linguistics Research on the Era of Artificial Intelligence – LREAI, Dalian, October 25–27, 2019, Dalian Maritime University (2019)
5. Alexandris, C.: Measuring cognitive bias in spoken interaction and conversation: generating visual representations. In: Beyond Machine Intelligence: Understanding Cognitive Bias and Humanity for Well-Being AI Papers from the AAAI Spring Symposium Stanford University, Technical Report SS-18-03, pp. 204-206 AAAI Press Palo Alto, CA (2018)
6. Alexandris, C., Nottas, M., Cambourakis, G.: Interactive evaluation of pragmatic features in spoken journalistic texts. In: Kurosu, M. (ed.) HCI 2015. LNCS, vol. 9171, pp. 259–268. Springer, Cham (2015). https://doi.org/10.1007/978-3-319-21006-3_26
7. Alexandris, C.: English, german and the international "semi-professional" translator: a morphological approach to implied connotative features. J. Lang. Transl. Sejong Univ. Korea 11(2), 7–46 (2010)
8. Arockiaraj, C.M.: Applications of neural networks in data mining. Int. J. Eng. Sci. 3(1), 8–11 (2013)
9. Austin, J.L.: How to Do Things with Words, 2nd edn. University Press, Oxford Paperbacks, Oxford (1962).(Urmson, J.O., Sbisà, M. (eds.) 1976)
10. Carlson, L., Marcu, D., Okurowski, M. E.: Building a discourse-tagged corpus in the framework of rhetorical structure theory. In: Proceedings of the 2nd SIGDIAL Workshop on Discourse and Dialogue, Eurospeech 2001, Denmark, September 2001 (2001)
11. Cutts, M.: Oxford Guide to Plain English, 4th edn. Oxford University Press, Oxford, UK (2013)
12. Evans, N.J., Park, D.: Rethinking the persuasion knowledge model: schematic antecedents and associative outcomes of persuasion knowledge activation for covert advertising. J. Curr. Issues Res. Advert. 36(2), 157–176 (2015). https://doi.org/10.1080/10641734.2015.1023873
13. Floros, V., Mourouzidis, D.: Multiple Task Management in a Dialog System for Call Centers. Master's thesis, Department of Informatics and Telecommunications, National University of Athens, Greece (2016)
14. Grice, H.P.: Studies in the Way of Words. Harvard University Press, Cambridge, MA (1989)

15. Grice, H.P.: Logic and conversation. In: Cole, P., Morgan, J. (eds.) Syntax and Semantics, vol. 3, pp. 41–58. Academic Press, New York (1975)

16. Hatim, B.: Communication Across Cultures: Translation Theory and Contrastive Text Linguistics. University of Exeter Press, Exeter, UK (1997)

17. Hedderich, M.A., Klakow, D.: Training a neural network in a low-resource setting on automatically annotated noisy data. In: Proceedings of the Workshop on Deep Learning Approaches for Low-Resource NLP, Melbourne, Australia, pp. 12–18. Association for Computational Linguistics-ACL (2018)

18. Hilbert, M.: Toward a synthesis of cognitive biases: how noisy information processing can bias human decision making. Psychol. Bull. **138**(2), 211–237 (2012)

19. Lewis, J.R.: Introduction to Practical Speech User Interface Design for Interactive Voice Response Applications, IBM Software Group, USA, Tutorial T09 presented at HCI 2009 San Diego. CA, USA (2009)

20. Liu, B.: Sentiment Analysis and Opinion Mining. Morgan & Claypool, San Rafael, CA (2012)

21. Ma, J.: A comparative analysis of the ambiguity resolution of two English-Chinese MT approaches: RBMT and SMT. Dalian Univ. Technol. J. **31**(3), 114–119 (2010)

22. Marcu, D.: Discourse trees are good indicators of importance in text. In: Mani, I., Maybury, M. (eds.) Advances in Automatic Text Summarization, pp. 123–136. The MIT Press, Cambridge, MA (1999)

23. Mourouzidis, D., Floros, V., Alexandris, C.: Generating graphic representations of spoken interactions from journalistic data. In: Kurosu, M. (ed.) HCII 2019. LNCS, vol. 11566, pp. 559–570. Springer, Cham (2019). https://doi.org/10.1007/978-3-030-22646-6_42

24. Nass, C., Brave, S.: Wired for Speech: How Voice Activates and Advances the Human-Computer Relationship. The MIT Press, Cambridge, MA (2005)

25. Nottas, M., Alexandris, C., Tsopanoglou, A., Bakamidis, S.: A hybrid approach to dialog input in the citzenshield dialog system for consumer complaints. In: Proceedings of HCI 2007, Beijing, People's Republic of China (2007)

26. Paltridge, B.: Discourse Analysis: An Introduction. Bloomsbury Publishing, London (2012)

27. Pan, Y.: Politeness in Chinese Face-to-Face Interaction. Advances in Discourse Processes series, vol. 67. Ablex Publishing Corporation, Stamford, CT, USA (2000)

28. Plutchik, R.: A psychoevolutionary theory of emotions. Soc. Sci. Inf. **21**, 529–553 (1982). https://doi.org/10.1177/053901882021004003

29. Poria, S., Cambria, E., Hazarika, D., Mazumder, N., Zadeh, A., Morency, L-P.: Context-dependent sentiment analysis in user-generated videos. In: Proceedings of the 55th Annual Meeting of the Association for Computational Linguistics, Vancouver, Canada, July 30-August 4 2017, pp. 873–88. Association for Computational Linguistics - ACL (2017). https://doi.org/10.18653/v1/P17-1081

30. Rocklage, M., Rucker, D., Nordgren, L.: Persuasion, emotion, and language: the intent to persuade transforms language via emotionality. Psychol. Sci. **29**(5), 749–760 (2018). https://doi.org/10.1177/0956797617744797

31. Sacks, H., Schegloff, E.A., Jefferson, G.: A simplest systematics for the organization of turn-taking for conversation. Language **50**, 696–735 (1974)

32. Searle, J.R.: Speech Acts: An Essay in the Philosophy of Language. Cambridge University Press, Cambridge, MA (1969)

33. Shah, K., Kopru, S., Ruvini, J-D.: Neural network based extreme classification and similarity models for product matching. In: Proceedings of NAACL-HLT 2018, New Orleans, Louisiana, June 1-6, 2018, pp. 8–15. Association for Computational Linguistics-ACL (2018)

34. Skonk, K.: 5 Types of Negotiation Skills, Program on Negotiation Daily Blog, Harvard Law School, 14 May 2020. https://www.pon.harvard.edu/daily/negotiation-skills-daily/types-of-negotiation-skills/. Accessed 11 Nov 2020

35. Stede, M., Taboada, M., Das, D.: Annotation Guidelines for Rhetorical Structure Manuscript. University of Potsdam and Simon Fraser University, Potsdam (2017)
36. Trofimova, I.: Observer bias: an interaction of temperament traits with biases in the semantic perception of lexical material. PLoS ONE **9**(1), e85677 (2014). https://doi.org/10.1371/journal.pone.0085677
37. Wardhaugh, R.: An Introduction to Sociolinguistics, 2nd edn. Blackwell, Oxford, UK (1992)
38. Williams, J.D., Asadi, K., Zweig, G.: Hybrid code networks: practical and efficient end-to-end dialog control with supervised and reinforcement learning. In: Proceedings of the 55th Annual Meeting of the Association for Computational Linguistics, Vancouver, Canada, July 30-August 4 2017, pp. 665–677. Association for Computational Linguistics (ACL) (2017)
39. Wilson, M., Wilson, T.P.: An oscillator model of the timing of turn taking. Psychon. Bull. Rev. **12**(6), 957–968 (2005)
40. Yu, Z., Yu, Z., Aoyama, H., Ozeki, M., Nakamura, Y.: Capture, recognition, and visualization of human semantic interactions in meetings. In: Proceedings of PerCom, Mannheim, Germany, 2010 (2010)
41. Zeldes, A.: rstWeb - a browser-based annotation interface for rhetorical structure theory and discourse relations. In: Proceedings of NAACL-HLT 2016 System Demonstrations. San Diego, CA, pp. 1–5 (2016). http://aclweb.org/anthology/N/N16/N16-3001.pdf

A Study on Universal Design of Musical Performance System

Sachiko Deguchi[(⊠)]

Kindai University, Higashi-Hiroshima Hiroshima 739-2116, Japan
deguchi@hiro.kindai.ac.jp

Abstract. This paper describes the development of a new UI of musical performance system based on the results of workshops in a care home, and describes the extension of the UI for non-Western music. The new UI has only 8 strings which are numbered or colored, and they can be tuned for most major or minor scales so that users do not need to use sharp/flat. A new function was added to the score display system to transpose keys in order to generate the scores which can be used for the new UI. The new UI was evaluated by an experiment, and the result indicates that the new UI is easier than keyboard for the people who have little musical experience. Also, the two notations of duration of scores were evaluated by an experiment to know which is easy for those people. The score DB is enhanced based on the result of workshops in a care home. The new systems (string UI of musical performance system and score display system) were developed for elderly people and people with little musical experience. Then, the string UI was extended so that users can choose a number of strings and each string can be any pitch. By using this function, some UIs of non-Western musical instrument can be implemented.

Keywords: Numbered notation · Colored notation · UI for elderly people · UI of non-western music · Musical scale · Tuning of strings

1 Introduction

Music therapy is commonly used to improve the quality of life of elderly people [1, 2]. It is difficult to use musical instruments for elderly people who have little experience of musical performance. Some instruments have been proposed and used for elderly people along with singing [3], however, people could play chords but they do not play melody on the instruments. Our aim is to provide a system on which people can play melody. Our previous research provided the musical performance system and the scores for the people who were not familiar with staff notation scores [4, 5]. Many musical performance systems have been proposed [6–9], however, the notation of scores have not been discussed enough. While, numbered notation scores are sometimes used for elderly people, children and beginners, and colored notation scores are exceptionally used for children, however, scientific and technological discussions are not enough. The aim of this research is to improve user interfaces of our musical performance system and

© Springer Nature Switzerland AG 2021
M. Kurosu (Ed.): HCII 2021, LNCS 12764, pp. 18–33, 2021.
https://doi.org/10.1007/978-3-030-78468-3_2

to enhance score display system. Also, the aim of this research is to use the performance system and score display system in some genres of non-Western music.

The following results were presented in HCII2019 [4].

(1) We developed a musical performance system on tablet PC. The system had several UIs (with note names, numbers, colors or shapes on keyboards, or without symbols on keyboards).
(2) We proposed several musical notations and developed a score database.
(3) We evaluated the UIs and scores and found that the numbered notation was most useful for the people who were not familiar with staff notation scores. Also, we found that colored notation would be useful for some people.

2 Utilization of UI and Scores of Numbered Notation

2.1 Utilization in 2018

Method. We had an extension course about musical performance at our university in Dec., 2018. We used commercial electric pianos (32 keys: 19 white keys and 13 black keys) and put the labels of numbers on the keys, and we used numbered notation scores. 28 people over 50 years old attended the course (Fifties: 1, Sixties: 17, Seventies: 9, Eighties: 1).

Numbered notation scores of 13 Japanese children's songs, 9 English children's songs and 3 pieces of classical music were used in the course. An instructor explained the scores and participants practiced the keyboard using the scores. The participants also sang the songs. Total time of explanation was around 30 min, and total time of practice was around 70 min. At the end of the course, the participants answered the questions by rating 4, 3, 2 or 1 (4:good, 3:a little good, 2:a little bad, 1:bad). Questions are as follows.

Q1: Are the scores easy to understand?
Q2: Is the keyboard easy to play?
Q3: Is it easy to play using the scores?
Q4: Is it easy to play and sing at the same time?

Table 1. Mean values of evaluation by participants of extension course.

	Q1	Q2	Q3	Q4
Sixties	3.94	3.71	3.71	3.53
Seventies	4.00	3.67	3.78	3.44
Eighties	3	3	1	2

Result and Discussion. The mean values of questions answered by people over 60 years old are shown in Table 1. A person in his eighties wrote in the questionnaire that he had difficulties in using the keyboard, while people in their seventies played well and did not wrote about the difficulties. Therefore, we understood that we should study the usage for aged people.

2.2   Utilization in 2019

Method. We used the same electric pianos used in the extension course in 2018 at three workshops in a care home in Oct. and Nov., 2019. The number of participants and the number of people who agreed to answer the questions at each workshop are as follows. 7 people attended all three workshops and answered the questions and 3 people attended two workshops and answered the questions.

– First workshop: 13 (attended), 10 (answered the questions)
– Second workshop: 12 (attended), 11 (answered the questions)
– Third workshop: 10 (attended), 9 (answered the questions)

The ages and the numbers of the participants who answered the questions are as follows.

First workshop: 75–79: 1, 80–84: 2, 85–89: 6, 90–94: 1
Second workshop: 75–79: 1, 80–84: 1, 85–89: 5, 90–94: 2, 95–99: 2
Third workshop: 75–79: 1, 80–84: 1, 85–89: 4, 90–94: 2, 95–99: 1

Numbered notation scores of 12 Japanese children's songs and 1 English children's song were used in the workshops. An instructor explained the scores and participants practiced the keyboard by using the scores. The participants practiced at their own pace. The participants also sang the songs. Total time of explanation was around 15 min, and total time of practice was around 30 min in each workshop. In the first workshop, participants practiced basic songs individually. In the second workshop, participants practiced basic songs again and other songs. Also, they practiced a song together. In the third workshop, participants learned several functions of electric keyboard and practiced some songs. At the end of each workshop, the participants answered the questions. Questions are as follows in each workshop.

First workshop

Q1: Are the scores easy to understand? Choose 4, 3, 2 or 1 (4:good, 3:a little good, 2:a little bad, 1: bad).
Q2: Is the keyboard easy to play? Choose 4, 3, 2 or 1.
Q3: Is it easy to play using the scores? Choose 4, 3, 2 or 1.

Q4: Is it easy to play and sing at the same time? Choose 4, 3, 2 or 1.
Q5: Did you enjoy this workshop? Choose 7, 6, 5, 4, 3, 2 or 1 (7:very good, 6:good, 5:a little good, 4: neither good nor bad, 3:a little bad, 2:bad, 1:very bad).

Second workshop

Q1-Q5 are the same as Q1–Q5 of first workshop.
Q6: Is it good for you to play with other people?

Third workshop

Q3–Q5 are the same as Q3–Q5 of second workshop.
Q7: Is it good to change tone colors? Choose 4, 3, 2 or 1.
Q8: Is it good to use the function of accompaniment? Choose 4, 3, 2 or 1.
Q9: Is it good to listen to the songs stored in the keyboard? Choose 4, 3, 2 or 1.
Q10: Is it good to use percussion button? Choose 4, 3, 2 or 1.

Result and Discussion. The mean values of questions Q1–Q6 are shown in Table 2. In the third workshop, some people could not answer all questions because they could not try all functions of keyboard or could not practice well because of the time limit. The mean values of Q3 in the 1st and 2nd workshops are 3.60 and 3.55 (max is 4), therefore, the participants could play the keyboard using numbered scores if they practice at their own pace. While, the mean values of Q4 in the 1st and 2nd workshops are relatively low. It would be difficult for aged people to play and sing at the same time. The mean value of Q5 is around 6 (max is 7) in each workshop, therefore, we think the participants almost enjoyed the workshops.

The mean values of questions Q7–Q10 are as follows.

Q7: 3.63, Q8: 3.50, Q9: 3.50, Q10: 3.29

The result indicates that participants were interested in changing tone colors, playing with accompaniment and listening to the music. Therefore, we should implement these functions in our system.

In these workshops, we also found the followings:

(a) People took time to play notes beyond one octave.
(b) People took time to play sharp or flat notes.
(c) People remembered children's songs well.

We decided to develop a new system based on these findings.

3 New User Interface

3.1 Development of Basic System

In our previous research, we developed several UIs on tablet PC [4]. We used HTML, CSS and JavaScript for implementing UIs. In this research we developed a simple UI

Table 2. Mean values of evaluation by participants of workshops at a care home.

	Q1	Q2	Q3	Q4	Q5	Q6
1st WS	3.90	3.80	3.60	3.30	5.90	
2nd WS	3.82	3.64	3.55	3.09	5.91	3.55
3rd WS			3.25	3.50	6.00	

based on the results of workshops at a care home in 2019. We found that "People took time to play notes beyond one octave", therefore, we provide a UI of 8 notes, because, many simple songs can be played within 8 notes (one octave and 1 note). This UI has eight strings which correspond 7 notes in one octave and 1 note next to the octave. e.g., {C4, D4, E4, F4, G4, A4, B4, C5} in C major. The numbers (1, 2,... 7) are written at the strings. This UI was designed referring to a shape of Lyre of ancient Greek music [10]. A user can choose the UI of colored strings. Figure 1 shows examples. The UI with colored strings without numbers are also provided.

We also found that "People took time to play sharp notes or flat notes" at the workshops, therefore, we provide a function to change keys. Most simple songs use notes on the scale, e.g., in G major, {G, A, B, C, D, E, F#} are used. If we play a song in G major on the keyboard, we have to use black key next to F for F#. While, if we play a song in G major on the string instrument which is tuned for G major, we don't have to use any black key. In our system, the pitches of strings can be transposed to most major keys and minor keys. Also, we provide two ways to transpose keys: (1) The first note is a keynote, or (2) The first note is always C4. E.g., in G major, a user can choose (1) The strings are tuned for {G4, A4, B4, C5, D5, E5, F#5, G5}, or (2) The strings are tuned for {C4, D4, E4, F#4, G4, A4, B4, C5}. In both cases, the sequence of string numbers is always {1, 2, 3, 4, 5, 6, 7, 1'}, or the sequence of string colors is always {red, orange, yellow, green, light-blue, blue, purple}. I.e., 1/red means the first string, 2/orange means the second string, and so on. A number/color does not mean pitch, but it means string number/color.

Since we use numbers or colors on strings, any pitches can be assigned to strings and we do not have to use sharp/flat to play the UI. To avoid using sharp/flat, we could transpose an original key to C major or A minor, however, the range of pitches is changed and it would be inconvenient to sing the song. It is important that we can use any key and that we can play without sharp/flat.

3.2 Outline and Method of Evaluation Experiment

An experiment to evaluate the new UI was carried out in 2020. Examinees were students because we could not make an experiment in a care home in 2020. This section describes the outline and method of experiment.

The aim of this experiment is to compare two UIs: UI of keyboard (using black keys) and UI of strings (tuned for a scale). We call the former UI-1, and the latter UI-2. UI-1 is shown in Fig. 2, and UI-2 used in pre-experiment is shown in Fig. 1 (left). UI-2 was modified after pre-experiment, which is described in Sect. 3.3.

Fig. 1. A simple UI of strings with numbers (left, UI-2 in the pre-experiment) and a UI with numbers and colors (right).

Parts of scores used in the experiment are shown in Fig. 3. The pitches are notated as numbers (1–7) and +/- symbols are used for sharp/flat. The duration is notated as the length of space in these scores. The melodies used in the experiment are generated as follows.

- First, the intervals of each notes on the scale are determined, e.g., (1 1 −1 2 1 −2 1...) in Score-1 (used for UI-1) and (2 −1 1 1 −2 1 2...) in Score-2 (used for UI-2). Both melodies are similar.
- Next, pitches of notes are determined based on the intervals, e.g. (2 3 4+ 3 5+ 6 4+ 5+...) in Score-1 and (1 3 2 3 4 2 3 5...) in Score-2.
- Quarter notes and eighth notes are used in these scores.
- The melody length is 8 bars in each score.

The procedure of the experiment is as follows.

Experiment 1:

- Examinees play UI-1 twice using Score-1 (including 3 sharps, A major).
- Examinees answer the questions.

Experiment 2:

- Examinees play UI-2 twice using Score-2 (UI is tuned for A major)
- Examinees answer the questions.

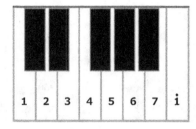

Fig. 2. A simple UI of keyboard with numbers (UI-1 in the experiment).

The questions are as follows.

Q1: Is the UI easy to understand? Choose 5, 4, 3, 2, 1, 0 (5:very good, 4:good, 3:a little good, 2:a little bad, 1:bad, 0:very bad).
Q2: Is the Score easy to understand? Choose 5, 4, 3, 2, 1, 0.
Q3: Is it easy to play using the scores? Choose 5, 4, 3, 2, 1, 0.

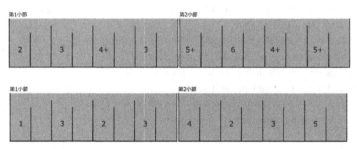

Fig. 3. A part of numbered notation score in A major used for UI of keyboard (above, Score-1 in the experiment) and for UI of strings (below, Score-2 in the experiment).

3.3 Pre-experiment and Modification of UI

Method. We made a preliminary experiment. Examinees were five lab students (male, age: 22–24). Experiment 1 and Experiment 2 were carried out as described in Sect. 3.2.

Result and Discussion. After the experiment, examinees said as follows.

- UI-2 (Fig. 1 left) was dark and it was difficult to read the numbers.
- The strings of UI-2 were thin, therefore, they felt uneasy when they played the system.
- They recognized the merit of UI-2 because they did not have to think about sharp (black key), however, the design of UI-1 (keyboard) was better.

Modification of UI. We decided to modify the design of UI-2 based on the discussion of pre-experiment. Figure 4 shows the new design of UI-2.

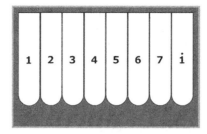

Fig. 4. A simple UI of strings with numbers, which was designed based on the result of pre-experiment (UI-2 in the experiment).

3.4 Evaluation Experiment

Method. The evaluation experiments were carried out several times in Dec. 2020. Total number of examinees were 33 (Male Students, Age 19–25). 31 Examinees had no experience with keyboard instrument. Experiment 1 and Experiment 2 were carried out as described in Sect. 3.2. UI-1 (Fig. 2) and the new design of UI-2 (Fig. 4) were used. score-1 (Fig. 3 above) and Score-2 (Fig. 3 below) Were used for UI-1 and UI-2.

Result and Discussion. The mean values of questions are shown in Table 3. The mean value of each question for UI-2 is higher than that for UI-1.

Table 3. Mean values of evaluation of UI-1 and UI-2.

	UI-1	UI-2
Q1	3.94	4.42
Q2	3.39	4.18
Q3	3.18	4.15

Paired sample t-test is used for the comparison of the mean values of each question for two UIs. The degrees of freedom is 32, and the critical value for significance level of 0.05 (two-tailed test) is 2.0369 and that of 0.01 is 2.7385. T-ratios of the comparisons are as follows.

Q1: -4.50 Q2: -7.54 Q3: -6.07

Therefore, there is a significant difference between the mean values of each question for UI-1 and UI-2. This result indicate that UI-2 would be easier than UI-1 to play the system. Because UI-2 can be tuned for any keys, we do not see any sharp/flat in scores. While, when we use UI-1, we have to use black keys corresponding to sharp/flat in scores.

We also asked the examinees: Which do you think is easier to play, UI-1 or UI-2? The numbers of examinees who answered UI-1, UI-2 or "Almost the Same" are as follows.

UI-1: 1 UI-2: 25 Almost the Same: 7

This result also shows that UI-2 would be easier to play for the people who have little experience with keyboard instrument.

The black keys on the keyboard are asymmetric, and this layout is helpful for a user to recognize the location where she/he is playing. One examinee pointed out that there should be some mark or color on the string UI so that he could recognize the location.

3.5 Development of Application System

Three Octave Version. We have extended the UI of strings (Fig. 1) for normal use. The system has 22 strings (for three octaves) and has scroll function. Figure 5 shows an example. The strings can be tuned for most major scales and minor scales. Users can choose normal size or wide size of strings. This UI also has some functions: recording user's performance, playing the recorded performance, and playing music using scores in score database. These functions could support the practices. Since we made sounds of 5 octaves, the UI of 5 octave version can be implemented if needed.

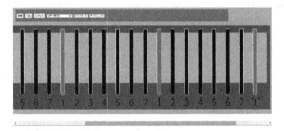

Fig. 5. A 3-octave UI of strings.

Any String Number and Any Pitches. For non-Western music, we are now developing a system in which users can choose any number (9–21) of strings and any pitches. E.g., UI of koto (Japanese harp) can be designed by choosing 13 strings and assigning the following pitches {D4, G3, A3, A#3, D4, D#4, G4, A4, A#4, D5, D#5, G5, A5} to the strings. People can use this function to customize the UI to their musical instrument and can play the UI using original scores. Also, composers can use this function to compose music in some musical genre, even if they are not familiar with the genre, e.g., a composer usually working on popular music could compose a piece of koto music using the UI of koto.

The numbered or colored UI is a universal design. The merits of using numbered or colored UI and scores instead of keyboard and staff notation scores are as follows.

- In previous research, we showed that it was easy to play numbered or colored UI with numbered or colored scores for the people who had little musical experience. The notation using note names would be also easy to play, however, note names would not be useful when people play and sing at the same time.
- In this research, we showed that numbered or colored UI enabled us to play musical performance system without treating sharp/flat by tuning strings and using corresponding scores.

This UI is also a cross-cultural design. Major or minor scales are commonly used in Western music and popular music in many countries today. However, 7 scales are theoretically possible and it is said that 6 scales were used in medieval music. Also, several genres of traditional music in the world use the scales other than major or minor scale. E.g., koto music uses different scale [11]. The sequences of intervals of major, minor, and koto scales are as follows, where, "w" means whole tone and "s" means semitone.

Major scale: w w s w w w s
Minor scale: w s w w s w w
Koto scale: s w w w s w w

Therefore, it is important to provide the functions to implement scales other than major or minor scales.

Also, tuning is usually complicated in traditional music. E.g., in koto music, there are several tunings, and 5 notes in the scale are assigned to strings and other 2 notes in the scale are played by pushing the strings (to increase the pitches). Therefore, the function to assign a pitch to each string is necessary along with some functions for playing methods.

In previous research, we provided musical notations for people with little musical experience based on koto scores, and used those notations for keyboard UI (with numbers, colors, or note names). In this research, we first developed a new UI for elderly people and people with little musical experience based on the design of ancient Greek Lyre. Then we noticed that this UI can be extended to non-Western music. It is interesting that a universal design would be a cross-cultural design and vice versa.

3.6 Sounds of Musical Performance System

As described in Sect. 2.2, people are interested in changing tone colors. This musical performance system provides the sounds (the pitches of 5 octaves) of piano and two electric pianos. We also made other sounds, which should be improved before being used in the system. Usually DTM systems use MIDI sounds, but it is slow to use MIDI sounds on tablet PC. Therefore, we developed a program using C language to generate WAVE data based on the additive synthesis. In previous system, we generated data of 44.1 kHz sampling and 16-bit length. Since the data size was big, we evaluated several sampling rates and data lengths. Then, we decided to use 10 kHz sampling and 16-bit length, therefore, the data size became 1/4.

Because of human auditory property, most speakers enhance the power of low frequency sounds. However, speakers of tablet PC which we are using do not implement this function. We implemented the function to enhance low frequency sounds by ourselves, and users can choose enhanced sounds or original sounds.

4 Score Display System

4.1 Improvement of the System and Evaluation of Two Notations of Duration

Staff notation is widely used in Western music today. It is the standard to notate music, and it is especially important for complex music. Also, it could be used as a support tool for performers. When performers play musical instrument, the pitches and the location of fingers are important for performers and staff notation is convenient because we can memorize and recognize the melody by glancing at notes on five lines. However, in some musical genres, some types of tablature are used. E.g., guitar music uses tablature scores. Koto music uses numbered notation scores and each number corresponds to each string of koto instrument.

We developed score display system in 2018 [4] and improved the system in 2019 and 2020. This system can display scores of 2/4, 3/4 and 4/4 time signatures. This score display system can generate four kinds of notations about pitches (numbers, note names, note names in Japanese, and colors), and can generate two types of notations about duration (space length and symbol). Figure 6 shows example scores: two notations of pitches and one notation of duration. We already compared the notations about pitches (numbers, note names, colors, and staff notation) in 2018. In 2018, the score display system was under development, therefore, we used the scores which were made manually by using Excel. While, in 2020, we compared the notations about duration using the scores generated by our system.

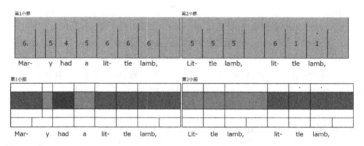

Fig. 6. A score of numbered notation (above) and a score of colored notation (below).

Method. The evaluation experiments of scores were carried out several times after the experiments of UIs. Total number of examinees were 33 (Male Students, Age 19--25).

The aim of the experiment is to compare two scores: Type-1 score represents the duration using space length, while, Type-2 score represents the duration using symbol. Type-1 score was designed based on the design of Ikuta-school koto score [12], while, Type-2 score was designed based on the design of Yamada-school koto score [13]. Figure 7 shows an example of each score. In Type-1 score of Fig. 7 (above), the first note is quarter note and the second note is 8th note. A user can know the duration of each note by the length of space where the note is placed. While, in Type-2 score of Fig. 7 (below), the first note is quarter note and the second note is 16th note. A quarter note has no symbol, an 8th note has an underline, and a 16th note has a double underline. We call the Type-1 score used in the experiment Score-3, and call the Type-2 score used in the experiment Score-4.

The melodies used in the experiment are generated as described in the experiment of UIs. In the scores of this experiment, 16th notes are used along with quarter notes and 8th notes.

In this experiment, UI-2 (Fig. 4) was used. The procedure of the experiment is as follows.

- After Experiment 1 and Experiment 2 to evaluate two UIs, examinees practiced Type-2 score twice (the same melody of Type-1 score used in Experiment 2).
- After the practices, Experiment 3 and Experiment 4 were carried out as follows.

Experiment 3–1:

- Examinees played UI-2 once using Score-3 (Type-1).

Experiment 4–1:

- Examinees played UI-2 once using Score-4 (Type-2).

Experiment 3–2:

- Examinees played UI-2 once again using Score-3 (Type-1).
- Examinees answered the questions.

Experiment 4–2:

- Examinees played UI-2 once again using Score-4 (Type-2).
- Examinees answered the questions.

Examinees used Score-3 and Score-4 alternately because they had to get used to 16th notes before they evaluated the scores.

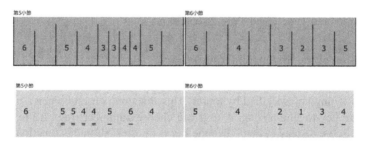

Fig. 7. A part of numbered notation score of Type-1 (above, Score-3 in the experiment) and Type-2 (below, Score-4 in the experiment).

The questions are as follows.

Q1: Is the Score easy to understand? Choose 5, 4, 3, 2, 1, 0 (5:very good, 4:good, 3:a little good, 2:a little bad, 1:bad, 0:very bad).
Q2: Is it easy to play using the scores? Choose 5, 4, 3, 2, 1, 0.

Result and Discussion. The mean values of questions are shown in Table 4. The mean value of each question for score-3 (Type-1) is slightly higher than that of score-4 (type-2). Paired sample t-test is used for the comparison of the mean values of each question for two scores. The degrees of freedom is 32, and the critical value for significance level of 0.05 (Two-Tailed Test) is 2.0369 and that of 0.01 is 2.7385. T-ratios of the comparisons are as follows.

Q1: 3.32 Q2: 2.20

Therefore, there is a significant difference (level of 0.05) between the mean values of each question for Type-1 score and Type-2 score. This result indicate that Type-1 score would be easier than Type-2 score for the people who have little experience of musical performance.

Table 4. Mean values of evaluation of Type-1 score and Type-2 score.

	Score-3 (Type-1)	Score-4 (Type-2)
Q1	3.73	3.00
Q2	3.39	3.00

We also asked the examinees: Which do you think is easier to play, Score-3 (Type-1, using space length) or Score-4 (Type-2, using symbol)? The numbers of examinees who answered Type-1, Type-2 or "Almost the Same" are as follows.

Type-1: 21 Type-2: 8 Almost the Same: 4

This result also shows that Type-1 score would be easier to play. However, 8 people preferred Type-2 score. If people practice Type-2 scores well, they would understand the symbols of duration well and it could be easier to use Type-2 scores. Also, the scores similar to Type-2 scores are used in Taisho-goto [14] in Japan. Therefore, we think we should provide both Type-1 and Type-2 scores.

4.2 Extension of the System for Transposition

We have added a new function to the score display system. This function transposes original key to any key specified by a user. This function is useful when a user wants to change the key to sing a song. A user can choose a number from -12 to 12 in the menu on the score display system, then the key is transposed. In this function, 1 means semitone (half step) and 2 means whole tone (whole step). E.g., if a user chooses 7, C major is transposed to G major, i.e., the note numbers $\{1, 2, 3, 4, 5, 6, 7\}$ on the score are changed to $\{5, 6, 7, 1', 2', 3', 4+'\}$. The key of a song is not always specified in the score data, and the system could not determine the key, therefore, this system changes note numbers and put + symbol for sharp automatically. A user should choose + (sharp) or - (flat) by her/himself. E.g., if a user choose 5 in the transposition menu (from C major to F major), the note numbers $\{1, 2, 3, 4, 5, 6, 7\}$ are changed to $\{4, 5, 6, 6+, 1', 2', 3'\}$ by the system, then a user can choose flat in the menu, and the numbers are changed to $\{4, 5, 6, 7-, 1', 2', 3'\}$.

As described in Sect. 3.1, the strings of new UI are tuned for the scale specified by a user. Therefore, users do not need to know the pitches of the strings. E.g., in G major, the strings are tuned for (1) {G4, A4, B4, C5, D5, E5, F#5, G5} or (2) {C4, D4, E4, F#4, G4, A4, B4, C5}, but users only see the string numbers {1, 2, 3, 4, 5, 6, 7}. Therefore, the corresponding scores should be provided.

In the former case (1), users need scores which are transposed from G to C, because in G major, the numbers {1, 2, 3, 4+, 5, 6, 7} are used in the scores of keyboard UI and {5, 6, 7, 1', 2', 3', 4+'} should be changed to {1, 2, 3, 4, 5, 6, 7} for the string UI.

For the latter case (2), another new function has been added. In G major, the numbers {1, 2, 3, 4+, 5, 6, 7} are used in the scores of keyboard UI, while the numbers {1, 2, 3, 4, 5, 6, 7} should be used in the scores of the string UI whose pitches are {C4, D4, E4, F#4, G4, A4, B4, C5}. Therefore, the score display system provides the function to delete sharp/flat from the original scores.

4.3 Score DB

The results of workshops in a care home showed that elderly people remembered children's songs well. Therefore, we decided to enhance score DB. We made score DB of 17 Japanese children's songs and 11 English children's songs in Humdrum format before. In this research, we encoded these songs in our original form as described below. We are adding some songs whose copyrights were expired. Especially, we should add scores within 8 notes. Also, we will add some children's songs in the world.

MusicXML [15] is commonly used for data exchange today. E.g., MuseScore (free software to generate staff notation scores) [16] uses original data format, but it can export data in MusicXML format. Several music encoding methods have been proposed and used. MEI [17] is used by researchers of Western music today. Humdrum [18] has been used for a long time and it is a simple encoding method. We had been using Humdrum format, however, we decided to use our original format in this research. Since we need to edit text files, we use a simple and readable format as Humdrum.

The following lines show examples of our format and Humdrum (**kern, **text).

Our format:A4 0 8 lit-

Humdrum (**kern, **text):8a lit-

In Humdrum (**kern), each note is encoded, where a number represents duration and an alphabet represents pitch. E.g., 8a means 8th note of pitch A4, 4cc means quarter note of pitch C5, 16f# means 16th note of pitch F#4, and so on. While, in each line of our format, the first element means pitch, the second element means sharp/flat (1:sharp, −1:flat, 0:without sharp/flat), the third element means duration, and the fourth element means syllable of lyric.

We have developed a program by using python, which can convert MusicXML format (which was generated by MuseScore) to our data format. We are adding scores to DB using MuseScore and our converting program. This program cannot convert all MusicXML data which is available on the internet. We have also developed a program which can convert Humdrum (**kern) format to our data format. Therefore, we could convert huge resources of copyright free music (mainly classical music) [19] to our format.

5 Conclusions and Future Work

We developed a new UI of musical performance system based on the results of the workshops in a care home. The new UI has only 8 strings and the strings can be tuned for most major or minor scales so that users do not need to use sharp/flat. The strings are numbered or colored. The evaluation experiments showed that the string UI without sharp/flat keys was easier than the normal keyboard with sharp/flat keys for the people with little musical experience. We also developed 3-octave version of string UI. We extended the system in which a user can choose string number and pitches for the strings, therefore, a user can use this system for non-Western music. We also compared the notations of duration: using space lengths, or using symbols. The result showed that both notations are usable. We added a new function to the score display system to transpose keys. This function provides scores for the string UI. We are enhancing score DB based on the result of the workshops in a care home.

In this research, we showed that numbered or colored UI enabled us to play musical performance system without treating sharp/flat by tuning strings and using corresponding scores. We developed a new UI for elderly people and people with little musical experience based on the design of ancient Greek Lyre. Then we noticed that this UI can be extended to non-Western music. A universal design would be a cross-cultural design and vice versa.

Future work includes the followings. As for the UI of musical performance system, we will develop vertical layout of UI, sharp function for koto UI, some functions to represent playing methods for the string UI, and a function to play with accompaniment. We would add harp sounds and some sounds of playing methods such as vibrato. The template of 6/8 time signature will be added to the score display system. Children's songs in the world should be added to the score DB. Also, the new simple UI should be evaluated by elderly people. The extended version of UI for non-Western music should be evaluated by the people who are familiar with some genre of non-Western music and by the composers who are not familiar with the genre.

Acknowledgments. The author would like to thank the manager of care home, the care staff and the coordinator of Kindai University for supporting the workshops of musical performance. The author would also like to thank N. Kimura, Y. Sugimoto, K. Sasaki, R. Takeuchi and S. Kaneda for their contribution to the development of the musical performance system.

References

1. Ridder, H.M., Wheeler, B.L.: Music Therapy for Older Adults: Music Therapy Handbook. The Guilford Press, New York (2016)
2. Davis, W.B.: Music Therapy and Elderly Populations: An Introduction to Music Therapy, 3rd edn. The American Music Therapy Association, Maryland (2008)
3. Götell, E., Brown, S., Ekman, S.L.: Caregiver-assisted music events in psychogeriatric care. J. Psychiatr. Ment. Health Nurs. **7**, 119–125 (2000)
4. Deguchi, S.: Multiple representations of the UI, score and scale for musical performance system and score DB. In: Kurosu, M. (ed.) HCII 2019. LNCS, vol. 11568, pp. 177–191. Springer, Cham (2019). https://doi.org/10.1007/978-3-030-22636-7_12

5. Deguchi, S.: A Study on the UI of musical performance system and score representation. In: AAAI 2018 Spring Symposium Series Technical Report, pp. 207–211 (2018)
6. Zbyszynski, M. et al.: Ten years of tablet musical inter-faces at CNMAT. In: Proceedings of the International Conference on New Interfaces for Musical Expression, pp. 100–105. NIME (2007)
7. Hochenbaum, J., et al.: Designing expressive musical interfaces for tabletop surfaces. In: Proceedings of the International Conference on NIME, pp. 315–318. NIME (2010)
8. Oh, J., et al.: Evolving the mobile phone orchestra. In: Proceedings of the International Conference on New Interfaces for Musical Expression, pp. 82–87. NIME (2010)
9. Brown, D., Nash, C., Mitchell, T.: A User experience review of music interaction evaluations. In: Proceedings of the International Conference on NIME, pp. 370–375. NIME (2017)
10. Mathiesen, T.J.: Apollo's Lyre: Greek Music and Music Theory in Antiquity and the Middle Ages, ACLS Humanities E-Book (2010)
11. Deguchi, S., Selfridge-Field, E., Shirai, K.: The temperament, scale and mode of Koto music, In: Proceedings of International Congress of Musicological Society of Japan 2002, pp. 434–438 (2002)
12. Miyagi, M.: Rokudan no Shirabe Koto Score of Ikuta School. Hogakusha, Tokyo (2005)
13. Nakanoshima, K.: Rokudan no Shirabe. Koto Score of Yamada School, Hogakusha, Tokyo (2008)
14. Hirano, K., et al.: Nihon Ongaku Daijiten (In Japanese). Heibonsha, Tokyo (1989)
15. MusicXML: https://www.musicxml.com/. Accessed 23 Jan 2021
16. MuseScore: https://musescore.com/. Accessed 23 Jan 2021
17. MEI: https://music-encoding.org/. Accessed 23 Jan 2021
18. Huron, D.: Humdrum Toolkit. https://www.humdrum.org/. Accessed 23 Jan 2021
19. CCARH: Kern Scores. http://kern.ccarh.org/. Accessed 23 Jan 2021

Developing a Knowledge-Based System for Lean Communications Between Designers and Clients

Yu-Hsiu Hung and Jia-Bao Liang[✉]

Department of Industrial Design, National Cheng Kung University, Tainan, Taiwan
idhfhung@mail.ncku.edu.tw

Abstract. Design is all about communication. Clients often have a difficult time expressing their needs to designers through the proper channels, leaving many designers struggling to meet the demands placed on them. The objective of this study was to improve designer-client communication by looking at the communication process with Lean Thinking, finding waste and eliminating it, and creating a knowledge base containing comprehensive product attributes that can be targeted to help designers and clients simplify the communication. An experiment was conducted to develop the children's electric toothbrush knowledge base with four main stages. The first stage was analyzing the attributes of toothbrush from several aspects includes function, behavior and structure. The second stage was surveying 10 designers by questionnaire and the results were analyzed qualitatively and quantitatively. The third stage was to import individual cases and filter attribute elements to establish mapping relationships. The fourth stage was the use of Django project structure and presentation of knowledge base. Based on the findings of this study, an augmented children's electric toothbrush knowledge base using the Kansei retrieval method was developed, the knowledge base contains comprehensive product attribute items and cases, which can be used by both clients and designers to improve the designer-client communication.

Keywords: Designer-client communication · Product knowledge base · Lean communication

1 Introduction

Design and communication are closely related. Maier, Eckert [1] have reviewed research on models of design communication and communication problems and divided them into mechanical and systematic arguments: the former is based on the five elements of communication proposed by Shannon and Weaver [2], pointing out that the problems in communication are mainly noise in the communication channel and incomplete communication information, etc. The latter uses Luhmann [3] conceptual model of the three elements of communication (information, expression and understanding) as an example, pointing out that the problems in communication are mainly due to the different interpretations of information by the communication subjects, and that the key to the communication process is the recipient of the communication and the process of understanding the information.

© Springer Nature Switzerland AG 2021
M. Kurosu (Ed.): HCII 2021, LNCS 12764, pp. 34–48, 2021.
https://doi.org/10.1007/978-3-030-78468-3_3

Designers always try to extract information from their communication with clients and turn it into a design language, however, there is a huge gap between designers and clients [4]. To solve the problem of information transfer during communication, Shen, Zhang [5] reviewed various models of communication between designers and clients, summarising the basic structure of these models and the eight key issues they cover: (i) Context and characteristics; (ii) Reflective representation; (iii) Interactive interpretation; (iv) Artefactual variation; (v) Mutual awareness; (vi) Consumer engagement; (vii) Collaborative production; (viii) Collective consumption. Therefore, the biggest problem in communication between designers and clients is that it is often difficult for clients to find appropriate channels to effectively communicate their needs to designers [6], thus making it difficult for many designers to meet their clients' requirements.

There has been much research into effective design communication, including effective communication between designers and designers, effective communication between designers and engineers, and effective communication between designers and customers. Graham, Wildes [7] suggest that communication with customers in design is an embodiment of user-centredness, related to the field of human-computer interaction (HCI), through such interaction, customers and designers can become more effective in communication (especially at the technical level). As customers and designers from different backgrounds need to communicate with each other for a common set of goals, they may have different perceptions of representations and convey different information, so effective communication plays a crucial role in the design process. Many researchers have used mathematical theories and models to analyse uncertain, incomplete or redundant user requirements in order to obtain the relationship between customer requirement sequences (e.g. fuzzy mathematics [8], QFD [9], statistical methods [10], and kano models [11], where the extraction or ranking of importance of communication information is considered, but there is no mention of how these rankings or extraction affects communication and how it affects design. In particular, with the exponential increase in the amount of information available to consumers today, it is worth investigating how to improve the efficiency of the organisation of recording and managing information in the design communication process to make two-way communication between designers and customers more efficient [12].

In the above-mentioned research on design communication, only one side (client side or designer side) of the information presentation problem is addressed, but not the two-way communication between designers and clients, nor does it examine the true cause of the problem in the process of finding communication and eliminating waste in the communication process to achieve efficiency. Lean thinking, as a method of improvement that has received more attention in recent years, has been shown to work well in many process improvements [13]. The documentation and management of information in processes is also an important part of lean thinking, as is the process of communication, which requires researchers to extract and manage effective information in the process of communication, so many studies have been conducted around lean communication, for example, Colazo [14] demonstrated that lean thinking can effectively change the effectiveness of communication in teams, even when faced with a lot of information and complex relationships. Most of these studies have looked at models and methods of lean communication in production organisations, and only a few have looked at the value of using lean communication in the product development process. For example, Ferreira and Barbosa [15] proposed Lean Communication-centred design and point out that, compared to traditional communication approaches, in each iteration of the solution's details, integrating pieces of the communication model created at different stages of the process, and the Lean A3 record captures these different stages, so that the design of a lean communication is easier for designers to review and reflect on. However, with the advent of artificial intelligence and the era of big data, consumers' consumption concepts and pursuits are constantly changing, so how can Lean Communication respond to this background, solve the stagnation and waste in the communication between the client and the designer, combine with a knowledge base to effectively manage the exponentially increasing complex design knowledge, methods and cases used in the product design process, so that designers and clients can communicate more effectively? It is worthwhile to further study and think about this in order to reduce the waiting time of customers in the design development process.

The aim of this paper is to (i) examine the two-way communication process between designers and clients based on lean communication, analyse the waste in designer-client communication and identify opportunities for improvement (ii) propose a lean-based knowledge base that can simplify the communication between designers and clients to improve design efficiency in the context of the information age.

This study has been designed to support the communication between designers and clients by building a framework model that combines lean communication and design communication in the information age, and by identifying and eliminating wastage in the analysis and identification of user requirements and communication in the design development process.

2 Literature Review

2.1 Problems in Design Communication

Design communication is the process by which information is passed and agreed between the clients and the designers, either individually or as a group, in order to achieve design objectives. In the process of design communication, there are many obstacles that affect the effectiveness of communication.

Maier collates research on design communication and divides the problems in design communication into two categories: (i) the mechanisms of communication [16], including the noise of the communication channel and the incompleteness of the communication information; and (ii) the systemic nature of communication [17], i.e. the different understandings of the information by the communication subjects and the key to the communication process is the receiver of the communication and the understanding of the information.

Based on the above two types of problems, three aspects of design communication can be summarised that may affect the efficiency of design communication: (i) the communication medium - the effectiveness and accuracy of information transfer and reception; Raaphorst, Duchhart [18] suggest that by using visual methodology, visual representation is the main medium of communication between stakeholders in the design process.

The authors propose the use of visual methodologies such as visual discourse analysis, iconographic content analysis and social symbolism analysis to investigate these representations at different stages of meaning formation and suggest that these research methods have the potential to address issues such as miscommunication between participants. (ii) the language of communication - the distortion of information; Judge, Randall [19] reviewed the literature to identify graphic symbols, tools, language or communication attributes that are currently available to support children's communication and inform decision making for those working with children. and (iii) the organisation of communication - the problem of transferring information at various levels of the organisation. Pedó, Brandalise [20] point out that because of the large number of internal and external stakeholders involved in the management design, a complex organisational structure is needed, i.e. an information system to support collaboration and coordination. The authors therefore examine the use of VM tools in design management and present an ongoing visual management tool developed in collaboration with a UK infrastructure design company.

8 Most of the solutions or frameworks mentioned in the above study are either specialist in nature or require prior knowledge or learning to reach consensus on certain representations before they can be used, and to some extent lack usability, ease of use and timeliness. Alternatively, there are a number of complementary approaches that attempt to improve the efficiency of design communication, but the research is often conducted with the aim of improving efficiency, without examining the issue of waste in design communication and improving its efficiency by eliminating it.

2.2 Lean Communication

Industry 4.0 has brought about a wave of digitisation, and if we do not eliminate waste but simply introduce technology, then it means autonomising waste as well, so we need clear thought to guide us to eliminate waste in communication.

Lean thinking, as an improvement approach that has received more attention in recent years, has shown to work well in many process improvements (Soares & Teixeira, 2014), for example, Iuga (2017) studied the role and importance of communication and types of communication for organisations and their employees, and what has remained consistent is the purpose of communication: communication for all sizes, types and cultures of organisations are critical to effectiveness and success. The authors validate the effectiveness of lean and visual communication by establishing visual communication methods on the internal shop floor of an automobile and subsequently investigating the effectiveness of the implementation of these methods.

Mostly models and methods of lean communication in production organisations have been explored, with only a small number of studies focusing on the value of applying lean communication in the product development process, e.g. Chang, Lee, and Huang (2018) found that newly formed interdisciplinary teams were slow and severely behind schedule when working on a new project with poor team communication and coordination. Ferreira and Barbosa (2016) propose a lean communication-centred design and show that, compared to traditional communication methods, the design process is more effective when In each iteration of a solution, the designer redefines the definition of the previous stage, integrating the pieces of the communication model created at different stages of the process, and the Lean A3 record captures the important details of these different stages, making the design under Lean Communication easier for designers to review and reflect on.

However, with the changing needs of customers, design and even production work is becoming less and less repetitive, if the lead time for product development and design is reduced, thereby reducing the lead time for production and increasing customer value is a question worth considering. The effective management of the exponentially increasing amount of complex design knowledge, methodologies and case studies used in the product design process allows designers and customers to communicate more effectively, thereby reducing the waiting time for customers in the design development process, and is worthy of further study and consideration.

2.3 Communication Tools for the Designer-Client

Although there are various types of product design processes, such as 'KJ method' [21], 'brainstorming' [22], 'Design ethnography' [23] or 'concept mapping' [24], they all treat the design process as usually starting from a briefing stage and ending with design sketches. Archer defines the design process as involving four interlinked phases: (1) problem analysis (2) solution synthesis (3) evaluation and (4) communication. The communication between different participants usually goes through the whole design process. Participants in a typical product design process usually include the designers, clients, and consultants from many other disciplines. During the briefing and design solution development process, the designer–client communication is intensive and significant. (Wu et al. 2013).

With the development of technology, computer-based tools facilitating designer–client communication gradually appear. Knowledge base (KB) also comes into being. The emergence of the knowledge base has benefited from the development of Web technologies, with the purpose of optimizing the results of search engines and improving the quality and experience of clients' searching. Since [22] Tim Bernes-Lee [25] invented the World Wide Web (Linked Information System) in 1989, the system has undergone a transition from hypertext links to semantic links. Later, the concept of the Semantic Web was introduced, emphasizing the use of semantic relationships to describe resources and data in the World Wide Web. Semantics refers to the rich meaning of the data itself. The Web links these data to form huge network information. In this development process, artificial intelligence scholars introduced "ontology" to characterize knowledge, defined Linked Data, and proposed a large number of Knowledge Representation (KR) methods. These unified forms of knowledge constitute a knowledge base (KB).

When building a knowledge base, it actually build a few basic components, including extracting concepts, instances, attributes, and relationships. From the way of construction, the construction of the knowledge base can be divided into manual construction and automatic construction [26]. Buchanan and Shortliffe [27] use expert knowledge to define computer programs that are able to solve complex problems. There are many ways to build a knowledge base by manual work. For example, by interviewing and transcript analysing to obtain case(Hart 1986); Manual construction relies on expert knowledge to write certain rules, collect relevant knowledge information from different sources, and build knowledge architecture [28]; by designing common fuzzy input space according to the expert knowledge [29]; by reading documents and visiting in the field to obtain cases [30].

Automated build is based on knowledge engineering, machine learning, artificial intelligence and other theories automatically collect and extract concepts, instances, attributes and relationships from the Internet [31, 32].Over the last decade, the construction of the knowledge base by automated work moving from pattern matching [33] and rule-based systems [34] to systems that use machine learning [35–37], DeepDive [38, 39], statistical inference [40] and so on [41, 42].

With the advent of the era of big data, more and more algorithms and data mining research are being carried out in the field of knowledge base, but often such projects are time consuming and costly, and require a long-term preparation process and post-maintenance. While manual construction can reduce the pre-learning time of knowledge base construction, it requires the expert knowledge used by the knowledge base to accurately describe the attributes and relationships of objects.

The aforementioned empirical KB research show the potential of KB in supporting product design. However, there are research gaps remaining. First, the object-oriented knowledge base was mostly unidirectional, but in the development process of product design, the communication between designers and clients are bidirectional. Second, most of the research focused on the theoretical and academic level but lacked the empirical research. These two gaps suggest that (i) The knowledge base can also be bidirectional. Taking the product knowledge base as an example, it can be used for both designers and clients. (ii) It is necessary to choose the right product and attribute organization strategy to verify that the product knowledge base construction method is feasible. The research questions are as follows:

- Can KB be bidirectional for both the designer and the consumer during the construction, thereby eliminating the current waste in communication and effectively simplifying the communication between designer and client?
- Is it possible to select a certain type of product and use the proposed construction method to construct the knowledge base, thereby confirming the mapping relationship of the internal attributes of knowledge?

3   Method of Product Knowledge Base Based on Expert Knowledge

3.1   Objective

In order to examine the whole process of communication, reduce the waste between designers and clients' communication, so as to improve the efficiency of design and client communication, and to solve the current situation of unidirectional construction of knowledge base and few empirical cases, this paper eliminates the wastage in the communication process before improving the communication efficiency, and avoids amplifying the waste when digitising the design communication knowledge base, and then adopts an expert knowledge and case reasoning The next step is to build a product knowledge base using a combined attribute organisation strategy. Helping customers to extract effective information accurately and efficiently from the vast amount of data, building a bridge between effective information, facilitating designers to accurately capture client needs, shortening the development and design cycle, and enabling consumers to search the knowledge base to find products that meet their needs.

3.2 Overview of the Method of Product Knowledge Base

As shown in Fig. 1, it is a model flow chart of a product knowledge base construction design method. Firstly, look at the whole process of communication and use the principle of lean thinking as a guideline to find and eliminate waste and to find reasonable solutions to improve the efficiency of communication. Secondly, the client demands need to be cognized, acquired and expressed, obtain product background knowledge and basic conditions, extract the Kansei words related to the product, filter the Kansei words through questionnaires, and obtain the final Kansei words related to the product after statistics; Thirdly, the client demands are transformed, the expert knowledge is used to analyze the product to obtain the internal properties. Questionnaires and statistical analysis may be performed at this stage. Finally, the clinet demands are presented. Through the mapping relationship established by the expert knowledge of the previous part, the product knowledge base is built by means of programming language. The construction of the knowledge base follows the expert knowledge rules and is combined with case analysis to quickly build knowledge for designers and consumers in a short period of time.

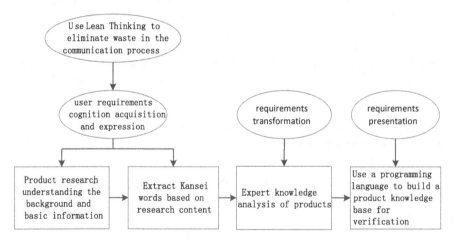

Fig. 1. A brief model flow chart of design method for product knowledge base

3.3 The Specific Technical Route of This Construction Method

As shown in Table 1, it is a detailed flow chart of a method for establishing a product knowledge base based on expert knowledge, and the specific steps are as follows:

- Improve the efficiency of the process with Lean Thinking

- By examining the designer-client communication process with Lean Thinking, we can see that there are many wastes, as summarised in the table below

Table 1. waste in communication processes and corresponding improvement measures.

Waste in the communication process	Improvements
Rework due to misunderstanding of requirement information	Establishing a mapping between user needs and design requirements
Rework due to a gap in expertise between client, designer and technician	Establishing a mapping between user language, design language and technical language
Rework due to discrepancies between the designer's presentation and practice	Presentations are made using the current product library and the basic solution is confirmed and then improved

- Cognition, acquisition and expression of clients demands.

Through the literature reading, market research, interviews, observation and other methods to summarize the background knowledge and basic conditions of the product, the Kansei words are extracted for the first time. Design a questionnaire, select product clients or designers related to the product to conduct a survey, and screen out a number of (fixed number) of emotional vocabulary based on the results.

- Transform user demands.

Select appropriate expert knowledge as the basis for rule construction. These rules can accurately analyze the attribute knowledge of the information inside the knowledge base and establish an effective relationship between these attributes. Next, a questionnaire needs to be designed, respondents have to score the matching degree of a certain attribute and a certain Kansei words by using the 5-point Likert scale from $1 = $ Strongly Disagree to $5 = $ Strongly Agree. Through the statistical results, the mapping relationship between Kansei words and attribute, and the mapping between attributes are established. In this way, the attribute relationship of the internal objects of the knowledge base can be constructed through expert knowledge.

- Presenting client demands.

Analyze the product case that needs to be stored in the knowledge base, and determine whether the product has a certain attribute. If the product case includes a certain attribute, a mapping relationship can be established between the Kansei words matching the attribute and the product case. Use the programming language to build the logical framework of the product knowledge base based on the analysis of the previous steps. Design and optimize the pages of the knowledge base so that clients can get specific products by searching for vague and Kansei words. This knowledge base can be aimed at both clients and designers. Clients can search for products that best meet their needs.

4 Mapping Construction of Children's Electric Toothbrush Knowledge Base

This article chooses FBS as the expert knowledge base and children's electric toothbrushes as the case for knowledge base construction. In 1990, Gero first proposed the Function-Behavior-Structure (FBS) [43] for the product design process. This model can accurately describe the attributes and relationships of objects by establishing models and mappings of products. As an emerging fast-moving consumer goods, demands for children's electric toothbrush are fuzzy and changes frequently, so it has certain representativeness in product design. Therefore, this paper takes children's electric toothbrush as an example to explain the design method of a sensory engineering product knowledge base based on FBS model.

4.1 Cognition, Acquisition and Expression of Client Needs of Children's Electric Toothbrushes

Through the literature reading, market research, interviews, observations and other methods, 20 Kansei words related to children's electric toothbrushes were summarized. 26 people were surveyed by questionnaires on industrial design-related professional backgrounds. Each person selected 10 representative descriptions. The emotional vocabulary of children's electric toothbrushes. The results are shown in Fig. 2. The results of the survey are analyzed and sorted. The adjectives of the high votes are selected and the results are checked and corrected. Finally, the emotional vocabulary of 10 children's electric toothbrushes is: intelligent, safe, lively, cute, light, reliable, client-friendly, concise, qualitative, novel, convenient and professional.

4.2 Transforming Client Demands for Children's Electric Toothbrush

The function of the children's electric toothbrush is expressed by the method of "verb+noun". The function, behavior and structure of children's electric toothbrush are subdivided from the functional expression of children's electric toothbrush, and they are modeled separately from function, behavior and structure. Finally, the functional unit base, behavior unit base and structural unit base model of the product are obtained.

As shown in Fig. 3, an example of the basic function modeling of a child's electric toothbrush is shown.

The questionnaire was designed to allow the respondents to score the matching degree of the children's electric toothbrush functional base in Fig. 4 and the 12 Kansei words obtained in Sect. 4.1. Take the "warn oral problems" in the basic functional unit of children's electric toothbrushes as an example.

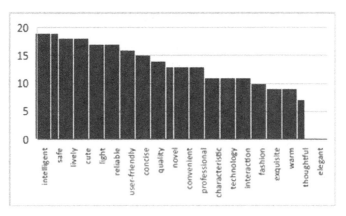

Fig. 2. Children's electric toothbrush questionnaire Kansei words intention bar chart

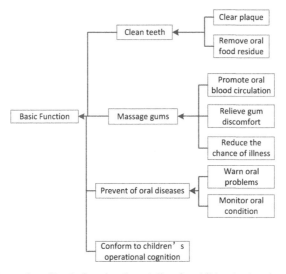

Fig. 3. Examples of basic functional modeling for children's electric toothbrush

The statistics of the recovered scores are shown in Table 2, Sensitive vocabulary with a mean value greater than 4.0 is: smart, safe, reliable, humanized, convenient, and professional. The smallest standard deviation is convenient, so the mapping between "convenient" and "warning oral problems" is established. relationship.

Establish a mapping relationship between children's electric toothbrush function-behavior-structure, match the behavioral base with the functional base, and then match the structural base with the behavioral base to finally complete the function, behavior and structure mapping. When the mapping relationship is established, Fig. 4 is a diagram showing the additional behavior-additional structure mapping relationship of the children's electric toothbrush.

Table 2. Numerical analysis of warning oral problems

	Mean	Standard deviation	A confidence interval estimate for 90% of the mean	
			Lower limits	Upper limits
intelligent	4.4	0.699	3.995	4.805
safe	4.4	0.843	3.911	4.889
lively	2.8	1.032	2.201	3.399
cute	3.0	1.247	2.277	3.723
light	3.2	1.398	2.389	4.011
reliable	4.1	0.876	3.592	4.608
user-friendly	4.0	0.817	3.527	4.473
concise	3.6	1.265	2.867	4.333
qualitative	3.9	1.197	3.206	4.594
novel	3.4	1.075	2.777	4.023
convenient	4.2	0.422	3.956	4.444
professional	4.2	0.789	3.743	4.657

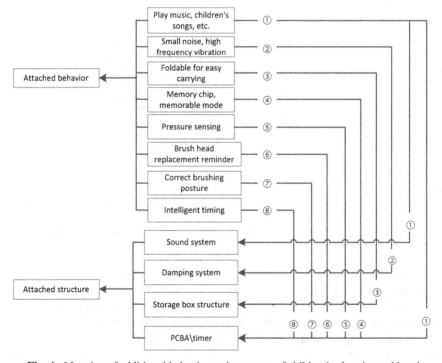

Fig. 4. Mapping of additional behavior and structure of children's electric toothbrush

5   Mapping Construction of Children's Electric Toothbrush Knowledge Base

After using the expert knowledge to construct the logical relationship of the internal objects of the knowledge base, it is necessary to construct the operational logic of the overall knowledge base. It is also the presentation of the clients needs of children's electric toothbrushes mentioned in Sect. 3.2. The operation process of the knowledge base is shown in Fig. 5.

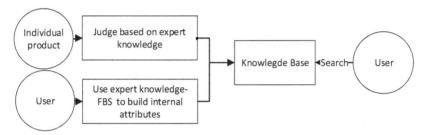

Fig. 5.   Operation flow chart of product knowledge base based on FBS model

Analyze a case of a child's electric toothbrush product that needs to be stored in the knowledge base, and determine whether the product has a unit base. If the product case includes a unit base, a mapping can be established between the Kansei word that matches the unit base and the product case.

Use the programming language to build the logical framework of the product knowledge base based on the analysis of the previous steps. The Django project is a Python custom framework used by the knowledge base site presented in this study. The logic code for implementing the knowledge base. The admin under /tooth/app is the code for the background administrator registration management page, the models are the code for defining the model (design database), the views are the code for implementing the view logic, the urls are the code for the distribution address, and the settings for /tooth/tooth are The configuration code for the knowledge base.

Design and optimize the pages of the knowledge base so that clients can get specific products by searching for vague and sensible words.

6   Conclusion

A product knowledge base establishment method based on expert knowledge has the following contributions compared with the existing research:

- Using Lean Thinking to guide designer-client communication to improve processes. Develop a product knowledge base based on expert knowledge to simplify designer-client communications.
- By combining expert knowledge with practical cases, the method covers the product attributes comprehensively and quickly establishes relationships between the various relationships, in order to map the relationship between clients, products and designers;

- Build a product knowledge base based on FBS model, which is fast and at the same time oriented to clients and designers. Clients can search for products that best meet their needs. Designers can design innovative products based on knowledge base products to greatly improve design efficiency.

Communication is the heart and soul of design and the total object of design is to communicate in some form. The study provided reference for using Lean Thinking to improve product design communication processes and develop product knowledge base. What's more, the development of the knowledge base transformed the fuzzy client demands to the clear design requirements and made the communication between designers and clients effectively.

References

1. Maier, A.M., Eckert, C.M., Clarkson, P.J.: A meta-model for communication in engineering design. CoDesign **1**(4), 243–254 (2005)
2. Shannon, C.E.: A mathematical theory of communication. ACM SIGMOBILE Mob. Comput. Commun. Rev. **5**(1), 3–55 (2001)
3. Luhmann, N.: What is communication? Commun. Theor. **2**(3), 251–259 (1992)
4. Crilly, N., Maier, A., Clarkson, P.J.: Representing artefacts as media: modelling the relationship between designer intent and consumer experience. Int. J. Des. **2**(3), 15–27 (2008)
5. Shen, W., et al.: The user pre-occupancy evaluation method in designer–client communication in early design stage: a case study. Autom. Constr. **32**, 112–124 (2013)
6. Lertlakkhanakul, J., Choi, J.W., Kim, M.Y.: Building data model and simulation platform for spatial interaction management in smart home. Autom. Constr. **17**(8), 948–957 (2008)
7. Graham, A.K., et al.: User-centered design for technology-enabled services for eating disorders. Int. J. Eat. Disord. **52**(10), 1095–1107 (2019)
8. Xue, L., et al.: An approach of the product form design based on gra-fuzzy logic model: a case study of train seats. Int. J. Innovative Comput. Inf. Control **15**(1), 261–274 (2019)
9. Büyüközkan, G., Güler, M., Mukul, E.: An integrated fuzzy QFD methodology for customer oriented multifunctional power bank design. In: Kahraman, C., Cebi, S. (eds.) Customer Oriented Product Design. SSDC, vol. 279, pp. 73–91. Springer, Cham (2020). https://doi.org/10.1007/978-3-030-42188-5_5
10. Oliveira, F., et al.: Identifying user profiles from statistical grouping methods. J. Inf. Syst. Eng. Manage. **3**(1), 06 (2018)
11. Ozalp, M., et al.: Integration of quality function deployment with IVIF-AHP and Kano model for customer oriented product. Customer Oriented Prod. Des. Intell. Fuzzy Tech. **279**, 93 (2020)
12. Redeker, G.A., Kessler, G.Z., Kipper, L.M.: Lean information for lean communication: analysis of concepts, tools, references, and terms. Int. J. Inf. Manage. **47**, 31–43 (2019)
13. Soares, S., Teixeira, L.: Lean information management in industrial context: an experience based on a practical case. Int. J. Ind. Eng. Manage. **5**, 107–114 (2014)
14. Colazo, J.: Changes in communication patterns when implementing lean. Int. J. Qual. Reliab. Manage. (2020)
15. Ferreira, D.V.C., Barbosa, S.D.J.: Lean communication-centered design: a lightweight design process. In: Kurosu, M. (ed.) HCI 2016. LNCS, vol. 9731, pp. 553–564. Springer, Cham (2016). https://doi.org/10.1007/978-3-319-39510-4_51
16. Cruz-Lozano, R., et al.: Determining probability of importance of features in a sketch. ASCE-ASME J. Risk Uncert. Eng. Sys. Part B Mech. Eng. **3**(4), 041003 (2017)

17. Zhang, Z., et al.: A design communication framework based on structured knowledge representation. IEEE Trans. Eng. Manage. (2020)
18. Raaphorst, K., et al.: The semiotics of landscape design communication: towards a critical visual research approach in landscape architecture. Landsc. Res. **42**(1), 120–133 (2017)
19. Judge, S., et al.: The language and communication attributes of graphic symbol communication aids–a systematic review and narrative synthesis. Disabil. Rehabil. Assist. Technol. **15**(6), 652–662 (2020)
20. Pedó, B., et al.: Digital visual management tools in design management (2020)
21. Scupin, R.: The KJ method: a technique for analyzing data derived from Japanese ethnology. Hum. Organ. **56**, 233–237 (1997)
22. Sutton, R.I., Hargadon, A.: Brainstorming groups in context: effectiveness in a product design firm. Adm. Sci. Quart. **41**, 685–718 (1996)
23. Salvador, T., Bell, G., Anderson, K.: Design ethnography. Des. Manage. J. (Former Series) **10**(4), 35–41 (1999)
24. Novak, J.D.: Concept mapping: a useful tool for science education. J. Res. Sci. Teach. **27**(10), 937–949 (1990)
25. Berners-Lee, T., Hendler, J., Lassila, O.: The semantic web. Sci. Am. **284**(5), 34–43 (2001)
26. Shi, Z.Z.: Knowledge Discovery. Tsinghua University Press, Beijing (2011)
27. Buchanan, B.G., Shortliffe, E.: The MYCIN Experiments of the Stanford Heuristic Programming Project. Addison-Wasley, Reading (1984)
28. Boose, J.H.: A knowledge acquisition program for expert systems based on personal construct psychology. Int. J. Man Mach. Stud. **23**(5), 495–525 (1985)
29. Guillaume, S., Magdalena, L.: Expert guided integration of induced knowledge into a fuzzy knowledge base. Soft. Comput. **10**(9), 773–784 (2006)
30. H.Q, W.F.Z.: Statistical analysis and coping strategies of cases of ethnic factors in China: based on the knowledge base of chinese national emergencies in 1980–2015. J. Intell. **35**, 122–128 (2016)
31. Zhong, X.-Q., Liu, Z., Ding, P.-P.: Construction of knowledge base on hybrid reasoning and its application. Jisuanji Xuebao (Chinese J. Comput.) **35**(4), 761–766 (2012)
32. Niu, F., et al.: Elementary: large-scale knowledge-base construction via machine learning and statistical inference. Int. J. Semant. Web Inf. Syst. (IJSWIS) **8**(3), 42–73 (2012)
33. Hearst, M.A.: Automatic acquisition of hyponyms from large text corpora. In: Coling 1992 Volume 2: The 15th International Conference on Computational Linguistics (1992)
34. Li, Y., Reiss, F., Chiticariu, L.: SystemT: a declarative information extraction system. In: Proceedings of the ACL-HLT 2011 System Demonstrations (2011)
35. Betteridge, J., et al.: Toward never ending language learning. In: AAAI Spring Symposium: Learning by Reading and Learning to Read (2009)
36. Carlson, A., et al.: Toward an architecture for never-ending language learning. In: Proceedings of the AAAI Conference on Artificial Intelligence (2010)
37. Nakashole, N., Theobald, M., Weikum, G.: Scalable knowledge harvesting with high precision and high recall. In: Proceedings of the Fourth ACM International Conference on Web Search and Data Mining (2011)
38. Chen, Y., Wang, D.Z.: Knowledge expansion over probabilistic knowledge bases. In: Proceedings of the 2014 ACM SIGMOD International Conference on Management of Data (2014)
39. Shin, J., et al.: Incremental knowledge base construction using deepdive. In: Proceedings of the VLDB Endowment International Conference on Very Large Data Bases. NIH Public Access (2015)
40. Niu, F., et al.: DeepDive: web-scale knowledge-base construction using statistical learning and inference. VLDS **12**, 25–28 (2012)

41. De Ville, B.: Applying statistical knowledge to database analysis and knowledge base construction. In: Sixth Conference on Artificial Intelligence for Applications. IEEE Computer Society (1990)
42. McCoy, A.B., et al.: Development and evaluation of a crowdsourcing methodology for knowledge base construction: identifying relationships between clinical problems and medications. J. Am. Med. Inform. Assoc. **19**(5), 713–718 (2012)
43. Gero, J.S.: Design prototypes: a knowledge representation schema for design. AI Mag. **11**(4), 26 (1990)

Learn and Share to Control Your Household Pests: Designing a Communication Based App to Bridge the Gap Between Local Guides and the New Users Looking for a Reliable and Affordable Pest Control Solutions

Shima Jahani$^{(\boxtimes)}$, Raman Ghafari Harivand, and Jung Joo Sohn

Purdue University, West Lafayette, IN, USA
{jahani,rghafari,jjsohn}@purdue.edu

Abstract. One of the most crucial steps to becoming independent for young people is leaving their parents' homes to study or get a decent job. Based on the current population reports, 4,208,601 young people from 20–24 leave their parents' house to live independently. When Young adults start their higher education or employment by living independently, they face many challenges with housekeeping specialty pest control. In this study, researchers tried to help young adults who move to a new place to start their higher education or employment to share their pest control experiences, access updated local information, and communicate better by designing a communication-based platform application. Community-based applications consist of one or many forums in which each member could be involved in the community.

Keywords: Pest control · Community-based strategy · Household pesticide · Pest management strategy · Communicative forum

1 Introduction

A nationwide survey by Home Team Pest Defense, the third-largest US residential pest control company, found that in the past 12 months, 84% of American homeowners have encountered a pest problem [1]. The health and well-being of house occupants can be hurt by the presence of pests [2], especially for young adults who start their higher education or employment by living independently, they face many challenges with housekeeping chores to keep it clean and hygienic [3]. Pest is any living creature or organism which could affect human wellbeing or economy negatively [4]. According to a consumer affairs report, most of the renters and owners in the US were nervous about ants, spiders, roaches, and bedbugs [5]. There are numerous integrated Pest Management (IPM) techniques for controlling pests; [2] Since pest control management strategies rely on a broad knowledge of pest's biology and ecology, it is very challenging to apply effective and efficient methods [6]. One of the well-known methods is using pesticides [7]; although most of them are harmful to home occupants and nature, 80–90% of households use

© Springer Nature Switzerland AG 2021
M. Kurosu (Ed.): HCII 2021, LNCS 12764, pp. 49–66, 2021.
https://doi.org/10.1007/978-3-030-78468-3_4

them [8–10]. This research aims to provide a communicative atmosphere for our target users who are college or university students with no pest control experience. Lack of knowledge and experience makes them unable to cope efficiently with pest issues. Having communication with the expert people in the pest management field could help users with no pest control background find efficient, effective, and affordable solutions.

2   Related Works

2.1   Importance of Knowing Pest Control Solutions

During screening the literature, the researchers decided to focus on the significant problems with pest control. Customers apply the solutions to exterminate the pests, but sometimes they are not aware of applying a given solution. Lack of knowledge, time, and budget leads the target users, young adults who move to a new place to start their higher education or employment and apply appropriate pest management solutions. In the following paragraphs, researchers provide evidence to show why the preexisting solutions could not always be useful.

World Health Organization (WHO) data (2010) showed that one household pesticide contains two active ingredients for distinct insecticide clusters, carbamates and pyrethroids [11]. These ingredients impact human well-being and pollute rivers and groundwater, which cause poisoning and numerous diseases [12]; the use of pesticides in the houses is dangerous for residents and can threaten public health [13]. It causes several health issues such as cancer, asthma, allergies (sensitive to chemicals), fetal disability, acceleration of bone calcification, hypertension, reproductive disorders, carcinogenesis [14] and Parkinson's [15].

People are exposed to pesticides when used in and around the home [16], and remaining pesticides are carried into the home on the residents' shoes or clothing from the outside or workplace [17]. Children are more subject to pesticides because they are at home most of the time. Also, they show given behaviors such as hand to mouth, playing on the floor. Moreover, the children's metabolism is immature, and their smaller size leads to greater consumption of pesticides from foods [18]. Pests cause diseases and physical damages and damnify human beings in terms of time and money. According to the United States Department of Agriculture (USDA), US "residents spend at least $1 billion on Formosan termite control and repairs each year. Some experts estimate the number is closer to $2 billion" [19].

2.2   Lack of Budget Effects Pest Management Strategies

Since our target users are young adults (students) with can earn 13,880 over the year, which means about 1,156 per month [20]. Spending money on pest management is not reasonable under this circumstance. This financial loss is not only associated with termites but also the other pests that can cause financial damages. In many cases, people need to call pest control agencies to solve their issues, which is very costly and time-consuming. Based on the HomeGuide website, the average cost for pest control is about 250$, and if the customers need to hire someone to exterminate the pest, they will charge between 250\$ to 400\$, which is more than one-fourth of the monthly income of our target users. It is worth mentioning that their price is different by region and even by zip code. Table 1 shows the average cost for pest control by agencies in Indiana. The prices are varied based on the type of pest and areas [21].

Table 1. Average cost of pest control in Indiana state [21].

Pest Type	Average Cost
Ants	$250+
Carpenter Ants	Starting at $500 for initial spray (plus cost of physical labor & any repairs).
Termite Control	Starting at $1000 for initial spray (plus cost of physical labor & any repairs).
Termite Inspection	$75 – $150
Bats	$250 - $500
Bees	$200 - $500 (for treatment only, not removal).
Bed Bugs	$200 – $400 per room
Cockroaches	$300+ for initial treatment
Fleas	$150 - $300
Ticks	$150 - $300
Spiders	$200+
Wasps	$200 - $500 (for treatment only, not removal).
Mice & Rats	Starting at $300
Weevils	$100-300 (for treatment only, not removal).
Carpet Beetles	$250+

2.3 Role of Time in Pest Control

Time plays an important role in the pest control process. Customers need to dedicate time to assess the situation, such as where the pest is living, how they are entering the home and finding the best strategy to exterminate them. US Bureau of Labor Statistics shows that college and undergraduate students have less than 4 h of free time [22]. It means spending time on pest control, which is a time-consuming process, is not rational for our target users.

The process of pest management typically costs \$300–\$550 per visit. The process of pest management typically costs \$300–\$550 per visit. Therefore, if the customer faces a seasonal pest, their house needs a periodic visit that is more expensive. A periodic visit can happen every month, every two months, or every three months, and lasts more than 2 h per visit. Here are the average cost breakdowns for each kind of periodic visit:

Every month: \$40 to \$45.
Every two months (semi-monthly): \$50 to \$60.
Every three months (quarterly): \$100 to \$300 [21].

Since the existence of pests in houses can cause various physical and biological problems, and lack of knowledge about the solutions like using chemical pesticides could be ended up in serious problems, the goal of this research is to provide a context that customers could diagnose their pest troubles efficiently and make the best solutions for choosing the solutions.

A communicative platform can lead people, whit pest issues to share their problems with the people who have appropriate pest control experiences.

2.4 Community-Based Strategy

A community-based approach is an appropriate tool for this study. Delgado, in Social work practice in nontraditional urban settings, explains that "Community-based program design is a social method for designing programs that enable social service providers, organizers, designers and evaluators to serve specific communities in their environment. This program design method depends on the participatory approach of community development, often associated with community-based social work, and is often employed by community organizations [23]."

Therefore, this research aims to help young adults who move to a new place to start their higher education or employment to share their pest control experiences, access updated local information, and communicate better by designing a communication-based platform application. Community-based applications consist of one or many forums in which each member could be involved in the community. In this research, we decided to adopt a communication-based design into the app design and engage the users to share their pest control experiences with the new users looking for a reliable and affordable solution [24].

3 User Research and Findings

3.1 User Study (Questionnaire Survey)

In order to collect first-hand data from users regarding pest control, the researchers have conducted a questionnaire survey. Through this survey, researchers tried to figure out the main problems the users face regarding pest control and the severity of the issue. It was also essential to understand how users cope with pest issues and their preferences when encountering pest issues. Understanding the type of the users' houses, pest problems, their possible solutions, and their experiences regarding pest controlling was the aim of this survey.

The questionnaire can be divided into two significant sections. The first section focuses on demographic questions and the second section is about the users' experiences regarding pest control issues. To collect the data that will lead to developing the app, researchers have provided different types of responses such as 10 points Likert, Multiple choice, and Open-ended questions. To collect the data that will lead to developing the app, researchers have provided different types of responses such as 10 points Likert, Multiple choice, and Open-ended questions. This would lead to more accurate results as it provides the responders a better degree of freedom in answering the questions.

Researchers considered the target users as students or employees between 18 and 32 years old, who have started to live independently for the first time. Out of all 32 individuals who fill out the form, 34.4% were students, and 65.6% were employees. Chart 1 shows the duration that the participants have started living independently.

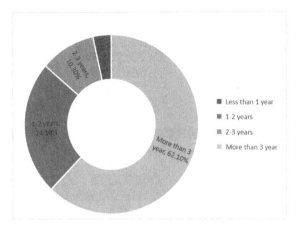

Chart 1: Living duration-independently

The survey shows that the majority - 62.5% - of the target users live in apartments (suite of rooms forming one residence, typically in a building containing a number of these.) Chart 2 depicts the distribution for the type of dwelling, based on the users' response.

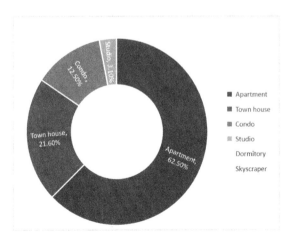

Chart 2: Users house types

Based on our survey, 71.9% of users have been infected with at least one kind of pests. Also, it states that 76.9% of users have faced pest infection between 0 to 5 times per season.

Users reported that the kitchen is the first place where they found most of the pests there, and their bedrooms were the second place which receives pests' damages mostly.

Chart 3 is revealing that pests damaged which parts of their houses. Based on the survey responses, the kitchen is considered the hardest place for exterminating the pest. (Chart 4)

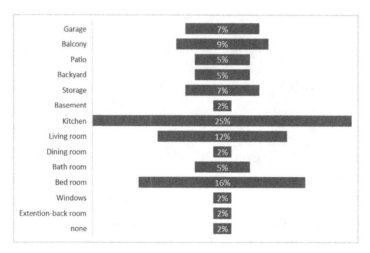

Chart 3: Affected places by pests

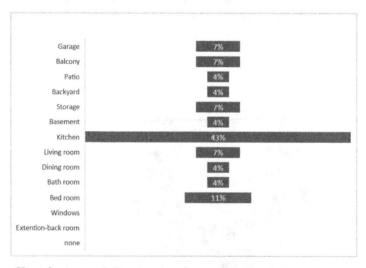

Chart 4: A most challenging place for exterminating the pest percentage

There are numerous signs and symptoms which the users figure out of the pest infestation in the house. The way users understand that pests have infected their houses is shown in the chart below (Chart 5). The responses show that 21 of the participants discovered the infestation by seeing the building's pests themselves.

When those were moving around, and nine responders found body parts in their houses. In this question, participants could select multiple responses.

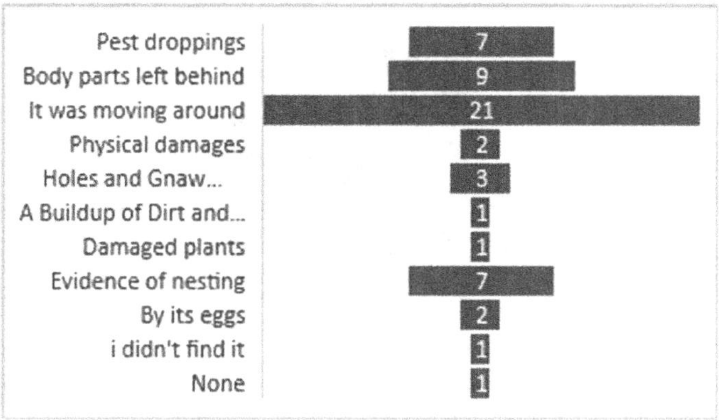

Pest droppings	7
Body parts left behind	9
It was moving around	21
Physical damages	2
Holes and Gnaw...	3
A Buildup of Dirt and...	1
Damaged plants	1
Evidence of nesting	7
By its eggs	2
i didn't find it	1
None	1

Chart 5: The ways that users found the pests.

The first reaction of users encounter with pests is the essential part of our survey. The majority of responses (15 responses) show that their first reaction when facing a pest issue is to seek advice from their family or their friends on the issue by sharing the problem. Chart 6 states that the second reaction uses commercial pesticides by the house owner to exterminate the pest directly.

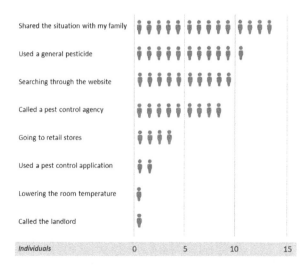

Chart 6: Distribution of responses for encountering pest issues

Researchers asked users about their preference regarding getting help from local advisors or pest control agencies. Based on the responses, 88.9% of users trust local advisors and 11.1% trust the pest control agencies. In addition, Chart 7 demonstrates their reasons of trust as well as the frequency of each reason.

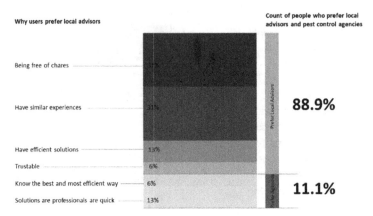

Chart 7: Why people can trust or cannot trust local advisors

Participants provided some solutions regarding pest controlling through open-ended questions. The variation of the solutions was limited. Therefore, researchers summarized them in Table 2. Among all the responses, using pesticides was the most popular solution among the participants, which means users prefer to do the pest controlling processes by themselves.

Table 2. solutions for pest control.

Ranking	Solutions
1	Using pesticide
2	Using DIY and non-chemical solutions
2	Setting mice trap
3	Waiting for season changing
3	Asking someone for help
4	Calling agencies
4	Searching on Google
5	Raiding

More than 53% of participants mentioned that their solutions did not work, and the pests appeared after a while. They provided why their strategies regarding pest control failed or passed (Table 3).

Throughout the survey participants were asked about the platforms (applications or websites) to control the pests. More than 89% of them have not any experience with pest

Table 3. Reasons of successful of unsuccessful solutions

Ranking	Solutions	Outcomes
1	Old house with many unsealed holes	Unsuccessful
2	New pests come back every season	Unsuccessful
2	Effective chemical pesticides	Successful
3	DIY (do it yourself) solutions worked	Successful
4	Hard to find their nests	Unsuccessful

control applications or websites. Reddit, Instagram, Bobvila.com, and Facebook were the platforms that less than 11% of participants have used for pest issues.

According to the responses, more than 83% of users think that the above-mentioned platforms were not helpful because their information was very general, or they did not have a chance to use them. Besides, 16% of users thought that the platforms were helpful because it was free and saved their time. Also, they believed that using the platforms was very easy and quick which made them needless to search on Google.

3.2 Conclusion of the Survey

Throughout this survey, the target users were asked about the type of house they live in and the pest issues they usually face. Researchers found that approximately 62% of target users are living in apartments for more than three years. Users stated that the kitchen and bedrooms are the two most infested areas of the home. Also, they mentioned that exterminating pests from these two places are considered harder than the other areas of the houses. Besides, users mostly notify about pest issues in their home when the pest moves around, making them easy to discover. The results state that half of the individuals shared their problems with their families or friends and used pesticides as the first reaction to pests. When target users solve the problems, they prefer to apply the local advisor's solution instead of asking pest control agencies to help. The possible reason for the users tending to apply the local advisors' suggestion vs. using pest control agencies was that local advisors 'services are free of charge and trustable. Although more than 11% of users prefer to get a service from a pest control agency, more than 88% think that local advisors have the same experiences with efficient solutions that could help pest control agencies. According to the survey, using chemicals and "Do It Yourself" pesticides are the practical solutions to cope with pest problems. However, these strategies are not always effective as the pests come back as the season changes or the users' houses are old enough to have many unsealed holes.

3.3 User Interview

Then after the questionnaire survey, 6 participants were recruited from the 32.

participants for the two rounds of interviews are for knowing the challenges users face during pest invasions and methods they use for pest control.

The interview questions are mixed and listed below:

- How would you rate the severity of the pest control situation at your place?
- Based on the questionnaire you submitted, you said you had a pest infection. Can you please tell me more about your past experiences with pests at your new location?
- Did you plan to prevent future incidents (pest invasions)? How?
- Did you try to identify the type of pest? How?
- Have you ever tried the pest controlling methods yourself? How?
- Have you ever asked for advice from your friend or family friend regarding the pest situation?
- Have you tried to ask your questions from local people and learn from their pest controlling experience? Would you trust their advice?
- Have you ever contacted a pest control agency or a professional for pest control? Why? What was the problem?
- Have you ever checked a website for pest control? Do you remember the situation? Did you find the information useful? If not, why?
- Do you use the general pesticide?
- Why did you start to cook? For what kind of reason?
- Do you inspect the house for the pest situation frequently?

After the interviews, we analyzed the interview scripts listed the findings, and selected the key findings. Here are our key findings from the interviews:

- In general, pest control situations are either simple or complex. There are distinct motivations for whom target users turn toward first based on the severity of their situation.
- DIY Solutions are proactive and not just reactive solutions.
- Climate and weather outside impact the pest control situation inside the home
- Users will use social media (Instagram story question/response feature, Facebook suggestions post) to assess who has been in a similar situation and what their solutions worked, and which ones did not work. Then they will contact those people directly for more information if necessary.
- Problems with finding information from search engines:

  – Information on the internet is scattered (too many sources)
  – Varying opinions
  – Difficult to refine your search to your specific situation
  – Which sources are trustworthy
  – Hard to identify the specific pest with personal identification through a search engine

- Solutions should be personal and customizable to fit the customer's needs.

- The cleanliness of one's home has a direct correlation with pest control.
- Cost is a major influence on what solution someone chooses to engage with.
- People trust their landlords because they are easily accessible, typically knowledgeable, and include this as part of the lease agreement (affordable)
- Local professionals/people with experience are useful.
- Tenants/homeowners may need emotional support from someone they trust that can soothe them if their pest control situation produces fear/anxiety and give them practical solutions that they know will work.
- Users ignore pest control situations and do not regularly inspect the house until it becomes a significant issue.
- Many users face short-term pest invasions, and they need efficient, cheap, and effective solutions.

After analyzing the findings, we identified the emerging themes. Based on the emerging themes, we created the ten insights statements.

3.4 Insights Gained from User Research

- Sharing pest control experience with the local community is effective, efficient, and affordable
- Users require quick, accurate responses in emergencies
- Trust is essential when giving recommendations for pest situations
- Complicated pest infections require professional expertise
- Solutions should be customizable to fit the customer's needs
- Comprehensive and valid pest information and methodologies provide convenience
- Future pest incidents can be prevented by appropriate cleaning and homecare
- Many pest infections are invisible, and users become aware when the situation is out of control
- Templates and communication guides make it easier to share the information

After listing general insights, we prioritized our insights based on our original Design Challenge and project goals, and we discarded any that do not directly relate to our challenge. We then refined the key insights and prioritized them based on the following criteria Well-informed research data point, memorable content, and actionable results.

Key Insights

- Sharing pest control experience with the local community is effective, efficient, and affordable.
- Trust is essential when giving recommendations for pest situations.
- Emergency pest situations require quick and accurate responses.
- Complicated/dangerous pest infections require professional expertise.
- The pest information on the internet is too general and does not help with identifying the pest and finding appropriate solutions.

4 Design Process

After the user research, we created product attributes for our application design. Creating a community-based platform application was our primary goal. Therefore, we created a social forum to let the people share their experiences and communicate. We also created ways for users to reach out to the professionals in a fast and affordable way. As for finding accurate and credible information, we also tried to add functions to our application.

We brainstormed many ideas and went through several rounds of brainstorming and ideation. For each round, we created low fidelity prototypes and refined the ideas several times. After the final product attributes were decided, we confirmed the user flow structure of our app. Afterward, we designed wireframes and the user interface and created a high-fidelity version of our application with interactive pages (Fig 1).

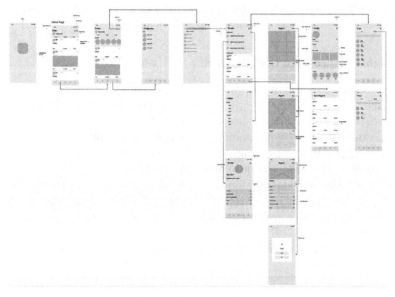

Fig. 1. User flow of Pesto

4.1   Main Features

There are five main features to help the user with the pest control process.

1. Creating a report
2. Search for finding the pest and the solutions
3. Posting on a Forum
4. Adding a link on News
5. User Profile
1. *Creating a report:* By this feature, users can create a post, link, or report. The new posts go to a given forum, the new link will be sent to the News page, and the report will be sent to the selected people, other media, or even a forum by users' selection (Fig. 2).

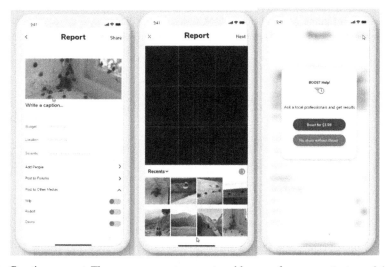

Fig. 2. Creating a report: The user can report any pest problems on forums, contacts, social media, or seek a quick answer from the local professionals.

2. *Search for finding the pest and the solutions:* The users can quickly identify the pest type by taking a picture of it or put some keywords, and the application will bring up the matched results based on the input of the user and location. The user can find specific details of the pest and share them with others. The search feature also provides relevant information on the posts shared by other users (Fig. 3).

Posting on a Forum: The users can post their questions or any external links in the forum. What they see in the forum are the general hot posts that local people have posted, and it is totally location-based but the Home page includes worldwide posts. They have organized based on users' favorite topics (Fig. 4).

Fig. 3. Search for finding pest and situations: Users can type the name of the pest in the search bar or upload a picture of it, if it is available, in order to identify the pest information

Fig. 4. Posting on a forum. The users have access to the forums to share their experience and learn from local professionals or ask a new question.

Adding a link on News: Users can add and share an external link from the other News agencies and read the outbreak news regarding pest issues (Fig. 5).

3. *User Profile.* The users receive a score from the application based on their activity on the forum pages and their rating from the other users. After passing a certain level, the user's membership will transform to "professional Member," and the user can receive Boost requests from the other users to answer them and get paid (Fig. 6).

Fig. 5. Adding a link on News.

Fig. 6. User Profile. The User has access to the archive of his/her pest controlling activities through the application.

5 User Testing to Evaluate the Prototype

In order to evaluate our application, we performed quantitative and qualitative user testing and used the "Think Aloud" approach. We hired 4 participants who were previously participated in the early stages of the design to test our prototype to find answers to the following questions: Effectiveness: Is it possible for the user to navigate and use the tools in the application's interface free of errors? Efficiency: What is the average time it takes for a user to complete each task? How long does it take to correct the errors? Satisfaction: Are users subjectively satisfied when using the application? Is the application pleasing to use? Is the user interface easy to use and learn?

Since the prototype was not fully functional, we filled the contents for some steps, and the user just needed to click on the page to process the application. For example, the user could not share something on social media, but when clicking on the share button, a screenshot of a social media post would be shown to the user to get his/her reaction.

We asked users to accomplish the tasks below in order to evaluate the application:

- Search for finding the information about a predefined pest by uploading a preexisting photo in the gallery and inserting given information.
- Sharing pest information on social media
- Report/Share a pest problem
- Creating a forum
- Adding a link on News

The feedback we received from the participants were generally positive. The final results were showing that the application is easy to understand and efficient to accomplish the tasks. The users finish most of the tasks with no problem and found the application effective as well. They found the "Report" feature very useful in emergencies. They also liked the forum page and how it's integrated into the search results. They also found it very useful to be able to find more information about the pest by taking pictures of it when it's hard to identify it and learn from other people's experiences in the forum pages.

There was some valuable negative feedback as well. Some users had a hard time understanding the scoring system and how they become a local professional and earning money. Some users also were not sure if networking and having connections on a pest control application is necessary and did not find it quite useful.

6 Discussion and Conclusion

This paper reported findings from 32 participants through surveys and six individual interviews for pest control. Researchers created questionnaires to understand various users' situations for each housing type during the primary research phase. We found great potential in sharing information among local community members and the importance of finding a problem early. Through the user research, we figured out five key insights and developed five main features.

We designed an application based on an information-sharing platform, built a community to connect with other users, and quickly reported to local professionals. By encouraging users to share information and solutions, we promoted the interaction among the users and their engagement in the community. To get a quick solution for an urgent case, we added the paid service 'Report' that can get quick advice from other users and quotes from local professionals. We believe that the report service is a win-win strategy for both community users and professionals. Other features of the app, such as posting on a forum and searching a database, also help users find a control pest solution and encourage sharing information with other community members.

In this study, most of the main features have no major problem, as the evaluation turned out. However, there are some details and the business model that could be polished.

Also, pest problems do not happen every day. This will affect the activity of the forum and the frequency of use. Our future work may focus on making a more detailed working prototype and solution for a more active community in the app.

References

1. Home Team Pest Deafense "Survey Results on Pests": https://pestdefense.com/hometeam-releases-survey-results-on-pests/. Accessed 24 Apr 2012
2. Centers for Disease Control and Prevention and U.S. Department of Housing and Urban Development: Healthy housing reference manual, Chapter 4. US Department of Health and Human Services, Atlanta (2006)
3. Murphy, R.G., Todd, S.: Minimizing pest risk in dwellings. Struct. Surv. **14**(1), 9–13 (1996). https://doi.org/10.1108/02630809610116197
4. Bateman, P.L.G.: Household pests. Struct. Surv. **2**(2), 115–123 (1984). https://doi.org/10.1108/eb006181
5. Parkman, K.: Pest control statistics and trends. https://www.consumeraffairs.com/homeowners/pest-control-statistics.html. Accessed 14 May 2020
6. Pélissié, B., Crossley, M.S., Cohen, Z.P., Schoville, S.D.: Rapid evolution in insect pests: the importance of space and time in population genomics studies. Curr. Opin. Insect Sci. **26**, 8–16 (2018)
7. Triwidodo, H., Mudikdjo, K., Panjaitan, N.K., Manuwoto, S., Yuliani, T.S.: Studies on the behavior housewives in home pesticide usage in Special Capital Region Jakarta. IPB (Bogor Agricultural University (2012). https://repository.ipb.ac.id/jspui/handle/123456789/54270
8. Armes, M.N., et al.: Residential pesticide usage in older adults residing in Central California. Int. J. Environ. Res. Public Health **8**, 3114–3133 (2011). https://doi.org/10.3390/ijerph8083114
9. Savage, E.P., et al.: Household pesticide usage in the United States. Arch. Environ. Health **36**, 304–309 (1981). https://doi.org/10.1080/00039896.1981.10667642
10. Stout II, D.M., et al.: American Healthy Homes Survey: a national study of residential pesticides measured from floor wipes. Environ. Sci. Technol. **43**, 4294–4300 (2009). https://pubs.acs.org/doi/full/10.1021/es8030243
11. World Health Organization: The WHO Recommended Classification of Pesticides by Hazard and Guidelines to Classification 2009, p. 8. World Health Organization (2010). https://apps.who.int/iris/bitstream/handle/10665/44271/9789241547963_eng.pdf?sequence=1
12. Den Hond, F., Groenewegen, P., van Straalen, N.: Pesticides Problems, Improvements, Alternative, pp. 1–17. Blackwell Sciences Ltd., Blackwell Publishing company (2003)
13. Raini, M., Isnawati, A., Herman, M.J.: Paparan propoxur pada anggota rumah tangga yang menggunakan anti serangga semprot di Jakarta, Tangerang, Bekasi dan Depok. Indonesian Bull. Health Res. **37**, 43–54 (2009). https://doi.org/10.22435/bpk.v37i1
14. Atkinson, H.C., Begg, E.J., Darlow, B.A.: Drugs in human milk. Clinical pharmacokinetic considerations. Clin. Pharmacokinet. **14**, 217–240 (1988). https://doi.org/10.2165/00003088-198814040-00003
15. Hileman, B.: The environment and Parkinson's: If exposure to chemicals causes this dread disease, regulators may have to alter approaches to neurotoxicity testing and risk assessment. Chem. Eng. News. **79**, 35–37 (2001). https://doi.org/10.1021/cen-v079n038.p035
16. Bradman, A., Whyatt, R.M.: Characterizing exposures to nonpersistent pesticides during pregnancy and early childhood in the National Children's Study: a review of monitoring and measurement methodologies. Environ. Health Prospect **113**, 1092–1099 (2005). https://doi.org/10.1289/ehp.7769

17. Coronado, G.D., Vigoren, E.M., Thompson, B., Griffith, W.C., Faustman, E.M.: Organophosphate pesticide exposure and work in pome fruit: evidence for the take-home pesticide pathway. Environ. Health Prospect **114**, 999–1006 (2003). https://doi.org/10.1289/ehp.8620

18. Steer, C.D., Grey, C.N.B., Alspac Study Team: Socio-demographic characteristics of UK families using pesticides and weed-killers. J. Expo. Sci. Environ. Epidemiol. **16**, 251–263 (2006). https://doi.org/10.1038/sj.jea.7500455

19. Kaplan, K.: Learning What "Wood" a Termite Prefers. https://www.ars.usda.gov/news-events/news/research-news/2015/learning-what-wood-a-termite-prefers/. Accessed 12 Nov 2015

20. Collage affordability: Working at the Minimum Wage. http://collegeaffordability.urban.org/covering-expenses/working-during-college/#/. Accessed 10 May 2016

21. Daniel, W.: How much does pest control service cost? https://homeguide.com/costs/pest-control-prices. Accessed 18 Mar 2020

22. U.S Bureau of Labor Statistics: Time use on average weekly for full time university and college students. https://www.bls.gov/tus/charts/students.htm. Accessed 20 Dec 2016

23. Delgado, M.: Social Work Practice in Nontraditional Urban Settings. Oxford University Press (1999)

24. Kazmi, S.S.: Create Community Based Mobile Apps. https://appsgeyser.com/blog/create-community-based-mobile-apps/. Accessed 8 Jul 2020

Developing User Interface Design Strategy to Improve Media Credibility of Mobile Portal News

Min-Jeong Kim[✉] [iD]

Sookmyung Women's University, Cheongpa-ro 47-gil 100, Yongsan-gu, Seoul 04310, Korea
min-jeong.kim@sookmyung.ac.kr

Abstract. According to various media phenomena appearing in Internet environment, portal news is becoming one of the most influential media in Korea. However, the media credibility of portal news is not very high compared to that of broadcast media or newspapers. Therefore, the focus of this study is to elicit insights for establishing strategies for improving the media credibility of portal news by relating the credibility of various news media and features of user groups. First, media credibility is identified through a factor analysis and user segments are obtained by a cluster analysis. Then, user interface design strategies of mobile portal news are provided according to characteristics of each group. The findings can contribute to classifying user groups by factor-specific media credibility and to suggesting design strategies for mobile portal news, depending on the features of user groups for improving media credibility.

Keywords: Mobile portal news · Media credibility · Factor analysis · Cluster analysis

1 Introduction

Journalism is undergoing a fundamental transformation, perhaps the most fundamental since the rise of the penny press of the mid-nineteenth century. In the twilight of the twentieth century and the dawn of the twenty-first, there is emerging a new form of journalism whose distinguishing qualities include ubiquitous news, global information access, instantaneous reporting, interactivity, multimedia content, and extreme content customization. At the core of transformation is the Internet. Digital technologies such as the Internet bring about not only the concept of news and media, but also structural changes such as supply and consumption of news [1].

Among the various press-related phenomena that emerged in the age of the Internet, portal news has established itself as one of the most influential journalism in Korea [2]. Portal news refers to the provision of news services through portal sites, which act as a gateway to Internet users. It differs slightly from news portals, which are the internet-enabled version of traditional news media. In portal news, the portal sites rely on other news media and news agencies for most of their news, and they retransmit the news articles of news media and news agencies. In other words, portal sites have

© Springer Nature Switzerland AG 2021
M. Kurosu (Ed.): HCII 2021, LNCS 12764, pp. 67–84, 2021.
https://doi.org/10.1007/978-3-030-78468-3_5

sufficient influence over consumers of news in the editing process, although the sites do not produce news of their own [3].

Whether portal news can be considered the news media has been a topic of debate since the beginning of news services by portal sites in Korea in the 2000s. The argument against considering portal sites as a type of news media is that they do not carry out the actual functions of the news media but instead mediate news commercially with profit-centric intentions. Furthermore, the media-related characteristics of portal sites reveal low entry barriers and communications media that involve communication and information exchange on a broad level immediately, making them fundamentally different from print media and broadcast news [4, 5]. On the contrary, the arguments put forth in favor of viewing portal sites as news media are that portal sites (a) engage in editing, one of the major functions of journalism; (b) carry out gatekeeping and agenda-setting functions while filtering and selecting news articles; and (c) influence the formation of public opinion. Hence, they can be regarded as performing the functions of journalism in Korean society [6–8].

While conflicting viewpoints exist regarding the status of portal sites as a form of news media, portal news has already become one of the influential journalism by carrying out journalistic functions through agenda setting and formation of public opinion in the process of social communication. An examination of the news utilization rates by medium revealed that the utilization rate of news through television reduced to 85.4% in 2018 from 95.2% in 2011; printed newspaper use fell by more than half, from 44.6% in 2011 to 17.7% in 2018. However, the population using the Internet via mobile devices and PCs to access news increased from 57.0% in 2011 to 82.3% in 2018; and among this population, mobile-enabled news access increased from 19.5% in 2011 to 80.8% in 2018 while PC-enabled news access dropped from 51.5% in 2011 to 31.7% in 2018 [9]. As such, there has been a decrease in the proportion of accessing news via TV, printed newspapers, and radio over the last 7 years, while the news-mediating functions of the Internet have expanded continuously, most notably, mobile news access. Furthermore, considering the high proportion of portal sites among mobile-enabled news access [10], the role of portal news has become more significant.

While an increasing number of people are using their mobile devices to access portal news in recent times, analysis has revealed that the media credibility of portal news is not very high compared to that of broadcast media or newspapers [9]. In other words, portal news users consume portal news even though its credibility is not as high as that of broadcast media or newspapers. Most of the domestic studies on portal news have focused on its legal regulation given the change in the importance of portal news. With the rising importance of portal news, there have been many studies on media credibility, similarities and differences in the credibility of various forms of media, including portal news. In addition, research on user interface design of portal news was conducted for both PC and mobile devices. However, research on user interface design in portal news has generally focused on advancing usability, and there have been hardly any studies on user interface design for improving media credibility. Therefore, this study aims to design a mobile user interface for improving the media credibility of portal news.

The objective of this study is to identify user groups based on the measurements of media credibility for various news mediums. It also aims to design the user interface of mobile portal news based on the characteristics of the identified groups. In the first phase of this study, factor analysis is used to identify common characteristics in the credibility of various news media, and the results are summarized into factor-specific media credibility. This is followed by cluster analysis, which is used to classify user groups by factor-specific media credibility. The next phase involves analyzing the demographic and social characteristics, frequency and method of portal news usage and providing user interface design strategies for each group based on the findings. Through the proposed user interface design strategies for mobile portal news, this study aims to improve the media credibility of portal news and contribute to creating a preferred user experience.

2 Background

2.1 Transformation in the Portal News Medium

With the spread of the Internet, Korean news media underwent major changes. The environment of news distribution through newspapers and broadcasting changed to digital-centric news distribution, and the existing news media companies strived to change by creating subsidiaries and engaging in online news distribution. In the 2000s, the existing news media companies began to supply news to portal sites along with their own online news distribution and thereafter failed to establish their own distribution methods, handing over the reins of news distribution to portal sites. This then led to dramatic changes in the importance of portal sites in Korea; news service users using portal sites in 2003 increased from 6.97 million in January 2003 to 10.97 million in November 2003 in the case of Naver (Korea's No.1 portal), and Daum (Korea's 2nd portal) saw an increase to 17.58 million users from 6.89 million over the same time period. Furthermore, 15 news media companies supplied news to portal sites at the beginning of the 2000s; this number then surpassed 100 in 2006, and in 2015 there were more than 200 news media distributing news through portal sites [11]. This signifies that portal sites, as platform operators, lead the online news distribution in Korea and have unparalleled influence on news media companies. Furthermore, a survey on 1,000 smartphone users aged between 20 and 60 in March 2018 to explore news utilization through portal sites confirmed that portal sites (93.3%) were the major source for news consumption. While news consumers who accessed news through terrestrial TV broadcasting and general programming channels were still significant at 81.8% and 61.6%, respectively, people accessing news through radio and print newspaper were 1.7% and 2.5%, respectively [10].

With the increasing importance of portal sites as news mediators, the Roh Moo-hyun Administration (2003–2008) began to take interest in the journalistic functions and public opinion formation functions based on portal sites. The government implicitly acknowledged that the Internet, including portal sites, functioned as the journalism in Korean society, by including the Internet in the laws and regulations governing the news media [12]. Furthermore, along with the institutionalization of regulation of the Internet through amendments in laws, the Ministry of Culture, Sports and Tourism established and announced the "Guidelines for News Use Agreement between news media and portals" to induce autonomous regulation of portal sites.

With the rising demand for the social responsibility of portal sites in Korea, the Korean Internet Self-governance Organization (KISO) has been launched as a tool for self-regulation in 2009. In 2012, three years after its launch, KISO enacted the "Autonomous regulation on the arrangement of articles of Internet news service providers" in partnership with the Korea Internet Corporations Association, to lay the foundation for improving the fairness and credibility of socially controversial Internet news [2].

2.2 Media Credibility

Studies on media credibility have been conducted in the United States since the early 1950s. The term "credibility" has been studied as two concepts: audience credibility and source credibility. Hovland and Weiss explained source credibility as a factor for enhancing communication effectiveness [13]. Gaziano and McGrath, who studied measurement the concept of credibility, showed that 12 items grouped together in a credibility factor and created newspaper and television credibility scores based on scores on the 12 items, which later formed the basic framework of research into credibility of newspapers and television news [14]. Meyer divided the 12 items of Gaziano-McGrath into 2 dimensions, which were news believability and community affiliation [15]. Among 2 dimensions, Meyer developed 5 believability indexes (fairness, bias, completeness, accuracy, and trustworthiness) to define and measure the credibility of newspapers [15], and studies that followed have since measured credibility based on Meyer's research. Starting in the late 1990s, research comparing the credibility of traditional media (newspapers, TV) and online media (Internet) was conducted; Johnson and Kaye compared Internet and traditional source on media credibility measure, and concluded that online media tended to be judged more credible than their traditional versions [16].

Media credibility research in Korea was spearheaded by the Korea Press Foundation with user surveys taken every two years since 1984 to assess overall media credibility; surveys after 2000 have since compared the credibility of newspapers, TV, and the Internet. According to the Korea Press Foundation, in 2004, credibility ranking was in the order of TV, radio, newspaper, Internet, and cable TV [17]. Recent results also indicate that the credibility of portal news is not higher than that of broadcast media and newspapers [9]. The reason for the poor credibility of portal news is because their coverage of news on politics and economics has reduced, which are traditionally considered important, to secure higher traffic through the distribution of sensational soft news on topics such as sports and entertainment [18]. Studies that measure media credibility have begun to include speed as an additional measure of credibility, along with other major items measuring media credibility with the development of new media [19, 20]; this is because, given the characteristics of online media, speed of information delivery is an important trust factor from a user's perspective.

2.3 User Interface Design of Online News

Studies on the user interface of online news services have been conducted since the late 1990s [21–24], and along with this, research on the usability of online news websites was also carried out. Generally, the standards for usability of online news websites are based on usability and web contents as defined in ISO documents such as ISO 9241-Part 11 [25].

As the use of news through smartphones and tablets is increasing, research on recommendation of news content according to personalization of interface and method of providing user interface personalization has been conducted [26]. As portal news became the dominantly used media in Korea, studies on the user interface of portal news became common: Park et al. used Focus Group Interview (FGI) in their study on the user interface of Korea's top portal news [27]; and Lee et al. comparatively analyzed the news portals of existing news media and portal news, suggesting a layout that could improve the accessibility and functionality of portal news [28]. Research on the service design of mobile portal news was conducted by evaluating news services of the two leading providers of portal news in Korea and presenting associated recommendations [29].

3 Research Method

3.1 Respondents

The data are drawn from the 2017 Survey on the Opinion of the Media Audience by Korea Press Foundation [30]. The Korea Press Foundation conducted a computer-aided personal interview (CAPI) survey using tablet PC of 5,010 citizens aged over 19 nationwide in order to establish data for media-related research. Usage behaviors and media credibility of news media based on the changes in the media environment are being investigated bi-annually since 1984 and are being surveyed every year since 2010. The 2017 Survey on the Opinion of the Media Audience covers 15 news media (regional daily newspapers, regional weekly newspapers, national newspapers, economic newspapers, news agencies, news magazines, news channels, general programming channels, terrestrial TV broadcasts, radio broadcasts, SNS, messaging services, portal news, Internet news, and websites of news media) and contains data on usage behaviors and media credibility of 15 news media and usage behaviors of portal news. In this study, 2,576 respondents who responded to the portal as a news media were first selected out of the total 5,010 respondents, and 2,084 among the 2,576 respondents were finally analyzed except those who responded 'I don't know' to a question on credibility of news media.

3.2 Analysis Method

We subdivide the finally selected 2,084 respondents by using the media credibility of 15 news media as variables. However, using 15 variables to derive cluster characteristics can lead to distribution of cluster characteristics, thus making it difficult to identify cluster-specific differentiators. Therefore, a factor analysis was conducted to reduce the number of variables through the elimination of redundancy and a cluster analysis was employed to classify the respondents into groups for the factor scores which were obtained from the factor analysis. In this way, there are studies in which factor analysis and cluster analysis are performed together for segmentation [31, 32]. These analyses in this paper were performed by SPSS. Additionally, the respondent distributions in segments (which were obtained from the two analyses) were examined in terms of socio-demographic characteristics and usage behaviors of portal news. In this section, the factor analysis and the cluster analysis for the data are described in detail.

Factor Analysis

As mentioned above, factor analysis is a method for investigating whether a number of variables of interest are linearly related to a smaller number of unobservable factors [33]. It constitutes a data analytics method that is most faithful to the principle of parsimony [34]. In this paper, factor analysis was employed for the purpose of reducing the number of variables (15 type of news media) to fewer significantly meaningful factors groups. Factor analysis was performed by evaluation of principal components and computing eigenvectors. Only the eigenvalues higher than 1 (Kaiser Criterion) [35], giving a cumulative percentage of the variance above 60%, were retained. Afterwards, the rotation of the principal components was carried out by a varimax rotation method. The results, presented as factor loadings of the rotated method enables to summarize variables into factors and to detect structures in the relationships between variables. In addition, in order to be used in the cluster analysis in the next stage, the factor scores for the respondents was calculated using the factor score coefficient obtained from the extracted factors.

Cluster Analysis

At this stage, cluster analysis was performed to classify respondent groups by factor-specific media credibility, which is summarized by multiplying media credibility of the respondents by factor score coefficient. Punj and Stewart examined several clustering methods used for marketing practices [36]. They concluded that iterative partitioning methods tended to outperform hierarchical methods, on the basis of an extensive review of numerous empirical studies. In particular, the iterative partitioning methods were widely used for a large number of data for clusters since their computational processes were faster than those of the hierarchical methods. There are a number of techniques in iterative clustering methods, but one of the most prominent is a K-means technique, which was employed as it is appropriate for our large-size data. Through this K-means technique, user segments based on the factor-specific media credibility were formed. After the segmentation, the information on influential variables such as socio-demographic factors and usage behaviors of portal news for each segment was analyzed to better characterize the segments. The results can be used in developing design strategies for mobile portal news, which could be customized for each user group.

4   Research Results

In this section, the results of applying the analytics methodology based on the respondents' survey data are summarized. The chapter begins by explaining the analysis of credibility of 15 news media from the respondents. Then, the credibility of the 15 news media was categorized into three factors through a factor analysis. Next, three segments for factor-specific media credibility was obtained through a cluster analysis with factor scores of the respondents' survey, and the user profiles and their characteristics in each segment were analyzed.

Table 1. Descriptive statistics of the raw data - mean (standard deviation).

News media	Mean (StDev)	News media	Mean (StDev)
Regional daily newspapers	3.44(0.804)	Terrestrial TV broadcasts	4.08(0.832)
Regional weekly newspapers	3.49(0.807)	Radio broadcasts	3.63(0.789)
National newspapers	3.58(0.812)	SNS	3.02(0.827)
Economic newspapers	3.64(0.841)	Messaging services	3.11(0.817)
News agencies	3.71(0.858)	Portal news	3.74(0.758)
News magazines	3.35(0.823)	Internet news	3.31(0.820)
News channels	3.99(0.791)	Websites of news media	3.38(0.838)
General programming channels	4.10(0.815)		

The basic statistics of the credibility of 15 news media are presented in Table 1. Media credibility was surveyed on a 5-point scale (1 point for Not credible at all – 5 points for Very credible), and general programming channels had the highest credibility at 4.10 points. This was followed by 4.08 points for terrestrial TV broadcasts and 3.99 for news channels, indicating high credibility for broadcasting media. In particular the credibility of terrestrial TV broadcasts is lower than that of general programming channels because the image of unfair and biased reporting has made a negative impression on viewers. Fourth on the list was portal news, with 3.74 points. This is because the survey respondents were selected only the respondents who answered the portal as a news media, and their media credibility of portal were relatively high. On the other hand, when we look at the news media with low scores, credibility of news from SNS had the lowest credibility with 3.02 points, followed by messaging services at 3.11 points, Internet news at 3.31 points, news magazine at 3.35 points, and websites of news media at 3.38 points. Among these classifications, websites of news media refer to media through which Korean news media distribute news online, and Internet newspapers refer to Internet-based online news companies that grew because of higher Internet penetration and installation of high-speed Internet [11] and both can be considered similar to news portals. The credibility of portal news is higher than that of other forms of online media such as websites of news media and Internet news because both websites of news media and Internet news supply portals with news, and thus portal news had higher credibility in terms of unbiasedness and objectivity compared to individual online news media, and it had the highest score for speed [19].

4.1 Factor Analysis of Media Credibility

As mentioned, the factor analysis aimed at categorizing the media credibility of 15 news media into fewer factors (factor-specific media credibility) based on responses for the degrees of media credibility. In this study, a principal component analysis was applied to group the 15 variables under consideration, and three major factors with eigenvalues of 1 or more were identified. The three factors accounted for 62.7% of the cumulative percentage of the variance. In general, the factors accounting for 60–70% or more of the variance can be considered to be a good fit to the data. A varimax rotation was then applied to the three factors, with 5 iterations. This procedure rotated the set of individual scores within the space defined by the principal component axes, thereby creating a new set of factor loadings for the factors that have already been found [33]. The rotated factor matrix is presented in Table 2 – in terms of factor loadings, eigenvalues, percent of variance (cumulative percent), and communality.

Table 2. Main factors underlying credibility of news media.

News media	Print media	Broadcast news	Internet	Communality
Regional daily newspapers	**0.818**	0.181		0.708
Regional weekly newspapers	**0.802**	0.197	0.153	0.705
National newspapers	**0.764**	0.192	0.157	0.646
Economic newspapers	**0.664**	0.316	0.255	0.605
News agencies	**0.510**	0.474	0.222	0.534
News magazines	**0.448**	0.420	0.358	0.505
News channels	0.187	**0.817**		0.711
General programming channels	0.139	**0.789**	0.169	0.671
Terrestrial TV broadcasts	0.274	**0.707**	0.155	0.599
Radio broadcasts	0.348	**0.587**	0.163	0.482
SNS	0.105		**0.875**	0.779
Messaging services	0.142		**0.862**	0.770
Portal news	0.183	0.359	**0.615**	0.540
Internet news	0.280	0.451	**0.540**	0.574
Websites of news media	0.419	0.407	**0.482**	0.573
Eigen value	3.367	3.252	2.793	
% of variance	22.446	21.680	18.623	
Cumulative %	22.446	44.126	62.749	

The nature of each factor was determined by the characteristics of the variables. The high loadings on the factors appear in bold font in Table 2. The first factor (Component 1) had heavy loadings for six variables (i.e., regional daily newspapers, regional weekly newspapers, nationwide newspapers, economic newspapers, news agencies, and news magazines), which were mainly related to print media. This factor was called "print media." The second factor (Component 2) was characterized by four variables (i.e., news channels, general programming channels, terrestrial TV broadcasts, and radio broadcasts) relating to broadcast news. This factor was called "broadcast news." The third factor (Component 3) centered on five variables (i.e., SNS, messaging services, portal news, Internet news, and websites of news media) for Internet. This factor was termed "Internet." As a result, we reduced media credibility of 15 news media to three factor-specific media credibility.

Table 3 shows the factor score coefficient matrix. This matrix was used to calculate the factor scores of all of the responses. As described above, the three main factors were extracted to ensure the quality of clustering instead of directly using the 15 variables. Using this matrix, the factor scores for the 2,084 respondents could be obtained and then used in forming segments.

Table 3. Factors score coefficient matrix.

News media	Print media	Broadcast news	Internet
Regional daily newspapers	0.383	−0.143	−0.107
Regional weekly newspapers	0.358	−0.143	−0.064
National newspapers	0.339	−0.136	−0.055
Economic newspapers	0.235	−0.052	−0.011
News agencies	0.110	0.091	−0.034
News magazines	0.073	0.054	0.057
News channels	−0.147	0.405	−0.117
General programming channels	−0.176	0.390	−0.064
Terrestrial TV broadcasts	−0.076	0.305	−0.076
Radio broadcasts	−0.003	0.213	−0.062
SNS	−0.080	−0.151	0.444
Messaging services	−0.067	−0.140	0.426
Portal news	−0.090	0.050	0.241
Internet news	−0.053	0.089	0.172
Websites of news media	0.044	0.033	0.129

4.2 User Segments Based on Factor-Specific Media Credibility

To obtain the factor scores, users' responses for the media credibility of 15 news media were multiplied by the factor score coefficients (see Table 3). The media credibility of three factors (i.e., print media, broadcast news, and Internet) obtained through the factor analysis were used as the input variables in a cluster analysis. A K-mean technique was employed for this analysis.

The cluster analysis with the 2084 × 3 matrix was performed for the values of the drawn factors. The analysis results for the factor scores of the respondents for media credibility are presented in Table 4. The number of clusters was set to three through a process of trial and error, taking into consideration the significance levels of the factors. The cluster centers mean are the center values of each cluster, that is, the set of the average factor scores. F tests should be used only for descriptive purposes because the clusters have been selected to maximize the differences among the clusters, and thus the significance levels cannot be used to test the hypothesis that the cluster means are different. Rather, if the observed significance level of a factor is high, it can be relatively assured that the factor does not contribute much to the separation of the clusters [37]. Because all the significance levels for the factors in Table 4 were less than .001 in case of the three clusters, the factors were meaningful in differentiating the clusters.

Table 4. Cluster analysis results.

	Final Cluster Centers			d.f	F	Sig
	1	2	3			
Print media	−.37764	−.49767	**.81813**	2	582.355	<.001
Broadcast news	**.85202**	−.99865	.07637	2	1332.119	<.001
Internet	−.50098	**−.16865**	.63995	2	321.637	<.001
Number of cases	704	656	724			

The highest score in each cluster is displayed in bold font in Table 4. For the first cluster (segment 1: 704 of 2,084 cases in total), the factor with the highest score was Broadcast news and the factor with the lowest score was Internet. Segment 1 was characterized as the group with the highest media credibility for Broadcast news factor and the lowest media credibility for Internet factor. The second cluster (segment 2: 656 cases) generally evaluated the media credibility to be low; however, contrary to segment 1, the Internet factor was considered the most credible and the Broadcast news factor the least. The third cluster (segment 3: 724 cases) was a group that evaluated the media credibility positively, unlike segment 2. This cluster was most associated with the Print media factor. These results showed the relative associations of these three factors with each segment.

4.3 User Profiles of Segments

To establish the user interface design strategies for mobile portal news that can lead to higher media credibility, it is necessary to consider the user profiles and distributions in each segment and to relate them to the factors of that segment. Table 5 presents the distribution of respondents for each segment. In this study, we have included subjective political orientation and class identification in user characteristics, and this is based on the findings that the types of media used differ according to political orientation and class identification [38].

Segment 1 had the highest concentration of individuals aged higher than 50 and with middle school or lesser level of education. Furthermore, it also had a high proportion of respondents with monthly income less than 2 million won, and a higher percentage of individuals residing in small and medium city and rural area rather than metropolitan

Table 5. User profiles of segments for media credibility.

		Segment1	Segment2	Segment3	Total
Gender	Male	372(.345)	355(.330)	350(.325)	1077
	Female	332(.330)	301(.299)	374(.371)	1007
Age	19–29	122(.269)	162(.357)	170(.374)	454
	30–39	148(.322)	147(.320)	165(.359)	460
	40–49	165(.324)	178(.349)	167(.327)	510
	50–59	159(.388)	118(.288)	133(.324)	410
	60s and above	110(.440)	51(.204)	89(.356)	250
Level of education	Middle school and below	56(43.1)	29(22.3)	45(34.6)	130
	High school diploma	274(35.0)	227(29.0)	282(36.0)	783
	University and above	374(31.9)	400(34.2)	397(33.9)	1171
Monthly income	Less than 1 million won	29(.387)	27(.360)	19(.253)	75
	1–2 million won	65(.392)	50(.301)	51(.307)	166
	200–300 million won	110(.331)	112(.337)	110(.331)	332
	3–4 million won	173(.335)	164(.317)	180(.348)	517
	4–5 million won	175(.359)	144(.296)	168(.345)	487
	5–6 million won	105(.315)	113(.339)	115(.345)	333
	More than 6 million won	47(.270)	46(.264)	81(.466)	174
Size of residential area	Metropolitan city	267(.269)	279(.281)	447(.450)	993
	Small & medium size city	366(.392)	329(.352)	239(.256)	934
	Rural area	71(.452)	48(.306)	38(.242)	157
Subjective Political orientation	Progressive	280(.332)	286(.339)	278(.329)	844
	Center	199(.334)	206(.346)	191(.320)	596
	Conservative	225(.349)	164(.255)	255(.396)	644
Subjective Class identification	Low	154(.346)	162(.364)	129(.290)	445
	Medium	440(.339)	416(.320)	442(.341)	1298
	High	110(.323)	78(.229)	153(.449)	341

city. The subjective political orientation and class identification were distributed more evenly than other segments. Segment 2 had lesser number of individuals aged above 50. It had the lowest proportion of those with high school education or below, and the highest proportion of those currently attending, or are graduates of, college. The percentage of respondents who answered that they were "conservative" was low (25.5%)

and the percentage of respondents who answered that they were "high" in subjective class identification was low (22.9%), while the percentage of respondents who answered that they were "low" was the high (36.4%). Segment 3 had a high proportion of high-income earners with more than 6 million won in monthly income (46.6%) and they were more likely to reside in metropolitan areas compared to other clusters. Furthermore, the percentage of respondents who answered their own political orientation as a conservative was high (39.6%) in this segment. Segment 3 showed high percentage of respondents (44.9%) who answered "high" and low percentage of respondents (29.0%) who answered "low" to subjective class identification.

4.4 Usage Behavior of Portal News of Segments

In addition, we analyzed the usage behavior of portal news usage by segment for user interface design of mobile portal news, which reflects the segment-specific user characteristics as derived from the cluster analysis. Table 6 shows the results of analyzing the frequency of portal news usage by segment. According to the results, 975 (46.8%) of the 2,084 respondents said they use portal news every day, while 289 (13.9%) said they do not use portal news at all. The proportion of respondents reporting that they did not use portal news at all was the highest in segment 1, and the lowest in segment 2. Those responding that they used portal news every day were similar in proportion across all segments; however, the proportion of segment 2 was comparatively higher.

Table 6. Frequency of portal news usage of segments for media credibility.

	Segment1	Segment2	Segment3	Total
Does not use at all	114(.394)	74(.256)	101(.349)	289
1–2 days	43(.323)	37(.278)	53(.398)	133
3–4 days	109(.280)	131(.337)	149(.383)	389
5–6 days	115(.386)	79(.265)	104(.349)	298
Daily	323(.331)	335(.344)	317(.325)	975

Table 7 is a table that explains a news usage method on portal sites by segment. The portal news usage methods were derived by asking the 2,084 survey respondents on how they read or watched the news on portal sites over the past week, and duplicate responses were allowed. The results pertaining to all respondents are as follows. The response that they "clicked on the news from the title or photos of the first page of portal sites" was the highest at 81.6%. This was followed by "Searched for people or incidents ranked in real-time search rankings" at 58.8%, "Utilized news related to the information I was searching for" at 55.2%, "Utilized news from categories and subjects of interest in the news homepages of portal sites" at 54.9%, "Searched for specific articles in the search bar" at 38.9%, and "Utilized news with high views and/or comments' at 35.2%.

When classifying portal news usage methods by segment, segment 1 showed the highest response rate of "Utilized news with high views and/or comments" compared

Table 7. Portal news usage methods of segments for media credibility.

	Segment1	Segment2	Segment3	Total
Clicked on the news from the title or photos of the first page of portal sites	564(.332)	551(.324)	585(.344)	1700
Searched for people or incidents ranked in real-time search rankings	394(.321)	412(.336)	420(.343)	1226
Utilized news related to the information I was searching for	376(.327)	382(.332)	393(.341)	1151
Utilized news from categories and subjects of interest in the news homepages of portal sites	357(.312)	405(.354)	382(.334)	1144
Searched for specific articles in the search bar	235(.290)	285(.352)	290(.358)	810
Utilized news with high views and/or comments	264(.360)	238(.324)	232(.316)	734
Searched for news articles from specific news media in the news homepages of portal sites	180(.283)	211(.332)	245(.385)	636
Searched the websites of specific news media websites	29(.188)	43(279)	82(.532)	154
Utilized news that I had pre-set as my preferences	15(.146)	29(.282)	59(.573)	103

to other segments, and the rate of using news through search on portal sites was low, such as "Searched for specific articles in the search bar," "Searched for news articles from specific news media in the news homepages of portal sites," and "Searched the websites of specific news media websites." Particularly, the proportion of respondents who answered that "Utilized news that I had pre-set as my preferences" was even lower. This shows that segment 1 mainly accessed news articles that have already been placed (particularly, articles with high views and comments) rather than actively using portal news. Segment 2 did not have any significantly differentiating usage methods compared to other segments; however, the users were more active compared to those in segment 1 and more passive than those in segment 3. Users in segment 3 were found to use portal news in a variety of ways. In particular, segment 3 shows the highest response rate of "Searched the websites of specific news media websites" and "Utilized news that I had pre-set as my preferences" compared to the other two segments.

5 Mobile Portal News Design Strategies

Using the user profiles and usage behavior of portal news of segments analyzed above, we could develop design strategies for mobile portal news for improved media credibility. On the basis of the results and findings above, each segment can be described in terms of user groups, design factors, and design strategies as shown in Table 8.

Since segment 1 has the highest rate of not using portal news at all, it is desirable to improve the accessibility of portal news by providing news push service at a certain time,

Table 8. Design strategies for segments.

	Segment1	Segment2	Segment3
User groups	• Highest level of credibility for broadcasting, and lowest for online • Old, low educational level, low income, and resides in small to medium cities • High proportion of those who do not use portal news at all; any usage is passive	• Low level of credibility for all media; highest for online among different media • High proportion of those in their 20 s; high educational level, high proportion of those earning 1 million won or less, subjective perception of hierarchy low • Highest proportion of those using portal news daily and lowest proportion of those that do not use portal news at all	• High credibility for all media, with highest for newspapers • High income, metropolis-residing, conservative political stance; subjective perception of hierarchy high • Active portal news users including search and setting functions
Design Factors	• Push services, including today's issues • News library by broadcast agencies • Ability to select font size	• Option to individualize topics	• News library by news agency • Option to individualize topics • Bookmarking functions for articles of interest • Sharing and blog services for selected articles
Design Strategies	From the perspective of design factors of segments • Select news library for broadcast or news agencies at the start page • News push service (as default, can be removed in news settings) • Option to individualize topics		

such as today's issue [39]. News push service exposes about three agendas with a large number of related articles to provide news notifications and provides a route to connect to portal news if user wants to see the detailed news articles. This push service, which can be set up so that the users receive alerts at a time convenient to them, can be set up in the following two modes. First is a manual mode, which is the mode that the user manually sets up in advance so that the users receive the news at a time of their preference - during breakfast, commute, prior to meetings, break-times, or prior to sleeping. Second is an automatic mode where the push service is connected to the scheduler application on the users' mobile, allowing them to receive notifications at appropriate times amid their busy schedules. Moreover, users of segment 1 answered that they trust the broadcast news factor most among media factors; therefore, the credibility of portal news of them can be improved, if video contents can be viewed directly in portal news by providing news libraries by broadcast news companies. For this service, users should be able to select, add, remove, and re-arrange their favorite broadcaster with the option to edit the broadcaster they want to subscribe to. Furthermore, it has the highest distribution of older individuals compared to other segments, and hence a font-size change function can benefit legibility.

While segment 2 has a lower degree of credibility for media itself compared to other segments, the credibility of the Internet factor is the highest for this segment among other factors. As a result, this cluster has the lowest proportion of those not using portal news at all, and the highest proportion of those using portal news daily. Therefore, providing a personalization option for topics would help improve news accessibility and legibility [26]. To provide the personalization option, users should also be given the option to edit the topic. The personalization option for topics can be selected, added, deleted, and rearranged by the user, but it can also provide the function of recommending the news topic based on the article previously read by the user [40]. Moreover, the selected topics can be used to provide users with topic-related news at a time of their preference in conjunction with the news push services.

Last, segment 3 is a group that utilizes portal news actively to the point that they utilize pre-set news settings; therefore, providing them with various functions would be reasonable. In other words, it is necessary to provide the personalization option for topics as in segment 2, and to enable users to use portal news in a variety of ways such as distinguishing articles into already read articles and later read articles through bookmarking function of interested articles [41]. Especially, for this group, functions such as bookmarking, sharing, emoticon, and comment should be provided. One of the reasons for the increase in the use of portal news services is because they can be used for other services such as search, mail, and blogging through portal sites [29]. It is considered that various interworking services are needed to be available with other services in using news services by highlighting these advantages of portal sites. Moreover, sharing and blogging functions for select articles can also be considered, allowing the portal news to act as a channel for social marketing [42]. Users of segment 3 responded that they trust the print media factor the most, and it can be recommended to provide news libraries in portal news by print media companies. Therefore, news libraries by print media companies should be provided on the initial screen, and users should be able to select, add, remove and rearrange their favorite newspaper with the option to edit the newspaper they want to subscribe to.

Finally, the initial screen of the mobile portal news is an extremely important screen that serves as gatekeepers for daily news. Therefore, two sub-parts for the initial screen is proposed: urgent breaking news part and the part that exposes the articles in the order of many related articles. Both parts are typical of mobile news representation, where selecting an article leads to another page where related articles are listed, and the users can select the article of interest from the page of related articles. The reason for exposing the articles in the order of the large number of related articles and presenting the number of related articles on the screen on the right side of the article text is because studies show that prioritizing news with a high number of comments is perceived as being focused on enjoyment and as stimuli-centric [29]. Therefore, exposing the articles according to the number of related articles demonstrates the objectivity and accuracy of news delivery.

6 Conclusion

This study used the credibility measurements of various news media to classify user groups based on media credibility and presented design strategies of user interfaces to advance the credibility of mobile portal news. Factor analysis and cluster analysis methodologies were used; for the factor analysis, the common characteristics between credibility variables by news media type were identified and cluster analysis was used to classify users based on the media credibility, by media type. This method was effective in formulating news media and classifying users based on the resulting form and identifying the characteristics of portal news usage methods by users in an environment of multiple news media.

Through factor analysis, the credibility of 15 news media could be summarized into three factors: newspaper, broadcasting, and online. Three clusters were derived using the resulting 3 factor variables as inputs for the cluster analysis. The 3 types of segmented user groups had differences in user profiles, frequency, and methodology of portal news usage, and they demonstrated that their design factors can be different by segments. User interface design strategies were proposed from design factors of segments. This design emphasized functionality to improve the media credibility as viewed by the segmented group. It was designed so that the functionality of editing news libraries by press and broadcasting agencies can take up a large proportion of the screen for the groups with high credibility for broadcasting and newspaper factors. Furthermore, a news push service was proposed for the group that used portal news in a passive manner. However, the news push service is expected to be effective for groups that actively use the portal news, given the functionalities of its linkage with scheduler apps and topic individualization.

From a methodological standpoint, this study classified the credibility of news media into several factors, conducted cluster analysis based on the factors, and provided design alternatives for mobile portal news by analyzing the usage characteristics of portal news, including the key factor characteristics and demographic characteristics. The unexpected results could not have been drawn by applying the existing demographic segmentation. For example, the results indicated that users in the same age group had different patterns of mobile portal news usage. Given this context, we could confirm that segmentation based on media credibility was effective in developing a user interface design strategy for mobile portal news.

Last, on the limitations and resulting research tasks, it is important to verify the validity of the designs of the mobile portal news screens stemming from this study. The Survey on the Opinion of the Media Audience, analyzed by this study, did not include research on the preferences for portal news layouts, making it difficult to understand the user needs on the portal news screens. Hence, a detailed analysis into the preferences for the designs presented herein can predict the likelihood of ideas in the designs that could be selected.

References

1. Pavlik, J.: Journalism and New Media. Columbia University Press (2001).
2. Bae, J.: Public accountability and self-regulation of internet portals. J. Commun. Res. **54**(4), 67–105 (2017)
3. Ahn, J.: A study on the characteristics of portal journalism: breaking news, interaction, and relative news with reference to Naver news and Yahoo media. J. Commun. Sci. **11**(1), 187–218 (2011)
4. Hur, J.: Study on the legal structure for the regulation of internet portals. J. Media Law Ethics Policy Res. **8**(2), 237–262 (2009)
5. Hwang, S.: A study on the nature of news service at the internet portal site as news delivery service provider and the liability of the portal site. J. Cybercommun. Acad. Soc. **21**, 197–232 (2007)
6. Chae, J.: Study on the viewpoint diversity of the portal sites news by a type of remediation: focused on the 18th election news. Korean J. Broadcast. Telecommun. Stud. **28**(5), 237–284 (2014)
7. Choi, M., Kim, W.: A study of the agenda setting function of news service at the web portal site: focused on the featured differences of the offered-news and the preferred-news. Korean J. Journal. Commun. Stud. **50**(4), 437–463 (2006)
8. Kim, K.: Online news diffusion and public opinion formation: a case study of controversy over Park Kyung Sin blog posting. J. Commun. Sci. **12**(4), 35–72 (2012)
9. Korea Press Foundation: Survey on the Opinion of the Media Audience. Korea Press Foundation (2018)
10. The Korea Economic Daily: https://www.hankyung.com/it/article/2018030716787. Accessed 30 Apr 2019
11. Song, H., Yang, J.: Online news portal service and changes in news distribution- big data analysis of Naver news in 2000–2017. Korean J. Journal. Commun. Stud. **61**(4), 74–109 (2017)
12. Lee, J., Sang, Y.: Establishing a proper measure of redeeming reputational damages in the portal media. J. Broadcast. Telecommun. Res. **66**, 265–296 (2008)
13. Hovland, C., Weiss, W.: The influence of source credibility on communication effectiveness. Public Opin. Q. **15**(4), 635–650 (1951)
14. Gaziano, C., McGrath, K.: Measuring the concept of credibility. Journal. Mass Commun. Q. **63**(3), 451–462 (1986)
15. Meyer, P.: Defining and measuring credibility of newspapers: developing and index. Journal. Mass Commun. Q. **65**(3), 567–574 (1988)
16. Johnson, T., Kaye, B.: Cruising is believing? Comparing internet and traditional sources on media credibility measures. Journal. Mass Commun. Q. **75**(2), 325–340 (1998)
17. Song, J.: Similarity and distinction of media credibility: a comparative analysis of audience and reporter. Korean J. Journal. Commun. Stud. **51**(2), 180–202 (2007)
18. Park, K., Ahn, J.: A study on the characteristic of the portal site's front-page: soft/hard news, sub-headline, hyperlink. Korean J. Journal. Commun. Stud. **50**(6), 199–226 (2006)
19. Ban, H., Kwon, Y.: The study of the usage correlation between portal and traditional news media. Korean J. Journal. Commun. Stud. **51**(1), 399–426 (2007)
20. Park, C.: Decomposing of news media credibility in the information age: the social goodness of news is a determinant to the publics perceived media credibility. Korean J. Broadcast. Telecommun. Stud. **15**(3), 129–154 (2001)
21. Chung, D.: Interactive features of online newspapers: identifying patterns and predicting use of engaged readers. J. Comput.-Mediat. Commun. **13**(3), 658–679 (2008)

22. Eriksson, C., Åkesson, M.: Introducing the e-newspaper – audience preferences and demands. In: Proceedings of ELPUB 2007 Conference on Electronic Publishing, pp. 65–74 (2007)

23. Li, X.: Web page design and graphic use of three U.S. newspapers. Journal. Mass Commun. Q. **75**(2), 353–365 (1998)

24. Massey, B., Levy, M.: Interactivity, online journalism, and english-language web newspapers in Asia. Journal. Mass Commun. Q. **76**(1), 138–151 (1999)

25. ISO 9241–11: Ergonomics Requirements for Office Work with Visual (VDTs) – Part 11: Guidance on Usability (1998)

26. Liu, J., Pedersen, E., Dolan, P.: Personalized news recommendation based on click behavior. In: Proceedings of the 2010 International Conference on Intelligent User Interfaces, pp. 31–40 (2010)

27. Park, S., Ryoo, H., Kim, Y.: Interface design research on news service user from domestic (Korea) Portal site-focused on the Naver news service. J. Digit. Des. **13**(4), 269–278 (2013)

28. Lee, K., Kim, Y., Kim, M.: The proposed layout of the portal site news page – focused on the lines, planes, formative principles of grid. J. Digit. Des. **16**(3), 137–146 (2016)

29. Kim, B., Kim, W.: The using case analysis of mobile news service design- use behavior centrally based on NAVER and NATE. J. Digit. Des. **13**(4), 729–737 (2013)

30. Korea Press Foundation: Survey on the Opinion of the Media Audience. Korea Press Foundation (2017)

31. Kim, M., Park, J.: Mobile phone purchase and usage behaviours of early adopter groups in Korea. Behav. Inf. Tech. **33**(7), 693–703 (2014)

32. Lee, S., Kim, M., Park, J., Shin, D.: Design strategies for idle screens of smartphones based on service usages. Hum. Factors Ergon. Manuf. Serv. Ind. **25**(4), 409–427 (2015)

33. Tryfos, P.: Method for Business Analysis and Forecasting: Text and Cases. Wiley (2005)

34. Child, D.: The Essentials of Factor Analysis. Bloomsbury Academic (2006)

35. Kaiser, H.: The application of electronic computers to factor analysis. Educ. Psychol. Measur. **20**, 141–151 (1960)

36. Punj, G., Stewart, D.: Cluster analysis in marketing research: review and suggestions for application. J. Mark. Res. **20**(2), 134–148 (1983)

37. Norušis, M.: IBM SPSS Statistics 19 Statistical Procedures Companion. Addison Wesley (2011)

38. Korea Press Foundation: Digital News Report 2017 Korea. Korea Press Foundation (2017)

39. Nielsen Norman Group: https://www.nngroup.com/articles/push-notification/. Accessed 27 May 2019

40. Oh, K., Lee, W., Lim, C., Choi, H.: Personalized news recommendation using classified keywords to capture user preference. In: Proceedings of the 16th International Conference on Advanced Communication Technology, pp. 1283–1287 (2014)

41. Flaxman, S., Goel, S., Rao, J.: Filter bubbles, echo chambers, and online news consumption. Public Opin. Q. **80**(S1), 298–320 (2016)

42. Zhao, D., Rosson, M.: How and why people twitter: the role that micro-blogging plays in informal communication at work. In: Proceedings of the ACM 2009 International Conference on Supporting Group Work, pp. 243–252 (2009)

Elderly-Centered Design: A New Numeric Typeface for Increased Legibility

Yu-Ren Lai and Hsi-Jen Chen[(✉)]

National Cheng Kung University, Tainan City 701, Taiwan
hsijen_chen@mail.ncku.edu.tw

Abstract. This study focuses on senior citizens as the target group for font design. It sets the field in the visual display terminal (VDT) operating environment. By referring to the existing literature and research results, we not only find the current fonts with better legibility but also understand the visual problems faced by senior citizens and what is suitable for In addition to finding the existing fonts with better legibility, we know the visual difficulties faced by the elderly and what is the appropriate graphic design for the elderly and explore the relevant criteria of font design in depth. Then, through experiments to find similar numerical combinations and computer simulations of older people's reading conditions, the strengths and weaknesses of existing fonts in mild and severe cataract environments were identified, and the elements of font design were analyzed and investigated. Finally, we hope to design an Arabic numeral font suitable for senior citizens and evaluate it through an actual operation.

Keywords: Elderly-centered design · Legibility · Typeface

1 Introduction

In an aging society, designing for the elderly is imperative. They are an oft-neglected and influential social group [1], as aging is an inevitable process in life. In other words, an in-depth study of the elderly is not only for them but also for us.

Reading plays an essential role in daily life. As people age, their information processing speed and efficiency in reading declines. Research has revealed that when reading text composed of very small or substantial characters, the elderly's reading speeds drop to about 70% of a young adult's [2].

Many scholars have researched the impact of text size and kerning on elderly reading ability. Pirkl (1988) stated that the larger the visual display, the better the optical performance of the elderly [3]. However, they added that overly large text size would reduce the amount of information obtained and inhibit visual performance [4]. Vanderplas and Vanderplas (1980) found that 12–14 point text size is better for the elderly [5]. Bernard et al. (2001) also suggested that the elderly use a 14-point text size [6].

In contrast, few scholars are researching the impact of typeface on elderly reading ability. This research project hopes to remedy that and conduct new typeface research. Due to time and study constraints, we will focus on Arabic numeral typefaces under the

© Springer Nature Switzerland AG 2021
M. Kurosu (Ed.): HCII 2021, LNCS 12764, pp. 85–96, 2021.
https://doi.org/10.1007/978-3-030-78468-3_6

VDT operation and design an Arabic numeral typeface that increases reading speed and efficiency for the elderly.

2 Literature review

With aging, five dimensions of human vision decline: visual processing speed, light sensitivity, dynamic vision, myopia, and visual search [7], and the spatial and temporal visible nerves associated with optics deteriorate, resulting in reduced reading speed [8], and not only in visual, auditory, and mental abilities but also in motor reaction time [9]. The present study is more relevant to the visible deterioration of the elderly and therefore focuses on the optical characteristics of the elderly and discusses the related problems faced by the elderly when reading.

2.1 The Vision of the Elderly

Visual Attention
A study examining whether some of the cognitive deficits associated with aging may be related to limited visual attention span showed that in trials with consistent display sizes, older subjects performed better on smaller display sizes, whereas younger subjects performed equally well on both measures; furthermore, older adults found it easier to shift from a large to a small area than to maintain attention in a large extent, and older subjects preferred to focus on a smaller spatial size compared to younger subjects [10]. Also, older adults find it easier to shift from a large to a small area than to maintain attention to a large extent, and older adults prefer to focus their attention on smaller spatial areas than younger adults [10]; therefore, given the visual characteristics of older adults, the display area should be minimized.

Reduced Reading Speed
The degree of crowding that does not recognize cluttered text is thought to affect reading speed. Compared to younger individuals, older adults read significantly slower, with more significant crowding and a reduced visual field, and crowding increases with age; age-related changes in crowding may partially explain the slower reading speed of older adults [11].

Environmental Illumination
The interaction between ambient illuminance and the type and age of the electronic display has a significant effect on users' visual performance. When using Ch-LC displays, elderly participants have significantly better visual understanding at ambient illuminance levels higher than 1500 lx than other illuminance settings. In contrast, illumination levels of 50 and 6000 lx appear to harm visual performance when older adults use conventional transmissive LCDs, suggesting that either too intense weak ambient illumination can harm older adults when using electronic displays [12]. In other studies, it has been shown that the ambient luminance around computer monitors is lower than that of younger people in situations where the illumination may reduce the visibility of the monitor (glare disability) and cause discomfort (uncomfortable glare) [11].

2.2 Collation of Font-Related Literature

Visibility, Legibility, and Readability

According to Sanders and McCormick (1993), three human factors, namely visibility, legibility, and readability, are used to evaluate font layout and font size in text design. Visibility, also known as visibility, refers to the property of properly separating words or symbols from the background; legibility, also known as legibility, refers to the property of being able to distinguish between words or symbols separated from the environment, depending on the form of the character, the thickness of the strokes, contrast, etc.; readability Readability, also known as comprehensibility, refers to the property of information content that can be understood or recognized by people, and is affected by words, grouping, line spacing, and surrounding white space [13].

Comparing Serif and Non-Serif Fonts

The effect of serifs and non-serifs on reading has been debated, with some studies suggesting that serif fonts have a positive impact on reading efficiency, others holding the opposite view, and some indicating that they do not affect text reading speed and comprehension [14]. It can be seen that the positive impact of serifs depends on the context of reading, text, case, original font, and spacing.

Arditi and Cho (2005) used lowercase fonts that varied in serif size (0%, 5%, and 10% maximum height) to assess legibility. The results show that 5% of serif fonts are more legible than non-serif fonts. Still, serifs may produce less legibility when the spacing between serif letters increases or when the text is smaller or further away. The study concludes by emphasizing that legibility does not vary between fonts but is affected by serifs' presence or absence [15].

Non-serif fonts are less suitable for reading in dense text. Still, they are ideal for situations where text is immediately legible and is often used in abrupt or brief places, such as advertising signage, headlines, or notes. Studies have shown that non-serif fonts improve various reading metrics such as speed of reading scientific abstracts [16].

The Effect of Font Type and Font Size

Pirkle and Babic (1988) showed that the larger the visual display, the better the visual performance of the elderly [3], but too large a font size reduces the amount of information obtained and reduces visual performance [4].

Kingery and Furuta (1997) experimented with four factors: font type (Times New Roman, Arial Book, Antiqua, and Century Gothic), font size (14, 20, 24), screen resolution (640*480, 1024*768), and display size (14″ and 19″) on legibility. The legibility experiment results on the effect of display size (14″ and 19″) showed that Times New Roman and Arial fonts had the best legibility. All the factors considered in the study interacted with each other, and the best visual performance for the 14″ display was found at 20 dots, while the poor performance at 14 dots was attributed to the fact that the font size was too small for the subjects to distinguish between the letters. The authors attribute the poor performance at 24 points because the letters occupy too much surface space and the eye gets too little information during each gaze [4].

Sheedy, Subbaram, Zimmerman, and Hayes (2005) used a threshold size approach to determine the effect of font design and electronic display parameters on text legibility. Six fonts, three smooth fonts, four font sizes, and a combination of 10-pixel heights were used to measure participants' visual acuity (the reciprocal of the minimum detected size, representing the threshold legibility in each case) and four-stroke widths using both upper and lower case letters. The results show that single letters play a prominent role in threshold word recognition, while word shapes play a more minor role. Pixel height, font, stroke width, and font smoothness have a significant impact on threshold legibility. The best clarity is obtained at 9 pixels (10 points), Verdana and Arial being the most explicit fonts, and Times New Roman and Franklin is the least clear. Sub-pixel rendering (ClearType(TM)) improves some fonts' threshold legibility and is the most legible condition when used in conjunction with Verdana. The increased stroke width (bold) improves threshold legibility, but only at the narrowest width tested [11].

3   Materials and Methods

3.1   VDT Workstation settings

An environmental illumination of 500lx is most suitable for the elderly when reading VDT. The stimulus will be displayed on an iPad Air 2020 10.9 inches with a resolution of 2360×1640 pixels. Kroemer and Grandjean (1997) suggested that the proper viewing distance for VDT should be 70 cm [2], while Hennings and Ye (1996) found that most people prefer to be slightly more than 60 cm [18]. By current ISO guidelines and the studies mentioned above, participants will view the monitor at a distance of approximately 70 cm [19].

3.2   Participants

To alleviate the burden our research poses on the elderly, the first experiment will invite 30 young adults under 60 with normal or corrected vision. The second experiment will invite 30 elderly participants between 60 to 80 years old who use visual terminal displays such as tablets.

3.3   Stimulus

Text size varies depending on the hardware and software settings of the VDT operation, so visual angle will be used to assess the extent.

$$VA = (3438 * H)/D \tag{1}$$

In this equation, VA is the visual angle in minutes, H is the text height, and D is the viewing distance. Sanders and McCormick (1993) suggested that the optimal text size in a VDT operation is $20'$ to $22'$ [13]. According to the ANSI/HFS-100 standard, the minimum text size should be $16'$ and suitable text size is between $20'$ to $22'$ [20].

Regarding typeface, a study by Kingery and Furuta (1997) shows that Times New Roman and Arial have the best legibility [4]. Tullis, Boynton, and Hersh (1995) posited that Arial and MS Saris have better readability [21]. Readability research also commonly uses the Helvetica typeface. When designing the typeface, we refer to the three human factors indicators proposed by Sanders and McCormick (1993), visibility, legibility, readability [13].

For our research, all stimuli are presented in the center of the screen. Three Arabic numerals with a $20'$ VA will be displayed in 0.05 s with masking of 0.02 s.

3.4   Procedure

This experiment is divided into two stages.

In the first stage, the similarity matrix is used to compare the similarity between the two numbers, and then cluster analysis is used to filter out similar and dissimilar groups of numbers.

In the second stage, the two sets of similar and dissimilar numbers were combined into 44 columns, and two fonts that had been shown to have better legibility in the previous study: Verdana and Arial, with Gaussian blur 8px and 10px, respectively, were used to simulate mild and severe cataracts for the young subjects to compare the best legibility performance (see **Error! Reference source not found.**) (Figs. 1 and 2).

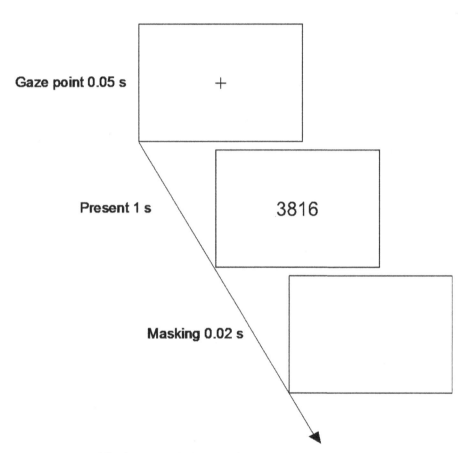

Fig. 1. Schematic diagram of the experimental procedure

Fig. 2. Schematic diagram of computer simulation of weakened vision of the elderly

4 Results

4.1 Similarity Matrix and Cluster Analysis

The similarity matrix was used to compare two numbers, from zero to one, zero to two, zero to three, and so on, to eight to nine. A table was obtained with the total score of each combination of numbers. Then three clusters of numbers were found by cluster analysis, namely, most similar, average, and least similar (see Fig. 3). We found that the numbers 38, 68, 09, and 89 were the most identical number combinations, and then we discovered an order problem in the number combinations. Then we did a simple experiment and found that the numbers were more similar when the open space was inward, i.e., less easily distinguishable (Fig. 4).

4.2 Typeface Experiment

Then we extracted the most similar eleven sets of numerical combinations randomly with the minor similar numerical combinations to form a group of four numerical combinations to start a series, and choose the best legibility font in the past literature: Arial and Verdana, and use Gaussian blur 8px and 10px to simulate the field of vision of mild and severe cataract patients, a total of 44 series to young people aged 19–21 years old to test, to determine the response time.

From the experimental results, we found that both Arial and Verdana have longer reaction times in the Gaussian blurred 10px environment, in the simulated field of severe cataract patients, with an average of 1.6 s and 1.5 s, respectively. The response time of Arial was even longer (1.52 s) than that of Verdana (1.51 s) in the Gaussian blur of 8 px (Tables 1 and 2).

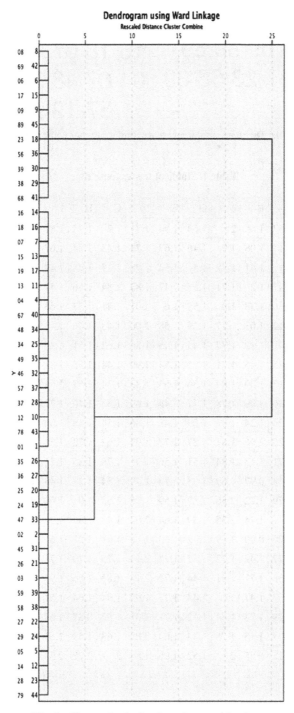

Fig. 3. Cluster Analysis of number combinations

Most Similar   Least Similar

38 68 09 89 69   16 18 07 13 19 15
08 06 17 23 56 39 04 67 48 34 49 46
                    57 12 78 01

Fig. 4. The most similar and least similar number combinations

Table 1. Table of the response time

A	B	c	D	E	F	G	H	I	J
1.57	1.66	2	1.64	1.94	1.71	1.7	1.72	1.81	1.66
1.1	1.08	1.9	1.46	1.67	1.74	1.43	1.54	1.67	1.38
1.1	1.41	1.82	1.5	1.54	1.78	1.25	1.74	1.47	1.23
1.47	1.2	1.71	1.53	1.47	1.83	1.34	1.56	1.57	1.37
1.36	1.38	1.9	1.55	1.6	2.01	1.41	1.53	1.63	1.39
1.12	1.03	1.77	1.29	1.58	2.06	1.43	1.46	1.48	1.59
0.9	1.15	1.77	1.45	1.45	1.86	1.62	1.51	1.46	1.11
1.23	1.45	1.71	1.25	1.54	1.99	1.44	1.52	1.81	1.27
1.13	1.29	1.84	1.56	1.53	1.83	1.34	1.57	1.61	1.54
0.86	1.09	1.78	1.47	1.48	1.69	1.53	1.46	1.77	1.44
1.24	1.24	1.8	1.59	1.48	1.86	1.54	1.48	1.56	1.67
1.23	1.06	1.81	1.27	1.77	1.97	1.62	1.72	1.22	1.45
1.71	1.13	1.84	1.51	1.56	1.91	1.78	1.35	1.21	1.41
1.43	0.97	1.69	1.33	1.72	1.79	1.34	1.27	1.48	1.42
1.79	1.22	2.56	1.57	1.59	1.95	1.63	1.91	1.68	2.31
1.17	1.44	2.35	1.39	1.64	2.03	1.43	1.3	1.96	1.58
1.26	0.99	1.69	1.32	1.63	1.88	1.43	1.27	1.6	1.21
1.77	1.42	1.72	1.37	1.75	2.13	1.75	1.79	1.74	1.72
1.38	1.71	1.81	1.44	1.72	2.19	1.83	1.56	1.94	2.2
1.57	1.47	1.63	1.44	1.77	1.92	1.94	1.64	1.51	1.45
1.29	1.23	1.64	1.62	1.71	2.01	1.52	0.57	1.64	1.83
1.37	1.45	1.73	1.43	1.63	2.08	1.63	1.59	1.61	1.64
1.18	0.85	2.1	1.52	1.95	1.84	2	2.72	2.23	1.42

(continued)

Table 1. (*continued*)

A	B	c	D	E	F	G	H	I	J
1.22	1.33	1.68	1.48	1.66	1.68	1.6	1.71	1.65	1.5
1.07	1.75	1.59	1.38	1.55	1.84	1.59	1.51	1.74	1.38
1.35	1.29	1.62	1.24	1.73	1.83	1.68	1.6	1.51	1.39
1.21	1.84	1.73	1.39	1.57	2	1.67	1.46	1.67	1.32
1.24	1.31	1.59	1.41	1.4	1.89	1.6	1.5	1.58	1.29
1.18	1.31	1.56	1.37	1.62	1.96	1.57	1.54	1.55	1.01
0.99	1.34	1.51	1.31	1.48	1.79	1.54	2.01	1.58	1.46
1.14	1.22	1.47	1.26	1.33	1.67	1.58	1.4	1.57	1.19
1.33	1.16	1.42	1.18	1.39	1.72	1.48	1.47	1.43	1.03
1.11	1.22	2.09	1.3	1.54	1.75	1.64	1.47	1.64	1.4
1.08	1.55	1.55	1.38	1.44	1.88	1.55	1.41	1.55	1.28
0.87	0.93	1.58	1.42	1.42	1.95	1.55	1.31	1.63	1.01
1.21	1.07	1.73	1.32	1.36	1.9	2.27	1.18	1.47	1.42
1.4	1.14	1.58	1.3	1.56	1.95	1.6	1.22	1.4	1.48
1.82	1.4	1.53	1.38	1.45	1.83	1.7	1.36	1.51	1.37
1.27	1.27	1.63	1.4	1.76	1.85	1.49	1.54	1.41	1.71
1.67	1.42	1.49	1.36	1.65	1.81	1.5	1.65	1.66	1.36
1.26	1.25	1.61	1.25	1.45	2.04	1.46	1.37	1.42	1.34
1.3	1.37	1.52	1.3	2.14	2.01	1.56	1.44	1.52	1.58
1.17	1.17	1.63	1.54	1.77	1.92	1.5	1.87	1.74	1.35
1.31	2.43	1.49	1.39	1.69	1.93	1.61	1.54	1.3	1.16

Table 2. Typeface and average reaction times

Typeface	Gaussian blur	Average reaction times (s)
Arial	8px	1.52
	10px	1.60
Vendana	8px	1.50
	10px	1.51

5 Discussion

In the next chapter, I will discuss Arabic numerals' characteristics and Arial and Verdana's font characteristics based on the experimental results to find out the design elements that may enhance legibility and help us have some direction when we do font design in the future.

5.1 Characteristics of Arabic Numerals

After analyzing the similarity matrix and clusters, we found that Arabic numerals with symmetric circular features are similar in length, such as 0, 3, 6, 8, 9, etc. Also, 1 and 7 are very similar, especially in some serifs. However, numbers with circular features are not easily confused with numbers with straight features like 1 and 7, which are very unlike each other. The number 4 is exceptional in that it is not very similar to any different number.

5.2 Characteristics of Arial and Verdana Typeface

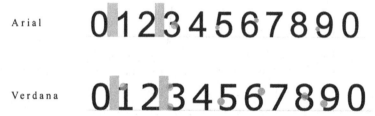

Fig. 5. Characteristics of Arial and Verdana

We found that the Arial font's reaction time was much longer than that for the Verdana font. After the experiment, we carefully compared the two fonts, Arial and Verdana. We found that the opening space of Arial is smaller than that of Verdana, which may be one of the reasons for its better legibility. Besides, Verdana's characters are more comprehensive, and the amplitude space is more significant, reducing blurring or preventing the visual perception of letters from being mixed. If we look more closely, we can see that Verdana retains some of the characteristics of serif fonts, such as the middle of the 3 is not vertical, and the middle of the 8 has two interlaced circular shapes (Fig. 5).

From the experiment results, it can be judged that if we want to carry out typeface design in the future, we should refer to the font characteristics of Verdana and use it as a starting point to explore more deeply, which will provide more legibility for senior citizens.

6 Conclusion

This research explores the problems when the elderly read existing Arabic numeral typefaces. We realized the critical point of typeface design to increase legibility through our research, and we will design an Arabic numeral typeface in response to these issues. We hope that this numerical typeface can be expanded into a complete set of English typefaces in the future with further research.

References

1. Design for the Real World: Making to Measure.
2. Akutsu, H., Legge, G., Ross, J., Schuebel, K.: Psychophysics of reading—X. Effects of age-related changes in vision. J. Gerontol. **46**, 325–331 (1991). https://doi.org/10.1093/geronj/46.6.P325
3. Pirkl, J.J.: Guidelines and Strategies for Designing Transgenerational Products: An Instructor's Manual (1996)
4. Kingery, D., Furuta, R.: Skimming electronic newspaper headlines: a study of typeface, point size, screen resolution, and monitor size. Inf. Process. Manag. **33**, 685–696 (1997). https://doi.org/10.1016/S0306-4573(97)00025-3
5. Vanderplas, J.M., Vanderplas, J.H.: Some factors affecting legibility of printed materials for older adults. Percept. Mot. Skills **50**, 923–932 (1980). https://doi.org/10.2466/pms.1980.50.3.923
6. Bernard, M., Liao, C.H., Mills, M.: The effects of font type and size on the legibility and reading time of online text by older adults. In: Proceedings of ACM CHI 2001, vol. II, pp. 175–176. ACM Press (2001)
7. Kosnik, W., Winslow, L., Kline, D., Rasinski, K., Sekuler, R.: Visual changes in daily life throughout adulthood. J. Gerontol. **43**, P63–P70 (1988). https://doi.org/10.1093/geronj/43.3.P63
8. Brussee, T., Van Den Berg, T.J., Van Nispen, R.M., Van Rens, G.H.: Associations between spatial and temporal contrast sensitivity and reading. Optom.Vis. Sci. **94**, 329–338 (2017). https://doi.org/10.1097/opx.0000000000001030
9. Pelosi, L., Blumhardt, L.D.: Effects of age on working memory: an event-related potential study. Cogn. Brain Res. **7**, 321–334 (1999). https://doi.org/10.1016/S0926-6410(98)00035-4
10. Kosslyn, S.M., Brown, H.D., Dror, I.E.: Aging and the scope of visual attention. Gerontology **45**, 102–109 (1999). https://doi.org/10.1159/000022071
11. Sheedy, J.E., Smith, R., Hayes, J.: Visual effects of the luminance surrounding a computer display. Ergonomics. **48**, 1114–1128 (2005). https://doi.org/10.1080/00140130500208414
12. Wang, A.-H., Hwang, S.-L., Kuo, H.-T., Jeng, S.-C.: Effects of ambient illuminance and electronic displays on users' visual performance for young and elderly users. J. Soc. Inf. Disp. 18 (2010). https://doi.org/10.1889/JSID18.9.629
13. Sanders, M.S., McCormick, E.J.: Human Factors In Engineering and Design. McGraw Hill Education, New York (1993)
14. Akhmadeeva, L., Tukhvatullin, I., Veytsman, B.: Do serifs help in comprehension of printed text? an experiment with Cyrillic readers. Vis. Res. **65**, 21–24 (2012). https://doi.org/10.1016/j.visres.2012.05.013
15. Arditi, A., Cho, J.: Serifs and font legibility. Vis. Res. **45**, 2926–2933 (2005). https://doi.org/10.1016/j.visres.2005.06.013
16. A matter of font type: the effect of serifs on the evaluation of scientific abstracts – PubMed. https://pubmed.ncbi.nlm.nih.gov/25704872/. Accessed 27 March 2021
17. Grandjean, E., Kroemer, K.H.: Fitting The Task To The Human: A Textbook Of Occupational Ergonomics, 5th edn. Taylor and Francis, London (1997)
18. Hennings, L.K., Ye, N.: Interaction of screen distances, screen letter heights and source document distances. Interact. Comput. **8**, 311–322 (1996). https://doi.org/10.1016/S0953-5438(97)83776-9

19. 14:00-17:00: ISO 15008:2009. https://www.iso.org/cms/render/live/en/sites/isoorg/contents/data/standard/05/08/50805.html. Accessed 22 October 2020
20. American National Standard for Human Factors Engineering of Visual Display Terminal Workstations (1988)
21. Tullis, T.S., Boynton, J.L., Hersh, H.: Readability of fonts in the windows environment. In: Conference Companion on Human Factors in Computing Systems, pp. 127–128. Association for Computing Machinery, New York (1995). https://doi.org/10.1145/223355.223463

Research on Interactive Experience Design of Peripheral Visual Interface of Autonomous Vehicle

Zehua Li[(✉)], Xiang Li, JiHong Zhang, Zhixin Wu, and Qianwen Chen

Nanjing University of Science and Technology, Nanjing 210094, China

Abstract. With the continuous development of intelligent technology, the technology of autonomous vehicles has matured day by day, and many manufacturers are carrying out batch experiments and production of real cars. In order to improve the safety of autonomous vehicles and interactive experience, will the existing autonomous vehicles peripheral visual interface interactive experience design research. First of all, starting from literature research and case analysis, research and analysis of the external visual interface interactive experience of UISEE autonomous driving "urban mobile box", Volkswagen unmanned driving car Sedric, Hong Qi smart minibus, and SEMCON smiling concept car Design, and then analyze and refine the hardware equipment and visual elements based on the peripheral visual interface design of these models, design the experimental plan to study the cognitive efficiency and psychological comfort of the peripheral visual interface, and analyze the experimental data to summarize the peripheral visual interface The design focus of visual elements to improve the safety and interactive experience of autonomous vehicles. The research and practice of this paper provide a more feasible theoretical reference for the design of the external visual interface interactive experience of autonomous vehicles.

Keywords: Autonomous vehicle · Interaction design · Human-machine interface · Interaction experience

1 The Current Status of the Edge Visualization Interface of Autonomous Vehicles

1.1 Research Background

With the continuous development of smart technology, the technology of Autonomous Vehicle has become more mature. After Google, Tesla and other companies first introduced self-driving systems, established automakers such as BMW, Mercedes and Audi have also joined the self-driving the system came to the camp and conducted a series of real vehicle tests. Autonomous driving technology has made great breakthroughs whether it is in the algorithm research to deal with complex scenarios or in the testing of enterprise actual vehicle projects, and the commercialization of autonomous vehicles is gradually accelerating.

© Springer Nature Switzerland AG 2021
M. Kurosu (Ed.): HCII 2021, LNCS 12764, pp. 97–107, 2021.
https://doi.org/10.1007/978-3-030-78468-3_7

After road users enter the public road network, they begin to exchange information continuously with the traffic environment and other road users in the same environment to deal with different emergencies. Human drivers use various formal methods to exchange information with other road users when driving vehicles, such as whistle, turn signal lights, brake lights, emergency double flashing lights, etc. In addition to these formal methods, many informal methods are used to exchange information with other road users, such as eye contact, facial expressions, and gestures. These formal and informal methods have played an important role in transportation tasks.

In the US SAE-J3016 self-driving level, autonomous vehicles are divided into six levels L0-L5, and fully autonomous vehicles are L5, which is the fifth level of autonomous vehicles. This level of autonomous vehicles can automatically drive through the vehicle's own automatic driving system combined with hardware, and can intelligently perform all the operations of the human driver, including dealing with various complex road scenarios. With the use of autonomous vehicles, in addition to setting the destination navigation before traveling, the entire driving task does not require a human driver or passenger to control the vehicle, which in a real sense liberates the operation of the human driver and can fully devote attention to work and entertainment Waiting for non-driving tasks. Based on this situation, autonomous vehicles can only communicate information with road users through formal methods when performing driving tasks, and traditional informal methods will disappear. This change will have a huge impact on the most vulnerable pedestrians among road users. In most cases, pedestrians exchange information with human drivers through informal methods to ensure the safety of crossing the road, such as gestures and eye contact. Therefore, the emergence of autonomous vehicles in the road network will challenge the comfort of pedestrians and create a trust problem. Therefore, it is very necessary to find a way for pedestrians to interact with autonomous vehicles, let pedestrians understand the expected behavior of autonomous vehicles, and improve the tolerance of autonomous vehicles and traffic safety. The latest solution at this stage is to equip the periphery of the autonomous vehicle with a visual interface. The autonomous vehicle transmits important driving information to the pedestrians on the road through the visual interface of the periphery of the car. Pedestrians recognize and judge the information displayed on the peripheral visual interface. Understand the expected behavior of the autonomous vehicle, and then perform the corresponding actions. Therefore, the peripheral visual interface is an important medium for the communication activities between autonomous vehicles and pedestrians, and it is of great significance to conduct research on the interactive experience design of the peripheral visual interface.

1.2 Current Theoretical Research

For the interactive experience design of the external visual interface of autonomous vehicles, there have been preliminary research results in the world. The purpose is to optimize the communication activities between people and autonomous vehicles to reduce the occurrence of traffic accidents. At present, the research in this direction mainly starts from the theoretical level, and conducts research and practice in the two dimensions of pedestrians and cars.

Research from the perspective of pedestrians, Including pedestrian behavior, perception psychology, etc. For example, Shuchisnigdha Deb et al. studied the influence of the design of the peripheral visual interface of autonomous vehicles on the safety of pedestrians when crossing the road and the psychological comfort; Yeti Li et al. Perceived urgency of different types of interface interaction design.

Research starting from the dimension of the car, Including the image of the car's interface design, the technology used, etc., for example, Lex Fridman and others provided the subjects with the form of related images, and found that the subjects were cognitive efficiency of different types of autonomous vehicle interface design; Lagstrom et al. studied the use of the LED display to indicate the mode of the vehicle in different states, such as the LED display making a gradual motion toward the center to indicate the vehicle's start; The concept car of the Swedish car company SEMCON added a "smile" pattern to the interface; Zhang et al. found that when a human driver is driving a vehicle, it is easy to associate green with a driving autonomous car, while red is the opposite.

1.3 Application Experiment Status

Four typical cases are selected from the existing autonomous vehicles for analysis. The interface interaction design integrates many elements, which is of great reference value. UISEE autonomous driving "urban mobile box", Volkswagen's autonomous vehicle Sedric, Hong Qi smart minibus, SEMCON The Smiling Car of Sweden.

UISEE Autonomous Driving "Urban Mobile Box": The interface consists of a smart display on the rear windshield of the car and an LED light strip on the roof; the smart display can show the running state of the vehicle, and the light strip can also be used with the smart display Show the same color, using a combination of image and light; the colors are red, green, white, and cyan (Fig. 1).

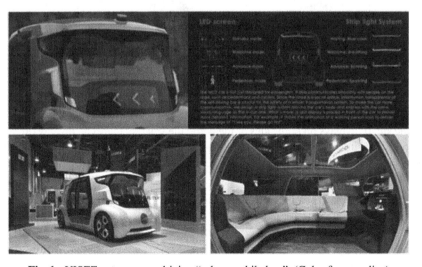

Fig. 1. UISEE autonomous driving "urban mobile box". (Color figure online)

Volkswagen autonomous vehicle Sedric: The interface consists of the rear windshield of the car and multiple smart displays on both sides of the body; the smart display can display different text and image information, and can send different types of signal information; the colors are white and Mainly blue (Fig. 2).

Fig. 2. Volkswagen autonomous vehicle Sedric. (Color figure online)

Hong Qi Smart Minibus: The interface is composed of the rear windshield of the car and multiple smart displays on both sides of the body; the smart display can display different text and image information, and the smart displays on both sides of the body can play videos such as advertisements and colors. Mainly red and blue (Fig. 3).

Fig. 3. Hong Qi Smart Minibus. (Color figure online)

SEMCON The Smiling Car, Sweden: The interface is placed on the front radiator grille and consists of a smart display that can transmit two driving modes: normal driving, slowing down and yielding, and an anthropomorphic smiling image; the color is white (Fig. 4).

Fig. 4. SEMCON The Smiling Car, Sweden.

2   Analysis of the Interface Design Composition of Autonomous Vehicles

From the analysis of the above four cases, it can be concluded that the interactive design of the peripheral visual interface of autonomous vehicles is mainly composed of hardware equipment and visual elements. The hardware equipment includes position and technology; the visual elements include text, images, and colors.

2.1   Hardware Devices

Position. At present, the peripheral visual interfaces of autonomous vehicles are mainly located on the front windshield, rear windshield, sides of the body and the door positions. For example, UISEE autonomous driving "urban mobile box" places the peripheral visual interface on the rear windshield of the car. Hong Qi smart minibuses place the peripheral visual interface on the smart display under the front windshield of the car and on the side of the car body.

Technology. At present, the peripheral visual interfaces of autonomous vehicles are extremely technological, using many high technologies. For example, the front and rear windshields of Volkswagen's autonomous vehicle Sedric and the side of the Hong Qi smart minibus use smart displays for information exchange.

2.2   Visual Elements

Text. At present, the peripheral visual interface of autonomous vehicles is used for information transmission. For example, the Hong Qi smart minibus displays its company slogan "Red Flag Let Ideal Fly", and also uses words such as "Please pass" and "Starting" when the car is driving.

Image. At present, the peripheral visual interface of autonomous vehicles displays common public transportation system logos. At the same time, it has also developed images of its company characteristics. For example, in the peripheral visual interface of UISEE autonomous driving "urban mobile box", "standby mode" is designed, "Welcome mode", "advance mode", "pedestrian mode".

Color. At present, the peripheral visual interface of autonomous vehicles uses many colors, such as red, green, blue, yellow, white, etc. Most peripheral visual interface designs use red and green in the public transportation system, and some use new colors. For example, the peripheral visual interface of UISEE autonomous driving "Urban Mobile Box" uses cyan-blue to represent its young and technological characteristics.

3   Research on Cognitive Efficiency and Psychological Comfort of Peripheral Visual Interface

3.1   Experimental Design

Using eye tracking technology and Likert scale method to design an experimental study to test the cognitive efficiency and psychological comfort of different peripheral visual interface design schemes of autonomous vehicles, and find the optimal design scheme. The data collection is divided into two groups: eye tracking technology-collecting pedestrian cognitive efficiency data, and Likert scale method-collecting pedestrian psychological comfort score data.

3.2   Participant

Fifty graduate students from Nanjing University of Science and Technology participated in this experimental study, and 50 valid subjects (25 males, 25 females). They are in good physical condition, with normal vision, no astigmatism and color blindness, and able to walk at a normal pace and gait. They are between 20 and 23 years old, with an average age of 21.5 years.

3.3   Experimental Site and Equipment

This experiment was carried out in the laboratory of the School of Design, Art and Media, Nanjing University of Science and Technology. The experimental equipment used in the experiment was a Tobii T120 eye tracker and a Lenovo laptop. The analysis and reporting platform of the experiment was the supporting Tobii Studio software.

3.4   Experimental Materials and Procedures

Using the visual component text information, image information, and color information of the peripheral visual interface of autonomous vehicles, the elements were combined, and 6 peripheral visual interface experimental materials were designed to test the optimal scheme for cognitive efficiency and psychological comfort. Among them, the color uses the red and green in the traditional public transportation system, and the blue in the visual interface of the existing autonomous vehicle; the image uses the graphics of "pedestrian" and "zebra crossing"; the text uses simple text "go". Then superimpose this visual information on the peripheral visual interface of the "Hong Qi Smart Minibus" and place it on the crosswalk waiting for the red light to determine the experimental scenario.

Before the start of the experiment, the participants were explained to the participants the instructions and procedures of the experiment, and invited to fill in the informed consent form and the basic situation survey form. The whole experiment process was quiet, and the subjects were done independently.

(1). Instruct the subjects to sit within an effective distance range of about 60–70 cm before the test screen, maintain a comfortable sitting posture, and adjust the horizontal eye position to be the same height as the screen.

(2). The five-point method is used to calibrate the sight line of the subjects to ensure that the visual accuracy of each subject is within the range of 1.0° in both the horizontal and vertical directions.

(3). The experiment is officially started: the computer screen will play the image of the autonomous vehicle parked at the crosswalk. You need to simulate and imagine that you are preparing to pass the crosswalk. Then, based on the information displayed on the visual interface of the autonomous vehicle, you can judge whether you can safely pass the crosswalk. During the whole process, the dominant hand is required to always hold the mouse lightly to facilitate quick response.

(4). After the 6 experimental materials have been played, score the psychological comfort of these 6 experimental materials. The scoring method is based on the Likert scale method: 5 points are very comfortable, 4 points are comfortable, 3 points are fair, and 2 points are not comfortable 1 point is very uncomfortable, and finally ends the experiment (Fig. 5).

Fig. 5. Experimental materials. (Color figure online)

3.5   Experimental Data Analysis

Eye tracking experiment, through the analysis of the eye movement experiment data of 50 subjects, the other elements are the same, the total visit time is 5.83 s when the color is red, the average visit time is 5.32 s when the color is blue, and the total visit when the color is green the average duration is 3.20 s, that is, when the color is green, the average access duration is the shortest and the cognitive efficiency is the highest. When there are only image elements, the average visit duration in red is 3.35 s, the total visit duration in blue is 3.05 s, and the total visit duration in green is 1.75 s, that is, the average visit duration in green is the shortest and the cognitive efficiency is the highest. With text elements, the total visit duration in red is 2.48 s, the total visit duration in blue is 2.27 s, and the total visit duration in green is 1.45 s, that is, the average visit duration in green is the shortest and the cognitive efficiency is the highest. In the same color (red, blue, green), only image elements are 0.87 s, 0.78 s, and 0.30 s longer than the total visit time with text elements, which means that the total visit time with text elements is shorter. Cognitive efficiency is higher (Fig. 6).

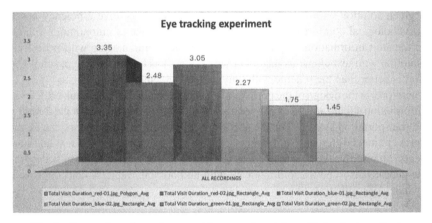

Fig. 6. Comparison chart of eye tracking experiment data. (Color figure online)

Likert scale method, after sorting and analyzing the score data of 50 subjects, green has the highest score with text elements (4.78) and the best psychological comfort, followed by green with only image elements (4.70) and blue. With text elements (3.73), blue only image elements (3.65), red with text elements (2.25), red only image elements have the lowest score (1.94) and the worst psychological comfort (Fig. 7).

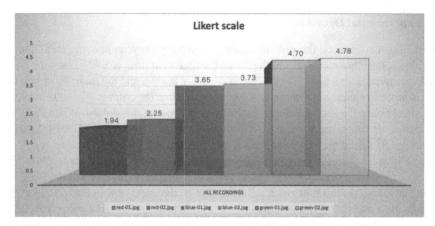

Fig. 7. Likert scale method scoring comparison chart. (Color figure online)

3.6 Experimental Results

The "green solution with text elements" has the highest cognitive efficiency and the best psychological comfort in the peripheral visual interface of autonomous vehicles. It can transmit information very accurately and better communicate with pedestrians. The solution with text elements the cognitive efficiency is higher and the psychological comfort is better than the scheme with only image elements.

Therefore, in the design of the peripheral visual interface of autonomous vehicles, the key information should still be expressed according to the green and red in the traditional public transportation system. For the secondary information, other colors can be used to express to meet different requirements. More use of a combination of text and image elements can improve the cognitive efficiency and psychological comfort of pedestrians, enable pedestrians to better communicate with autonomous vehicles, and improve the safety index of traffic travel.

4 Conclusion

In recent years, automakers and related technology researchers have become more and more enthusiastic about commercializing autonomous vehicles and pushing them into the consumer market. Although it is impossible to complete the popularization in a short time, the popularization of autonomous vehicles will change our lifestyle. At present, researchers should continue to research on the technical level and visual interface design. This article summarizes the organization of the peripheral visual interface through literature and case analysis, and designs experiments for data analysis to provide more feasibility references for peripheral visual interface design. To ensure the successful implementation of autonomous vehicles in the existing public transportation system.

References

1. van Brummelen, J., O'Brien, M., Gruyer, D., et al.: Autonomous vehicle perception: the technology of today and tomorrow. Transp. Res. Part C: Emerg. Technol. **89**, 384–406 (2018)

2. Zhang, N.: Analysis of "Idriverplus" driverless delivery vehicle [EB/OL]. http://kuaibao.qq.com/s/20180424G18OST00?refer=cp 1026. Accessed 11 November 2020. (in Chinese)
3. SAE International. SAE J3016™, Taxonomy and Definitions for Terms Related to on road Motor Vehicle Automated Driving Systems. SAE International, New York (2018)
4. Deb, S., Strawderman, L.J., Carruth, D.W.: Investigating pedestrian suggestions for external features on fully autonomous vehicles: a virtual reality experiment. Transp. Res. F: Traffic Psychol. Behav. **59**, 135–149 (2018)
5. Li, Y., Dikmen, M., Hussein, T.G., et al.: To cross or not to cross: urgency-based external warning displays on autonomous vehicles to improve pedestrian crossing safety. In: Proceedings of the 10th International Conference on Automotive User Interfaces and Interactive Vehicular Applications. ACM (2018)
6. Fridman, L., Mehler, B., Xia, L., et al.: To walk or not to walk: crowdsourced assessment of external vehicle-to-pedestrian displays. In: Proceedings of the Transportation Research Board 98th Annual Meeting (2019)
7. Lagstrom, T., Lundgren, V.M.: AVIP-Autonomous Vehicles Interaction with Pedestrians. Chalmers University of Technology, Goteborg (2015)
8. Snyder, J.B.: This self-driving car smiles at pedestrians [EB/OL]. https://www.autoblog.com/2016/09/16/this-self-driving-car-smiles-atpedestrians/. Accessed 11 November 2020
9. Zhang, J., Vinkhuyzen, E., Cefkin, M.: Evaluation of an autonomous vehicle external communication system concept: a survey study. In: Stanton, N.A. (ed.) Advances in Human Aspects of Transportation, pp. 650–661. Springer International Publishing, Cham (2018). https://doi.org/10.1007/978-3-319-60441-1_63
10. Likert, R.: A technique for the measurement of attitudes. Arch. Psychol. **22**(40), 1–55 (1932)

Human-Centered Design Reflections on Providing Feedback to Primary Care Physicians

Ashley Loomis[✉] and Enid Montague

DePaul University, Chicago, IL 60604, USA
aloomis1@depaul.edu

Abstract. To better understand physicians' current and desired feedback experiences on their interactions with patients, this qualitative study applied design thinking methods to facilitate discussions and produce artifacts. Nine primary care physicians and one medical resident participated in a design workshop to understand experiences, needs, and opportunities for design. Thematic analysis found that, 1) Feedback, received in many forms, is important to physicians' practice and patient well-being, 2) there are concerns about the impact of certain types of feedback, and 3) experience and system-related factors can impact physicians' workflow and interactions. Tools to improve feedback should take into account these considerations. While residents may desire immediate, direct feedback, concerns about the potential impact on patient care and their current workflow are important.

Keywords: Feedback · Design thinking · Primary care

1 Introduction

1.1 Feedback in Primary Care

Feedback is a valued tool for improving physician-patient interactions. It can cover a wide range of interactions from visits, including both the clinical and social aspects of provider communication [13]. Previous research has assessed and provided guidelines for administering feedback. A study on Veteran's Affairs physicians' perceptions of performance feedback showed that the process and receipt of feedback was one that garnered emotion and that acceptance of the feedback was impacted by directness [17]. In the context of validating recommended feedback guidelines on medical interviewing, physicians noted the preference for non-judgmental feedback directed towards specific skills and aligned with their personal goals [11].

Yet feedback is a complicated process to understand and implement. While many studies have evaluated the quality and impact of feedback, variations in efficacy demonstrate a need for further research on implementation and communication [5]. Additional research is needed to understand the method and nature of feedback that would be useful for and accepted by physicians.

© Springer Nature Switzerland AG 2021
M. Kurosu (Ed.): HCII 2021, LNCS 12764, pp. 108–118, 2021.
https://doi.org/10.1007/978-3-030-78468-3_8

1.2 Design Thinking Framework

To understand primary care providers' experiences and needs around feedback, a design workshop was conducted to understand how physicians receive feedback and how new designs might be integrated into their work. This human-centered design approach allows experts and end users to add experience-driven insight and ideas to developing concepts through various activities in an interactive workshop setting [12]. The application of this method with inclusion of potential users has been documented positively in health technology design [14, 19].

While not commonly appearing in medical education interventions, participatory design workshops and its collaborative nature are becoming more frequently encouraged [4]. Workshop methods allow for user participation in creating or improving designs. Previous studies about understanding physicians' perceptions of and experiences with feedback have used interviews as a methodology [6, 17]. The use of human-centered design methods in this study allows for further collaboration in design; it actively involves working with potential users through every phase of the process in medical education, from understanding the problem to creating a solution.

The research described in this paper is part of a larger study to understand physician feedback through the human-centered design approach involving end users in participating in the design process. The primary aim of this workshop was to understand the experiences and desires of primary care providers around feedback. Workshop goals were: 1) Understand current provider experiences with feedback, preferences for feedback, and interactions with patients, 2) Gain a sense of workflow, pain points, and opportunities to improve interactions with patients, and 3) Use a participatory approach to learn how physicians may envision a feedback system and brainstorm initial design concepts.

2 Methods

A design thinking workshop and qualitative thematic analysis of the results were the primary methods used in this research study. The study was approved by the IRB committee at DePaul University.

2.1 Design Workshop

Participants were recruited from a family medicine residency program at a clinical facility in Chicago, IL. The residents in this program see patients in inpatient and outpatient settings at the clinic. The 10 total participants in the workshop consisted of nine residents and one medical student. Of these participants, half identified as female, half as male. Six were under age 30 and four were ages 31–40 years old. Five identified as Asian/Pacific Islander and five as white.

The design workshop lasted 2.5 h and consisted of three activities: poster prompts, journey mapping, and prototyping. These activities were sourced from the researchers' own experiences in design thinking. The aim of these activities was to not only produce artifacts to describe physicians' experiences and needs, but also to act to start discussions. Participants worked individually for the first activity and in groups of 3–4 for the second

Table 1. The three activities during the workshop.

Activity	Description	Research question
Poster prompts	Participants wrote individual responses on sticky notes to four prompts	How might physicians experience feedback and interactions with patients?
Journey mapping	Participants detailed tasks, interactions, and emotions of typical work weeks in timeline format	How might we understand physicians' short- and long-term workflow?
Prototyping	Participants created paper versions of their feedback concepts	How might physicians envision a feedback tool?

and third activities. After each activity, there was a share-out and discussion of the results of the activity. Table 1 describes the activities and goals.

For the poster prompt activity, participants were given post-it notes and ten minutes to respond to four prompts: *How do you typically receive feedback, how do you prefer to receive feedback, describe a negative interaction you've had with a patient, and describe a positive interaction you've had with a patient.* Participants were encouraged to write one thought or response per post-it note; they could contribute as many responses as they liked during the time period. Figure 1 shows the result of the poster prompt activity.

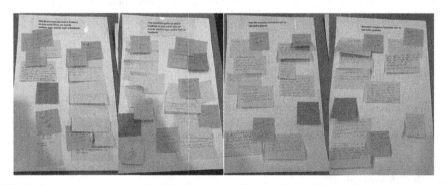

Fig. 1. Responses to prompts detailing the nature of patient interactions and current and desired feedback in the first activity.

Participants were divided into groups of 3–4 for the journey mapping activity and given highlighters, crayons, tape or glue, notecards, and plain paper. They were instructed to create a timeline of typical events, actions, interactions, and feelings before an appointment, during an appointment, and after an appointment. Participants were encouraged to consider the responses from the previous activity in creating their journey maps. The journey maps are shown in Fig. 2.

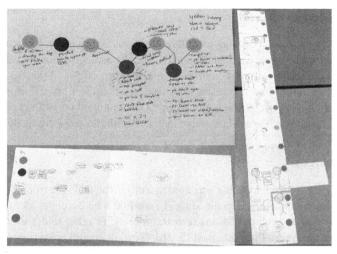

Fig. 2. The three journey maps showing tasks, interactions, and emotions included in a typical appointment experience.

To create the prototypes, participants were instructed to use the materials given to them to create basic designs for a feedback system that could be used before, during, or after appointments to improve their interactions with patients. There were no requirements for how or when the tool would operate, or the type of feedback the system would produce, but they were encouraged to consider all responses and products from the first two activities. The prototypes from this activity are shown in Fig. 3.

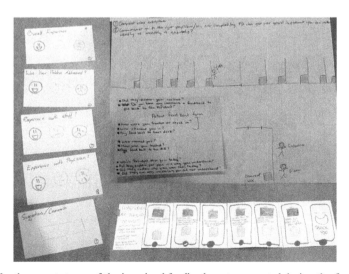

Fig. 3. The three prototypes of the imagined feedback system created during the final activity.

2.2 Data Collection

Data consisted of video recordings from three cameras set up at the back and sides of the room, notes taken by research staff, photos, and the artifacts from the activities: the artifacts from the poster prompts, journey maps, and prototypes. After the workshop, videos were transferred to a secure network folder and audio from the share-outs and group discussions was paraphrased into a script. Observational notes and relevant notes from and descriptions of the artifacts were included with the script for analysis.

2.3 Data Analysis

Thematic analysis with open coding was used to analyze the dialogue from the workshop using focus group techniques. Open coding is a method where a coder identifies labels, themes, keywords, and interpretations of text, artifacts, or other relevant data without use of a predetermined coding scheme [15, 16]. Next, the codes were transformed into digital post-it notes using the web application *Stormboard* to create an affinity diagram: notes were grouped into themes and a hierarchy of themes was created through several rounds of axial coding: grouping notes and creating keywords to summarize each group [1]. See Fig. 4 for a screenshot of the affinity diagram in Stormboard. The final themes were sent to two research staff that assisted with the workshop for validity and feedback.

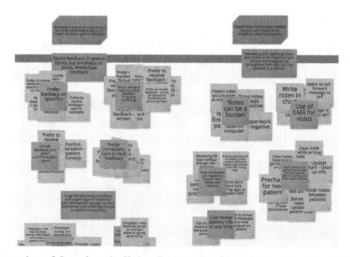

Fig. 4. Screenshot of Stormboard affinity diagram showing axial themes and subthemes from transcript, notes, and artifacts.

3 Results

Open coding the script and observational notes from the session and artifacts produced 228 codes. From these codes, three primary themes were derived from axial coding: 1)

Feedback, received in many forms, is important to physicians' practice and well-being, 2) There are concerns about the impact of certain types of feedback, and 3) Experience and system-related factors can impact physician workflow and interactions.

3.1 Feedback, Received in Many Forms, is Important to Physicians' Practice and Patient Well-Being

Participants described many ways in which they currently receive feedback in their work. Feedback from staff and patients are received in several mediums (written, verbal), for various targets (clinical, interactions), and at various intervals (specific and immediate, summarized later). The written and oral mediums refer to the fact that physicians may receive feedback that is recorded and delivered in a written or digital evaluation. Verbal feedback may or may not contain similar information but is orally communicated. Clinical feedback is focused on the technical diagnoses, treatment, and other medical advice physicians give their patients, whereas evaluations on interactions describe the interpersonal aspect of visits. Feedback that is given during or right after is referred to in the results as 'immediate', and often tends to be quite specific. 'Delayed' feedback is usually complied into a summary of multiple visits or interactions and delivered days, weeks, or months after the interactions occurred. This information is displayed in Table 2.

Table 2. Summary of feedback received

Timing	Feedback from clinical staff	Feedback from patient
Intermediate	Face-to-face evaluation of patient plan Verbal advice on patient care and management Notes and corrections in patients' charts	Emotional response to care during visit Health status of patient
Delayed	Written and oral evaluations on clinical, interpersonal, and professional performance	Summary of post-visit surveys on satisfaction

The participants reported variations in the formality of feedback from the clinical staff they were mentored by. Formal evaluations were often received at set intervals, such as quarterly or annually. This included appointment reviews, one-on-one meetings reviewing milestones, strengths, and weaknesses, and summarized evaluations viewable online. Informal feedback typically consisted of advice or corrections regarding specific interactions with patients throughout the workday.

Aside from receiving summarized patient satisfaction surveys in their evaluations, feedback from patients was often more ad hoc, during or after appointments. Direct feedback from patients often occurred during the appointment, frequently from patients communicating emotion. Patients might verbally communicate their satisfaction with their provider. Participants also viewed the patients' health status as a form of feedback:

"In the immediate, it's how the patient is doing overall...Am I seeing changes in their health? That's good, positive feedback."

Time with patients was described as generally positive, but interactions could be impacted by patients' current health or emotional status or care plan compliance. Negative interactions occurred when patients were non-compliant with treatment plans, did not listen, or came in sick or unhappy. Participants described an intentionality around creating positive interactions and patient well-being. As both a method of caring for patient health and receiving feedback, one resident noted checking in on patients after the visit or if they were in the hospital. Another noted that they were the ones to do the follow-up calls to patients (as opposed to the medical assistants), as they were sometimes able to resolve negative interactions that way.

3.2 There are Concerns About the Impact of Certain Types of Feedback

Similar to the ways in which they receive feedback, participants noted a variety of ways in which they desired to receive feedback: written, verbal, immediate, or summarized.

Many participants expressed a desire for face-to-face, targeted feedback. Receiving feedback later meant that they would likely receive more generalized feedback, which was less desirable. As one participant stated, "I prefer one-on-one verbal feedback. It's easier to get more specific details on feedback. If you have to wait four months, it's usually more generic...instead of the specific aspects that I do well or things that need more work."

Each group independently produced a prototype of a post-visit patient survey. These surveys focused on experience and satisfaction measures, with the ability for this feedback to be sent to the physician the patient had seen that day. According to the participants, surveys have the potential to provide more honest feedback, as patients are not being watched. Cultural norms sometimes prevent critical feedback of doctors. Alternatively, some noted that they may instead receive less valuable feedback through surveys, as patients may tend to provide mean, instead of helpful, feedback.

Participants expressed mixed feelings about anonymity of feedback. Negative feedback from a patient could impact how they give care. Anonymity allows for honest feedback without repercussions from the physician. A resident noted that, "And now the fact that I know you gave that feedback, it's going to make me feel crappy, and the next time I see you despite me wanting to treat you the right way, I may not be able to, or there's a little bit of bitterness."

3.3 Experience and System-Related Factors Can Impact Physician Workflow and Interactions

Participants' workflow, mood, and interactions with patients and faculty were shaped by a variety of factors, from clinical experience to interactions with the EHR system.

Residents have constant access to the EHR via smartphone. They viewed this access as both positive and negative as they interact with this system throughout their day for various reasons. One participant noted the advantage of being able to check the EHR system on the way from their car into the medical center. Another expressed frustration with the number of messages received through the system, "it's annoying to have your phone keep going off."

Another way in which the EHR system may act as a burden on their workflow is during charting. Chart review and updates are necessary to patient care and woven throughout their workdays. Participants noted the difficulty of trying to update a patient's chart during appointments if they have a long list of medical issues and the negative feelings they have around charting.

Experience impacts the efficiency and nature of residents' work. One participant described having to make many notes to themselves; more experienced residents do this less as they become better at filtering what information is important. Multitasking with the patient and EHR became easier with more experience. Additionally, those further along in their residency see more patients than junior residents and have less time with each patient. A larger patient load impacts their ability to conduct follow-up calls, instead having patients schedule follow-up appointments.

4 Discussion

Participants were eager to receive feedback and improve or maintain their patients' health. Residents receive feedback in many ways throughout their career, both in informal ways and in formal evaluations determined by the medical center. Findings from the workshop align with previous work on the topic of feedback and provide additional insights to help guide further research and design.

From the findings, three reflections on feedback for physicians in primary care settings are as follows: 1) Feedback is welcomed and important, but not all is viewed as helpful or trustworthy. Feedback should be provided in a way that supports physician growth, 2) Critical feedback may be difficult for physicians to receive and react to appropriately in the moment; a system should provide feedback in a way that won't impact patient care, 3) Physician workflow should be considered when implementing a feedback system; feedback should be integrated naturally into the short- and long-term flow of work as to not add to workflow or distract from their clinical work.

Feedback is important to participants' improvement of their own practice, which in turn improves their patients' health. They demonstrated willingness to actively seek feedback from clinical staff with more experience than them. Much of the feedback received as part of their routine evaluations were seen as beneficial, particularly specific, immediate feedback. However, they expressed skepticism over anonymous survey data, despite mostly creating prototypes of that nature. Similarly, one study in the UK found that general practitioners valued patient feedback but questioned the validity and utility of survey feedback when interviewed about their thoughts on patient surveys [6]. Given this result, surveys may not be the best tool for providing feedback to physicians. Any tools that aim to provide feedback to physicians should consider these frustrations and preferences to ensure that feedback provided is useful and trusted.

Participants expressed the difficulties of receiving negative feedback in a non-anonymous manner. They were concerned that their ability to continue to provide unbiased and proper care might be hampered by knowing that a specific patient has criticisms of their care. A system that provides feedback to a physician will provide critical evaluations in order to assist them in improving their practice. Given the concerns noted by participants, the delivery and timing of feedback should consider how their interactions with patients might be impacted.

To support the participants' desire for immediate and specific feedback, real-time feedback is a mode that could be considered in future design and evaluations. Studies that have looked at the implications of real-time feedback in the primary care space have found opportunities for this type of system. On evaluating a system providing live visualizations during telehealth calls, physicians noted an increased awareness around non-verbal interactions such as eye gaze [7]. In a simulated environment, a sun-moon visual provided feedback on affiliation and control based on non-verbal cues. Although participants noted the potentially distracting nature of the tool, they found an increased awareness of their behavior [10]. There is evidence that automated, real-time feedback may be acceptable and useful for improving physician-patient interactions. However, additional research and evaluation is needed to determine how these tools may be effective in naturalistic settings with a diversity of patients and clinicians.

Day-to-day tasks provide interruptions to workflow and opportunities for feedback. These factors should be considered in when and how feedback should be communicated to physicians. This is important not just for efficiency, but also for physician well-being. It is documented in previous research the impact EHR systems can have on burnout and physician's work [8]. Excess messages and notifications, stress associated with use of the systems, and the amount of time spent on paperwork outside of office visits, EHRs and other health technology may be contributing to burnout [8, 9]. Burnout has several negative impacts to both the physician and the patient, including physical and mental health issues, decreased patient satisfaction, and clinical errors [18].

Workshop participants noted the adverse impact that updating patient charts had on their own work, including the burden of time from these tasks. Furthermore, patients may also feel negatively about their providers' focus on the computer screen during the visit [3]. Experience may impact workflow as well. Even within EHR use, physicians have individual workflow styles [2]. Additional work should not be added to physician's schedules. Feedback systems should consider how workflow may vary between physicians, in addition how the feedback might fit into their workflow.

5 Conclusions

Determining the most effective approach for providing feedback to clinicians in a clinical setting is a complex issue with great potential for innovation through design thinking methods. The workshop with medical residents highlighted the need for more rigorous design approaches to determine how to best provide feedback.

A limitation to this research is the homogenous nature of the participants. All participants were in their early years of practice at the same medical center. Those with more years of practice or those practicing at different medical centers or clinics may have different experiences, as well as variations in needs and desires for feedback shared by those experiences. Additionally, the patient perspective was not considered in this study, as the physician-side improvement of interactions was the primary focus.

Additional research should investigate further the themes uncovered in this workshop and design implications surrounding those themes. As the prototypes appeared to focus primarily on the existing structure for feedback from patients in the form of surveys, future research should encourage participants to explore alternate forms of feedback. Further prototyping and testing of prototypes focusing on real-time, automated feedback is needed.

References

1. n.d. Stormboard.
2. Asan, O., Chiou, E., Montague, E.: Quantitative ethnographic study of physician workflow and interactions with electronic health record systems. Int. J. Ind. Ergon. **49**, 124–130 (2015). https://doi.org/10.1016/j.ergon.2014.04.004
3. Asan, O., Kushner, K., Montague, E.: Exploring residents' interactions with electronic health records in primary care encounters. Fam. Med. **47**(9), 722–726 (2015)
4. Badwan, B., Bothara, R., Latijnhouwers, M., Smithies, A., Sandars, J.: The importance of design thinking in medical education. Med. Teach. **40**(4), 425–426 (2018). https://doi.org/10.1080/0142159x.2017.1399203
5. Baines, R., et al.: The impact of patient feedback on the medical performance of qualified doctors: a systematic review. BMC Med. Educ. **18**(1), 173 (2018). https://doi.org/10.1186/s12909-018-1277-0
6. Farrington, C., Burt, J., Boiko, O., Campbell, J., Roland, M.: Doctors' engagements with patient experience surveys in primary and secondary care: a qualitative study. Health Expect. **20**(3), 385–394 (2017). https://doi.org/10.1111/hex.12465
7. Faucett, H.A., Lee, M.L., Carter, S.: I should listen more: real-time sensing and feedback of non-verbal communication in video telehealth. Proc. ACM Hum.-Comput. Interact. 1(CSCW), Article 44 (2017). https://doi.org/10.1145/3134679
8. Gardner, R.L., et al.: Physician stress and burnout: the impact of health information technology. J. Am. Med. Inform. Assoc. **26**(2), 106–114 (2019). https://doi.org/10.1093/jamia/ocy145
9. Gregory, M.E., Russo, E., Singh, H.: Electronic health record alert-related workload as a predictor of burnout in primary care providers. Appl. Clin. Inform. **8**(3), 686–697 (2017). https://doi.org/10.4338/ACI-2017-01-RA-0003
10. Hartzler, A.L., et al.: Real-time feedback on nonverbal clinical communication. Methods Inf. Med. **53**(05), 389–405 (2014)
11. Hewson, M.G., Little, M.L.: Giving feedback in medical education: verification of recommended techniques. J. Gen. Intern. Med. **13**(2), 111–116 (1998). https://doi.org/10.1046/j.1525-1497.1998.00027.x
12. ISO 2019: Human-centred design for interactive systems (ISO 9241–210:2019) in Ergonomics of human-system interaction. https://www.iso.org/obp/ui/#iso:std:iso:9241:-210:ed-2:v1:en
13. Jackson, J.L., Kay, C., Jackson, W.C., Frank, M.: The quality of written feedback by attendings of internal medicine residents. J. Gen. Intern. Med. **30**(7), 973–978 (2015). https://doi.org/10.1007/s11606-015-3237-2
14. Lamonica, H.M., et al.: Technology-enabled mental health service reform for open arms – veterans and families counselling: participatory design study. JMIR Form. Res. **3**(3), e13662 (2019). https://doi.org/10.2196/13662
15. Miles, M.B., Huberman, A.M., Saldaña, J.: Qualitative Data Analysis : A Methods Sourcebook. SAGE Publications Inc., Thousand Oaks (2014)
16. Patton, M.Q.: Qualitative Research & Evaluation Methods : Integrating Theory and Practice. SAGE Publications Inc., Thousand Oaks (2015)

17. Payne, V.L., Hysong, S.J.: Model depicting aspects of audit and feedback that impact physi-cians' acceptance of clinical performance feedback. BMC Health Serv. Res. 16(1), 260 (2016). https://doi.org/10.1186/s12913-016-1486-3
18. Salyers, M.P., et al.: The relationship between professional burnout and quality and safety in healthcare: a meta-analysis. J. Gen. Intern. Med. 32(4), 475–482 (2016). https://doi.org/10.1007/s11606-016-3886-9
19. Woods, L., Duff, J., Roehrer, E., Walker, K., Cummings, E.: Design of a consumer mobile health app for heart failure: findings from the nurse-led co-design of Care4myHeart. JMIR Nurs. 2(1), e14633 (2019). https://doi.org/10.2196/14633

Interaction with Objects and Humans Based on Visualized Flow Using a Background-Oriented Schlieren Method

Shieru Suzuki[1](✉), Shun Sasaguri[1], and Yoichi Ochiai[1,2]

[1] University of Tsukuba, Ibaraki 3058577, Japan
{wasdkey,shun.sasaguri}@digitalnature.slis.tsukuba.ac.jp
[2] Pixie Dust Technologies, Inc., Tokyo 1010041, Japan
wizard@slis.tsukuba.ac.jp

Abstract. Air flow is a ubiquitous phenomenon that can provide important insights to extend our perceptions and intuitive interactions with our surroundings. This study aimed to explore interaction methods based on flow visualization using background-oriented schlieren (BOS) in three case studies. Case 1 involved visualization of the airflow around humans or objects, which demonstrated that visualized flow provides meaningful information about the human or object under investigation. Case 2 involved the testing of a prototype sensor, where visualized flow was used to sense fine airflow. Stabilization of the flow was required for operation of the sensor. Case 3 involved the testing of a prototype system to investigate the use of flow as an input interface for playing a video game. The system did not operate as expected, but the design of the flow can be improved. Overall, interaction using flow visualization allows for the perception of air flow in a broad sense, and presents new opportunities in the field of human computer interaction.

Keywords: Flow visualization · Input interface · Affordance

1 Introduction

Air flow is a ubiquitous phenomenon throughout our living space, as we are in contact with air the majority of the time. Flow is generated due to the influence of various objects and phenomena, as well as the activities of the human body, where common examples included the flow of breath caused by human breathing and hot air generated from a cup containing a hot drink. Thus, this flow behavior can provide insights regarding the state and phenomena of the related human body or object. In turn, methods to obtain information from flow are required to expand our perception and intuitive interactions with objects.

This study explored interaction methods based on a flow visualization method. Although interaction methods based on wind have been widely reported in human computer interaction (HCI) [2,3,6,19,21], few studies have investigated flow visualization methods. Background-oriented schlieren (BOS) techniques [11,12,17] allow for optical visualization of a flow field based on density

© Springer Nature Switzerland AG 2021
M. Kurosu (Ed.): HCII 2021, LNCS 12764, pp. 119–137, 2021.
https://doi.org/10.1007/978-3-030-78468-3_9

gradients. Specifically, this method calculates changes in the refractive index of a medium to quantitatively visualize the flow in a non-contact manner. This approach has been used to visualize flow field phenomena such as shock waves, a supersonic free jet, and blade tip vortices of a helicopter during flight [17,18]. However, to the best of our knowledge, no studies have applied BOS techniques in the field of HCI. Analysis based air flow shows great promise, as it is a common and natural phenomenon that can be interpreted to gain various types of information. Thus, interaction based on flow visualization for the perception of air flow in a broad sense presents new opportunities in the field of HCI.

The main purpose of this research was to explore interaction methods based on visualized flow information, and discuss the possible application of such methods. Prototypes for several applications were investigated using case studies, where the performance, usefulness, and usability was discussed based on the results. Specifically, the information regarding the state of the human body and objects obtained from flow visualization videos using the BOS method are presented, as well as the affordances offered by the various objects and human body. A sensor was prototyped for the sensing of fine airflow, and the performance of a user interface for a video game based on a real-time flow visualization system was evaluated.

2   Related Work

2.1   Interaction with Wind

Many studies have investigated interactions using wind, as wind is related to many visual and olfactory display systems. For example, studies have proposed fog displays using breath [2], and propelled soap bubbles filled with scent and fog to deliver scent to humans and display projected images, respectively [19]. Wind can also be used to levitate and transport objects [3,19], and has been proposed as an interaction method for presenting tactile sensations, such as introducing tactile sensations via a vortex ring [21] and adjusting temperature [6]. However, previous research on interaction has not included the visualization of air flow.

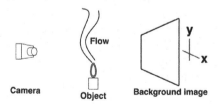

Fig. 1. BOS setup with a camera and background image fixed opposite each other to measure the flow between them.

2.2   Flow Visualization Methods

The interaction between objects, humans, and computers was explored in this study using BOS, where the density gradient of a flow field was measured in a non-contact manner for quantitative visualization. Conventional contact methods include the application of an oil film to the surface of an object to physically visualize the flow on the surface [10]), but BOS offers several advantages over contact methods, such as superior scalability, the ability to measure a flow not facing the object, and no physical interaction with the object. The implementation of BOS is simple, and only requires a background image and a camera (Fig. 1). Further, the complex optics required for some of the other non-contact methods (e.g., the Schlieren method) are not required. Unlike particle image velocimetry (PIV), particle tracking velocimetry (PTV), and laser Doppler velocimeter (LDV), BOS does not involve the scattering of particles in the air or laser irradiation.

BOS was first proposed by Meier in 1999 [11], and aimed to partially replace the optical processing aspect of the Schlieren method with computer calculation. The continued advancements in computer performance have recently enabled real-time processing [23]. BOS visualizes the flow occurring within a three-dimensional space and represents it two-dimensionally. However, three-dimensional visualization methods for BOS has also been proposed [4,9,13].

A method called Simplified BOS (S-BOS) [1] was used in this study. Conventional BOS is computationally expensive due to the use of a cross-correlation algorithm, while S-BOS reduces the computational complexity by devising a background image and computation method. Conventional BOS visualizes the density gradient in two directions (x-axis and y-axis) simultaneously (Fig. 1), while S-BOS is limited to visualization of flow in a single direction (either x-axis or y-axis). This is similar to the Schlieren method. Although methods have been proposed to overcome this limitation [7,15], these developmental methods were not used to ensure that calculation and implementation was as simple as possible.

Various applications of BOS have been proposed, including the evaluation of jettison motor plumes, turbines for airplanes and power generation, and wake flows in linear turbine cascade facilities [17]. Further, it has been used to study flow in a supersonic free jet, a turbulent flame, and a helicopter in flight [18]. The use of BOS for temperature estimation has also been proposed [22]. However, applications in the field of HCI have not yet been reported.

2.3   Affordance

Affordance is an actively discussed concept in the field of HCI [8]. The term was defined by Gibson in 1977 [5], and was later interpreted by Norman and widely adopted in the field of design. Norman's interpretation explains that "affordances define what actions are possible", and that "affordances are relationships between object and user" [14]. Based on Norman's interpretation of affordance, the action possibilities offered to a human observer when viewing an object or a human body surrounded the visualized flow have been considered. The appearance of an object changes dynamically when the flow is visible, thus the observed can adjust their interaction based on this new appearance of the object.

The affordances that a human body offers as an object may also be considered for interactions based on verbal communication, as a common action between two people is talking. Thus, the human body also offers affordances, and affords a human observer conversational behavior (e.g., the appropriate tone or word choice).

3   Methodology

The visualization procedure using BOS involves the measurement and visualization of the density gradient of a medium based on the behavior of light passing through a region of the medium, where changes in density gradient lead to changes in refractive index (Fig. 2) [11]. The operator acquires an initial image of the physically displayed background image with a camera in the absence of the test object and its density gradient. The object is subsequently placed between the camera and the background image and video of the object is acquired, where the background image observed by the camera is distorted by the measured density gradient. The density gradient is calculated in each video frame based on the initial image. This data can be used to produce a visualized movie. The code used for this methodology is available at https://github.com/DigitalNatureGroup/SimplifiedBOS.

Displacement (d) is an important parameter in terms of sensitivity, and is defined as the distance between the point at which the light from the background image passes through to the image sensor in the presence of a test object and the point at which it reaches the image sensor when there is no test object between the background and image sensor. The displacement determines the minimum density gradient that can be measured, and has the following relationship [12]:

$$d \sim af\,grad(n)/g \tag{1}$$

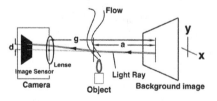

Fig. 2. Optical scheme for the BOS technique.

Fig. 3. Example background pattern for the S-BOS technique.

where a is the distance between the background image and the measured density gradient, f is the focal length of the camera, n is the refractive index, and g is the distance between the background image and the camera lens (Fig. 2).

The implementation of S-BOS for the visualization of a flow field was explored in this study, where a background pattern of vertical stripes was used to measure and visualize flow in the horizontal direction (i.e., direction of color change) (Fig. 3). A number of parameters were determined before images were acquired, including the width of the stripes in the background pattern, the distance between the camera and the measured flow, the distance between the camera and the background image, the resolution and frame rate of the camera, the focal length, the aperture (i.e., f-number), the light sensitivity (i.e., ISO value), and pixel size of the image sensor. It is also important that the camera and background image are physically fixed and that the camera is focused on the background image.

4   Case Studies

4.1   Case 1: Visualization of Flow Around the Human Body and Objects

The possibility of interaction between objects and humans based on visualized flow was explored. Specifically, visualization experiments using S-BOS were conducted to determine the types of information that a human can obtain when the flow around a human body or objects is visualized.

Set-Up. The implementation of S-BOS was conducted by placing a camera and monitor opposite each other at a distance of 570 cm (Fig. 4). A human body and various objects were placed between them at a distance of 390 to 430 cm from the camera, and the flow generated by the human or object was visualized

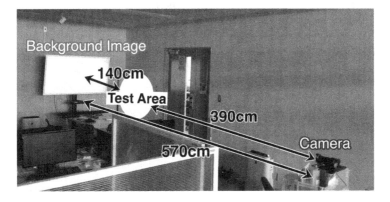

Fig. 4. Implementation of S-BOS, where an object or human body is placed in the test area to measure the surrounding flow.

Table 1. Key settings for the implementation of S-BOS for the visualization of flow around the human body and objects.

Width of stripes in background pattern	6.0 mm
Distance between camera and flow	390~430 cm
Distance between camera and background image	570 cm
Camera resolution	3840 × 2160 pixels
Camera frame rate	30 fps
Camera focal length	200 cm
Camera f-number	2.8
Camera ISO value	100
Image sensor specifications	Exmor RS CMOS sensor (13.2 × 8.8 mm; 21 megapixels)

with high sensitivity. A single-lens reflex camera (Sony DSC-RX10M2, Exmor RS CMOS sensor, 13.2 8.8 mm, 21 megapixels) with a focal length of 200 cm, f-number of 2.8, ISO100, 30 fps, and resolution of 3840 2160 pixels was used to capture the visualization videos. The background image was displayed on a 65-in. 4K ultra-high definition (UHD) liquid crystal display (LCD) monitor to visualize the horizontal component flow, where the physical width per stripe of the displayed background pattern was 6 mm (Table 1).

Visualization of the Flow from a Soldering Iron, Computer, and Human Profile. The flow surrounding a human profile, soldering iron, and desktop computer placed in close proximity was visualized (Fig. 5). Specifically, the resulting videos mainly visualized the flow generated by the hot air and exhalation from the surface of the body, the heat soldering iron, and the exhaust of the computer, where different flow generation was observed for each (Fig. 6).

Human Profile During Various Activities. The flow around a human profile was visualized before and after the exercise (Fig. 7). The video of the flow generated by the breath and body surface was visualized, where the momentum and spread of the breath, and the amounts of breath coming from the nose and mouth differed when the person was breathing before exercise, laughing before exercise, breathing after exercise, and coughing (Fig. 8).

Cup of Hot Water. The flow around a polypropylene cup filled with hot water was visualized (Fig. 9). The video clearly exhibited the flow from the exposed liquid surface exposed at the top of the cup, while flow from the side of the cup was also observed (Fig. 10). However, flow from the cool handle of the cup was hardly visualized.

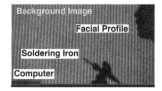

Fig. 5. Positioning of a human profile, soldering iron, and computer between the displayed background pattern and the camera.

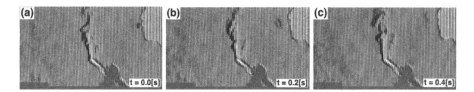

Fig. 6. Visualization of the flow generated by human breath, heat from a soldering iron, and computer ventilation.

Fig. 7. Human profile positioning between the displayed background pattern and the camera.

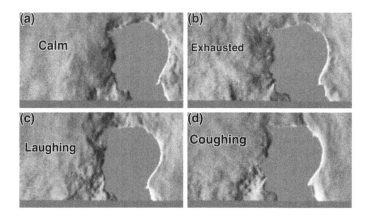

Fig. 8. Visualization of flow around a person during (a) pre-exercise breathing, (b) post-exercise breathing, (c) laughing, and (d) coughing.

Cans of Hot and Iced Water. The flow around two cans filled with boiling and iced water was visualized (Fig. 11). The video of the generated flows revealed that the flow from the hot can moved upwards, while the flow from the cold moved downwards (Fig. 12).

Application and Drying of Spray Paint. Spray paint was applied to an A4 sheet of copy paper using an acrylic resin sprayer, and the drying process was imaged to visualize the flow from the paper surface (Fig. 13). The video revealed that the flow from the sprayer and applied paint disappeared with time (Fig. 14). The gas flow from the paint was stagnant facing the paint, but blowing air from the side during the drying process led to movement of the gas. Gas was subsequently generated from the paint surface when blowing was removed, and stagnated again. The stagnated gas gradually disappeared over approximately 4 min. The operator touched the paint once all gas had disappeared to confirm that the paint was dry.

Fig. 9. Cup filled with boiling water positioned between the displayed background pattern and the camera.

Fig. 10. Visualization of the flow around a cup of boiling water, where the flow due to the heat of the water was clearly visualized around the cup except at the handle.

Fig. 11. Cans of iced (**left**) and boiling water (**right**) positioned between the displayed background pattern and the camera.

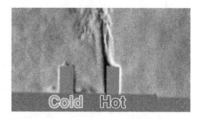

Fig. 12. Visualization of the flow of the warmed and cooled air around the two cans.

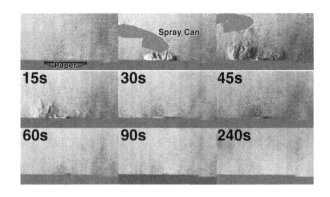

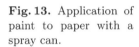

Fig. 13. Application of paint to paper with a spray can.

Fig. 14. Visualization of the spray jet during the application of paint to paper using a spray can (**top**) and the flow of volatile gases from the applied paint during drying (**middle and bottom**).

4.2 Case 2: Sensing System with Hot Air Plumes from Heat Sources

The potential of computer-object interaction was explored by detecting fine airflow to sense information regarding its source. The hot air plumes generated by lit candles were observed to establish whether the hot plumes were affected by the fine airflow around the lit candles.

Direct visualization of the fine airflow based on S-BOS without considering the flow from the flames can lead to practical issues during implementation. The direct measurement and visualization of fine airflow with S-BOS rely on highly sensitive measurements, which are associated with more noise due to the detection of fine density gradients in the area surrounding the measurement target. Further, large variations in the size of the density gradient of the measurement target must be accommodated by adjusting the S-BOS settings accordingly, which leads to inefficiency of the sensing method. However, indirect detection of fine airflow from the hot air plumes does not lead to these issues.

Setup. A prototype system was used to visualize the hot air plumes from ten lit candles arranged in two rows of five candles spaced 20 cm apart (Fig. 15). A single-lens reflex camera (SONY α7S II ILCE-7SM2, Exmor CMOS sensor, 35.6 23.8 mm, 12.4 megapixels, SIGMA 35 mm f/1.4 DG HSM lens) with a focal length of 35 cm, f-stop of 2.0, ISO 100, 60 fps, and resolution of 1920 1080 pixels was used to capture the visualization videos. The distance between the camera and the candles was 40 cm, and the distance between the camera and the background image was 100 cm. The background image was displayed on three 23.8-in. full high definition (HD) LCD monitors placed around the candles to visualize the horizontal component flow. The displayed background pattern had a physical width of 4.5 mm per stripe. Marionettes were used to create a fine airflow

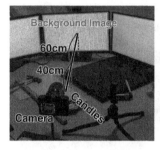

Fig. 15. Implementation of S-BOS to sense hot air plumes from lit candles placed between the camera and the monitor.

Fig. 16. Marionette used create a fine airflow around the lit candles (**left**) and the view from the camera perspective (**right**).

Table 2. Key settings for the implementation of S-BOS for the sensing of hot air plumes from heat sources.

Width of stripes in background pattern	4.5 mm
Distance between camera and flow	40 cm
Distance between camera and background image	100 cm
Camera resolution	1920 × 1080 pixels
Camera frame rate	60 fps
Camera focal length	35 cm
Camera f-number	2.0
Camera ISO value	100
Image sensor specifications	Exmor CMOS sensor (35.6 × 23.8 mm; 12.4 megapixels)

around the candles without requiring a large space, where the marionette was manipulated and made to walk around the candles (Fig. 16) (Table 2).

Results. The visualization of the hot air plumes from the lit candles revealed that the flow from the flames fluctuated to various sizes and was generally unstable, regardless of the motion of the marionette (Fig. 17). Further, the upper section of the flow from the lit candles became turbulent.

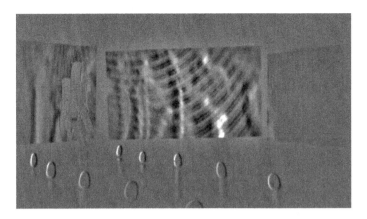

Fig. 17. Visualization of the hot air plumes from the lit candles, where flow was unstable regardless of the motion of the marionette.

4.3 Case 3: User Interface for Playing the Video Game "Flappy Bird"

The potential for interaction between computers and humans was explored, where a prototype input interface based on the BOS method was used to play a simple video game. The game was played for 3 min, and the highest score was noted.

Setup. A user interface was assembled for the real-time measurement and visualization of the plume flow from a lit candle to play a simple video game (Fig. 18). The built-in camera of a laptop computer was used (MacBook Air, 13-in., 2017). Some of the specifications of the camera, namely f-number, image

Fig. 18. Prototype user interface based on S-BOS (**left**) and a user interfering with the plume flow of a lit candle by using his hands and breath to play a simple video game (**right**).

Table 3. Key settings for the implementation of S-BOS for playing a video game.

Width of stripes in background pattern	2.5 mm
Distance between camera and flow	15 cm
Distance between camera and background image	65 cm
Camera resolution	1280 × 720 pixels
Camera frame rate	6∼12 fps
Camera focal length	Undisclosed
Camera f-number	Undisclosed
Camera ISO value	Auto
Image sensor specifications	Undisclosed

sensor specification, focal length, were not disclosed. ISO was automatically adjusted by the source code, the resolution was 1280 720 pixels, and the frame rate fluctuated between 6 and 12 fps. The distance between the camera and the candle was 15 cm, and the distance between the camera and the background image was 65 cm. The background image was displayed on a 27-in. full HD LCD monitor to visualize the horizontal component flow. The displayed background pattern had a physical width of 2.5 mm per stripe (Table 3).

"Flappy Bird" is a video game in which a bird on the screen must rise and fall as it travels at a constant speed between upper and lower obstacles. The player can only control the height of the bird, and cannot control its speed. The score is based on the number of obstacles that the bird successfully passes before touching one obstacle. The source code of the game was based on the following: https://github.com/ikergarcia1996/NeuroEvolution-Flappy-Bird.

The prototype system was able to adjust the height of the bird once per cycle. This jumping motion was chosen instead of switching to take advantage of the continuity of the flow. The cycle of the jump was dependent on the sum of the pixel values in the visualized image. The game screen and the real time image of the visualized flow were displayed on the same screen, and the player manipulated the height of the bird by interfering with the plume flow by the lit candle from the side with either their breath or hands while watching the screen. The game was played by adjusting the scale of the variation of the bird's jumping period with respect to the variation of the sum of the pixel values of the visualized image. The time spent changing the settings was not included in the playing time.

Results. An image of the game screen during play was obtained (Fig. 19), where the game screen appeared on the left with the corresponding real-time visualized flow on the right. The maximum game score was 0 points.

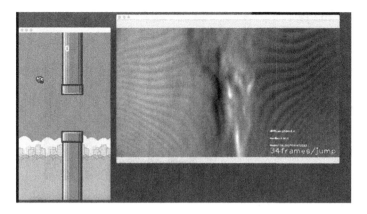

Fig. 19. Image of the screen during game play, where the user interferes with the flow while watching the real-time visualization image on the right. The sum of the pixel values in the visualized image changed the period time of the bird's jumping motion in the game screen on the left.

5 Discussion

5.1 Flow Visualization with BOS

Flow measurement using BOS does not offer sufficient accuracy for some applications. BOS techniques measure and visualize density gradients in a medium based on the refraction of light travelling through the region with the density gradients. The orientation of a straight line passing from the background image to the camera sensor may be considered as the z-axis in a xyz coordinate space (Fig. 20), where the light is bent under the influence of all the xy components (i.e., multiple density gradients of the medium) as it travels along this line. Specifically, the light is bent the position Δx in the x-axis direction and Δy in the y-axis direction (Fig. 20) away from its position on the straight line A parallel to the z-axis. However, the exact coordinate of the density gradient on the z-axis is unknown. Several solutions to this issue in the BOS method have been proposed [4,9,13], where three-dimensional measurement of the density gradients has been shown to provide a more accurate visualization of flow.

The density gradient of a gas visualized by BOS is determined by the distribution of its temperature, pressure, and humidity, as well as the distribution of the type and constituents of the gas [16,20]. However, this study assumed that the density gradient is predominantly determined by temperature distribution, except for the density gradient visualized around the spray paint in the Case 1 attributed the organic solvent volatilized from the paint.

Background Image

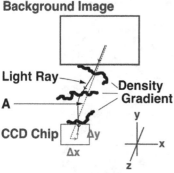

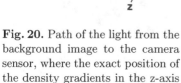

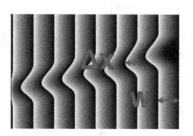

Fig. 20. Path of the light from the background image to the camera sensor, where the exact position of the density gradients in the z-axis is unknown.

Fig. 21. Example of an image resulting from light that travelled through a region of air with a density gradient between the background image and the camera sensor, where the light was bent due to the changes in refractive index.

The size of the density gradient must correspond to the size of pattern of the background image used in S-BOS to ensure accurate measurements. The S-BOS method in this study was performed using a periodic gradient pattern as the background image, where a narrower pattern width (W) (Fig. 21) allows for a more precise density gradient measurement. However, a displacement (Δx) (Fig. 21) wider than W cannot be measured. Therefore, the pattern of the background image must be adjusted according to density gradient under investigation.

5.2   Visualization of Flow Around the Human Body and Objects

Common visualized flows include steam, smoke, fire dust, and confetti, where these substances are carried within a flow to visualize it. Humans can obtain meaningful information by observing these visualized flows. For example, steam rising from food indicates that the food is warm and not dry, the number of the sparks from a fire is related to the intensity of the fire, and drifting smoke indicates the momentum of the wind in the localized area. Similarly, the visualization of invisible flow shows promise for the extraction of meaningful information.

The BOS technique extends flow visualization, where the flows around a human profile, a soldering iron, and a desktop computer provided insights into the mixture of hot air and exhalation generated from the body, the air flow and heat from the soldering iron, and the exhaust from the computer, respectively. Each of these samples had a different shape, movement, and characteristics. Specifically, the stream of breath from the mouth became invisible soon after its occurrence, the soldering iron produced a distinct stream from its tip, and the computer's exhaust flowed indistinctly near its surface.

The visualization of the flow around the human profile before and after the exercise highlighted the differences in the momentum and spread of the breath and the amounts exhaled through the nose and mouth depending on the person's state. For example, nasal breathing was predominant before exercise, while mouth breathing was predominant afterwards. The visualized flow was wider during laughing compared to that at rest, and the momentum of the flow out of the mouth was greater during coughing. Therefore, the visualized flow of breath provided information regarding the physical and psychological state of human subject.

The visualized flow around the cans of boiled and iced water revealed that flow from the hot can moved upward, while that of the cold can moved downwards. This demonstrated that the flow around a can indicated whether the water inside is hot or cold. This difference was attributed to the expansion of air with a higher temperature than the surrounding air, which leads to a decrease in density and, in turn, rising. Conversely, air with a lower temperature contracts, where the increased in density causes it to fall.

The visualized flow revealed volatilized gases leaving the paint during drying. The gas was blown away by wind, but continued to accumulate until no new gas was generated. Once no flow was observed, the paint was found to be dry to the touch. Thus, the absence of visualized gases from the paint provides an indication that paint is dry. Conversely, the observation of gas generated from paint indicates that the paint was not completely dry.

5.3   Affordances of Visualized Flow

The visualization of flow around objects and human bodies offers several affordances by providing information to a human observer. This creates the possibility of actions. The flow generated by the heat of the cup filled with hot water occurred everywhere but the handle. Thus, the cup and its flow afforded the action of holding its handle. Further, the spray-painted paper produced volatile gases as the paint dried, which gradually disappeared. Thus, the flow of volatilized gases from the paint afforded the behavior of placing the dried paper in a file (Fig. 22).

Fig. 22. Paper with dried paint was stored in a file once the emission of volatile gases from the paint was no longer observed because the visualized gas afforded storage of the paper.

The human body offers affordances in the form of conversational behavior. The flow around a human profile visualizes the rhythm, volume, and jet speed of their exhalations, as well as the amount of breath from the nose and mouth. The visualized breath differed depending on the physical and psychological state of the person, such as mood and level of fatigue. Therefore, the visualized breath of a person afforded an indication of how this person should be spoken to or treated, and informs the tone of voice used to talk to them. For example, when a person is laughing, one should talk to them in a friendly manner. When they are fatigued, the conversation should begin by offering a word of encouragement. In addition, the momentum and rough spread of the breath during coughing was visualized. This visualized flow afforded the actions of physical distancing from the person for sanitary reasons. This visualization of breath may encourage people to distance themselves from one other appropriately, which has the potential to improve behavior for infection control of Covid-19.

5.4   Sensing with Visualized Flow

The usefulness of the BOS system based on visualization of the hot air plumes from lit candles as a sensor of fine air flow was evaluated. The flow visualization videos demonstrated that the flow did not maintain a stable shape, and had some degree of turbulence. This obscured the changes in the movement of the flow from the flames against the surrounding fine airflow, which reduced the usefulness of the sensor. The hot air plumes from the lit candles became turbulent at a relatively far point from the heat source (i.e., the flame). The flame itself also fluctuated, and the source of the surrounding fine airflow was not limited. A better experimental environment in which these factors are removed should be explored further.

It is important that sensors used in human living spaces have an aesthetic appearance. Candles possess aesthetic values, as they are commonly used for both lighting and decoration. Thus, this study attempted to find a function for candles as sensors of the environment while benefitting from their aesthetic value. The use of decorative objects as sensors is important in the internet of things (IoT), which is based on the integration of sensors into human living space.

5.5   Input Interface Based on Visualized Flow

Real-time visualized flow from the BOS system was investigated as an input interface to play a video game. However, it was not possible to manipulate the bird on the game screen as desired. The plume flow from the lit candle tended to rise by itself, leading to irregular and turbulent flow. Manipulation of the flow with a user's hand or breath increased this turbulence, and the shape and movement of the flow could not be manipulated as desired. Further, the flow was only displayed on the screen as a visualized image. Therefore, physical interference of the flow by the user indirectly led to responses of the flow movement while watching the real-time visualization image on the screen, which was not intuitive. In addition, the user could feel the warmth of the flow from the flame, but had minimal response to the tactile sensation.

The presence of the hand in the visualized image affected the input data. The interval at which the bird jumped was determined by the sum of each pixel value in the visualized image. The hand had a considerable effect on the sum value, thus factors other than the flow affected the operation of the interface. The use of the player's breath showed promise for overcoming this issue.

Overall, the unpredictability of the flow behavior, the ambiguity of the tactile feedback, and the indirect visualization of the physical flow limited the usability of the input interface based on visualized flow using the BOS method. Instead, the flow behavior and flow visualization should be controlled more directly (i.e., physically).

6   Conclusion

An interaction method based on visualized flow using S-BOS was explored in three case studies. Case 1 demonstrated that the flow of gas around a human body or object can be visualized with high sensitivity. Meaningful information was obtained from the visualized flow around objects, and could be used to vaguely characterize the nature of things, such as the state of objects and the human body. This case study also demonstrated that the visualization of the flow around objects or a human body extends affordances.

Case 2 explored a prototype sensor for sensing fine airflow, and its usefulness was discussed. Hot air plumes from the lit candles were visualized within an environment of fine airflow around the candles. The response of the visualized flow from the flames to the surrounding fine airflow was obscured due to the instability and fluctuations of the visualized flow. Thus, the usefulness of this sensor was questionable. However, stabilization of hot air plumes would allow for the development of a sensing method. Specifically, a future system based on machine learning to obtain information regarding the factors that cause the fine airflow around the candles shows promise.

Case 3 aimed to play the video game "Flappy Bird" using an input interface based on real-time visualization of flow. The player manipulated the shape and movement of the visualized flow with their hands and breath to control the game. However, sufficient usability was not achieved because the player could not control the system as intended. The use of visualized flow as an input interface relies of the development of a technology that enables the design of the flow.

Overall, the findings of this study demonstrated the possibility of natural, unconscious, and ubiquitous interaction for humans using flow visualization. Further research is recommended to construct a sufficiently evaluable interaction model.

Acknowledgments. We would also like to thank Assistant Professor Fushimi for his supervision of the experiment in Case 2.

References

1. Akatsuka, J., Nagai, S.: Flow visualization by a simplified BOS technique. In: 29th AIAA Applied Aerodynamics Conference, p. 3653 (2011). https://doi.org/10.2514/6.2011-3653
2. Alakärppä, I., Jaakkola, E., Colley, A., Häkkilä, J.: BreathScreen: design and evaluation of an ephemeral UI. In: Proceedings of the 2017 CHI Conference on Human Factors in Computing Systems, pp. 4424–4429 (2017). https://doi.org/10.1145/3025453.3025973

3. Alrøe, T., Grann, J., Grönvall, E., Petersen, M.G., Rasmussen, J.L.: Aerial tunes: exploring interaction qualities of mid-air displays. In: Proceedings of the 7th Nordic Conference on Human-Computer Interaction: Making Sense Through Design, pp. 514–523 (2012). https://doi.org/10.1145/2399016.2399095
4. Atcheson, B., et al.: Time-resolved 3D capture of non-stationary gas flows. ACM Trans. Graph. (TOG) 27(5), 1–9 (2008). https://doi.org/10.1145/1409060.1409085
5. Gibson, J.J.: The theory of affordances. Hilldale USA 1(2), 67–82 (1977)
6. Han, P.H., et al.: AoEs: enhancing teleportation experience in immersive environment with mid-air haptics. In: ACM SIGGRAPH 2017 Emerging Technologies, pp. 1–2 (2017). https://doi.org/10.1145/3084822.3084823
7. Hatanaka, K., Hirota, M., Saito, T.: 0407 visualization of free jet with BOS method using colored grid back ground pattern containing two frequency components (in Japanese). In: JSME Fluids Engineering Conference 2012, pp. 203–204. The Japan Society of Mechanical Engineers (2012). https://doi.org/10.1299/jsmefed.2012.203
8. Kaptelinin, V.: Affordances and Design. The Interaction Design Foundation, Aarhus (2014)
9. Le Sant, Y., Todoroff, V., Bernard-Brunel, A., Le Besnerais, G., Micheli, F., Donjat, D.: Multi-camera calibration for 3DBOS. In: 17th International Symposium on Applications of Laser Techniques to Fluid Mechanics (2014)
10. Loving, D.L., Katzoff, S.: The fluorescent-oil film method and other techniques for boundary-layer flow visualization (1959)
11. Meier, G.E.: Hintergrundschlierenverfahren. Germany Pat., DE 19942856 A 1 (1999)
12. Meier, G.E: On the origin of BOS. In: Proceedings 18th International Symposium on Flow Visualization. ETH Zurich (2018). https://doi.org/10.3929/ethz-b-000279170
13. Nicolas, F., et al.: A direct approach for instantaneous 3D density field reconstruction from background-oriented schlieren (BOS) measurements. Exp. Fluids 57(1), 13 (2016). https://doi.org/10.1007/s00348-015-2100-x
14. Norman, D.A.: The Psychology of Everyday Things. Basic Books, New York (1988)
15. Ota, M., Hamada, K., Kato, H., Maeno, K.: Computed-tomographic density measurement of supersonic flow field by colored-grid background oriented schlieren (CGBOS) technique. Meas. Sci. Technol. 22(10), 104011 (2011). https://doi.org/10.1088/0957-0233/22/10/104011
16. Picard, A., Davis, R., Gläser, M., Fujii, K.: Revised formula for the density of moist air (CIPM-2007). Metrologia 45(2), 149 (2008). https://doi.org/10.1088/0026-1394/45/2/004
17. Raffel, M.: Background-oriented schlieren (BOS) techniques. Exp. Fluids 56(3), 1–17 (2015). https://doi.org/10.1007/s00348-015-1927-5
18. Richard, H., Raffel, M., Rein, M., Kompenhans, J., Meier, G.: Demonstration of the applicability of a background oriented schlieren (BOS) method. In: Laser Techniques for Fluid Mechanics, pp. 145–156. Springer, Heidelberg (2002). https://doi.org/10.1007/978-3-662-08263-8_9
19. Seah, S.A., et al.: SensaBubble: a chrono-sensory mid-air display of sight and smell. In: Proceedings of the SIGCHI Conference on Human Factors in Computing Systems, pp. 2863–2872 (2014). https://doi.org/10.1145/2556288.2557087
20. Shelquist, R.: Equations - air density and density altitude. https://wahiduddin.net/calc/density_altitude.htm. Accessed 02 Aug 2021
21. Sodhi, R., Poupyrev, I., Glisson, M., Israr, A.: AIREAL: interactive tactile experiences in free air. ACM Trans. Graph. (TOG) 32(4), 1–10 (2013). https://doi.org/10.1145/2461912.2462007

22. Taberlet, N., Plihon, N., Auzémery, L., Sautel, J., Panel, G., Gibaud, T.: Synthetic schlieren—Application to the visualization and characterization of air convection. Eur. J. Phys. **39**(3), 035803 (2018). https://doi.org/10.1088/1361-6404/aaa791
23. Wernet, M.P.: Real-time background oriented schlieren: catching up with knife edge schlieren (2019)

Research on Aging Design of News APP Interface Layout Based on Perceptual Features

Zhixin Wu[✉], Zehua Li, Xiang Li, and Hongqian Li

Nanjing University of Science and Technology, Nanjing 210094, China

Abstract. Objective Based on the perception characteristics of the elderly and the analysis of news APP interface layout, by changing the design of news APP interface layout, to study the influence of graphic presentation mode of interface layout on information retrieval efficiency of the elderly. Methods According to the analysis results of the corresponding relationship model between the perceived characteristics of the elderly and the layout of news APP interface, the research method of combining subjective user experience data analysis with objective eye movement experiment analysis was carried out, and finally the aging design strategy of news APP interface layout was summarized. Results (1) Using graphic layout of news information can increase the information retrieval time of the elderly, while using plain text layout can reduce the information retrieval time; (2) The subjective user experience data of interface layout shows that the elderly tend to graphic interface layout; (3) According to the eye movement experiment results, the visual browsing time of the elderly on the left layout boundary of the right picture is obviously higher than that on the left layout. Conclusion The effective layout of news APP interface is helpful to improve the information retrieval efficiency of the elderly, and further stimulate the enthusiasm of the elderly users to retrieve information. The research results can be used to optimize and innovate the interactive design of news APP interface layout.

Keywords: News APP · Interface layout · Elderly people · Perceptual features · Suitable for aging · IR

1 Introduction

With the acceleration of social aging, society needs more products suitable for aging. After entering the Internet era, information APPlications have shown explosive growth, and news app has become the main source for most mobile phone users to obtain news information. However, there are still many problems in APP reading, such as unreasonable layout of pictures and texts, too complicated content of text information, etc., which seriously affect the reading enthusiasm of the elderly. Therefore, how to make the interface layout attract the elderly users, make the elderly accustomed to interface reading, and then improve the efficiency of information retrieval for the elderly has become a new challenge for the aging design of news APP interface layout. Therefore, in order to achieve the best effect of information interface aging design, it is necessary to pay

© Springer Nature Switzerland AG 2021
M. Kurosu (Ed.): HCII 2021, LNCS 12764, pp. 138–152, 2021.
https://doi.org/10.1007/978-3-030-78468-3_10

attention to the study of cognitive characteristics of the elderly. From the perspective of graphic layout, this paper focuses on analyzing the perception characteristics of the elderly in three aspects: sight, hearing and touch, and paying attention to the influence of news APP interface layout on the use experience and cognitive efficiency of the elderly, which will help to further optimize the graphic layout structure of news APP and enhance the overall user experience of news applications.

2 Interpretation of the Perception Characteristics of the Elderly Group

2.1 Visual Features

Visual perception is an important perception channel for human beings, and about 80% of external information is obtained by visual means. With the increase of age, people's visual organs will age and their visual ability will decline obviously. For example: (1) The field of vision becomes smaller, and the pupils of the elderly become smaller, which will reduce the field of vision compared with the young people. (2) The ability to distinguish colors is weakened, and the cornea of the elderly becomes flat and thick, which will lead to the deterioration of the ability of the elderly to distinguish red, blue and yellow. (3) Visual acuity declines, which leads to the weakening of the accuracy of receiving external information.

2.2 Auditory Features

Attenuation of hearing ability is a common phenomenon among the elderly. The decline of hearing perception of the elderly is mainly manifested as: (1) hearing loss, which is caused by aging of the hearing organs of the elderly; (2) The language comprehension ability declines, and the elderly people's language processing ability weakens under normal speech speed and quiet environment. Studies show that even normal elderly people have lower language comprehension ability than young people. According to research data, the language recognition rate of the former is about 85.7%, while that of the latter is about 95%. Due to the decline of temporal processing and frequency resolution, as well as the extension of information capture time, its ability to summarize context and content before and after communication is reduced. (3) The sensitivity of voice decreases, and the ability to recognize language in noisy environment or competitive signal decreases with age, with an average of about 90% at the age of 65, and an average of about 60% at the age of 75.

2.3 Tactile Features

The decline of tactile perception of the elderly is mainly manifested as the decrease of tactile sensitivity, which leads to the decrease of tactile sensitivity of the elderly due to the decrease of sensory nerve fibers on the skin, resulting in a series of conditions such as slow behavior.

3 Correspondence Model Between Perceived Characteristics of the Elderly and Page Layout of News APP

When people enter the old age, the sensitivity of each sensory organ will gradually decrease, which makes it more difficult for the elderly to complete some basic interface operations. Compared with young people, the rate of misoperation will be higher. Donald a Norman pointed out three levels of design in emotional design, namely, instinct level, behavior level and reflection level. Among them, instinctive needs are the most basic needs of the elderly, which are mainly reflected in perceptual needs, that is, visual, auditory and tactile needs. In the aging design of news APP interface layout, the main performance is to bring better reading experience to the elderly users through the overall page layout, so as to improve the information acquisition efficiency of reading news APP.

3.1 Relationship Model Under Visual Demand

The decline of visual perception leads to higher requirements of interface layout, icons, characters and colors for the elderly. The key of information interface design under visual demand lies in interface layout and color contrast. Yuan Lei found that enlarging interface picture elements, selecting long wave colors (red, etc.), reducing brightness difference and designing details can meet the visual perception needs of the elderly, thus reducing the discomfort of users in the process of information retrieval. Yao Jiang, Mary Zajicek and other scholars have studied the interactive design of product information interface for the elderly, and found that interface layout structure and graphic distribution have an important impact on the interface interaction of information products for the elderly. The interface structure should be clear, the fonts should be slightly larger, the pictures should be simple and the overall layout should conform to the visual cognitive habits of the elderly. More complex interface layout will further increase the burden and difficulty of reading for elderly users, so the information interface layout pays more attention to the need of concise layout.

3.2 Relationship Model Under Auditory Demand

The key of interface design based on auditory perception lies in language broadcasting and voice input supported by news APP. The elderly users have visual impairment or typing difficulties due to the weakening of perception ability. Under normal circumstances, the elderly have certain difficulties in inputting and outputting news information. If we reduce the efficiency of information retrieval from the perspective of auditory perception, we can help elderly users to read news information efficiently to a certain extent, and at the same time reduce the difficulty of interface operation. Liu Kang and other scholars believe that sound is mostly used for information feedback. When old users operate products, they can feedback the right or wrong of operation through the types of sound. For example, soothing and pleasant sound means that the operation is correct and can be continued, while urgent warning sound means that the operation is wrong and stopped.

3.3 Relationship Model Under Tactile Demand

The key of interface design based on tactile sensation lies in obvious tactile sensation and low fault tolerance. Due to the popularity of touch-screen mobile phones, a large number of elderly users are interested in using touch-screen mobile phones. With the increase of age, the tactile sensitivity of old people's fingers will decrease. Therefore, the enhancement of tactile sensation and the increase of tactile area can improve the effect of information feedback, thus reducing the frequency of misoperation of old users when operating the interface.

4 Experimental Study on Aging Resistance of News APP Interface Layout Based on Perceptual Features

4.1 Graphic Layout Structure Analysis

There are many researches on the layout of information search feedback interface at home and abroad, among which scholars such as White are famous. They have established rich information search and retrieval results interface layout based on multiple representation theory, which can present information retrieval results from multiple angles. Traditional retrieval interface texts tend to display title information, while multiple feedback interfaces pay more attention to enhancing implicit related feedback, which is conducive to reducing the uncertainty of information retrieval interaction between users and intelligent interfaces. The news information interface based on multiple feedback can not only display the target information in words, but also in pictures, audio and video. Through investigation, it is found that the popular news apps in China, such as Tencent News, Today's Headlines and Netease News, basically adopt the structure of left picture, right picture, left picture and right picture, and pure text. Therefore, based on the theory of multiple representations, this study will analyze the influence of the above three graphic layout designs on the information retrieval efficiency of the elderly.

4.2 Eye Movement Experimental Analysis of Information Retrieval Performance

There are two main behaviors of elderly users when using mobile news APP for information retrieval: visual search and visual browsing. Visual search refers to the purposeful retrieval of news information, while visual browsing refers to viewing news information without a destination. Among them, visual search can better reflect the interaction process between elderly users and information interface. Many domestic scholars, such as Zhang Lulu and Huang Kun, comb the influence of emotional load theory at home and abroad on the information interaction process. Comparing the interactive process of purposeful and non-purposeful retrieval information, it is found that the interface layout has obvious influence on the interactive process and retrieval efficiency of users' purposeful retrieval information. Therefore, this study takes the visual search efficiency of elderly users as the main reference index of information performance. In the research of user subjective feedback information retrieval, eye movement experimental research has been favored by more and more scholars. Eye tracking technology is helpful to analyze the information performance and attention distribution of users in the process of information search, and can also be used to test the effectiveness and usability of interactive interface in the process of human-computer interaction. Wu Dan and other scholars put forward four application trends of eye tracking in interactive information retrieval research: (1) research on cognitive differences in interactive information retrieval (2) research on mobile search based on eye movement (3) research on eye movement of interactive information retrieval behavior in natural environment (4) combination of eye tracking method and other diversified analysis methods. It shows that the eye movement experimental study provides a basis for the result analysis of user information retrieval efficiency, can more accurately study the cognitive behavior of elderly users in the process of visual search, and has guiding significance for the aging design of news APP interface layout.

4.3 Research Questions

Based on the analysis of graphic layout structure, this study divides the layout design of news APP interface into two categories, namely graphic display interface and text display interface, and tries to discuss the following research questions: first, whether the change of interface layout will have a significant impact on the information retrieval efficiency of the elderly, and how; Second, whether the change of interface layout has a significant impact on the subjective feelings of the elderly when reading news, and how. By answering these two research questions, we can understand the behavior preference of the elderly in reading the news APP interface, and provide the basis for the aging design of the news APP interface layout.

4.4 Experimental Research

Experimental Design. In this experimental study, a single variable experiment will be carried out by combining subjective measurement table with objective eye movement experimental data analysis. According to multiple representation theory and graphic layout analysis, the interface layout of news APP is set to three structural modes, namely, left picture, right text layout, right picture, left text layout and plain text layout. Each subject needs to search for the target in the mobile phone interface according to the keywords given by the experimenter in each test interface, and complete three information retrieval tasks in sequence. After the experiment is completed, the experimenter guides the subjects to fill in the subjective feeling measurement form.

In order to facilitate the analysis of eye movement data after the experiment, the graphic interface layout is divided into two interest areas: picture interest area and text interest area, and the information retrieval efficiency of the elderly is compared and studied through different page layout forms. The hot zone map, first fixation time, fixation points in interest area, fixation time and blink rate are taken as important evaluation indexes to measure the information retrieval efficiency of the elderly. After the experiment, the subjects evaluated the information retrieval process of news interface from usability, effectiveness, ease of use, satisfaction and comfort. A brief experimental design is shown in Fig. 1.

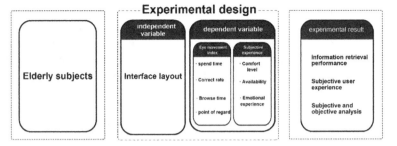

Fig. 1. Detailed experimental design flow chart

Experimental Environment and Materials. This experiment was completed in the laboratory of Nanjing University of Science and Technology, and the indoor lighting was normal. X3-120 model of Tobii Pro company was used in the experiment, which can record the eye movement track, gaze point, gaze time and other characteristics. The subjects sat in front of the display screen, keeping their eyes about 60–70 cm away from the display screen, and the equipment calculated the eye movement information such as eyeball position and fixation through corneal reflex mode and other information. In order to avoid the interference caused by the large changes in the interface structure, the interface layout of the same kind of news is being modified. The interface information of 15 mobile news clients was selected as the experimental material, and then the design was carried out according to three layout structures: left right text, right left text and plain text. In order to ensure the validity of the experimental results, the selected experimental material picture format is made to conform to the screen size of the secondary experimental equipment (iPhone 8), so as to ensure that the materials that the subjects see during the experiment are consistent with the actual mobile news materials. Experimental material display as shown in Fig. 2.

Fig. 2. Experimental material display

Experimental Subjects and Experimental Indicators. A total of 18 elderly subjects (all living in residential areas of Nanjing University of Science and Technology) were recruited in this experiment, aged between 60 and 70 years old, including 10 male subjects and 8 female subjects. All the subjects have no perceptual behavior defects, all the subjects have a high school education level or above, and all of them have the experience of using mobile phones to browse news apps to retrieve information. In this experiment, a single variable paradigm is adopted, with the layout of interface graphics and text as an independent variable and the retrieval time of subjects as a dependent variable. Other variables remain unchanged, and hot zone map, first fixation time, fixation points in interest area, fixation time and blink rate are important evaluation indexes for measuring information retrieval efficiency of the elderly. By analyzing the above evaluation indexes, we can find out how the layout of interface graphics and text will affect the information retrieval efficiency of elderly users.

Experimental Process and Data Collection

(1) In order to ensure that the subjects can successfully complete all experimental tasks, before the formal experiment, the subjects browse the experimental task arrangement under the guidance of experimenters, and familiarize themselves with the tasks that need to be completed in the experimental process in advance. The tasks of this experiment are as follows: First, the subjects should browse each sample picture for 15000 ms, and the stimulation interval between each picture is 2000 ms. Then search the browsed news information, that is, inform the news headlines, specific release time and other basic information, and find the target news by entering the headlines. The specific tasks are shown in Table 1.

Table 1. Experiment task content arrangement

Left picture and right text layout	Right picture and left text layout	Plain text layout
Find "Trump Tweet, World Wide Web, 9044 Comment" and open the interface	Search for "No vaccine for New York State? World Wide Web, 168 reviews" and open the interface	Search "New important position of the US Department of Commerce to promote dialogue tough? International Online, 729 reviews", open the interface
Find "Surge in New Coronary Cases, Beijing Daily Client, 110 Comments" and open the interface	Find "Pompeo arrives in Paris for embarrassing journey, reference message, 87 comments", and open the interface	Search "97-year-old Kissinger talks about Sino-US relations, Observer Network, 13,000 comments", and open the interface
Search "Obama denies that he will serve in the new US government because it is related to his wife, overseas website, 168 comments", open the interface	Search for "11 million confirmed diagnoses in the United States, Beijing Daily client, 61 reviews" and open the interface	Find "Supporters marching into Washington demonstration, 73 comments on the observer network", open the interface

(2) The experimenter explains the experimental process and points for attention to ensure that the subjects start the experiment after understanding the experimental process and operation.

(3) Connect the eye tracker, run the experimental software, and enter the eye movement calibration stage.

(4) Show the news interface pictures to the subjects in turn. First, the subjects should browse each sample picture for 15000 ms, and the stimulation interval between each picture is 2000 ms. Then, when the target interface is displayed, the subjects search for target words according to the task requirements, click the area where the target items are located after completing the task, and switch to the next target interface.

(5) After the subjects complete the information retrieval task of eye movement experiment, they collect subjective user experience data under the leadership of experimenters. It mainly includes three dimensions: comfort, usability and emotional changes. The comfort scale is adapted from reading comfort scale [13], which includes three questions. The availability measurement table is adapted according to the System Availability Questionnaire (SUS) [14], including ten questions. With reference to the Positive and Negative Emotion Scale (PANAS) [15], the emotional measurement table screened out 10 emotional options which are consistent with this study. Details of subjective user experience data tables in the above three items are as follows 2, 3 and 4 (Tables 2 and 4).

Table 2. User comfort measurement table—left picture and right text/right picture and left text/plain text

(1) The interface layout makes my eyes comfortable	(2) The content of the interface layout is clear	(3) The interface layout is easy to read

All items and tables adopt a satisfaction scoring system of 1–5, the higher the satisfaction, the higher the score.

Table 3. User usability measurement items—left picture and right text/right picture and left text/plain text

(1) General information search tasks can be completed in the interface layout	(2) In this interface layout, people are satisfied with the time it takes to complete the information search	(3) Satisfied with the assistance of this interface layout action
(1) This interface layout allows me to browse information more efficiently	(2) This interface layout makes it easier for me to accomplish what I want to do	(3) This interface layout makes my browsing purpose clearer
(6) This interface layout can meet my needs	(8) This interface layout is very useful	(9) This interface layout makes it easy to find the information you want
(10) I am satisfied with this layout		

Table 4. User sentiment measure—left picture and right text/right picture and left text/plain text

Item	Slight or no	Kind of	Moderate	Very strong	Extremely strong
(1) Interested in	1	2	3	4	5
(2) Disgust	1	2	3	4	5
(3) Excited	1	2	3	4	5
(4) Impatient	1	2	3	4	5
(5) Inspired	1	2	3	4	5
(6) Pleasure	1	2	3	4	5
(7) Trembling	1	2	3	4	5
(8) Worry	1	2	3	4	5
(9) Optimism	1	2	3	4	5
(10) Depressed	1	2	3	4	5

4.5 Experimental Results

Influence of Graphic Layout on Time and Accuracy of Information Retrieval for the Elderly. In this experiment, by changing the layout of news APP information interface, we explore the efficiency of elderly users in the process of information retrieval. By changing the layout of single variable graphics and text, and doing variance analysis of single variable. In the interface layout on the left and right, the average information retrieval time of 18 subjects is about 156.4 s, with the longest time and the lowest correct rate, which is 88.8%; In the layout of the left interface on the right, the average information retrieval time is about 128.3 s, and the correct rate is 91.3%; In plain text interface layout, the average information retrieval time is about 120.7 s, which takes the shortest time and the highest accuracy rate is 92.6%. See Table 5 for detailed data.

Table 5. The average time and accuracy of information retrieval in different news APP interface layouts.

	Task completion time (s)	Task completion rate
Left picture and right text layout	156.4 s	88.8%
Right picture and left text layout	128.3 s	91.3%
Plain text layout	120.7 s	92.6%

Influence of Graphic Layout on Subjective Experience of Information Retrieval of Elderly Users. The visual browsing time of elderly users in this experimental study refers to the time spent browsing information in the area of interest. The longer browsing time means that elderly users are more interested in the information in the area of interest. The gaze points of the interest area are the gaze points of the elderly users browsing information in the area. Through eye movement technology, the browsing time and fixation points of subjects in each interest area were recorded, and the browsing time and fixation points were compared and analyzed by post-data processing. The statistical results show that the browsing time ratio of the left text in the right picture is higher, while the right text in the left picture is lower. Details are shown in Table 6.

Table 6. Browsing time and gaze ratio of elderly users under different page layouts (standard deviation)

Ratio (%) and standard deviation	Browse time ratio	Fixation ratio
Left picture and right text layout	9.19 (12.66)	16.12 (8.11)
Right picture and left text layout	23.45 (12)	36.1 (8)

Further analysis of Table 3-1 shows that the ratio of fixation points of elderly users in the left interface layout of the right figure is about 11% higher than that in the right one of the left figure, which shows that the change of picture position has obvious influence on fixation points of elderly users in information retrieval, that is to say, the change of news information interface layout leads to the change of information retrieval time and browsing path of elderly users, thus affecting information retrieval efficiency.

Influence of Graphic Layout on Subjective Experience of Information Retrieval of Elderly Users. In exploring the influence of graphic layout on the subjective experience of elderly users, comfort, usability and emotional experience are taken as dependent variables, graphic layout of news interface is taken as independent variable, and single variable variance analysis is done. The results show that graphic layout has a significant impact on user experience comfort, usability and emotional experience, and elderly users have obvious emotional preference for different graphic layout structures. Detailed data are shown in Table 7.

Table 7. The impact of the interface layout on the user's subjective experience on the single variable analysis of variance

Dependent variable	Comfort	Availability	Emotional experience
Mean variance	16.62	32.12	40.53
Degree of freedom	2	2	2
F value	12.01	22.08	18.12
P value	0.001	0.001	0.001

The subjective experience of information retrieval of elderly users is further analyzed: (1) It is found that the average score of elderly users on the right text of the left picture is lower than that on the right picture (2.23, 3.45), and the comfort of plain text is the lowest (1.65); (2) It is found that the average score of the usability of the right text in the left picture is lower than that in the right picture, and the comfort of plain text is the lowest; (3) It is found that the average score of elderly users on emotional experience in the left picture is lower than that in the right picture, and the emotional experience in plain text is still the lowest. From the user's subjective experience, the elderly prefer the left text on the right picture, and the evaluation degree of news information retrieval is obviously higher than that of the left picture, right text and plain text. Comprehensive analysis shows that elderly users are more inclined to graphic layout, which shows that pictures can improve their reading experience. In the setting of interface picture position, elderly users prefer the structure of the left text on the right picture. This graphic layout based on users' subjective experience can reduce users' reading burden in information retrieval and improve users' reading efficiency. Detailed data are shown in Table 8.

Table 8. Average user comfort, usability, and emotional experience under different page layouts

	Mean comfort	Mean availability	Emotional experience
Left picture right text	2.23	2.15	2.12
Right picture left text	3.45	3.49	3.83
Plain text	1.65	1.89	1.97

5 Aging Design Strategy of News APP Interface Layout Based on Perceptual Features

According to the interpretation of the perception characteristics of the elderly and the layout structure of news interface, and the analysis of experimental data. The aging design strategy of news APP interface layout can be put forward from three aspects: emotional demand, interactive interface and operation mode.

5.1 Suitable Aging of Emotional Expression

Emotional expression mainly refers to the process that the interface layout can arouse the emotional memory and spiritual sustenance of elderly users in the process of information retrieval using news APP, thus establishing a kind of emotional cognition. First of all, the conscious or unconscious prompt design of different colors and shapes on the interface layout should conform to the perceptual characteristics of the elderly users, reduce the distance between information and users, and improve the emotional experience of the elderly users. Secondly, the design of different interface modes is interesting and easy to use. In addition, we can use situational and quasi-materialized design reasonably, which can arouse the resonance of users' hearts. Finally, by adding some personalized settings, elderly users can have their own preferences to sort and delete information levels, and can freely match interface colors and styles, which not only gives users a complete sense of participation, but also reduces the cognitive load brought by the information interface to elderly users.

5.2 Aging of Interactive Interface

Interactive interface mainly refers to the interaction between elderly users and information interface. In designing an aging interactive interface, we should focus on the design of information input and output, page adjustment and pointing settings. First of all, due to the decline of perception ability of the elderly, for some complex interface operations, multi-sensory cooperation is needed to successfully complete information retrieval. Secondly, due to the lack of information coverage, the elderly often have a longer time to understand the information and pictures displayed in the information interface, so it is necessary to set some information tips for the elderly users to help them successfully complete the information retrieval. Finally, the information interface should be smooth and smooth when switching, so as to reduce the interactive burden of elderly users in the process of searching and obtaining information.

5.3 Aging Adaptation of Operation Mode

Operation mode refers to the process and feedback of the old users' operation interface. Reasonable and effective operation mode helps the old people to know their own operation behavior, thus reducing operation errors and improving the emotional experience of information retrieval. First of all, the core idea of designing operation mode should be user-centered. Secondly, the operation mode should follow the principle of conciseness, intuition and clarity, and reduce the cognitive difficulty of elderly users as much as possible. Finally, the operation mode is diversified, providing the elderly with multi-sensory operation mode, and providing cancellable options after operation errors, thus reducing the fault-tolerant rate of operation.

6   Conclusion

This study is based on perceptual features to explore the aging of news APP interface layout, and to explore the influence of interface layout change on information retrieval efficiency of elderly users. According to the experimental results, we can see that: (1) the layout structure of news information interface has obvious influence on the reading efficiency of the elderly, and the reading efficiency of plain text interface layout is the highest; (2) Users with graphic interface layout have higher subjective experience scores, while plain text interface layout has the lowest scores. (3) The layout structure on the left of the right figure is the most satisfactory interface form for elderly users, which increases the time for users to browse information and also enhances the experience of users' information retrieval. Finally, based on experimental research and theoretical analysis, the aging design of news APP interface layout based on perceptual features should comprehensively consider the actual information retrieval efficiency and subjective experience evaluation of elderly users. The conclusion of this study can provide some help for the aging design of news APP interface layout and provide some effective ideas for the optimization and upgrading of news information interface design.

References

1. Scott, G.G., Hand, C.J.: Motivation determines Facebook viewing strategy: an eye movement analysis. Comput. Hum. Behav. **56**, 267–280 (2016). 409–449, 742
2. Yuan, Q., Hou, W.: Research on typical interface structure of mobile phone based on eye movement browsing law. J. Beijing Univ. Posts Telecommun. (Soc. Sci. Edn.) **16**(1), 25–30 (2014)
3. Hassenzahl, M., Monk, A.: The inference of perceived usability from beauty. Hum.-Comput. Interact. **25**(3), 235–260 (2010)
4. Zhang, L., Kun, H.: Research on information retrieval behavior of digital library users based on cognitive style. J. Inf. Sci. **11**, 1164–1174 (2018)
5. Kun, H., et al.: A summary of emotional load theory and application research in information behavior research. Libr. Inf. Sci. **12**, 116–124 (2018)
6. Mi, L., Zhong, N., Lu, S.: Eye movement research on visual search and browsing strategies of Web pages. J. Beijing Univ. Technol. **37**(5), 773–779 (2011)
7. Qing, K., Zhou, H.: Research on Interactive Behavior of Information Retrieval Based on User Cognitive Style Differences, pp. 9–10. Science Publishing House, Beijing (2017)
8. Yuan, L.: Perception-based interaction interface design and operation flow research of smart phones for the elderly. Art Des. (Theory) **5**, 92–94 (2016). Yuan, L.: Based on perception research on mobile phone interface design and operation of elderly. Art Des. (Theory) **5**, 92–94 (2016)
9. Mary, Z.: Interface design for older adults. In: Proceedings of the 2001 EC/NSF Workshop on Universal Accessibility of Ubiquitous Computing: Providing for the Elderly (2001)

10. Kang, L., Jiang, X., Li, S.: Application of feedback mechanism in product interaction design. Packag. Eng. **30**(22), 123–125 (2009)
11. Dan, W., Liu, C.: Eye tracking analysis in interactive information retrieval research. J. Libr. Sci. China **2**, 109–128 (2019)
12. White, R.W.: Using searcher simulations to redesign a poly representative implicit feedback interface. Inf. Process. Manag. **42**(5), 1185–1202 (2006)
13. Hou, G., et al.: Larger Chinese text spacing and size: effects on older users' experience. Aging Soc. **40**(2), 389–411 (2020)
14. Tellegen, A.: Development and validation of brief measures of positive and negative affect: the PANAS scales. J. Pers. Soc. Psychol. **54**(6), 1063–1070 (1988)
15. Brooke, J.: SUS—A quick and dirty usability scale. Usab. Eval. Ind. 189–194 (1996)
16. Eileen, K.: Eye movements: the past 25 years. Vis. Res. **13**(1), 1457–1483 (2011)
17. Lund, H.: Eye tracking in Library and Information Science: a literature review. Libr. Hi Tech **34**(4), 585–614 (2016)
18. Mostafa, J., Gwizdka, J.: Deepening the role of the user: neuro-physiological evidence as a basis for studying and improving search. In: ACM on Conference on Human Information Interaction and Retrieval, pp. 63–70. ACM (2016)
19. Lorigo, L., Haridasan, M., Brynjarsdóttir, H., et al.: Eye tracking and online search: lessons learned and challenges ahead. J. Assoc. Inf. Sci. Technol. **59**(7), 1041–1052 (2014)
20. Katti, H., Kankanhalli, M.: Eye-tracking methodology and applications to images and video. In: ACM International Conference on Multimedia, pp. 641–642. ACM (2011)
21. Papoutsaki, A., Laskey, J., Huang, J.: SearchGazer: webcam eye tracking for remote studies of web search. In: Proceedings of the 2017 Conference on Conference Human Information Interaction and Retrieval, pp. 17–26. ACM (2017)
22. Joachims, T., Granka, L., Pan, B., et al.: Accurately interpreting click through data as implicit feedback. ACM SIGIR Forum **51**(1), 4–11 (2017)
23. Zhang, X., Gu, L.: Research on information architecture and interface design of medical APP for the elderly. Design **21**, 146–147 (2015)
24. Lin, W., Rao, P.-L.: Investigation on the factors affecting the elderly's acceptance of information technology. Ind. Eng. **13**(5), 85–88 (2010). Lin, W., Rao, P.-L.: Elders information technology acceptance. Ind. Eng. J. **13** (2010)
25. Wang, J., Li, J., Yu, S.: Research on cognitive decline of elderly users based on cognitive load. Soc. Psychol. Sci. **1**, 31–36 (2017). Wang, J., Li, J., Yu, S.: Cognitive decline of elderly users based on cognitive load. Soc. Psychol. Sci. **1**, 31–36 (2017)
26. Ping, H.: Research on electronic product interaction design under the background of aging society. Tianjin University of Technology, Tianjin (2015). Ping, H.: Electronic product interaction design in the aging society. Tianjin University of Technology, Tianjin (2015)
27. Liu, A., Yang, Y., Sun, T.: Product design for the elderly based on human-computer interaction. Ind. Eng. **5**, 92–97 (2010)
28. Liu, L., Yang, Y., Sun, T.: Design of elderly products based on human-computer interaction. Ind. Eng. **5**, 92–97 (2010)
29. Wang, F.: Mobile phone interface design for the elderly based on modern lifestyle. Hebei University of Technology, Tianjin (2014). Wang, F.: Design of mobile phone interface for the elderly based on modern life style. Hebei University of Technology, Tianjin (2014)
30. Liu, X., Ding, H., Wei, X.: Research on the interface design of information APP based on the cognitive demand model of the elderly. Design **280**(1), 28–29 (2018). Liu, X.-L., Ding, H., Wei, X.: Design of information APP interface based on cognitive need model of elderly. Design **280**(1), 28–29 (2018)

31. Zhang, H., Tu, D., Zhang, G.: The design of human-computer interaction channel and interface suitable for the change of cognitive ability of the elderly. Ergonomics **19**(1), 67–71 (2013). Zhang, H., Tu, D.-W., Zhang, G.: Human-computer interaction channel and interface design suitable for the change of cognitive ability of the elderly. Chin. J. Ergon. **19**(1), 67–71 (2013)
32. Chen, Z.: Application of cognitive psychology in UI interface design. Packag. Eng. **38**(16), 42–45 (2017). Chen, Z.: Application of cognitive psychology in the UI design. Packag. Eng. **38**(16), 44 (2017)
33. Yin, K.: Innovation and realization of user-based service design. Packag. Eng. **36**(2), 9–12 (2015). Yin, K.: Design and implementation of user-based service design. Packag. Eng. **36**(2), 9–12 (2015)

Research on Modular Design of Children's Furniture Based on Scene Theory

Junnan Ye, Wenhao Li, and Chaoxiang Yang(⊠)

East China University of Science and Technology, Shanghai 200237, China

Abstract. Modular children's furniture can meet the needs of children's growth for sustainable use due to the diversification of functions and the variability of forms, which has become the main research object in the children's furniture market. Specifically, modular design, as a systematic design method, can effectively shorten the product design cycle, quickly respond to market demands, and extend the product life cycle. Thus, it can help companies quickly grab market share and achieve commercial success. However, through the investigation of the existing modular children's furniture in the market, it is found that most of the products are only for functions, ignoring the emotional needs of users during the interaction with products, such as the satisfaction of intelligence and interest. Scenario theory is a business development concept that understands and interprets user needs from the perspective of users' scenario and accurately adapts services and information, thereby helping companies gain reputation and commercial profits by shaping a higher service experience and service conversion rate. This paper studies the design of modular children's furniture based on the research method of scene theory. This study applies scene theory into the design of modular children's furniture, which can effectively help designers more accurately grasp the relationship between products and users and their needs, thereby further improving product rationality and product satisfaction, and also providing a new and effective exploration for modular children's furniture design.

Keywords: Scene theory · Modular design · Children's furniture · Furniture design · User experience

1 Introduction

With the growth of global urban population, residents' income and investment in the construction industry, coupled with the continuous consumption upgrades and parents' increasing attention to the growth environment of their children, the global children's furniture market continues to expand, with a market share of approximately 100 billion. Modular children's furniture can meet the needs of children's growth for sustainable use due to the diversification of functions and the variability of forms, which has become the main research object in the children's furniture market. Specifically, modular design, as a systematic design method, can effectively shorten the product design cycle, quickly respond to market demands, and extend the product life cycle. Thus, it can help companies quickly grab market share and achieve commercial success. However, through

© Springer Nature Switzerland AG 2021
M. Kurosu (Ed.): HCII 2021, LNCS 12764, pp. 153–172, 2021.
https://doi.org/10.1007/978-3-030-78468-3_11

the investigation of the existing modular children's furniture in the market, it is found that most of the products are only for functions, ignoring the emotional needs of users during the interaction with products, such as the satisfaction of intelligence and interest.

Scenario theory is a business development concept that understands and interprets user needs from the perspective of users' scenario and accurately adapts services and information, thereby helping companies gain reputation and commercial profits by shaping a higher service experience and service conversion rate. This paper studies the design of modular children's furniture based on the research method of scene theory. First of all, through literature research, observation, interview, and scene analysis, the types of children's furniture, usage scenarios, children's use behaviors, and parents' consumption concepts are investigated, thus creating the objective scene of users' demand for modular children's furniture, with three major functions of "safety and firmness, intelligence and interest, flexibility and durability". On this basis of the objective scene, through the KJ analysis method and AHP analytic hierarchy process, this paper defines the five design requirements for the modularization of children's furniture (reasonable size, fun, versatility, unified style, safety), as well as the order of importance of the five design elements. Furthermore, based on the design principle of furniture modularization, focusing on functional requirements analysis and scene adaptation theory, a set of children's furniture modular system is constructed, with support module and bearing module as the basic modules, graffiti module and game module as special modules and other adaptation modules as the main content. The furniture modular system adopts plug-in module connection mode, square and round geometrical module form, and module size in line with ergonomics. Besides, natural materials such as solid wood are used as the main materials. Finally, DFMA technology is introduced to analyze and evaluate the modular combination mode, manufacturing process and production characteristics of the children's furniture modular system to verify the feasibility and effectiveness of the design practice.

This study applies scene theory into the design of modular children's furniture, which can effectively help designers more accurately grasp the relationship between products and users and their needs, thereby further improving product rationality and product satisfaction, and also providing a new and effective exploration for modular children's furniture design.

2 Theoretical Research

2.1 Scene Theory

Scene theory is a user-centered design method inspired by several disciplines, such as anthropology, psychology, and design [1]. Its core is to understand and interpret user needs from the perspective of the user's scene, and to accurately adapt services and information to provide the users with creative solutions. Scene theory is characterized by flexibility, rationality, co-rationality, landing and standardization. There are mainly two ways to classify scene types in scene theory. The first one is to classify according to structured scenes, which can be divided into value scenes, activity scenes, and interactive scenes. The other is to divide the scene into objective scenes and target scenes, simulation scenarios, application scenarios according to the different stages of design.

2.2 Children's Furniture

Children's furniture is designed specifically for children to sit, lie down, or support and store items in their life, works or social practice. It needs to meet children's physical and psychological needs. Furniture is more than a simple functional material product, but is an important part in the daily life [2]. It must meet certain specific uses and provide certain aesthetic pleasure to arouse the associations in the process of contact and use.

2.3 Modular Furniture

Modular furniture design indicates the combination of a series of furniture functional modules through standardized interfaces [3]. It is applied in the design of the entire furniture product system, and is a standardized and modular design. The modular design of furniture mainly includes two aspects: module establishment and module combination.

3 Modular Children's Furniture Design Method and Process Based on Scene Theory

The scene design theory is composed of four stages [4]: (1) collection of scene user data; (2) the integration of data and construction of the scene model structure; (3) using data to prototype product and service concepts; (4) testing and improving the product concept. The procedures are shown in Fig. 1.

Fig. 1. Design method of scenario theory

3.1 Project Initiation Phase-Collecting Objective Scene Data

During the start-up phase of the project, the data collection of objective scenarios is required to understand the background of the target product. The intrinsic needs of users can be identified by collecting user-related data. Quantitative methods, such as questionnaire surveys or content analysis, and qualitative methods, such as interviews or observation can be used for data collection.

3.2 Structured Scenario-Build the Target Scenario Model

Before the scene model is constructed, the collected scene data should be sorted out, and the user settings under the target scene should be summarized. After that, a value scenario model will be created to fulfill the user's internal needs. The purpose of the value scenario model is to show the product goals in the scenario and provide the keywords in the design. Subsequently, an activity scenario model based on value scenario and user settings will be created to visually display the collected user activity information, construct the tasks and goals that should be completed, and to determine the product opportunity points. Finally, an interactive scene model based on the activity scene and user settings will be created to explain the required operations and interactions for the tasks and goals in the activity scene model. It is necessary to combine the characteristics of the hardware and the user to provide a feasible system solution to the manufacturing of the product.

3.3 Product Design-Design Simulation Scenarios

It is difficult to imagine the specific image of the product and the process structured in the scene based on the description of the text. At this stage, it is necessary to design a specific solution and to visualize the needs of the user in the scene through the prototype of the scheme and the design of the product.

3.4 Program Usability Evaluation-Test Actual Application Scenarios

By using the design method based on scenario theory, the structured scenarios provide a process of "evaluation" and "visualization" for each stage. After each stage of the structured scene is completed, a scene model evaluation will be required. After all the construction target scenes are constructed and the visualization scheme is completed, a complete round of overall feasibility evaluation of the scheme will be carried out.

4 Research on the Functional Requirements and Use of Children's Furniture

4.1 Research Purpose and Content

(1) Research purpose
   The purpose of this survey is to clarify the specific functional requirements and the problems with the furniture in children's rooms to help with the construction of children's furniture modular systems.
(2) Research content
   The content of the survey is mainly divided into two parts: ❶ Observe the usage of children's furniture, such as tables and chairs, bed cabinets, and storage, including the interaction between children and furniture and the occurrence of problem. ❷ Conduct interviews with children's parents to understand the consumption tendency of children's furniture and the demand for the product.

4.2 Research Method and Process

(1) Research methods: observation, unstructured interview
(2) Research process: The investigation of the using of children's furniture is divided into six steps (see Fig. 2).

Fig. 2. Investigation and research process

4.3 Research Places and Users

(1) Research site
A field survey is conducted on the households of middle-income families with children aged 0–12 in Huangshi City. The children's rooms in 5 residential communities were visited, mainly in the Nanjing Road Community, Tianfang Rose Garden, Huangshi Port District. Hubin Avenue No. 34 Community, Huangshigang Bridge South Community.
(2) Research users
The subjects of this survey include 30 children and their parents.

4.4 Usage of Children's Furniture for Children Aged 0–12

The user pattern of children's furniture is mainly obtained by observing the behavior of children and their parents in using the furniture in the following two scenarios:

(1) Children and parents use tables, chairs, bed cabinets, and storage furniture;
(2) Children's spontaneous behaviors when using tables, chairs, bed cabinets, and storage furniture.

By summarizing children' pattern in the above two scenarios, the behavior and problems of three types of children's furniture are extracted, and the individual functional needs for children's furniture is listed in Table 1.

Table 1. Functional requirements and usage of children's furniture

	Behavior	Functional needs	Usage and problems
Tables and chairs	Sit and learn	Load bearing	Unreasonable size, unable to adjust flexibly
	Stationery, toys placement	Item placement	Insufficient free space on desktop
	Doodle on the desktop	Doodle game	The graffiti traces on the desktop are difficult to clean up
Bed cabinets	Go to bed	Safe and comfort	The distance between the railings of the children's bed is not appropriate, some cannot protect it, and some are easy to jam the child
	Clothing storage	Organize storage	Unreasonable size and capacity, unable to adjust flexibly
	Cabinet door graffiti	Doodle game	Graffiti traces are difficult to clean
	Space organization	Environment layout	If the furniture is too large and the center of gravity is unstable, it will cause the children's furniture to fall and hurt children
Storage	Books and toys placement	Item placement	The storage unit is too small and it is inconvenient to get things

4.5 Functional Requirements of Children's Furniture

The furniture usage in Table 1 is sorted and classified based on the needs of both parents and children. The functional requirements of children's furniture system can be obtained, which can be divided into three categories:

(1) Safe and firm. Given children's low awareness of self-protection and their active nature, safety is the primary factor in the design of children's furniture. It includes structural safety, material safety, and color safety [5].
(2) Flexible and durable. Many existing children's furniture are only brightly-colored miniature of adult furniture, without considering the characteristics of children's physical and psychological growth [6]. Therefore, singular function and style, unreasonable scale, and lack of sustainability are the main problems that obstruct the development of children's furniture [7]. The modular design of children's furniture not only expands the use of children's furniture, but also solves the problem of homogeneity in design.

(3) Puzzle and interesting. Children's furniture must first be safe to use, and should meet certain requirements for guidance, education and intellectual development. In early childhood education, "play" is used as a cognitive means to form a thinking mode [8]. Games are the lifestyle of children, and designing furniture is about presenting a lifestyle [9]. Meanwhile, the design of educational furniture can attract children's attention and improve their practical ability and coordination in the process of using the furniture. Therefore, children's furniture should be educational and interesting.

5 Construction of the Target Scene Model of Modular Furniture for Children

5.1 Research on the Design Requirements of Modular Furniture for Children

Before carrying out the modular design, it is necessary to clarify the specific constraints and the design requirements [10]. Based on the observations and interviews in Chapter 3, we use the KJ analysis method to collect information from the perspective of the designer and clarify the requirements. The specific research process is as follows:

(1) Decide the theme: KJ analysis is applied to explore the design requirements of modular furniture for children.
(2) Method of collecting information: collective BS method.
(3) The process of information collection: ❶ Determine the members of the discussion group, including a furniture industry designer, a furniture manufacturer, a professional with a master's degree in furniture, and two doctoral students. ❷ Define goals. ❸ Build consensus. ❹ Start a brainstorming: gather the group members to brainstorm on the design requirements of furniture modularization, and to summarize the proposed furniture modularization into phrases. Record these notions on the cards, and eliminate the cards with the same meaning. The remaining card is called the "basic card" (see Fig. 3).

Fig. 3. Basic card   **Fig. 4.** Team title card   **Fig. 5.** Large group of title cards

(4) Marshalling

1. Put all "basic cards" on the desktop;
2. All the members form a card group to discuss the requirements according to the cards with similar meanings;

3. Analyze and summarize the content of the cards in the group, and use an appropriate title to review the common points of the cards in the group. Write this title on a card as a "group title card" (see Fig. 4);

4. Regard the "group title card" as an individual, merge the "group title cards" with similar content again, and name the appropriate title as the "large group title card" (see Fig. 5);

5. Draw the conclusion.

The specific content of the three-level cards are summarized, and the information is shown in Table 2. The content of the "big group title card" indicates the modular design requirements of children's furniture. It includes ① scientific and reasonable modular size; ② educational and interesting elements in the modular; ③ universality of the modular; ④ unified style of the module; ⑤ safety. Since the hierarchy between the five requirements is not yet clear, it is necessary to conduct AHP analysis into these five design requirements.

Table 2. Modular design requirements for children's furniture

Basic card	Subtitle card	Headline card
The structural proportions of the modular furniture size and the child's body size are coordinated	Scientific and reasonable modular size	Scientific and reasonable modular size
The module has the ability to grow, and the furniture size can be adjusted, which can extend the life cycle		
The size of the module meets the ergonomic requirements of children of the target age, and is comfortable		
Modular modeling cartoon	Modular form interesting	Educational and interesting elements in the modular
Module modeling biomimetic		
The modular shape design has a sense of rhythm and rhythm, and follows the principle of order		
The module has strong practicability, multi-purpose, modular combination of diversified functions, customizable, and can meet the needs of individual customization	Module function puzzle and interesting	
The module has complete functional configuration to meet the differences in the functional needs of children at different ages		
Modular furniture meets children's play behavior		

(*continued*)

Table 2. (*continued*)

Basic card	Subtitle card	Headline card
Module assembly can cultivate children's hands-on and practical ability, stimulate children's imagination, and exercise creative thinking		
Module assembly can strengthen parent-child interaction and enhance the emotional communication between parents and children		
Module technology and structure are standardized and highly versatile	Universality of the modular	Universality of the modular
The module is easy to use, convenient for children to use		
Systematic modular design, recyclable, reusable, and interchangeable		
Modular style conforms to children's natural nature, individuality, freedom and authenticity	Unified style of the module	Unified style of the module
The style of the module is unified with the style of children's living environment		
Module color matching is overall coordinated and soft		
Modular furniture decoration and beautification are compatible with the use function, and does not affect the normal use function		
The module structure has strong stability, ensuring safety in any state of use	Module structure safety	Safety
Module combination should use hardware reasonably, so as not to cause noise pollution to children		
The module should have a safe design that guides children to use correctly		
The modular furniture switch is closed with a protective device, and ventilation is carried out in a confined space		
The surface of the module material is easy to clean and wear-resistant	Module material safety	
Module material meets the comfort of children's touch		

Table 2. (*continued*)

Basic card	Subtitle card	Headline card
The module material has strong chemical stability, no irritating odor, and does not cause children's olfactory hypersensitivity		
The base material and auxiliary materials of the modular furniture are all green materials, no pollution		
Modular shape modeling uses soft curves, and the edges and corners are rounded	Module form safety	
The module form has strong visual stability		
Modular furniture should have warning signs for dangerous behaviors to help children avoid danger		
The color of the module is not over-stimulating, prevents visual fatigue and protects the development of the optic nerve	Module color safety	
Color selection is in line with the characteristics and preferences of the target child's age group		

5.2   Level Analysis of Modular Design Requirements for Children's Furniture

AHP analytic method is used to analyze the modular design requirements of children's furniture, and the importance of the five-point design requirements is ranked in accordance with expert scoring and rational data weight analysis. The details are as follows:

The 5 points of modular design requirements obtained in 4.1 were drawn into a design requirement importance score sheet, and a total of 10 designers were invited as the experts to evaluate the importance of the design requirements from the perspective of furniture design by applying the scoring standards (Table 3).

Table 3. The scoring standards of the importance of furniture modular design requirements

I is absolutely important to J. Fill in "5:1" in the corresponding box
I is very important compared to J, fill in "4:1" in the corresponding box
I is obviously more important than J, fill in "3:1" in the corresponding box
I is slightly more important than J, fill in "2:1" in the corresponding box
I is as important as J, fill in "1:1" in the corresponding box

(2) According to the above-mentioned scoring standards, a score sheet for the modular design requirements of children's furniture can be obtained. It has a total of 10 copies. Table 4 is a diagram of the score sheet.

Table 4. An example of the scoring sheet of modular design requirements

I	J				
	The scientific and reasonable size of the module	Safety	Universality of the modular	Unified module style	Educational and interesting elements in the modular
The scientific and reasonable size of the module	1	1/4	2	2	1/2
Safety	4	1	2	4	2
Universality of the modular	2	1/3	1	2	1
Unified module style	1	1/5	1	1	1/2
Educational and interesting elements in the modular	2	1/2	2	2	1

(3) According to the scoring sheet of the modular design requirements of children's furniture, the importance evaluation matrix B can be obtained. The eigenvector W of the matrix can be calculated.

$$B = \begin{bmatrix} 1 & 1/4 & 2 & 2 & 1/2 \\ 4 & 1 & 2 & 4 & 2 \\ 2 & 1/3 & 1 & 2 & 1 \\ 1 & 1/5 & 1 & 1 & 1/2 \\ 2 & 1/2 & 2 & 2 & 1 \end{bmatrix}$$

B_{ij} represents the degree of importance of the modular design requirement i relative to the modular design requirement j, $B_{ij} = 1/B_{ij}$.

The importance of the modular design of children's furniture is calculated according to the following formulas:

$$\overline{w_i} = \sqrt[m]{\prod_{j=1}^{m} B_{ij}}$$

$$w_i = \overline{w_i} / \sum_{i=1}^{m} \overline{w_i}$$

Where Wi is the weight required for modular design of children's furniture.

Afterwards, the weights required for modular design of children's furniture are shown in Table 5.

Table 5. Weights required for modular design of children's furniture

Expert number	Element				
	The scientific and reasonable size of the module	Safety	Universality of the modular	Unified module style	Educational and interesting elements in the modular
01	0.1606	0.4004	0.1541	0.0847	0.2002
02	0.1301	0.5004	0.0932	0.0587	0.2176
03	0.1623	0.3840	0.2047	0.1126	0.1364
04	0.1418	0.3925	0.2808	0.0827	0.1022
05	0.0921	0.4166	0.1339	0.0905	0.2669
06	0.1741	0.4521	0.1053	0.0720	0.1966
07	0.1269	0.3387	0.2168	0.1322	0.1853
08	0.1295	0.4122	0.1440	0.1251	0.1892
09	0.2204	0.4330	0.1080	0.0721	0.1665
10	0.0795	0.1867	0.1320	0.0641	0.5377
Average weight	0.14173	0.39166	0.15728	0.08947	0.21366

By comparing the weight values in Table 5, we can see that the modular design requirements of children's furniture can be ranked in the descending order of importance. ① Safety; ② educational and interesting elements in the modular; ③ universality of the modular; ④ the scientific and reasonable size of the module; ⑤ unified module style.

5.3 Decomposition of Requirements for Modular Design of Children's Furniture

Generally, modular furniture design can be divided into three steps: (1) modular overall design; (2) modular design; and (3) modular product design [11]. The above-mentioned five-point design requirements should also correspond to the specific design content in the requirements (Table 6), so that it can guide the directional and purposeful implementation of modular design.

Table 6. The corresponding requirement and solutions in the design stage

Corresponding to the design stage	Claim	Solution
Overall module design	Universality of the modular	Module function analysis
Modular design	The scientific and reasonable size of the module	Module size meets ergonomic requirements
Modular product design	Safety Unified module style Educational and interesting elements in the modular	Reasonable design according to specific design requirements

6 Modular Children's Furniture Design and Evaluation

6.1 Construction of Modular System for Children's Furniture

When carrying out the modular design of children's furniture, a modular system, and the framework of the modular furniture system should be constructed in a standardized and systematic way of thinking. Modular system construction is mainly composed of three parts: modular object division, module function integration and module division.

Object Division of Children's Furniture Modules. There are many types of children's furniture. Before building the modular system, the objects of modular furniture implementation should be clarified to select the individual type of furniture that is suitable for modular design. Children's furniture mainly includes three types: tables and chairs, bed cabinets, and storage. The requirements of modules should be universally combined. In this study, we put bed cabinets and storage furniture in the same modular furniture system.

Functional Integration of Children's Furniture Modules. The division of children's furniture should be based on the function of the furniture [12]. Therefore, the function of the furniture should be analyzed and integrated. In view of the importance of the function of furniture, the total function of the furniture can be decomposed into basic functions, installation functions, special functions, adaptive functions and user functions.

Division of Children's Furniture Modules. The modules of children's furniture corresponding to the above five functional types can be divided into basic modules, special modules, interface modules, adaptive modules, and non-deterministic modules.

(1) Basic module. The basic module corresponds to the basic function, which is mostly the bearing function [13]. Therefore, the basic module of children's furniture includes two furniture modules: bearing module and support module.
(2) Special modules. Special modules correspond to special functions. The game function is a special function setting up to meet the special needs of children [14]. Therefore, special modules include game modules such as peeping module and graffiti module.

(3) Interface module. The interface module corresponds to the installation function and is used to connect the basic module to realize the functional combination of the module. In view of the different connection modules, the interface modules can be divided into a bearing module interface module, a support module interface module and a game module interface module.

(4) Adaptation module. The adaptation module corresponds to the adaptation function. Due to the different needs of children with different body sizes for furniture, children's furniture needs to be equipped with adaptation modules to meet the needs of children at different ages.

(5) Non-deterministic module. Non-deterministic modules correspond to user functions. For children's furniture, the functional modules that can satisfy children's potential game behaviors are non-deterministic modules, which belong to the extended part of the modular system and should be enriched in the subsequent research.

In accordance with the above analysis, the framework of the modular system of children's furniture is shown in Fig. 6.

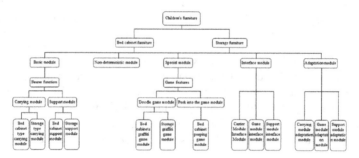

Fig. 6. Children's furniture modular system

6.2 Design Scheme Display

Module Display. Based on the design principle of furniture modularization, focusing on functional requirements analysis and scene adaptation theory, a set of children's furniture modular system is constructed, with support module and bearing module as the basic modules, graffiti module and game module as special modules and other adaptation modules as the main content (see Tables 7 and 8). Different support modules are connected through the interface module to construct a furniture frame, and then load-bearing modules, game modules, are placed to form a modular furniture unit. The furniture modular system adopts plug-in module connection mode, square and round geometrical module form, and module size in line with ergonomics. Besides, natural materials such as solid wood are used as the main materials.

Table 7. Support module icon

Single-layer bidirectional support module	Single-layer three-way support module	Double-layer three-way support module
Single layer bidirectional support module 2	Single layer bidirectional module support 3	Single-layer three-way module support 2

Table 8. Diagrams of other modular parts

Load-bearing module/Tuya module	Interface module	Adaptation module	Peek into the game module

Modular Furniture Display. The children's furniture in the modular furniture system includes cribs for 0–3 years old, beds for 3–6 years old and for 6–12 years old, bookcases and wardrobe for 3–6 years old, and growth Style wardrobe for 0–12 years old. The furniture is obtained through the combination of various modules, as shown in Table 9.

Modular Furniture Scene Display. The above modular can be combined and matched to form the furnishings of children's room, which is shown in Fig. 7.

6.3 DMFA Technical Analysis of Modular Children's Furniture

Design for manufacturability (DFM) manifests the essence of improving the current manufacturing process of the product [15]. The application of DFM technology mainly focuses on analyzing the manufacturability of design information, evaluating the rationality of manufacturing, and making improvement in the design [16]. Therefore, it is necessary to consider the relevant characteristics of the product, such as assemblability and manufacturability, in the design.

Table 9. Modular furniture

Cribs for 0-3 years old	
Use part modules: Load-bearing module, support module, interface module, peeping game module, adaptation module	Combination method: Double-layer three-way support module + peeping game module + interface module = guardrail Load-bearing module = bed board Adaptation module*4=bed leg
Beds for 3-6 years old	
Use part modules: Load-bearing module, support module, interface module, adaptation module	Combination method: Single-layer three-way support module 3 + single-layer two-way support module * 2 + interface module = guardrail Load-bearing module = bed board Adaptation module*4=bed leg
Beds for 6-12 years old	
Use part modules: Load-bearing module, support module, interface module, adaptation module	Combination method: Single-layer three-way support module + single-layer two-way support module*2+single-layer two-way support module 3*4+single-layer two-way support module 2*4+adaptation module*4+load-bearing module*10=bed Load-bearing module = bed head

(*continued*)

Table 9. (*continued*)

Bookcases for 3-6 years old	
Use part modules: Load-bearing module, support module, interface module, adaptation module	Combination method: Single-layer two-way support module*6+Single-layer three-way support module*3+bearing module*4=bookcase 　　Adaptation module*4=cabinet feet
Wardrobe for 3-6 years old	
Use part modules: Load-bearing module, support module, interface module, adaptation module	Combination method: Double-layer two-way support module*2+Double-layer three-way support module 2+Single-layer three-way support module*3+Load-bearing module*3+Adaptation module*6=Wardrobe Adaptation module*4=cabinet feet
growth Style wardrobe for 0-12 years old	
Use part modules: Load-bearing module, support module, interface module, adaptation module	Combination method: Four-layer three-way support module*2+Double-layer three-way support module 2*2+Single-layer three-way support module*8+Load-bearing module*9+Adaptation module*16=Wardrobe

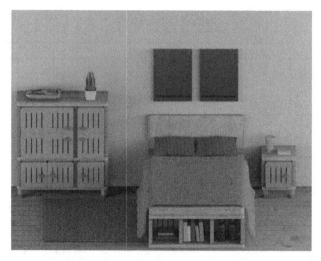

Fig. 7. Children's furniture scene display

Manufacturability Analysis and Optimization. By determining the specific production size of modular furniture, adjusting the proportions, determining the small-scale model manufacturing plan, selecting the three-plywood as the main model processing ingredients, processing raw materials such as running-in and cutting, and selecting the smallest-size hardware connectors for assembly, we can verify the manufacturability of modular furniture [17].

Assemblability Analysis and Optimization. The evaluation of assemblability should consider three aspects: cost, efficiency and technology [18]. Since the design has not been put into mass production, this study cannot obtain the cost and efficiency of the assembly unit. We can predict that these aspects are affected by the following factors: the number of parts, the type of parts, and the reasonable unit product structure, the assembly steps, the difficulty of assembly, the quality of each assembling step, the reasonable degree of assembly plan and resource planning. In the entire assembly process of the product, the technical characteristics should be improved to ensure that the technology is easy to use.

Although the quantitative evaluation index of the actual data cannot be obtained due to the lack of objective data, the qualitative evaluation of the assembly of children's furniture can be carried out by taking the above-mentioned influencing factors into account [19]. In other words, the less the number of parts, the greater the variety; the more reasonable the unit product structure, the fewer the assembly steps; the simpler the assembly action, the more reasonable the assembly plan and resource planning; the lower the cost of assembly action and the less the time wasted in the design, the higher the assemblability. Modular children's furniture should follow the principle of universality. The modules are simple and unified, the structure is reasonable, so that the design can be assembled more easily.

7 Summary and Forward

This paper studies the design of modular children's furniture based on the research method of scene theory. The main achievements are as follows:

(1) Through literature research, observation, interview, and scene analysis, the types of children's furniture, usage scenarios, children's use behaviors, and parents' consumption concepts are investigated, thus creating the objective scene of users' demand for modular children's furniture, with three major functions of "safety and firmness, intelligence and interest, flexibility and durability".

(2) On this basis of the objective scene, through the KJ analysis method and AHP analytic hierarchy process, this paper defines the five design requirements for the modularization of children's furniture (reasonable size, fun, versatility, unified style, safety), as well as the order of importance of the five design elements.

(3) Furthermore, based on the design principle of furniture modularization, focusing on functional requirements analysis and scene adaptation theory, a set of children's furniture modular system is constructed, with support module and bearing module as the basic modules, graffiti module and game module as special modules and other adaptation modules as the main content. The furniture modular system adopts plug-in module connection mode, square and round geometrical module form, and module size in line with ergonomics. Besides, natural materials such as solid wood are used as the main materials.

(4) Finally, DFMA technology is introduced to analyze and evaluate the modular combination mode, manufacturing process and production characteristics of the children's furniture modular system to verify the feasibility and effectiveness of the design practice.

Meanwhile, due to the limited depth of scientific research and constraints of time, this research has certain deficiencies that calls for further effort.

(1) Since the main body of the article is about modular children's furniture, the research on scene theory should be conducted;

(2) The sample size is not sufficient, and the summary of children's behavior is not comprehensive enough. These will result in the division of furniture modules, which cannot meet the needs of all children. In the future study, children's furniture environment life, and game activities should be included to expand and update the module library;

(3) The exploration of the connection mode between the modules is not profound enough, as it is impossible to conduct a systematic study on the connection mode. The subsequent research on the modularization of children's furniture might start from analyzing the connection method of the modules, specifically the combination and connection methods of the modules, to improve the modular design of children's furniture.

References

1. Holtzblatt, K., Wendell, J.B., Wood, S.: Rapid contextual design: a how-to guide to key techniques for user-centered design. Ubiquity **2005**(March), 3 (2005)
2. Wen, Q.K.: Research and design of smart high-speed rail travel products based on scenario theory. Master, South China University of Technology (2019)
3. Chen, Z.: Research on the market analysis of children's furniture design. Master, Nanjing University of Science and Technology (2007)
4. Lin, H., Hua, Y.C., Yang, W.J.: On the modular design of mass-customized furniture. China Forest Prod. Ind. **3**, 10–12+42 (2004)
5. Cao, Y.F., Mu, Y.P., Duan, H.Y.: Humanized design of children's furniture. J. Northwest Forest. Univ. **24**(01), 173–176 (2009)
6. Huang, W.H., Yang, C.: Children's furniture explore innovative applications. Arts **12**, 197–198 (2012)
7. Liu, X.H., Zeng, H.: Domestic children furniture market analysis. Furniture **3**, 53–56 (2005)
8. Zhang, H.Y., Wang, F.H.: Design of biological furniture in the child amusement park. Furniture Inter. Des. **3**, 22–23 (2010)
9. Ji, X.D.: Preschool children furniture modeling design. New Technol. New Prod. China **16**, 97 (2010)
10. Dai, X.: Modular design of kindergarten children's furniture based on activity area division. Master, Nanjing University of Science and Technology (2018)
11. Ning, X.: Research and design practice of modular children's cardboard furniture. Master, Beijing Forestry University (2015)
12. Wang, S.: The application of modular design in product design. Furniture Inter. Des. **1**, 22–23 (2018)
13. Wu, Q., Jia, K., Liu, Y.: Sustainable design of children's bed based on Modularization. Packag. Eng. **40**(18), 140–144+175 (2019)
14. He, W.: A new probe into the design of interesting children's furniture. Packag. Eng. **40**(10), 294–296 (2019)
15. Qu, Y.T.: Research on the design of customized furniture modular system based on DFMA technology. Master, China Academy of Art (2019)
16. Sun, X.F.: DFA technology and application research. Master, Liaoning Technical University (2004)
17. Ye, W., Zhu, Y.: Design research on the shape and structure of customized furniture. Furniture Inter. Des. **3**, 14–15 (2018)
18. Du, J.W.: Food machinery design for manufacturing and assembly. Mach. Equip. **1**, 34 (2017)
19. Jeffrey: Assembly Automation and Product Design. Mechanical Industry Press, Beijing (2009)

A Design Method of Children Playground Based on Bionic Algorithm

Fei Yue$^{(\boxtimes)}$, Wenda Tian$^{(\boxtimes)}$, and Mohammad Shidujaman

Academy of Arts and Design, Tsinghua University, Beijing 100030, China

Abstract. A reasonable and healthy playground is an important guarantee for children to develop cognition through physical games. [] However, due to the influence of early childhood psychology and the popularity of stereotypes, the existing industrialized production of children's play space has been defined and designed from the perspective of adults. With the help of interdisciplinary thinking and tools, based on the theory of child psychology and the circular game system, we propose a new method of children's playground design. At first, we reviewed the fallacies of the past children's playground design and their causes and summarized the elements of ideal children's playground construction. Secondly, we introduced the Physarum polycephalum algorithm and brought this algorithm to the path generation of different terrains and environments. Third, we analyze the path and introduce the amoeba bionic algorithm tool to determine the facilities, and then generate a series of play facilities. Finally, we brought this result into the case and discussed its potential applications in interactive design.

Keywords: Space design · Child-playground interaction · Algorithm design · Children psychology · Interactive design

1 Introduction

Education is an activity that is not limited to location, and sometimes it even exceeds the scope of the school. Various institutions or places such as playgrounds and museums are responsible for educating children. Especially playgrounds can be regarded as vital in terms of releasing children's high energy, positive self-development, exploring children's skills, self-esteem and success, as well as children's cognitive, physical and mental development. We need playgrounds to enhance these skills and provide children with options to learn new things [1]. Studies have shown that children are more likely to play in areas where more play facilities is installed, and the density of children in facilities areas is 3.3 to 12.6 times that of open grasslands [2]. In areas with goals and a fixed play structure, children are more likely to be very active than in open areas. Therefore, the facilities on the playground has a great influence on where children play. In order to enable children to carry out the maximum physical exercise, the playground should be designed with enough varied play facilities. In addition, the diversity of plants and terrain corresponds to functionally related structures, providing multiple functions. According to research, there is also a close relationship between landscape structure and

© Springer Nature Switzerland AG 2021
M. Kurosu (Ed.): HCII 2021, LNCS 12764, pp. 173–183, 2021.
https://doi.org/10.1007/978-3-030-78468-3_12

play functions. The diversity of terrain and environmental elements may be regarded as a dimension of the quality of natural play facilities. It can improve children's athletic ability through a full range of games and exploring the natural game environment [3, 9]. Therefore, diverse children's play facilities and environments are important guarantees for children's games. However, most children's playgrounds in China still use traditional set play facilities. This may bring about a series of issues. Traditional set play facilities only provide a single game mode designed for children. In addition, this kind of facilities usually randomly placed on the playground and has no contact with the surrounding environment. In order to allow children to obtain more diversified games and maximize the benefits of reasonable playground space planning. Here we propose a way to help design a children's playground through bionic algorithms. In this method, terrain and surrounding environment can be taken into consideration as elements of the bionic algorithm. Different terrains will generate different paths, and then designers can choose the next step to generate specific rides based on the path. It is realizing to increase the diversity of children's games, and it can better correspond to the surrounding environment. We hope that this method can provide designers with different needs with a variety of choices and references.

2   The Importance of Children's Play

2.1   The Stereotypical Playground Mode

In China, most kindergartens and communities use complete sets of play facilities including slides, swings, and climbing equipment as playing facilities in children's playgrounds. Such facilities provide children with a fixed game mode. At the same time, these facilities are placed in the space according to the spatial arrangement. For example, this is often seen in kindergartens, where play facilities are usually placed in corner to ensure that the other area of the open space is sufficient for other functions. We analyze the cause of the massive popularity of this design as a misunderstanding of early psychology for children's games. The nineteenth-century psychologist Herbert Spencer advocated the "Residual Energy Theory" in the book "Principles of Psychology", which means that the main reason for children's play is to get rid of excess energy. This popular view has lasting influence on the design of children's outdoor play environment. The playground is regarded as a place for sports activities when children are recuperating. Children are "burning" here, not for other development or learning areas [4]. Based on the lack of understanding of children's games, the designers of children's play facilities have also been shaped into playgrounds based on this theory. It should be designed to manage children and not to stimulate children. In this context, the playground with "slides, swings, and climbing" considered a reasonable mode by most adults has been continued. What most designers do is to change their colors from the perspective of an adult.

2.2   The Importance of Play in Children Psychology

Although the theory of residual energy affects the design of children's amusement facilities. But the psychology of children's play has been developing. Piaget pointed out that games are the most basic way of communication that occurs before language and art. Games are also a means for children to explore and understand the world. Studies have shown that 'active' toys make children tend to be inactive, the smarter the toys, the less room for imagination and creativity for children. Some toys with established patterns may cause children to fall into a single mindset. The traditional complete set of playground equipment has a fixed game setting. It gives children less room for self-development games. It should be noted that this does not mean that children can start creating games on their own without the help of any tools or any outside guidance. Children still need a platform to play games, and this platform needs to provide game possibilities, but there is no certain game setting.

2.3 Circular Play Systems

Japanese landscape architect Mitsura Senda has many large-scale children's space design works. By observing the children, he found that children like to chase and run around. In a place suitable for playing, the flow of the game is cyclic. On the other hand, he found that in cities, places where children can play games are generally selected in blocks that can circle around, and there are shortcuts that can be copied. Mitsura Senda suggested that the play space designed for children should base on circle path. Under the premise of safety, this ring can be full of changes, allowing children to experience the excitement that is so happy and dizzy. The circle must contain a landmark place, large and small gathering places for children to play games, need to have a shortcut route, and be designed as a "porous" space for children to pass through [5].

2.4 Our Ideal Playground Mode

Based on the theory of child psychology and the inspiration of Mr. Mitsura Senda, we hope that through our new method, we can generate a playground space that provides children with game opportunities instead of specific game modes. We hope that the generated space has the following characteristics: connected with surrounding environment, in other words, the game facilities need to be related to the environment. This can inspire children to discover more ways to play. Then the circulation road in the space should be smooth and varied. This is an important guarantee for the safety of children. And it adds fun to the children's game process. The whole space is composed of porous structure. The hole structure is similar to the structure in nature and can bring many game methods. For example, a small hole can be used as a passage for children to observe, while a large hole can become a "short path" for children.

3 The Paths of Playground Space

3.1 Slime Mold Algorithm

Slime mold is a representative of swarm intelligence: individuals are single cells, but the colony's reproduction and movement seem to be intelligent and can find the shortest path between foods. Researchers have shown that Physarum Polycephalum, a widespread eukaryotic microbe growing in nature, can solve several spatial planning problems. A group of studies from Japan used oatmeal to let Physarum Polycephalum find the shortest path in a maze [6]. What is more widely known is the experiment of drawing Tokyo's transportation network using Polycephalum polycephalum in 2010. Scientists took advantage of the light-shielding properties of slime molds, simulated Japanese terrain with light spots, and placed food at the corresponding locations of several important subway stations in Tokyo [7]. The results show that slime mold can spread the path in the most time-saving way to form a network, which is almost exactly the same as the complicated Tokyo subway route. We will apply the slime mold algorithm to draw grid paths in different terrains (Fig. 1).

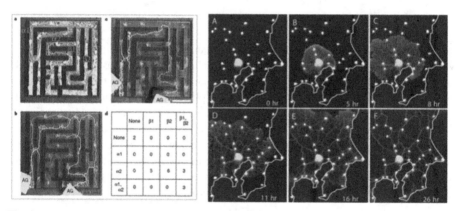

Fig. 1. Polycephalum polycephalum find food in the maze with the shortest path (left). Slime Mold Grows Network Just Like Tokyo Rail System (Right)

3.2 Different Terrain and Environment

Here we have established six sets of terrain to illustrate the application of slime mold algorithm to different grid generation. They are the indoor group (which may have load-bearing structures) and the outdoor group (with undulating terrain and irregular venues). According to the characteristics of different terrains and environments, we set up entrances suitable for them. Use the entrance as a starting point for food and slime mold. In practical applications, designers can create 3D topographic maps by using red lines and geographical features. At the same time, the surrounding environment can be taken into consideration. Designers can avoid obstacles in the surrounding environment, such as buildings and green belts, by adjusting the position of the entrance to the playground. If there is an indoor space with a weighing structure, the pillars can also be built into the terrain (Fig. 2).

3.3 Route Generation

We set up different entrances for different terrain and environmental characteristics and used them as food points and slime mold starting points. After multiple iterations of

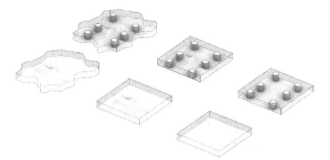

Fig. 2. Six different terrains will be brought into the algorithm to generate paths. They include regular and irregular contours, flat ground and special undulating terrain, and indoor terrain with load-bearing structures.

slime molds, they draw grids that respond to different terrains. These grids show the best path connecting several entrances, that is, the smooth traffic flow pattern in the space. The designer may consider placing the facility in a transportation hub. Here, we use the path as a design element for the next design step (Fig. 3).

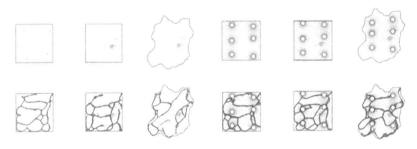

Fig. 3. The terrain and its corresponding path are generated under the slime mold algorithm.

4   Construction of Playground Facilities

4.1   Find the Basic Form

First, we convert the obtained path into a volumetric shape, and then we select the denser part of the path as the basis for our target facility. Next, we take this section of modeling as the basic model, and then use artificial methods to design and intervene this section of basic model. We will use three basic design ideas to demonstrate facility design to provide designers with reference (Fig. 4).

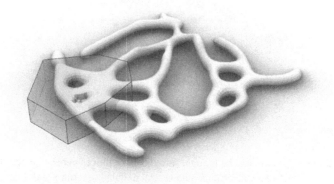

Fig. 4. For the entity transformed from the path, the more parts of the route are selected for design on this basis.

4.2 Trans Path to Entity

Here, we provide three different ideas to transform based on the path. Based the intercepted path of the certain part we plan to generate three different heights, which can divide the space and create more short-circuit porous ring facilities.

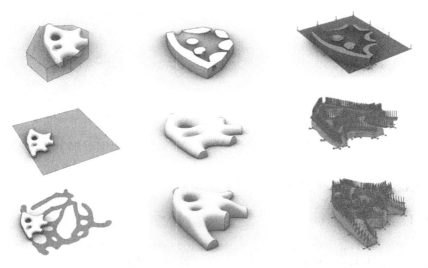

Fig. 5. Generate shapes of three heights for the same path which corresponding to different game modes.

First, we obtain the basic geometric shape according to the outline of the intercepted path, and use the positive and negative shapes to subtract the path. This results in a geometry with path channels as the basic model. Then use the amoeba plugin to optimize its topology. The top part and the part of the runway are regarded as the direction of the force load. For the second one, we hope to generate a low terrain where children can crawl in it. We cut out this section of the path and stretched this shape to make it more suitable for the ups and downs of the terrain. In the third example, we raise and deform the intercepted path to establish continuity with other parts of the terrain and create a slope at the same time. This is a relatively complex shape. We designed it with two layers up and down, so that children can pass through the lower layer, and the resulting bionic structure provides children with climbing and shuttle functions (Fig. 5).

4.3 Two-Way Progressive Algorithm

The basic concept of the progressive structural optimization method is to continuously reduce the inefficient materials in the structure. Through this process, the structure will evolve into an optimized topology and shape. We bring the obtained shape into the ESO algorithm for material reduction iteration. Some materials that do not affect the force of the structure are deleted in this process. The shape of the ESO algorithm can not only save materials under the premise of ensuring the load capacity, but also generate holes with a bionic structure, which meets our vision for children's playground facilities (Figs. 6 and 7).

Fig. 6. Finite element stress analysis of three different facilities.

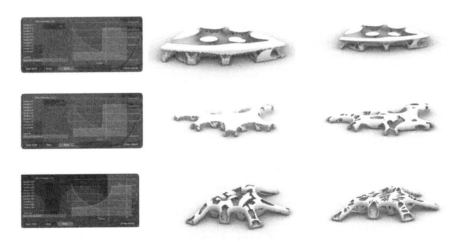

Fig. 7. The BESO algorithm optimizes the structure

5 Application and Outlook

5.1 The Composition of the Playground

We obtained several other basic shapes by intercepting the path and brought them into the ESO algorithm. After the equipment is generated, they are placed on the original path position to form a series of playground facilities [8]. In this playground, we set up the most suitable open space entrance for people to flow in and out according to the surrounding environment and generated a path according to the shape and undulation of the terrain. Based on the path, a porous ring structure suitable for children's play is generated (Figs. 8 and 9).

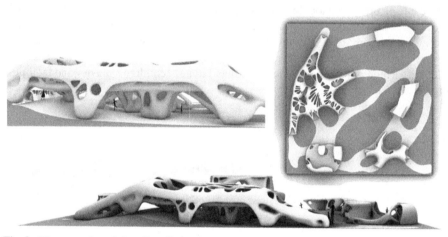

Fig. 8. Playground rendering. Detailed. (Upper left) top view (Top right). The overall renderings (Bottom)

Fig. 9. Whole playground rendering.

5.2 Applications in Interaction Design

Here we propose several interactive applications based on the generated playground equipment. The illumination lights connected to the sensors can be placed in playgrounds and facilities. A series of actions such as running, touching and sound of children will trigger different lighting effects. This can turn playground facilities into public art at night. At the same time, different lighting interaction mechanisms bring more different kinds of games to children (Fig. 10).

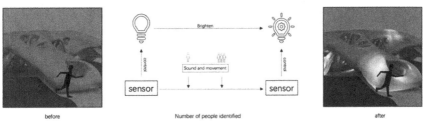

Fig. 10. Conceptual design of interactive function design that can sense different human actions.

The method we introduced is in not only applied in the generation of playground facilities. It can also be applied to the development of other children's spaces. For example, in China, children's science and technology museums are mostly displayed on shelves and window displays, accompanied by caption in text and pictures. This mode is obscure and boring for children. Many Western science museums have developed some experiential games to replace words caption to help children understand scientific knowledge. We can combine projection to design exhibition halls with different themes, such as ocean, desert, space, etc. Children have an immersive experience in different spaces (Figs. 11 and 12).

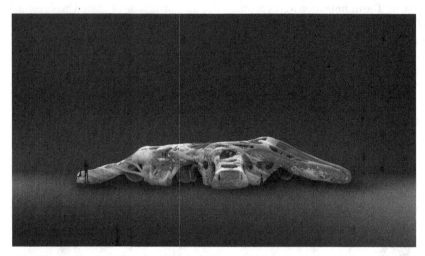

Fig. 11. The combination of the facilities and the ocean theme projection can be used as a theme exhibition hall.

Fig. 12. Interior structure diagram of the theme exhibition hall

6 Conclusion

The design of children's playgrounds has undergone several changes in developed countries. There are also many studies on how to build a playground that is more conducive to the physical and mental development of children. However, design practices and methods are still insufficient for playgrounds in China that fully consider children's psychology and needs. We propose a new design method. The purpose is to provide a reference for those designers who want to develop non-standard playground facilities. This method uses bionic algorithms to generate a three-dimensional playground based on factors such as natural environment, terrain changes, and traffic flow in the layout configuration.

References

1. Unal, M.: The place and importance of playgrounds in child development. Inonu Univ. J. Fac. Educ. (INUJFE) 10(2), 95–98 (2009)
2. Ingunn, F., Jostein, S.: The natural environment as a playground for children: landscape description and analyses of a natural playscape. Landsc. Urban Plan. 48(1–2), 83–97 (2000)
3. Farley, T.A., Meriwether, R.A., Baker, E.T., Rice, J.C., Webber, L.S.: Where do the children play? The influence of playground equipment on physical activity of children in free play. J. Phys. Act Health 5(2), 319–331 (2008)
4. Malone, K., Tranter, P.: Children's environmental learning and the use, design and management of schoolgrounds. Child. Youth Environ. 13(2) (2003)
5. Senda, M.: Design of Children's Play Environments. McGraw-Hill, New York (1992)
6. Nakagaki, T., Yamada, H., Tóth, Á.: Maze-solving by an amoeboid organism. Nature 407, 470 (2000)
7. Tero, A., et al.: Rules for biologically inspired adaptive network design. Science 439(42), 439 (2010)
8. Xie, Y.M., Steven, G.P.: A simple evolutionary procedure for structural optimization. Comput. Struct. 49(5), 885–896 (1993)
9. Chen, W., Shidujaman, M., Jin, J., Ahmed, S.U.: A methodological approach to create interactive art in artificial intelligence. In: Stephanidis, C., et al. (eds.) HCI International 2020 – Late Breaking Papers: Cognition, Learning and Games. HCII 2020. LNCS, vol. 12425, pp.13–31. Springer, Cham (2020). https://doi.org/10.1007/978-3-030-60128-7_2

Bias in, Bias Out – the Similarity-Attraction Effect Between Chatbot Designers and Users

Sarah Zabel$^{(\boxtimes)}$ (iD) and Siegmar Otto(iD)

University of Hohenheim, Stuttgart, Germany
sarah_zabel@uni-hohenheim.de

Abstract. Biases in algorithmic systems tend to discriminate against certain user groups. In order to ensure that the decisions made by these systems are fair, it is necessary to understand how biases in human cognition and language find their way into a system and affect user perception. In this study, we examined the emergence of such biases in the development and design of chatbots by focusing on the gender identities of chatbot designers and users. Therefore, 13 different participants designed chatbot dialogues, which were then presented to 421 participants in an online survey. There was an effect of the interaction between designers' and users' genders on users' affective reactions. When the genders of users and designers matched, users showed more positive and less negative affect. Designers' experience did not reduce this similarity-attraction effect of gender identity, and gender-fair language was not more positive or less negative for women. The results underline the need to consider the gender identities of designers and their impact on language so that non-discriminatory systems can be designed.

Keywords: Gender bias · Algorithmic discrimination · Similarity-attraction effect · Chatbots

1 Introduction

More than 70 years ago, the United Nations declared gender equality a fundamental human right and one of their core values [1]. However, the development and design of products is often still based on a supposedly gender-neutral model, which in fact possesses characteristics that tend to reflect the average man [2–4]. One does not have to look hard to find an example of this: During the COVID-19 pandemic in 2020, many women, and perhaps some men, expressed frustration that standard face masks did not fit their faces very well as most were adapted to fit the average man's head. While the consequences of this bias are not always this easy to see, the result is often a systematically reduced product fit and lower intentions to use the product for any people who deviate from the model [5].

The cause of this bias often lies in incorrect implicit assumptions about gender equality or inequality [6] and implicit representation techniques in the development process

© Springer Nature Switzerland AG 2021
M. Kurosu (Ed.): HCII 2021, LNCS 12764, pp. 184–197, 2021.
https://doi.org/10.1007/978-3-030-78468-3_13

[5]. Designers and developers[1] often implicitly rely on their own needs and preferences, thereby creating products and systems that are particularly likely to please or attract especially users who are similar to themselves [5, 7]. The emergence of this bias is favored by an uneven gender distribution in some occupational fields, such as the ICT sector, which is still predominantly male [4]. This industry is often referred to as a driver of innovation, generating a large number of new technologies. A growing sector within this field engages in the development of AI technologies, that is, algorithmic systems that influence our decisions by suggesting what products to buy, what films to watch, or what employee to hire. While the technologies that are already embedded in our cars, smartphones, and computers become more and more popular, cases of systematically biased decisions and predictions have been revealed [8, 9]. Because algorithmic systems are trained on existing data, they inherit the biases and societal stereotypes that are embedded in these data and eventually the implicit biases of designers [10]. As many machine-learning algorithms interact via natural language [11], it is necessary to consider the biases that are embedded in language in order to prevent algorithms from carrying forward and reinforcing such biases. While a bias in the context of algorithms is simply a deviation from a standard that does not necessarily include disadvantageous treatment [10], many biases result in discrimination against certain people. Similarly, male individuals are overrepresented in language [12–14], and language is part of the design of any product that needs language (e.g., textbooks, chatbots, websites). In addition, gender differences have been found in the style and use of language [15, 16].

In this study, we focused on the design of chatbots (also known as text-based conversational agents, CAs), which are programs that enable human-computer interaction via natural language [17, 18]. They are frequently used, for example, as personal agents in customer service where they have been found to increase user satisfaction through their social presence [19, 20]. Chatbots follow a rule-based architecture in order to provide preprogrammed text modules as responses to users' text input [17]. Therefore, they replicate the conversational style and implicit biases that exist in the language of their designers.

Generally, computer programs that interact via natural language are perceived as social actors [21, 22]. Therefore, humans activate the same schemas and apply the same social scripts as in human-human interactions [23, 24]. Even minimal gender cues, such as a gender-specific synthesized voice or name, are likely to activate gender stereotypes among users [25, 26]. Baxter et al. [23] commented on the consequences: "This can prove detrimental as users can be inclined to measure the success of a system based on their biases and emotional connection with the agent rather than on the actual system performance" (p. 1). Among humans, the initial emergence of such an emotional connection is triggered by the similarity of the actors [27, 28]. While most research on this so-called similarity-attraction effect has focused on attitudinal similarity between humans, the effect has also been found for demographic similarity, for example, in customer-salesperson relationships [29–31]. In human-computer interactions, a

---

[1] Designers are those who participate in the designing of products, and developers are those who participate in the development of technological systems. Hereinafter, we do not distinguish between the two and use the word designers to refer to people who play either of these roles.

similarity-attraction effect of gender has been found in the context of voice-based computer systems [32] and anthropomorphic agents [33, 34]. For example, Lee, Liau & Ryu [35] found that children evaluated a synthesized voice more positively when it matched their gender. Animated avatars with matching gender were more effective in changing users' attitude [36]. Furthermore, women were more likely to accept recommendations from agents that matched their gender [34]. Studies on pedagogic conversation agents found that students were more likely to choose agents with younger avatars [37]. However, other studies did not find demographic similarity-attraction effects between humans and agents [e.g., 38]. While these inconsistent results might be due in part to insufficient statistical power or different outcome variables, it is still not clear which gender cues trigger demographic similarity-attraction effects in interactions with CAs. Furthermore, most studies have measured attraction via intention to use, predictability, or social presence [e.g., 32, 36, 39]. Although affective experiences are essential for the quality of a user's experience [40], the affective reactions to gender matching in CAs are largely unknown. Thus, researchers have stressed the need to consider the gender identity of designers to promote the design of products and systems that do not contain barriers for certain user groups [5]. To our knowledge, no one has answered these calls yet. Therefore, on the basis of the similarity-attraction paradigm, we explored how the similarity between designer and user in terms of gender influences users' affective reactions to a chatbot and whether it translates into intentions to use the chatbot. While a similarity-attraction effect of gender has been found for anthropomorphic agents and computer-based voices, to our knowledge, studies have yet to investigate whether such an effect naturally occurs on the basis of plain text when the gender identities of designers and users match.

While other studies have explicitly manipulated similarity or relied on users' ratings of the chatbot's communication style as similar to their own style [39], in our study, the chatbot dialogues were created by designers who were blind to our hypothesis. Thus, our experiment is unique in the sense that all potential biases were created implicitly – comparable to the practical design processes. We did not externally manipulate or normatively evaluate any of the content created by the designers. While we focused on the consequences of matching gender identities, we also considered designers' and users' age. Language is a product of socialization; therefore, generation-specific language patterns might also have an impact on users' affective reactions. In order to unravel the emergence of biases in chatbot interactions, we also considered designers' experience in the design of chatbots. Professional experience might reduce the application of implicit representation techniques (i.e., the unconscious reliance on personal experience and needs, see [7]) in the design and development process, shifting the focus to the users' personas and their specific preferences. We further considered a specific bias in language, that is, the use of masculine generics instead of gender-fair language (GFL). In German, masculine role nouns can be used to describe groups of mixed or unknown gender (e.g., Lehrer refers to a (male) teacher as well as a group of teachers) [14]. Feminine forms are used to describe women only (e.g., Lehrerin is a female teacher, while Lehrerinnen refers to a group of female teachers) [14, 41]. The use of GFL aims at reducing this asymmetry by using either neutral forms (e.g., Lehrkräfte) or explicitly including women and individuals with non-binary gender identities when referring to groups (e.g., Lehrer:innen, which includes the male and female form, while the colon visualizes individuals with non-binary gender identities). We therefore explored whether the degree of GFL a chatbot used had an influence on users' positive and/or negative affective reactions.

2 Method

In order to explore the interaction of designers' and users' gender identities through a chatbot conversation, our survey consisted of two parts. In the first study, we conducted interviews to obtain the stimulus material for the second study. Because gender differences in German were the focus of our research, all of our participants were fluent in German.

2.1 Study I

For the test of the gender-matching hypothesis, seven chatbot dialogues were created by 13 interviewees (7 female; 22 to 46 years old). They worked together in dyads that were homogenous with respect to gender, age, and professional experience. One person was interviewed alone. Gender and professional experience were fully crossed between the groups. One additional dyad – consisting of women who actively promote gender equality in politics and in their professions – was interviewed in order to obtain a gender-fair version of a chatbot. To test the influence of age differences between designers and users on users' perceptions, we conducted one more interview with a gender-mixed dyad consisting of a 52-year-old woman and a 53-year-old man. Table 1 provides an overview of the 8 bot versions created by the interviewees. While bot 7 is a version that uses gender-neutral language, none of the designers explicitly included women and individuals with non-binary gender identities through language. In order to examine the influence of varying degrees of gender-fair language, we created an additional bot (not included in Table 1) based on bot 7.

Table 1. The gender, age, and experience of the interviewees who designed the different chatbots

		Experience in the design of chatbots		
		None	Theoretical	Practical
Gender	Male	Bot 1: 35 & 38 years	Bot 2: 33 & 33 years	Bot 3: 22 & 24 years
	Female	Bot 4: 22 & 25 years Bot 7: 37 & 39 years	Bot 5: 42 & 46 years	Bot 6: 29 years
		Bot 8: m, 53 & f, 52 years		

Note. Bots 1–7 were utilized for all hypotheses, while bot 8 was considered only for the analyses of age differences and GFL.

Participants were asked to design four dialogue modules for a service chatbot from a fictional travel company. The dialogue was supposed to include messages on the following topics: 1. Welcoming, 2. Providing further information, 3. Referring to other services, and 4. Saying goodbye. The interviewees received graphical and verbal instructions for each module. Figure 1 shows the instruction slide for the last dialogue module. Besides this, the interviewees did not receive further information about the company.

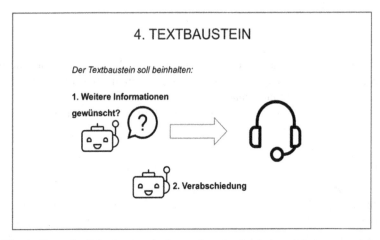

Fig. 1. Example slide showing the instructions for the design of dialogue modules

For the next study, the dialogue modules were prepared so that they looked like screenshots of real chatbot conversations, as Fig. 2 illustrates.

Fig. 2. Example of a chatbot dialogue module used in Study II

2.2 Study II

We tested the gender-matching hypothesis using a 2×3 between-subjects design with matching gender between designers and users (yes/no) and the professional experience (none/theoretical/practical) of the designers as independent variables and users' affective reactions as the dependent variable.

Sample and Procedure. An online questionnaire was distributed via e-mail and social media among German-speaking participants between August 6, 2020 and September 6, 2020. From the 458 responses, we had to exclude 38 due to implausible completion speeds [42] or wrong answers to the attention check. The answers of $N = 421$ subjects (62.5% female, 1.9% inter/diverse; age: $M = 27.2$; $SD = 8.93$) were utilized for the study. For the test of the gender-matching hypothesis, only the participants who rated bot versions 1–7 from Table 1 were considered ($n = 320$, 63.64% female, age: $M = 27.25$, $SD = 9.04$). To test the age-difference effect between designers and users, bots 1–8 were considered ($n = 343$, 62.10% female, 1.75% inter/diverse, age: $M = 27.41$, $SD = 9.23$). In order to explore the impact of GFL on users' affective reactions, the full sample was considered. In the study, participants were randomly assigned to one of the nine bot versions and received all four of their bot's dialogue modules. Subsequently, they rated their affective reactions to the chatbot.

Measures. All dependent variables were self-reported on 5-point Likert scales ranging from 1 *(do not agree at all)* to 5 *(fully agree)*.

Positive and Negative Affect. Users' affective reactions were assessed with 20 items from the German version of the Positive and Negative Affect Schedule [43]. The scale captures momentary affect via different adjectives such as "active" for positive and "ashamed" for negative affect.

Intention to Use. To assess participants' intention to use the chatbots, we modified two items from Diers [17]. Participants indicated whether they would use the chatbot in the future if they had the opportunity.

Gender-Fair Language. To compare the degree of GFL in the chatbots, an index of the frequency of gender-fair forms was calculated. Gender-neutral language was coded 0, while including women and individuals with non-binary gender identities through language was categorized as +1. The use of masculine nouns to describe groups was coded −1. The resulting values ranged from −3 to +5.

Control Variables. We controlled for participants' gender. Furthermore, we asked participants to estimate the gender and age of the chatbot designer in order to test whether they were conscious of the reasons behind a potential similarity-attraction effect. Some of the designers created a name for their chatbot. As this might act as a gender cue, we controlled for participants' perception of the name as specific to one gender.

Additional Variables. We provide documentation of all variables assessed in this project (https://doi.org/10.17605/osf.io/s9jnw).

Data Analysis. Before testing our hypothesis, we tested the different bot versions and conditions for parallelism. There were no significant differences in participants' affective reactions between the different chatbot versions. Also, the mean affective reaction did not differ between chatbot versions created by male vs. female dyads or between dyads with different levels of experience in the design of chatbots.

3   Results

Table 2 presents descriptive statistics, intercorrelations, and reliability coefficients for all variables relevant for our analysis. There was a small negative correlation between positive and negative affect. Furthermore, there was a correlation between intention to use and positive affect but not negative affect. Participants' gender was correlated with gender matching and negative affect, therefore, it was included as a control variable in the analyses. Of the independent variables, only gender matching was correlated with positive and negative affect.

Table 2. Descriptive statistics, reliabilities, and Pearson correlations.

Variable	N	M	SD	1	2	3	4	5	6	7
1. Gender	413	.64	.48	–						
2. Age	419	27.20	8.93	.05	–					
3. Gender matching	320	.53	.50	.15**	.08	–				
4. Age diff	370	12.14	9.11	.08	.16**	.08	–			
5. GFL	421	0.38	2.43	−.03	−.01	.02	−.22***	–		
6. Positive affect	421	2.88	0.71	−.08	.10*	.14*	.03	−.01	–	
7. Negative affect	421	1.54	0.60	−.15**	−.09†	−.15**	.01	.01	−.12	-
8. Intention to use	421	2.92	1.25	.15**	.00	.02	−.01	−.04	.15	−.05

Notes. Gender matching was coded 0 (unmatching gender) or 1 (matching gender). Participants' gender was coded 0 (male) or 1 (female).
† $p < 0.10$, * $p < 0.05$, ** $p < 0.01$, *** $p < .001$.
Age diff refers to the age difference between designers and users.

3.1   Similarity-Attraction Effect of Gender

Before analyzing the similarity-attraction effect of gender, we tested for multicollinearity of the predictor (gender matching) and the control variable (participants' gender). The variance inflation factor was below 1.1, that is, our variables were not affected by multicollinearity. The mean levels of affect for designers' and users' gender are presented in Table 3. A multiple regression analysis with gender matching and participants' gender revealed a significant influence of gender matching on positive affect, $F(2, 317)$ $= 4.66, p = .01, B = 0.21$, SE$(B) = 0.08, \beta = .15, p = .01$, 95% CI for B [0.06, 0.37]. The influence of gender was marginally significant, $B = -0.15$, SE$(B) = 0.08, \beta = -.10, p = .07$. Thus, a similarity-attraction effect between participants and designers was found for positive affect. We further found an effect of gender matching on negative affect, $F(2, 317) = 5.46, p = .005, B = -0.16$, SE$(B) = 0.07, \beta = -.14, p = .02$, 95% CI for B [$-0.30, -0.03$]. Again, participants' gender did have a marginally significant influence on negative affect, $B = -0.13$, SE$(B) = 0.07, \beta = -.11, p = .06$. Gender matching accounted for 2% of the variance in both positive and negative affect.

To test whether this effect translated into intention to use, we performed two mediation analyses. The significance of the models was tested via bootstrapping (5,000 iterations). There were no significant mediation effects for positive affect, $F(2, 317) = 2.72$, $p = .07$, 95% CI [0.00, 0.04], or for negative affect, $F(2, 317) = 2.09, p = .80$.

Table 3. Mean levels of positive and negative affect for designers' and users' gender

| | | Users' gender | | | | | |
| | Designers' gender | Male (n = 115) | | Female (n = 204) | | Inter/diverse (n = 7) | |
		M	SD	M	SD	M	SD
Positive affect	Male	3.12	0.82	2.75	0.60	2.83	0.71
	Female	2.85	0.62	2.92	0.73	1.87	0.99
Negative affect	Male	1.53	0.54	1.57	0.66	2.23	0.65
	Female	1.69	0.68	1.40	0.50	1.63	0.40

3.2 The Role of Professional Experience and User-Centered Design

We further tested whether designers' professional experience reduced the effect of matching gender identities on users' affective reactions. The results of the analyses are presented in Table 4. The model was significant due to the gender matching effect, $F(6,313)$ $= 2.79, p = .01$ for positive affect, $F(6,313) = 2.53, p = .02$ for negative affect. However, there was no significant influence of either theoretical or practical experience on positive or negative affect. Furthermore, there were no interaction effects of gender matching and experience. Designers' experience did not reduce the effect of matching gender identities on users' affective reactions.

Table 4. Results of the regression analyses for gender matching and designers' experience

	Positive affect			Negative affect		
	B	SE(B)	β	B	SE(B)	β
Constant	2.82	0.09		1.76	0.08	
Gender	−0.19	0.08	−.13*	−0.10	0.07	−.09
Gender matching	0.37	0.12	.27**	−0.32	0.10	−.27**
Theoretical exp.	0.06	0.14	.04	−0.17	0.11	−.13
Practical exp.	0.21	0.14	.14	−0.12	0.12	−.09
Gender matching × Theoretical exp.	−0.32	0.19	−.16†	0.30	0.16	.18†
Gender matching × Practical exp.	−0.23	0.19	−.11	0.24	0.16	.14
R^2 corr.		.03*			.03*	

Notes. Designers' experience was included as a dummy variable (theoretical exp. and practical exp.).
† $p < 0.10$, * $p < 0.05$, ** $p < 0.01$.

3.3 Age Difference

To test whether an age difference between designers and users had an influence on users' affective reactions, we computed two regression analyses for positive and negative affect with participants' gender. There was no influence of an age difference on participants' positive affect, $B = .00$, SE(B) $= .00$, $p = .73$; $F(2, 367) = 2.27$, $p = .10$, or negative affect, $B = .00$, SE(B) $= .00$, $p = .64$; $F(2, 367) = 2.47$, $p = .09$.

3.4 Gender-Fair Language

We computed a regression analysis to test whether the degree of GFL had an influence on users' positive or negative affect. We further tested whether the interaction between gender and GFL had an effect on affective reactions. There was no significant effect of the interaction between frequency of GFL and gender on positive affect ($B = 0.03$, SE(B) $= 0.03$, $p = .29$ for females and $B = 0.15$, SE(B) $= 0.10$, $p = .13$ for participants with a non-binary gender identity), while the overall model was significant due to the main effect of gender, $F(5, 415) = 2.62$, $p = .02$. We further found no significant effect of the interaction between GFL and gender on negative affect ($B = 0.01$, SE(B) $= 0.02$, $p = .72$ for females and $B = 0.05$, SE(B) $= 0.09$, $p = .58$ for participants with a non-binary gender identity), with the overall model also being significant due to the main effect of gender, $F(5, 415) = 2.59$, $p = .03$.

4   Discussion

We were able to detect a similarity-attraction effect of gender on positive and negative affect, that is, participants reading a dialogue created by a person of their own gender showed more positive and less negative affect – even without any intentional manipulation. These results go beyond the findings of studies that provided explicit cues to suggest the gender of the CA and explicitly written texts to activate similarity-attraction effects [34, 39]. While Nass et al. [26] postulated that minimal gender cues in a computer program would be sufficient to activate social scripts, this study showed that even without consciously generated gender cues, the effects of similarity and attraction prevailed. This result calls into question the assumption that a CA has to have a visual presence in order to provoke an affective reaction [44]. The effect of matching gender identities on users' affective reactions was independent of designers' professional experience in the design of chatbot dialogues. Even experienced designers let their perceptions and biases in language slip into the development of dialogues and eventually based their chatbot on their own needs. However, the effect of matching gender identities did not translate into a higher intention to use.

The age difference between designers and users did not influence users' affective reactions. However, results from other studies on this effect have been inconsistent and have often been based on samples of children or adolescents [e.g., 37]. One possible explanation is that users expect a CA to use an informal communication style rather than a style that is specific to their generation (i.e., consistency-attraction effect). For the same reason, the designers might have fulfilled the expectations of a consistent language style for a chatbot in our study.

The use of discriminatory vs. gender-fair language did not influence positive or negative affect among users with different gender identities. This indicates that these subtle biases that find their way into chatbot design cannot easily be manufactured and captured explicitly but nevertheless have an impact on affective outcomes.

4.1   Limitations and Further Research

Our first exploration of this implicitly elicited similarity-attraction effect comes with several limitations. First, we did not control for many potentially confounding factors (e.g., designers' personality), and our samples were not representative or stratified with respect to any populations of designers or users. Thus, further studies should control for confounding factors and replicate these findings with a larger sample of designers and a stratified sample of users.

Furthermore, it would be interesting to capture the actual semantic differences that are responsible for the bias and the factors that lead to these semantic differences in men and women. To answer these questions, a mixture of methods including qualitative analyses of the texts or analyses of existing chatbots could help.

4.2   Practical Implications

While most studies have focused on visible gender biases in CAs, gender-matching effects can occur even without avatars or gender-specific names. The similarity-attraction effect could be used deliberately to trigger a more positive affective reaction to the CA among users and to address groups with a lower initial affinity for algorithmic systems. This could help reduce existing imbalances in technology acceptance and use. Our results underline the need to consider the gender identities of designers and their impact on the outcome or product and to be aware of potential gender biases in product design [e.g., 5]. In ICT, where 82.7% of the employees in Europe are male [45], these seemingly small similarity-attraction effects can otherwise add up and result in discrimination against any users with other gender identities.

An immediately actionable step against biases would be to increase diversity in the teams that design and develop such algorithms [19]. However, it will certainly not be a quick and easy task to increase diversity in ICT. Another approach would be to explicitly represent different users in design and development projects. Different user personas could be used to bring about a change in perspective even in homogeneous design and development teams and to take different users into account. However, critical reflection on one's own biases during design and development is also indispensable here so that the personas do not merely represent stereotypes [46].

The effect we generated was on an implicit level and was about a well-known issue that people tend to have varying attitudes toward. However, from a broader perspective, there are many societal issues that can have strong impacts because people tend to disagree about them and express a wide range of different attitudes about them. For instance, in the judicial system, implicit stereotypes have influenced and biased people's decisions, but with respect to climate change or sustainable development, attitudes also tend to diverge substantially. Such differences and biases are nothing new, but if they find their way into the algorithms that drive automated decisions – through either coding or training material – these biases might get cemented and, in many cases, scaled up and even intensified [47]. If ignored, even small imbalances, such as a systematically better product fit for men, can add up and lead to discrimination against any people who deviate from the male model – in most cases women [48]. Thus, we need to conduct experiments similar to the one presented here so that we can carefully uncover biases, particularly implicit biases.

Finally, technology evolves and apart from producing bias-free, neutral versions of services and products, customization could help to match different versions of the product or service with different users to avoid discrimination. Such matching, at least in terms of content, is already in place, for instance at social networks, where the users are known. However, matching of language style might even work with unknown users after a short interaction based on certain cues such as users' language or "metadata" (e.g., device, operation system, and browser).

References

1. United Nations: Universal declaration of human rights (1948)
2. Hielscher, N.: Geschlechtergerechtigkeit in Disease Management Programmen für koronare Herzkrankheiten. In: Bessenrodt-Weberpals, M., Gransee, C., Doleschall, D., Menzel, B., Lorenz, J., Seibt, A., Verch, U. (eds.) Gender in den Gesundheitswissenschaften - Geschlechtsdifferenzen aus sozio-kultureller Perspektive, vol. 7. Gender Studies in den Angewandten Wissenschaften. Hochschule für Angewandte Wissenschaften Hamburg, Hamburg (2013)

3. Kuhlmann, E.: Gender Mainstreaming in den Disease Management-Programmen – das Beispiel koronare Herzkrankheiten. In: Expertise im Auftrag der Bundeskoordination Frauengesundheit des Arbeitskreises Frauengesundheit, gefördert durch das Bundesministerium für Familie, Senioren, Frauen und Jugend. Bundeskoordination Frauengesundheit des Arbeitskreises Frauengesundheit (2004)

4. Schiebinger, L., Klinge, I., Arlow, A., Newman, S.: Gendered innovations: mainstreaming sex and gender analysis into basic and applied research. Meta-analysis of gender science research - Topic report. European Commission, Brussels (2010)

5. Oudshoorn, N., Rommes, E., Stienstra, M.: Configuring the user as everybody: gender and design cultures in information and communication technologies. Sci. Technol. Hum. Values **29**, 30–63 (2004). https://doi.org/10.1177/0162243903259190

6. Ruiz-Cantero, M.T., et al.: A framework to analyse gender bias in epidemiological research. J. Epidemiol. Commun. Health **61**(Suppl. 2), ii46–ii53 (2007). https://doi.org/10.1136/jech.2007.062034

7. Akrich, M.: User representations: Practices, methods and sociology. In: Rip, A., Misa, T.J., Schot, J. (eds.) Managing Technology in Society: The Approach of Constructive Technology Assesment. Printer Publishers, London (1995)

8. Buolamwini, J., Gebru, T.: Gender shades: intersectional accuracy disparities in commercial gender classification. In: Friedler, S.A., Wilson, C. (eds.) Proceedings of the 1st Conference on Fairness, Accountability and Transparency, vol. 81, pp. 77–91. PMLR, (2018)

9. Lambrecht, A., Tucker, C.: Algorithmic bias? An empirical study of apparent gender-based discrimination in the display of STEM career ads. Manage. Sci. **65**, 2966–2981 (2019). https://doi.org/10.1287/mnsc.2018.3093

10. Criado, N., Such, J.M.: Digital discrimination. In: Algorithmic Regulation, chapter Digital Discrimination. Oxford University Press (2019)

11. Aran, X.F., Such, J.M., Criado, N.: Attesting biases and discrimination using language semantics. Auton. Agent. Multi-Agent Syst. (in press). https://arxiv.org/abs/1909.04386v1

12. Baker, P.: Sexed Texts: Language, Gender and Sexuality. Equinox, London (2008)

13. Stahlberg, D., Braun, F., Irmen, L., Sczesny, S.: Representation of the sexes in language. In: Fiedler, K. (ed.) Frontiers of Social Psychology. Social Communication, pp. 163–187. Psychology Press (2007)

14. Sczesny, S., Formanowicz, M., Moser, F.: Can gender-fair language reduce gender stereotyping and discrimination? Front. Psychol. **7**, 1617 (2016). https://doi.org/10.3389/fpsyg.2016.00025

15. Iosub, D., Laniado, D., Castillo, C., Morell, M.F., Kaltenbrunner, A.: Emotions under discussion: gender, status and communication in online collaboration. PLoS ONE **9**(8), (2014). https://doi.org/10.1371/journal.pone.0104880

16. Pennebaker, J.W., King, L.A.: Linguistic styles: language use as an individual difference. J. Pers. Soc. Psychol. **77**, 1296–1312 (1999). https://doi.org/10.1037//0022-3514.77.6.1296

17. Diers, T.: Akzeptanz von Chatbots im Consumer-Marketing: Erfolgsfaktoren zwischen Konsumenten und künstlicher Intelligenz. Springer, Gabler (2020). https://doi.org/10.1007/978-3-658-29317-8

18. Zue, V.W., Glass, J.R.: Conversational interfaces: advances and challenges. Proc. IEEE **88**, 1166–1180 (2000). https://doi.org/10.1109/5.880078

19. Feine, J., Gnewuch, U., Morana, S., Maedche, A.: Gender bias in chatbot design. In: Følstad, A., et al. (eds.) CONVERSATIONS 2019. LNCS, vol. 11970, pp. 79–93. Springer, Cham (2020). https://doi.org/10.1007/978-3-030-39540-7_6

20. Verhagen, T., Van Nes, J., Feldberg, F., Van Dolen, W.: Virtual customer service agents: using social presence and personalization to shape online service encounters. J. Comput. Med. Commun. **19**(3), 529–545 (2014). https://doi.org/10.1111/jcc4.12066

21. Nass, C., Steuer, J., Tauber, E., Reeder, H.: Anthropomorphism, agency, and ethopoeia: computers as social actors. In: CHI '93: Conference on Human Factors in Computing Systems, pp. 111–112 (1993)

22. Sundar, S.S., Nass, C.: Source orientation in human-computer interaction: programmer, networker, or independent social actor. Commun. Res. **27**, 683–703 (2000). https://doi.org/10.1177/009365000027006001

23. Baxter, D., McDonnell, M., McLoughlin, R.: Impact of chatbot gender on user's stereotypical perception and satisfaction. In: Proceedings of the 32nd International BCS Human Computer Interaction Conference (HCI), pp. 1–5 (2018). https://doi.org/10.14236/ewic/HCI2018.154

24. Nass, C., Moon, Y.: Machines and mindlessness: social responses to computers. J. Soc. Issues **56**, 81–103 (2000). https://doi.org/10.1111/0022-4537.00153

25. Brahnam, S., De Angeli, A.: Gender affordances of conversational agents. Interact. Comput. **24**, 139–153 (2012). https://doi.org/10.1016/j.intcom.2012.05.001

26. Nass, C., Moon, Y., Green, N.: Are machines gender neutral? Gender-stereotypic responses to computers with voices. J. Appl. Soc. Psychol. **27**, 864–876 (1997). https://doi.org/10.1111/j.1559-1816.1997.tb00275.x

27. Berscheid, E., Reis, H.T.: Attraction and close relationships. In: Gilbert, D.T., Fiske, S., Lindzey, G. (eds.) The Handbook of Social Psychology, pp. 193–281 (1998)

28. Byrne, D.: The Attraction Paradigm. Academic Press, New York (1971)

29. Binning, J.F., Goldstein, M.A., Garcia, M.F., Scattaregia, J.H.: Effects of preinterview impressions on questioning strategies in same-and opposite-sex employment interviews. J. Appl. Psychol. **73**, 30–37 (1988). https://doi.org/10.1037/0021-9010.73.1.30

30. Dwyer, S., Orlando, R., Shepherd, C.D.: An exploratory study of gender and age matching in the salesperson-prospective customer dyad: testing similarity-performance predictions. J. Pers. Sell. Sales Manage. **18**(4), 55–69 (1998)

31. Tsui, A.S., Xin, K.R., Egan, T.D.: Relational demography: the missing link in vertical dyad linkage. In: Jackson, S.E., Ruderman, M.N. (eds.) Diversity in Work Teams: Research Paradigms for a Changing Workplace, pp. 97–129. American Psychological Association (1995)

32. Nass, C., Lee, K.M.: Does computer-synthesized speech manifest personality? Experimental tests of recognition, similarity-attraction, and consistency-attraction. J. Exp. Psychol. Appl. **7**, 171–181 (2001). https://doi.org/10.1037/1076-898X.7.3.171

33. Ozogul, G., Johnson, A.M., Atkinson, R.K., Reisslein, M.: Investigating the impact of pedagogical agent gender matching and learner choice on learning outcomes and perceptions. Comput. Educ. **67**, 36–50 (2013). https://doi.org/10.1016/j.compedu.2013.02.006

34. Benbasat, I., Dimoka, A., Pavlou, P.A., Qiu, L.: The role of demographic similarity in people's decision to interact with online anthropomorphic recommendation agents: evidence from a functional magnetic resonance imaging (fMRI) study. Int. J. Hum.-Comput. Stud. **133**, 56–70 (2020). https://doi.org/10.1016/j.ijhcs.2019.09.001

35. Lee, K.M., Liao, K., Ryu, S.: Children's responses to computer-synthesized speech in educational media: gender consistency and gender similarity effects. Hum. Commun. Res. **33**, 310–329 (2007). https://doi.org/10.1111/j.1468-2958.2007.00301.x

36. Guadagno, R.E., Blascovich, J., Bailenson, J.N., McCall, C.: Virtual humans and persuasion: the effects of agency and behavioral realism. Media Psychol. **10**(1), 1–22 (2007)

37. Johnson, A.M., DiDonato, M.D., Reisslein, M.: Animated agents in K-12 engineering outreach: preferred agent characteristics across age levels. Comput. Hum. Behav. **29**, 1807–1815 (2013). https://doi.org/10.1016/j.chb.2013.02.023

38. Qiu, L., Benbasat, I.: A study of demographic embodiments of product recommendation agents in electronic commerce. Int. J. Hum.-Comp. Stud. **68**, 669–688 (2010). https://doi.org/10.1016/j.ijhcs.2010.05.005

39. Li, M., Mao, J.: Hedonic or utilitarian? Exploring the impact of communication style alignment on user's perception of virtual health advisory services. Int. J. Inf. Manage. **35**, 229–243 (2015). https://doi.org/10.1016/j.ijinfomgt.2014.12.004
40. Yang, X., Aurisicchio, M., Baxter, W.: Understanding affective experiences with conversational agents. In: Proceedings of the 2019 CHI Conference on Human Factors in Computing Systems, pp. 1–12 (2019)
41. Bußmann, H., Hellinger, M.: Engendering female visibility in German, vol. 3. Gender Across Languages. The Linguistic Representation of Women and Men. John Benjamins Publishing Company, Amsterdam/Philadelphia (2003)
42. Leiner, D.J.: Too fast, too straight, too weird: post hoc identification of meaningless data in internet surveys. In: Survey Research Methods, pp. 229–248 (2013)
43. Breyer, B., Bluemke, M.: Deutsche Version der Positive and Negative Affect Schedule PANAS (GESIS Panel). In: Zusammenstellung sozialwissenschaftlicher Items und Skalen (2016)
44. Baylor, A.L.: Promoting motivation with virtual agents and avatars: role of visual presence and appearance. Philos. Trans. R. Soc. B **364**, 3559–3565 (2009). https://doi.org/10.1098/rstb.2009.0148
45. Eurostat: Girls and women under-represented in ICT (2018)
46. Erharter, D.: Gendergerechtes Forschungsdesign für digitale Medien. In: Aigner, W., Blumenstein, K., Iber, M., Moser, T., Zeppelzauer, M., Schmiedl, G. (eds.) 10th Forum Media Technology and 3rd All Around Audio Symposium, St. Pölten (2017)
47. Dastin, J.: Amazon scraps secret AI recruiting tool that showed bias against women. In: Reuters (2018)
48. Valian, V.: The cognitive bases of gender bias. Brooklyn Law Rev. **65**, 1037–1962 (1999)

Research on Immersive Virtual Reality Display Design Mode of Cantonese Porcelain Based on Embodied Interaction

Shengyang Zhong, Yi Ji[✉], Xingyang Dai, and Sean Clark

School of Art and Design, Guangdong University of Technology, Yuexiu District of Dongfeng East Road No. 729, Guangzhou 510000, China

Abstract. In recent years, the development of Immersive Virtual Reality (IVR) provides new opportunities for the protection and inheritance of traditional handicrafts. Cantonese porcelain (CP) is one of the most important intangible cultural heritages in China based on its special cultural content and unique form of expression. However, according to the survey, we found that it is difficult for people to acquire the knowledge of CP because cultural connotation of CP is metaphorical, and it is difficult for people to have a profound cognition and understanding of it. To address the problems, this paper proposes an IVR display design mode of CP based on embodied interaction, and proves the availability of the mode with design practice. According to this mode, the knowledge of CP in IVR can be delivered to people through virtual roaming and interaction from three levels: physical embodiment, imaginary embodiment and knowledge construction. Through tests for participants, this method has been proved to be helpful for people to quickly establish the knowledge framework of CP. Furthermore, it provides a method reference for other development of traditional handicrafts.

Keywords: Embodied interaction · Immersive virtual reality · Cantonese porcelain · Traditional handicraft

1 Introduction

In recent years, immersive virtual reality (IVR) experience has become more and more popular around the world. Many commercial exhibitions, cultural communication and education institutions have begun to adopt IVR, which has attracted a large number of audiences and learning experiencers [1]. With the rapid development of digital protection and innovation inheritance, the research and application of IVR has provided new opportunities for intangible cultural heritage [2]. For example, Marcelo Carrozzinod et al. proposed the classification of virtual reality devices for cultural heritage applications according to interactivity and immersion. By summarizing and analyzing examples, they provide a tool for building virtual reality systems and provide indicators for the cost, availability and quality of sensory experiences. Finally, they put forward some suggestions on how to use IVR more widely and effectively for culture [3].

© Springer Nature Switzerland AG 2021
M. Kurosu (Ed.): HCII 2021, LNCS 12764, pp. 198–213, 2021.
https://doi.org/10.1007/978-3-030-78468-3_14

Traditional handicraft is a very important part of intangible cultural heritage. Traditional handicraft is the carrier of national emotion, personality and national cohesion, as well as a manifestation of the diversity of human culture. It carries a very rich knowledge system [4]. People often start from the understanding of its corresponding tangible traditional handicrafts and then learn its intangible handicrafts to have a deep cognition of its cultural background and national characteristics. Traditional handicrafts come from the people, so the significance of protection and inheritance is not only to keep people interested in traditional handicrafts but also to enable people to use their personality and creativity and become protectors and inheritors.

In this paper, we will take the Cantonese porcelain (CP), a kind of traditional handicraft of China, as a case study to carry out related research and testing. CP is a kind of decorative porcelain art in Guangzhou. It is an important carrier of Lingnan culture and has a high reputation at home and abroad. Since CP was listed as a national intangible cultural heritage in 2008, there has been a significant breakthrough in its inheritance. New digital technology [5] and new teaching mode [6] have been reasonably applied to the spread of CP. The design of cultural and creative products of CP is also being researched and developed [7, 8]. Most of those researches aimed at CP enthusiasts and cultural researchers. These groups already have certain cognition and understanding of the knowledge of CP, and even have the ability to re-innovate the content of CP. However, for people who come into contact with CP for the first time, IVR is a useful form that helps them quickly recognize history, culture and crafts of CP. Through offline research and interviews, it can be seen that there are an endless number of cases of displaying traditional handicrafts with IVR, but the efficiency in conveying the cultural content of traditional handicrafts is not obvious. People's understanding of traditional handicraft has been significantly improved in terms of vision, but lack of cognition of its connotation and innovative ways. Through offline research and participants interviews, it can be seen that participants who come into contact with CP for the first time can quickly establish a cognition for its histories, culture and crafts by IVR. However, it is difficult for them to enhance their participation and improve their cognition levels of CP. The specific reasons may be reflected in the following two aspects:

(1) Compared with the tangible artworks, knowledge of traditional handicraft is invisible and its cultural connotation is metaphorical [9]. Metaphorical knowledge includes the implication of the forms of traditional handicrafts in each period of historical development, as well as the historical background and the evolution of human consciousness reflected by the influencing factors of different forms. Although the metaphorical knowledge can be displayed in the visual form in IVR, the lack of embodied cognition makes people feel difficult to understand of the knowledge of traditional handicraft deeply. Therefore, it greatly affects the systematization and effectiveness in the protection and inheritance of traditional handicrafts.

(2) The lack of professional theories to guide the IVR display design of traditional handicrafts makes it difficult to give full play to the advantages of IVR technology, which leads to the lack of participation in the experience and learning process.

In order to solve the above problems, this research proposed an IVR display design mode based on embodied interaction to improve the participants' cognition level of CP and enhance their participation in the innovative application of CP. Finally, the case and offline exhibition are design based on this mode, and the effectiveness of this model is verified by the test to the participant.

2 Embodied Interaction

Dourish takes the concept of embodied cognition into interaction design for the first time in Where The Action Is and introduces the concept of embodied interaction [10]. He thinks that embodiment is a way for people to confront the world, and embodied interaction is a combination of physical computing and social computing [11]. Embodied cognition is an emerging research field and it is one of the theories of the second generation of cognitive science, which is still under development [12]. The objectivity of embodied cognition has been proved in the experimental research of multidisciplinary fields such as psychology, which makes it a new research boom. Embodied cognition theory emphasizes that the body plays an important role in the process of cognition, and cognition is formed by the behavior and experience of the body. In addition, embodied interaction may increase learners' learning motivation. For example, physical exploration of the environment can generate student attitudes to new knowledge, and students' ability to learn about manipulable and explorable material objects will increase. Other researches have found that body-based experiences are more immersive and lead to a greater sense of presence, so that learners may feel they are in a more real and meaningful learning space [13]. The designers of the Smallab at Arizona State University (ASU) identified three key elements that must be considered in technology-enabled embodied interaction: (1) The degree of sensorimotor involvement. (2) Consistency of posture and movement (The degree of mapping between the induced posture and the content to be learned).(3) Perception of immersion [14].

There are many researches that use embodied interaction theory to propose a series of design frameworks for complex classroom knowledge or simple teaching environments. Satinder P.Gill studies the area of rhythm in human interaction, music and language, focusing on movement of body and voice and establishing a research framework based on embodied interaction [15]. Dor Abrahamson studies the role of automatic feedback in the construction of sensorimotor and proposes a heuristic embodied interaction design framework for children's participation in embodied interactive vignettes [16]. John B.Black proposes an embodied interaction design framework applied to teaching, which provides learners with two embodied interaction modes: physical embodiment and imaginary embodiment. The purpose of this framework is to facilitate learners' cognition of knowledge and concepts from both physical and psychological perspectives [17]. Among them, physical embodiment includes direct embodiment, proxy embodiment and augmented embodiment. Based on physical embodiment, imaginary embodiment perceive and act through the individual's imagination. Physical embodiment promotes the generation of cognition and imaginary embodiment promotes the transfer of knowledge. Combined with digital technology, knowledge transmission with embodied interaction greatly improves learners' immersion in learning traditional handicrafts. The focus is not only on the direct display of images through technology, but also on the interaction between learners and traditional handicrafts through equipment. In this way, the metaphorical knowledge in traditional handicraft can be accurately and effectively conveyed to learners through the embodied interaction [18]. This research aims to establish a knowledge transmission mode based on embodied interaction for the protection and inheritance of CP. In this mode, learners will learn the knowledge of CP through the interaction between the body and the environment, to overcome their difficulties of cognition in the invisible metaphorical part of the knowledge of CP.

3 Methodology

3.1 A Framework of IVR Display Design Based on Embodied Interaction

An IVR can be defined as a technical system consisting of a computer and a display, with rich sensory fidelity and immersion. By blocking out the physical world, it allows participants to mentally feel like they are in a simulated environment. Helmet-mounted displays (HMD) are a virtual reality device that places a screen in front of a participant's eyes, blocking out other visual stimuli. It can provide different levels of visual scenes in stereo or single view, by integrating sensors, eye tracker, data gloves and big data and other fields of technology to generate three-dimensional virtual world, realizing human-computer interaction through the handle or data glove, as well as using computer simulation technology to expand the boundaries of human perception [19]. VR technology is the core of IVR. Through the research and analysis of VR technology, it can be concluded that the basic characteristics of VR can be summarized as Immersion, Interaction and Imagination [20]. In a VR experience, immersion is the premise, interaction is the process, and the final desired result is to make participants produce cognition and imagination.

Through comparison and analysis, it can be seen that the three key elements of embodied interaction are consistent with the basic characteristics of virtual reality. Therefore, this research combines embodied interaction and IVR technology to help participants build a systematic cognition of the knowledge of CP, and proposes a framework of IVR display design of CP based on embodied interaction. This framework is composed of two parts, one is the embodied interaction mode for participants, and the other is a design framework of IVR display for constructing participants' knowledge system in IVR. Among them, the three process of embodied interaction can correspond to the three key steps of IVR display design. (1) Physical embodiment: Through the interaction between the body and the environment in the IVR, participants' physical senses are mobilized to form the sensory experience when they just enter the scenario. (2) Imaginary embodiment: Participants interact in IVR through previous experience to generate imagination for the content of CP. (3) Knowledge construction: Tasks set in the IVR are used to drive participants to construct knowledge of CP (see Fig. 1).

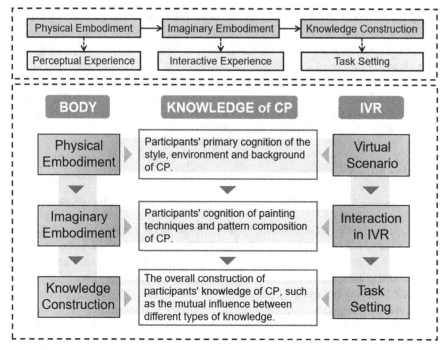

Fig. 1. A framework of IVR display design of CP based on embodied interaction.

3.2 Knowledge of CP Built by Embodied Interaction in Three Key Steps

The three key steps of embodied interaction do not mean the process in the IVR display design, but design indicators for participants to obtain different degrees of cognition of CP in the three steps. The cognition degree of participants can be divided into primary cognition, deep cognition and the construction of cognitive system. The knowledge of CP contained in each level of cognition can be obtained through corresponding embodied interaction steps.

Physical Embodiment (Immersion and Interaction). Participants' primary cognition of the knowledge of CP includes style, era, environment and so on. In the physical embodiment, participants' primary cognition of CP in IVR came from the sensory stimulation of virtual scene, virtual objects and simulated sounds when they just entered the environment. For people who have never had contact with CP, roaming in the scene can quickly enable them to learn the knowledge of CP. In this step, simple interactions, such as browsing the scene, roaming, opening and closing doors, turning off lights and touching objects, can help participants adapt to the virtual environment and get a primary understanding of the style, history and existing environment of CP.

Imaginary Embodiment (Interaction and Imagination). In imaginary embodiment, participants can interact more deeply with the virtual objects in the IVR. For example, they can open reference books or play videos in scene to systematically understand CP. They can pick up or classify the virtual porcelains and other objects. They can also pick up the porcelain to view the details of the pattern and consult the floating graphical user interface in the virtual scene. With the more diversified interaction, participants can gradually build a deeper cognition of CP, such as their painting techniques, firing techniques and pattern composition. At the same time, participants can also generate ideas on the innovation and creativity of CP, such as the recombination of two different elements on a virtual porcelain, so that it can become a new pattern without breaking away from the original style.

Knowledge Construction (Immersion and Imagination). Participants need to complete the knowledge acquisition in IVR under the guidance of certain tasks. These tasks can arouse the participants' interest and curiosity in CP, and enable them to spontaneously establish a knowledge framework of CP. This knowledge framework represents a deeper cognition, such as the reasons for the formation of different styles of CP, and the mutual influence between the era, policy, technique and aesthetic.

4   Cantonese Porcelain as a Case Study

4.1   Equipment and Platform

In this case study, the virtual scene and 30 virtual samples of typical CP are all produced by 3Dmax software. The content of interaction in IVR is developed by Unity3D software, and the offline experience is carried out with the help of HTC Vive equipment (see Fig. 2). The head-mounted display (HMD) of HTC Vive adopts an OLED LCD screen, and the exclusive positioning system consists of two Lighthouse. The screen has an effective resolution of 2160 * 1200 pixels, which can reduce dizziness when used. Participants can use a HMD and a pair of operating handles in a fixed area to interact in the IVR and get cognition of CP.

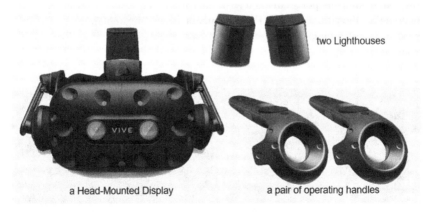

Fig. 2. HTC vive (a HMD, a pair of operating handles and two Lighthouse).

4.2 IVR Display Design Based on Embodied Interaction in Three Key Steps

Physical Embodiment: Roaming in IVR

The IVR display design in physical embodiment requires participants to form a primary cognition of CP through roaming in the virtual scene (see Fig. 3). In this step, the key problem is how to establish a virtual scene that can express the knowledge of CP. According to offline museum research, in the middle of the 18th century, the ship, carrying items including tea, porcelain, silk and rattan ware, hit a reef and sank on its way home. Starting in the 1980s, the salvage operation continued for nearly 10 years and brought up more than 400 pieces of complete porcelain and 9 tons of porcelain fragments. Most of these porcelains have traditional Chinese designs and patterns, while a few are painted with European style patterns. It is obvious that they are CPs specially ordered by Gotheborg I for a specific customer.

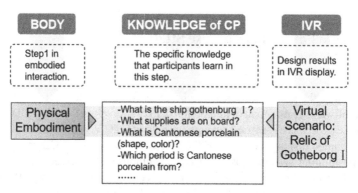

Fig. 3. IVR display design in physical embodiment.

Different from using porcelain factory or museum as the scene, choosing the relic of "Gotheborg I" as the virtual scene of IVR not only facilitates the implantation of historical background, but also makes the interaction of participants in the scene diversified and personalized (see Fig. 4).

Fig. 4. Virtual scene: relic of Gotheborg I.

With the help of a HMD, participants are able to view the virtual relic scene of the "Gotheborg I" in all directions, and move freely with the help of operating handles, as well as open or close doors and grasp virtual objects and other actions. Roaming in the virtual scene, participants could see worn wooden furniture and tools scattered on the ground, objects such as CP stored in certain areas, and could hear the voice of their walking and opening or closing doors. This near-reality scenario can quickly bring participants to a state of immersion.

Imaginary Embodiment: Interaction in IVR

Participants need to get a deeper cognition of CP, such as its composition elements and arrangement rules, through the interaction between their bodies and IVR (see Fig. 5). In this step, a relatively effective method of knowledge transmission is to operate the handle to control the virtual porcelain in the scene, so that it can be moved to various positions by the participants. The control of single or multiple virtual porcelain patterns and other details is also very important. It is also important to control the details, such as the patterns or models of virtual porcelains. In the imaginary embodiment, the content of interaction should be enriched as much as possible and the freedom of operation should also be improved under the condition of ensuring the authenticity and effectiveness of the conveyed content.

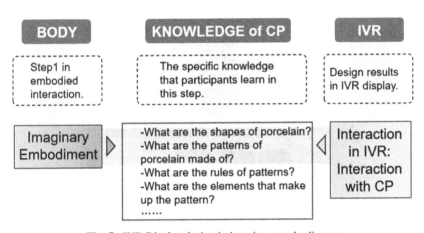

Fig. 5. IVR Display design in imaginary embodiment.

The degree of operation freedom and the scene reality are key factors in determining immersion, which requires participants to be able to interact in the virtual scene based on their existing experience in reality. However, the operating handles make the gesture of grasping and other actions not exactly the same as in reality. We can take advantage of the convenience of operating handles in IVR to ensure that participants can interact differently and get different content by using the same action with operating handles. In the IVR of this case study, the pair of operating handles plays the role of a mouse in the three-dimensional space, which enables the participants to complete all the instructions during interaction with a simple action. They can find the intact CPs in the wooden box in the virtual scene, and pick them up or down. They can also click the virtual buttons around the virtual porcelain to open the corresponding text and voice introduction (see Fig. 6).

In an imaginary embodiment, the redrawing and arrangement of CP patterns reflect the imagination. We set up a database of pattern elements of different types of CP, and participants can redraw patterns through a tangible user interface (see Fig. 7). In this interaction process, participants can observe the real-time changes of the elements corresponding to different positions on the virtual porcelain. Through this method, participants can not only recognize and distinguish the pattern elements, but also have a certain cognition of the pattern composition rules of CP. In addition, the consistency of posture and movement is noteworthy in this interaction process. In terms of interaction, moving the porcelain with the operating handles requires a relatively slow speed, otherwise the porcelain will be thrown rudely. Through the interaction, participants can simulate "Fengjin", the final and special step in making a CP, by moving the operating handles across the edge of the porcelain.

Fig. 6. Interaction in IVR.

Fig. 7. Innovation of CP.

Knowledge Construction: Task Setting

Setting a task for the embodied interaction in the IVR helps participants form a knowledge construction of CP (see Fig. 8). The task may be an archaeological treasure hunt type of storyline, a simple painting process of porcelain or a serious game of answering questions. The purpose is to make participants in IVR not interact aimlessly in virtual scenes, but to scientifically establish the knowledge framework of CP through a systematic process.

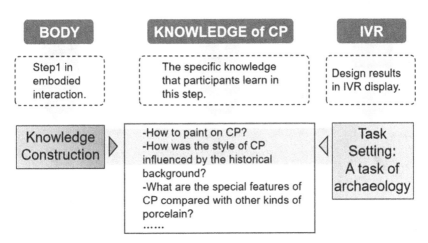

Fig. 8. IVR display design in knowledge construction.

Based on the complexity of knowledge of CP and the close combination of factors such as style, history, background and era changes, this case study sets a story-oriented task to involve all aspects of CP knowledge, which helps participants to build an overall knowledge framework in embodied interaction. As participants put on the HMD to begin their interaction, they will watch a short 50-s video describing the historical background to the sinking of the "Gotheborg I", followed by an animated statement of the task. Correspondingly, at the end of the whole interaction process, there will be an 8-s short video, taking participants from the virtual world to the reality (see Fig. 9). In this case study, the task is to find the porcelains in the virtual relic of Gotheborg I, according to the traditional patterns shown on a CP order (see Fig. 10). This order contains introduction to the various classical patterns of CP, which are the most important components of the porcelain and an important proof that it is a "custom made porcelain". Participants are required to find the porcelain painted with the classical patterns in the virtual scene, and they are also required to actively modify the patterns to meet the conditions on the order. After collecting these porcelain, they can pass the task and get a reward.

Fig. 9. Screenshots of the animations in task start and task end.

Fig. 10. CP order in the task.

4.3 Practice and Testing

The offline practice of this research is carried out in the comprehensive exhibition hall of School of Art and Design, Guangdong University of Technology. A fixed activity area for participants is set on the exhibition site, and posters and electronic display screens are provided for other visitors to watch (see Fig. 11). In order to prove the reliability and effectiveness of this design framework and design practice, we select 20 participants as subjects. The subjects are all students from all grades and academic backgrounds at the Guangdong University of Technology, and none of them have ever known anything about CP. The subjects are divided into two groups, among which 10 subjects in group A successively experience the IVR project in this study, while the other 10 subjects in group B only learned the knowledge of CP by roaming in IVR. While one subject is experiencing in the IVR, other subjects cannot observe the process or result of interaction. After they all finish their experience, we test these subjects though questionnaires to understand their knowledge of CP. The question of the test is the knowledge of CP displayed in this IVR project (see Fig. 12 in appendix). The forms of the questions include judgment questions, multiple choice questions and subjective questions. The questionnaire should be scored according to the three steps of embodied interaction, so as to check the subjects' mastery of the knowledge of CP at three different levels of cognition. The following Table 1 shows the title numbers in the three embodied interaction steps and the mean scores and scoring rates of the two groups.

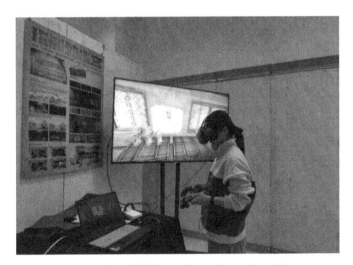

Fig. 11. Offline exhibition and experience of participants.

The test result shows that: (1) The subjects in both groups have a correct cognition of the primary knowledge of CP. (2) In terms of cognition of composition rules and element details of CP, the subjects in Group A perform better. (3) In terms of the knowledge construction of CP, the subjects in Group A obviously get more correct answers and think more deeply. This test result proves that the framework of IVR display design of CP based on embodied interaction proposed in this research is reasonable and effective.

Table 1. The title numbers in three steps and the scores of two groups.

Three steps	Physical embodiment	Imaginary embodiment	Knowledge construction
Title numbers in three steps	1, 2, 3, 4, 8	4, 5, 6, 7, 8, 9, 10	11, 12
Scoring average of Group A	28/30, 93%	50/55, 91%	24/30, 80%
Scoring average of Group B	25/30, 83%	40/55, 73%	16/30, 53%

5 Conclusions and Future Work

Chinese traditional handicraft is an important representative of Chinese culture. As a typical technology in the digital age, virtual reality has made great progress in the protection and inheritance of traditional handicrafts. Aiming at the relative inefficiency of IVR in the display of traditional handicrafts, this research matches the behavior and knowledge gained by participants in IVR, and proposes an IVR display design framework according to the three key steps of embodied interaction. In order to verify the rationality of the design mode and framework, we design an IVR display of CP based on Unity3D software and HTC Vive equipment. In the three key steps of embodied interaction, participants can acquire the corresponding knowledge of CP from the shallow to the deep, and establish their knowledge systems. The test result proves that this mode and framework have certain rationality in assisting the design of IVR display of traditional handicraft.

In the future research, we will continue to transmit the knowledge of CP with IVR, and further push it into the field of individuation. In addition, we also need to inspire participants with different levels of knowledge of CP to have innovative cognition and generate creation of CP. The ultimate goal of the research is to adapt the digital preservation method of traditional handicraft with IVR to various user groups, so that they can individualize to fill their knowledge gaps or generate creations, so as to maximize the efficiency of preservation and innovation of traditional handicraft.

Acknowledgments. This research was supported by the Humanities and social sciences research project of the Ministry of Education (20YJA760031).

Appendix

Knowledge of Cantonese Porcelain

*1. 广彩瓷是清代康熙晚期诞生的外销瓷。
Cantonese porcelain was an export porcelain born in the late period of Emperor Kangxi of the Qing Dynasty

○ T

○ F

*2. 部分广彩瓷上绘制有欧洲皇室的场景或家族徽章。
Some Cantonese porcelain are painted with scenes of European royalty or family insignia.

○ T

○ F

*3. 广彩瓷风格独具清雅，多为淡青色，没有过多的金色装饰。
Cantonese porcelain style is unique and elegant, mostly light blue, without too much gold decoration

○ T

○ F

*4. 广彩瓷的瓷胎产自广州本地。
The mould of Cantonese porcelain is made locally in Guangzhou.

○ T

○ F

*5. 广彩瓷的组织图案一般绘制在斗方内，也可绘制在瓷器的其他空白处。
The pattern of Zuzhi of Cantonese porcelain is usually drawn in the square(Doufang) or other blank parts of the porcelain

○ T

○ F

*6. 广彩瓷的主题图案一般叠加绘制在锦地之上。
The theme pattern of Cantonese porcelain is usually overlaid and painted on the brocade

○ T

○ F

*7. 绘制广彩瓷的第一步？
What is the first step in the painting of Cantonese porcelain?

○ Fengjin(封金)   ○ Kaifu(开幅)   ○ Doucai(斗彩)   ○ Miaoxian(描线)

Fig. 12. Questionnaire.

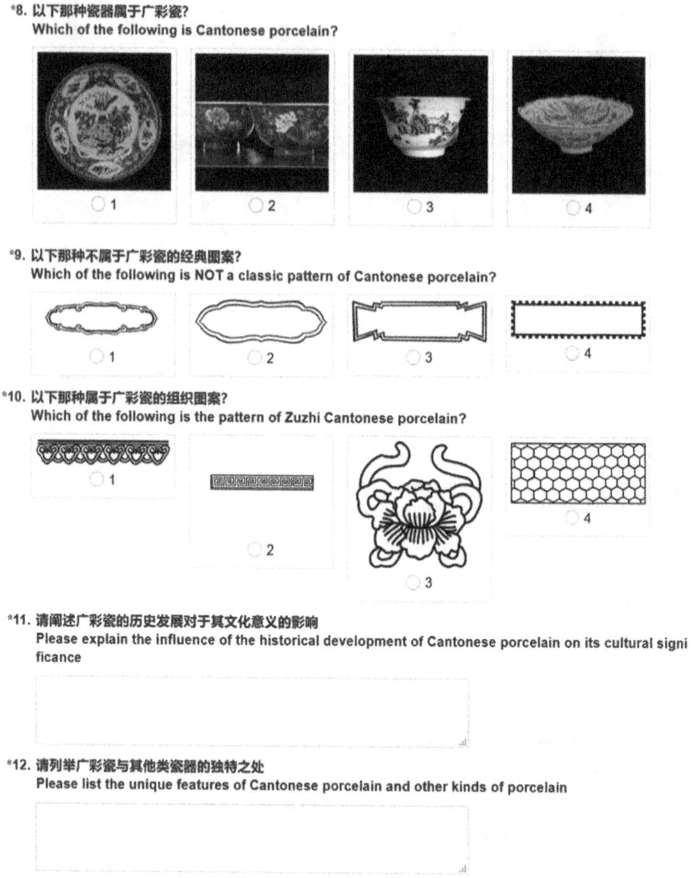

*8. 以下那种瓷器属于广彩瓷?
Which of the following is Cantonese porcelain?

○ 1   ○ 2   ○ 3   ○ 4

*9. 以下那种不属于广彩瓷的经典图案?
Which of the following is NOT a classic pattern of Cantonese porcelain?

○ 1   ○ 2   ○ 3   ○ 4

*10. 以下那种属于广彩瓷的组织图案?
Which of the following is the pattern of Zuzhi Cantonese porcelain?

○ 1

○ 2

○ 3

○ 4

*11. 请阐述广彩瓷的历史发展对于其文化意义的影响
Please explain the influence of the historical development of Cantonese porcelain on its cultural significance

*12. 请列举广彩瓷与其他类瓷器的独特之处
Please list the unique features of Cantonese porcelain and other kinds of porcelain

Fig. 12. (*continued*)

References

1. Slater, M., Sanchez-Vives, M.V.: Enhancing our lives with immersive virtual reality. Front. Robot. AI **3**, 1–47 (2016). https://doi.org/10.3389/frobt.2016.00074
2. Selmanović, E., et al.: Improving accessibility to intangible cultural heritage preservation using virtual reality. J. Comput. Cult. Herit. (2020). https://doi.org/10.1145/3377143
3. Carrozzino, M., Bergamasco, M.: Beyond virtual museums: experiencing immersive virtual reality in real museums. J. Cult. Herit. **11**, 452–458 (2010)
4. Managment, F.: National heritage and development of traditional handicraft centres. Soc. Stud. **2236**, 1457–1471 (2012)
5. Tan, P., Hills, D., Ji, Y., Feng, K.: Case study: creating embodied interaction with learning intangible cultural heritage through WebAR. In: Conference on Human Factors in Computing Systems - Proceedings (2020). https://doi.org/10.1145/3334480.3375199
6. Ji, Y., Tan, P.: Exploring personalized learning pattern for studying Chinese traditional handicraft. In: ACM International Conference Proceedings Series, pp. 140–143 (2018). https://doi.org/10.1145/3202667.3202691

7. Ji, Y., Tan, P., Chen, S.-C., Duh, H.B.-L.: Kansei engineering for e-commerce cantonese porcelain selection in China. In: Kurosu, M. (ed.) HCII 2019. LNCS, vol. 11566, pp. 463–474. Springer, Cham (2019). https://doi.org/10.1007/978-3-030-22646-6_34

8. Zhong, S., Tan, P., Fu, T., Ji, Y.: Product design model for e-commerce cantonese porcelain based on user perceptual image in China. In: Kurosu, M. (ed.) HCII 2020. LNCS, vol. 12183, pp. 350–364. Springer, Cham (2020). https://doi.org/10.1007/978-3-030-49065-2_25

9. Ji, Y., Fu, T., Tan, P., Sun, X.: Research on learning experience of intangible cultural heritage workshop from the perspective of innovation. In: ACM International Conference Proceedings Series, pp. 109–112 (2019). https://doi.org/10.1145/3332169.3332260

10. Dourish, P.: Where the Action Is: The Foundations of Embodied Interaction. Where action is Found. Embodied Interact (2001). https://doi.org/10.1162/leon.2003.36.5.412

11. Dourish, P.: Embodied interaction: exploring the foundations of a new approach to HCI. Work (1999)

12. Holton, D.L.: Constructivism + embodied cognition = enactivism: theoretical and practical implications for conceptual change (2010)

13. Lindgren, R., Tscholl, M., Wang, S., Johnson, E.: Enhancing learning and engagement through embodied interaction within a mixed reality simulation. Comput. Educ. **95**, 174–187 (2016). https://doi.org/10.1016/j.compedu.2016.01.001

14. Johnson-Glenberg, M.C., Birchfield, D.A., Tolentino, L., Koziupa, T.: Collaborative embodied learning in mixed reality motion-capture environments: two science studies. J. Educ. Psychol. **106**, 86–104 (2014). https://doi.org/10.1037/a0034008

15. Gill, S.P.: Rhythmic synchrony and mediated interaction: towards a framework of rhythm in embodied interaction. AI Soc. **27**, 111–127 (2012). https://doi.org/10.1007/s00146-011-0362-2

16. Abrahamson, D., Trninic, D.: Toward an embodied-interaction design framework for mathematical concepts. In: Proceedingsof IDC 2011 - 10th International Conference on Interaction Design and Children, pp. 1–10 (2011). https://doi.org/10.1145/1999030.1999031

17. Black, J.B., Segal, A., Vitale, J.M., Fadjo, C.L.: Embodied cognition and learning environment design. In: Theoretical Foundations of Learning Environments (2012)

18. Ji, Y., Tan, P.: Chinese traditional handicraft education using AR content. Leonardo **53**, 199–200 (2020). https://doi.org/10.1162/leon_a_01863

19. Bryson, S.: Virtual reality. In: Computer Science Handbook, 2nd edn. (2004). https://doi.org/10.6017/ital.v38i4.11847

20. Sheridan, T.B.: Interaction, imagination and immersion some research needs. In: Proceedings of the ACM Symposium on Virtual Reality Software and Technology, VRST (2000). https://doi.org/10.1145/502390.502392

Design and Research of Children's Robot Based on Kansei Engineering

Siyao Zhu, Junnan Ye[✉], Menglan Wang, Jingyang Wang, and Xu Liu

East China University of Science and Technology, Shanghai 200237, People's Republic of China

Abstract. Under the background of the spread of COVID-19, there has been a shift from offline education to online education. Online education is rapidly becoming large-scale in a short time, and its related hardware and software markets are expanding rapidly. The development of this kind of online education hardware carrier represented by children's robot has become a hot spot in the industry at this time, but there are still some problems in its design, such as ignoring the emotional needs of users. This study first focuses on the user's function and emotional needs through market research and user research, then uses the method of Kansei engineering to select a certain sample of existing children's robots, conducts Kansei vocabulary research through SD method, and analyzes the data results through SPSS, so as to summarize the modeling semantic keywords. Finally, from the perspective of Kansei Engineering, a new practical design scheme of children's accompanying robot is proposed. The feasibility and effectiveness of the design practice are verified by the satisfaction survey.

Keywords: Kansei Engineering · Online education · Semantics product design · Children's robot

1 First Section

1.1 A Subsection Sample

In 2020, COVID-19 spread all over the world, and the educational pattern of the whole world has changed greatly. Students of all ages have experienced the change from offline education to online education. Online education expands rapidly in a short time and forms a certain market scale. Even if the current epidemic situation has improved, the education model will gradually return to offline. But online education has not faded out, and gradually become a part of students' life. Online education is rapidly becoming large-scale in a short time, and its related hardware and software markets are expanding rapidly. Especially for the younger students who need more guidance, the market demand for carrier hardware is rising. Children's robot is an important hardware carrier of online education for young students. It is based on artificial intelligence, Internet technology, speech recognition technology, a combination of hardware and software products. In the online education during the epidemic period, children's robots can guide and supervise the learning of young students, and also can accompany young students to alleviate their

© Springer Nature Switzerland AG 2021
M. Kurosu (Ed.): HCII 2021, LNCS 12764, pp. 214–225, 2021.
https://doi.org/10.1007/978-3-030-78468-3_15

loneliness. Most of the existing modeling design and research of children's robot in the market focus on the function, and ignore the emotional needs of users in the process of interaction with the product. But today's product design research shows that in the process of product design, we should not only meet the good realization of product functions, but also pay attention to the emotional output of target users [1] especially in children's products. At the same time, more and more studies show that the appearance design of products should avoid the subjective emotions of designers and emphasize user centered innovation. As a mature design theory, Kansei engineering theory has been widely used in all aspects of design. In the process of product design, the application of this systematic research and design method is effective and feasible. Based on the perceptual experience of consumers, the methods and technical means of perceptual engineering are applied to the design and development of children's accompanying robot. With the perceptual data model of the audience as the reference, the design and development is combined with the development of engineering technology and modern information technology, which not only meets the needs of modern development, but also improves the efficiency of design [2].

Therefore, this paper uses Kansei Engineering, a quantifiable, scientific and systematic design tool to help understand users' perceptual needs and visual transformation, to study the appearance design of children's accompanying robot, and to produce the design practice results after the research [3].

2 Kansei Engineering

2.1 Kansei Engineering

Kansei originated from the Japanese transliteration of "カ ン セ イ", which refers to the psychological feelings and product image cognition brought by the commercialized products. Kansei engineering is a kind of human factors engineering technology based on human beings. It combines it with engineering technology to study users' perceptual needs, quantify people's emotional information, find out the relationship between perceptual quantity and engineering physical quantity, and transform perceptual information into specific design form to develop new products that meet consumers' needs [4].

The service object of design is people rather than things, so we need to design products according to people's preferences and physiological characteristics. And the purpose of design is to design the products that let users have a sense of satisfaction and pleasure. But because of the complexity and change of human sensibility, different people will have different feelings for specific objects in different states and scenes [5]. Therefore, how to design a product to make customers feel positive is a problem worthy of study. The essence of Kansei engineering is to scientifically quantify people's abstract emotions and concrete materials, so as to establish an equivalent logical relationship between them, and express all kinds of emotions and feelings brought by products through product semantics. This is the research paradigm of Kansei engineering.

2.2 Application of Kansei Engineering in Product Design Research

From the perspective of Kansei Engineering, product research is a scientific and rigorous analysis process, and it has been a relatively mature methodology. According to the Kansei engineering based product design framework of Chen Jinliang's research on Kansei engineering based product design method [6], the specific process and method are as follows:

Clear Product Market and Product Positioning: First of all, it is necessary to conduct research on the relevant product market, and then position the product after the research. This determines the product development prospects and goals [7]. In addition, we need to make clear the target users of the product, which is not only to further clarify the product, but also to clarify the follow-up research object.

To Determine the Typical Samples of Products: Before establishing the typical samples of products, a large number of sample types need to be selected. In the selection of samples, there are mainly the following methods: A. browsing the relevant websites; B. visiting the physical stores; C. consulting literature and so on. Through the above several methods of extensive collection and establishment of sample library, and then through expert evaluation and other forms of analysis and selection of typical product samples. The selection of samples has a crucial impact on the extraction of perceptual vocabulary and the scientificity and effectiveness of data analysis.

Determine Perceptual Vocabulary: Perceptual vocabulary is the text expression of users' subjective feelings, and accurate perceptual vocabulary is conducive to accurately obtain the effective psychological feedback of users in the follow-up research. Therefore, the establishment of perceptual vocabulary should be the same as too many kinds of methods, such as: A. design research; B. check the text data related to products to summarize perceptual vocabulary; C. collect a large number of perceptual vocabulary through brainstorming, and then further screen to establish refined, representative and highly relevant perceptual vocabulary.

Design the Questionnaire of Semantic Difference Method: Use the semantic difference method (SD) to design the questionnaire. The semantic difference method is a kind of language measurement method, which was established by American psychologist Osgood in 1957 and applied in the field of psychology. It is a scientific measurement method which takes a pair of antonyms as the two ends of the scale. The scope of the scale is divided into n grades, and the number of grades must be odd. The tester can score the sensory intensity with a scale. Researchers can then quantify users' feelings through rating data [8].

Typical Sample Perceptual Semantic Evaluation: Select the appropriate research object to collect evaluation, because the research object has an important impact on the research results, so in the selection of research object, we must choose the relevant typical object.

Data Analysis and Design Guidance: Use data analysis software to analyze the sensory intensity data. Get intuitive results and analyze the results, and finally draw a conclusion and use it in the follow-up design practice guidance.

3   Design of Children's Accompanying Robot Based on Kansei Engineering

3.1   Market Research of Children Accompany Robot

Before the Kansei Engineering Research of children's accompanying robot, we need to investigate the existing children's robot market and user needs. Through the collection of network information and the distribution of questionnaire, we found that there is still a lot of time gap and communication space between parents and children. The accompanying robot can not only fill the loneliness of children when they are alone, but also become a bridge between parents and children. This also proves that the children accompany robot has its extensive market and social significance. At the same time, the survey of users shows that "safety" and "accompany" have become the high-frequency words in the needs of users for children's accompanying robots. We need to take these keywords into account to meet the inner needs of consumers to a greater extent.

3.2   Product Design Orientation

Social development is also accompanied by the emergence of some social problems, in which children's physical and mental development has become an important part. At this time, the development of children's accompanying robot has become a hot spot in the industry. In addition to establishing the communication media between parents and children and some additional functions, children's accompanying robot should also try to consider the emotional needs of users for products. The shape, color and material of children's accompanying robot will have an impact on users' perception and preferences. However, the existing children's robots on the market obviously lack of research on this factor. Therefore, this paper focuses on the main positioning of "safe accompany", and researches and designs the children accompany robot from the perspective of Kansei engineering. "Accompany" is that the robot can relieve children's loneliness by telling stories and chatting, so as to accompany children to a certain extent. The "protection" is that the robot will be equipped with lidar, motion recognition and other technologies to monitor the safety of children and ensure their safety. The target user group of this child care robot is children aged 6–12, who have obvious product selection tendency and emotional needs.

Table 1. Five typical samples of children's robots.

Sample 1	Sample 2	Sample 3	Sample 4	Sample 5

3.3 Determination of Typical Product Samples

According to a variety of typical sample collection methods, the sample collection of children's robot is carried out, and 40 children's robot samples are preliminarily obtained. And through the guidance and analysis of professional groups and experts, according to the appearance characteristics of the robot, such as the type, style, overall shape and material, the collected samples of children's robots are classified and deleted, and five typical samples of children's robots are obtained (as shown in Table 1).

3.4 Determine Product Perceptual Vocabulary

In this paper, 60 perceptual words are collected and sorted into 30 pairs of antonym phrases (as shown in Table 2).

Table 2. 30 pairs of perceptual words.

Number	Perceptual vocabulary	Number	Perceptual vocabulary	Number	Perceptual vocabulary
1	Simple——Miscellaneous	11	Hign End——Low End	21	Affinity——Icy
2	Elegant——Bright	12	Lovely - Boring	22	Energetic——Steady
3	Textured——Shoddy	13	Friendly——Rigid	23	Intellectual——Ordinary
4	Technological——Staid	14	Innovative——Old	24	Durable——Vulnerable
5	Modern——Traditional	15	Systematic——Messy	25	Round——Angular
6	Interesting——Boring	16	Flexible - Mechanical	26	Safe——Dangerous
7	Soft——Stiff	17	Smart——Clumsy	27	Stable——Risky
8	Smart——Dull	18	Gentle——Frosty	28	Refined——vulgar
9	Special——Common	19	Simple——Complex	29	Changing——Single
10	Luxurious——Plain	20	Intuitive——Abstract	30	Warm——Cold

By classifying and summing up the words in Table 3, the group words with similar meaning and little relevance are deleted, and six groups of effective perceptual words are selected.

Table 3. Six pairs of effective perceptual words.

Number	Perceptual words
1	Simple——Miscellaneous
2	Modern——Traditional
3	Safe——Dangerous
4	Lovely——Boring
5	Smart——Clumsy
6	Affinity——Cold

Table 4. The specific semantic difference questionnaire of child care robot.

Simple	-3	-2	-1	0	1	2	3	Miscellaneous
Modern	-3	-2	-1	0	1	2	3	Traditional
Safe	-3	-2	-1	0	1	2	3	Dangerous
Lovely	-3	-2	-1	0	1	2	3	Boring
Smart	-3	-2	-1	0	1	2	3	Clumsy
Affinity	-3	-2	-1	0	1	2	3	Cold

Simple	-3	-2	-1	0	1	2	3	Miscellaneous
Modern	-3	-2	-1	0	1	2	3	Traditional
Safe	-3	-2	-1	0	1	2	3	Dangerous
Lovely	-3	-2	-1	0	1	2	3	Boring
Smart	-3	-2	-1	0	1	2	3	Clumsy
Affinity	-3	-2	-1	0	1	2	3	Cold

Simple	-3	-2	-1	0	1	2	3	Miscellaneous
Modern	-3	-2	-1	0	1	2	3	Traditional
Safe	-3	-2	-1	0	1	2	3	Dangerous
Lovely	-3	-2	-1	0	1	2	3	Boring
Smart	-3	-2	-1	0	1	2	3	Clumsy
Affinity	-3	-2	-1	0	1	2	3	Cold

Simple	-3	-2	-1	0	1	2	3	Miscellaneous
Modern	-3	-2	-1	0	1	2	3	Traditional
Safe	-3	-2	-1	0	1	2	3	Dangerous
Lovely	-3	-2	-1	0	1	2	3	Boring
Smart	-3	-2	-1	0	1	2	3	Clumsy
Affinity	-3	-2	-1	0	1	2	3	Cold

Simple	-3	-2	-1	0	1	2	3	Miscellaneous
Modern	-3	-2	-1	0	1	2	3	Traditional
Safe	-3	-2	-1	0	1	2	3	Dangerous
Lovely	-3	-2	-1	0	1	2	3	Boring
Smart	-3	-2	-1	0	1	2	3	Clumsy
Affinity	-3	-2	-1	0	1	2	3	Cold

"Simple or Miscellaneous" refers to whether the modeling language of the child care robot is simple or not, which is the most basic design language judgment; "Modern or Traditional" refers to whether the children's accompanying robot gives people the feeling of modern fashion or the feeling of traditional obsolescence on the whole; "Safety or Danger" is a very important feeling for children's accompanying robot. Whether a product can bring intuitive "safety" feeling to users in modeling is the key of children's products; "Lovely or Boring" refers to whether the modeling of children's accompanying robot can touch users' emotional points and make them interested; "Smart or Clumsy" refers to the whole process In terms of body shape, it gives users a kind of flexibility in following activities; "Affinity or cold" refers to that the product produces a sense of closeness rather than a sense of distance.

3.5 Questionnaire Design Based on Semantic Difference Method

Semantic difference method (SD) was used to design the questionnaire. The final five children robot samples were arranged with serial numbers [9], and 6 groups of perceptual words were used to establish a scale of level 7. The perceptual setting values are -3, -2, -1, 0, 1, 2, 3 respectively, where -3 represents the leftmost perceptual vocabulary and 3 represents the rightmost perceptual vocabulary. Users score according to their perception of product modeling [10]. The specific semantic difference questionnaire of child care robot is shown in the following Table 4:

3.6 Perceptual Semantic Evaluation of Typical Samples

A total of 55 valid questionnaires were collected, and the average feeling values of six groups of perceptual words in five samples were obtained (as shown in Table 5).

3.7 Data Analysis and Design Guidance

According to the data obtained from the questionnaire survey, the average value of perceptual vocabulary is poured into SPSS analysis software, and the perceptual vocabulary intention line chart among the samples is drawn. According to the intention line chart, the following analysis results can be obtained: A. the simple shape formed by such stretching curve in sample 1 and sample 2 products is more likely to make people feel simple and generous; B. samples 2 and 4 with scientific and technological elements (such as light band) are more likely to make people feel modern science and technology; C Sample 2 and sample 5, which are more mellow and solid anthropomorphic modeling languages, are more likely to make users feel safe and reliable; D. sample 3, which is an abstract animal bionic modeling language, is more likely to make users feel lovely; e. sample 2 and sample 4, which have been cut and divided in a certain proportion, often give people a more flexible feeling; D. sample 3, which is from the reality, can make users feel more comfortable The free modeling language evolved from state is easier to bring users a friendly feeling (Fig. 1).

Table 5. Average score of perceptual vocabulary.

Sample	Modeling	Simple	Modern	Safe	Lovely	Smart	Affinity
Sample 1		-1.02	-0.8	-0.78	-0.84	-0.62	-0.64
Sample 2		-0.18	-0.75	-0.49	-0.27	-0.31	-0.24
Sample 3		-0.09	-1.04	-0.65	-1.05	-0.69	-1.11
Sample 4		0.62	-1.07	-0.4	-0.58	-0.36	-0.41
Sample 5		0.31	-0.38	-0.47	-0.15	-0.55	-0.33

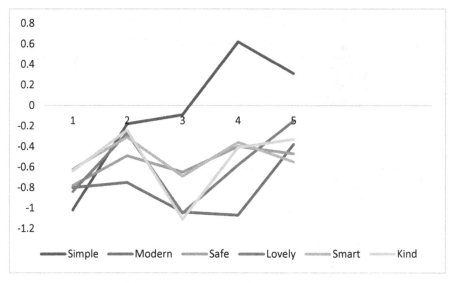

Fig. 1. Perceptual lexical intention line chart.

4 Design Practice

Based on the previous market research and user research, it is determined that the main selling points of this children's accompanying robot are "safety" and "accompanying". Therefore, whether the modeling language can bring a sense of security and affinity to users should be considered in the product modeling design. At the same time, combined with the perceptual semantic research of the five sample products, the design languages of "body segmentation", "solid", "mellow", and "bionic" are summarized. Cubort, a child care robot, is designed (as shown in Figs. 2, 3).

This scheme integrates the design theme of "safe escort" into the product, presenting a round and solid pagoda shape on the whole. The division of facial and neck lines is an abstract bionic for the image of "bodyguard", giving people a safe and reliable image. There are motion sensors on both sides of the body, and the shape design of this part is also integrated with the overall shape, which is of great significance in design A sense of wholeness. The position of the rear universal wheel adopts the detail treatment of the turning surface, which makes the product function highly combined with the shape. The actual visual effect of the product is shown in Fig. 4.

Fig. 2. The modeling design of children's robot.

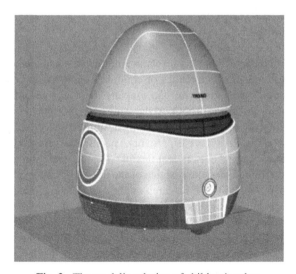

Fig. 3. The modeling design of children's robot.

Finally, through the form of questionnaire survey, in the form of 30 target users of the product design satisfaction survey, collected the target user perception of the product modeling elements and satisfaction. 81.9% of the users perceived the "security" element; 69.8% of the users perceived the "affinity" element. The average score of satisfaction with the product is 7.89.

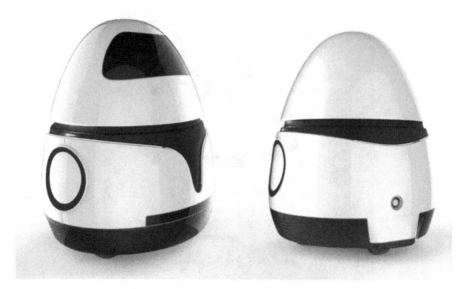

Fig. 4. Children's robot design renderings.

5   Summary and Prospect

In this paper, we use Kansei engineering to study the product design of children's accompanying robot. Combined with market research and user demand analysis, we scientifically summarize the modeling semantics of children's accompanying robot. Through the research, it is found that "safety" and "accompany" are the key words of users' needs when designing a child accompany robot. At the same time, through the scientific method of Kansei Engineering, the key words of modeling design are analyzed. For example, the round and solid pagoda modeling is easier to make people feel safe, and the flexible segmentation of the body can make users feel flexible. Finally, the optimal design scheme of the product is determined, and the practice of the design of children's accompanying robot is implemented. Applying the research method of Kansei engineering to product design can effectively help designers evaluate users' emotional preferences and modeling preferences in a scientific way, and further enhance the identity of products among consumers. However, in practice, this method will be affected by the sample selection in the questionnaire survey and the uncertainty of the respondents, which will have a certain impact on the results. This problem will be improved by using more accurate research methods (such as artificial interview, psychological test, etc.) in the follow-up research.

References

1. Chen, J.: Host's remarks on research topic of kansei engineering. Hum. Packag. **33**(03), 11 (2018)
2. Cui, Y., Shen, J., Yin, H.: Design of front face of micro electric vehicle based on kansei engineering. J. Taiyuan Univ. Tech. **51**(03), 471–477 (2020)

3. Wang, Y., Zhang, S.: Research on perceptual elements in elderly bathtub design. Packag. Eng. **41**(10), 168–174 (2020)
4. Li, H., Zhang, S., Chen, J.: Research progress of Kansei engineering methodology and its application in product design process. Hum. Packag. **31**(04), 23–27 (2016)
5. Peng, D., Bian, Z., Huang, Z.: Hesitant fuzzy Kansei TOPSIS evaluation method for product design scheme. Syst. Sci. Math. 1–17(2020)
6. Chen, J., Zhao, F., Li, Y., Zhang, Q.: Research on product design method based on kansei engineering. Packag. Eng. **40**(12), 162–167 (2019)
7. Zhang, X.: Research on lamp design based on kansei engineering. North Univ, Tech (2016)
8. Xu, X., Jiang, Z.: Research on intelligent sound design based on Kansei Engineering. West. Leather **41**(16), 36–37 (2019)
9. Chen, Y., Wan, Z., Yu, D., Ye, J.: Research on innovative design of domestic drinking water dispenser based on users' perceptual needs. Packag. Eng. **41**(08), 173–179 (2020)
10. Zhou, J., Zhang, Y., Zhou, J.: Perceptual quantitative evaluation of the application effect of geometric patterns on swimsuit. Knit. Indus. **05**, 67–72 (2020)

User Experience and Technology Acceptance Studies

Exploring Citizens' Attitudes Towards Voice-Based Government Services in Switzerland

Matthias Baldauf[✉], Hans-Dieter Zimmermann, and Claudia Pedron

Eastern Switzerland University of Applied Sciences, Rosenbergstrasse 59,
9001 St. Gallen, Switzerland
{matthias.baldauf,hansdieter.zimmermann,claudia.pedron}@ost.ch

Abstract. Voice-based applications might become a promising novel channel for governments to engage with citizens and to provide easy-to-use and always available administrative services. To learn about citizens' attitudes towards this "conversational e-government", we conducted an online survey among Swiss residents (n = 397). While half of the participants tended towards not using such prospective services, 38% were positive about them. Regular users of voice assistants and participants with interest in technology showed a significantly higher willingness-to-use. The top-rated service was looking up government-related information. Advanced services (such as ordering certificates by voice) were perceived more skeptically. As trustworthy service providers the municipality and national tech companies were clearly favored over major international ones due to privacy concerns.

Keywords: E-government · Conversational government · Online survey · Voice-based citizen services

1 Introduction

E-government, i.e. the delivery of government information and services online through the Internet or other digital means [15], has made great advances over the last years. Today, governments around the world provide respective Web platforms and/or dedicated mobile apps for citizens to access government services 24/7. Following related developments in e-commerce ("conversational commerce" [13]), one latest trend in the domain of e-government is the integration of so-called "conversational user interfaces" [11] which exploit natural human language with the goal to improve citizen engagement and enable quicker and easier interaction with digital government services. In particular, "chatbots" for the public sector (supporting requests in natural written language) have been gaining interest in academia (cf. [3,12]). Several cities have started to provide

© Springer Nature Switzerland AG 2021
M. Kurosu (Ed.): HCII 2021, LNCS 12764, pp. 229–238, 2021.
https://doi.org/10.1007/978-3-030-78468-3_16

chatbots to answer citizens' frequent questions, such as St.Gallen[1], Hamburg with its *Frag-den-Michel*[2] service or Vienna with its *WienBot*[3] app (cf. Fig. 1).

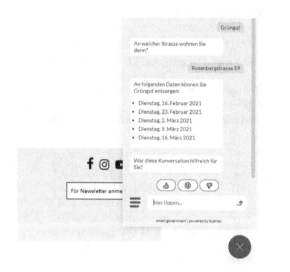

Fig. 1. Two examples of chatbots recently launched by cities: integrated into the official website (St. Gallen, left) and as mobile app (Vienna, right).

In contrast, voice-based e-government services and corresponding scientific knowledge are still scarce. Early scientific work mainly focused on technological fundamentals and includes a voice-enabled personal assistant to support civil servants advising citizens in an e-government multi-agent system [6]. Examples of more recent research addressing available commercial voice platforms is work by Lafia et al. [9] who proposed voice assistants for discovering open public data and work by Baldauf and Zimmermann [5] who derived implications and considerations for both providing the fundamentals as well as designing and implementing conversational e-government services from interviews with e-government experts.

As a pioneer, the UK government has been launching a conversational e-government service for *Alexa* and *Google Assistant* which provides more than 12,000 pieces of governmental information via the respective voice assistants [8].

To learn about citizens' attitudes towards such voice-based e-government services, we conducted an online survey among Swiss residents (n = 397). We investigated the overall willingness-to-use voice-based e-government services (RQ1), desirable types of conversational e-government services (RQ2), and preferred trustworthy providers of such services (RQ3). The results of this initial survey provide a first step towards understanding the requirements of voice-based conversa-

---

[1] https://www.stadtsg.ch/chatbot.

[2] https://www.hamburg.de/fragdenmichel/.

[3] https://play.google.com/store/apps/details?id=at.gv.wien.wienbot.

tional e-government and can inform the design and introduction of future digital citizen services.

2   Method

Our online survey started with an explanation of current mass-market voice assistants and questions on the participants' usage behavior regarding voice assistants (frequency and common applications). Then, we introduced the concept of "conversational e-government" services by describing the example of the UK government.

Participants were asked to state their overall willingness to use voice-based e-government services in Switzerland on a five-point Likert scale from *"I would definitely not use such services."*) (1) to *"I would definitely use such services."*) (5) as well as to give a reason for their rating in a free text field. Furthermore, we asked participants to rate their willingness to use specific voice-based services. For each service, they could state the degree of their agreement on a five-point Likert scale (no, rather no, I don't know, rather yes, yes). The list of services was inspired by related e-government services currently provided by the university's municipality via Web pages. Additionally, we asked participants to propose additional voice-based e-government services they considered useful.

Finally, we were interested in the preferred provider(s) of voice-based e-government services. Since trust has been shown to be an important catalyst of e-government adoption [14], we asked the participants whether they considered a respective service trustworthy if it was offered by the participant's home municipality, a national tech company from Switzerland, or a major international tech company (with the examples of *Apple, Google* and *Microsoft*). These alternatives are deliberately not exclusive. Again, the three questions could be answered on five-point Likert scales (no, rather no, I don't know, rather yes, yes). Optionally, participants could state the reasons for their decisions. The survey closed with demographic questions regarding age and sex as well as a self-assessment regarding interest in new technologies (five-point Likert scale from not interested at all (1) to very interested (5)).

The survey was distributed via social media and university mailing lists in December 2019. Filling out the survey took about 10 min. Participation was anonymous, yet participants who completed the survey, could submit their e-mail address to took part in a draw for three vouchers for an online electronics shop.

Overall, 621 participants took part in this survey. For the analysis we only considered the ones who completed the entire questionnaire, i.e. 397 respondents. These participants (156 male, 241 female) were between 18 and 67 years old ($M = 26.6$; $SD = 8.1$). Regarding their current usage behavior, 5% of the participants stated to use voice assistants on a daily base, 9% weekly, 5% monthly, and 47% more rarely. 34% stated to have not used a voice assistant so far.

3   Results

In the following, we present the survey results with regard to our three research questions.

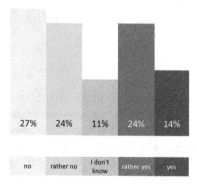

Fig. 2. Participants' agreement to the statement "When voice-based e-government services will be available in Switzerland, I will use them." (numbers indicate percentage of participants).

3.1   RQ1. Willingness-to-Use

Figure 2 shows the results of the participants' ratings regarding their overall willingness-to-use (M = 2.76; SD = 1.43). More than half of the participants (51%) did not confirm the overall statement "When voice-based e-government services will be available in Switzerland, I will use them." 27% of the participants answered "no", 24% "rather no". In contrast, 38% of the participants were positive towards such services: 14% answered "yes", 24% "rather yes". The remainder of 11% was indecisive ("I don't know").

Mean difference comparisons for participants interested in new technologies (i.e. with a corresponding self-assessment of 4 or 5) and ones with less or no interest by a Mann-Whitney test showed a significantly higher willingness-to-use (p < .001) by the technology-savy participants. Furthermore, the willingness-to-use of the participant group who uses voice assistants on a daily or weekly base, was significantly higher than that of the remaining participants with infrequent or no usage (p < .001). No significant differences of the willingness-to-use could be found for age and sex.

The participants' reasons for using a respective voice assistant were mainly related to a more convenient, easier, and quicker access to governmental services. Several participants referred to negative prior experiences with offices (bad service, long waiting times, limited opening times) and expected digital voice-based services to be more simplified and citizen-oriented. Several participants anticipated an improved accessibility of such services for handicapped people.

The main arguments for refusing voice-based e-government services included the lack of personal contact and advice as well as concerns regarding data protection and privacy. Some participants mentioned their fear of misunderstandings and harmful actions triggered respectively. A few participants explicitly referred to similar Web-based services and could not see an advantage over such available offers.

3.2 RQ2. Desirable Types of Services

Figure 3 depicts the participants' ratings regarding different types of voice-based e-government services, ordered by the number of positive (i.e. "rather yes" and "yes") answers. The service most preferred by the participants (with positive answers by 66% of the participants) was getting overall (static) information such as opening hours. Second-ranked was looking up dates for garbage collection (54%).

Fig. 3. Participants' agreement to use different types of prospective conversational e-government services (numbers indicate percentage of participants).

Making an appointment with a civil servant via a voice-based service was perceived positive by 42% of the participants. Also, 42% were positive towards ordering certificates (for officially proving the current residence, e.g.) via a voice assistant. A similar number of positive ratings received voice-based services for ordering printed extracts from the debt enforcement registers (35%), reporting address changes after a relocation (34%), and, as offered by some municipalities in Switzerland, ordering reduced tickets for public means of transport (34%).

The voice-based service with the fewest positive ratings (31% of the participants) was ordering a printed extract from the judicial records (as required by some employers, e.g.). Only the two top-ranked services received positive feedback by more than the majority of the participants.

Fig. 4. Participant ratings for potential providers of voice-based citizen services (numbers indicate percentage of participants).

The participants came up with additional services they considered a voice assistant suitable for. Among the most frequently mentioned services were requesting extensions for official documents (such as passports, e.g.) and for forms to be handed in (such as tax declarations, e.g.). Furthermore, the participants envisioned voice-based assistant services providing information on the naturalization procedure, tax declarations, recent election results, administrative duties after a relocation, and public municipal events.

3.3   RQ3. Trust in Service Provider

Figure 4 depicts the participants' responses regarding their trust in potential providers of voice-based citizen services. 57% of the participants state to (rather) trust services provided by their municipality, 33% to (rather) not, 20% were indecisive (M = 3.14; SD = 1.40). 43% of the participants would (rather) trust in a local tech company as service provider, 34% (rather) not, 23% were indecisive (M = 3.05; SD = 1.32). Finally, 16% said to (rather) trust a major international tech company, 66% to (rather) not, 18% were indecisive (M = 2.18; SD = 1.21).

Pairwise Wilcoxon tests showed highly significant differences (p < .001) in the trustworthiness of a municipality and a major international tech company as well as of a Swiss tech company and a major international tech company.

Reasoning their positive ratings for municipalities as service providers, several participants supposed that those would thoroughly evaluate respective services and publish them only in accordance with latest data protection regulations. Furthermore, participants expected that municipalities would provide such services *"to the benefit of the citizens"* and without any commercial interest. Negative remarks on municipalities were related mainly to the lack of their knowledge of and experience with such recent technologies as voice-based services and the participants' corresponding concerns regarding data protection.

Regarding local companies, many participants explained their trust by the assumption that voice data would be held in national data centers and that these companies had to comply with strict national data protection laws. Furthermore, comparing to municipalities, they appreciated their technical expertise and professional working. On the negative side, several participants mentioned the commercial interest: Companies are profit-oriented and thus, the collected data might be used for purposes beyond the actual government service.

Almost all negative remarks regarding major international technology companies contained concerns regarding data protection and privacy. A majority of the participants feared the exploitation of their data and referred to recent privacy scandals around audio recordings by voice assistants.

Several participants criticized that *"these companies already possess too much data and they know too much about us"* and large tech companies would use gathered data for further profit-making services. Participants who were more positive about these major players explained that *"they can't afford to lose the trust of their customers"*. Additionally, participants related to own experiences with respective technology and appreciated the technology expertise of large international companies. Only very few participants differentiated between companies and, for example, preferred Apple over Google due to privacy concerns.

4   Discussion

In this section, we refer back to our research questions and critically reflect on the survey results.

4.1   RQ1. Willingness-to-Use

Overall, the participants were skeptical regarding voice-based citizen services: only 38% stated that they would (rather) use such services. More technology-savy participants rather were positive towards conversational e-government. Similarly, participants who are more experienced with voice assistants and use them on a daily or weekly base had a higher willingness to use voice-based e-government services. Peoples' prior experiences with voice assistants seem to have a crucial impact on the acceptance of respective governmental services.

While in Switzerland popular voice assistants such as *Siri* and *Google Assistant* are available on smartphones, several smart speakers such as *Amazon Echo* can be bought via retailers, yet are not officially marketed by their producers. Overall, our participants thus were less experienced with voice-based services than US citizens (with 24% owning at least one smart speaker[4], for example. This might partly explain the scepticism by the majority of our participants. International comparisons with countries with a higher penetration of voice assistants due to the availability of smart speakers (such as the US) and with countries where first basic voice-based e-government services are available (such as the UK) could help to study the impact of prior experiences in detail and to identify the relevance of regional characteristics on the overall willing-to-use.

---

[4] https://www.nationalpublicmedia.com/insights/reports/smart-audio-report/.

4.2   RQ2. Desirable Types of Services

The two top-rated conversational e-government services were applications for looking up information by voice. Some of these questions can be answered by today's mass-market voice assistants since the related information (e.g., opening hours of offices) can be found on the Web. Answering more specific questions requires dedicated extensions (such as the services provided by the UK government). This preference for information look-up is in line with prior research on frequent applications of voice assistants (cf. [2]).

More advanced voice-based citizen services such as ordering certificates or extracts from official records were rated less positively. According to the participants' remarks, participants were concerned about privacy issues or had doubts about the benefit over today's Web-based solutions. To address the latter concern, we conclude that for a follow-up experiment prototypes of concrete services should be developed in order to let participants experience potential advantages and identify promising candidates for pilot studies.

When selecting services and designing such prototypes, it must be ensured to simplify formerly extensive administrative processes while not increasing complexity caused by the voice channel. For example, advanced conversational e-government services will require an authentication of the user. Respective authentication techniques for voice-based services must be efficient and easy-to-use. Additionally, when prioritizing services to be implemented, the navigation flow and necessary vocabulary should be considered. For example, related prior work on conversational user interfaces recommends well-structured use cases to ease natural language understanding and reduce recognition errors (cf. [7]).

4.3   RQ3. Trust in Service Provider

The best ratings of the three options received the municipality; 47% stated to trust a service provided by a municipal entity. Second-ranked (positive rating by 43% of the participants) were national tech companies. Major international tech companies as providers of voice-based e-government services were considered less trustworthy (with negative ratings by 66%).

The results indicate that trustworthy conversational e-government services could be officially offered by a municipality with the underlying technology provided by a national technology specialist. Custom conversational engines would enable voice-based citizen services on Web pages and in mobile apps. However, to reach a broad mass of citizens, respective services need to be integrated into popular voice assistants available on major mobile platforms and smart speakers.

Our results imply that if governmental services are realized on top of the major voice platforms such as *Alexa* and *Google Assistant*, municipalities can have an important role in publishing and promoting these services in order to establish citizens' trust. Prior related research has been showing that users have incomplete mental models of voice assistants. For example, many of them do not know which of the involved data is processed where and they are not aware whether they are using built-in functions (such as asking for the time) of a voice assistant or a third party extension (cf. [1,10]). Based on our participants' feedback, we conclude that conversational government services should clearly communicate which data is (persistently) stored and processed. This might particularly be true in case of advanced voice-based services beyond looking up public information.

5   Conclusion and Outlook

Half of the participants of our survey tended towards not using respective services, 38% were positive. Regular users of voice assistants and participants with interest in technology were significantly more positive towards such services. Looking up government-related information via voice was among the top-rated services, for more advanced services such as ordering certificates the majority of the participants were skeptical. As trustworthy service providers our participants clearly favored the municipality and national tech companies over major international ones due to privacy concerns.

Promising future research includes international comparisons of the citizens' willingness-to-use of (advanced) conversational e-government services in order to investigate and obtain a deeper understanding of the relevant acceptance factors. In our future work, we plan to conduct participatory workshops with citizens to collaboratively design prototypes for selected voice-based e-government services. As proposed by some of our participants, special consideration could be given to impaired user groups which might particularly benefit from simplified voice-based government services (cf. [4]). Finally, results from user studies involving functional prototypes will provide in-depth insights into promising and user-accepted conversational e-government services.

References

1. Abdi, N., Ramokapane, K.M., Such, J.M.: More than smart speakers: security and privacy perceptions of smart home personal assistants. In: Proceedings of the Fifteenth USENIX Conference on Usable Privacy and Security, SOUPS 2019, pp. 451–466. USENIX Association, USA (2019)
2. Ammari, T., Kaye, J., Tsai, J.Y., Bentley, F.: Music, search, and IoT: how people (really) use voice assistants. ACM Trans. Comput.-Hum. Interact. **26**(3) (2019). https://doi.org/10.1145/3311956
3. Androutsopoulou, A., Karacapilidis, N., Loukis, E., Charalabidis, Y.: Transforming the communication between citizens and government through ai-guided chatbots. Government Information Quarterly (2018). https://doi.org/10.1016/j.giq.2018.10.001
4. Baldauf, M., Bösch, R., Frei, C., Hautle, F., Jenny, M.: Exploring requirements and opportunities of conversational user interfaces for the cognitively impaired. In: Proceedings of the 20th International Conference on Human-Computer Interaction with Mobile Devices and Services Adjunct, MobileHCI 2018, Barcelona, Spain, 03–06 September 2018, pp. 119–126. ACM (2018). https://doi.org/10.1145/3236112.3236128

5. Baldauf, M., Zimmermann, H.-D.: Towards conversational e-government. In: Nah, F.F.-H., Siau, K. (eds.) HCII 2020. LNCS, vol. 12204, pp. 3–14. Springer, Cham (2020). https://doi.org/10.1007/978-3-030-50341-3_1
6. Cabrera Paraiso, E., Barthès, J.-P.A.: A voice-enabled assistant in a multi-agent system for e-government services. In: Ramos, F.F., Larios Rosillo, V., Unger, H. (eds.) ISSADS 2005. LNCS, vol. 3563, pp. 495–503. Springer, Heidelberg (2005). https://doi.org/10.1007/11533962_45
7. Fiore, D., Baldauf, M., Thiel, C.: "Forgot your password again?": acceptance and user experience of a chatbot for in-company IT support. In: Paternò, F., Jacucci, G., Rohs, M., Santoro, C. (eds.) Proceedings of the 18th International Conference on Mobile and Ubiquitous Multimedia, MUM 2019, Pisa, Italy, 26–29 November 2019, pp. 37:1–37:11. ACM (2019). https://doi.org/10.1145/3365610.3365617
8. Government Digital Service: Government uses Alexa and Google Home to make services easier to access (2019). https://bit.ly/32mamSv. Accessed 03 June 2020
9. Lafia, S., Xiao, J., Hervey, T., Kuhn, W.: Talk of the town: discovering open public data via voice assistants. In: 14th International Conference on Spatial Information Theory, COSIT. LIPIcs, vol. 142, pp. 10:1–10:7 (2019). https://doi.org/10.4230/LIPIcs.COSIT.2019.10
10. Major, D.J., Huang, D.Y., Chetty, M., Feamster, N.: Alexa, who am i speaking to? understanding users' ability to identify third-party apps on Amazon Alexa (2019). http://arxiv.org/abs/1910.14112
11. McTear, M., Callejas, Z., Griol, D.: Introducing the conversational interface. In: McTear, M., Callejas, Z., Griol, D. (eds.) The Conversational Interface, pp. 1–7. Springer, Cham (2016). https://doi.org/10.1007/978-3-319-32967-3_1
12. Porreca, S., Leotta, F., Mecella, M., Catarci, T.: Chatbots as a novel access method for government open data. In: Proceedings of the 25th Italian Symposium on Advanced Database Systems, p. 122 (2017). http://ceur-ws.org/Vol-2037/paper_19.pdf
13. Tuzovic, S., Paluch, S.: Conversational commerce – a new era for service business development? In: Bruhn, M., Hadwich, K. (eds.) Service Business Development, pp. 81–100. Springer, Wiesbaden (2018). https://doi.org/10.1007/978-3-658-22426-4_4
14. Warkentin, M., Gefen, D., Pavlou, P.A., Rose, G.M.: Encouraging citizen adoption of e-government by building trust. Electron. Mark. 12(3), 157–162 (2002). https://doi.org/10.1080/101967802320245929. https://www.tandfonline.com/doi/abs/10.1080/101967802320245929
15. West, D.M.: E-government and the transformation of service delivery and citizen attitudes. Public Adm. Rev. 64(1), 15–27 (2004). https://doi.org/10.1111/j.1540-6210.2004.00343.x

Too Hot to Enter: Investigating Users' Attitudes Toward Thermoscanners in COVID Times

Alice Bettelli[1]([⊠]), Valeria Orso[2], Gabriella Francesca Amalia Pernice[2], Federico Corradini[3], Luca Fabbri[3], and Luciano Gamberini[1,2]

[1] Department of General Psychology, University of Padova, Padova, Italy
alice.bettelli@studenti.unipd.it
[2] Human Inspired Technology Research Centre, University of Padova, Padova, Italy
[3] SMACT Competence Center, Venezia, Italy

Abstract. One of the most evident symptoms of the SARS-CoV-2 infection is fever. In response to the ongoing health emergency, Thermoscanners are becoming more and more popular to measure citizens' body temperatures in many public places. Indeed, they can be a useful tool for preventing the spreading of Covid-19. Most of the current research focused on understanding people's decisions in the use of protective behaviors related to physical health and health risk perceptions, but still the acceptance and the user-experience related to the adoption and use of thermoscanner is unexplored. This paper explores the attitudes and behaviors towards a thermoscanner located at a public office in two different scenarios: a larger office accessible to employees and visitors and a smaller office with only employees. To this end, data in the field were collected, including self-reported quantitative ratings (i.e., questionnaire) and behavioral observations. Overall, participants (N = 206) showed a general positive attitude toward using the thermoscanner in public spaces and a propensity to comply with the rule of measuring temperature. Interestingly, external users report to perceive the public environment safer thanks to presence of the thermoscanner compared to employees. This finding suggests that employees have clearer the preventive role of the termoscanner. Finally, this study provides a series of guidelines for implementing an efficient large-scale monitoring tool on the territory, enhancing a correct users behavior.

Keywords: Thermoscanner · Temperature · SARS-CoV-2 · Risk perception · Users attitudes · Public space

1 Introduction

The coronavirus (Sars-Cov-2) is a very infectious virus that soon led to a health emergency worldwide starting from December 2020. More specifically, in Italy the first positive cases were found in February 2020 [1].

The Sars-Cov-2 outbreak has wholly reshaped our habits and behaviors. In this emergency, almost all the World governments have taken restrictive measures to stop the virus spread. Indeed, there are different specific recommendations on infection prevention and control during the coronavirus (COVID-19) promoted by World Health Organization

© Springer Nature Switzerland AG 2021
M. Kurosu (Ed.): HCII 2021, LNCS 12764, pp. 239–252, 2021.
https://doi.org/10.1007/978-3-030-78468-3_17

and based on new scientific findings as the epidemic evolved [2]. In particular, the most important protective measures, still in force, include social distancing, wearing Personal Protective Equipment (PPE; such as wearing a mask in public), and adopting personal protective measures (such as handwashing and self-isolation) [3].

In addition to respiratory symptoms, one of the most obvious signs for the early detection of flu is body temperature. The fever typically appears few days (2–14) after the contagion, thus being an early sign of the COVID-19 infection [4]. Therefore, the alert to flu-related symptoms is increased. Intercepting people with high body temperature (higher than 37.5 °C) and preventing them the access to public spaces was soon introduced as a further measure to contain the contagion [5]. Since April 2020 in Italy this screening is mandatory for all workers and public employees at the workplace entrance, which has rapidly become a common practice in many other public venues [6].

Thermoscanners have become increasingly popular because, they allow large-scale and rapid measurements [7]. However, measuring one's body temperature can reveal sensitive health data, which may not be welcomed by everybody. Additionally, this practice can raise employees' negative feelings because monitoring activities unrelated to working performance can be perceived as privacy-invading [8].

Most of the current COVID-19 research focused on physical health and people's risk perceptions for understanding decision about the adoption of protective behaviors, but research on the acceptance of using the thermoscanner during the COVID-19 pandemic are still lacking. This article explores attitudes towards a thermoscanner located in public buildings. Two different scenarios have been studied: a large public structure with a big turnout (employees and customers) and a smaller one accessible to a small group of people (employees). The aim is to investigate in-field users' perception about these devices that remotely detected body temperature, with-out involving any operator directly, understanding their behavior and their attitudes in adopting these prevention's systems to access public spaces.

2   Covid Risk Perception

Nowadays, there are a growing number of studies focusing on the risk perception to contract COVID-19, with the aim to gather insights for the management of the pandemic [4, 9, 10].

Typically, implementing preventive behaviors on a regular basis is directly linked to people's perception of health risk. Still, because COVID-19 was an unfamiliar risk as it began to spread across the world, the information available was limited and constantly evolving [11]. Additionally, there was no certainty no certainty regarding how long protective measures will be active [3].

In their study, Lanciano and collaborators [12] revealed that in Italy the health risk perception is related to how people perceive and imagine the ongoing events and future scenarios. Italians perceive higher risks related to institutional-economy and work, and lower related to health. Yet, one of the workers' most common concern is to return to work and contract COVID-19, despite the prevention measures adopted [13].

This pandemic changed working conditions for the workforce. Many companies have reorganized their work in remote adopting dedicated technology [14]. However, this does

Too Hot to Enter: Investigating Users' Attitudes Toward Thermoscanners in COVID Times

Alice Bettelli[1]([⊠]), Valeria Orso[2], Gabriella Francesca Amalia Pernice[2], Federico Corradini[3], Luca Fabbri[3], and Luciano Gamberini[1,2]

[1] Department of General Psychology, University of Padova, Padova, Italy
alice.bettelli@studenti.unipd.it
[2] Human Inspired Technology Research Centre, University of Padova, Padova, Italy
[3] SMACT Competence Center, Venezia, Italy

Abstract. One of the most evident symptoms of the SARS-CoV-2 infection is fever. In response to the ongoing health emergency, Thermoscanners are becoming more and more popular to measure citizens' body temperatures in many public places. Indeed, they can be a useful tool for preventing the spreading of Covid-19. Most of the current research focused on understanding people's decisions in the use of protective behaviors related to physical health and health risk perceptions, but still the acceptance and the user-experience related to the adoption and use of thermoscanner is unexplored. This paper explores the attitudes and behaviors towards a thermoscanner located at a public office in two different scenarios: a larger office accessible to employees and visitors and a smaller office with only employees. To this end, data in the field were collected, including self-reported quantitative ratings (i.e., questionnaire) and behavioral observations. Overall, participants (N = 206) showed a general positive attitude toward using the thermoscanner in public spaces and a propensity to comply with the rule of measuring temperature. Interestingly, external users report to perceive the public environment safer thanks to presence of the thermoscanner compared to employees. This finding suggests that employees have clearer the preventive role of the termoscanner. Finally, this study provides a series of guidelines for implementing an efficient large-scale monitoring tool on the territory, enhancing a correct users behavior.

Keywords: Thermoscanner · Temperature · SARS-CoV-2 · Risk perception · Users attitudes · Public space

1 Introduction

The coronavirus (Sars-Cov-2) is a very infectious virus that soon led to a health emergency worldwide starting from December 2020. More specifically, in Italy the first positive cases were found in February 2020 [1].

The Sars-Cov-2 outbreak has wholly reshaped our habits and behaviors. In this emergency, almost all the World governments have taken restrictive measures to stop the virus spread. Indeed, there are different specific recommendations on infection prevention and control during the coronavirus (COVID-19) promoted by World Health Organization

© Springer Nature Switzerland AG 2021
M. Kurosu (Ed.): HCII 2021, LNCS 12764, pp. 239–252, 2021.
https://doi.org/10.1007/978-3-030-78468-3_17

not appear to be a viable long-term solution. Many researchers have studied people's attitudes towards telework, showing an increase of health issues, such as anxiety, sleep problems, and depression [15]. Indeed, a decrease in motivation and quality of work emerged, suggesting the workforce need to return to work in the office [16].

On the other hand, workplaces have reorganized to accommodate the new needs of health safety. More specifically, the measures improve the safety of physical environments and the hygiene. These are a priority for many nations because of the personal risk and exposure has reached high levels [17]. A clear communication and making risk mitigation efforts well visible will be key to address the psychological hurdle that employees face when they get back to work [10].

3 Thermoscanner in Covid Pandemic

After SARS-CoV infection from 2002 to 2004, research on body temperature measurement has rapidly advanced, and today it is possible to use thermal scanners almost all over the world [18] thanks to the to the possibility to screen a lot of people in a very short time [6].

The term 'thermoscanner' indicates an electronic device through which it is possible to measure the body temperature at a distance without the need to be in direct contact with it [19].

Infrared thermometers need to be pointed at a part of the user's body (for example, the forehead or wrist), to detect the temperature [18]. These devices were used during the triage in the hospital, but healthcare workers reported to perceive to be more exposed to the risk of being in contact with potentially infected subjects because of the proximity with the patient [7, 20]. Differently, thermal imaging cameras show the distribution of the body temperature on a display without involving operators directly. Some systems with thermal imaging cameras use facial recognition algorithms, that allow to see the temperature value for each individual [21].

Workers must be subjected to temperature measurement in order to access their workplace. Very important is the training of the operators that have to use these systems, especially in those places where there is no specific experience prior. However, the safety protocols do not indicate the need for an operator to ensure the correctness of the measurement, this can also be done autonomously [6].

To make the best use of thermoscanner is recommended to have the better accuracy in measurement of body temperature [22], measuring the temperature of one person at a time [21]. In general, special attention should be paid to the installation site in a place with a steady temperature-controlled environment.

4 Experimental Design

The experiment followed a between-subjects design, where the location (larger office vs. smaller office) and the user group (employees vs. external users) were the independent variables.

4.1 Setting and Equipment

The experiment took place at the premises of a public office which is meant to assist citizens for a variety of bureaucracy issues. The data collection was conducted at two different locations, a larger one with a higher number of employees and frequently accessed by users (Location 1), and a smaller one attended only by employees (Location 2). In both cases, a thermoscanner was located in between the entrance and the reception, following the recommendations previously described and the implementation of supportive graphic signage. In case the thermoscanner detected a temperature above the threshold, the receptionist invited the person to leave the building.

The implemented thermoscanner consisted of three distinct parts: the monitor for displaying information and system status (25 cm × 17 cm), the thermal cameras used for temperature measurements and a column support. To facilitate the user in measuring the temperature, the graphic interface had a dial indicating where the user's face should be positioned for the facial recognition. In addition, aids were provided to help the user in determining the position (e.g., take a step forward). At the end of the temperature measurement, confirmation to the user takes place via auditory feedback and visual feedback represented on the screen. Finally, the device was able to recognize the use of the mask.

The research was conducted when Italy was again allowed access to customers in public spaces, adopting the appropriate security measures in order to contrast the virus spread.

4.2 Materials and Experimental Procedure

A post-experience questionnaire was devised *ad hoc* to investigate the following 7 dimensions (16-item).

The *information awareness* (2 item) explored the level of awareness of the role and function of the thermoscanner [8].

The *perceived usefulness* (4 items) assessed how much participants found the thermoscanner was helpful for limiting the COVID-19 pandemic and for protecting personal and social health [23].

The *perceived usability* (3 items) evaluated the extent to which respondents thought that using the support was effortless and efficient [24].

Credibility, (1 item) investigated how reliable are informations provided by the thermo-scanner by users [25]. The *emotional impact* (3 items) investigated users' affective reactions to the tool [26]. The *perceived safety* (2 items) explored whether shared indoors public spaces are conceived as safer thanks to the thermoscanner [27]. Finally, one item investigated the extent to which users *trust* the thermoscanner company in fairly treating the data collected [8]. Respondents were asked to answer on a 5-point Likert scale.

Indeed, a section of the questionnaire investigated participants' demographic characteristics, including gender, age, education, and professional role. This section also included information about the frequency of access to the location, if they downloaded mobile applications to contain and contrast COVID-19, and previous experience with temperature screening to access public spaces.

Furthermore, during the data collecting, two researchers independently annotated participants' behavior at the buildings' entrance. In particular, using an observation grid, they collected observed: if they needed to be worn by security personnel to use the thermoscanner; how many users didn't notice the thermoscanner; how many times users had to adjust their position to measure the temperature.

The questionnaire was administered right after users had measured the temperature using a tablet (Fig. 1). More specifically, a trained experimenter approached the user, introduced the research and asked them if they would like to partake. Those who decided to participate, were handed the tablet with the full information on the data collection aim, procedure, storage and treatment. If they agreed, they could proceed to the questionnaire. On average, it took 5 min to complete the questionnaire. Respondents received no compensation for taking part in the study.

Fig. 1. (a) a participant is measuring the temperature through the thermoscanner (Location 2); (b) a participant is completing the post experience questionnaire (Location 1).

4.3 Participants

The final sample consisted of 206 respondents (F = 101) with an average age of 46.65 ($SD = 10.96$). Employees who worked inside the analyzed locations were 83 (average age 47.01; $SD = 9.37$). Visitors who accessed the locations were 123 (average age 46.39; $SD = 11.95$). At Location 1, 56 users (average age 46.48; $SD = 9.53$) were employees and 123 visitors (average age 46.39; $SD = 11.95$), while at Location 2 all the 27 users were employees (average age 48.11; $SD = 9.12$).

Concerning professional role, 42% of users (n = 86) reported that they work as personnel (e.g., work as administrative personnel or technical staff). A percentage of 33% of users (n = 67) said that they were specialized practitioners (such as executive managers, lawyers, or businessmen), while 21% (n = 43) declared to work in the field of commerce, craft, or other services. There were 9 users (4%) that reported to work as a non-specialized staff.

Considering the total sample (N = 206) referring to the education, almost half of them had a university degree (47%; n = 98), a percentage of 40% of users (n = 82) had a high school education. 12% of users (n = 24) reported to have middle school diploma. Finally, only 1% (n = 2) reported to have a doctoral degree.

Concerning professional role, 42% of users (n = 86) reported that they work as personnel (e.g., work as administrative personnel or technical staff). 33% of users (n = 67) said that they were specialized practitioners (such as executive managers, lawyers, or businessmen), while 21% (n = 43) declared to work in the field of commerce, craft, or other services. There were 9 users (4%) who reported to work as non-specialized staff.

Regarding the frequency of access at the public offices, 39% (n = 80) attended the locations every week. 9% of users (n = 18) attended the locations every month. A large percentage of users (55%; n = 98) visited the locations once a year. For the 5% of users (n = 10) it was the first time they had access to the locations.

About the app promoted by the Italian Ministry of Health to help monitor and contrast the COVID-19 pandemic in Italy, most of the sample reported not have downloaded it yet (79%; n = 163).

Finally, most of the sample (96%; n = 197) have already screened their body temperature entering public places (e.g., restaurants or shops).

4.4 Analysis

To analyze the participants' impression regarding the thermoscanner, a series of one-sample Wilcoxon tests applying Benjamini-Hochberg (BH) correction were run. In particular, we compared the scores that participants assigned to each dimension of post-experience questionnaire with the median value of the scale ($Mdn = 3$), which indicates a neutral attitude. Moreover, to compare the reactions of different user groups (employee's larger office vs. employee's smaller office, employees vs. external users) a series of Mann-Whitney Tests (BH correction) were run. In addition, it was tested if there were differences related to education, profession, having or not downloaded the mHealth application among users through a series of Mann-Whitney Tests (BH correction) and Kruskal-Wallis test.

Regarding observations, two independent judges identified the behavior and assigned a code. Then they compared the codes and discussed those differing until consensus was reached. Cases that remained uncertain were removed from the sample.

5   Results

5.1   Post-experience Questionnaire

Comparison Between Locations (Location 1 and Location 2). Results indicate that the thermoscanner was positively received at both locations. Participants reported to be well aware and informed about the thermoscanner. Moreover, they considered it useful, easy to use, and providing a credible measurement. They reported that thermoscanner did not evoke negative emotions and they showed trust in the company regarding data protection. Finally, users in Location 2 perceived the thermoscanner as tool that doesn't protect their safety (Table 1).

Table 1. Values of one-sample Wilcoxon tests comparing score with median (Mdn = 3); values means, standard deviations and medians of the post-experience questionnaire reported for the Location 1 and Location 2.

Dimension	Location 1					Location 2				
	Z	p(BH)	M	SD	Mdn	Z	p(BH)	M	SD	Mdn
Information awareness	−12.00	<.001	4.70	0,56	5	−4.66	<.001	4.69	0.65	5
Perceived usefulness	−11.30	<.001	4.40	0.76	4.75	−4.39	<.001	4.32	0.69	4.5
Perceived usability	−12.00	<.001	4.76	0.45	5	−4.63	<.001	4.58	0.60	5
Credibility	−9.78	<.001	4.08	0.92	4	−3.89	<.001	4	0.83	4
Emotional impact	−9.59	<.001	3.96	0.91	4	−3.81	<.001	3.74	0.7	3.66
Perceived safety	−0.38	.70	2.94	1.24	3	−2.39	0.02	2.44	1.06	2
Trust	−10.62	<.001	4.35	0.89	5	−3.69	<.001	4.14	0.99	4

In addition, a series of Mann-Whitney test (BH corrections) showed no statistically significant differences comparing the answers provided by the users at Location 1 and Location 2.

Comparison Between User Group (Employees and Visitors). Considering the sample divided by employees and visitors, the results show a positive attitude by both groups. They reported that they understand the reason and the purpose of the thermoscanner. The thermoscanner was considered useful and easy to use. Also, they perceived its measure as credible. They did not feel embarrassed or insecure about using the thermoscanner, without fear of having a fever and they showed trust in the company regarding data protection (Table 2).

Table 2. Values of one-sample Wilcoxon tests comparing score with median (Mdn = 3); values means, standard deviations and medians of the post-experience questionnaire reported by workers employees and visitors.

Dimension	Employees					Visitors				
	Z	p(BH)	M	SD	Mdn	Z	p (BH)	M	SD	Mdn
Information awareness	−8.32	<.001	4.77	0.50	5	−9.83	<.001	4.65	0.62	5
Perceived usefulness	−8.32	<.001	4.40	0.72	4.75	−9.83	<.001	4,38	0.77	4.75
Perceived usability	−8.32	<.001	4.66	0.56	5	−10.02	<.001	4.79	0.41	5
Credibility	−6.68	<.001	4.02	0.88	4	−8.12	<.001	4.11	0.92	4
Emotional impact	−6.52	<.001	3.89	0.80	4	−8.04	<.001	3.97	0.94	4
Perceived safety	−6.53	<.001	2.51	1.09	2.5	−1.38	0.17	3.13	1.26	3
Trust	−3.75	<.001	4.46	0.80	3	−8.34	<.001	4.24	0.96	5

In addition, comparing the scores provided by the two groups, a series of Mann-Whitney test (BH corrections) showed a statistically significant difference in perceived safety ($U = 6525.5, p < 0.01$). Interestingly, the employees ($M = 2.68, SD = 1.66, Mdn = 3$) did not consider the thermoscanner as a tool capable to make spaces healthier than the visitors ($M = 2.51, SD = 1.085, Mdn = 2.5$) (Fig. 2).

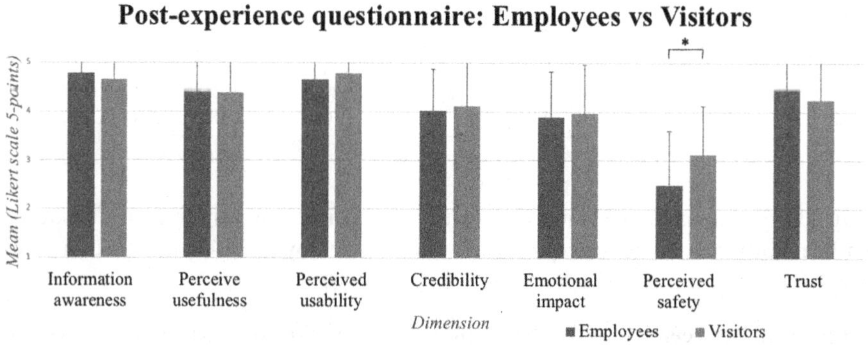

Post-experience questionnaire: Employees vs Visitors

Fig. 2. Values of mean of the post-experience questionnaire dimensions regarding Employees (n = 83) and Visitors (n = 123); (* p < 0.01).

Indeed, similar results emerged considering only the Location 1: external users perceived the thermoscanner as tool protecting their safety ($U = 2531.5, p = 0.03; M = 3.13, DS = 1.26, Mdn = 3$) compared to internal users ($M = 2.546, SD = 1.10, Mdn = 2.5$).

Finally, a series of Mann-Whitney test (BH corrections) showed no statistically significant differences and the answers provided by the workers employed at the two different locations.

Comparison Between Different Professions. It was tested whether there were any differences in the attitude towards the thermoscanner with respect to the profession of the users: personnel; specialized practitioners; field of commerce, craft or other service (n = 196). The non-specialized staff category was excluded from the analyzes due to the small sample size. The Kruskal-Wallis tests showed a statistically significant difference for perceived usability ($H(2) = 12.05, p = 0.01$). *Post-hoc* comparisons indicated that specialized practitioners (M = 4.86, SD = 0.37, *Mdn* = 5) believe that the perceived usability of the thermoscanner is greater than the users who works in the field of commerce, craft or other service ($p = 0.03; M = 4.71, SD = 0.45, Mdn = 5$) and personnel ($p = 0.01; M = 4.65, SD = 0.55, Mdn = 5$). Furthermore, the Kruskal-Wallis tests showed a statistically significant difference for the perception of safety ($H(2) = 11.21, p < 0.01$). *Post-hoc* comparisons indicated that employees ($M = 2.51, SD = 1.07, Mdn = 2.5$) consider the spaces less safe than other professional categories in the field of retail, craft or other service ($p = 0.01; M = 3.16, DS = 1.11, Mdn = 3$) and specialized practitioners ($p = 0.02; M = 3.10, SD = 1.35, Mdn = 3$); (Fig. 3).

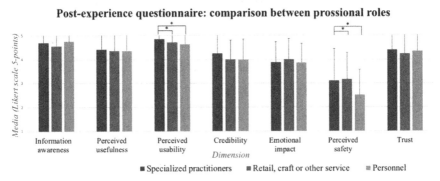

Post-experience questionnaire: comparison between prossional roles

■ Specialized practitioners   ■ Retail, craft or other service   ■ Personnel

Fig. 3. Values of mean of the post-experience questionnaire dimensions regarding Specialized practitioners (n = 67), Retail, craft or other service (n = 43) and Personnel (n = 86); (* p < 0.05).

Comparison Between Different Levels of Education. Regarding the differences related to the level of education between users, we compared participant with high school education and those holding a university degree (n = 180). The categories of doctoral degree (2%) and middle school diploma (12%) were excluded from the analyzes of the total sample due to the small sample size. A series of Mann-Whitney Tests (BH corrections) highlight that users with a degree ($M = 4.83, SD = 0.36, Mdn = 5$) are more aware and informed about the thermoscanner at the entrance of the offices ($U = 3197, p = 0.02$) than who have a high school education ($M = 4.53, SD = 0.74, Mdn = 5$); (Fig. 4).

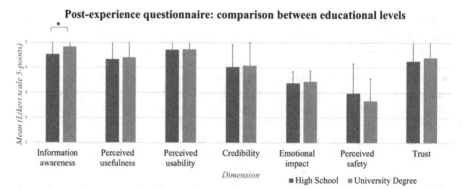

Fig. 4. Values of mean of the post-experience questionnaire dimensions regarding High School (n = 82), Degree (n = 98); (* p < 0.05).

Comparison of who Downloaded Free mHealth Application for COVID-19 Management. Finally, any differences between those who downloaded the app for COVID-19 contrast and those who didn't. From Mann-Whitney Test (BH correction) emerged that users who downloaded free mobile application for COVID-19 containing ($M = 4.63$, $DS = 0.65$, $Mdn = 5$) consider the input temperature measurement more useful ($U = 2562$ $p = 0.03$) than users who did not download the app ($M = 4.32$, $SD = 4.32$, $Mdn = 4.5$) (Fig. 5).

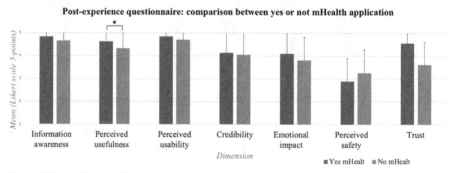

Fig. 5. Values of mean of the post-experience questionnaire dimensions who downloaded (n = 43) or not the free mHealth application for COVID-19 management (n = 163); (* p < 0.05).

5.2 Behavioral Observations

The final sample consisted of 123 respondents. Employees who worked inside the analyzed locations were 54 while visitors were 69. At Location 1, 27 users were employees and 69, while at Location 2, all the 27 users were employees.

Results showed that 49% of users (n = 60) were invited by security personnel to use the thermoscanner to measure the body's temperature once they entered the building, while 50% autonomously use the thermoscanner (n = 62). Just one-time security personnel had to draw user attention because one user didn't measure his body temperature.

Regarding the number of postural adjustments made by users in front of the thermoscanner to obtain the temperature, for the 70% (n = 86) any adjustments was necessary for the measurement. The 20% (n = 25) have done just a single movement (a step forward or backward), while the 10% of them (n = 12) have done more than a single movement (2 o more) until they received feedback of correct measurement.

Furthermore, from the Spearman Correlation it emerged the presence of an association between the behavioral data relating to the measurement attempts carried out by users and the self-report data concerning the perception of usability ($rs = -0.19$, $p = 0.04$): users who made fewer postural adjustments provided more positive comments regarding the use of the thermoscanner. However, from the Mann Whitney test no significant differences emerge considering perceived usability ($U = 1898$, $p = 0.05$) between those who adjusted ($M = 4.60$, $SD = 0.68$, $Mdn = 5$) and didn't adjusted ($M = 4.76$, $SD = 0.46$, $Mdn = 5$) to measure the temperature.

6 Discussion and Conclusions

This study aimed to investigate how users perceived the position of thermoscanner at the entry of public office to monitoring the access gate.

Results indicate an overall positive attitude toward the use of the thermoscanner in public spaces, regardless of the size of the office and whether respondents were employed at the location or were visitors. These data are in line with what emerged from the observations: the propensity of users who access the offices is to comply with the safety protocol, measuring the temperature without being called back by the security operator.

Users considered as well as being easy and fast the screening of the temperature, also to detect the right positioning in front of the thermoscanner was easy. In addition, they perceived the relieved measurements as accurate and they did not evoke negative emotions related to the thermoscanner. Moreover, they reported to be informed about the thermoscanner and consider it useful for the protection of their and others health.

In general, previous studies report that instruments related to health monitoring can be perceived as an invasion of privacy by the company, especially for the employee [8]. The user showed confidence in the management and anonymity of the temperature data. This can be motivated by the extraordinary situations related to pandemic [28] and a lot of promotion about containment and prevention measures by different authorities (e.g. governance, medical) around the world [2].

Furthermore, for those who visit temporarily the building, the presence of the thermoscanner made them perceived the environment as more secure, while employees considered the thermoscanner a preventive rather than a protective device, in line with its function. This aspect also emerged considering the professional role.

These findings highlight how the importance of users' awareness regarding the behaviors to be kept in offices and public places, where it is necessary to comply with the security protocols. Although the thermoscanner has a positive value for users, it must not be taking as an excuse for lowering attention to the contentive measures to be maintained to protect personal and social health as much as possible in the public spaces. The user must be well aware that asymptomatics can access the structures [3] and cannot not detect them. This indicates the key role played by the information material to encourage citizens to behave correctly, congruently with containment safety protocols.

The data were collected in two different public offices, but only the biggest one allowed the access to visitors with a large turnover. Future research could focus on investigating public offices that admit not only the employees. Additionally, this research investigated offices that assist citizens for a variety of bureaucracy issues. It would be interesting to explore other kind of public spaces where there is the highest risk of contagion as care services [7] or public spaces that do not offer essential services or that require mandatory physical presence for certain activities.

6.1 Thermoscanner Guidelines for Proper Monitoring user's Safety

This study provides information on guidelines relating adopting the thermoscanner in public spaces to enhance user's safety, based on recommendations found in the literature and our findings:

- It would be necessary screening one person at a time to provide an accurate temperature's measurement [18].
- If there are operators (not necessarily healthcare) who do surveillance of the temperature screening using the device, it is necessary to perform training [19].
- The thermoscanner must be positioned at the entrance of public buildings to be able to perform temperature screening by preventing access to people who have a temperature higher than 37.5 C [21].
- The thermoscanner must be place in a space where there are no temperature changes to allow an accurate measurement of the temperature [19].
- If the thermoscanner is placed inside a building, it would be necessary to create an internal path avoiding errors in temperature's screening [6].
- To have an adequate temperature measurement, thermoscanner should be placed in a suitable place to avoid interference caused by the environmental elements (for example, away from mirrors or reflective material such as glass) [19].
- To use thermoscanner must be followed guidelines dictated by current standards, to allow its own functioning and protect the health and safety of people who use it [22].
- Every thermoscanner has its own usage protocol which must be applied [21].
- It would be necessary to have indications to inform users about the main preventive function of the thermoscanner and remind users to comply with security protocols.
- The thermoscanner should provide multimodal indications to help the user find the correct positioning.
- The thermoscanner should include functions to help the users to wear Personal Protective Equipment correctly.

References

1. Spina, S., Marrazzo, F., Migliari, M., Stucchi, R., Sforza, A., Fumagalli, R.: The response of Milan's emergency medical system to the COVID-19 outbreak in Italy. Lancet **395**(10227), e49–e50 (2020)
2. World Health Organization, WHO: Coronavirus disease (COVID-19) advice for the public. World Health Organization (2020). https://www.who.int/emergencies/diseases/novel-corona virus-2019/advice-for-public. Accessed 4 June 2020
3. Krsak, M., Johnson, S.C., Poeschla, E.M.: COVID-19 serosurveillance may facilitate return-to-work decisionns. Am. J. Trop. Med. Hyg. **102**(6), 1189–1190 (2020)
4. Haghani, M., Bliemer, M.C., Goerlandt, F., Li, J.: The scientific literature on Coronaviruses, COVID-19 and its associated safety-related research dimensions: a scientometric analysis and scoping review. Saf. Sci. **129**, 104806 (2020)
5. Decreto del Presidente del Consiglio dei Ministri (2020). https://www.lavoro.gov.it/docume nti-e-norme/normative/Documents/2020/DPCM-26-aprile-2020.pdf
6. Dell'Isola, G.B., Cosentini, E., Canale, L., Ficco, G., Dell'Isola, M.: Noncontact body temperature measurement: uncertainty evaluation and screening decision rule to prevent the spread of COVID-19. Sensors **21**(2), 346 (2021)
7. Spagnuolo, G., De Vito, D., Rengo, S., Tatullo, M.: COVID-19 outbreak: an overview on dentistry. Int. J. Environ. Res. Public Health **17**(6), 2094 (2020)
8. Carpenter, D., McLeod, A., Hicks, C., Maasberg, M.: Privacy and biometrics: an empirical examination of employee concerns. Inf. Syst. Front. **20**(1), 91–110 (2016). https://doi.org/10. 1007/s10796-016-9667-5
9. Flesia, L., Fietta, V., Colicino, E., Segatto, B., Monaro, M.: Stable psychological traits predict perceived stress related to the COVID-19 outbreak (2020). https://doi.org/10.31234/osf.io/ yb2h8
10. Lohiniva, A.L., Sane, J., Sibenberg, K., Puumalainen, T., Salminen, M.: Understanding coronavirus disease (COVID-19) risk perceptions among the public to enhance risk communication efforts: a practical approach for outbreaks, Finland, February 2020. Eurosurveillance **25**(13), 2000317 (2020)
11. de Bruin, W.B., Bennett, D.: Relationships between initial COVID-19 risk perceptions and protective health behaviors: a national survey. Am. J. Prev. Med. **59**(2), 157–167 (2020)
12. Lanciano, T., Graziano, G., Curci, A., Costadura, S., Monaco, A.: Risk perceptions and psychological effects during the Italian COVID-19 emergency. Front. Psychol. **11**, 2434 (2020)
13. Eikenberry, S.E., et al.: To mask or not to mask: modeling the potential for face mask use by the general public to curtail the COVID-19 pandemic. Infect. Dis. Model. **5**, 293–308 (2020)
14. Parker, L.D.: The COVID-19 office in transition: cost, efficiency and the social responsibility business case. Account. Audit. Account. J. (2020)
15. Robelski, S., Keller, H., Harth, V., Mache, S.: Coworking spaces: The better home office? A psychosocial and health-related perspective on an emerging work environment. Int. J. Environ. Res. Public Health **16**(13), 2379 (2019)
16. Tovmasyan, G., Minasyan, D.: The impact of motivation on work efficiency for both employers and employees also during COVID-19 pandemic: case study from Armenia. Bus. Ethics Leadersh. **4**(3), 25–35 (2020). https://doi.org/10.21272/bel.4(3).25-35.2020
17. Beaudoin, C., Georgules, J., Raicht, T.: Tenant needs in a post-pandemic world 2020 forecast. JLL (2020). https://www.us.jll.com/en/trends-and-insights/research/2020-first-look-nav igating-post-COVID-19
18. Ring, E.F.J., McEvoy, H., Jung, A., Zuber, J., Machin, G.: New standards for devices used for the measurement of human body temperature. J. Med. Eng. Technol. **34**(4), 249–253 (2010)

19. Censi, F., Mattei, E., Calcagnini, G., Abbenda, F., Cecere E., Onder G.: Indicazioni rel-ative alla scelta e alla gestione dei termoscanner per il controllo della temperatura cor-porea (2020). https://www.iss.it/notiziario//asset_publisher/OhHfyMRQ6V0V/content/vol ume-33-n.-10-ottobre-2020-2
20. Ndiaye, M., Oyewobi, S.S., Abu-Mahfouz, A.M., Hancke, G.P., Kurien, A.M., Djouani, K.: IoT in the wake of COVID-19: a survey on contributions, challenges and evolution. IEEE Access **8**, 186821–186839 (2020)
21. Food Drug Administration: Thermal Imaging Systems (Infrared Thermographic Sys-tems/Thermal Imaging Cameras) (2020). https://www.fda.gov/medical-devices/general-hos pital-devices-and-supplies/thermal-imaging-systems-infrared-thermographic-systems-the rmal-imaging-cameras
22. ISO/TR 13154: 2017: Medical electrical equipment — Deployment, implementation and operational guidelines for identifying febrile humans using a screening thermograph. https://www.iso.org/obp/ui/#iso:std:iso:tr:13154:ed-2:v1:en
23. Alhasan, A., Audah, L., Ibrahim, I., Al-Sharaa, A., Al-Ogaili, A.S., Mohammed, J.M.: A case-study to examine doctors' intentions to use IoT healthcare devices in Iraq during COVID-19 pandemic. Int. J. Pervasive Comput. Commun. (2020)
24. Mital, M., Chang, V., Choudhary, P., Papa, A., Pani, A.K.: Adoption of internet of things in India: a test of competing models using a structured equation modeling approach. Technol. Forecast. Soc. Chang. **136**(11), 339–346 (2018)
25. Fogg, B.J.: Tecnologia della persuasione. Un'introduzione alla captologia, la disciplina che studia l'uso dei computer per influenzare idee e comportamenti. Apogeo, Milano (2005)
26. Theng, Y.-L., Teo, P.F., Truc, P.H.: Investigating sociability and affective responses of elderly users through digitally-mediated exercises: a case of the Nintendo Wii. In: Forbrig, P., Paternó, F., Mark Pejtersen, A. (eds.) HCIS 2010. IAICT, vol. 332, pp. 152–162. Springer, Heidelberg (2010). https://doi.org/10.1007/978-3-642-15231-3_16
27. Lee, Y., Li, J.Y.Q.: The value of internal communication in enhancing employees' health information disclosure intentions in the workplace. Public Relat. Rev. **46**(1), 101872 (2020)
28. Chen, H.Y., Chen, A., Chen, C.: Investigation of the impact of infrared sensors on core body temperature monitoring by comparing measurement sites. Sensors **20**(10), 2885 (2020)

Teens' Conceptual Understanding of Web Search Engines: The Case of Google Search Engine Result Pages (SERPs)

Dania Bilal[1(✉)] and Yan Zhang[2]

[1] University of Tennessee, Knoxville, TN 37996, USA
dania@utk.edu
[2] University of Texas, Austin, TX 78701, USA
yanz@ischool.utexas.edu

Abstract. We explored teens' (aged 15–17) conceptual understanding of search engines (SEs), emphasizing search engine result pages (SERPs). In an online survey, we asked teens to articulate how a search engine (SE) finds, generates summaries of, and ranks search results; identify the structural components of search results; comment on learning in school about SEs; as well as provide suggestions for improving SEs. Of one-hundred and ten teens, twenty-two completed the survey. Analyses revealed that teens' conceptual understanding of SERPs is more perceptual than conceptual and guided by incidental and experiential learnings rather than systematic instruction in school. We found a gap between teens' understanding of the design and representation of the structural components of search results and Google designers' conceptual model (interface design) of these components, suggesting the need for design that is more transparent and with better affordances and signifiers. Teens suggested three categories of design improvements in Google (SERPs, Search and Retrieval, and Privacy) in support of enhancing their experiences. Practical and theoretical implications are discussed.

Keywords: Search engine result page · Teenagers · Children · Information retrieval

1 Introduction

People's conceptions of how a system works guide their interaction behavior [1]. Search Engine Result Pages (SERPs) display listings of search results in a ranked order. Part of a search result is the summary or snippet, which is a description of or an excerpt from the webpage... or the description portion of a search listing," excluding the title and URL address (https://searchengineland.com/anatomy-of-a-google-snippet-38357). Search engines (SEs) generate search engine result pages (SERPs) in response to search queries. SERPs play a key role in user interaction, experience, and success. Numerous studies have paid attention to various aspects of SERPs, including effectiveness of summaries [e.g., 2, 3]; length [e.g., 4, 5]; modified layouts [e.g., 6, 7]; utility and cost [e.g., 8], and readability [e.g., 9, 10]. Much of this research concerned adult users.

© Springer Nature Switzerland AG 2021
M. Kurosu (Ed.): HCII 2021, LNCS 12764, pp. 253–270, 2021.
https://doi.org/10.1007/978-3-030-78468-3_18

Work that focused on young users (children, pre-teens, and teens) has examined their interaction with SERPs, including click behavior [e.g., 11, 12]; reading strategies [e.g., 13, 14, 15, 16]; and query formulation and reformulation [e.g., 17, 18, 19, 20, 21]. Studies have also addressed young users' relevance judgment and credibility assessment of web information [e.g., 22, 23, 24, 25, 26, 27, 28, 29]; and collaborative information seeking on the web [e.g., 30]. Researchers have developed child-centered query suggestion assistance to support effective query formulation in SEs [e.g., 31, 32, 20]; while others designed child-centered interfaces [e.g., 18, 33, 34]; and assessed the readability of SERPs [35–37].

Understanding young users' web knowledge is important. As [28] found, young users' (aged 11–18) belief that a website is a hoax site significantly influenced their credibility assessment of websites. Similarly, believing that the web has accurate information significantly influenced how students select relevant search results [6]. One may assume that due to high exposure, today's teens possess good understandings of SEs. Nonetheless, to the best of our knowledge, no studies validate this assumption. In the present study, we explore teens' conceptual understanding of key aspects of SERPs, including how SEs find, create summaries of, and rank search results; identification of the design components of search results on SERPs; as well as learning in school about SEs. Additionally, we elicit teens' suggestions for improving the design of SEs with a focus on Google.

The findings have implications for providing innovative pedagogical SE literacy programs in schools to support teens' understanding and knowledge. They also serve as a new lens to inform the transparency of Google interface design and representation of SERPs. Finally, the findings have theoretical directions for examining teens' conceptualization of SEs in combination with their interaction behaviors with SERPs, an area that has been under-investigated.

2 Background

2.1 Conceptual Framework

Exploring teens' conceptual understanding of SEs and aspects of SERPs is situated within the user-centered design perspective [1]—that is, the extent to which a user's conception of a system matches with the designer's conceptual model of the system. Explicably, a mismatch could create difficulties, confusion, error, and uncertainty for the user, especially when the design of the system is not transparent [1]. Thus, exploring teens' understanding of the design and representation of SERPs will reveal whether such design provides affordances and signifiers [1] that are self-explanatory or self-evident [38] for teens, and subsequently, informs of whether a gap exists between the teens' epistemic knowledge of SERPs, particularly the components of search results, and the designer's conceptual model of these components.

2.2 Design and Representation of SERPs

Numerous studies focused on improving SERPs to support user interaction. One strand of research examined users' reactions to SERP information organization. For example,

[39] organized web search results into hierarchical categories using text classification algorithms and found that participants liked the category interface much better than the list interface and were 50% faster at finding information organized into categories. [6] compared a grid format list to a standard list format, concluding that users of the grid interface spent an equivalently long time on all search results, whereas users of the list format spent most of the time examining top results.

Another strand of research investigated how users reacted to SE summaries or snippets. Studies generally concurred that participants preferred longer result summaries, and these were perceived to be more informative than shorter ones [5, 40]. [4] created three search interfaces that varied by number of SERPs (i.e., three, six, and ten). They found that those who interacted with three results and six results per page spent more time viewing the top-ranked results than those who interacted with ten results per page. [5] designed four layouts of SERP snippets (title only, title and one snippet, title and two snippets, and title and four snippets). They found that while participants preferred longer snippets, their identification of relevant documents was similar across the four layouts, with participants clicking on relevant results with longer summaries and on those that were non-relevant. [41]'s study revealed that longer snippets increased participants' search time and were not as effective for mobile users as they were for desktop users, while the study by [3] indicated that snippets enriched with metadata from corresponding webpages captured users' attention.

A third line of research explored users' reactions to the linguistic features of summaries. [42] found that participants were more likely to identify relevant documents when using query-biased summaries (i.e., summaries generated with respect to the query rather than by extracting representative sentences from a document). Query-based summaries were also preferred on mobile devices [43]. A fourth line of research focused on the readability of SERPs, revealing that poor readability affects users' judgement of relevance and click behaviors [9, 10]. These research efforts involved adult users.

2.3 Young Users' Interaction with SEs

Young users engage in complex web activities as early as six years of age [44]. Studies showed that children (aged 11–13) experienced difficulties with formulating search queries in SEs and hardly found documents relevant to their queries [23]. In using Google, young children (aged 7, 9, and 11) struggled with constructing effective search queries [e.g., 18, 14, 45, 46]. Query reformulation is a consistent problem among young users. A child aged 13, for example, reformulated a search query in Google nine times in order to find relevant information on a self-selected search task to no avail [17]. While query suggestions or auto-complete features in SEs have been designed to scaffold users' selection of search terms and phrases, studies revealed inconclusive results about the use of these features. For example, [18] found that young children did not pay attention to the auto-complete feature while typing their search queries in Google, whereas older children made effective use of this feature [20].

2.4 Eye-Tracking Studies

Few eye-tracking studies have involved young users (for a review of eye-tracking studies, see [47, 48]). [13] examined children's behavior on web search results, concluding that children in 5th and 7th grade fixated their eyes on the bolded keywords in snippets, whereas those in the 9th - and 11th -grades read each individual search result. [14]'s eye-tracking study focused on young children's (average age 9–10 years) information behavior and perception of interface elements on SERPs in Google and a German search engine designed for children. They found that children paid more attention and were more attracted to visual representations (thumbnails of media) than textual summaries. [11] found differences between children's eye fixations on search results on SERPs. Children aged 11 fixated 25% less frequently on the Google SERPs they visited per search query than did children aged 13. [16] eye-tracking study concluded that nearly 17% of the children (aged 12–13) only looked at the title of the search result, 50% looked at the titles and snippets but occasionally viewed URLs, and 33% looked almost always at the three components (title, URL, and snippet). Ability to decode words and understand lexical representations [49] and reading comprehension combined with cognitive frames influence young users' task performance [30]. None of these reviewed studies examined children's understanding of the components of search results on SERPs.

2.5 SE Ranking

The ranking position of results on SERPs and their perceived relevancy affect users' click selection decisions, regardless of age [50]. An early study of children's (aged 12–13) interaction with SEs showed that they did not go beyond the first page of search results, clicked on the top search results above the fold, and hardly examined other results on a page [23]. This behavior has been found to be consistent over different search engines and over time. For example, on Google, studies revealed that children (aged 7, 9, and 11) clicked on the top ranked results and stopped at the sixth-ranked result on a SERP [18, 51, 52]. [15] reported that children's click behavior on Google search results was more frequent on the first-and second-ranked results and that this behavior varied by age. Children aged 11, for example, clicked more frequently on first- and second-ranked results, compared to children aged 13 whose clicking ranged from the first- to the sixth-ranked result. [12] found that children (aged 6–13) considered the top three-ranked results as the most relevant to their search queries. Reversing the ranking order of search results on a SERP did not affect users' selection of top-ranked results [6, 7, 53].

In sum, numerous studies have examined the design and representation of SERPs with adult users. Work that investigated young users' interaction with SERPs has mainly focused on ages 10–14 years. While [16] investigated the effect of young users' prior knowledge of the web on their viewing and selection of search results on SERPs, it ignored their conceptual understandings of the structural components of these results. While one study found that the visual representation in a search result on a SERPs is more attractive to young users than textual information, it did not examine the users' conceptual understanding of the structural components and design representation of results. To the best of our knowledge, no study has investigated teens' conceptual understanding of SEs functionality and, specifically the design representation of the components of search results on SERPs. Thus, in this study, we addressed the following research questions:

RQ1. What conceptual understanding do teens have of SERPs in relation to: (a) how SEs find search results; (b) how SEs generate summaries/snippets of search results; c) how SEs structure or design the components of search results; and (d) how SEs rank search results?

RQ2: What Are the Differences Between Teens' Conceptual Understanding of the Design of the Structural Components of Search Results on SERPs and the Google designer's Conceptual Model or Design of These Components?

RQ3: What do teens learn in school about SEs?

RQ4: What do teens suggest for improving the design of Google?

3   Method

This study is exploratory and employed the survey method to collect data from teens. Exploratory research is often conducted in new areas of inquiry where researchers seek to "scope out the magnitude or extent of a particular phenomenon, problem, or behavior" ([54], p. 5); or to tackle a new problem or behavior on which little or no previous research exists. This exploratory study allowed us to develop an initial understanding of the nature of teens' conceptual understandings of SEs and various aspects of SERPs. While exploratory research may not lead to a highly accurate understanding of this topic, or to generalizing the findings, it is "worthwhile and serves as a useful precursor to more in-depth research." ([54], p. 6).

3.1 Instrument

The initial survey instrument was tested with six teen participants in multiple iterations, based on which modifications were made. The final instrument included nine open- or close-ended questions. The questions pertaining to the present study include: demographics, prior experience with the internet and SEs, use of SEs, specific aspects of SERPs (including how an SE finds, generates summaries of, and ranks search results), identification of the structural components of snippets, learning in school about the internet and SEs, and suggestions for improving SEs.

3.2 Search Results on SERP

We extracted a search result from Google consisting of four components (title, URL, snippet, and a video thumbnail, Fig. 1).

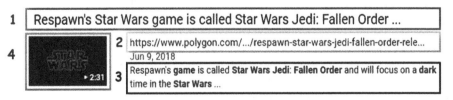

Fig. 1. Search result shown to teens in the survey

3.3 Participants

We contacted 110 parents among whom 38 had children aged 15–17 attending high schools. We sought participants up to age 18 but no responses were obtained from that age group. Typically, in the US, high school begins at age 15 and ends between ages 17–18 and the teens in this study fell within this age range. The majority (83%) attended schools in different districts located in four different geographic areas (names are kept confidential). Of the 38 who took the survey, 22 provided completed responses.

3.4 Procedures

The survey was implemented in Qualtrics. We collected data between February and April 2019. Following our university Institutional Review Boards (IRBs) of the study, we contacted our personal networks, regional and state professional association listservs, researchers' universities, colleges' and departments' listservs, and used word-of-mouth to identify parents with youth in the desired age range. As minors, teens (aged 15–17) must obtain parental consent and provide their own assent to participate in this study. We sent an email invitation to the parents who expressed willingness to allow their teens to participate. This email described the purposes of the study and contained the survey URL. Once the URL is clicked, the parental consent form appears in Qualtrics and a parent has the option to agree (clicking Yes) or disagree (clicking No) to their teen's participation. By clicking Yes, the teen's consent form is displayed describing the study and providing instructions on completing the survey. Teens have the option to click Yes or No. Upon clicking Yes, the survey questions will be displayed one screen at a time. Teens could opt out of the survey at any time without penalty. We followed up twice with the teens' parents. Our recruiting was limited to the U.S. and had no exclusion criteria.

4   Data Analysis

We analyzed the quantitative data using descriptive statistics, facilitated by Microsoft Excel. We analyzed the qualitative data collected by the open-ended questions using the qualitative content analysis method [55], facilitated by MAXQDA 2018 (VERBI Software GmbH). We read all the responses and coded them based on the research questions. New themes were allowed to emerge from the data. The codes were then compared and contrasted, and, thereafter, organized into categories. We validated the codes by double-checking the codes against the participants' responses.

In order to identify the extent to which teens' understanding of the structural components of a search result (Fig. 1) matches with the Google designer's conceptual model or interface design of these components, we assigned a score of "1" to a correct answer and of "0" to an incorrect answer for each of the four components (Fig. 1). We calculated the percentage of correct answers a teen provided on the four components. For example, a teen who gave a correct answer to all four components received a score of 4 or (S = 4), resulting in a 100% match with the designer's model or interface design of these components. Conversely, a teen who had no correct answers on any of the components received (S = 0), resulting in a total mismatch with the designer's model.

5 Results

5.1 Participant Demographics

A total of 22 high school teens (7 females and 15 males) from three states completed the survey (one from Florida, two from Washington, and 19 from Tennessee). Their ages ranged from 15 to 17 years old, with 12 being 15, three being 16 and seven being 17 (Mean = 15.8; SD = 0.92). Their grades spanned from high school freshmen to sophomores. The teens from Tennessee were from four different school districts in different geographic areas and attended different schools within a district (Names are kept confidential).

5.2 Experience and Use of SEs

All teens used the internet to find information on a daily basis, with 12 reporting doing so more than 6 times a day, five 4–6 times a day, and five 2–4 times a day. All except one teen (21, 95.5%) used the internet without parents' help. The majority of the teens considered themselves very experienced (14; 63.6%) or moderately experienced (6; 27.3%) or experienced (2; 9.9%).

Google is the most favored SE among all teens, with 77% indicating using Google to find information for research and other classroom assignments.

5.3 RQ1a: Teens' Conceptual Understanding of How SEs Find Search Results

Nearly 41% of teens (9, 40.9%) indicated that they do not know how SEs find results. Among the remaining teens (n = 13), 9 (69.2%) pointed out that SEs pull results based on keyword match. For example, one teen commented: "It uses keywords and compiles all the websites that contain those keywords." Two among the nine teens (22%) demonstrated a bit more sophisticated understanding by mentioning additional search mechanisms. One teen mentioned, "location of the computer" and "recent search history," but did not elaborate on either mechanism. The other teen pointed out that SEs look for similar topics. The teen commented: "[A web search engine] combs various sources for keywords and phrases as well as websites which focus on similar topics." One teen did not mention search mechanisms but commented on the feature of search results. The teen indicated: "I guess it searches a data base and brings up the most relevant result." The other teen did not mention keyword match, but touched upon on what SEs examine to pull up results, commenting that SEs "scan[s] the titles and the website to generate a page of websites for you to decide on."

Three teens had misconceptions. One teen mentioned, "It takes years of programming into account and comes up with a result." The second teen wrote that SEs find results based on, "Research off of other sites or news articles or professionals." The third teen perceived that the search results "are created based on the degree of importance and relevance of information on a webpage."

5.4 RQ1b: Teens' Conceptual Understanding of How SEs Generate Summaries of Search Results

About 30% of the teens (7, 31.8%) could not articulate how SEs create the summaries or snippets. Among the remaining teens, eight (53.3%) thought that the summary was constructed based on certain parts of webpages, including (the numbers in the parentheses refer to the number of teens; one teen could mention multiple points): "lines directly surrounding the keywords" (2); "first paragraph, first few sentences, or first few lines of text of the webpage" (3); "a paragraph or sentence with most of the keywords you searched for" (2); and "sentences with the searched keywords" (2).

Two teens were not able to go into this detail. They only commented that the summary is created based on keywords, specifically "from what you searched up and what they found in the article," "matches to what you searched for," and "based off of keywords in one's search." Four teens described features of summaries, unable to speculate how they were generated. Among them, one teen described a summary as "a paragraph or so that includes the keywords for which you searched." One teen mentioned that a summary "highlights keywords that are [in] the original search." The other teen noted that a summary shows "the most relevant piece of information." One other teen thought it was the retrieved websites that created the summary, saying, "I think the website creators make the snippets."

5.5 RQ1c: Teens' Conceptual Understanding of the Design of the Structural Components of SE Search Results on SERPs

Teens described the numbered components (items) in Fig. 1 in the following ways:

Item 1. Two teens (9%) reported not knowing how to name this item. Fifteen teens (75%) properly described Item 1 as *title*, *headline*, or *heading*. The remaining five teens (25%) provided non-optimal descriptions (i.e., *hyperlink, snippet*), or simply described the content in Item 1: "what the game is called."

Item 2. One teen (4.5%) reported not knowing how to name this item. Twenty teens (95.2%) properly described Item 2 as a *link, URL, website*, or an *address*. The remaining one teen labeled it wrongly as *title*.

Item 3. Two teens (9%) reported not knowing how to name this item. Thirteen teens (65%) properly indicated Item 3 as *summary* and *description*. The remaining seven teens (35%) described it incorrectly as *the name of the game, an introduction*, and a *Star Wars movie*.

Item 4. Two teens (9%) reported not knowing how to name this item. Fourteen teens (70%) properly described Item 4 as *a video*. However, only four of them were able to speculate why it is part of the snippet. They noted, for example, it is *the main video of the page* and it is *from a video website*. The remaining six teens described it incorrectly as *image, picture*, or *thumbnail*.

5.6 RQ1d: Teens' Conceptual Understanding of How SEs Rank Search Results on SERPs

Among the 22 teens, three (13.6%) were not able to speculate on how SEs rank search results. The remaining teens (19; 86.4%) mentioned four criteria by which SEs do the ranking, as shown next. One teen could mention multiple criteria.

Popularity. The most widely held criterion (13; 68.4%) is *popularity*, referring to how many people have clicked, chosen, or used that result. An example is: *I believe the search engine orders the results based on the popularity of the website. In other words, I believe it is based on how many clicks it usually gets by users.*

Relevance. Nine teens (47.4%) mentioned *relevance* based on keywords, referring to whether or not a result contains keywords, all keywords in the query, the highest number of keywords, most of the number of keywords, a number of keywords, or keywords that are in the same order as they appear in search queries. For example, one teen mentioned, *whichever mentions the keywords the most or seems most relevant [ranks higher].*

Fee. Three teens (15.8%) indicated that SEs rank results by fee. An example is: *Some websites pay to have their site show first, others are popularly visited.*

Publishers. One teen thought that results are ranked based on *features of information providers* and that results that came from *large publishers* are ranked higher. The teen commented:

If it's the most used, biggest publisher, or how much a company pays the search engine workers to make their result the first.

5.7 RQ2: Differences between Teens' Conceptual Understanding of the Design of the Structural Components of Search Results on SERPs and the Google Designer's Conceptual Model (Interface Design) of these Components

Six teens (27%) correctly named/described all four components of the extracted Google search result (Fig. 1; S = 4), matching 100% with the designer's model; 7 teens (~32%) correctly named/described three components (S = 3), matching 75% with the designer's model; 5 teens (22%) correctly named/described two components (S = 2), matching

Table 1. Teens' identification of components of search results versus Google design

No. of Teens (N = 22)	Correct identification of components of search result (S = 4 = 100%)	Match with designer's model/interface design (S = 4; %)
6	4	100
7	3	75
5	2	50
3	1	25
1	0	0

50% with the designer's model; 3 teens correctly named/described one component (S = 1), matching 25% with the designer's model; and one teen had incorrect answers to all four components of the search result (S = 0), resulting in a none-match with the designer's model (Table 1).

5.8   RQ3: Teens' Learning in School About the Internet and SEs

Two of the 22 teens mentioned a feature related to SE searching skills (Table 2). Over half of teens learned how to assess source reliability (54.5%) and to ensure safety in using the internet (18.2%). Surprisingly, 6 (27.3%) teens indicated learning nothing about the internet and SEs. Note that some teens reported on more than one area of learning.

Table 2. Teens' learning in school about SEs

Area of learning	No. of Teens (N = 22)	Percent
How to cite source	1	4.5
Should not plagiarize	1	4.5
Nothing	6	27.3
Safety	4	18.2
Be careful about source reliability	12	54.5
Search skills	2	9.1

5.9   RQ3: Teens' Suggestions for Improving Google Design

Nine teens (9, 40.9%) were not able to provide any suggestions for improving SEs. The remaining teens expressed desire for SEs to improve on three aspects: (1) SERPs, (2) search and retrieval functions, and (3) privacy. Table 3 summarizes the results.

SERPs. All the remaining 13 teens wanted to see improvement on search results. They wished to be exposed to fewer or no advertisements (particularly fraudulent advertisements), be able to filter results based on location and to filter out non-credible sources, and be able to sort sources by credibility and reliability. Additionally, they wished to see a rating system indicating the level of helpfulness of a result in relation to a search. One teen also expressed desire not to highlight the top result. The teen may be referring to the featured snippet that provides an answer to a question. Not knowing the difference between the "organic" and highlighted or boxed snippet, the teen commented:

"There is often a "highlighted result" that appears at the top of the page with large font, a longer summary than other results, and an accompanying image, and then this result ends up being the first in the following list of regular results anyway. I don't think it's necessary to highlight the top result if it's also going

to be displayed first in the list. It usually distracts me from more helpful results because it takes up so much of the page that I click on it automatically, even if it clearly doesn't contain the information I'm looking for."

Table 3. Teens' suggestions for improving Google design

Aspect	Specific suggestions	No. of teens (N = 22; percent)
SERPs	*Highlighting top search result* - Unnecessary to highlight top search result *Ads* - Limit ads.; fewer ads.; remove fraudulent ads, no ads *Filtering* - Filter out non-credible sources - Need a location filter *Sorting* - A known fact to be the first source of information - More credible sources at the top of search results - Sort by reliability *Displaying* - A rating system to indicate whether a suggestion is helpful - Not highlight the top result	13 (100%)
Search and retrieval functions	*Find best results* - Use AI to find the best results for the search - Have the keywords work better *Specific functions* - In-text search - To be able to use + or − signs - To be able to pick up on keywords - To be able to search not based on previous search history	8 (61.5%)
Privacy	- Stop keeping my information - Stop selling information to commercial entities	2 (15.4%)

Search and Retrieval Function. Teens expressed a desire to find better, more relevant search results, presumably through Artificial Intelligence (AI) technologies and keyword search technologies. They also suggested specific functions, including in-text search, supporting + and − signs, freedom in choosing keywords, and search not shadowed by prior search history.

Privacy. Two teens also expressed a desire to see tighter protection of their personal information from SEs. One wished that SEs not keep or sell their personal information.

6 Discussion

Google is the favorite SE for teens in this study. We found that over half of teens (54%) did not know how SEs find search results and 13% had misconceptions to that effect. Although this is a high percentage, it is not surprising given that teens were not exposed to formal learning about this "backend" process in school. Teens who mentioned that SEs use a variety of ways to find results (i.e., keyword match in a page, location of the computer, or recent search history) may have incidentally learned about these processes through informal channels, such as peer, family members, or other media (incidental learning) [56]; or through trial-and-error (experiential learning) [57].

The study findings showed that nearly 54% of the teens recognized that the summary is generated based on certain parts of webpages, but provided simplistic explanations to that end (i.e., based on keywords of one's search; lines surrounding the keywords; sentences with the search keywords, and a paragraph or sentence with most of the keywords you searched for). Bolded keywords in snippets provide cues as to a match between a user's search query and retrieved results; thus, providing some transparency to the user. Nonetheless, one-third of the teens could not articulate at all how SEs generate the summaries or provide examples illustrating their understanding of this process. This deficiency is attributed to a minimal or lack of exposure to effective instruction about SEs in school.

While all teens identified the URL correctly, the majority of them had limited understanding of one or more components of the search result presented to them (Title, Snippet, and video). The gap we found between teens' conceptual understanding of the structural components of the search result and Google designers' conceptual model (interface design) of these components challenges assumptions of the self-explanatory nature or transparency of human-centered design. As [1] notes, a gap between the designer's conceptual model of a system and that of the user could create confusion, errors, and difficulties in using a system. This problem can be further exacerbated by absence of or very limited instruction in school about SEs beyond safety and credibility assessment.

Teens are aware that paid ads are ranked first on a SERP. The majority of them are also cognizant of two of the several factors SEs use in ranking results aside from ads, popularity and relevance, but their explanations were not optimal. Three teens, however, did not know how result ranking works, and three other teens had misconceptions about it. This is expected as teens' understanding of SERPs is mostly perceptual and founded on "incidental" or "experiential learnings" [56].

The finding that teens attended schools that provided minimal exposure to searching skills or no formal instruction about SEs seems to be consistent across different schools in Tennessee. In a study of children's (aged 11 to 13) interaction with Google, [15] found that the majority of the children learned about Google ranking from "peers," "family members," or "somewhere" and were unable to recall the learning source.

Teens' suggestions for improving Google emphasized filtering non-credible results, sorting SERPs by credibility and reliability, and providing a rating system of result usefulness based on which to rank SERPs. Apparently, judging the reliability and credibility of SERPs is a tedious task for teens. This is especially true given that the majority of schools that the teens attended focus on these two evaluation criteria in teaching about SEs. In light of today's abundant fake information on the internet, including fake URLs, a credibility filter associated with the usefulness or relevancy of SERPs vis-à-vis search queries could reduce teens' cognitive load in judging SERPs while supporting their emotional experience during the interaction. Additionally, Advertisements appearing at the top of a SERP seem to be frustrating and distracting for a few teens. Advertisements are a revenue generator for SE companies. Nonetheless, offering an advertisement filter could reduce or eliminate teens' negative affect and provide a more positive experience.

It seems that teens are not satisfied with the nature or retrieval of Google SERPs, as evident in the comments, "find best results" and "have the keywords work better." One teen suggested that SEs use AI to improve search results, implying desire to see improvement in search results. The "in-text search" suggestion may imply that teens want to be able to search by keyword within web pages. This search feature is available in web browsers using the (CTRL F) keys. Apparently, the teens who mentioned this were not aware of the Find function in the browsers. The operators (+ and -) to which one teen referred are already supported in Google, although not explicitly. Additionally, the suggestion "not use search history" to find information for a search query indicates that personalization is another feature that seems to frustrate some teens. Google designers should reconsider the personalization feature and possibly make it optional. Nonetheless, this functionality may be effective for another teen population. Therefore, this feature should be explored with teens in future studies to identify reasons for its non-optimal liking.

Privacy is of concern to the two teens who asked that SEs "stop keeping [my] information" and "stop selling information to commercial entities." These comments clearly reflect on those teens' awareness of SEs' practices in terms of sharing one's personal information with other companies. How to use browser functions (e.g., Incognito) to protect one's personal or behavioral information needs to be conveyed to the teens in schools.

6.1 Limitations

This study is exploratory, and the findings are not generalizable. The data were self-reported and tended to be subjective and possibly prone to inaccuracy. However, it sheds light on a less explored area, teens' conceptual understanding of SERPs, and generates some interesting and important hypotheses for more in-depth research.

6.2 Implications

This study revealed that teens' conceptual understanding of various aspects of SERPs is more perceptual than conceptual and is mostly guided by "incidental" and "experiential learnings" rather than systematic instruction in school. The gap between teens' understanding of the components of search results and Google designers' conceptual model (interface design) of the components is critical. The findings have practical and theoretical implications.

Practical. We urge information practitioners in schools to provide innovative pedagogical SE literacy programs that go beyond safety and credibility assessment to include various retrieval aspects of SERPs. Exposure to systemic instruction is essential for adjusting teens' conceptual understanding of specific aspects of SE functionality to scaffold their thinking and learning and prepare them for successful academic work as they transition to college.

The significant gap between teens' conceptual understanding of the structural components of a Google search result and the designer's model of these components is contrary to the designer's belief that *one-size-fits-all*. Not all teens are able to decipher, understand, name, or identify the purpose of these components. Thus, we urge designers to consider a design with better affordances and signifiers [1]. For example, using hover over text to present details about each component could make these components more self-explanatory and transparent [38].

Theoretical. The findings provided initial insights into the *nature of conceptual understanding* teens hold about SERPs and the nature of their learning in school about SEs. These findings call for new theoretical directions in future studies that integrate teens' interaction behavior in using SEs alongside their conceptions of these tools so that we develop a more coherent, nuanced understanding of their needs, and develop design solutions that meet those needs.

7 Conclusion

This study explored the nature of teens' conceptual understanding of web search engines (SEs), emphasizing key aspects of Google SERPs. Teens' understanding of SERPs is more perceptual than conceptual and is mostly founded on "incidental" and "experiential learnings." Teens possessed limited understanding, inaccurate understanding, or no understanding of key aspects of SERPs. This is attributed to two main factors, minimal or lack of exposure to SE information literacy in school beyond assessing credibility and reliability of search results, and to limited transparency in the design and representation of SERPs, particularly the components of search results. Exploring teens' conceptual understanding of SEs and, specifically SERPs, is a worthwhile area of study to investigate more in-depth in future research. Detecting teens' effective and efficient interaction behavior with Google alongside conceptual understanding of SERPs will provide a new lens for validating whether conceptual understanding has an effect on teens' task performance and overall experience with the search engine.

In this study, we collected data using the survey approach. Incorporating a mixed research design will heighten our understanding of the validity of teens' claimed experiences with SEs vis-à-vis their interaction behavior and performance in context. Future research should investigate the level of information literacy programs provided in school for various aspects of SEs not only from teens' perspectives, but also from those of school librarians in order to gauge an analysis and evaluation of these programs and correlate with teens' conceptual understandings, interaction behaviors, performance, and emotional experiences.

References

1. Norman, D.: The Design of Everyday Things. Basic Books, New York (2013)
2. Lewandowski, D.: The retrieval effectiveness of web search engines: considering results descriptions. J. Doc. **64**(6), 915–937 (2008)
3. Marcos, M.-C., Gavin, F., Arapakis, I.: Effect of snippets on user experience in web search. In: Proceedings of the XVI International Conference on Human Computer Interaction, pp. 1–8 (2015)
4. Kelly, D., Azzopardi, L.: How many results per page? A study of SERP size, search behavior and user experience. In: Proceedings of the 38th International ACM SIGIR Conference on Research and Development in Information Retrieval, pp. 183–192 (2015)
5. Maxwell, D., Azzopardi, L., Moshfeghi, Y.: A study of snippet length and informativeness: behaviour, performance and user experience. In: Proceedings of the 40th International ACM SIGIR Conference on Research and Development in Information Retrieval, pp. 135–144 (2017)
6. Kammerer, Y., Gerjets, P.: The role of search result position and source trustworthiness in the selection of web search results when using a list or a grid interface. Int. J. Hum.-Comput. Interact. **30**(3), 177–191 (2014)
7. Pan, B., Hembrooke, H., Joachims, T., Lorigo, L., Gay, G., Granka, L.: In Google we trust: users' decisions on rank, position and relevancy. J. Comput.-Mediat. Commun. 1, **12**(3), 801–823 (2007)
8. Azzopardi, L., Thomas, P., Craswell, N.: Measuring the utility of search engine result pages: an information foraging based measure. In: The 41st International ACM SIGIR Conference on Research and Development in Information Retrieval, pp. 605–614 (2018)
9. Kanungo, T., Orr, D.: Predicting the readability of short web summaries. In: Proceedings of the Second ACM International Conference on Web Search and Data Mining, pp. 202–211 (2009)
10. Collins-Thompson, K.: Computational assessment of text readability: a survey of current and future research. Int. J. Appl. Linguist. **165**(2), 97–135 (2014)
11. Bilal, D., Gwizdka, J.: Children's eye-fixations on Google search results. Proc. Assoc. Inf. Sci. Technol. **53**(1), 1–6 (2016)
12. Gossen, T.: Search Engines for Children: Search User Interfaces and Information-Seeking Behaviour. Springer, New York (2016)
13. Dinet, J., Bastien, J.C., Kitajima, M.: What, where and how are young people looking for in a search engine results page? Impact of typographical cues and prior domain knowledge. In: Proceedings of the 22nd Conference on l'Interaction Homme-Machine, pp. 105–112 (2010)
14. Gossen, T., Höbel, J., Nürnberger, A.: A comparative study about children's and adults' perception of targeted web search engines. In: Proceedings of the SIGCHI Conference on Human Factors in Computing Systems, pp. 1821–1824 (2014)

15. Gwizdka, J., Bilal, D.: Analysis of children's queries and click behavior on ranked results and their thought processes in google search. In: Proceedings of the 2017 Conference on Conference Human Information Interaction and Retrieval, pp. 377–380 (2017)

16. Hautala, J., Kiili, C., Kammerer, Y., Loberg, O., Hokkanen, S., Leppänen, P.H.: Sixth graders' evaluation strategies when reading internet search results: an eye-tracking study. Behav. Inf. Technol. **37**(8), 761–773 (2018)

17. Bilal, D., Gwizdka, J.: Children's query types and reformulations in Google search. Inf. Process. Manag. **54**(6), 1022–1041 (2018)

18. Druin, A., et al.: How children search the internet with keyword interfaces. In: Proceedings of the 8th International Conference on Interaction Design and Children, pp. 89–96 (2009)

19. Foss, E., Druin, A., Yip, J., Ford, W., Golub, E., Hutchinson, H.: Adolescent search roles. J. Am. Soc. Inform. Sci. Technol. **64**(1), 173–189 (2013)

20. Kammerer, Y., Bohnacker, M.: Children's web search with Google: the effectiveness of natural language queries. In: Proceedings of the 11th International Conference on Interaction Design and Children, pp. 184–187 (2012)

21. Rutter, S., Ford, N., Clough, P.: How do children reformulate their search queries? Inf. Res. Int. Electron. J. **20**(1), 149–157 (2015)

22. Agosto, D.E.: Bounded rationality and satisficing in young people's web-based decision making. J. Am. Soc. Inform. Sci. Technol. **53**(1), 16–27 (2002)

23. Bilal, D.: Children's use of the Yahooligans! Web search engine: I. Cognitive, physical, and affective behaviors on fact-based search tasks. J. Am. Soc. Inf. Sci. **51**(7), 646–665 (2000)

24. Braasch, J.L.: Advances in research on internal and external factors that guide adolescents' reading and learning on the Internet. J. Study Educ. Dev. **43**(1), 210–241 (2020)

25. Cole, C., Beheshti, A., Abulhimd, D., Lamoureux, I.: The end game in Kuhlthau's ISP model: knowledge construction for grade 8 students researching an inquiry-based history project. J. Soc. Inf. Sci. Technol. **66**(11), 2219–2266 (2015)

26. Julien, H., Barker, S.: How high-school students find and evaluate scientific information: a basis for information literacy skills development. Libr. Inf. Sci. Res. **31**(1), 12–17 (2009)

27. Large, A., Beheshti, J.: The web as a classroom resource: reactions from the users. J. Am. Soc. Inf. Sci. **51**(12), 1069–1080 (2000)

28. Metzger, M.J., Flanagin, A.J., Markov, A., Grossman, R., Bulger, M.: Believing the unbelievable: understanding young people's information literacy beliefs and practices in the United States. J. Child. Media **9**(3), 325–348 (2015)

29. Subramaniam, M., Taylor, N.G., Jean, B.S., Follman, R., Kodama, C., Casciotti, D.: As simple as that?: tween credibility assessment in a complex online world. J. Doc. **71**(3), 550–571 (2015)

30. Meyers, E.M.: When search is (mis) learning: analyzing inference failures in student search tasks. Proc. Assoc. Inf. Sci. Technol. **55**(1), 357–366 (2018)

31. Azpiazu, I.M., Dragovic, N., Anuyah, O., Pera, M.S.: Looking for the movie seven or sven from the movie frozen? A multi-perspective strategy for recommending queries for children. In: Proceedings of the 2018 Conference on Human Information Interaction & Retrieval, pp. 92–101 (2018)

32. Fails, J.A., Pera, M.S., Anuyah, O., Kennington, C., Wright, K.L., Bigirimana, W.: Query formulation assistance for kids: what is available, when to help & what kids want. In: Proceedings of the Interaction Design and Children, pp. 109–120 (2019)

33. Gossen, T., Nitsche, M., Vos, J., Nürnberger, A.: Adaptation of a search user interface towards user needs: a prototype study with children & adults. In: Proceedings of the Symposium on Human-Computer Interaction and Information Retrieval, pp. 1–10 (2013)

34. Large, A., Nesset, V., Beheshti, J., Bowler, L.: "Bonded design": a novel approach to intergenerational information technology design. Libr. Inf. Sci. Res. **28**(1), 64–82 (2006)

35. Bilal, D.: Comparing Google's readability of search results to the Flesch readability formulae: a preliminary analysis on children's search queries. Proc. Am. Soc. Inf. Sci. Technol. **50**(1), 1–9 (2013)

36. Bilal, D., Huang, L.-M.: Readability and word complexity of SERPs snippets and web pages on children's search queries. Aslib J. Inf. Manag. **71**(2), 241–259 (2019)

37. Vajjala, S., Meurers, D.: On the applicability of readability models to web texts. In: Proceedings of the Second Workshop on Predicting and Improving Text Readability for Target Reader Populations, pp. 59–68 (2013)

38. Krug, S.: A Common Sense Approach to Web Usability, 3rd edn. New Riders, Indianapolis (2014)

39. Chen, H., Dumais, S.: Bringing order to the web: automatically categorizing search results. In: Proceedings of the SIGCHI Conference on Human Factors in Computing Systems, pp. 145–152 (2000)

40. Chen, W.-F., Hagen, M., Stein, B., Potthast, M.: A user study on snippet generation: text reuse vs. paraphrases. In: The 41st International ACM SIGIR Conference on Research & Development in Information Retrieval, pp. 1033–1036 (2018)

41. Kim, J., Thomas, P., Sankaranarayana, R., Gedeon, T., Yoon, H.-J.: What snippet size is needed in mobile web search? In: Proceedings of the 2017 Conference on Conference Human Information Interaction and Retrieval, pp. 97–106 (2017)

42. Tombros, A., Sanderson, M.: Advantages of query biased summaries in information retrieval. In: Proceedings of the ACM SIGIR Conference on Research and Development in Information Retrieval, pp. 2–10 (1998)

43. Spirin, N.V., Kotov, A.S., Karahalios, K.G., Mladenov, V., Izhutov, P.A.: A comparative study of query-biased and non-redundant snippets for structured search on mobile devices. In: Proceedings of the 25th ACM International on Conference on Information and Knowledge Management, pp. 2389–2394 (2016)

44. Spink, A., Danby, S., Mallan, K., Butler, C.: Exploring young children's web searching and technoliteracy. J. Doc. **66**(2), 191–206 (2010)

45. Jochmann-Mannak, H., Huibers, T., Lentz, L., Sanders, T.: Children searching information on the Internet: performance on children's interfaces compared to Google. In: SIGIR Workshop on Accessible Search Systems, vol. 10, pp. 27–35 (2010)

46. Kodama, C., Jean, B.S., Subramaniam, M., Taylor, N.G.: There's a creepy guy on the other end at Google!: engaging middle school students in a drawing activity to elicit their mental models of Google. Inf. Retrieval J. **20**(5), 403–432 (2017)

47. Lewandowski, D., Kammerer, Y.: Factors influencing viewing behaviour on search engine results pages: a review of eye-tracking research. Behav. Inf. Technol. 1–31 (2020)

48. Strzelecki, A.: Eye-tracking studies of web search engines: a systematic literature review. Information **11**(6) (2020). https://www.mdpi.com/2078-2489/11/6/300

49. Vibert, N., et al.: Adolescents' developing sensitivity to orthographic and semantic cues during visual search for words. Front. Psychol. **10**, Article 642 (2019)

50. Lorigo, L., et al.: Eye tracking and online search: lessons learned and challenges ahead. J. Am. Soc. Inform. Sci. Technol. **59**(7), 1041–1052 (2008)

51. Druin, A., Foss, E., Hutchinson, H., Golub, E., Hatley, L.: Children's roles using keyword search interfaces at home. In: Proceedings of the SIGCHI Conference on Human Factors in Computing Systems, pp. 413–422 (2010)

52. Foss, E., et al.: Children's search roles at home: Implications for designers, researchers, educators, and parents. J. Am. Soc. Inform. Sci. Technol. **63**(3), 558–573 (2012)

53. Schultheiß, S., Sünkler, S., Lewandowski, D.: We still trust in Google, but less than 10 years ago: an eye-tracking study. Inf. Res. **23**(3) (2018). https://files.eric.ed.gov/fulltext/EJ1196314.pdf

54. Bhattacherjee, A.: Social science research: Principles, methods, and practices. Global Text Project (2012). http://scholarcommons.usf.edu/oa_textbooks/3
55. Zhang, Y., Wildemuth, B.M.: Qualitative analysis of content. In: Wildemuth, B.M. (ed.) Applications of Social Research Methods to Questions in Information and Library Science, 2nd edn, pp. 318–329. Libraries Unlimited (2017)
56. Marsick, V.J., Watkins, K.: Informal and Incidental Learning in the Workplace. Routledge, New York (1990)
57. Kolb, D.A.: Experience as the Source of Learning and Development. Prentice Hall, River (1984)

What Futuristic Technology Means for First Responders: Voices from the Field

Shaneé Dawkins(✉) , Kerrianne Morrison , Yee-Yin Choong ,
and Kristen Greene

National Institute of Standards and Technology, Gaithersburg, MD 20899, USA
{shanee.dawkins,kerrianne.morrison,yee-yin.choong,
kristen.greene}@nist.gov

Abstract. The public safety communication technology landscape in the United States (U.S.) is evolving to supplement the use of land mobile radios with a broader spectrum of communication technologies for use on the newly created Nationwide Public Safety Broadband Network. The goal of the multi-phase research study presented here was to understand the use of communication technologies by the population of first responders—Communications (Comm) Center & 9-1-1 Services; Emergency Medical Services; Fire Services; and Law Enforcement. The sequential, exploratory mixed methods study consisted of an initial exploratory qualitative phase followed by a larger quantitative phase. The qualitative data collection was via in-depth interviews with 193 first responders across the U.S.; the quantitative survey was completed by 7,182 first responders across the U.S. This paper presents the results of the study related to first responders' perceptions about the future of public safety communication technology. Discussed are the technologies first responders think would benefit their individual user populations, as well as communication technologies that would be useful across user populations within the public safety domain. Results show that first responders are open to new and exciting technologies, but their needs are utility driven; to have the biggest impact, their communication technology must be tailored to their needs and contexts. This paper will present the needs of first responders, in their own voices, to aid in the research and development of public safety communication technology.

Keywords: Usability · User survey · UX (user experience) · User requirements · Public safety · First responders · Incident response

1 Introduction

The public safety communication technology landscape in the United States (U.S.) is evolving. With the newly created Nationwide Public Safety Broadband Network (NPSBN), the public safety community is supplementing the use of land mobile radios with a broader spectrum of communication technologies. The public safety community has identified User Interfaces and User Experiences (UI/UX) as one of the key areas for research and development of these rapidly advancing technologies [1]. As such, the

© Springer Nature Switzerland AG 2021
M. Kurosu (Ed.): HCII 2021, LNCS 12764, pp. 271–291, 2021.
https://doi.org/10.1007/978-3-030-78468-3_19

Public Safety Communications Research (PSCR) Program at the National Institute of Standards and Technology (NIST) conducts research focusing on the end users – first responders [2]. Under this program, the NIST PSCR Usability Team performs research and provides guidance to ensure that communication technology in the public safety domain helps first responders achieve their goals and objectives with effectiveness, efficiency, and satisfaction in their specified contexts of use [3]. To this end, the NIST PSCR Usability Team has studied the public safety field to gain a better understanding of the user population of first responders—Comm Center & 9-1-1 Services (COMMS); Emergency Medical Services (EMS); Fire Services (FF); and Law Enforcement (LE). These four first responder disciplines, COMMS, EMS, FF, and LE, use different types of tools for different purposes; they experience different problems and have different communication technology needs. This is why it is crucial to understand the different public safety user groups and the communication technology they currently use, the problems they experience with current technology, and the technology they would like to have access to in the future.

NIST's PSCR Usability Team conducted a multi-phase, mixed methods research project in order to provide greater understanding of first responders, their experiences, and their communication technology problems and needs. The goal was to understand what first responders believe is necessary to facilitate communication and address their communication technology needs. Phase 1 of the project was a qualitative examination of first responder contexts of work [4]; interviews were conducted with first responders across the country from the four first responder disciplines—COMMS, EMS, FF, and LE. Phase 2 of the project utilized data from the qualitative interviews conducted in Phase 1 to create a large-scale, nationwide survey. The Phase 2 survey was designed to augment understanding of the types of communication technology first responders have, use, and want, and the problems they currently experience with their technology [5]. Understanding the use of communication technology by the four disciplines is critical to the success of the technology developed for the NPSBN.

Given the breadth and depth of the data collected, this paper focuses on a subset of the results from the Phase 2 survey related to the future of public safety and the NPSBN, presenting Phase 1 interview data throughout as appropriate. Previously analyzed results from the study are presented in [4–11]; additional data will be examined in future publications. The forward-looking communication technology needs of first responders presented here specifically focus on the potential usefulness of current devices first responders do not have, futuristic devices, and virtual reality (VR).

2 Methodology

2.1 Overview

The project consisted of a study with a sequential, exploratory mixed methods design, where an initial exploratory qualitative phase was followed by a larger quantitative phase. Phase 1 – the qualitative phase – examined first responders' communication technology use via in-depth interviews [4, 7]. The data from the interviews were the basis of the survey design used in Phase 2 – the quantitative phase [5]. In Phase 2, a large-scale, nationwide survey was conducted in order to gain a more comprehensive understanding of communication technology in the public safety community [5]. Data from both phases was integrated for analysis to provide for a more holistic understanding of first responders and their communication. For ease of exposition, this paper will refer to the research phases as "interviews" and "survey" henceforth (for the Phase 1 qualitative interviews and the Phase 2 quantitative survey, respectively).

Overarching Sampling Goals. To provide a representative sample of first responders in the U.S., multiple variables were considered to develop the sampling strategy in both phases of the study. The sampling strategy included first responders in a variety of positions within the four public safety disciplines – COMMS, EMS, FF, and LE. Due to the varied public safety issues faced in different parts of the country, geographic and cultural diversity were also primary considerations. Across the U.S., urban (U), suburban (S), and rural (R) districts were sampled to ensure that cities and districts of different sizes and different economic realities were represented. Another consideration was jurisdictional diversity, including federal, state, county and local jurisdictions; however, local jurisdictions had higher priority, as incident response typically starts at the local level. Other variables considered in the sampling strategy were career and volunteer FF, public and private EMS, and civilian and deputized COMMS. With the wide range of different types of first responders, their roles and responsibilities, and their different communication and technology needs, this approach provided insight into the many different experiences of public safety communication across the U.S., ensuring coverage of both typical and unique experiences.

The NIST Research Protections Office reviewed the protocol for this project and determined it met the criteria for "exempt human subjects research" as defined in 15 CFR 27, the Common Rule for the Protection of Human Subjects.

2.2 Interview Methodology

The interviews were conducted with first responders across the U.S. in 2017 and 2018. There were three research questions:

1. How do public safety personnel describe the context of their work, including their roles and responsibilities as well as process and flow?
2. How do public safety personnel describe their communication and technology needs related to work?
3. What do public safety personnel believe is working or not working in their current operational environment related to communication and technology?

These research questions guided the interview protocol design and analysis, as [4] extensively reported.

Interview Sampling. Since demographic factors such as age, years of service, and gender may play a role in participants' views related to public safety communication, purposive sampling was applied in Phase 1. The sampling involved seeking participants who represented the full range of first responder experiences, as previously mentioned. Areas for in-person interviews were chosen that provided reasonable coverage of the depth and breadth of geographic and cultural diversity in the U.S., as well as the broad types of incidents that first responders face, aligning with eight of the ten U.S. Federal Emergency Management Agency (FEMA) regions [12].

Data Collection and Analysis. The data collection and analysis followed a rigorous qualitative research process. First, the in-depth interviews with first responders in the COMMS, EMS, FF, and LE disciplines were conducted in 45-min sessions with first responders at their convenience (typically one-one-one at their station or department). These interviews were then audio recorded and transcribed. Two code lists were generated in order to label, or tag, participant statements: one for EMS, FF and LE, and one for COMMS, given the unique environment and primary tasks within that discipline. Then, the transcripts were coded according to the code lists, and the data were extracted (i.e., the data associated with a code from each transcript was exported into a separate document). Finally, themes were identified; relationships were examined among the codes, and between and within the four disciplines. This iterative process facilitated the identification of themes, trends, and outliers and provided an overall impression and understanding of the data. The themes, along with communication technology problems and needs findings, were used as the basis for the survey design in the second phase of the study.

2.3 Survey Methodology

The survey development began at the conclusion of the interviews; Greene, et al. extensively reported details about the survey instrument and survey methodology [5]. The following research questions served as guides for the development of the survey.

1. What are first responder needs related to communication and technology as they engage in their user-identified primary tasks?
    a. What communication tools and technology do first responders believe currently work, or do not work, for them?
2. What are the problems that first responders experience as they use communication technology?

The survey collected a wide variety of data related to communication technology use by first responders, from their day-to-day technology use, problems, and needs, to the technology that would be more suitable for use in larger, out of the ordinary incidents. Survey questions and response options were grounded in research from the previously collected empirical interview data, as well as from content and survey expert reviews during survey development. One of the driving ideals in the design of the survey was to keep it short out of respect for first responders and their time, and to encourage survey completion.

Survey Instrument Design. After a rigorous design process that included content and survey expert reviews, and given the myriad of different types of communication technology utilized and needed for the individual disciplines, it became clear there would need to be four different surveys, tailored for each discipline. The overall survey structure and flow were largely similar across the four survey versions: all began with a section on demographics, followed by a section on use of technology for day-to-day incident response (including questions on applications/software), and concluded with a section on use of technology in large events. The survey questions for EMS, FF, and LE were nearly identical, while differing somewhat more for COMMS, due to the different nature of their working environment [9]; for example, COMMS respondents were asked questions about call centers and Next Generation 9-1-1 (NG 911) [13, 14]. For all four disciplines, lists of technologies were used for questions about responders' use of day-to-day devices and devices used for large events. The lists of technologies used in the survey were catered to each discipline as the result of a thorough review of the problems and requested functionality identified in the interviews [7]. The goal was to not have first responders go through questions or lists of technologies that did not pertain to their work, as part of the effort to keep the survey short out of respect for first responders and their time. Greene et al. reported detailed descriptions of survey logic, branching, and all questions and response options [5].

As this paper focuses on a subset of the survey data, the remainder of this section describes the details of the survey design solely related to the questions from which results are discussed. These questions, related to the potential usefulness of futuristic technologies for day-to-day incident response, are: 1) futuristic technologies; 2) NG 911 (COMMS only), and 3) VR.

Futuristic Technologies Question. The futuristic technology question was framed with the text, "We know there is no such thing as a "typical" day in public safety. However, for this set of questions, focus on the kinds of things you use in your daytoday work." The question stem was "Which of the items below **would also be useful** for your **DAYTODAY** work." Respondents were presented with a list of technologies and asked to "Check all that apply." The goal here was solely to identify those items that respondents believed would be useful in daytoday incident response, not to have them rank these items or indicate whether they were more or less useful than other items.

The list of technologies in this question was populated from two sources. The first source was a preset list of technology based on PSCR research priorities and derived from the results of the interviews. Note that as previously mentioned, different first responder disciplines saw different lists of futuristic technologies, because the survey was driven by the interview data and the technologies that first responders discussed as potentially important for their work. The second source was a list of items that were piped forward based on a participant's previous survey responses about their day-to-day technology use. On a previous question, participants were asked about how often or not they use existing technologies. Every device for which they made no selection or selected "do not have" was piped forward to the future technology list. The items that were piped forward allowed respondents to select items they thought would be useful even if they did not currently have them.

In addition to the "Check all that apply" question, respondents were also provided with an open-ended text box where they could list additional technologies they thought would be useful or provide additional information.

Next Generation 9-1-1 Question. NG 911 is a digital or Internet Protocol (IP)-based 911 system that has several key capabilities, including: the ability for voice, photos, videos and text messages to be sent from the public to the 911 network; the transfer of emergency calls, location information, and multimedia to another PSAP; and the exchange of voice and data with other state or federal entities involved in the response via internetworking technologies based on open standards [13, 14]. After the broader futuristic technology section, COMMS participants were asked two questions specifically about NG 911:

1. "Have you ever heard of Next Generation 9-1-1?"
2. "Next Generation 9-1-1 is a system that will allow the public to send texts, pictures, and video to 9-1-1 call centers. Do you think this will help you in your job?"

The response items for these questions were: Yes, No, or Not Sure. Interview data drove the design of the survey and indicated that some first responders did not know what NG 911 was or how it would apply to their work. The survey intentionally used a simplified definition of NG 911 in the second question listed above; content expert reviewers of the survey believed it better captured how COMMS participants would define and understand it.

Virtual Reality Question. Given its importance to PSCR's initial research agenda [15], all participants were asked specific questions about the use of VR for training and for other purposes. The two questions asked were:

1. "Do you think VR (virtual reality) would be useful for training in your work?"
2. "Do you see VR as useful in other ways for your work?"

The response items for these questions were: Yes, No, or Not Sure. An open-ended text box was also provided to give participants the opportunity to respond with additional details about their answers to the VR questions listed above.

Survey Sampling and Dissemination. In order to reach a large number of first responders, outreach occurred at the department/agency level. The sampling frame consisted of an online database with contacts in all 10 U.S. FEMA Regions [12] and a variety of first responder departments and agencies. Other means of outreach were via public safety organizations and through previous points of contact within the public safety community. Individuals contacted were asked to forward the survey to their first responder communities and colleagues in order to reach as many departments and agencies as possible, and through them to reach first responders, in order to have broad representation. The survey was disseminated to first responders across the U.S. for approximately 5 months between 2018 and 2019.

3 Participants

The first responder population sample for the interviews and survey accounted for geographic and cultural diversity; different area types (urban, suburban, and rural); and various levels in the chain of command within the COMMS, EMS, FF, and LE disciplines. The participants in the interviews represented 13 states in eight FEMA regions; the survey had representation from all 50 states and Washington D.C. Other demographic variables of interest—such as jurisdictional level (local, county, state, federal), years of service, and age—also showed good variability in both the interview and survey data. 193 first responders participated in the interviews; 7,281 first responders completed the survey.

The 193 first responders interviewed resulted in 158 interview transcripts. Some interviews included multiple participants; five participants opted to not be recorded [4]. Each of the four disciplines was represented in the sample; Fig. 1 below shows a breakdown of interview participants by discipline and area type.

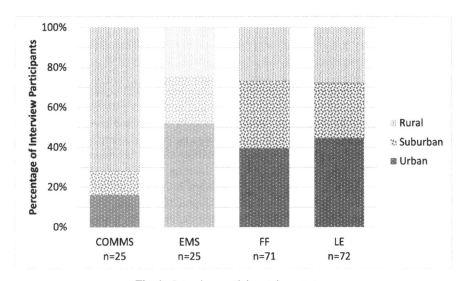

Fig. 1. Interview participants by area type

Likewise, the survey sample included diverse representation of the first responder population in all four disciplines. Figure 2 shows a similar breakdown for the survey data – participants who completed the survey by discipline and area type.

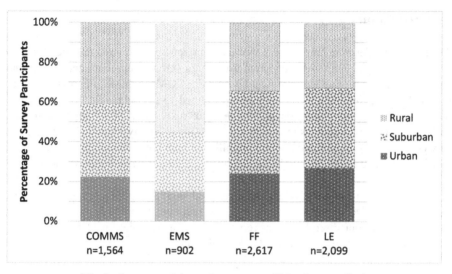

Fig. 2. Survey participants by area type (Color figure online)

4   Results

The results presented here are quantitative survey data supported by qualitative data from both the survey (from open-ended survey questions) and interviews. Quotes from the qualitative data are verbatim and are indented in blue text with a reference notation following each quote. The reference notation represents a particular participant response and is composed of three parts: the first represents the discipline of the response (COMMS; EMS; FF; LE), the second represents the area of the response (Urban = U; Suburban = S; Rural = R), and the third is the record ID number. Interview quotes are distinguishable from survey quotes in their notations; "INT" precedes the three-part notation for interview quotes. For example, (FF:U:1234) represents the survey responses for record ID #1234, from a fire service respondent in an urban area; (INT-LE-U-006) refers to an LE interview, from an urban location, who is law enforcement interviewee number 006. It is important to highlight that these notations are not connected to specific participants, as survey and interview data are anonymous.

As previously stated, this paper focuses on a subset of the survey data that are the results of the analysis of three survey questions: 1) futuristic technologies; 2) NG 911 (COMMS only), and 3) VR. Due to the relationships between the responses to these questions and the complexities in the data, the presentation of the results is structured as follows. Examined first is the usefulness of existing devices to which first responders do not have access (deeming them "futuristic"), both across and within the four disciplines (see Sect. 4.1). Second, technologies that are typically considered futuristic both within the public safety domain and externally (e.g., VR) are explored across disciplines (see Sect. 4.2). Finally, the paper presents the discipline-specific communication technologies that first responders think would be most useful for incident response, including, for COMMS, NG 911 (see Sect. 4.3).

The analyses yielding these results was performed on unweighted survey data (see Appendix). Survey responses are representative of the first responders who completed the survey; weighting of the data should be applied prior to making any generalizations about the results to the broader public safety population. The full dataset from the interviews and survey are available online [16].

4.1 Access to Existing Technologies

As noted in the survey methodology section, some devices currently used for public safety communication are not used universally; while many devices currently exist for first responders use, not all first responders use or even have access to the same types of technology. Those devices that survey participants indicated that they did not have were piped forward in the survey to the list of technologies for the futuristic technology question. As expected, these devices varied across disciplines and demographic measures, including technologies that are often considered to be more mainstream in the public safety domain today. Perhaps of most importance here are all the basic items that respondents still do not have, but that they believe would be useful, e.g., radios and mobile data terminals (MDTs).

Across the four disciplines, survey respondents consistently identified work-issued smartphones as something that would be useful in their day-to-day work; 21.08% of COMMS thought they would be useful, 31.11% of EMS, 30.41% of FF, and 39.34% of LE. While smartphone technology exists, many first responders do not currently have access to work-issued smartphones. In contrast to the usefulness of work-issued smartphones, much lower percentages of participants thought personal smartphones would be beneficial; 8.96% of COMMS, 13.40% of EMS, 19.34% of FF, 8.05% of LE. Dawkins, et al. posited that the concerns over the cost of smartphones could explain the discrepancy between work-issued and personal smartphones in the perceived benefits of their use [11]. The interview data mirrored these findings, showing the lack of access is often due to the cost of the devices as well as the additional costs beyond the technology itself, such as maintenance and data plans.

> At this point, I would love to buy officers smart phones, but I don't have the funding for it. So right now the only communication device that the department supplies is the radio. (INT-LE-U-029)

In addition to cost, particularly for personal smartphones, research findings suggest that major detractors from smartphones' usefulness to first responders were due to the necessity for personal data plans, the lack of adequate (if any) subsidies, and the possibilities for the subpoena of a first responder's personal smartphone [11].

Aside from smartphones, the only other technology existing in the public safety domain that crossed all four disciplines in a similar manner was desktop computers. Desktop computers are not typically considered a futuristic technology, yet like work-issued smartphones, are a technology that not all first responders currently have access to in their day-to-day work. While the percentages of EMS and FF who chose this item were somewhat low (EMS—11.65%, FF—9.58%), far more LE and COMMS respondents chose this item (19.39% of LE and 38.46% of COMMS).

Several other technologies were included in the list for three of the four first responder disciplines—EMS, FF, and LE—those public safety disciplines that are in the field. At least 20% of participants in each of these three disciplines thought the following devices that they do not currently have would be useful for their work:

- Laptop computer
- Mobile Data Terminal (MDT) or Mobile Data Computers (MDCs)
- Portable radio
- Tablet
- Vehicle radio
- Work-issued wireless earpiece

These devices, particularly MDTs and radios, represent critical public safety communication devices – something identified in the interviews as very important to first responders [4]. Again, these do not represent new or especially futuristic technology, but they are items that many first responders do not currently have but identify as potentially useful for their day-to-day incident response.

In addition to these cross-cutting technologies are those discipline-specific technologies to which first responders do not currently have access. These discipline-specific items were often those chosen by the largest percentage of respondents within the disciplines who use them. Fingerprint scanners (45.59%) and license plate readers (46.11%) were the top two devices chosen by LE respondents, with body cameras also chosen by a large percentage (31.96%). Thermal imaging cameras (TIC) for FF (27.15%) and headsets (32.47%) for COMMS also represent discipline-specific items that were selected by large percentages of their corresponding respondents. While these represent discipline-specific needs, large percentages of respondents who did not have access to them identified them as useful for their day-to-day work.

As public safety looks toward the use of more cutting-edge technologies, it is important to consider ways to make the existing technologies presented to this point more accessible to first responders in order to appropriately address the needs of the public safety community.

4.2 Technologies Useful for All

The majority of the technologies listed for the futuristic survey question were predetermined during survey development (see Sect. 2.3). Several of the technologies listed for all four disciplines – COMMS, EMS, FF, and LE – were selected by high percentages of respondents. The one item that over 50% of respondents in each discipline chose was "one login" (instead of many different usernames and passwords). While not yet ubiquitous, the use of one login, or single sign-on (SSO), is becoming increasingly widespread for the general public, but is still uncommon in public safety—for first responders, one login is still "futuristic" technology. One login was the top overall item checked for FF and LE, and the second overall item for COMMS and EMS, demonstrating its importance across all four disciplines (see Fig. 3). This mirrors the findings from the interview data – a major source of frustration for many first responders was the requirement to use multiple logins and passwords on their devices [4, 11]. The open-ended survey responses also indicate that SSO would be of tremendous benefit for first responders.

> One login would be at the top of everybody's list here. It is ridiculous the number of passwords and log-ins that have to be used and waste the time of first responders in their preparation and continuous log-in status. (LE:R:5075)
> I need to purchase an app just to remember all of the id's and passwords I need for each program I need to use. This is very frustrating and time-consuming. Where is the fob that allows me to log into anything I want? Biometrics? Bring it! (FF:S:4460)
> ONE LOGIN!!! Gosh, I spend an inordinate amount of brainspace and time tracking all my logins. (COMMS:U:3213)

These open-ended survey responses highlight the quantitative survey data about the importance of having one login, showing that first responders believe SSO would save time and lead to less frustration.

Three other technologies garnered relatively high percentages from first responders in all four disciplines, making them the desired future, in part, of the broader public safety domain: real-time on-scene video, indoor mapping, and voice controls for hands-free input (see Fig. 3).

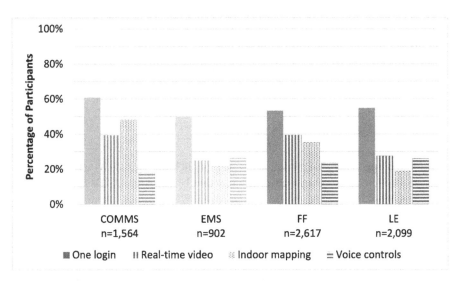

Fig. 3. Top futuristic technologies across all four disciplines

While these technologies were identified by all four disciplines as potentially useful for their day-to-day work, there were some differences amongst the disciplines. For example, COMMS and FF respondents chose indoor mapping and real-time on-scene video more often than their EMS and LE colleagues, while there was greater consistency across disciplines for voice controls for hands-free input.

As with the data presented in the previous section, some technologies cut across the three disciplines for which first responders work in the field —EMS, FF, and LE. When asked if drones would be beneficial in their day-to-day work, large percentages of FF and LE thought they would, while fewer EMS thought drones would be beneficial (see Fig. 4). However, in each of these three disciplines, including EMS, drones were one of the technologies that intrigued first responders during the interviews. First responders expressed how both aerial drones (e.g., to give "a live feed 360 view of [the scene]" (INT-FF-S-033)) and ground drones (e.g., "the BB-8 character from Star Wars...get that little ball with the camera... [for] reconnaissance." (INT-LE-U-013)) would be useful for incident response [7].

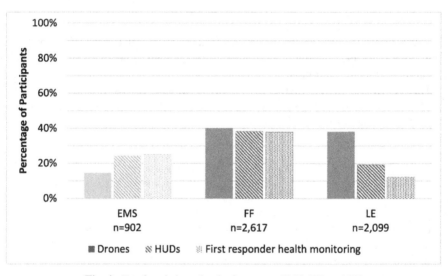

Fig. 4. Top futuristic technologies across EMS, FF, and LE

The highest percentage of participants who thought heads-up displays (HUDs) would be beneficial were in FF. Interview data show that FF envision HUDs built-into their face pieces, where they "can glance down at that HUD and look through the thermal imager if the smoke is too thick [to] be able to see through otherwise" (INT-FF-S-040). The status of first responder health and vitals is also a critical piece of information in high-risk environments; many FF and EMS respondents thought the health monitoring of first responders would be beneficial to their work. EMS and FF first responders' priority is preservation of life, but this information would also be especially helpful for incident commanders managing an incident.

Finally, the survey asked participants about the use of VR in multiple ways. First, VR was included in the list of technologies for the futuristic question. Second, the survey asked if VR would be useful for training. Lastly, participants were asked about the potential use of VR for other purposes. Results show that the usefulness of VR to first responders was tied to the way it would be used in their work contexts.

When asked about general VR benefits in their day-to-day work and about other uses for VR, respondents either did not think it would be helpful or were unsure about its usefulness. A very low percentage of respondents selected VR in the list of futuristic technologies; less than 7% in each discipline thought VR would be useful in their day-to-day work (4.92% COMMS, 3.33% EMS, 6.84% FF, 5.81% LE)[1]. In comparison with the other futuristic technologies listed, these data suggest that there are far more technologies that first responders think would be useful in their day-to-day work than VR (see Appendix). This is demonstrated further in the results of the question asking participants if VR would be useful in their work for purposes other than training. Over 50% of respondents in each discipline responded, "Not sure," indicating that first responders were unsure if VR would be useful in other ways for their work. In fact, more respondents in all four disciplines chose "No" than "Yes" in response to this question.

While respondents had difficulty imagining other situations in which VR might be useful, when asked to think specifically about VR and training, they were more able to recognize its potential utility. Responses on the use of VR for training show more than 50% of respondents from EMS (50.28%), FF (51.54%), and LE (58.83%) said they believe VR would be useful for training in their discipline (see Fig. 5). For COMMS, this percentage was slightly lower at 33.78%, but still higher than the percentage of COMMS respondents who indicated they did not see VR as useful for training in their work. While high numbers of respondents supported the use of VR for training in their discipline, it must be noted as well that over 30% of respondents from all four disciplines indicated they were not sure if VR would be useful for training in their work. These data show that many first responders need additional information about the potential capabilities and value of VR to their work if VR is to be used in public safety.

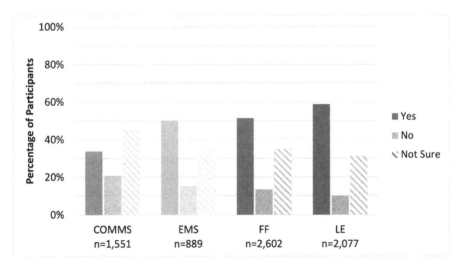

Fig. 5. Usefulness of VR for training

---

[1] Similarly, low percentages of respondents thought augmented reality (AR) would be useful in their day-to-day work: 4.80% of COMMS, 4.55% of EMS, 5.88% of FF, 4.95% of LE.

The higher percentage of LE respondents who saw VR as useful for training may be due to their familiarity with simulation-based training in general, while the COMMS percentage may be lower since their work is often based on audio rather than video or in-person interaction. While some first responders see the benefits of VR for training, there are others who feel VR would be a hinderance to the work of first responders, especially in an operations capacity.

> Training, but I am not yet able to see the applicability of VR in the day-to-day operations. (EMS:S:2482)
> I do not see its practical application. (FF:S:250)
> So far, everything I've seen about VR seems gimmicky - more of a toy than a useful technology. (LE:R:4511)
> VR, to me, seems to be a system for gaming and entertainment… I unfortunately see little practical application it could be used for in 9-1-1 dispatch at this time. (COMMS:S:46)

Overall, the quantitative survey data related to VR show support across all four first responder disciplines for the use of VR for training in public safety. However, as these quotes show, the open-ended data are somewhat more qualified, with first responders noting other factors that affect VR's utility, even for training.

4.3   Discipline-Specific Technologies

For the futuristic survey question, some of the technologies listed were discipline-specific due to the various types of needs of first responders (see Sect. 2.3). These technologies provide specific functions and support for first responders and are of tremendous importance to the disciplines that use them. The subsequent sections here are centered around a single discipline in presentation of these data.

COMMS. First responders in Comm Center & 9-1-1 Services have unique roles in unique environments within public safety. As such, the communication technology used in COMMS is quite different than the other disciplines, which is reflected in the survey design as well as the results. 71.23% of COMMS respondents thought automatic caller location would be useful in their day-to-day work, far more than the other futuristic technologies listed for the futuristic survey question. A key component of the day-to-day work in COMMS is interacting with 9-1-1 callers and relaying their information to first responders in the field. With the ever-increasing number of 9-1-1 calls from mobile devices, accurate location of callers is essential to their work. Another technology that a high percentage of COMMS thought would be useful is first responder tracking; 60.55% of respondents selected this technology. As COMMS represents both call taking and dispatching responsibilities, first responder tracking would have a major impact on the day-to-day work of COMMS dispatchers.

As discussed in Sect. 2.3, the COMMS survey was uniquely positioned to include questions about NG 911. Figure 6 depicts results showing that COMMS respondents overwhelmingly said they had heard of NG 911 (89.72%) and believed it will be helpful in their work (74.47%). The fact that almost 20% of respondents (19.55%) said they were not sure that NG 911 will be helpful in their work may demonstrate a lack of clarity about NG 911 and the ways in which it might benefit COMMS workers.

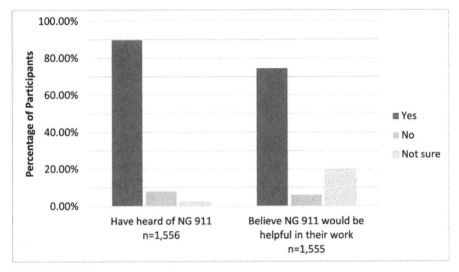

Fig. 6. COMMS survey responses to NG 911 questions

EMS. For EMS, more than half of respondents thought automatic transmission of patient vitals and information to the hospital would be useful in their day-to-day work (56.43%). Nearly 40% also thought health/vitals monitoring of patients and automatic vehicle location (AVL) would be useful (39.47% and 39.36%, respectively). The primary task for day-to-day work in EMS is treating patients. It is understandable that improvements to the health monitoring of EMS patients, as well as automating their communication tasks while treating those patients, are desirable technologies for the future of EMS.

FF. The fire service is unique in that many of FF first responders are cross-trained in EMS – their responsibilities include both fire-related and health-related service. As a result, there is some overlap in the future of communication technology with EMS and FF. This is reflected in the discipline-specific survey results, where nearly half of FF thought AVL – technology that enables COMMS to dispatch the closest vehicle to an incident, rather than just the closest station – would be useful in their day-to-day work (49.41%); a high percentage of EMS also thought AVL would be useful.

LE. Two discipline-specific technologies were selected by nearly 40% of LE – facial recognition and thermal imaging. In their day-to-day work, first responders in LE regularly need to identify persons of interest. Results suggest that first responders think technology may help in this task, as 38.69% of LE respondents thought facial recognition software would be useful in their day-to-day work.

As previously stated, some technologies listed for the futuristic survey question are more commonly used by the general public, but not as widely used in public safety; other technologies are used by some agencies and departments in public safety, but their use is not universal. Thermal imaging falls into the latter category of technology – TICs are more common in FF (but still not universally used), but not as prevalent in LE. First responders in LE think it may be beneficial for this to change, with 38.40% indicating that thermal imaging would be useful in their day-to-day work.

5   Conclusion

First responders were asked about their vision of the future of communication technology for incident response. While some of the futuristic technologies used in the survey may not be considered futuristic in some arenas, these items have often not made their way into the world of public safety. One of the best examples of this is single sign-on (SSO). Across all four disciplines – COMMS, EMS, FF, and LE – over half of participants indicated that SSO for their devices would be most useful in their everyday work. While SSO is commonly used in industry, it addresses a universal pain point in public safety, where its use is less common.

Other, more futuristic technologies first responders thought would be useful include real-time on-scene video, indoor mapping, and voice controls for hands-free input. In addition to these technologies, first responders also envisioned the usefulness of futuristic technologies specific to their individual disciplines. COMMS thought automatic caller location would be the most beneficial for their work, while also recognizing the potential of NG 911 as the future of 9-1-1 technology. EMS saw technology to automatically send patient vitals to a hospital as the most potentially useful. Automatic vehicle location (AVL) was considered by FF as the futuristic technology with the most benefit. Lastly, LE thought drones, thermal imaging, and facial recognition to identify a person of interest would be equally beneficial in their day-to-day work.

While the survey results generally showed favorability towards futuristic technologies, the open-ended survey data revealed that first responders consistently emphasized that an obstacle to the use of futuristic technologies was cost [11]. In the interviews as well, many participants cited issues of cost and price as prohibitive factors related to the adoption of new forms of technology.

> ...throw in the fact that most of us have inadequate funding (FF:S:5094)
> ...the technology is there, it just costs so much. (INT-LE-U-010)
> Technology is very expensive. You don't just buy it and you're good.
> You've got to maintain it... You've got to upgrade it. (INT-EMS-R-008)

As noted by the EMS interviewee quoted above, it is not just the initial cost of technology that makes it unattainable, there are often auxiliary costs beyond the technology itself, such as associated maintenance, certification, technical support and training. Cost may be one reason that respondents did not see some of this technology as useful for their day-to-day incident response. Improving current technology and meeting current needs rather than buying into (literally and figuratively) totally new technology was an important consideration for the first responders who participated in both the interviews and the survey. The best technology in the world is not useful if those who need it cannot afford it.

Additionally, when asked about futuristic technology, first responders often cited the need to focus less on cutting edge technology, like VR, and more on basics and current technology needed by first responders rather than on new technology.

> Until rural areas have a comms infrastructure that can support BASIC communications the rest is a fantasy. (EMS:R:2434)
>
> None of [the futuristic technologies] sound particularly useful and some could be disruptive to our normal work processes in dispatch. (COMMS:S:1545)
>
> Instead of introducing all this extra new stuff let's, one, make sure what we have actually works better. And then, two, let's not rely on it so much. (INT-FF-U-042)

If first responders are going to accept and adopt new technologies, they need to have a better understanding of how those technologies will help them accomplish their primary tasks and provide better efficiency, effectiveness, and satisfaction than what they currently use. As reported in the findings from the interview data, "New technology is exciting, and the possibilities for it are endless. While new technology may sound good and make sense to researchers and developers, adoption requires buy-in from first responders" [4].

As technology for the NPSBN is being developed, researchers, designers, and developers alike need to focus on the needs of the users – the first responders. As we learned in our interviews, there is no room in public safety to develop "technology for technology's sake" [4]. The interviews and survey both suggest that "one size does not fit all" – first responders are open to new and exciting technologies, but their needs are utility driven; to have the biggest impact, their communication technology must be tailored to each discipline's needs and contexts.

Acknowledgements. NIST would like to thank the many first responders, public safety personnel, and publicsafety organizations who graciously gave their time and input for this project.

Appendix

Table 1 and Table 2 show the results from the responses to the survey question on futuristic technology. The number of respondents, n, for each technology and the corresponding discipline is the following, unless otherwise noted: COMMS, n = 1,564; EMS, n = 902; FF, n = 2,617; and LE, n = 2,099.

Table 1. Participants who selected preset futuristic technology

Futuristic technology	COMMS	EMS	FF	LE
AR (augmented reality)	4.80%	4.55%	5.88%	4.95%
Automatic caller location	71.23%			
Automatic transmission of patient vitals and information to hospital		56.43%		
AVL (automatic vehicle location)		39.36%	49.41%	
Drones		14.52%	40.20%	38.21%
Facial recognition software	16.05%			38.69%
First responder tracking	60.55%			21.30%
Health/vitals monitoring of first responders		25.17%	37.87%	12.15%
Health/vitals monitoring of patients		39.47%	19.07%	
HUDs (heads-up displays)		24.39%	38.29%	19.39%
Indoor mapping	48.15%	21.51%	35.27%	18.87%
One login (instead of many different usernames and passwords)	60.93%	50.11%	53.31%	54.88%
Real-time on-scene video	39.51%	24.94%	39.47%	27.49%
Remote sensing (by aircraft or satellite)			10.58%	
Robots		2.00%	4.93%	7.86%
Self driving cars		6.21%	3.97%	3.53%
Smart buildings		6.98%	12.99%	7.58%
Smart glasses		8.98%	8.06%	7.86%
Smart watch	7.23%	16.41%	12.95%	15.39%
Thermal imaging				38.40%
Vehicle tracking				26.39%
Voice controls for hands-free input	17.90%	26.27%	23.42%	25.96%
Voice recognition for identification		15.52%	13.11%	16.77%
VR (virtual reality)	4.92%	3.33%	6.84%	5.81%

Table 2. Participants who selected existing technology

Existing technology	COMMS	EMS	FF	LE
Body camera				31.96%; n = 1214
Computer: desktop	38.46%; n = 26	11.65%; n = 103	9.58%; n = 240	19.39%; n = 196
Computer: laptop		31.62%; n = 136	35.93%; n = 501	38.66%; n = 476
Dash camera				25.43%; n = 1266
Earpiece: wireless (self purchased)		3.03%; n = 661	9.32%; n = 1931	4.67%; n = 1799
Earpiece: wireless (work issued)		21.67%; n = 812	28.95%; n = 2297	34.74%; n = 1802
Earpiece: with cord		4.47%; n = 694	4.81%; n = 1890	6.63%; n = 1147
Fingerprint scanner				45.59%; n = 1349
Flip phone: work issued		2.66%; n = 788	1.77%; n = 2369	2.47%; n = 1906
Foot pedal	10.87%; n = 276			
Headset	32.47%; n = 231			
License plate reader				46.11%; n = 1644
MDT/MDC (mobile data terminal/computer)		32.95%; n = 516	38.98%; n = 1116	28.46%; n = 615
Microphone: desktop	7.16%; n = 433			
Microphone: handheld or clip-on	9.08%; n = 859			
Mic: wireless		15.04%; n = 791	19.50%; n = 2251	19.40%; n = 1696
Mic: with cord		4.33%; n = 393	3.46%; n = 752	3.08%; n = 746
Monitor (at your personal workstation)	25.00%; n = 56			
Monitor (for shared viewing)	20.46%; n = 391			

(*continued*)

Table 2. (*continued*)

Existing technology	COMMS	EMS	FF	LE
Pager	1.33%; n = 1125	6.27%; n = 383	2.97%; n = 1178	0.55%; n = 2002
Phone: landline	16.67%; n = 42			
Radio	11.94%; n = 67			
Radio: in-vehicle		21.62%; n = 111	35.68%; n = 213	24.38%; n = 320
Radio: portable		32.79%; n = 61	34.88%; n = 43	11.83%; n = 93
Smartphone: personal	8.96%; n = 201	13.40%; n = 97	19.34%; n = 331	8.05%; n = 410
Smartphone: work issued	21.08%; n = 887	31.11%; n = 601	30.41%; n = 1391	39.34%; n = 816
Tablet		36.50%; n = 326	33.88%; n = 856	23.33%; n = 1380
TIC (thermal imaging camera)			27.15%; n = 291	

References

1. Public Safety Communications Research: Research Portfolios. https://www.nist.gov/ctl/pscr/research-portfolios. Accessed 11 Jan 2021
2. Public Safety Communications Research: User Interface/User Experience Portfolio. https://www.nist.gov/ctl/pscr/research-portfolios/user-interfaceuser-experience. Accessed 11 Jan 2021
3. ISO 9241-210:2010: Ergonomics of human-system interaction – Part 210: Human-centred design for interactive systems, ISO, Geneva, Switzerland (2010). http://www.iso.org/
4. Choong, Y., Dawkins, S., Furman, S., Greene, K.K., Spickard Prettyman, S., Theofanos, M.F.: Voices of First Responders – Identifying Public Safety Communication Problems: Findings from User-Centered Interviews. Phase 1, Volume 1. NISTIR 8216 (2018). https://doi.org/10.6028/NIST.IR.8216
5. Greene, K.K., et al.: Voices of First Responders—Nationwide Public Safety Communication Survey Methodology: Development, Dissemination, and Demographics. Phase 2, Volume 1. NISTIR 8288 (2020). https://doi.org/10.6028/NIST.IR.8288
6. Greene, K.K., et al.: Characterizing first responders' communication technology needs: towards a standardized usability evaluation methodology. In: Mattson, P., Marshall, J. (eds.) Homeland Security and Public Safety: Research, Applications and Standards, pp. 23–48. ASTM International, West Conshohocken (2019). https://doi.org/10.1520/STP161420180048
7. Dawkins, S., et al.: Voices of First Responders – Examining Public Safety Communication Problems and Requested Functionality, Findings from User-Centered Interviews. Phase 1, Volume 2.1. NISTIR 8245 (2019). https://doi.org/10.6028/NIST.IR.8245

8. Dawkins, S., et al.: Public safety communication user needs: voices of first responders. In: Proceedings of the Human Factors and Ergonomics Society's Annual Meeting, Philadelphia, PA, 1–5 October 2018.
9. Greene, K.K., et al.: Voices of First Responders—Examining Public Safety Communication from the Rural Perspective, Findings from User-Centered Interviews, Phase 1, Volume 3. NISTIR 8277 (2019). https://doi.org/10.6028/NIST.IR.8277
10. Steves, M., et al.: Voices of First Responders – Examining Public Safety Communication from the Perspective of 9-1-1 Call Takers and Dispatchers Findings from User-Centered Interviews, Phase 1, Volume 4. NISTIR 8295 (2020). https://doi.org/10.6028/NIST.IR.8295
11. Dawkins, S., Greene, K., Spickard-Prettyman, S.: Voices of First Responders – Nationwide Public Safety Communication Survey Findings, Mobile Devices, Applications, and Futuristic Technology. Phase 2, Volume 2. NISTIR 8314 (2020). https://doi.org/10.6028/NIST.IR.8314
12. Federal Emergency Management Agency (FEMA): Regions (2020). https://www.fema.gov/about/organization/regions. Accessed 11 Jan 2021
13. Joint Program Office for Intelligent Transportation Systems: Next Generation 9-1-1 (NG9-1-1) System Initiative Concept of Operations. U.S. Department of Transportation, April 2007. https://rosap.ntl.bts.gov/view/dot/4025. Accessed 11 Jan 2021
14. National 911 Program. Next Generation 911. Office of Emergency Medical Services, National Highway Traffic Safety Administration, U.S. Department of Transportation. https://www.911.gov/issue_nextgeneration911.html. Accessed 11 Jan 2021
15. Feldman, H., Leh, M., Felts, R., Benson, J.: Public Safety User Interface R&D Roadmap. NIST Technical Note 1961 (2017). https://doi.org/10.6028/NIST.TN.1961
16. NIST PSCR Usability Team: PSCR Usability Results Tool: Voices of First Responders. NIST (Revised 2020). https://publicsafety.nist.gov/. Accessed 11 Jan 2021

Blinking LEDs: Usability and User Experience of Domestic Modem Routers Indicator Lights

Massimiliano Dibitonto[✉]

9Bit A.P.S. Rome, Rome, Italy

Abstract. Smart home devices are starting to be widespread in our homes, becoming an important element in our daily life. For this reason, a good level of usability and user experience is an important factor in the adoption and acceptance of these systems. The home modem router is a crucial element and a potential weakness in such systems. This work analyses the relationship between users and the physical interfaces of such devices and especially the usability of LED indicator lights. In this work, research was carried out in order to identify the usability of this interface. The methodology adopted includes 3 steps: benchmark of widespread and new products identified among big with innovative interaction concepts; a questionnaire to identify how the device is used and the common pain points; a guessability study to identify the comprehensibility of the conventions (icons and colours) used on the products examined. The results show that there are some difficulties to understand the icons and that and that this can lead to interaction problems. The new concepts proposed by big players reveal a different communication paradigm based on colours that briefly indicate the modem statuses. This confirms a general need for simplification but also for a more pleasant aesthetic.

Keywords: Usability · Smart home · Modem/Router

1 Introduction

The Internet of Things (IoT) is a technological paradigm that has led to the emergence of a new generation of connected and sentient products and services. Beyond the technological side, the most important element is perhaps the pervasiveness [1] of this technological paradigm as is impacting a vast range of human activities, by changing the way we live cities, our homes, education, work and many other daily activities. This pervasiveness makes clear the need to evaluate different aspects about the relationship between human beings and "smart" technologies and environments. For example, the usability and the experience of use of a smart home system influences not only a single task but also our life experience. Furthermore, consumer products are meant for people who do not have technical skills or training to operate on complex technological systems, which is why ease of use acquires a fundamental role [2].

Smart home applications are an important sector in the Internet of Things (IoT) market [3]. The term "smart home" refers to a set of hardware and software products ("smart products") which, thanks to the use of sensors, actuators, internet connection and

© Springer Nature Switzerland AG 2021
M. Kurosu (Ed.): HCII 2021, LNCS 12764, pp. 292–302, 2021.
https://doi.org/10.1007/978-3-030-78468-3_20

local and remote processing capabilities, can enable a large number of "smart" services such as automation systems (e.g. close the shutters if it starts to rain, turn on the heating when you are about to return home), energy efficiency, surveillance, security, etc.

A crucial element and a potentially critical point of the usability of a Smart Home system is represented by the need of connecting a multitude of devices to the Internet in a simple way [4–6].

In this context, the modem router or home gateway plays an important role, allowing devices (depending on the type of technology) to exchange data both locally and remotely. It could be perceived as a passive device due to the low interactivity required during a normal use [7]. It has a limited physical interface (usually a set of LED indicator lights) and a web page or, sometimes, an app for richer interactions. However, the interaction with this device becomes crucial when the user needs to configure something (e.g. a port forwarding for a security camera) or to understand the reason why something is not working properly. The user, indeed, can look at indicator lights when he/she wants to get information on the status of the connection (e.g. why can't I surf the Internet? Why can't the PC connect to the Wi-Fi?) or to have a look at the graphical interface through the local website or the app.

To the best of our knowledge, most of the literature is focused on application use cases, networking strategies or on the usability of web interfaces used to configure smart home systems. This work focuses on on a particular aspect of the home modem/router/gateway interface: the indicator lights that communicate the device's status.

The goal of this work is to understand how users use their home modem router and the usability of the physical interface, with a particular regard to the indicator lights intelligibility. The research was developed through a heuristic evaluation of different kind of devices, widespread on the Italian market, and on some "new generation" devices. Initial findings were subsequently deepened through a questionnaire and a guessability study [8].

1.1 Related Works

A first literature research was focused on deepening the relationship between users and smart home systems with particular regard to potential adoption limits in relation to usability and networking issues. In this context, modem routers play an important role.

There are some barriers that hinder the adoption of such systems, such as the perception of certain risks (i.e. privacy, security, reliability, trust) as well as the technological skills required for their use [9, 10].

In their work, Yan and colleagues [6], categorize smart home gateway in three generations according to different features such as speed, processing power plus other technical features, and human-computer interaction aspects like Quality of Experience (QoE). The authors deem QoE and data awareness as key aspects of new generation smart gateways. They point out that in a smart home context usability, compatibility (with different protocols), scalability, security and privacy are critical challenges.

A similar approach is shown by Aldossari and Sidorova [11] which draw the attention to the the ease of use ("effort expectancy" in the proposed model) as a key factor for the adoption of smart home system/IoT system. Also Grinter et al. [12, 13] states that the tools used to create a home network should be designed to support and be integrate in domestic life taking into account the collaborative and social interactions happening in a domestic context.

Furthermore another research was carried out to deepen the usability and comprehensibility aspects of the indicators lights present on modem routers. To the best of our knowledge, while there is a large number of studies regarding the usability of icons on GUIs, we have found fewer studies addressing indicator lights and symbols on a domestic appliance. In this domain, we have found some design guidelines [14] for electronic devices and studies on specific use cases. For example, Meier and colleagues [15] investigates on the usability of a smart home thermostat, pointing out inconsistence of indicators and symbols as a major issue.

However, another approach could be to apply weel-known usability to this context. We can find a guide in the seminal, but still current, of Norman [16], in which he suggests that products should offer users controls and feedbacks. Indeed, for the user is important to understand the status of a device, what kind of actions he/she can perform and the effects that it might produce. According to the Norman's taxonomy, a modem router is essentially a passive device with an "internal representation" (data flows in an invisible way and user have no idea of what is happening inside the "black box"). Hence there is the necessity of a "surface representation" that gives a human-centered and a visible information about elements that are important to him/her e.g. absence of connection or successful device pairing while using the WPS function.

In the study conducted by Jakobi [17] and his colleagues about a smart home system, comes to the light the importance to provide awareness about system status besides the data sensed. Moreover they underline how this could influence user acceptance and trust. This information is useful to accomplish the task of controlling, maintaining, and potentially debugging systems. Moreover, the authors noticed that, after the initial period of adoption and appropriation, the information need changed with as users were asking to be informed only in case, if something went wrong.

2 Research

2.1 Methodology

The methodology adopted includes 3 stages:

- A benchmark of the most popular patterns on the market, analyzing both best-selling products (Amazon statistics) and new products identified among big players (Amazon, Google) that present innovative concepts;
- A questionnaire to identify how the device is used and the common pain points;
- A guessability [8] study to identify the comprehensibility of the conventions (icons and colours) used with the examined products.

2.2 Benchmark

A benchmark was conducted among several devices chosen from the best-selling ones in Italy (Amazon Italy, 2020) [18] and those provided by major telephone operators.

In particular, the following devices were defined as "mainstream" in the context of this research (both for the level of adoption and the use of similar conventions): TP-Link TD-W8961N, TP-Link VR1210v, AVM Fritzbox 7590, ZTE FastGate (Fastweb operator), TIM Hub (TIM operator), Sercomm Home & Life Hub (Wind 3 operator). Another category of devices, defined as "new generation" in this study, were evaluated. This kind of devices are still not very widespread but present innovative paradigms with respect to the use of indicator lights: Google On-Hub, Google Nest Router, Io Zyxel Multy U AC2100, Orbi Netgear and Linksys Velop AC1300. The objective of the study was to evaluate: comprehensibility and consistency of the representation of the states (evaluated between the various devices). The user manuals of the devices were used as a reference for the study.

The "mainstream" devices have a similar number of lights and states represented. In fact, almost all of them represent the following states with dedicated lights: ADSL synchronization, Internet connection, Wi-Fi network presence (possibly on 2.4 GHz and 5 GHz frequencies), connection of one or more devices, and WPS. The indicator lights are used in the on, off or flashing state.

As can be seen from the Table 1, there are "standard" icons for some common states as the Wi-Fi signal, while proprietary symbols are used for other indications. Using standards and labels underneath the icons might help users recognize rather than remember. The use of flashing can be inconsistent between the various states. For example, the blinking ADSL light means that a connection is being established but the modem still cannot surf the Internet, while the blinking WiFi light indicates that data is being transmitted correctly whithin the local network. It can also be underlined how some icons require a certain level of technical skill from the user: distinguishing between ADSL and the Internet connections requires knowledge of how the modem connects to the telephone exchange and can subsequently enable Internet access. The distinction between the two WiFi frequencies also requires prior technical competence, as well as the possible ambiguity of the 5G label/symbol, also used for mobile phone networks.

An exception in this category is represented by the FastGate modem that has indicator lights without labels or icons, relating to: connection status, Wi-Fi and WPS. The lights can be red (problem/no signal), green (problem solved), white (normal operation). This peculiarity makes it analysable together with the modems of the "new generation" category.

In "new generation" devices, the greatest discontinuity is represented by the use of a single indicator light capable of assuming various colours. Such devices have only the function of router, therefore having to represent a smaller number of states.

The criterion used is to represent states through color, with a more refined aesthetic. The use of colors requires simplifying and reducing the number of states represented. From the manuals we can see how the lights synthesize states eg. "everything is fine" or "there is a problem", referring to the configuration interface (web or app) for details. The arbitrariness of the color-state correspondence represents a weakness of this solution. Furthermore, color can create problems for color blind people, not compensated by the use of separate lights (recognizable by position). Comparing the colors used on the various devices, the only "strong" consistency detected is red = error. Another common pairing is: white = correct operation, pulsing white = booting. We see that the consistency decreases on other colors such as yellow, in some cases combined with factory-reset, firmware upgrade or connection problems (this difference also appears in products of the same brand). Blue is also used in some cases to indicate correct operation or configuration.

The observations collected in this benchmark were subsequently deepened with a questionnaire to detect the level of comprehensibility of these approaches.

2.3 Questionnaire

A quali-quantitative questionnaire has been created with multiple choice and open questions. The first part of the questionnaire collects demo-graphic data and data on the use of digital technologies and in particular of modem router devices and home connections.

A guessability study was conducted taking into consideration the methodology proposed by Wobbrock et al. [8] and by Kackmar and Carey [18]. As reference, we used the symbols shown on the modems analysed in the previous paragraph. In particular, the devices supplied by the main network provides were chosen, assuming that the respondents to the questionnaire use their personal knowledge, based on the devices previously used. Moreover, the reference to commonly used devices was also useful to analyse the actual/real understanding of the indicator lights of the devices currently in use.

On the basis of the benchmark carried out, both symbols common to the various manufacturers (e.g. the symbol of the Wi-Fi network) and specific symbols (e.g. the ADSL alignment symbol of TP-Link modems) were chosen. The user manuals were examined in order to have an exact correspondence between symbol and referent.

Inside the questionnaire, the participants were asked to choose between three possible answers for each symbol: one correct, one likely (based on semantic proximity of the symbol) and one unlikely. The possibility of not indicating answers was provided too ("I don't know" option). For the analysis of devices equipped with a single multicolored light, a matching grid between states and colours was proposed. A smaller number of questions has been entered relating to "new generation" devices.

A symbol was deemed understandable if the majority of users matched it to the correct meaning (selection accuracy) [18].

The "wrong" answers were further analysed. In fact, if a large number of users have identified a certain link between a symbol and a referent, albeit incorrect for the specific device, this may mean that the symbol may be misleading or suggest something else. Among the available answers on the questionnaire, it was chosen to insert features that were absent on all the devices analysed (for example, the indication of the connection speed) to discover if there was any desired function yet not present.

The last part of the questionnaire was about the wishes of users for any upgrades and changes to indicator lights, interaction modes and physical design of their current home modems.

Questionnaire Results The questionnaire was answered by 71 people, 40 women and 31 men with an average age of 37 (sd. 8). Most participants reported medium or high confidence with new technologies. The most popular connected devices within the respondents' homes are (see Fig. 1): PCs and smartphones 97%, smart TVs 73%, smart home devices 49%, voice assistants 39% and gaming consoles 25%. This data is interesting since it confirms the trend of the Italian market as it was measured by the Internet of Things Observatory of the Politecnico di Milano [19], with a strong penetration of smart home devices and voice assistants.

This also demonstrates the aptitude of most of the interviewees to rely on their home connection for advanced services too, and not only to surf the Web. This behaviour may suggest that users also used setup or troubleshooting procedures, which may sometimes be required to set up smart devices. In fact, 46% of the sample confirms that they have proceeded to configure the modem router on their own even if there is no agreement on the perceived ease of use. In fact, 32% deemed easy to interact with the modem router, 19% very easy, 26% quite easy and 16% not very easy. The rest of the sample (7%) deemed it difficult.

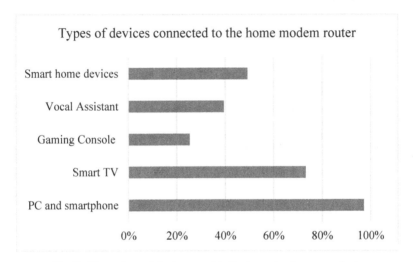

Fig. 1. Type of smart devices used in the home by the respondents

61% of the sample reported having the modem positioned in a visible point of the house but the majority did not believe that the LEDs of the device are a nuisance.

Regarding the usefulness, most of the respondents believe that the indicator lights are quite useful and clear and 91% says they look at them mainly when there are connection problems to understand the cause while only 10% says they look at them for other reasons as well (for example a visual check of the operation of the device).

The guessability study made it possible to verify whether users were actually able to match correctly the symbols shown on the indicator lights of the modem with their meanings. Table 1 shows the correct answers and the most voted answer among the proposed alternatives, even if incorrect.

From Table 1 it is possible to note that users have correctly matched the meanings to the symbols only in 4 cases, plus 1 ex-aequo (symbol 7, WPS function). It should be noticed that there are multiple symbols for the same meaning: symbols 2 and 10 (double frequency Wi-Fi network), 5 and 7 (WPS), 6 and 9 (LAN). This is because different manufacturers use different symbols for the same function. No clear correlation was

Table 1. Guessability study results for "mainstream" devices.

	Symbol	Meaning	%	Alternative	%
1		Wi-Fi network is on or off	**73,24%**	Connection speed	18,31%
2		Wi-Fi 2.4G and 5G networks are on or off	18,31%	Wi-Fi signal power	**57,75%**
3	* blinking	Wi-Fi network is on and transmitting	22,54%	Wi-Fi connection error	**46,48%**
4		Status of ADSL synchronization	25,35%	Don't know	**70,42%**
5		Status of WPS function	16,90%	Don't know	**43,66%**
6		Devices connected and trasmitting on the Ethernet ports	**61,97%**	Don't know	26,76%
7		Status of WPS function	**30,99%**	Don't know	**30,99%**
8		Availability of Internet connection	18,31%	Don't know	**50,70%**
9		Devices connected and trasmitting on the Ethernet ports	**70,42%**	Don't know	23,94%
10	2.4G 5G	Wi-Fi 2.4G and 5G networks are on	**45,07%**	The modem connects to the internet via 2.4G and 5G	21,13%
11	ADSL led is on and Internet led is off	ADSL synchronization has been established but cannot connect to the Internet	43,66%	Don't know	**69,01%**

found between owned devices and recognized symbols. For example, users with TP-LINK modems that use icon 5 for WPS were unable to recognize it. The same observation is valid for icon 7, used on almost all modems owned by respondents. A further study, not feasible with the available data but possible in future works, could be done on the connection between the ability to recognize a symbol (memory) and the frequency of use of the function. There was a high rate of "Don't know" responses for symbols 4, 5, 8 which are characteristic of a single manufacturer (TP-LINK). This may lead to the use of standards as suggested in the benchmark. Regarding symbols 2 and 10, we might argue that the presence of the labels increases the percentage of correct answers. However, it should be considered that the 5GHz Wi-Fi network is recently introduced and not present on the devices of some respondents,. Filtering this data gives a positive response rate of about 60%.

Table 2. Guessability study results for "new generation" devices. The correct combination of colour and status is shown in the coloured cells.

	Cross-fading	White	Blinking white	Red	Blinking yellow	Off
Working correctly	15,49%	**77,46%**	15,49%	9,86%	7,04%	8,45%
Connection problem	19,72%	0,00%	21,13%	22,54%	**35,21%**	8,45%
Error	4,23%	2,82%	9,86%	**59,15%**	7,04%	1,41%
Device updating	23,94%	2,82%	21,13%	0,00%	30,99%	0,00%
Device booting	**36,62%**	8,45%	**32,39%**	4,23%	18,31%	2,82%
Device off	0,00%	8,45%	0,00%	4,23%	1,41%	**78,87%**

A further question was related to the comprehensibility of the colours used instead of icons. As for the previous analysis, colours used on the modems / routers on the market examined in the benchmark were proposed. Since some devices have different functions (e.g. presence of Bluetooth connectivity) only some states and colours, common to the various selected products, have been chosen.

Table 2 shows the colour-state pairing guessed by respondents. The correct combination of colour and status is shown in the coloured cells. Depending on the device some colours correspond to different states. We can see that there is a strong agreement (>50%) about binding the white colour to the correct operation of the device, the red colour to an error, and the absence of light to the device-off status. In the other cases we have a weak agreement (<50%), a sign of uncertainty in deciding and, consequently, of incorrect symbol-meaning associations. Both cases can be related to the arbitrariness of the binding between colours and states but also to to colour conventions used in other circumstances eg. red = danger and white = on.

Table 3. How respondents would match colours and statuses.

	White	Blinking white	Red	Blinking red	Yellow	Blinking yellow	User defined	Off
Working correctly	**78,87%**	15,49%	2,82%	2,82%	8,45%	4,23%	**49,30%**	7,04%
Connection problem	0,00%	18,31%	22,54%	**52,11%**	23,94%	19,72%	14,08%	7,04%
Error	1,41%	1,41%	**67,61%**	38,03%	11,27%	8,45%	5,63%	2,82%
Device updating	1,41%	18,31%	1,41%	2,82%	**33,80%**	**36,62%**	11,27%	0,00%
Device booting	5,63%	**42,25%**	0,00%	2,82%	18,31%	25,35%	14,08%	2,82%
Device off	11,27%	2,82%	4,23%	0,00%	2,82%	4,23%	4,23%	**78,87%**

To the questions about how users would like the modem to be, most respondents replied that they would like the indicator lights to clearly indicate the presence/absence of a connection (67%) and speed (52%). A minor part of users requested the a signal of security problems (36%). Regarding device integration within home environment, the majority of preferences (53%) was for a more pleasant aesthetics. 25% of the sample indicated that they would like the modem router to have other useful functions such as a lamp, radio or clock. 24% indicated that they would like a device capable of being hidden while 18% would not change anything. Even in the open answers, respondents more frequently expressed the need for clearer icons, an indication of speed and the presence of other useful features in the home environment (eg lamp or clock). 28% found it very useful and 21% quite useful to be able to configure the switching of the indicator lights of their device while 26% found it neither useful nor useless. 53% expressed that it would be useful to replace the classic indicator lights with a single coloured one and, of these, 24% specified that they would like to be able to configure the combination between status and colour. Regarding this the Table 3 shows the desired combination between colours and functions. It is possible to find a correspondence with the default matching shown in Table 2. This is probably related to the presence of stronger conventions for states such as on-off and errors on other devices (but, it should be noted, that on many home appliances the red colour is used for stand-by status).

3   Conclusion and Future Works

In this work we wanted to examine in depth the relationship between users and devices which, although often "invisible", represents an enabling element of services and products for the smart home and, more generally, of the Internet of Things in domestic environment. The results of the research show us that the icons currently used by home modems routers have problems of comprehension, are often incorrectly interpreted and, in some cases, are superfluous. The use of standards and clear labelling, as well as symbols, helps in understanding. However, in some cases there is still the lack of standard references, such as in the use of colours for the representation of states. This is also due to the different technologies integrated into these devices (eg mesh networks, bluetooth, voice assistant, etc.). The results indicate that users need a simpler system to understand the modem router states, to solve any problems, but also a more pleasant appearance and, possibly, the addition of other features (e.g. clock, lamp) for a better integration of the device with the aesthetics of the home environment.

This is confirmed also by the new concepts proposed by some big players that show a different communication paradigm based on colours to indicate the status of the modem in a synthetic and aesthetically pleasant way.

Further developments in the work will explore the relationship with the user and the acceptance of new products and services for the smart home. We will investigate especially on how the physical and digital interfaces, of such systems, can help to build up trust between user and service, with particular regard to privacy protection and security.

References

1. Atzori, L., Iera, A., Morabito, G.: Understanding the Internet of Things: definition, potentials, and societal role of a fast evolving paradigm. Ad Hoc Netw. **56**, 122–140 (2017)
2. Leitner, G., Ahlström, D., Hitz, M.: Usability—key factor of future smart home systems. In: Home Informatics and Telematics: ICT for The Next Billion. ITIFIP, vol. 241, pp. 269–278. Springer, Boston, MA (2007). https://doi.org/10.1007/978-0-387-73697-6_20
3. Statista. Smart Home - Statistics and Facts (2020). https://www.statista.com/topics/2430/smart-homes/
4. Moallem, A.: Why should home networking be complicated? Advances in Usability Evaluation: part II. CRC Press (2013)
5. Moallem, A.: Home networking: Smart but complicated. In: Kurosu, M. (ed.) HCI 2014. LNCS, vol. 8512, pp. 731–741. Springer, Cham (2014). https://doi.org/10.1007/978-3-319-07227-2_70
6. Yan, W., Wang, Z., Wang, H., Wang, W., Li, J., Gui, X.: Survey on recent smart gateways for smart home: Systems, technologies, and challenges. Trans. Emerg. Telecommun. Technol. e4067 (2020)
7. Rowland, C., Goodman, E., Charlier, M., Light, A., Lui, A.: Designing Connected Products: UX for the Consumer Internet of Things. O'Reilly Media Inc., Sebastopol (2015)
8. Wobbrock, J.O., Aung, H.H., Rothrock, B., Myers, B.A.: Maximizing the guessability of symbolic input. In CHI 2005 extended abstracts on Human Factors in Computing Systems, pp. 1869–1872 (2005)
9. Hong, A., Nam, C., Kim, S.: What will be the possible barriers to consumers' adoption of smart home services? Telecommun. Policy **44**(2), 101867 (2020)
10. Shin, J., Park, Y., Lee, D.: Who will be smart home users? An analysis of adoption and diffusion of smart homes. Technol. Forecast. Soc. Chang. **134**, 246–253 (2018)
11. Aldossari, M.Q., Sidorova, A.: Consumer acceptance of Internet of Things (IoT): smart home context. J. Comput. Inf. Syst. **60**(6), 507–517 (2020)
12. Grinter, R.E., et al.: The ins and outs of home networking: the case for useful and usable domestic networking. ACM Trans. Comput. Hum. Interact. (TOCHI) **16**(2), 1–28 (2009)
13. Baumann, K.: User interface design of electronic appliances. CRC Press, Boca Raton (2001)

14. Meier, A., Aragon, C., Perry, D., Peffer, T., Pritoni, M., Granderson, J.: Measuring the usability of appliance controls. Lawrence Berkeley National Laboratory (2017). https://escholarship.org/uc/item/2c60m2k1
15. Norman, D.A.: Design principles for cognitive artifacts. Res. Eng. Design **4**, 43–50 (1992)
16. Jakobi, T., et al.: Evolving needs in iot control and accountability: a longitudinal study on smart home intelligibility. Proc. ACM Interact. Mob. Wear. Ubiquit. Technol. **2**(4), 1–28 (2018)
17. https://www.amazon.it/gp/bestsellers/pc/460165031. Accessed 20 Dec 2020
18. Kacmar, C.J., Carey, J.M.: Assessing the usability of icons in user interfaces. Behav. Inf. Technol. **10**(6), 443–457 (1991)
19. https://www.osservatori.net/it/prodotti/formato/video/valore-mercato-smart-home-italia-est ero-video. Accessed 5 Jan 2021

The Smaller the Better? A Study on Acceptance of 3D Display of Exhibits of Museum's Mobile Media

Xinhao Guo, Jingjing Qiao, Ran Yan, Ziyun Wang, and Junjie Chu[(⊠)]

Ocean University of China, Qingdao 266100, China
chujunjie@ouc.edu.cn

Abstract. In the context of the mature development of mobile media and mobile interaction, many museums have built their own mobile media to digitally display their collections, but the user's acceptance of this mobile media is not known. Based on the interactive attributes and information display attributes of the museum's mobile collections, this article has compiled a scale to select the most convincing research object from the 204 national first-class museums in China: the Mini Program of the Palace Museum, Digital Forbidden City, and conduct user acceptance research on the 3D display function of its collections. This research is based on the technology acceptance model, adding new influencing factors to obtain a more accurate model for questionnaire surveys, and using the structural equation model to analyze the data. A total of 200 valid questionnaires were collected in this study. The analysis results revealed some problems with the 3D display function of the museum's mobile collections: high learning costs, poor user interaction experience, and incomplete collection information. The study results have a very novel reference value for museums to improve the 3D display function of the mobile terminal and directly help museums to optimize users' experience of using mobile terminal media.

Keywords: Mobile media · Museum · User experience · TAM

1 Introduction

The museum is a public space for the collection and exhibition of human natural and cultural heritage. Collecting is the basic function of the museum, and exhibition is the way the museum exports culture to society. Alexander believes that as a cultural and educational institution, the purpose of the museum is not only to collect cultural relics but also to serve the society and promote the development of society and itself [1]. The 21st International Council of Museums (ICOM) Congress held in Vienna in 2007 defined museum as: A museum is a non-profit, permanent institution in the service of society and its development, open to the public, which acquires, conserves, researches, communicates, and exhibits the tangible and intangible heritage of humanity and its environment for education, study and enjoyment [2]. For museums, the display of collections is always the most powerful way to output information to society, that is, the information

© Springer Nature Switzerland AG 2021
M. Kurosu (Ed.): HCII 2021, LNCS 12764, pp. 303–324, 2021.
https://doi.org/10.1007/978-3-030-78468-3_21

flow that museums can provide to the public is relatively fixed. YIN Kai (Chinese) sum-marizes this relationship between museums and society as a relatively stable relationship model composed of exhibition planners (producers), exhibitions (products), audiences, or society (consumers) (In Chinese with English Abstract) [3]. Under such a definition and relationship model, museums can only achieve cultural education to the public by changing the way people interact with exhibits, that is, the way museum collections are displayed.

At present, the rapid growth of the amount of social information has led to an increase in people's requirements for information quality. At the same time, they are eager for efficient information acquisition methods and more direct information flow relationships. Corresponding to this is the new interaction of mobile phones and the wide application of new interactive methods under the restriction of media and mobile small screens. Such changes will bring about changes in the mode of Museum knowledge dissemination, that is, the speed, breadth, and depth of knowledge dissemination will be revolutionary improved [4], which makes museums reconsider the way of interaction between exhibits and audiences. And establish a new interactive media to realize the online display of collections to adapt to the current faster-paced information exchange, reduce the cost of users' viewing of the exhibition, and improve the efficiency of users' viewing of the exhibition. To provide users with a satisfactory online experience, it is becoming more and more important to understand the needs of online users [5]. This article aims to obtain user acceptance of the 3D display system of museum mobile collections through voluntary user acceptance surveys, and explore the rationality of current museum mobile interaction.

1.1 Museum Mobile Media

To adapt to the interactive mode of mobile and improve their user stickiness and social influence, most museums build mobile media, put collection information (video, audio, modeling, etc.) in their own official websites or mobile phone applets for the public to more easily watch the collections through mobile phones. Different from the original display mode in which the exhibits are trapped in the display cabinet, mobile media provides a variety of interactive ways between the exhibits and the audience, emphasizing the importance of user experience [3]. The emergence of mobile media in museums has broken the stereotyped impression that the museum is a destination that must be specially planned for time, which is conducive to the realization of the public education significance of the museum. It also makes the exhibition fewer time restrictions and place restrictions, greatly improving the efficiency and freedom of viewing exhibitions. At the same time, touch-screen gesture interaction on mobile media can help museums attract more users by leveraging people's operating habits for touch screens, who are motivated to take action by using familiar touch screens to actively explore exhibits and are eager to discover more [6].

However, how to correctly use gesture interaction under the restriction of a small screen to build a clear interaction structure to meet user needs for exploring exhibit information and other needs (sharing, commenting, etc.) is the problem that museums must solve. At present, the lack of evaluation system and design criteria for its mobile media results in the user experience not being guaranteed, and how acceptable users are to the new interactive system remains a problem to be verified. Joan Beaudoin, in his study of U.S. art museums' online collections, found that little is known about the overall state of online access to U.S. art museum collections, and how users interact and experience with it [7]. These problems confirm the lack of attention to mobile media in museums and illustrate the need for a representative user acceptance survey to reveal possible problems at this stage to attract the attention of museums while providing a possible reference for the improvement of mobile media in museums.

1.2 3D Display

The screen properties of the mobile terminal are naturally adapted to the display of two-dimensional exhibits, but how to effectively interactively display three-dimensional exhibits is a problem that all major museums are solving. The biggest difference between displaying collections in the form of illustrations (2D) and visualization (3D) is that the illustrations (2D) have no data (unless manually input), while visualization (3D) is a fusion of data [8]. The study found that the network People who experience 3D images in the environment also have a greater degree of enjoyment than those who experience traditional 2D images [9]. For museums, the 3D digital display can improve the problem of single display mode in the traditional museum on the one hand, and on the other hand, it can also enrich the exhibition content. Cultural relics, buildings, and archaeological sites that could not be displayed before can be displayed using new technical means., Fully demonstrate the integrity and authenticity of the collection and the diversity of information. Existing three-dimensional display methods can generally be divided into the following three categories: experiential exhibition based on VR technology, experiential exhibition hall based on panoramic texture, and exhibit display interface based on 3D modeling. The three methods give users different degrees of freedom to explore and information integrity, and the interaction structure between collections and users is also different. For a referenceable user acceptance survey, an objective evaluation standard is needed to select a representative research object, and the way of 3D display represented by it is relatively more suitable for the collection display of the Museum mobile media.

2   Research Subjects

2.1   National First-Class Museums in China

China's national first-class museum is the highest level of national museums divided by scores from all domestic museums that meet the standards after the comprehensive meeting of the National Museum Evaluation Committee (in Chinese with English Abstract) [10]. On the evening of December 21, 2020, China Museum Association announced the results of the fourth batch of National Museum grading evaluation, adding 74 national first-class museums, with a total of 204 [11]. To study the development of the 3D display function of Museum mobile terminal collections, this article decided to select the museum with the most complete function, the relatively high social impact, and the relatively high acceptance degree as the representative research object from the 204 national first-class museums recently evaluated.

2.2   Scoring Table

To select representative research objects from 204 first-class museums, we need a complete, objective, and theoretically supported standard system to evaluate. The existing evaluation of Chinese museums can be defined as "operation evaluation", "experience evaluation" and "education evaluation", of which "experience evaluation" only accounts for less than 20% of the total, and the existing experience evaluation is not aimed at the exhibition of Museum mobile media (in Chinese with English Abstract) [12], Antonella Basso's model for Museum evaluation, which combines DEA (the data envelopment analysis), BSc (Balanced Scorecard) and AHP (the analytical hierarchy process) based on previous research, also focuses on the performance of museums [13] but does not involve the analysis of 3D display function of collections. Therefore, we need a complete, objective, and theoretically supported evaluation standard system for this function, which can comprehensively, objectively, and truly reflect the comprehensive strength of the 3D display of collections in museum mobile media. This set of standards shall meet the following requirements:

1. The standard must have corresponding theoretical support, such as the citation of related papers.
2. The standard should be applicable and accurate results of yes or no can be obtained.
3. Standards that all museums meet or do not meet should not be set.
4. The standard system should reflect the comprehensive strength of the museum as a whole
5. Standards need to consider the impact of mobile media, such as different interaction modes

Based on meeting the above requirements and the two basic characteristics of the 3D display of the Museum mobile collection: the interactivity of mobile media and the integrity of collection information given by the display interface, this paper sorts out a scoring table (see Table 1).

Interactive Standards. Such standards refer to a series of standards-based on the inter activity of mobile media. The particularity of the research object makes the interaction model of the mobile terminal have a great impact on user experience. The screen size of the mobile device is limited, so we need to ensure that all the information on the interface is useful and intuitive to meet the needs of users faster. The interaction of mobile terminal is mainly gesturing interaction, so different gesture interaction rules will affect the user's experience of the function. Huiyue Wu classifies user-defined gesture interaction into three dimensions: form, semantics, and kinematics, including click, double click, slide, and other operations [14], which is defined as the basic gesture interaction between user and mobile screen. Although the interaction is still conducted in a 2D environment, the interaction between the user and the collection should be understood as the direct interaction between the user and a 3D object. In this kind of interaction, the multi-touch interaction represented by RST style (multi-touch rotation, scaling, translation) is still a more efficient interaction mode [15]. Besides, the purpose of user interaction is to operate the exhibits and display interface. We combine the basic interaction of gesture interaction, multi-point interaction of 3D objects, characteristic objects, and purposes of interaction, and sort out a series of interactive standards to select research subjects.

Functional Standards. This kind of standard used to measure the collection information integrity given by the display interface is called functional standard, which is directly expressed as the function provided by the display interface to the user. Museums can provide different exhibit information such as cultural relic model, size, audio, and video. The degree of information detail affects the diversity of information interaction between users and exhibits and then affects the user experience. Therefore, the function richness of the Museum mobile collection 3D display system is an important part of screening Museum standards. To measure the information integrity provided by users, we sorted out a series of functional standards for screening.

2.3 Scoring and Confirmation of Research Subjects

All the criteria are scored according to the two-level evaluation of yes or no. If they meet the criteria, one point will be given. Otherwise, zero points. After the scores are added up, the 3D display function of the mobile museum collection with the highest score will become our final research subject. The mobile experience of museums mainly focuses on two platforms: WeChat or the official website, all official websites browsed by Google when scoring. After that, the 3D display interface of the Palace Museum's digital collection is the research subject of this study with the highest score of 13 points. The scoring scale is also appropriately deleted according to the scoring situation. The invalid standards and subjective standards that are not available in all museums are deleted, and the final scoring table is obtained. The following Table 1 gives the score of the Palace Museum (based on the final scoring table).

Table 1. The score of the Palace Museum

The standard of marking	Score	The standard of marking	Score
Exhibits can be rotated at any angle	1	Video information for exhibits	1
Reset on the screen by single finger double-click	1	Exhibits can be rotated and displayed by themselves	1
Drag and drop exhibits with two fingers	1	Provide dimensional data of exhibits	1
Enlarge and shrink exhibits with two fingers stretch and contract	1	Exhibits are measurable in size	0
Control the rotation of light and shadow with three fingers dragging at the same time	1	Provide a virtual presentation environment	1
Voice explanations for exhibits	0	The interaction is guided by navigation	1
Text information for exhibits	1	The interface has forwarding and sharing functions	1
Text information is available in audio version	1		
Aggregate score		**13**	

As the largest museum of ancient culture and art in China, the Palace Museum is the pinnacle of Chinese museums. Its influence and social and cultural output are obvious to all. Social acceptance and public familiarity are also the first. In recent years, the international influence of the Palace Museum has been expanding in the process of holding "forum on the protection of world ancient civilization" for four consecutive times (in Chinese) [16], and it has also actively built its own mobile media applet digital Palace Museum, which has become one of the more complete mobile end media for museums. Therefore, taking the three-dimensional display function of the collection of the digital Palace Museum as the research object, its rationality and representativeness can be verified.

3 Research Model and Hypothesis

To conduct a comprehensive and rigorous user acceptance study to get the public's acceptance and use intention of the 3D display function of the digital Palace Museum app, and analyze the rationality and shortcomings of the current 3D display technology of the museum mobile media, to put forward the reference value for the existing display interface combined with the needs of users exposed in the survey Suggestions. This article will expand the Technology Acceptance Model (TAM), propose a more suitable expansion model with other characteristic factors that affect the public's behavioral intention to use the 3D display function of digital Palace Museum collections, and verify this model to explore the future of 3D display technology of collections in museum mobile media.

3.1 Technology Acceptance Model

In 1986, after the adaptation of the theory of reasoned action (TRA), Davis proposed the technology acceptance model (TAM) [17]. Its basic goal is to provide a reasonable and universal explanation for the factors that determine computer acceptance. This explanation should also be able to explain and predict the user's behavior when operating the computer widely [18]. With the wide application of TAM, it is more likely to be used to measure the determinants of the acceptance of a technology system by users, and in turn to explain the user behavior of consumers of this system in many similar systems and people, while maintaining the simplicity and rationality of the theory [19]. TAM believes that perceived usefulness and perceived ease of use have always been two powerful determinants of behavioral intention to use and external variables indirectly affect behavioral intention to use by influencing the two [20].

Perceived Usefulness and Perceived Ease of Use. As the two most direct factors affecting behavioral intention to use, perceived usefulness is defined as the probability that a user can use a technology system to improve his or her work efficiency in the work organization. Perceived ease of use is defined as the degree to which a user feels that a technology system can be easily used. Whether a system can be easily learned and used for work by users determines whether a user can use this technology system to work and improve work efficiency, so to a large extent, perceived ease of use will have a positive impact on perceived usefulness [18]. For the 3D display function of the Museum mobile collection, perceived usefulness usually refers to the degree that users know what they want through using this function, or that this function improves the efficiency of viewing online exhibition for the audience. Perceived ease of use should be defined as the degree that users can skillfully use this function, and do not lose or misoperate in the use process. Previous studies have found that when users think that technology is easy to use, they tend to accept and use it [21], and when users think that technology can meet their learning or work needs, they are more willing to use it, both of which will affect users' willingness to use the collection display function.

The external variables that affect perceived usefulness are some basic features of the 3D display function of this collection. In Venkatesh's previous research, the factors influencing perceived ease of use were defined as the different variables of users themselves and the basic rules of computer and computer use [22]. These influencing factors in the collection 3D display function are whether the user is familiar with the function, whether he has used the interaction structure with the display interface before, and the interaction mode provided to the user. This study focuses on the collection display interface and does not make too much analysis on the user's own differences. Other influencing factors will be mentioned below. In conclusion, it is hypothesized:

H1. Perceived usefulness has a positive impact on the behavioral intention of Museum mobile collection 3D display function.

H2. Perceived ease of use has a positive impact on the behavioral intention of Museum mobile collection 3D display function.

H3. Perceived ease of use of Museum mobile collection 3D display function has a positive impact on its perceived usefulness.

Perceived Enjoyment. In Davis's previous research, perceived enjoyment is defined as the degree of pleasure users feel about the use of the technology system in addition to the expected work results, and it is found that it is one of the important factors driving users to adopt the technology system [23]. TAM usually needs to be extended to propose a more comprehensive model, and perceived enjoyment is one of the most added structures in the extended TAM [24], which has been verified as an important attribute of technology theory in the past research [25]. It has also been proved that perceived enjoyment can affect the use of computers, the Internet, websites, and mobile applications, and has become an important variable for understanding and adopting new technologies [26]. As a classic mobile application, the 3D display function of Museum mobile collections can bring users a sense of pleasure in the process of use, which will greatly affect the behavioral intention to use. The realization of museum educational significance should also be based on the user's enjoyment of the exhibition process. Therefore, it is hypothesized:

H4: Perceived enjoyment has a positive impact on the behavioral intention of Museum mobile collection 3D display function.

3.2 Common Features of Mobile Media and Cultural Relics Display

Interactivity. Interactivity is defined as the ability of a technology system to allow users to more easily participate in the interaction with content [27]. It is considered as one of the core concepts of mobile digital technology, so it attracts users [28]. For the 3D display of the Museum mobile collection, interactivity refers to the diversity of interaction between users and exhibits in the interface, which is reflected in whether the types of interaction with exhibits are diverse and whether there is a high degree of interaction freedom. Different from reality, the interaction between users and collections, as the interaction in the virtual world, far exceeds the interaction with commercial websites, and the range of user interaction options greatly affects the user experience [27]. The simpler the interaction rules between users and exhibits, the easier it is to be familiar with this function, which is reflected in the perceived ease of use. The more diverse the interaction between users and exhibits, the higher the degree of freedom, the easier it is to meet the needs of exploration for the collection, and the more enjoyable the use process is. Although only users who use this function can generate interaction [26], a well interactive technology system requires the lower cost of user learning and exploration, which makes it easier for users to interact with this technology system efficiently and generate dependence and loyalty [29]. And good interaction will promote users' next use. Therefore, it is hypothesized:

H5: Interacticvity of Museum mobile collection 3D display function has a positive impact on its perceived enjoyment.

H6: Interacticvity of Museum mobile collection 3D display function has a positive impact on its perceived ease of use.

Shareability. Shareability is defined as the ease of sharing the collection's 3D display pages. The addition of this feature is based on the realization of the value of the museum. The core value of the museum is embodied in the collection, and the value of the collection needs to rely on the social sharing and education activities carried out by the museum to reflect and spread (in Chinese with English Abstract) [30]. Andrew J. Pekarik also mentioned in his research that museums provide accommodation for the shared value of cultural relics or geospatial space, and spread it through public exhibitions [31]. Relying on mobile media, user can share exhibits information by sharing a mobile screen or sending exhibition pages to other users, which is more convenient than the traditional offline exhibition. It is conducive to the museum to realize the value and increase the public's information acquisition efficiency, making online exhibition more convenient. Therefore, it is hypothesized:

H7: Shareability of Museum mobile collection 3D display function has a positive impact on its perceived ease of use.

H8: Shareability of Museum mobile collection 3D display function has a positive impact on its perceived usefulness.

3.3 Features Based on the Mobile Media

Mobility. Mobility is proposed as a basic property of mobile media. In previous research, it is defined as the unrestricted degree that the corresponding technology system can be used or accessed at any time and place, and the more users regard this technology system as a mobile technology, the more they will tend to use it [32]. In this study, the technology system refers to the 3D display function of collections in museum mobile media. The mobility of this function, as a basic attribute, allows users to watch exhibitions online at any time and place, which greatly improves the efficiency and convenience of users, enhances the willingness of existing users, and helps museums attract more attention. Therefore, it is hypothesized:

H9: Mobility of Museum mobile collection 3D display function has a positive impact on its perceived enjoyment.

H10: Mobility of Museum mobile collection 3D display function has a positive impact on its perceived ease of use.

H11: Mobility of Museum mobile collection 3D display function has a positive impact on its perceived usefulness.

3.4 Features Based on the Museum Collections Display

Information Quality. Information quality is defined as two aspects: the authenticity of exhibit modeling and the integrity degree of exhibit information. The purpose of 3D modeling of real exhibits is to make up for the lack of real touch through the interaction between users and 3D models [33]. The vividness and authenticity of 3D digital models of exhibits stimulate the formation of the user's sensory perception and psychological image [34]. We recognize it as the museum's efforts to make the display of mobile collections as close to the offline exhibition as possible strive. Users with different needs will have different expectations for the integrity of exhibits information. The higher the integrity, the greater the probability of meeting users' needs, and the higher the overall satisfaction of users. Therefore, it is hypothesized:

H12: Information quality of Museum mobile collection 3D display function has a positive impact on its perceived enjoyment.

Response Time. In the past research, response time was defined as the timeliness of the system responding to the user's information request or operation [35]. Response time was once regarded as a dimension of website interactivity [36]. In this study, when users experience the 3D display function of Museum mobile collection, they will interact directly with the 3d model of exhibits(Rotation, scaling, etc.), so response time can be independent of interactivity and become a significant factor. The response time reflects the sensitivity of the model change and the fit degree with the user's operation. A shorter response time can give the user a better interactive experience, otherwise, it will cause the user's waiting, affect the impression, and at the same time it is easy to bring misoperation. It is a very bad user experience, which is not conducive to the expansion of its influence. Therefore, it is hypothesized:

H13: Response time of Museum mobile collection 3D display function has a positive impact on its perceived enjoyment.

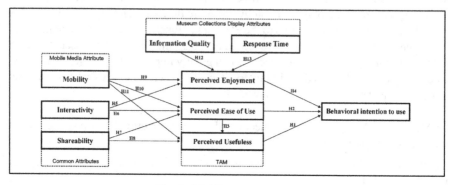

Fig. 1. Mobile-museum TAM

3.5 Research Model

In this study, we add the concept of perceived enjoyment, response time, information quality, interactivity, mobility, and shareability to expand TAM. Based on the two characteristics of the research object (Museum and mobile media), we named it mobile-museum TAM: (mm-TAM). This research is based on mm-TAM to investigate the user acceptance of the 3D display function of the Museum's mobile collection. Figure 1 shows the final research model (mm-TAM) after extending TAM. And Table 2 shows the measurement items corresponding to each factor in the model.

Table 2. Factors and measurement items

Factor	Measurement items
Perceived usefulness	This function will improve the efficiency of my exhibition
	This function is useful for me to understand the exhibits information
	This function makes it easy for me to watch exhibitions online
Perceived ease of use	I can easily use this function very skillfully
	I think this function is clear and easy to understand
	This function is easy to use
	I didn't misoperate in the process of using
	I've never been confused in the process of using this function

(continued)

Table 2. (*continued*)

Factor	Measurement items
Perceived enjoyment	I find it a pleasure to use this function in online exhibition
	I was pleasantly surprised by this feature when viewing the exhibition online
	The user experience of this function is very good
	This function is not boring to use
Response time	When using this function, the delay between operation and response is very small
	I hardly need to wait for the model to load
	I think this function runs smoothly
	I don't feel stuck when I operate the model of the exhibit
Information quality	This function can provide me with the information I want
	This function provides me with multi-mode information display of exhibits (pictures, text, video, etc.)
	The exhibits information (pictures, text, video, etc.) provided by this function is very delicate
	There is almost no difference between the model and the real exhibits
Interactivity	I can interact with this function flexibly and smoothly
	In the process of using, I can easily find the specific information I want
	I interact with the exhibits in various ways
	My interactive feedback with the exhibits is in line with my habits
Mobility	I can watch the exhibits online at any time and place I want
	I can use this function to watch the exhibition online while doing other things
	Watch the exhibition online to reduce the restrictions of time and place on me
Shareability	I can share this page during watching
	I can share through simple operation
	In the use process, I can easily share the exhibits page to other software or mobile media
Behavioral intention to use	Next time I watch the exhibits online, I will choose this function
	If I can continue to use it, I will use it later
	I would like to recommend this function to my friends

4 Data Collection and Analysis

4.1 User Data

This survey was conducted by using online and offline methods to recruit users mainly collects the experience data of undergraduates, educators, people with museum work, or volunteer experience. A total of 288 questionnaires were collected and 200 valid questionnaires were selected. According to the statistical results, the majority of the samples were young people aged 19–25 years (61%), students (66.5%), most of them did not have museum-related work experience (84%). As for the awareness of the museum mobile media, most people are at the stage of having heard (36.5%) and having used (38.5%). The above data show that young people are the majority of the respondents, have experienced a certain number of online visits to the museum, and have a preliminary understanding of the mobile side of the museum. Since most people do not have experience with museums, their attitudes towards the mobile end of museums are more representative of the attitudes of the general public. Generally speaking, the sample of the questionnaire is well represented.

From the result, more than half of users say the interaction and information provided by the display interface is difficult to satisfy when user needs are elicited. The results of the whole questionnaire show that the learning cost of mobile interaction in museums is too high, and there is a significant gap between the interactive experience of users at different levels.

4.2 Data Analysis

This study uses the Likert Five-Point Scale for data analysis. After data collection is completed, we do confirmatory factor analysis (CFA) on the measurement model to obtain a better measurement model through analysis and modification, which facilitates subsequent path analysis and structural equation model validation. The results are shown in Table 3 and Table 4.

Table 3. Parameters of the significant test and reliability

Factor	Items	Estimate	S.E.	Est./S.E..	P-Value	R-square
Perceived usefulness (PU)	PU 1	0.810	0.039	20.930	***	0.656
	PU 2	0.966	0.035	27.979	***	0.933
	PU 3	0.751	0.053	14.182	***	0.564
Perceived ease of use (PEU)	PEU 1	0.762	0.036	21.069	***	0.581
	PEU 2	0.887	0.028	31.445	***	0.787
	PEU 3	0.900	0.024	37.277	***	0.810
	PEU 4	0.672	0.050	13.504	***	0.452
	PEU 5	0.728	0.049	14.761	***	0.530

(continued)

Table 3. (*continued*)

Factor	Items	Estimate	S.E.	Est./S.E..	P-Value	R-square
Perceived enjoyment (PE)	PE 1	0.835	0.034	24.672	***	0.697
	PE 2	0.749	0.042	17.695	***	0.561
	PE 3	0.871	0.027	31.719	***	0.759
	PE 4	0.760	0.052	14.571	***	0.578
Response time (RT)	RT 1	0.811	0.035	23.161	***	0.658
	RT 2	0.819	0.036	22.896	***	0.671
	RT 3	0.901	0.024	38.126	***	0.812
	RT 4	0.748	0.045	16.476	***	0.560
Information quality (IQU)	IQU 1	0.675	0.051	13.302	***	0.456
	IQU 2	0.815	0.038	21.433	***	0.664
	IQU 3	0.894	0.026	33.833	***	0.799
	IQU 4	0.670	0.054	12.325	***	0.449
Interactivity (IN)	IN 1	0.733	0.037	19.561	***	0.537
	IN 2	0.812	0.030	26.697	***	0.659
	IN 3	0.916	0.023	40.686	***	0.839
	IN 4	0.730	0.038	19.388	***	0.533
Mobility (MO)	MO 1	0.818	0.052	15.793	***	0.669
	MO 2	0.680	0.054	12.588	***	0.462
	MO 3	0.676	0.054	12.474	***	0.457
Shareability (SH)	SH 1	0.828	0.029	28.709	***	0.686
	SH 2	0.912	0.023	38.897	***	0.832
	SH 3	0.828	0.029	28.749	***	0.686
Behavioral intention to use (BI)	BI 1	0.875	0.022	40.477	***	0.766
	BI 2	0.954	0.016	58.034	***	0.910
	BI 3	0.837	0.025	33.376	***	0.701

***P-Value < 0.001

An Estimate of more than 0.6 is acceptable for an item in a dimension, and an Estimate of more than 0.7 is ideal. The standardized estimating coefficients for each topic in Table 1 are all greater than 0.6, most of which is greater than 0.7, proving that the recommended standards have been met. Significance Estimation Divided by Standard Error (S.E.) yields a significant Z-Value (Est. /S.E.), greater than 1.96 indicates a significant presence, and P-Value < 0.05 indicates a significant presence. The Z-Value of each topic in Table 1 is greater than 1.96. The P-VALUE values are less than 0.001, which means that all measures are significant. Item reliability is the dimension's ability to interpret the items. Its judgment index is the square of standardized estimate (R-Square). More than 0.36 statements are acceptable. More than 0.5 statements have good item reliability. R-Square values in Table 3 are all greater than 0.36, most of them are greater than 0.5, proving that title reliability is up to standard, and most of them have good title reliability.

Table 4. Composite reliability, convergence validity, and discriminate validity

	CR	AVE	PU	PEU	PE	RT	IQU	IN	MO	SH	BI
PU	0.883	0.718	**0.847**								
PEU	0.894	0.632	0.595	**0.795**							
PE	0.880	0.649	0.670	0.606	**0.806**						
RT	0.892	0.675	0.423	0.575	0.629	**0.822**					
IQU	0.851	0.592	0.544	0.603	0.689	0.572	**0.769**				
IN	0.877	0.642	0.458	0.812	0.661	0.631	0.706	**0.801**			
MO	0.770	0.530	0.804	0.591	0.538	0.401	0.444	0.408	**0.728**		
SH	0.892	0.734	0.378	0.527	0.519	0.412	0.527	0.545	0.247	**0.857**	
BI	0.919	0.792	0.677	0.557	0.887	0.501	0.603	0.528	0.514	0.464	**0.890**

The Composite Reliability of the item in the component reliability dimension, with CR greater than 0.7, indicates that the component reliability is ideal. The CR values in Table 4 are all greater than 0.7, indicating that the reliability of composition is good. AVE is the average variance extraction quantity, which refers to the average explanatory power of the dimension to the topic. The higher AVE, the stronger the average explanatory power of the dimension to the topic. AVE > 0.5 indicates that the dimension has good explanatory power, greater than 0.36 indicates acceptable explanatory power, all dimensions in Table 4 meet the recommended standards and have good explanatory power. For discriminatory validity analysis, the reliability and convergence validity of Table 4 are both greater than 0.7 and 0.5. Based on the suggestions of Fornell, C. and Larcker, D.F., the difference validity AVE has a diagonal root sign value and the lower triangle is the Pearson correlation coefficient between dimensions. If the AVE root sign value is larger than the Pearson correlation coefficient of the corresponding dimension rows and columns, the difference validity between dimensions is good. After comparison, it is found that most of the open-root values of the dimensions are larger than the corresponding Pearson correlation coefficients, and a few are smaller than but still within the acceptable range, so there is a certain degree of difference validity between the dimensions.

Table 5 shows the goodness of fit of the model, each index meets the recommended value, indicating that the model fits well and can be used for subsequent research model hypothesis analysis. Table 6 shows the establishment of the study model hypothesis, P-Value < 0.05 indicates that the influence between dimensions is significant, that is, the hypothesis is valid. As shown in Table 6, there are 13 hypotheses in the model, 11 of which are valid and 2 of which are not: perceived ease of use affects perceived usefulness, and perceived ease of use affects behavioral intention to use.

Table 5. Model fitting degree

	Recommended value	Index	
χ^2/df	$1 < \chi^2$/df < 3	1.701	Matched
CFI	>0.9	0.918	Matched
TLI	>0.9	0.909	Matched
RMSEA	<0.08	0.059	Matched
SRMR	<0.08	0.063	Matched

The MLM method in Mplus is used to analyze.

Table 6. Hypothesis analysis

DV	IV		Est./S.E.	P-value	R^2	Hypothesis
BI	PU	Perceived usefulness - Behavioral intention to use	3.580	***	0.783	Support
	PEU	Perceived ease of use - Behavioral intention to use	18.195	***		Support
	PE	Perceived enjoyment - Behavioral intention to use	$-$ 0.575	0.565		Not Support
PU	SH	Shareability - Perceived usefulness	2.741	0.006	0.732	Support
	MO	Mobility - Perceived usefulness	13.604	***		Support
	PEU	Perceived ease of use - Perceived usefulness	1.083	0.279		Not Support
PEU	MO	Mobility - Perceived ease of use	6.255	***	0.739	Support
	IN	Interactivity - Perceived ease of use	12.985	***		Support
	SH	Shareability - Perceived ease of use	2.083	0.037		Support
PE	MO	Mobility - Perceived enjoyment	4.899	***	0.626	Support
	IQU	Information quality - Perceived enjoyment	4.644	***		Support
	RT	Response time - Perceived enjoyment	3.335	0.001		Support
	IN	Interactivity - Perceived enjoyment	2.638	0.008		Support

*** P-Value < 0.001

Explore the reasons why the hypothesis is not valid, from the user level, it is shown that some people think this function is easy to use, but they are not interested in viewing exhibits online. And some people find this not very useful, but they are interested in enjoying the display. These two types of users are mostly represented by ordinary users, which confirms that different levels of demand for different users are different. From the perspective of the research subject, we propose a hypothesis: the 3D display functional interface has the following characteristics: small size, concentrated function, and few levels of interaction. Factors such as interactivity, information quality, and response time have fully summarized the characteristics of the study subjects. Perceived ease of use is a very general factor. It is more appropriate for a complete system or app to talk about ease of use, while for such small-scale and few-level subjects, it seems that there is no need to process perceived ease of use. Based on this hypothesis, we believe that such results are acceptable. Besides, a previous study by Venkatesh and Bala suggested that the impact of perceived ease of use on behavioral intention to use will be moderated by experience. As experience increases during multiple uses, users become more familiar with functional systems and develop usage habits. Once more knowledge of the system is acquired, the impact of perceived ease of use on behavioral intention to use disappears [25]. Based on this theory, we guess that in the process of experience, to allow users to fully experience the function, we set the task to require users to observe multiple exhibits, which is equivalent to using the function system several times. After experience is gradually generated, users become familiar with such a small and interactive functional system and fully understand how to use it. The effect of perceived ease of use on behavioral intention to use is no longer significant.

5 Conclusion and Limitations

5.1 Research Conclusions

This study on the acceptance of users of the 3D display of mobile collections in Museums Based on the digital Palace Museum applet exposes the current lack of attention of museums to their own mobile media construction, which is manifested as ordinary users will obviously show more difficult to adapt than expert users. For all users, the current 3D display of mobile collections has a single interactive mode, an unnatural user interaction process, and insufficient information provided by the museum. This lack of attention to user experience has brought the current development of museum mobile media into a vacuum. It is necessary to make corresponding improvements in response to user needs and expectations. The results highlight the characteristics of this functional system, such as small volume, concentrated functions and few interaction levels, which provide a possible direction for future design improvements. This study also makes the needs of users clearer, the users can be divided into three main categories: professional scholars, hobbyists, and general audience. For the latter two types of users with higher demand for mobile media, our improvement should be to reduce the learning cost of the functional system and enhance the interactive feedback to enhance the user experience. Combining features of the functional system with users themselves, and considering that improvements will be limited by the permissions of the exhibit information provided by the museum, possible improvements will focus on simple page operation guidelines, interactive optimization, and fast operation.

Operational Guidelines: An interface with concentrated functions but few interaction levels requires clear interaction guidance so that users are not confused when interacting with the collections or exploring other information about the exhibit and can reduce user misoperation. When the user enters the display interface, an interactive guide page pops up and can be simplified to an icon that is called out whenever the user needs it.

Interactive optimization: In this interface, the user is directly in contact with collections. Therefore, improvements can be made in the following ways: more timely interaction and feedback, more in line with daily operation logic, more freedom of interaction, more diverse feedback, and so on, which can better arouse users' desire to explore.

Quick operation: When users view exhibits, they often need some automated built-in operation to make their interaction clearer and get information faster. Therefore, it is recommended to set up shortcut functions such as auto-rotation, one-click restore, etc. so that users can have more choices in the exploration process and not get lost.

In addition to the improvements to existing functions, we can also add new features with social attributes based on the realization of Museum value, such as setting up a commentary area on the display interface, allowing users to express their opinions and participate in discussions, or increasing poster sharing for individual exhibits, reducing sharing costs and expanding influence. These are the improvements which combines the social nature of most mobile apps with the cultural and educational significance of museums and the social dissemination properties of museums. They can help museums realize their own cultural and educational significance online.

5.2 Limitations

This study clarifies the basic needs of the museum audience for the 3D display function of mobile collections and has novel reference value and clear improvement direction for the optimization of the function system. The limitation of this study is that we are affected by the epidemic situation, which makes us focus on college students and educators when recruiting subjects. Although these two types of users constitute the majority of museum audiences, based on the value of cultural education for the public, museums should focus on the user experience in all aspects of society and clarify the special needs of different types of users to make more universal improvements.

Acknowledgement. We would like to express our deepest gratitude for this study is supported by the 2021 Student Research Developing Program of the Ocean University of China (OUC-SRDP).

Appendix. The Scores of All National First-Class Museums with the 3D Display Function of Mobile Media Collections.

Museum	Score	Museum	Score	Museum	Score
The Palace Museum	13	Henan Museum	6	Chifeng Museum	5
Hebei Museum	11	The Shenyang Palace Museum	6	Wuxi Museum	5
Qinghai Province Museum	11	Changzhou Museum	6	Lushan Museum	5

(continued)

(*continued*)

Museum	Score	Museum	Score	Museum	Score
Palace Museum of the Manchurian Regime	10	Guangdong Folk Arts Museum	6	National Museum of Chinese Writing	5
Luoyang Museum	9	Chifeng Museum	6	Ganzhou Museum	5
Nantong Museum	9	Suizhou Museum	6	Zhangqiu District Museum, Jinan City	5
Weifang Museum	8	The Military Museum of the Chinese People's Revolution	5	Changsha Museum	5
Capital Museum,China	8	Liaoning Provincial Museum	5	Guangzhou Museum of Art	5
Sanxingdui Museum	8	Hubei Provincial Museum	5	Yunnan Provincial Museum	4
Dalian Natural History Museum	8	Wuhan Museum	5	Yunnan Nationalities Museum	4
Heilongjiang Provincial Museum of Nationalities	8	Tibet Museum	5	Tianjin Museum	4
Anhui Museum	7	Quanzhou Maritime Museum	5	Xibaipo Museum	4
National Museum of China	7	Han Yangling Museum	5	Chengdu Wuhou Shrine Museum	4
Xuzhou Museum	7	Shenzhen Museum	5	China Museum for Fujian-Taiwan Kinship	4
Linyi Museum	7	Jinsha Site Museum	5	The Guyuan Museum of Ningxia	4
China (Hainan) Museum of the South China Sea	7	Xi'an Museum	5	Ningxia Museum	4
Chongqing China Three Gorges Museum (Chongqing Museum)	6	Chen Yun Memorial	5	Ningbo Museum	4
Jiangxi Provincial Museum	6	Nanjing Museum Administration	5	China National Silk Museum	4
Qingdao Municipal Museum	6	Wenzhou Museum	5	Jinggangshan Revolution Museum	4
Shanxi Museum	6	Wuhan Zhongshan Warship Museum	5	Chongqing Hongyan Revolution History Museum	4

(*continued*)

(*continued*)

Museum	Score	Museum	Score	Museum	Score
Shaanxi History Museum	4	Zhejiang Provincial Museum	3	Dalian Modern Museum	2
Emperor Qinshihuang's Mausoleum Site Museum	4	Emperor Qinshihuang's Mausoleum Site Museum	3	Anthropology Museum of Guangxi	2
Hunan Museum	4	Prince Kung's Mansion	3	Linfen Museum	2
Central Soviet Area (MinXi) history Museum	4	Hangzhou Museum	3	Longhua Martyr Cemetery of Shanghai	2
Beijing Auto Museum	4	China Huizhou Culture Museum	3	Imperial Examination Museum of China	2
Yuhuatai Martyrs Memorial Hall	4	Chongqing Museum of Natural History	3	Ningbo Tianyige Museum	2
Wuxi Museum	4	China National Film Museum	3	Zhoushan Museum	2
Changshu Museum	4	Shanxi Museum of Geology	3	Qi Heritage Museum	2
China National Tea Museum	4	China National Tea Museum	3	Jinan City Museum	2
Hangzhou Arts and Crafts Museum	4	Revolutionary Memorial Hall of South Lake	3	Chengdu Museum	2
Ningbo Tianyige Museum	4	Anhui Geological Museum	3	Comrade Zhu De's Former Residence Memorial	2
China Port Museum	4	Badashanren Memorial Hall	3	Guizhou Provincial Museum	2
Tengzhou Museum of Han Carved Stones	4	Jingdezhen China Ceramics Museum	3	Tso-Ngon(Qinghai) Tibetan Culture Museum	2
Pingdingshan Museum	4	Confucius Museum	3	Zunyi Conference Memorial Hall	1
5·12 Wenchuan Earthquake Memorial Museum	4	Anyang Museum	3	The Memorial Hall of the Victims in Nanjing Massacre by Japanese Invaders	1
Suzhou Museum (Jiangsu)	4	Wuhan Revolutionary Museum	3	Shandong Museum	1

(*continued*)

(*continued*)

Museum	Score	Museum	Score	Museum	Score
Dunhuang Academy	3	The Opium War Museum	3	Shanghai Science and Technology Museum	1
Zhengzhou Museum	3	Guilin Museum	3	Zhejiang Museum of Natural History	1
Beijing Luxun Museum and the New Cultural Movement Memorial of Beijing	3	Jianchuan Museum	3	Ruijin Central Revolutionary Base Memorial Hall	1
Lvshun Museum	3	Crossing the Chishui River Four Times Memorial	3	Nanchang August 1st Memorial Hall	1
The Museum of the Nanyue King of Western Han Dynasty	3	Taihang Memorial Museum of the Eighth Route Army	2	Gansu Provincial Museum	1
The Museum of Dr.Sun Yat-sen	3	Liaoning Provincial Museum	2	Zigong Salt Making Industry History Museum	1
The 9.18 Historial Museum	3	Beijing Planetarium	2	Tianshui Museum	1
Site of the first National Congress of the Communist Party of China	3	Zigong Dinosaur Museum	2	Museum of the War of the Chinese People's Resistance Against Japanese Aggression	1
Fujian Museum	3	Northeast China Revolutionary Martyrs Memorial Hall	2	Tsinghua University Art Museum	1
Qingzhou Museum	3	Forest of Stone Steles Museum	2	Peking-Tianjin Campaign Memorial Museum	1
Jilin Provincal Museum	3	Museum of Heilongjiang Province	2	Chongqing Three Gorges Immigrant Memorial Hall (Chongqing Wanzhou District Museum)	1
Tianjin Natural History Museum	3	Shaanxi History Museum	2		
Shanghai Museum	3	Ordos Museum	2		

References

1. Alexander, E.: Museums in Motion: An Introduction to the History and Functions of Museums (1979)
2. Zheng, Y.: Research on Museum Educational Activities. Fudan University (2012)
3. Yin, K.: The principle of changing: discussion on the history and functions of museums; a review. In: Museums in Motion: An Introduction to the History and Functions of Museums. Southeast Culture (03) 114–119 (2015)
4. Qi, Q.: Relationship between digital construction and improvement of social service capacity of museums. In: Beijing Association of Science and Technology Information Center, Beijing Digital Science Popularization Association (eds.) Creative Technology Assisted Digital Museum, pp.68–74. Communication University of China Press (2011)
5. Villaespesa, E.: Museum collections and online users: development of a segmentation model for the metropolitan museum of art. Visit. Stud. **22**(2), 233–252 (2019)
6. de Vet, M., van Kregten, J.: Touch van gogh and be touched – how new media are transforming the way we present complex research. In: MW2014: Museums and the Web 2014, 31 January 2014.https://mw2014.museumsandtheweb.com/paper/touch-van-gogh-and-be-touched-how-new-media-are-transforming-the-way-we-present-complex-research/. Accessed 3 Feb 2021
7. Beaudoin, J.: Art museum collections online: extending their reach. In: MW20: MW 2020, 15 January 2020. https://mw20.museweb.net/paper/art-museum-collections-online-extending-their-reach/. Accessed 9 Feb 2021
8. McNulty, R.: The value of a 3D asset and the future of museums of costume. In: MW20: MW 2020, 17 February 2020. https://mw20.museweb.net/paper/the-value-of-a-3d-asset-and-the-future-of-museums-of-costume/. Accessed 3 Feb 2021
9. Yim, M.Y.C., Drumwright, M., Cicchirillo, V.: How advertising works in new media: Consumer media experience model. In: Proceedings of American Marketing Association at its Annual Summer Marketing Educators' Conference, Chicago, IL (2012)
10. Yu, M.: Research on the Operation Evaluation of National First-class Museum. Northwestern University (2019)
11. Announcement on the List of the Fourth Batch of National First, Second and Third Class Museums. http://www.chinamuseum.org.cn/a/xiehuigonggao/20201221/13535.html. Accessed 21 Dec 2020
12. Zhao, X.: The development and tendency of museum visitor studies in China—based on the perspective of visitor research, evaluation, theory and method. J. Nat. Sci. Museum Res. **5**(04), 20–30+94 (2020)
13. Basso, A., Funari, S.: A three-system approach that integrates DEA, BSC, and AHP for museum evaluation. Decis. Econ. Finan. 1–29 (2020). https://doi.org/10.1007/s10203-020-00298-4
14. Wu, H.: User-defined gestures for dual-screen mobile interaction. Int. J. Hum. Comput. Interact. **36**(10), 978–992 (2020)
15. Wobbrock, J.O.: User-defined gestures for surface computing. In: Proceedings of the SIGCHI Conference on Human Factors in Computing Systems (CHI 2009), pp. 1083–1092. Association for Computing Machinery, New York (2009)
16. Yan, H.: Inheritance and exploration of the world cultural heritage and conservation site of the palace museum. Dunhuang Res. (06), 9–10 (2020)
17. Davis, F.D.: The technology acceptance model for empirically testing new end-user information systems: theory and results. Ph.D. thesis. Ph.d. dissertation Massachusetts Institute of Technology (1986)

18. Davis, F.D.: User acceptance of computer technology: a comparison of two theoretical models. Manag. Sci. **35**(8), 982–1003 (1989)
19. Manis, K.T.: The virtual reality hardware acceptance model (VR-HAM): Extending and individuating the technology acceptance model (TAM) for virtual reality hardware. J. Bus. Res. **100**, 503–513 (2019)
20. Venkatesh, V.: A theoretical extension of the technology acceptance model: four longitudinal field studies. Manag. Sci. **46**(2), 186–204 (2000)
21. Chatzoglou, P.D.: Investigating Greek employees' intention to use web-based training. Comput. Educ. **53**(3), 877–889 (2009)
22. Venkatesh, V.: Determinants of perceived ease of use: integrating control, intrinsic motivation, and emotion into the technology acceptance model. Inf. Syst. Res. **11**(4), 342–365 (2000)
23. Davis, F.D.: Extrinsic and intrinsic motivation to use computers in the workplace1. J. Appl. Soc. Psychol. **22**(14), 1111–1132 (1992)
24. Pantano, E.: Enhancing the online decision-making process by using augmented reality: a two country comparison of youth markets. J. Retail. Consum. Serv. **38**, 81–95 (2017)
25. Venkatesh, V.: Technology acceptance model 3 and a research agenda on interventions. Decis. Sci. **39**(2), 273–315 (2008)
26. McLean, G.: Shopping in the digital world: examining customer engagement through augmented reality mobile applications. Comput. Hum. Behav. **101**, 210–224 (2019)
27. Hoffman, D.L.: Flow online: lessons learned and future prospects. J. Interact. Mark. **23**(1), 23–34 (2009)
28. Javornik, A.: Augmented reality: research agenda for studying the impact of its media characteristics on consumer behaviour. J. Retail. Consum. Serv. **30**, 252–261 (2016)
29. Ratchford, B.T.: Online pricing: review and directions for research. J. Interact. Mark. **23**(1), 82–90 (2009)
30. Yana, C.: People-oriented and object-centered—what collections mean for a museum's social functions. Res. Nat. Hist. Museum **4**(00), 103–109 (2017)
31. Pekarik, A.J.: The long horizon: the shared value of museums. Curator Museum J. **54**(1), 75–78 (2011)
32. Merhi, M.I.: Factors influencing higher education students to adopt podcast: an empirical study. Comput. Educ. **83**, 32–43 (2015)
33. Raed, a.: Using authentic 3D product visualisation for an electrical online retailer. J. Custom. Behav. **9**(2), 97–115 (2010)
34. Cheng, L.-K., Chieng, M.-H., Chieng, W.-H.: Measuring virtual experience in a three-dimensional virtual reality interactive simulator environment: a structural equation modeling approach. Virtual Real. **18**(3), 173–188 (2014). https://doi.org/10.1007/s10055-014-0244-2
35. Wixom, B.H.: A theoretical integration of user satisfaction and technology acceptance. Inf. Syst. Res. **16**(1), 85–102 (2005)
36. Wu, G.: Conceptualizing and measuring the perceived interactivity of websites. J. Curr. Issues Res. Adv. **28**(1), 87–104 (2012)

Research on Information Visualization Design for Public Health Security Emergencies

Wenkui Jin[1](✉), Xurong Shan[1], and Ke Ma[2]

[1] School of Furniture and Industrial Design, Nanjing Forestry University, Xuanwu Area,
Nanjing 210037, China
[2] School of Design, Hunan University, Yuelu Area, Changsha 410082, China

Abstract. Information visualization design is closely related to statistics, computer science, visual image design and other scientific fields and professions, and is used to provide the public with epidemic prevention and health information during the epidemic. Relevant data and information are provided by health, industry and information technology, transportation, customs, immigration management, civil aviation, railway, etc. The purpose is to analyze various information visualization cases for public health emergencies and how to convey information to the public. We analyze how to deal with the three user elements of user participation subject, user cognitive psychology and user interaction behavior in the excellent information visualization design cases. Combined with the above analysis, the development of the epidemic situation can be presented in a rich and intuitive way, so that the public can understand the transmission route of the epidemic and the number of cases, and the public will have less panic about it. At the same time, the correlation between data should be mined to help the audience to establish an effective logical thinking in the face of massive information. Moreover, attention should also be paid to the different ways of information visualization to bring different psychological feelings to the viewers. Through these three approaches, the effect of information visualization in public security emergencies in the era of big data can be improved, and the information of public health emergencies can be more accurately and dynamically controlled, which is conducive to improving the ability of relevant organizations to predict and respond to public health emergencies.

Keywords: Public health security emergencies · Information visualization · Epidemics

1 Introduction

In recent years, along with the rapid economic and social development, the scale of urban modernization has been increasing, and metropolitan areas gather more people than ever before. As a result, the extent and scope of disaster events affecting cities' normal functioning have increased. It tests the response capacity of global metropolitan areas facing public health emergencies [1].

© Springer Nature Switzerland AG 2021
M. Kurosu (Ed.): HCII 2021, LNCS 12764, pp. 325–336, 2021.
https://doi.org/10.1007/978-3-030-78468-3_22

Since 2020, the impact of the epidemic on people's production and life has swept almost the whole world during the public health crisis of coronavirus. Although the form of excellent visual visualization designs are different around the world in the face of epidemic prevention and control, they have similar design purposes and information visualization principles. After the sudden outbreak of the new crown epidemic [2], people can openly access and interact with a large amount of data through the daily release of domestic and international epidemic data by media and institutions [3]. Intuitive and clear visualization of information presentation can effectively help the public understand the development of the epidemic situation and establish a correct knowledge of the coronavirus. At the societal level, it would be beneficial to strengthen the population's psychological construction to face the epidemic [4]. Through horizontal comparison and cluster analysis of a large number of information visualization design cases that emerged during the epidemic period, it will be helpful to find and summarize the operation mechanism and application methods of information visualization of the epidemic.

2 Background

Information visualization design is a means of visual expression that enhances people's cognitive abilities by studying abstract data's visual representation [5]. It is highly interdisciplinary and involves knowledge from several specialized fields such as statistics, computer science, and visual image design [6]. It is one of the effective ways for non-expert users to navigate data and share information. The core of information visualization design lies in the use of visual techniques for data narrative [7]. Designers need to thoroughly consider user needs, determine the best format for organizing information and what visual elements to use to improve usability [8]. In this way, information and developments are presented in an intuitive and efficient way, helping users to establish effective logical thinking before the mass of information [9].

With technological progress, the accuracy of data collection and processing has dramatically improved. In academic research and business practice, information visualization is defined as "an effective means of using the extensive information channels of human perception system to transmit large amounts of data" (Thomas & Cook 2005). With the help of information visualization, people can obtain, understand and explore data more efficiently and conveniently in daily life [10]. Additionally, they can achieve a higher quality of life through data and obtain an excellent user experience [11].

In the process of epidemic prevention, information visualization tools can help users compare different numerical values, track data trends and understand different relationships between variables [12]. Typical forms of visualization include heat maps, column chart, scatter plots, and chord diagrams. Relevant data are provided by transportation, health, customs, and other institutions. They are widely used in transportation such as airports, railway stations, buses, subways, taxis, and public places such as communities, shopping malls, office buildings, and parks.

Many well-known information visualization cases in history are related to infectious diseases. For instance, the John Snow Cholera Map is an early classic visual point map (Fig. 1). It used small bars to mark the number of cholera deaths in every household in the city block near London, and then judged the specific city block set based on the density and length of the bar graph. The designer wondered why the death trend was higher in one place than in other places through the information visualization. The survey results indicated that the families with the worst cholera all used the same well to drink water. It was a breakthrough discovery at that time and provided a useful reference for the prevention and control of the spread of cholera in the future. This visualization is considered successful mainly because it reveals the root cause of cholera and inspires solutions to prevent cholera spread [13].

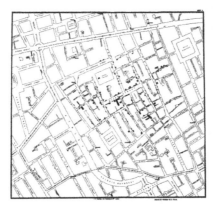

Fig. 1. Broad 1854 Street cholera outbreak

Accordingly, it follows that a successful visualization needs to clarify the specific requirements of four dimensions. First, define the design theme and clearly express the data and information; Secondly, the concept is vividly depicted through readable and interesting visual means; Then, select a reasonable visualization to meet the goal; Finally, highlight key elements in the design and structure.

Information visualization is becoming more and more popular today. Advanced tools and technologies allow for better interactive functionality and enhanced user experience [14]. Through the use of computers and mobile devices, people can drill down into the charts' details, manipulate and process data in real-time in an interactive way. It allows even common users to view topics of interest from different perspectives and access data information more easily.

3   Research Methods

After an emergency public health security incident occurs, it is necessary to sort out and construct a large amount of information reasonably, build an information model that can realize high-speed dissemination, in order to meet most people's psychological needs in the big data era. We analyze the information visualization design for public health emergencies from three aspects: user participation subject, user cognitive psychology, and user interaction behavior.

3.1   User Participation Subject

Stakeholders. The data sources for information visualization of public health and safety emergencies are relatively broad. Among them, overseas data sources include the Centers for Disease Control and Prevention, the World Health Organization, official notifications from national (regional) government health departments and authoritative media reports. Domestic data mainly come from national and local health commissions and research groups.

Stakeholders can be divided into three main categories: Government-centered coordinating body; Information subject with hospitals, CDC and other departments as the core; Information processing subject with multiple parties involved. With the development of the Internet and information technology, public safety and health information has shifted from "one-way communication" to "multi-directional communication." Stakeholders such as non-governmental organizations, media, self-media, and the public have also expanded the depth and breadth of public health safety information dissemination. In the construction of information and data visualization. On the one hand, the person in charge should fully collect, analyze and utilize the information of these groups, and encourage them to take the initiative. On the other hand, it is necessary to do an excellent job of management and positive guidance to maintain social stability and enhance public confidence. For the information collected through different channels, corresponding technical means should be adopted for information collection, such as data collection and text analysis.

Audience. Due to their different cognitive ability and understanding, users will actively choose different ways to obtain information. As a consequence, their initiative to obtain information and demand for information visualization also differ. According to these characteristics, the information audience mainly comprises three types of users: general users, interested users and professional users.

The general public's basic needs for information during an epidemic mainly include a scientific introduction, epidemic facts, and policy propaganda. A clear and intuitive presentation of information can enable people to understand and access the information they need quickly. When designing information visualization for general users, designers need to consider the information's accuracy and immediacy fully. Besides, they need to avoid inappropriate representation triggers ambiguity among users, which may cause negative emotions such as panic and anxiety among people. Proper nouns and unique concepts should be explained to avoid the cognitive bias of users.

Desire drive interested users, but they have less knowledge of information visualization than professional users. Driven by their interest in visualization, they actively search for information related to data visualization [15]. They usually have a certain knowledge reserve and are willing to spend more time exploring and analyzing data visualization content to obtain the required information. With the continuation of the epidemic, attention to the epidemic data should consider not only increments and increases, but also the addition of provinces as a dimension. Besides, long-term and high-density epidemic information bombardment can easily make people feel numb to the data. Therefore, the simplified presentation of epidemic information and data can make complex data more concise and understandable, so that it is easy to arouse users' interest in the experience. A visualization research team developed the epidemic change barometer by Peking University (Fig. 2). The data include the daily number of new confirmed cases for each province in China and each city in Hubei. The pixel visualization represents the number of new confirmed cases per day. The square area and color respectively symbolize the specific number and the increase or decrease of new cases from the previous day. This innovative visualization method not only provides a clear picture of the epidemic situation over time, but also allows for direct comparison. The use of small squares with different colors makes it easy for users to identify information related to changes in the epidemic, minimizing the difficulty of understanding and making it more intuitive and efficient.

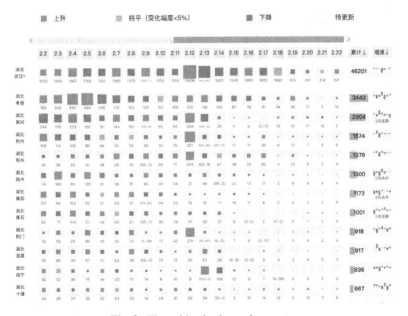

Fig. 2. The epidemic change barometer

Professional users mainly include managers of epidemic prevention and related government departments, data analysts, doctors, and other companies and social organizations closely related to epidemic prevention. This group has a high demand for information visualization. Information visualization is beneficial for them to explore data on the interactive information visualization. Users can get answers faster by querying and exploring data independently, which helps democratize access to data without waiting for data experts. Through exploration, users can find possible relationships in the data and make better decisions based on the data. Viewing data from different perspectives may inspire users to generate new ideas or concepts, enhancing their autonomous creativity.

3.2 User Cognitive Psychology

Gestalt Psychology. It values the holistic nature of experience and behavior. The theory holds the view that the whole is not equal to the sum of its parts. Moreover, the eye-brain action is the continuous process of organizing, simplifying, and unifying, which produces a harmonious and easy-to-understand whole. In the process of information visualization design, it is necessary to use the reorganization and expression of graphics, in order to influence the user's mental cognition and perception in receiving visual information. In this process, as a whole or apart, graphic elements have a significant role in the human receiving and understanding information. Therefore, the principles of Gestalt psychology can be used in the analysis and design of information visualization.

Take the analysis of novel coronavirus as an example (Fig. 3). The designers analyzed the generation process, transmission route, infection symptoms, and virus comparison of COVID-19. As an information visualization design of the epidemic, information presentation is the main body, which graphic should be perceptual. It requires highlighting the central part's characteristics so that it should have a clear outline, lightness and darkness, and unity. The background uses a clean and straightforward light blue pattern in this visualization design, while the graphics are mainly in gray. As a consequence, the focus of this visualization design is prominent, and the content is exact. The first part is the main content, using biological illustrations with text to explain the infection process and dissect the virus structure. Symmetry gives a sense of solidity and order, so that people usually give higher visual priority to the centrally symmetrical shape of a homogeneous object. In this case, the author chose a centrally symmetrical figure as the subject, giving a sense of balance and order. As a result, the viewer's eyes are focused on the main content that the author wants to convey. In addition, it is worth mentioning that the functional partitioning mainly reflects the principle of similarity. People tend to combine things with common characteristics and treat them as a whole, such as shape, movement, direction, color, size and others. The remainder is divided by the designer into two major parts, with each smaller part using the same style matrix, composition and color scheme. Such a design naturally divides the functional areas with clarity and clarity.

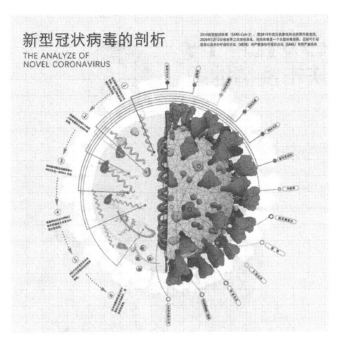

Fig. 3. The analyze of novel coronavirus (Designed by Xiangqiu LIN, Jie WANG) (Color figure online)

Visual Encoding. Visual encoding mainly refers to the establishment of mapping relations between the meanings of numbers and different visual representation attributes of graphics, and realizes the perception and understanding of visualization through visual channels [16].

This information visualization design focuses on the infection of the COVID-19 in Chongqing (Fig. 4), which uses Chongqing's map as a carrier for visualization. By constructing visual variables such as color, size, height and saturation of design elements on the map, the epidemic's location and extent can be intuitively expressed. Through the visual coding, the use of high expressive visual channel for more important data coding, improve the accuracy, differentiation, separation of visual channel encoded information, make its visual prominent.

3.3 User Interaction Behavior

Immediate Feedback. Immediate feedback means that when the user continues to input, the related output is visible simultaneously—for example, display data on mouse hover. It is a heat map of the COVID-19 risk level designed by the center for systems science and engineering at Johns Hopkins University in the United States (Fig. 5). When the mouse hovers over a color block with a state abbreviation, the state's full name, risk level, daily cases, and detailed information of new cases per person per day will be displayed. Among them, to make the daily changes of the data smoother, the daily cases are averaged over seven days.

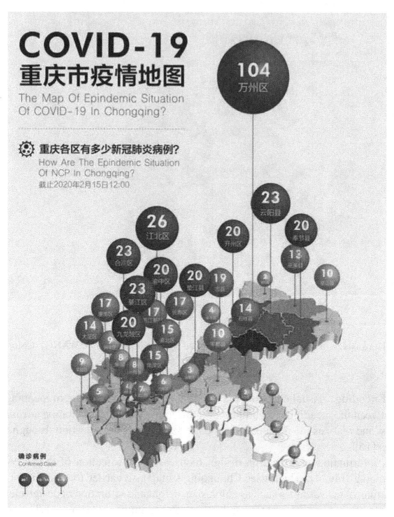

Fig. 4. Epidemic Map of Chongqing (Designed by Hongzhu LAI)

Trace the Path. In the process of interaction, attention should be paid to the user's trajectory, and the different operation options gradually appear to map the user's operation behavior. Based on the guided information on the visualization page, users can clearly recognize where they are in the interface. For example, reminding by positioning, sensitivity, peripheral information, information smell. The navigation effect should be sufficiently noticeable. Common forms include breadcrumb navigation. The interactive dashboard belongs to one of this interaction applications (Fig. 6). The case uses tag to vividly illustrate different information, enriching users' knowledge of the epidemic and enhancing their understanding of epidemic change.

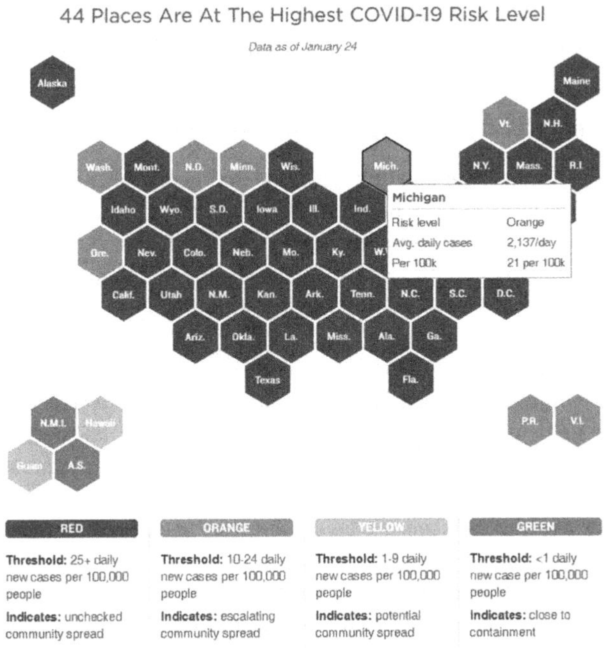

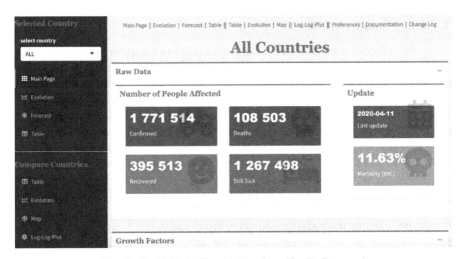

Fig. 5. COVID-19 in the United States

Fig. 6. Covid-19 dashboard (Developed by De Brouwer)

4 Discussion

Data has become an essential strategic resource for public health emergencies, in which case, information visualization provides a critical support role for epidemic prevention and control. We combine the above analysis and proposes a visualization strategy for handling massive information in public safety emergencies in the era of big data.

4.1 Clarify Application Scenarios and Core Semantics

In different scenarios, users have different needs and goals for information. It requires designers to gain insight into the problems to be solved in the scene, extract reliable data and features to transmit information, and solve problems. As to information visualization design for public health security emergencies, the main application scenarios include two categories: information processing and information expression. For information processing charts, this type of chart is often used to reveal hidden information and turn unobvious clues into visual information forms. The most important characteristics are truthfulness, accuracy, legibility and clarity. The expression chart of data information is usually used as a narrative method. As a substantial "communication and expression" tool, information visualization should center on a core semantics that needs to be transmitted.

When processing the information layer by layer, each processing will produce a certain amount of redundancy and lose part of the original information. In order to successfully transmit information, it is necessary to increase information redundancy instead of increasing signal strength. In general, present the epidemic's development more richly and intuitively, let the public understand the pathogenicity, transmission route, number of cases of infectious diseases and their pathogens, and then the less panic and fear there will be.

4.2 Mining Data Correlation

The data has a certain complexity. For example, change in the number of infected people is independent data, while the number of infected people in different areas changes over time, that is, multivariate data. For the viewer, the correlation between the different dimensions of data lies in the fact that the process of understanding these relationships will create a mental interaction. In this process, the user's mental model is continuously changing and evolving. Information visualization can help audiences establish practical, logical thinking in the face of massive information, bring out the patterns and inherent characteristics of complex data, and deeply explore the potential values behind the data.

4.3 Provide Emotional Care

Different presentation methods of information visualization will bring different psychological feelings to viewers. Designers should pay attention to user psychology and user experience and provide humanized visual design and emotional care. But we should know that having a large amount of available data is both a positive and negative thing. Nowadays, we have an unprecedented demand for more straightforward and accurate information visualization design to prevent misunderstanding and misleading. For information visualization designers, it means that they need to assume specific social responsibilities for the processing, organization, and dissemination of public health security emergencies information and design with a more cautious attitude.

At the same time, charts have always been a tool to help people convey and disseminate information. As humans we are not driven by numbers, but driven by emotions. People have reported on public health and safety events many times at the statistical and journalistic level. Nevertheless, only truly human information visualization can extend the meaning to a deeper level. The number of infected people and deaths are not just a number, but both represent lives. Designers should attempts to provoke thought about human nature, rather than just numbly receiving data.

Besides, visualization can also convey hope and temperature. The shapes and colors reflect the daily changes in the number of confirmed cases, cures and deaths across the country. The comfortable and natural green color may be chosen as the primary color to give people a sense of hope. By highlighting the cure rate, the design conveys warmth to achieve emotional healing.

5 Conclusion

By analyzing and summarizing mainstream media and classic global information visualization design cases, this paper has sorted out people's information visualization needs related to epidemic prevention and control in different scenarios during public health and safety emergencies. The operating mechanism and usage methods of information visualization in this context are analyzed in terms of visual cognitive psychology and interaction patterns. It has implications for developing visualization strategies for public health and security emergencies. Simultaneously, more accurate and dynamic control of information about public health emergencies can facilitate relevant organizations to improve their ability to predict and respond to public health emergencies. In the future, in order to realize the systematization, standardization and humanization of information visualization, further enhance user experience and alleviate social anxiety, it is still necessary for several related subjects to jointly think and explore.

Acknowledgment. This research was financially supported by MOE (Ministry of Education in China) Youth Project of Humanities and Social Sciences Fund, 2020: "Study on ergonomic design and evaluation mechanism based on 3D scanning technology" (No. 20YJCZH061).

References

1. Hong, L.: Visual design path of epidemic data from the perspective of the public. Pack. Eng. **41**(10), 221–227 (2020)
2. Wang, W., Xinangyang, X.: Influence of information and knowledge visualization on medical decision making. Pack. Eng. **36**(20), 8–11 (2015)
3. Reeder, B., Turner, A.M.: Scenario-based design: a method for connecting information system design with public health operations and emergency management **44**(6), 978–988 (2011)
4. Tuo, L.: Information visualization: a design method of making the epidemic 'visible' to the public. Art Des. **02**, 38–45 (2020)
5. Fuling, J., Yong, W.: Data analysis and expression methods in epidemic visualization design: taking data visualization analysis of covid-19 epidemic in Chongqing as an example. Ind. Eng. Des. **2**(02), 32–38 (2020)

6. Haiyan, J., Hui, X., Cheng, Z., Jingyi, Z.: Design and implementation of analysis and visualization of shared bicycle information. J. Phys. Conf. Ser. **1**, 1629 (2020)
7. Tyrvainen, L., Gustavsson, R., Konijnendijk, C., et al.: Visualization and landscape laboratories in plannin. design and management of urban woodlands. Forest Policy Econ. **8**(08), 811–823 (2008)
8. Xindi, W., Dongyuan, W., Kaiming, Z.: Research on the application of information visualization in interface design—taking the "real-time dynamics of coronavirus 2019" system interface as an example. Design **33**(08), 93–95 (2020)
9. Zhenyu, Q.: Reference and integration of information visualization design and industrial design. Create. Des. **01**, 5–13 (2020)
10. Qin, X., Luo, Y., Tang, N., Li, G.: Making data visualization more efficient and effective: a survey. VLDB J. **29**(1), 93–117 (2019). https://doi.org/10.1007/s00778-019-00588-3
11. Chris, Y.Y., Franz, S., Kwan-Liu, M., et al.: A user-centered design study in scientific visualization targeting domain experts. IEEE Trans. Vis. Comput. Graph. **26**(6), 2192–2203 (2020)
12. Lu, M., et al.: Frontier of information visualization and visual analytics in 2016. J. Vis. **20**(4), 667–686 (2017)
13. Horton, S., Nowak, S., Haegeli, P.: Enhancing the operational value of snowpack models with visualization design principles. Nat. Hazards Earth Syst. Sci. **20**(6), 1557–1572 (2020)
14. Samantha, S., Tiffany, P., Rebecca, S.: Patient preferences for visualization of longitudinal patient-reported outcomes data. J. Am. Med. Inform. Assoc. **27**(2), 212–224 (2020)
15. Yuanbo, S., Zhiyi, W., Ruige, X., Fei, L., Ge, L.: Data visualization design of COVID-19 epidemic. Pack. Eng. **41**(08), 51–62 (2020)
16. Qiansheng, L.: Discovering the beauty of data: teaching practice of information visualization design course at art school. Art Des. **01**, 112–114 (2017)

Comparative Study of the Interaction of Digital Natives with Mainstream Web Mapping Services

Marinos Kavouras[1(✉)], Margarita Kokla[1], Fotis Liarokapis[2,3],
Katerina Pastra[4], and Eleni Tomai[1]

[1] Cartography Laboratory, National Technical University of Athens,
Zografou Campus, 15780 Zografou, Athens, Greece
{mkav,mkokla,etomai}@mail.ntua.gr

[2] Research Centre on Interactive Media, Smart Systems and Emerging Technologies,
1011 Nicosia, Cyprus
f.liarokapis@cyens.org.cy

[3] Cyprus University of Technology, Faculty of Engineering and Technology,
3036 Limassol, Cyprus
fotios.liarokapis@cut.ac.cy

[4] Institute for Language and Speech Processing, ATHENA Research Center,
151 25 Maroussi, Athens, Greece
kpastra@athenarc.gr
http://www.survey.ntua.gr

Abstract. We present the results of a comparative study among four well-known web mapping services. The study explored how digital natives (young people under 30 years old who were born and raised with technology and smart devices) interact with web mapping services. The sample consisted of 167 University students in the field of Engineering and was conducted entirely online. Results indicate that the nature of tasks performed using mapping services affect both effectiveness and efficiency even when users interact with the same service. Among services, study results also indicate differences between task success rates as well as between successful task completion times. Finally, comparison between male and female participants showed no difference in either effectiveness or efficiency between genders.

Keywords: Comparative study · Web mapping service · Efficiency · Effectiveness · Usability · Digital natives

The research work was supported by the Hellenic Foundation for Research and Innovation (H.F.R.I.) under the "First Call for H.F.R.I. Research Projects to support Faculty members and Researchers and the procurement of high-cost research equipment grant" (ProjectNumber: HFRI-FM17-2661). This research was also partially supported by the project that has received funding from the European Union's Horizon 2020 research and innovation programme under grant agreement No 739578 (RISE–Call: H2020-WIDESPREAD-01-2016-2017-TeamingPhase2) and the Government of the Republic of Cyprus through the Directorate General for European Programmes, Coordination and Development.

M. Kurosu (Ed.): HCII 2021, LNCS 12764, pp. 337–350, 2021.
https://doi.org/10.1007/978-3-030-78468-3_23

1   Introduction

The current study aims at exploring the ways digital natives [1] interact with well-known web mapping services; Google Maps, Bing Maps, MapQuest, and HERE WeGo. Digital natives were selected because they belong to the Millennials; the generation born and raised with technology. Digital Natives are overexposed to information and communications technologies and to the use of smart devices, thus according to Prensky (ibid.), they exhibit special skills and characteristics such as enjoying multitasking, processing information fast and in parallel, feasting on technology and so on. If we are to adopt this view, digital natives present the ideal subjects for evaluating usability of web mapping services in an era of ever-increasing digital applications and environments.

ISO 9241-11 (1998) in [2] defines usability as "the extent to which a product can be used by specified users to achieve specified goals with effectiveness, efficiency, and satisfaction in a specified context of use". The revised version (ISO 9241-11, 2018) in [3] adds to the term product the terms system and service. By definition, usability is essentially defined as the combination of three components: (a) effectiveness, refers to whether users can complete tasks and accomplish goals using this system, product or service; (b) efficiency, the degree to which users spend resources to achieve their goals and (c) satisfaction, the level of comfort that users feel when achieving their goals [2].

The study presented herein measures two components of usability; efficiency and effectiveness. Effectiveness refers to whether participants correctly completed the tasks they had to perform using the services, while efficiency refers to their speed in performing a task.

The paper is organized as follows: Sect. 2 presents related work on the usability of web mapping services. It seems that regarding mapping services excessive usability studies have not been conducted, although a vast global population uses them on their desktops, laptops, and smart devices. Section 3 presents the study methodology detailing the procedure and the questionnaires given to participants. Section 4 provides information of the sample's demographics and Sect. 5 presents results of the analysis. Finally, the last section discusses general conclusions.

2   Related Work

As more and more users worldwide use web mapping services either through mobile devices or on a personal computer, evaluating the usability of these services is useful and imperative. Indeed, in recent years, efforts have been made to evaluate well-known and widely used web mapping services (e.g., Google Maps, Yahoo Maps, etc.) without, however, proceeding to large-scale evaluations of these services, especially recently. The following paragraphs present related surveys focusing on the adopted research/ experimental process of defining and measuring usability of web mapping services.

The usability study of [4] aimed at identifying possible usability problems of web mapping services with the objective of collecting quality information and of proposing guidelines for the future design of relevant services. The survey evaluated four services: Google Maps, MSN Maps & Directions (Bing Maps ancestor), MapQuest and Multimap (merged by Bing Maps). To conduct the study, a typical scenario of web mapping services use was presented to participants: "A tourist plans to visit London and uses a web mapping service to plan the trip in advance". A total of 24 participants (8 general users, 8 cartographers, and 8 usability engineers) made 32 different assessments. Users were given a predefined task at a time, which they would complete using one of the services under review that they had not used before. Users were encouraged to "think aloud" and to describe the rationale behind their actions. During the endeavors, the user's computer screen was recorded with a video camera to facilitate the subsequent analysis. General users had to perform seven tasks. Expert users, on the other hand, received both the scenario and the same list of tasks. After performing the tasks, they were asked to list all usability problems they identified. Usability problems were grouped into four different categories depending on the severity of the problem.

A usability framework for web mapping services was proposed with four levels of usability by Wachowicz et al. [5]: (1) usability typology (includes the content of the service, the functions and the way of interaction as well as the objects through which the interaction is achieved), (2) usability variables (related to the user and the purpose of using the application, the tasks performed through the use of the application, and the skills that users must have in order to use it), (3) usability data (also referred to as usability characteristics/properties, which are the measurable components of the usability concept), and (4) usability measures (those characteristics that can be quantified and therefore directly measured or observed during a usability test). Applying this framework, the researchers conducted a survey to investigate the relationship between web mapping services and user satisfaction. The selected services were: Map24.com (operational until 2011 considered the forerunner of the HERE WeGo) and Mappy.com (launched in France in 1997, covering all of Europe) and user interaction was based on windows, icons, menus, pointers allowing the user to navigate and search for information with the mouse or keyboard (Level 1). For Level 2, a pre-test two-fold questionnaire was designed that allowed the collection (a) of user profile information (occupation, age, and gender) and (b) of web mapping services usage information (e.g., user preferences and usage purposes). Participants performed 3 tasks related to finding a route and locating an object. As a usability element (Level 3) in usability research, "user satisfaction" was measured as the combination of three parameters (Level 4): (1) execution speed, (2) degree of interaction, and (3) error rate. The usability survey was conducted by eight participants and their entire interview and interaction with the services was recorded.

The survey on usability of web mapping services conducted by [6] consisted of the evaluation of: Google Maps, Bing maps, MapQuest, and Yahoo Maps. The services were evaluated by 42 people, with different skills of Geographic Information Systems (ordinary users but also experts), regardless of gender, age, and nationality. The sample was divided into groups and performed various tasks using the services. The research consisted of three parts: the pre-test which concerned the collection of the sample's basic information (age, gender, level of familiarity with GIS, etc.), the execution of various tasks, and one post-test questionnaire. The scenario of the experiment was as follows: participants were travellers visiting for the first time the US capital, Washington, DC. In this context they had to perform five tasks. The final quantitative results were obtained partly on the basis of the average time for the execution of each task in the four services and the percentage of successful execution of the tasks.

3   Methodology

3.1   Study Research Question

Our study comprises a large-scale evaluation of four web mapping services by undergraduate University engineering students constituting an age group that could provide interesting insights on how youth in the digital era explores and interacts with geo-services, as they are the so-called "digital natives". The study design (Sect. 3.4) allowed exploring also gender differences, if any, between male and female participants in their interaction with web mapping services.

3.2   Procedure

The study was undertaken online during the spring semester of the Academic Year 2019–2020. Due to special conditions, related to the COVID19 outbreak, the study was conducted in the framework of distance learning environments. Participants had been connected to the course team on Microsoft Teams and instructions for the study procedure were given to them orally by the research team. They were asked to perform the survey using their own laptops and PCs. The research team was present during the study to assist participants in any problem they faced either with the understanding of the tasks they had to perform or with any internet connection issues and all interactions were made on Microsoft Teams. The study was conducted in a time frame of one hour and half, so that all participants could take part in the study simultaneously. Data were collected and processed anonymously.

3.3   Pre-test Questionnaire

The pre-test questionnaire was designed to collect data on sample demographics such as gender, year of birth, familiarity with computers and smart devices etc. Details on sample demographics as derived from this initial questionnaire are given in Sect. 4.

3.4   Web Mapping Services Usability Questionnaire

We evaluated the four web mapping services in pairs, so three versions of the web mapping services questionnaire were designed. All participants evaluated Google

Maps, since it is the most used mapping service worldwide [7]. The remaining three services are: Bing Maps, MapQuest, and Here WeGo. Therefore, the sample was equally and randomly divided into three groups that each evaluated two services with Google Maps being the benchmark evaluated by all.

The tasks the participants were asked to perform are:

1. identifying a location (point) given its geographical coordinates and
2. locating the nearest point of interest (such as a hotel, a stadium, a library) to a specific point given to participants by its name, address, and coordinates.

The students were given the following "scenario": You have been admitted to Harvard University to attend some classes during a summer school. Before you leave, you want to plan your trip and see which places you will visit. This scenario made the survey process more appealing to the students but also Boston as a US city presented a safe choice since our students would have to perform the task in an unfamiliar environment and because all four mapping services are fully functional for this part of the world.

For each task, the following data were recorded and analysed:

- task completion score (1 for successful execution, 0 otherwise) and
- the response time (time it took for participants to complete the task regardless of whether it was successful or not).

4   Sample Demographics

The sample consists of 167 University students, below the age of 30 years old, of which 113 (68%) are males and 54 (32%) females. The mean age of participants is 21.80 (2.06) years old.

Participants' degree of familiarity with computers and smart devices is quite high since almost 50% of the sample responded that they are very familiar and almost 27% that they are extremely familiar. Only 22% considered themselves as moderately familiar. Table 1 details participants' answers and percentages regarding familiarity with computers and smart devices by gender as well as for the sample as a whole.

Table 1. Male, female and total participants' answers and percentages to their degree of familiarity with computers and smart devices.

Degree of familiarity	Males (%)	Females (%)	Total (%)
Slightly familiar	2 (1.8%)	0 (0.0%)	**2 (1.20%)**
Moderately familiar	26 (23.0%)	11 (20.4%)	**37 (22.1%)**
Very familiar	51 (45.1%)	32 (59.3%)	**83 (49.7%)**
Extremely familiar	34 (30.1%)	11 (20.4%)	**45 (27.0%)**

Answers to the question that explores the reasons why participants use computers and smart devices (they were enabled to choose multiple answers) are depicted on Table 2. Entertainment, education and social networking are the three most prevalent reasons for using these media regardless of gender, with similar percentages between men and women. In fact, these percentages in all cases exceed 25% of the answers, with the highest percentage of them being the answers of female participants related to education (28.2%). As expected, the percentage of answers related to work is much lower (17.8% of the sample) since the sample consists of active students, the majority of whom do not have a regular job yet. Finally, regarding the degree of familiarity with Boston, 90% of the sample states having slight or no familiarity with the city. As foreseen, results satisfy the prerequisite that the sample is not familiar with the area where the "scenario" takes place so that participants would use the four web mapping services to perform the tasks in an unknown environment as a means to homogenise the sample further but also to ensure maximum exploration when performing the tasks.

Table 2. Male, female and total participants' answers and percentages on the reasons for using computers and smart devices.

Reasons of use	Males (%)	Females (%)	Total (%)
Work	72 (18.5%)	29 (16.4%)	**101 (17.8%)**
Education	107 (27.5%)	50 (28.2%)	**157 (27.7%)**
Entertainment	109 (28.0%)	49 (27.6%)	**158 (27.9%)**
Social networking	99 (25.4%)	48 (27.2%)	**147 (26.0%)**
Other	3 (0.5%)	2 (0.5%)	**1 (0.5%)**

5   Study Results

Analysis of the collected data was performed per task and service. The analysis was undertaken for: (a) correctness of the participants' responses (effectiveness) and (b) response time (efficiency). Moreover, since all participants evaluated Google Maps, data for this service were analyzed to identify gender differences in performance, if any. Section 5.3 presents the results of such analysis.

All variables have been tested for normality and for the majority of cases, data collected do not follow a normal distribution, thus, all statistical analyses pursued is conducted using non-parametric tests.

5.1   Task 1: Point Identification

Within Groups Comparison. Regarding the correctness of participants' answers (effectiveness), Tables 3 and 4 depict accuracy (effectiveness) of groups in executing Task 1. Table 3 shows that according to the Chi-square tests performed, there is statistically significant moderate correlation between the

Table 3. Correlations between answers per pair of services for Task 1.

Groups	χ^2	Sig.	r_s
1. Google Maps/Bing Maps	1.27	p = .268	**0.152**
2. Google Maps/MapQuest	5.45	**p = .019**	**0.312**
3. Google Maps/HERE WeGo	5.67	**p = .017**	**0.318**

answers provided by participants of group 2 for Google Maps and MapQuest. The same holds for participants of group 3 for Google Maps and HERE WeGo.

Table 4 depicts that, according to the McNemar Tests performed, there is a statistically significant difference between the task's success rate of group 2 participants in Google Maps (better) and MapQuest. On the contrary, for the other two groups no difference can be deduced from the results.

Table 4. Task 1 success rates per group and service.

McNemar test ($\alpha = 0.05, \chi^2 = 3.81, df = 1$)		
Groups	X^2	Sig.
1. Google Maps (85.45%)/Bing Maps (87.27%)	0.02	p = .880
2. Google Maps (89.29%)/MapQuest (73.21%)	**5.56**	**p = .018**
3. Google Maps (91.07%)/HERE WeGo (80.36%)	3.03	p = .082

Regarding response time and successful completion time (efficiency), Tables 5 and 6 present results of the Wilcoxon matched-pairs signed rank test between response time and successful completion time respectively per pair of services in all three groups. The only statistically significant difference is between Google Maps and Bing Maps for group 1 participants on both cases, where participants seem to be faster on Bing Maps. Finally, there is statistically significant difference of the successful completion time of Task 1 between Google Maps and HERE WeGo, with participants being faster in the latter than the former.

Table 5. Differences between response times for Task 1 in service pairs per group.

Wilcoxon matched-pairs signed-rank test			
Groups	N	z	Sig.
1. Google Maps (Mdn = 220)/Bing Maps (Mdn = 98)	55	3.44	**p = .001**
2. Google Maps (Mdn = 232.5)/MapQuest (Mdn = 253.5)	56	0.60	p =.546
3. Google Maps (Mdn = 185.5)/HERE WeGo (Mdn = 125.5)	56	1.42	p =.157

Table 6. Differences between successful completion times for Task 1 in service pairs per group.

Wilcoxon matched-pairs signed-rank test			
Groups	N	z	Sig.
1. Google Maps (Mdn = 235)/Bing Maps (Mdn = 82.5)	42	3.89	**p<.001**
2. Google Maps (Mdn = 194)/MapQuest (Mdn = 254)	39	1.12	p = .264
3. Google Maps (Mdn = 181)/HERE WeGo (Mdn = 110)	43	2.46	p = .014

Among Groups Comparison. Comparing among Bing Maps, MapQuest, and HERE WeGo, regarding the correctness of participants' answers (effectiveness), a Chi-square test of independence was performed to examine if there is a relationship between the web mapping service and the ability of the respondents to give a correct answer to the Point Identification task. This relation is non-statistically significant since, $X^2(2, N = 167) = 3.46 < \chi^2(2, 0.05) = 5.99, p = .177$. Thus, the service used each time for the execution of the task is not related to the ability of each group to provide a correct answer for the specific task. On the other hand, regarding the successful completion time (efficiency), the Kruskal-Wallis H test shows that the service on which the task was performed has a significant effect on the time of its successful execution (H(2) = 25.09, p<.001). The Conover post-test shows that the difference between Bing Maps (Mdn = 91.5) and MapQuest (Mdn = 254) (p<.001) and the one between MapQuest and HERE WeGo (Mdn = 105) (p<.001) are significant, with participants successfully performing Task 1 on Bing Maps and HERE WeGo faster than those performing it on MapQuest. In contrast, between Bing Maps and HERE WeGo there is no statistically significant difference regarding the successful completion time (p = .407).

5.2 Task 2: Locating the Nearest Point of Interest

Within Groups Comparison. Table 7 shows no statistically significant correlation between answers per service pairs in all three groups for Task 2, according to the Chi-square tests performed. However, regarding success rates, there is statistically significant difference between Google Maps and MapQuest and Google Maps and HERE WeGo for groups 2 and 3 respectively with Google Maps success rates being very low (below 20%) for both groups (Table 8), according to the McNemar Tests performed. It should be noted that for Task 2, success rates of group 1 are low for both services; Google Maps and Bing Maps.

Table 7. Correlations r_s between answers per pair of services for Task 2.

Groups	χ^2	Sig.	r_s
1. Google Maps/Bing Maps	0	p = .990	-0.002
2. Google Maps/MapQuest	0.58	p = .445	0.102
3. Google Maps/HERE WeGo	1.10	p = .294	0.140

Table 8. Task 2 success rates per group and service.

McNemar test ($\alpha = 0.05, \chi^2 = 3.81, df = 1$)		
Groups	X^2	Sig.
1. Google Maps (23.64%)/Bing Maps (30.91%)	0.56	p = .456
2. Google Maps (14.29%)/MapQuest (50.00%)	**14.63**	**p<.001**
3. Google Maps (16.07%)/HERE WeGo (75.00%)	**30.18**	**p<.001**

Regarding response time and successful completion time (efficiency), statistically significant difference was found only for response time between Google Maps and Bing Maps for group 1 participants; they seem to be faster on Google Maps than on Bing Maps (Table 9). Finally, there is no statistically significant difference of the successful completion time of Task 2 in any service pair in any group, partly because no such comparison can be performed for groups 1 and 2 participants since those that successfully executed the task on both services for both groups 2 are very few; 4 and 5 respectively (Table 10).

Table 9. Differences between response times for Task 2 in service pairs per group.

Wilcoxon matched-pairs signed-rank test			
Groups	N	z	Sig.
1. Google Maps (Mdn = 242)/Bing Maps (Mdn = 402)	**55**	**3.77**	**p<.001**
2. Google Maps (Mdn = 231.5)/MapQuest (Mdn = 205)	56	1.37	p = .172
3. Google Maps (Mdn = 225)/HERE WeGo (Mdn = 216.5)	56	0.80	p = .424

Table 10. Differences between successful completion times for Task 2 in service pairs per group.

Wilcoxon matched-pairs signed-rank test			
Groups	N	z	Sig.
1. Google Maps/Bing Maps	4	NA	NA
2. Google Maps/MapQuest	5	NA	NA
3. Google Maps (Mdn = 199)/HERE WeGo (Mdn = 152.5)	9	0.21	p = .834

Among Groups Comparison. Comparing among Bing Maps, MapQuest and HERE WeGo, to assess accuracy, initially, a Chi-square test of independence was performed. This showed statistically significant difference among the three services since, $X^2(2, N = 167) = 21.76 < \chi^2(2, 0.05) = 5.99$, p<.001. Hence, the mapping service used each time to perform Task 2 seems to be related to the ability of each group to find the right answer to the specific task.

Table 11. Exact Fisher test results to compare accuracy in performing Task 2.

Services	Exact fisher test (p)
Bing Maps/MapQuest	.053
Bing Maps/HERE WeGo	<.001
MapQuest/HERE WeGo	<.011

Exact Fisher tests showed statistically significant difference between HERE WeGo and the other two (Table 11), with HERE WeGo (42 correct answers; 75% accuracy) exhibiting the best performance (group 3) followed by MapQuest (28 correct answers; 50% accuracy, group 2) and lastly by Bing Maps (17 correct answers; 31% accuracy, group 1). Regarding successful completion time, the Kruskal-Wallis H test among successful completion times on the three services, shows that the service on which the task was performed has a significant effect on the time of its successful execution (H(2) = 10.36, p = .006). The Conover post-test shows that the difference between Bing Maps (Mdn = 368) and MapQuest (Mdn = 201) (p = .002) and between Bing Maps and HERE WeGo (Mdn = 223.5) (p = .018) is significant, with participants using MapQuest and HERE WeGo successfully completing the task faster than when using Bing Maps. On the contrary, between MapQuest and HERE WeGo there is no difference in the successful completion time for Task 2 (p = .233).

5.3   Gender Performance

The entire sample of the study interacted with Google Maps as mentioned in Sect. 3.4. Hence, it was decided to make use of these sample data to assess whether there are any differences in performance (effectiveness and efficiency) between genders. In what follows, we present the results of the comparison between male and female participants in both tasks regarding effectiveness and efficiency.

Initially, a Chi-square test of homogeneity was performed to examine the homogeneity of the three groups in terms of the correctness of the answers to both tasks on Google Maps. Results indicate homogeneity of the three groups for both tasks (Task 1: $X^2(2, N = 167) = 0.90 < \chi^2(2, 0.05) = 5.99$, p = .636, and Task 2: $X^2(2, N = 167) = 1.85 < \chi^2(2, 0.05) = 5.99$, p = .396). Therefore, results of the three groups indicate that they come from the same population and they can be used as a whole to examine how male and female participants interacted with Google Maps.

Task 1: Point Identification. Before proceeding with comparing performance between genders, correlations between answers and time taken to respond have been calculated.

Table 12 shows point-biserial correlations between answers and response time of male and female participants for Task 1. For male participants as well as for female ones, the correlation between answers and time taken to perform the task is almost zero and non-statistically significant. This practically means that effectiveness of both groups (males and females) was not affected by the time they took to perform the task. As proved by the results (Sect. 5.1), Task 1 is quite easy, thus participants could perform the task correctly if we take into consideration the success rates independently of the time they took to complete the task, hence the zero correlation. Regarding the correctness of participants' answers (effectiveness), results of the Chi-square text indicate a non-significant difference in the correctness of 91% (103 out of 113) of male participants, compared to the 83% (45 out of 54) correctness of female participants $X^2(1, N = 167) = 2.21 < \chi^2(1, 0.05) = 3.84$, p = .137). While, regarding the response time and successful completion time (efficiency) the Mann-Whitney test performed, leads to the conclusion that male participants (Mdn = 190) were statistically significantly faster in their response time than females (Mdn = 264.5) (U = 2475.5, p = .025). The same holds when comparing between successful completion time; male participants (Mdn = 184) who performed the task correctly, did it faster than female participants (Mdn = 264) (U = 1873.5, p = .032).

Table 12. Point-biserial correlation between answers and response time for Task 1 for male and female participants

Participants	N	r_{pb}	Sig.
Males	113	−0.145	p = .125
Females	54	−0.196	p = .163

Task 2: Locating the Nearest Point of Interest. Again, as an initial step, correlations between answers and time taken to respond have been calculated.

Table 13 shows point-biserial correlations between answers and response time of male and female participants for Task 2. For all participants regardless of gender, the correlation between answers and time taken to perform the task is almost zero and non-statistically significant, similarly to Task 1. This practically means that effectiveness of both groups (males and females) was not affected by the time they took to perform the task. As proved by the results (see Sect. 5.2), Task 2 was not successful, meaning that participants, even those who took more time to complete the task, could not improve their effectiveness, hence the zero correlation.

Table 13. Point-biserial correlation between answers and response time for Task 2 for male and female participants

Participants	N	r_{pb}	Sig.
Males	113	0.026	p = .783
Females	54	0.084	p = .547

As for the correctness of participants' answers (effectiveness), results of the Chi-square test indicate a non-significant difference in the correctness of 19% (22 out of 113) of male participants, compared to the 15% (8 out of 54) correctness of female participants $X^2(1, N = 167) = 0.54 < \chi^2(1, 0.05) = 3.84$, p = .524). The same holds, for both response and successful completion times (efficiency), since according to the Mann-Whitney test, there is no statistically significant difference between male (Mdn = 228) and female (Mdn = 239) participants response time (U = 2707, p = .240). The same holds when comparing between successful completion time; there is no difference between successful completion time of male (Mdn = 189) and female (Mdn = 314) participants (U = 52.5, p =.101).

6   Overall Discussion and Conclusions

Study results show that although digital natives are familiar with the use of computers and smart devices, they have difficulties when exploring functionalities of web mapping services. This is indicated by the success rates in the two tasks they had to perform.

Specifically:

- Task 1 seems to be easier for the participants since for all services success rates are between 73%–91%. For group 2 participants though, there is a statistically significant difference in their success rates; participants performed better on Google Maps than on MapQuest. Moreover, considering genders' performance in interacting with Google Maps, no difference is indicated through the survey's sample for Task 1; the task seems to be equally easy to perform successfully by both males and females.
- Success rates for Task 2 are quite low since in two services (Google Maps and Bing Maps), they are below 31%. However, MapQuest and HERE WeGo present higher success rates (50% and 75% respectively) than the other two showing that for this task, the service used to perform the task was decisive for achieving successful results as also proven by the Chi-square test of independence. On Google Maps, both male and female participants reached similar success rates indicating no difference in effectiveness related to gender.

Regarding response time and time of successful task completion, the following are observed:

– In Task 1, response times and times of successful task completion, were shorter on Bing Maps and on HERE WeGo than those on Google Maps (statistically significant differences calculated, see Tables 5 and 6) but that does not hold for MapQuest. This result is partly consistent with the trial-by trial sequential effect [8] which argues that survey respondents who are required to use a series of tools or applications, tend to perform faster each time they perform the tasks they are called to, since they become familiarized with the process the following times. However, if we consider the results for Task 2, this is also partly supported but does not constitute a statistically significant difference in favor of the second map service used by each group (see Tables 9 and 10).

– Numerous studies have shown that effectiveness tends to increase especially when there is no time pressure, as it is in this case, where participants had no time limit for completing a task. However, the accuracy curve does not always seem to increase with response time [9]. Something similar seems to be happening in the present study as indicated by the almost zero correlation between the answers' correctness of both male and female participants and the time they took to perform the tasks on Google Maps.

– Finally, regarding to what is referred to as "rapid guessing" [10] observed due to lack of motivation or interest by the survey participants, after analysing the fifth percentile of response times, we can say that "rapid guesses" are correct for Task 1 in all four services, while mostly wrong for Task 2. This highlights once again the low degree of difficulty that Task 1 presented to participants. On the other hand, the degree of difficulty of Task 2 affected quick responses correctness to such extent that they can be characterized as "rapid guesses" on the part of the participants.

Gender performance results do not indicate any significant difference between male and female participants. Both groups are similar in accuracy in both tasks performed. A slight difference in speed favoring male participants in Task 1 alone is inconclusive for stating whether there is a systematic faster performance of males versus females, especially since no such difference exists for the "difficult" Task (Task 2).

As an overall conclusion, this study highlighted that significant part of participants' performance and interaction with web mapping services are mostly task-driven than service- or gender- driven; a difficult task downplays any difference among services usability issues and between genders and it seems to be the overarching factor of participants' performance.

Acknowledgements. Authors would like to thank all students who participated to the user study.

References

1. Prensky, M.: Digital natives, digital immigrants part 1. Horizon **9**(5), 3–6 (2001). https://doi.org/10.1108/10748120110424816
2. Brooke, J.: SUS: a retrospective. J. Usab. Stud. **8**(2), 29–40 (2013)

3. Bevan, N., Carter, J., Harker, S.: ISO 9241-11 revised: what have we learnt about usability since 1998? In: Kurosu, M. (ed.) HCI 2015. LNCS, vol. 9169, pp. 143–151. Springer, Cham (2015). https://doi.org/10.1007/978-3-319-20901-2_13
4. Nivala, A.-M., Brewster, S., Sarjakoski, T.L.: Usability evaluation of web mapping sites. Cartograph. J. **45**(2), 129–138 (2008). https://doi.org/10.1179/174327708X305120
5. Wachowicz, M., Cui, L., Vullings, W., Bulens, J.: The effects of web mapping applications on user satisfaction: an empirical study. In: Peterson, M.P. (ed.) International Perspectives on Maps and the Internet. Lecture Notes in Geoinformation and Cartography. Springer, Heidelberg (2008). https://doi.org/10.1007/978-3-540-72029-4_25
6. Wang, C.: Usability evaluation of public web mapping sites. Int. Arch. Photogram. Remote Sens. Spat. Inf. Sci. **60**(4), 285–289 (2014). https://doi.org/10.1179/174327708X305120
7. Panko, R.: The Popularity of Google Maps: Trends in Navigation Apps in 2018. The Manifest (2018). https://themanifest.com/mobile-apps/popularity-google-maps-trends-navigation-apps-2018. Accessed 03 Feb 2021
8. Baayen, H., Milin, P.R.: Analyzing reaction times. Int. J. Psychol. Res. **3**(2), 12–28 (2010). https://doi.org/10.21500/20112084.807
9. De Boeck, P., Jeon, M.: An overview of models for response times and processes in cognitive tests. Front. Psychol. **10**(102) (2019). https://doi.org/10.3389/fpsyg.2019.00102
10. Ratcliff, R.: Methods for dealing with reaction time outliers. Psychol. Bull. **114**, 510–532 (1993)

Success is not Final; Failure is not Fatal – Task Success and User Experience in Interactions with Alexa, Google Assistant and Siri

Miriam Kurz[1], Birgit Brüggemeier[2]([✉]) [iD], and Michael Breiter[2] [iD]

[1] Friedrich-Alexander-University Erlangen-Nuremberg, Erlangen, Germany
miri.kurz@fau.de
[2] Fraunhofer Institute for Integrated Circuits, Erlangen, Germany
{birgit.brueggemeier,michael.breiter}@iis.fraunhofer.de

Abstract. Speech assistants exhibit a high error rate with about one in three user requests resulting in an error. Nonetheless, speech assistants are adopted rapidly with about 1.8 billion users expected in 2021. Given the relatively high task failure rate of speech assistants this may be surprising and raises the question how much user experience (UX) is affected by task success in these devices. We measure user experience with four metrics of UX and evaluate task success in interactions with the speech assistants Alexa, Google Assistant, and Siri. We find that task success only explains between 13% and 28% of the variance of UX. This suggests that a majority of UX is not explained by whether an assistant successfully completes tasks. Moreover, we find that the three assistants do not significantly differ in task success rate, but differ in UX, which supports the conclusion that task success and UX possess limited alignment. We discuss our results and point out limitations and potential future work.

Keywords: User experience · Task success · Voice user interfaces · Measuring · SUS · SASSI · SUISQ · AttrakDiff · Alexa · Siri · Google Assistant

1 Introduction

Speech assistants are becoming increasingly popular [15] and are expected to have 1.8 billion users in 2021 [20]. This is not surprising, considering that voice interaction has advantages such as hands-free operation and intuitive use [9]. However, product reviews of speech assistants such as Google Assistant, Siri, and Alexa, criticize their ability to understand users [5]. This is supported by the finding that on average between one in three (Google Assistant) to two in three requests (Siri) is not understood or not fully and correctly answered by voice assistants [10]. This suggests that the adoption of speech assistants does not only depend on their ability to understand users. In our work, we investigate

© Springer Nature Switzerland AG 2021
M. Kurosu (Ed.): HCII 2021, LNCS 12764, pp. 351–369, 2021.
https://doi.org/10.1007/978-3-030-78468-3_24

how much the ability of speech assistants to successfully complete tasks affects user experience. We therefore correlate global measures of user experience with task success in interactions with speech assistants.

The quality of human-computer interaction can be measured with usability, which, according to the ISO 9241 definition, consists of *effectiveness, efficiency,* and *satisfaction* [13]. User experience (UX), compared to usability, goes beyond the mere use but also includes "a person's perceptions and responses that result from the use and/or anticipated use of a product, system or device" [13]. There are numerous different metrics of user experience, but there is no gold standard for measuring UX with modern speech assistants [18]. For our study, we selected four UX metrics that are commonly used in studies of conversational user interfaces [16–18], namely the *System Usability Scale (SUS,* positive version, for more details refer to [7]), the *Subjective Assessment of Speech System Interfaces (SASSI),* the *Speech User Interface Service Quality questionnaire – Reduced Version (SUISQ-R)* and *AttrakDiff.*

UX reflects the subjective experience of users. In order to make objective statements on system performance, Walker et al. suggested a task-based success measure in their framework *PARADISE* [21]. Task success can be compared to a subjective criterion like UX and the influence of task success on UX can be measured. The *PARADISE* framework is based on the idea that task success can be calculated by Cohen's Kappa and a confusion matrix, which represents task performance of the machine and the user. With linear regression it is possible to determine how predictive task success is of user experience.

To investigate the influence of task success on UX, participants in the present study were asked to play music with the speech assistants Amazon's Alexa (dot version), Google Home Pod (version 1.42.171861), and Apple home pod (version 12.4). One group of participants completed single tasks, which are one-off commands, e.g. requesting a song. The second group handled multi-turn tasks. As the name implies, these are multi-turn interactions between human and machine. For example, requesting a song and then asking for similar music (for more details on the task types, see [14]).

1.1   Research Questions

With this study, we want to find out how much user experience is affected by task success in speech assistants, leading to the following research questions:

1. To what degree are task success and UX metrics correlated?
2. How much of the variance in UX metrics is explained by task success?

In a previous study [7], we found that UX differs between task types and speech assistants. Analogously, we investigate potential differences in task success between task types and assistants in this study with our third research question:

3. Are there differences in task success between task types or speech assistants?

2   Methods

2.1   Participants

Participants were recruited within our institute and on the social network Facebook and with an advertisement on our institute's website and among one of the author's friends and acquaintances. The resulting sample included 51 participants of which three had to be excluded from further analysis. These exclusions were due to technical difficulties with the speech assistants (one male and one female were excluded) as well as a conspicuous answering pattern shown by one male (for more details see [7]). This leads to a final sample of $N = 48$. Twenty-four (50%) of them performed single tasks, 24 (50%) performed multi-turn tasks. The sample consisted of 22 females (46%) and 26 males (54%). On average, the subjects were 26.63 years old ($SD = 6.81$) and mostly non-native English speakers (96%). Two participants (4%) stated English to be their mother tongue. The experiment was conducted in English and we specified in our study advertisement and in our correspondence with participants that they should have a good command of English (B2 according to CEFR) in order to participate.

2.2   Procedure

The laboratory room was equipped with an Amazon Alexa, a Google Home Pod, and an Apple Home Pod, as well as with a notebook that was used to fill out questionnaires. Beforehand, participants knew that they would interact with different speech assistants and fill out questionnaires. The experimenter presented the three assistants and explained the procedure of the experiment. In all tasks, users were asked to control music with a speech assistant, e.g. by playing a song or getting more information on the album they were listening to [7]. Participants did not have to successfully complete every task, they were asked to answer the questionnaires spontaneously, even if some items might seem odd, and, for the sake of time, they were asked to play all songs for a few seconds only.

Before starting the experiment, participants were assigned to one of two groups: users with an odd number were assigned to single tasks, which consist of only one query and one answer (e.g. requesting a single song), whereas users with an even number were selected to complete multi-turn tasks, which include several sub-goals (e.g. asking for a rock song and then for the arist's name of that song, see [14]). For multi-turn tasks "the ability of the intelligent assistant to maintain the context of the conversation" is crucial [14]. In addition, multi-turn tasks are more difficult to accomplish than single tasks, possibly leading to a higher number of requests the user has to make. Thus, including single and multi-turn tasks adds variability in interaction difficulty, which may also affect system performance and user experience.

To be able to process the tasks by interacting with the speech assistant, participants were given written instructions (see Appendix 1). The problem with instruction however is, that people might just read the phrase out loud instead of forming their sentences and realistically interacting with the interface. That is why, for the presentation of tasks, we referred to [22], who indicated that a list-based method biases participants the least and thus we incorporated list-based instructions in our experiment.

2.3 Assessing Task Success

The framework *PARADISE* [21] was used as a basis to assess the system's performance and obtain an objective measure of task success. This framework displays task success in a confusion matrix. Walker et al. [21] present confusion matrices for structured dialogs that include only a limited number of possible requests a user can make. In their confusion matrix, they list all possible requests a user can make and what the system understood.

In this study, participants were asked to play music, and we did not set a limit on the songs they could ask for. This is why we decided to alter the confusion matrix such that it does not include all possible songs a participant can ask for. Instead, we decided to categorize requests into the categories *user correct, user wrong* and *system correct, system wrong*. Furthermore, as users made requests that could not clearly be assigned to either correct or wrong, a third category *unclear* for both system and user was established (see Table 1 and 2).

A user, for example, was assigned to the third category *unclear* if they did not follow the order of tasks that were presented to them. For instance, in one multi-turn task, users were supposed to play their favorite song and after accomplishing this, ask the speech assistant to play similar music. The outcome of this task was categorized as *user unclear* if, for example, instead of asking to play similar songs, a user asked for more information on their favorite song. Based on the confusion matrix, we calculated Cohen's *Kappa* (κ) as a performance measure. Kappa takes into account that correct system responses can occur by chance and controls for this.

$$\kappa = \frac{P_a - P_e}{1 - P_e} \tag{1}$$

While P_a is the proportion of correct responses, P_e is the percentage of correct responses expected by chance. We used two approaches to compute P_a, a conservative (see Table 1) approach and a liberal approach (see Table 2). In the conservative approach, P_a is defined as the proportion of times users and systems are categorized as correct. In the liberal approach, P_a is defined as the proportion of times users and systems are categorized as either correct or unclear. P_e is the proportion of correct requests and responses as expected by chance. For P_e, [21] suggested assuming agreement by chance due to weighted equal distribution. We decided to compute P_e assuming a uniform distribution. The formula to do so was obtained from [3] who mention the following formula, where $|A|$ describes "the number of favorable cases" and $|\omega|$ describes "the number of all possible cases". P_e in both approaches, liberal and conservative, equals 1/9.

$$P_e = \frac{|A|}{|\omega|} \tag{2}$$

Table 1. Diagram to illustrate our classifications in the **conservative approach**. To compare this confusion matrix with classifications made by Walker et al. please refer to [21]. Grey fields indicate cases that were considered correct in the conservative approach, whereas white fields indicate cases that were considered incorrect.

	System correct	System wrong	System unclear
User correct			
User wrong			
User unclear			

Table 2. Diagram to illustrate our classifications in the **liberal approach**. To compare this confusion matrix with classifications made by Walker et al. please refer to [21]. Grey fields indicate cases that were considered correct in the liberal approach, whereas white fields indicate cases that were considered incorrect.

	System correct	System wrong	System unclear
User correct			
User wrong			
User unclear			

Annotation. The procedure to obtain a confusion matrix, which is the basis for our calculation of Cohen's Kappa, was as follows. We recorded every participant's interaction with the assistants, and a colleague automatically transcribed the recordings using Google Cloud Speech-to-Text. We then reviewed the automatic transcriptions while listening to the original recordings and corrected transcription mistakes, where necessary. For every request the user had made, we decided whether both the user and the system were correct or wrong. For 8 participants (16%), another colleague reviewed the audio data as well and rated the dialogs independently. According to [2], calculating the percentage of agreement between two raters is a good enough measure of agreement. Therefore, in this study, an agreement of 89% with the independent rater was obtained by calculating the inter-rater agreement that "quantifies the closeness of scores assigned by a pool of raters to the same study participant. The closer the scores, the higher the reliability of the data collection method" [11].

For most inquiries, categorization was fairly clear. For example, if the user's task was to play a song that they like, and they asked for "Diamond on a Landmine" by Billy Talent, the user was correct. The system was correct if it played the requested song and wrong if it did not respond at all, played a different song or did not understand what to do and responded with an error message. For another task, the user was correct when they asked the assistant to create a playlist. The system was wrong if it answered by saying "Sorry, I can't create playlists" (Siri), or "Here is Create Me on Spotify" (Google). Some cases were unclear. For example, if the users corrected themselves, if the system asked the user to repeat their request, or if the user did not follow the task descriptions. For these cases, we established classification rules which can be found in Appendix 2. Based on the confusion matrix, we calculated Cohen's Kappa as a performance measure. To estimate whether there was a difference between the conservative and the liberal approach of defining P_a, all further analyses were conducted with both values.

2.4   Statistical Analysis

We computed average UX scores per participant and per questionnaires as described in [7].

Correlations. We calculated pairwise Pearson correlations between UX and task success metrics. The underlying assumption of correlating UX and task success is that there is a positive relationship between the two [21].

Explained Variance R^2 of UX. To investigate our second research question on how much variance of UX metrics is explained by task success κ, we computed coefficients of determination R^2. Note, that our experimental design involved multiple measures of UX per participant. In addition, all participants interacted with three speech assistants. This repeated measures approach requires multi-level modelling, which can be thought of as an extension of linear regression. For a detailed overview on multi-level modelling and tests of the appropriateness of this approach for our UX metrics, please refer to [7].

R^2 represents which proportion of the total variance can be explained by a model. However, in multi-level models classical R^2 can not be used. Multi-level models contain fixed and random factors and it can be argued that random factors should be included or excluded into the computation of explained variance. Therefore, Nagawa et al. [19] introduced two versions of R^2: marginal R^2, which excludes random factors, and conditional R^2, which includes random factors into the computation of explained variance. Importantly, in our models, κ is a fixed factor, which suggests that marginal R^2 is a meaningful metric when asking how much UX variance is explained by κ.

Our multi-level model can be written as:

$$y_{rig} = \beta_0 + \sum \beta_\kappa \cdot x_{\kappa rig} + y_g + \alpha_{ig} + \epsilon_{rig} \tag{3}$$

where y_{rig} is the average response r of individual i belonging to group g. We computed y_{rig} for each of the four UX metrics that we evaluated, i.e. SUISQ-R, SUS, AttrakDiff and SASSI. The intercept is indicated by β_0 and β_κ represents the regression coefficients (slopes) of the predictors liberal and conservative κ. The values of κ are shown as $x_{\kappa rig}$. The group specific random effects are specified by y_g. In our models y_g corresponds to the three assistants, as participants interacted with each of them. Moreover, α_{ig} is the individual-specific random factor introduced by multiple measures. Finally, ϵ_{rig} is the error term.

Group Comparisons. We tested pair-wise differences in κ between groups. First we tested normal distribution of values per group and found that κ values are not normally distributed for all groups. Hence we used a non-parametric approach, namely Wilcoxon Rank-Sum tests, for analyzing differences between groups.

3 Results

3.1 Correlations Between Task Success and UX Metrics

Figure 1 shows pair-wise Pearson correlation coefficients between all UX and task success metrics. Correlations across assistants are shown in Fig. 1a. The correlation between conservative κ and liberal κ is almost perfect with $r = .97$. Correlations between UX metrics are high with the lowest $r = .69$ between SUS and AttrakDiff and the highest $r = .84$ between SASSI and AttrakDiff. Correlations between task success and UX metrics are lower with the highest $r = 0.54$ between SASSI and liberal κ and the lowest $r = 0.35$ between SUISQ-R and conservative κ.

Figure 1b depicts a heatmap of pair-wise correlations for interactions with the speech assistant Alexa. A similar pattern as for the pooled correlations in Fig. 1a can be observed. Correlations between UX and task success are lower still with the highest $r = .4$ between AttrakDiff and liberal κ and the lowest $r = .22$ between SUISQ-R and conservative κ.

Figure 1c depicts a heatmap of pair-wise correlations for interactions with the speech assistant Google. A similar pattern as for the pooled correlations in Fig. 1a can be observed. However, correlations between UX and task success are somewhat higher than for the pooled data. The highest $r = .65$ between SASSI and liberal κ and the lowest $r = .48$ between SUISQ-R and conservative κ.

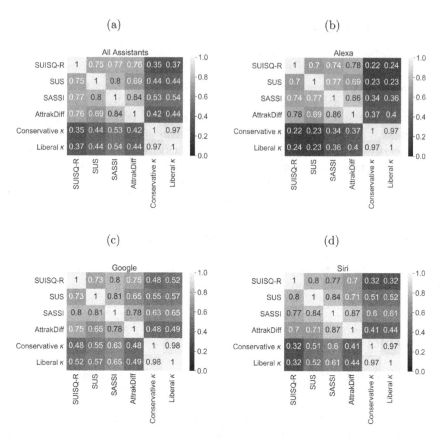

Fig. 1. Heatmap presentations of pairwise Pearson correlations between UX metrics and task success measures κ. **(a)** Correlations across all tested assistants. Correlations between UX metrics are higher than correlations between UX metrics and task success metrics κ. This plot is generated with data displayed separately for each assistant in subplots **(b)** – **(d)**. **(b)** Correlations for Alexa. Correlations between UX metrics are higher than correlations between UX metrics and task success metrics κ. **(c)** Correlations for Google Assistant. Correlations between UX metrics are higher or equal to correlations between UX metrics and task success metrics κ. **(d)** Correlations for Siri. Correlations between UX metrics are higher than correlations between UX metrics and task success metrics κ.

Figure 1d depicts a heatmap of pair-wise correlations for interactions with the speech assistant Siri. Again, the pattern of correlations is similar to the pooled correlations as well as to the correlations for the other two assistants. The highest $r = .61$ for correlations between UX and task success metrics is between SASSI and liberal κ and the lowest $r = .32$ between SUISQ-R and conservative κ (the correlation between SUISQ-R and liberal κ has the same r).

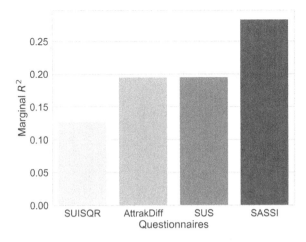

Fig. 2. Marginal R^2 for linear mixed models explaining each of the four evaluated questionnaires with conservative κ. The percentage of explained variance of liberal κ is similar and not displayed for redundancy. Marginal R^2 is the amount of variance explained by the fixed effects in the model. In this model κ is a fixed effect. For more information on the linear mixed models, see the Methods Section.

3.2   UX Variance Explained by Task Success

Marginal R^2 values are displayed in Fig. 2 for each of the four UX metrics we evaluated. These R^2 values give an indication of how much of the variance in UX scores is explained by task success, as measured by conservative and liberal κ. For more information on the models we computed marginal R^2 for, please refer to Sect. 2.4. Additional information on the rational and computation of marginal R^2 can be found in [19].

Both κ task success metrics explain 28% of the variance in UX scores of SASSI, about 20% of SUS and AttrakDiff and about 13% of SUISQ-R.

3.3   Comparisons of Task Success Between Groups

Figure 3 presents boxplots of conservative κ across the two types of groups we investigated: task type and speech assistant. There is a significant difference in task success κ between multi-turn tasks and single tasks ($p < .001$, $U = 7.34$). Single tasks are completed more successfully than multi-turn tasks.

In contrast, there is no significant difference in κ between the three tested speech assistants, which suggests that success rates are similar across these speech assistants.

(a)   (b)

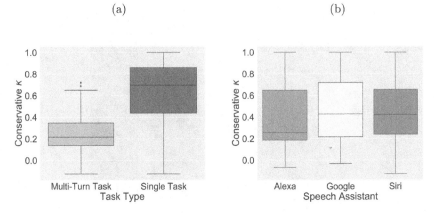

Fig. 3. Conservative κ by groups. In the boxplots, horizontal lines indicate the group median, boxes indicate the group inter-quartile-range (IQR), whiskers indicate $1.5 \times IQR$ for each group, and asterisks outliers larger than $1.5 \times the IQR$. Results for liberal κ are similar to conservative κ. One reason may be the high correlation between the two (see Fig. 1). Results from liberal κ were left out due to redundancy. **(a)** Conservative κ by task type. κ is significantly higher in single tasks than in multi-turn tasks ($p < .001$, $U = 7.34$). **(b)** Conservative κ by speech assistant. There is no difference in κ between the evaluated speech assistants ($p > .2$).

4   Discussion

4.1   Correlations

Correlations Between Kappa Conservative and Kappa Liberal. Our results suggest that Kappa conservative and Kappa liberal correlate almost perfectly. Kappa conservative is the proportion of times that both user and system are categorized as "correct" and Kappa liberal is the proportion of times that user and system are categorized "correct" or "unclear". Hence, the difference between the two metrics is whether unclear cases were counted as successful task completion. The high correlation between Kappa liberal and conservative shows that, in our study, the effect of unclear cases is negligible. This might be due to our experimental design, in which we assigned half of the participants to solving single tasks and most of those were clearly successfully completed. Single tasks are easier to process for speech assistants than multi-turn tasks [7,14] which may be why, most interactions were categorized as correct for this group.

Correlations Between UX Metrics. Correlations between UX metrics are larger than $r = .60$ in our study. This supports the findings in [6] and suggests that the UX metrics that were used, measure similar constructs for interactions with speech assistants.

Correlation Between UX and Kappa. Correlations between UX and Kappa are equal or lower than correlations between UX metrics. This suggests that UX metrics measure constructs that are not covered by task performance alone. Rather brand image, user expectations, trust and privacy concerns may influence user experience as well [4]. This is true across all speech assistants used in our study.

However, as can be seen in Fig. 1, correlations between UX and task success appear higher for Google Assistant than for Alexa and Siri. Interestingly, participants rate Google Assistant's UX as in-between the UX of Alexa (lowest UX ratings) and Siri (highest UX ratings) (see [7]). In our experiment, we used an Echo Dot (small version of Alexa), a HomePod (large, heavy Apple speaker) for Siri and a Google Home, which lies in-between HomePod and Echo Dot in size and weight. It could be, that users make snap-judgments of speech assistants based on their appearance which might influence their subsequent user experience. A user who sees the small Echo Dot, might get the impression that this product must be poor quality and evaluate the following interaction with this negative bias. Similarly, a large and heavy HomePod might create the impression that Siri is a high quality product, hence biasing their judgement of user experience positively. Indeed, Brüggemeier et al. [7] find that Siri is rated as significantly higher in UX than Alexa, which may be surprising, considering that we find that task success rates are similar across speech assistants.

Google Home, which in size is in-between the other two tested products, may have created the least appearance-based bias, allowing users to focus more on its actual task performance. This might explain, why we see the highest correlations between UX and task success for Google Assistant. If true, this would suggest that speech assistants can be subject to prejudices and snap-judgment biases. This idea should be further investigated. For example, one and the same speech assistant (e.g. Alexa) exists as different products, that differ in size and value (Echo Dot, Echo Studio, Echo Plus, see [1]). The UX and task performance of these products could be compared. If the appearance of the speech assistants affects UX, these different versions of Alexa may create different UX. In contrast, if biases are due to brand image [4] the UX of these different Alexa Amazon products may be similar.

4.2 Explained Variance

The variance of UX that Kappa explains is low with less than 30% across all UX metrics. This suggests that further research is necessary to identify other factors that influence UX of speech assistants. There are a lot of potential factors that may affect UX, for example brand image, expectations and their confirmation, trust and privacy concerns [4]. In our study, we found that UX metrics differ in the amount of variance explained by task performance, with SASSI being explained best by task success (28%) and SUISQ-R being explained least (13%). Notably, SUISQ-R covers voice attributes like "The system seemed professional in its speaking style", "The system's voice sounded like a regular person", and "The system's voice sounded natural" that are not covered by the other UX metrics. This may suggest that one of the UX-factors that task success does not measure is user perception of assistant voice.

About 20% of variance of both SUS and AttrakDiff are explained by task success. Interestingly, SUS and AttrakDiff differ in their construct scope, with SUS focusing on usability, which is a pragmatic factor as defined by Hassenzahl [12]. AttrakDiff also contains pragmatic factors, but in addition includes non-pragmatic, hedonic factors like fun when using the product [12]. It is important to note, that even though task success explains the same amount of variance in SUS and AttrakDiff, this does not suggest that these constructs measure the same thing, which is supported by the correlation between these constructs, which is the lowest between UX metrics that we tested (see Fig. 1).

4.3   Differences in Kappa Between Groups

As expected, there is a difference in task success between single and multi-turn tasks. Multi-turn tasks are known to be more difficult to successfully complete for speech assistants [14], hence it is unsurprising to see that task performance for multi-turn tasks is significantly worse than for single tasks. Moreover, this reflects product reviews that suggest that these speech assistants are apt in dealing with one-off requests, however have difficulties holding a conversation [8]. Thus, there is more work to be done for developers of these devices in order to enable them to hold conversations.

There are no differences in task success between the three tested speech assistants. This is in contrast to the differences in UX participants report for these assistants [7]. This observation supports the finding that task success explains only a small amount of UX variance. This is an important finding for developers as differences in UX of speech assistants may not be determined by task performance but by other, potentially more elusive factors. Thus, it may not be sufficient to optimize task success rates to achieve improvements in UX. Notably, UX predicts customer satisfaction and customer loyalty [23]. Hence, identifying factors that affect UX is relevant for business and should be studied further.

Acknowledgements. Our work is funded by the German Federal Ministry for Economic Affairs and Energy as part of their AI innovation initiative (funding code 01MK20011A). We want to thank Kim Wagener for being a second rater and annotating the audio data and Philip Lalone for providing a software solution to automatically transcribe the audio data.

Appendix 1: Task Instructions

Appendix 1 shows instructions for participants of our study. Words that were highlighted in bold face in the participants' instructions are also highlighted here. Half of the participants received instructions for single tasks and half of the participants received instructions for multi-turn tasks.

1.1 Single Tasks

You are given a set of tasks to perform with three speech assistants: **Amazon's Alexa**, **Google Assistant**, and **Apple's Siri** (order may differ).
After talking to each assistant, we ask you to rate your experience on four short questionnaires. That is, we ask you to:

1. interact with assistant A
2. fill out questionnaires for assistant A
3. interact with assistant B
4. fill out questionnaires for assistant B
5. interact with assistant C
6. fill out questionnaires for assistant C

The type of tasks you will be performing are "**single tasks**", which can be managed with one sentence. For each task, we provide you with a list and specify a goal that the assistant may be able to help you with. We'd like you to talk to the assistants in a natural manner and try to construct a sentence in your own words based on what the task says.

There is no time limit. If you are stuck, rephrase your request or move on to the next goal. It is important for you only to interact with the assistants, not to accomplish all goals.

Don't forget to start the conversation by saying "Alexa", "Okay Google" or "Hey Siri".

Single Tasks

1. Goal: **play a song**
   Song: choose one you like
2. Goal: **play an artist**
   Artist: choose one that was popular during your childhood
3. Goal: **play a playlist**
   Playlist: choose one that suits an activity you plan on doing today
4. Goal: **play a genre**
   Genre: choose one you like

1.2 Multi-turn Tasks

You are given a set of tasks to perform with three speech assistants: **Amazon's Alexa**, **Google Assistant**, and **Apple's Siri** (order may differ).
After talking to each assistant, we ask you to rate your experience on four short questionnaires. That is, we ask you to:

1. interact with assistant A
2. fill out questionnaires for assistant A
3. interact with assistant B
4. fill out questionnaires for assistant B
5. interact with assistant C

6. fill out questionnaires for assistant C

The type of tasks you will be performing are **"multi-turn tasks"**, which are designed to accomplish one final goal with a series of questions. For each task, we provide you with a list and specify a goal that the assistant may be able to help you with. We'd like you to talk to the assistants in a natural manner and try to construct a sentence in your own words based on what the task says.

There is no time limit. If you are stuck, rephrase your request or move on to the next goal. It is important for you only to interact with the assistants, not to accomplish all goals.

Don't forget to start the conversation by saying "Alexa", "Okay Google" or "Hey Siri".

Multi-tasks

1. Goal: **keep up to date with music**
   Sub-goal 1: play music
   type: popular
   Sub-Goal 2: get more information (e.g. song's name, artist's name, genre,..)
2. Goal: **build your own playlist**
   Sub-goal 1: create new playlist
   Playlist name: your choice of feeling (e.g. happy, melancholic, hungover,..)
   Sub-goal 2: play music
   Type: same feeling as above
   Sub-goal 3: add first song to your playlist
3. Goal: **get music recommendations**
   Sub-goal 1: play your favourite song
   Sub-goal 2: play music
   Type: similar

Appendix 2: Rules for Annotation

Appendix 2 depicts rules that we followed when manually annotating dialogues between users and speech assistants. Our annotation categories included *user correct, user unclear, user wrong, system correct, system unclear* and *system wrong*. For more details on annotation see Sect. 2.2. We appreciate that other rules are possible and may be more appropriate for annotations and this is especially true in experimental settings that differ from ours. We present these rules therefore not as recommendations for dialog annotation, but as a means to reconstruct and potentially replicate our analysis.

1. Requests in which the user fails to say the wake word correctly are considered as *user wrong*, except if users correct themselves within the request.
2. Requests like "Louder.", "Quieter.", "Turn up the volume.", "Stop playing the song.", "Hello.", "Next song.", "Can you hear me?", "Another sad song.", "Add song to library.", or requests that involve insults are not included in calculating *Kappa*.

3. User requests that are not music related, are not included in calculating *Kappa*.
4. If a speech assistant continues to play music when a user makes a new request, we consider the user as correct and the system as wrong.
5. If a speech assistant announces that it is about to start playing the requested song, but then does not actually play it, we consider the user as correct and the system as wrong.
6. When a user corrects him- or herself during their request, we consider
   (a) the user as correct, if the correction attempt takes place within the same sentence, that is to be corrected,
   (b) the user as wrong, if their correction attempt takes place in a new sentence and after an incorrect sentence.
7. If a user asks for chart songs and assistant plays a song that is called "Chart" or "Charts", we recognize the user as correct and the system as wrong.
8. If a user asks for music recommendations not as part of a task, or if they just ask for music and thereby they do not follow task instructions, we label the user as wrong. In these cases, we consider
   (a) the system as correct, if it responds by saying what music it can play,
   (b) the system as wrong, if it responds by saying "I couldn't find any songs that match your request".
9. If a system asks for user confirmation, even though the user request was clear, we label the user as correct and the system as wrong. For example a user may say "Hey *[system]*, can you play the latest charts?" and a system may respond "What do you want to hear?" or a user may say "Hey *[system]*, play ballet!" and a system may answer "Was that ballet?".
10. If a system asks for user confirmation after a user makes an unclear request we recognize both system and user as correct. For example a user may say: "play Bohemian Rhapsody" and a system may respond "Which one?". However, if a system interrupts a user while they are still making a request, we label the system as wrong.
11. If a user request is clear and asks for specific music and a system responds with "Here is Spotify" we label the user as correct and the system as wrong.
12. We consider users as correct independently of whether they follow the order we outlined for single tasks or not.
13. If a user does not follow the order we outlined for multi-turn tasks, we label
   (a) the user as correct, if they changed the order within a task goal,
   (b) the user as unclear, if they mix subgoals from different task goals.
14. If an annotator can not hear whether a system response is correct or wrong, for example because they do not know a song or genre:
   (a) we consider the system as wrong, if the user repeats their request,
   (b) we do not include this interaction in the computation of *Kappa* if the user does not repeat their request.
15. If a user asks for Classical Music and an assistant plays Classical Rock etc., we label the user as correct, and the system as wrong.
16. If a user requests the same piece twice, we include both requests in computing *Kappa*.

17. If a user requests a genre instead of a mood (i.e. the user does not follow our task description), we consider the user as wrong.

18. If a user requests a mood instead of a genre (i.e. the user does not follow our task description), we label the user as wrong.

19. In the task, in which users are supposed to create a playlist, if a user requests something else than creating a playlist, we label the user as wrong.

20. If a user requests e.g. "relaxing songs" without saying that they want to create a playlist, we consider the user as correct.

21. In the task, in which users are required to request their favorite song, if a user asks for "German music" instead of a specific favorite song, we label the user as wrong.

22. In the task, in which users are required to request their favorite song, if a user names an artist instead of asking for a favorite song, we consider the user as correct.

23. If a system plays a song or an album with the same name as stated in the user request, we recognize the system as correct.

24. In the task, in which users are supposed to create a playlist, if a user asks for playing songs of a certain mood, we label the user as correct.

25. If a user asks "Is song already added to my playlist?" we consider the user as wrong.

26. Requests that are being made while already filling out the questionnaires are included in calculating *Kappa* as it was not always possible to determine if the user had already begun to fill out the questionnaires.

27. Requests that are being made during the interaction with another assistant are included in calculating *Kappa*.

28. If a system does not process a user request because the request is too long, we label the user as correct and the system as wrong. For example a user may say: "Hey *[system]*, can you please play some popular music ... not the one that you played just now." and a system may respond: "I looked for popular music not the one that you played just but it either isn't available or can't be played right now".

29. If a request is not clear and a system responds by saying they can not help we consider the user as wrong and the system as correct.

30. After a user makes a request to play similar music and the annotator can tell that the music is not actually similar to the previously played song, we label the system as wrong.

31. If a user asks to play "independent music" and a system plays "independent women", we label the user as correct and the system as wrong.

32. If the system continues to play the song that had been played before, even though the user has made a new request, we consider the system as wrong. For example, the user may ask for their favorite song, which the system then plays. Subsequently, the user wants to listen to similar music, but the system responds to that request simply by continuing to play the user's favorite song.

33. If a user says "Play a genre.", "Play my music." or "Play a playlist.", that is they make generic requests, that do not follow our task descriptions, we

consider the user as wrong. If the system starts playing any music after such user requests, we label the system as correct.

34. Here we outline a specific dialog and our annotation. User says: "Add this song to a playlist". We label user as correct. System responds: "What is the name of the playlist?". We consider the system to be correct in their response. User responds: "Classical music", which we recognize as correct user response. Then the system answers: "Hm, I didn't find a playlist called classical music", which we label as wrong system response.

35. If a system responds by citing a Wikipedia article, we consider the system as wrong.

36. If a system does not respond by giving the easiest possible answer, we label the system as wrong. For example a user may ask "Who is the artist?" of a specific song that is playing. The system may respond: "the first two are *name 1* and *name 2*. I have nine answers in total. Let me know if you want to hear more."

37. If a system says that it adds a song to a music library instead of a playlist, we consider the system to be correct.

38. If a system is asked to play rock music and responds by saying "Shuffling Legendary from Spotify." we label the system as wrong as neither the playlist's name nor its description include the word *rock*.

39. We consider the following types of music as genre:
    (a) Rock, Pop, Classical, R&B, Rap, Metal, Blues, Soul, Folk music, etc.
    (b) Charts,
    (c) German, Italian, etc. music,
    (d) Children Rhymes,
    (e) and Bollywood music.

40. We do not consider "Soft pop hits" as popular music and label the system as wrong when playing those in response of a user asking for popular music.

41. If a user asks for classical music, the request is considered as correct. If the system responds by playing "Epic Piano", we recognize the system response as wrong as neither the playlist's name nor its description include the word *classical*.

42. If the user is asked to build a playlist and play music linked to a specific feeling, e.g. happy, and they ask for "Weihnachtslieder" (Christmas Carols), we label the user as wrong. If a system responds to that request by playing Christmas carols, we recognize that system response as correct.

43. When required to play a genre, and a user asks for Local FM, their request is considered wrong. A system is labeled correct, if it plays local FM, wrong if it plays other music, or unclear if it lets the user know that it is not able to fulfil the request.

44. When users make requests in German, we label
    (a) the system as correct, if it does not respond or responds by saying that it is not sure how to help,
    (b) the system as wrong, if it gives an unrelated response,
    (c) and user as wrong in both of the above cases.

45. If a user asks the system how to create a playlist, we label the user as unclear.

References

1. Albanesius, C.: Amazon's Echo Lineup: What's the Difference? https://uk.pcmag.com/features/94664/amazons-echo-lineup-whats-the-difference (2019). Accessed 29 Dec 2020
2. Artstein, R., Poesio, M.: Inter-coder agreement for computational linguistics (2008)
3. Bortz, J., Schuster, C.: Statistik für Human-und Sozialwissenschaftler: Limitierte Sonderausgabe. Springer, Heidelberg (2011). https://doi.org/10.1007/978-3-642-12770-0
4. Brill, T.M., Munoz, L., Miller, R.J.: Siri, Alexa, and other digital assistants: a study of customer satisfaction with artificial intelligence applications. J. Mark. Manag. (2019). https://doi.org/10.1080/0267257X.2019.1687571
5. Brown, M.: Best smart speakers: which deliver the best combination of digital assistant and audio performance? https://www.techhive.com/article/3252155/best-smart-speakers.html (2020). Accessed 22 Jan 2021
6. Brüggemeier, B., Breiter, M., Kurz, M., Schiwy, J.: User experience of Alexa when controlling music: comparison of face and construct validity of four questionnaires. In: ACM International Conference Proceeding Series (2020)
7. Brüggemeier, B., Breiter, M., Kurz, M., Schiwy, J.: User experience of Alexa, Siri and google assistant when controlling music – comparison of four questionnaires. In: Stephanidis, C., Marcus, A., Rosenzweig, E., Rau, P.-L.P., Moallem, A., Rauterberg, M. (eds.) HCII 2020. LNCS, vol. 12423, pp. 600–618. Springer, Cham (2020). https://doi.org/10.1007/978-3-030-60114-0_40
8. Collins, K., Metz, C.: Alexa vs. Siri vs. Google: Which Can Carry on a Conversation Best? https://www.nytimes.com/interactive/2018/08/17/technology/alexa-siri-conversation.html (2018). Accessed 29 Dec 2020
9. Dasgupta, R.: Voice User Interface Design. Apress (2018)
10. Enge, E.: Rating the Smarts of the Digital Personal Assistants in 2019 (2019). https://www.perficient.com/insights/research-hub/digital-personal-assistants-study#smarttest. Accessed 29 Dec 2020
11. Gwet, K.L.: Computing inter-rater reliability and its variance in the presence of high agreement. Br. J. Math. Stat. Psychol. (2008). https://doi.org/10.1348/000711006X126600
12. Hassenzahl, M., Burmester, M., Koller, F.: AttrakDiff: Ein Fragebogen zur Messung wahrgenommener hedonischer und pragmatischer Qualität. In: Szwillus, G. and Ziegler, J. (eds.) Mensch & Computer 2003, pp. 187–196. B. G. Teubner (2003)
13. International Organization for Standardization: ISO 9241–210: Ergonomics of human-system interaction - Part 210: Human-centred design for interactive systems (2019)
14. Kiseleva, J., Williams, K., Hassan Awadallah, A., Crook, A.C., Zitouni, I., Anastasakos, T.: Predicting user satisfaction with intelligent assistants. In: Proceedings of the 39th International ACM SIGIR conference on Research and Development in Information Retrieval - SIGIR 2016 (2016)
15. Klemmer, S.R., Sinha, A.K., Chen, J., Landay, J.A., Aboobaker, N., Wang, A.: SUEDE: a wizard of Oz prototyping tool for speech user interfaces. In: UIST (User Interface Software and Technology): Proceedings of the ACM Symposium (2000)
16. Kocaballi, A.B., Laranjo, L., Coiera, E.: Measuring user experience in conversational interfaces: a comparison of six questionnaires. In: HCI 2018 (2018)
17. Kocaballi, A.B., Laranjo, L., Coiera, E.: Understanding and measuring user experience in conversational interfaces. Interact. Comput. 31, 192–207 (2019). https://doi.org/10.1093/iwc/iwz015

18. Lewis, J.R.: Standardized Questionnaires for Voice Interaction Design. Voice Interact, Des (2016)
19. Nakagawa, S., Schielzeth, H.: A general and simple method for obtaining R2 from generalized linear mixed-effects models. Methods Ecol. Evol. (2013). https://doi.org/10.1111/j.2041-210x.2012.00261.x
20. Richter, F.: Siri und Co. - Stets zu Diensten (2016). https://de.statista.com/infografik/5627/nutzung-von-digitalen-virtuellen-assistenten/. Accessed 31 Dec 2020
21. Walker, M.A., Litman, D.J., Kamm, C.A., Abella, A.: PARADISE: A Framework for Evaluating Spoken Dialogue Agents. arXiv Prepr. C. (1997)
22. Wang, W.Y., Bohus, D., Kamar, E., Horvitz, E.: Crowdsourcing the acquisition of natural language corpora: Methods and observations. In: 2012 IEEE Workshop Spoken Language Technology SLT 2012 - Proceedings, pp. 73–78 (2012). https://doi.org/10.1109/SLT.2012.6424200
23. Zhou, R., Wang, X., Shi, Y., Zhang, R., Zhang, L., Guo, H.: Measuring e-service quality and its importance to customer satisfaction and loyalty: an empirical study in a telecom setting. Electron. Commer. Res. **19**(3), 477–499 (2018). https://doi.org/10.1007/s10660-018-9301-3

Research on the Usability Design of HUD Interactive Interface

Xiang Li[✉], Bin Jiang, Zehua Li, and Zhixin Wu

Nanjing University of Science and Technology, Nanjing 210094, China

Abstract. In the context of the Industry 4.0 era, with the rise of artificial intelligence technology and autonomous driving of automobiles, automobile companies are carrying out extensive technology research and development, product deployment and commercial layout around technologies such as autonomous driving, car networking, and human-computer interaction. In the development stage of automobile intelligence, a large amount of information and data such as entertainment and social interaction enter the in-vehicle system. The interactive information inside and outside the vehicle collected with physical components such as on-board sensors enriches the driver's driving experience to a certain extent, but at the same time it is easy to let The driver is distracted and affects driving safety. Head-up display (HUD), as a new driving assistance safety system, is considered to be the main way of presenting in-vehicle information in the future. However, the HUD information display system supported by technology lacks specific research on the design of human-computer interaction interface. This article will clarify the specific design based on the eye movement experiment to achieve the purpose of usability.

Keywords: HUD · Safe driving · Interface interaction

1 Research Background

In the context of the Industry 4.0 era, with the rise of artificial intelligence technology and autonomous driving of automobiles, automobile companies are carrying out extensive technology research and development, product deployment and commercial layout around technologies such as autonomous driving, car networking, and human-computer interaction. In the development stage of automobile intelligence, a large number of information and data such as entertainment and social interaction enter the in-vehicle system. The interactive information inside and outside the vehicle collected with physical components such as on-board sensors enriches the driver's driving experience to a certain extent, but it is easy to make the person be distracted and affect driving safety.

As a new type of driving assistance safety system, the head-up display is considered to be the main way of presenting in-vehicle information in the future. However, the HUD information display system supported by technology lacks specific research on the design of human-computer interaction interface. This article will be based on eye movement experiments with the help of the human-machine driving information transmission relationship model and other methods are clearly designed to achieve the purpose of usability.

© Springer Nature Switzerland AG 2021
M. Kurosu (Ed.): HCII 2021, LNCS 12764, pp. 370–380, 2021.
https://doi.org/10.1007/978-3-030-78468-3_25

2   Interface Visual Design and Application

2.1   Interactive Interface Design Principles

Compared with traditional interaction methods, the interaction design of automobiles has the biggest difference that it changes based on different situations. The car is always in a changeable and complex situation, far different from the stable interactive environment in the past. Therefore, we need to combine interface design principles with specific driving environment characteristics, and use this as a basis to design automobile interactive interface principles.

(1) **Rationalization Principle of Information Selection Layout.** According to the research results of vehicle ergonomics, about 60% of the visual attention during driving will be focused on maintaining the state of the vehicle and coping with emergencies.

Therefore, the vehicle interface should not occupy too much visual channels, but needs to ensure that users can quickly Get information and perform operations. therefore, in the limited visual channel, it is necessary to classify the information, divide the information priority, retain the necessary information according to the frequency and importance of use, and discard irrelevant information barriers. At the same time, in the information layout, more use of graphics and text forms, as far as possible to enable users to complete most of the information acquisition and operation behavior on the main page.

(2) **Information Feedback Principle.** To change the default, adjust the template as follows.The information feedback principle is based on the feedback mechanism to guide the interaction design, in order to ensure that users get instant feedback in the context of use, confirm operations, and improve the success rate of operations. Context-based vehicle interaction interface information is complex and variable, so it is particularly important to feedback this information immediately.

The specific performance of information feedback is: timely feedback the changes and status of objects and programs; provide feedback to remind users whether there are errors, and help users correct in time during operation; special symbols and graphics should be used to indicate where there is a need to increase attention The meaning of it; when the user is resting or working, the message should be used to remind the user in a softer way.

(3) **The Principle of Interface Simplicity.** In today's choice of car interaction methods, the functions of physical buttons and knobs are gradually shifted to touch-sensitive interactive screens, which undoubtedly increases the difficulty of interface design. A simple interactive interface with clear instructions can shorten the human-computer interaction time and increase the accuracy of the interactive content, ensuring driving safety.

The interface design should be concise but not simple. The semantic design of information should clearly express icons, scales and numbers to avoid ambiguity in visual understanding. The design and arrangement of buttons should consider the consistency of coding, which is conducive to memory and enables users to perform blind operations after familiarization.

2.2 Interactive Interface Content

Refer to the relevant content of the vehicle driving system, the system information can usually be divided into five categories: basic vehicle information, navigation system, driving safety warning, social entertainment information, and auxiliary imaging system, as shown in Table 1 shows:

Table 1. Assisted driving system information classification

Basic vehicle information	Navigation system	Driving safety warning	Social entertainment information	Auxiliary imaging system
Speed	Road indication trajectory	In-car safety warning information	Bluetooth button control	Reversing camera system
Rotating speed	Distance to destination	Obstacle information	Voice control	Visual blind zone imaging
Mileage	Road name	Lane information	Gesture Recognition	
Water temperature		Identification information	We Chat	
Oil temperature			SMS	
			Music	

However, in addition to the basic principles of interaction design, the interface design should also focus on the cognitive load of the driver during the driving process and the real-time dynamics and multi-dimensional complexity of the driving situation in the selection of content. Excessive occupation of visual channels and receiving cumbersome interactive information will often lead to a certain difference between the conceptual model of the system and the user's mental model, which will affect driving safety.

Therefore, it is necessary to construct a hierarchical HUD security prompt information model. This study is based on the principle of information classification, and the information priority is divided according to the importance of interactive content and frequency of use, as shown in Fig. 1 below. The content with higher priority is status information display and context information display. The status information display interface includes basic driving information, warning information, and social entertainment information; the context information display interface includes collision avoidance instructions and navigation instructions. Therefore, the interface usability design will be expanded on such interactive interface content.

First priority   Second priority   Third priority   Fourth priority   Fifth priority

Fig. 1. Information visualization chart

2.3 Interface Usability Design

The interface information of the assisted driving system is closely related to the driving environment and user driving behavior. In the design process, it is necessary to comprehensively consider the font, functional layout and color tendency of the visual elements.

(1) **Font.** MIT's Age Lab, the University of New England Transportation Center, and Monotype conducted a study on the reading efficiency of sans-serif fonts due to different line spacing widths and different font thicknesses. It was found that Square Grotesque fonts increase the reading time by 12% compared with Humanist fonts, which makes cars in the braking distance when driving at the same average speed differs by 50 feet, and a distance of 50 feet means the difference between safe driving and a serious accident. Monotype proposes to use human-oriented sans-serif fonts, among which Roboto fonts are generally considered to be the most accurate and efficient fonts for reading, and have been verified by Google to read information in the car, as shown in Fig. 2.

Fig. 2. Information priority classification

(2) **Information Layout.** The functional layout of the HUD interface is based on the content of the interface information. After priority classification, the five functional module information of basic driving information, anti-collision instruction information, navigation instruction information, warning information and social entertainment information are obtained. In order to further determine the location of the module, the study uses the driver to look straight ahead as the first perspective, and divide the interface into regions, as shown in Fig. 3:

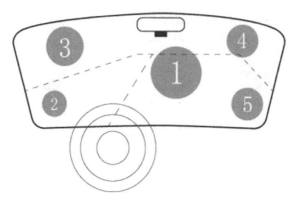

Fig. 3. Module area division

First of all, the middle position of the interface occupies most of the driving angle of view. This area (position 1) mainly presents basic road conditions, and is associated with the anti-collision indication information, such as detecting the distance, speed, safety distance, pedestrians and other information of the vehicle ahead.

Secondly, the information that needs to be recorded is the basic driving information. In the simplest mode, this area mainly presents the vehicle speed value and unit information. It has a small area and does not need to occupy too much area, so it is more appropriate to place it in position 2.

Furthermore, the area with a larger interface area and more scattered information is the navigation indicator information module, which has strong display flexibility, and most systems support user-defined display content; the similar area is the warning information module, it contains random auxiliary driving information such as road speed limit information, cruise control information, vehicle distance prompts and other information. The purpose of both is to display the information in the driving process more intuitively and concisely, avoiding the occurrence of dangerous situations due to distraction. Therefore, these two module areas are suitable for 3 and 4 parts.

Finally, place the social entertainment information area with the lowest priority at position 5, which is in the lower right quadrant in human visual cognitive habits, and is in the area with the lowest recognition rate. This requirement is just in line with the low frequency and unimportant information characteristics of social entertainment information in driving.

(3) **Color Tendency.** Color is very important in interface design. In completing visual tasks, color coding is beneficial to enhance the efficiency of information recognition, thus shortening the information processing time. The visual interface of the HUD assisted driving system is a virtual image projected on the front windshield of the vehicle. The visibility of interface elements will be affected by factors such as light, weather, road conditions, and environment. Therefore, it is necessary to fully ensure that the clarity of the element display is not disturbed when selecting colors.

At the same time, this research needs to select the color of HUD in combination with the traffic safety color system. In the road traffic safety color system, most of the high-visibility color designs and applications are based on green, yellow and red. Among them, the red system means prohibition and stop, the green system means safe and feasible; the yellow system means warning and buffering to distinguish different safety prompts.

Refer to the color matching of the existing HUD in the current market, as shown in Fig. 4. The HUD interface design of this study uses blue as the main color, and red, yellow, and green as auxiliary colors to display information prompts. The specific basis will be explained in the eye movement experiment verification in Sect. 3.

Fig. 4. HUD Color Matching

3   Eye Movement Experiment and Verification

3.1   Experimental Study

Purpose. The core task of the HUD assisted driving system is to assist the driver to effectively complete the driving task and improve driving safety. The study focuses on the specific design of the usability of the interactive interface, and clarifies the size, color and location of the interface elements. According to the design description in the third part, in order to verify the effectiveness of the HUD system design, the purpose of this experiment has two points:

Experiment 1: Through the accuracy test of the interface safety prompt information, it is verified that the HUD system visual interface of the information layout described in the third part has the best cognitive performance.

Experiment 2: Through the sensitivity test to potential hazards in complex driving situations, it is verified that the color selection of the HUD system visual interface described in the third part has the best response ability to the driver's danger.

(1) Experimental Method. This experiment conducts an objective evaluation of driving safety from the accuracy of interface cognition and the driver's ability to react dangerously. It mainly adopts eye movement experiment method and spoken language analysis method.

Eye Movement Experiment: Aiming at the interface information cognitive efficiency and driver's risk response ability test, the eye movement experiment method is mainly used to record the information cognitive situation and driving behavior response of the subjects under different information layout and color selection interfaces.

Oral Analysis: For the test of the accuracy of interface information cognition, in addition to the eye movement experiment, the oral analysis method is mainly used, which can externalize the results of the implicit process such as the user's information cognition stage and cognitive strategies. After the experiment process is over, the subjects are asked to give oral answers to the specific information content that appears, so as to judge the driver's information cognition efficiency under different information layouts.

(3) **Experimental Variables**

Independent Variable:

Experiment 1: Information layout of system interface
Experiment 2: HUD system visual interface color

Dependent Variable:

Experiment 1: Cognitive performance
Experiment 2: Risk factor sensitivity

3.2   Experimental Design

(1) **Participant Selection.** In order to prevent the participants from having insufficient knowledge of the driving interface information, using experience, and lack of basic information cognitive ability of the HUD system functional interface, this experiment selects participants with a certain driving experience, and minimizes the participants' exposure to the HUD. Factors such as cognitive bias caused by system unfamiliarity. There are 12 participants, 9 males and 3 females, with driving experience in the range of 2–10 years.

(2) **Experimental Material.** The experimental instrument of the eye movement experiment adopts the portable eye tracker of Tobii Pro's X3–120 model, which can record the trajectory of human eye movement, fixation point, fixation time and other characteristics. At the same time, according to different experimental purposes, this study also selected and produced two sets of experimental materials according to experimental requirements, as follows:

Experiment 1: Make HUD visual interface materials with different information layouts. According to the difference of independent variables, the experiment produced three kinds of experimental materials with different information layouts, as shown in Fig. 5 below. The different information layout interfaces displayed by the experiment materials were sequentially changed, and different subjects were required to memorize the specific information content and answer related questions after the experiment. The questions are as follows:

- In the current situation, how far is the vehicle from the position of the vehicle ahead?
- In the current situation, what is the driving speed of the vehicle?
- In the current situation, how far is the left turn from the navigation prompt?
- In the current situation, what kind of warning message is there for the distance ahead?
- In the current situation, who is making the voice call?

Fig. 5. Information layout interface material

Fig. 6. Visual color interface material

Experiment 2: Make different HUD visual color interface materials. According to the difference of independent variables, the experiment produced four different color interface materials, as shown in Fig. 6. The experiment requires the subjects to freely watch the assisted driving interface of different colors in turn, and arrange relevant risk factors in the actual situation in the interface, such as: Side pedestrians, distance to the vehicle ahead, lane location, etc. After the experiment, the gaze hot zone of the eye movement experiment parameters was observed to record the subjects' sensitivity to risk factors during the test.

(3) Cognitive Performance Evaluation

Cognitive Performance Evaluation: The inspection and evaluation of the cognitive performance of visual interface information mainly focus on the speed and accuracy of cognitive information. In this experiment, the latter is selected as the cognitive performance indicator, and the correct rate of the driver's question answer after the completion of the test is defined as the cognitive accuracy rate. Failure to answer or failed to answer is defined as an error. Finally, the number of correct cognition and the ratio of the total times is the cognitive accuracy rate.

Risk Sensitivity Evaluation: Improving driving safety is the purpose of the HUD assisted driving system. Therefore, prompting of potential hazards in complex driving situations is an important part of HUD. For the driver, the degree of subjective sensitivity to hazard warnings determines the ability to react to hazards. Therefore, this experiment defines the driver's hazard sensitivity as an important indicator to verify driving safety efficiency under different visual color interfaces.

3.3 Data Processing and Analysis

(1) **Cognitive Performance Analysis.** Through the experiment, a pair of 12 subjects' cognitive efficiency was recorded and analyzed, and the result of the accuracy

Table 2. Information layout interface and cognitive accuracy

Participant serial number	Material number	Number of correct answers (times)	Cognitive accuracy (%)
1	Material 1	5	100%
2	Material 2	1	20%
3	Material 3	3	60%
4	Material 1	3	60%
5	Material 2	2	40%
6	Material 3	4	80%
7	Material 1	5	100%
8	Material 2	1	20%
9	Material 3	3	60%
10	Material 1	4	80%
11	Material 2	1	20%
12	Material 3	3	60%

of the information layout on the cognition was calculated, as shown in Table 2. From the data in the figure, the interactive interface of different information layouts There is an impact on the efficiency of knowledge. The cognitive accuracy rate (85%) of the information layout interface reflected by the material is better than the other two groups (25% and 65%), indicating that the information layout HUD visual interface designed in this experiment is conducive to the same situation, the reading and understanding of driver information at the same time conforms to the law of driver information recognition.

(2) **Risk Sensitivity Analysis.** Through the experimental records of the 12 subjects in Experiment 2, the driver's eye movement hot zone diagrams under different visual color interfaces are obtained, as shown in Fig. 7. Under no experimental task, with the same experimental situation and equal experimental time, driving the gaze of the interactive interface of different visual colors is different.

According to the evaluation index, the visual interface with blue as the main color tends to pay the most attention to potential hazards in the road in the driving task, especially for pedestrian elements, showing red hot spots; the interface with yellow as the main color has the gaze of the vehicle in front The highest, low attention to pedestrians; the red and purple color interface hot zone is messy, indicating that the driver's gaze is scattered during driving and driving danger is prone to occur.

From the analysis results, it can be seen that under the premise of the same driving situation, the HUD system with a blue-based visual interface can improve the driving safety of the driver, has a good role in assisting driving, and is more sensitive to danger in driving other HUD vision systems.

Fig. 7. HUD color matching

3.4 Experimental Results

Through objective experimental evaluation, the hypothesis of the purpose of this experiment was fully verified:

1. In the performance evaluation of information cognition in experiment 1, the cognition accuracy rate of the information indicators of each group of the experiment was analyzed. The data results showed that the information cognition accuracy rate of material 1 was better, which verified the rationality of the information layout design results. That is, the HUD visual interface with this information layout has the highest cognitive performance.
2. In the evaluation of the risk sensitivity of experiment 2, the color interface of each group of the experiment was analyzed for the risk sensitivity. The data results show that the HUD system with a blue-based visual interface can play a good auxiliary role and improve the driving safety of drivers. This color-oriented HUD visual interface has the highest color sensitivity.

References

1. Zheng, X.: Research on the design of automotive central control infotainment system based on user experience. Guangdong University of Technology (2019)
2. Ye, S., Li, J.: Study on the design of auto interactive adaptive interface based on context. Des. Art Res. **10**(04), 78–81+105 (2020)
3. Yang, X.: Research on the design principles of the vehicle-mounted AR-HUD road safety prompt information interface. South China University of Technology (2017)
4. Chahine, N., Reimer, B., Dobres, J.: Branding und Lesbarkeit von Schriften in Displays. ATZelektronik **10**(1), 64–69.Y (2015)
5. He, X.: Research on mobile phone adaptive user interface design based on context awareness. Beijing University of Posts and Telecommunications, Beijing (2012)
6. Hou, Y.: Visual performance analysis of mobile phone interface based on user experience. Packaging Eng. **37**(10), 151–154 (2016)
7. Yue, Y.: Comparison of time measurement method and oral analysis method. J. Nanjing Normal Univ. (Soc. Sci. Ed.) **03**, 35–40 (1994)

Current Problems, Future Needs: Voices of First Responders About Communication Technology

Kerrianne Morrison[✉] [iD], Shanee Dawkins[✉] [iD], Yee-Yin Choong[✉] [iD],
Mary F. Theofanos, Kristen Greene[iD], and Susanne Furman

National Institute of Standards and Technology, Gaithersburg, MD 20899, USA
{kerrianne.morrison,shanee.dawkins,yee-yin.choong,
mary.theofanos,kristen.greene,susanne.furman}@nist.gov

Abstract. With advances in network technologies, there has been increasing interest in developing new communication technology for first responders that utilizes wireless broadband networks. In order to develop new communication technology, user requirements are needed to ensure new technology is usable; however, capturing user requirements for first responders has been challenging due to the diversity of its users' contexts and needs. This paper aims to provide guidance and insight into developing user requirements for communication technology developed for first responders by exploring first responders' communication technology problems and needs. Qualitative interviews with 193 first responders across four disciplines (Communications (Comm) Center & 9-1-1 Services; Emergency Medical Services; Fire Service; Law Enforcement) revealed that they often encountered problems with their communication technology's reliability, usability, and interoperability. Their primary need for their communication technology was for solutions to their current problems, rather than development of new technology. Many were also interested in communication technology that can provide them with real-time information. This study underscores that communication technology for first responders should be designed and developed for and with first responders.

Keywords: Cognition · First responders · Psychology · Public safety · Social sciences · Usability · User requirements · UX

1 Introduction

First responders play a critical role in maintaining public safety, as they are the front-line responders in emergencies and major crises. During these incidents, first responders rely on communication technology such as radios, cell phones, and computer-aided dispatch (CAD) to gather information and coordinate appropriate incident response. Historically, first responders have used land mobile radios (LMR) to communicate and share information during incident response [1]. Although first responders have primarily relied upon LMR technology for their incident response, first responders have increasingly begun to utilize technology compatible with wireless broadband network solutions to communicate and transmit information [2].

© Springer Nature Switzerland AG 2021
M. Kurosu (Ed.): HCII 2021, LNCS 12764, pp. 381–399, 2021.
https://doi.org/10.1007/978-3-030-78468-3_26

Until recently, there was no dedicated wireless broadband network infrastructure for first responders in the United States (U.S.). Fortunately, in 2012, the Middle Class Tax Relief and Job Creation Act provided funding to support the creation of the Nationwide Public Safety Broadband Network (NPSBN) [3]. This system, currently being deployed, will allow for long-term evolution (LTE) data-based solutions to supplement LMR. Utilizing data-based technology has the potential to improve the efficiency and effectiveness with which first responders respond to incidents, as research suggests that new devices connected through the broadband network may allow them to transmit and access data and information more quickly [4–6] and access new types of information and functions previously not available to them (e.g., Internet of Things devices [7]).

Although the technological benefits first responders may derive from communication technology and other types of network-enabled technology are clear, the user requirements needed for this new technology have yet to be determined. Determining appropriate user requirements is a challenging task due to the specific and unique needs of the first responder user population. First responders require communication technology and equipment that will perform specific functions (e.g., push-to-talk) in a variety of environments (e.g., fires, rural areas) and scenarios (e.g., emergency crisis, major disasters) [2, 8]. An added challenge to developing user requirements for first responders is the diversity of disciplines within the first responder population. Disciplines such as Communications (Comm) Center & 9-1-1 Services (COMMS), Emergency Medical Services (EMS), Fire Service (FF), and Law Enforcement (LE) have different needs due to the variety of duties they perform and contexts in which they work [2, 8]. First responders also have unique infrastructure, functionality, and economic (e.g., market size and budgets) needs for technology. These needs differ greatly from other populations such as the general public or even the military population, who often respond to similar scenarios (e.g., major disasters) [2]. Therefore, the distinctive needs of the first responder population often preclude developers from simply retrofitting user requirements and technology from other populations for first responders' use [2]. Research and development are needed to develop unique and specific user requirements and technology for first responders that account for the contexts they work within and the needs they have.

To develop these user requirements, a user-centered design approach is needed. This approach posits that to develop technology, it is important that the characteristics, experiences and needs of the users of technology are taken into account, considering their environments, context of work, and needs when developing technology for them [9, 10]. Ultimately, taking users into account helps to ensure new technology is usable, enabling users to complete their desired tasks with effectiveness, efficiency, and satisfaction [9, 10]. Although some work has used user-centered design approaches when developing and designing technology for first responders (e.g., [4]), less work to date has comprehensively examined the context and needs of the first responder population.

The National Institute of Standards and Technology (NIST) Public Safety Communications Research (PSCR) program focuses on improving first responders' communication technology by conducting research and development efforts (see [11]), with User Interfaces and User Experiences (UI/UX) as one of the key areas for research and development [12]. To support UI/UX research and development, the NIST PSCR Usability

Team utilizes human factors and user-centered design principles to produce guidance and insight for gathering user requirements for researchers, developers, and designers [13]. As part of this effort, an exploratory, sequential, mixed-methods study was conducted with first responders. In this multi-phase study, an initial qualitative phase (Phase 1) was followed by a quantitative phase (Phase 2) to investigate first responders' experiences with and perceptions of communication technology [8, 14]. The research questions for this project were:

1. How do public safety personnel describe the context of their work, including their roles and responsibilities as well as process and flow?
2. How do public safety personnel describe their communication and technology needs related to work?
3. What do public safety personnel believe is working or not working in their current operational environment related to communication and technology?

In Phase 1 of the project, interviews were conducted with first responders to understand their context of work and their communication technology experiences, including their most pressing problems and needs [8]. Results from initial analyses of the Phase 1 interviews suggested that first responders' needs are specific to their environments and tasks, and that a "one size fits all" approach to developing communication technology is ill-suited to improving first responders' communication technology [8, 15].

Phase 1 data analysis also included gaining an in-depth understanding of what first responders' current problems are with their communication technology as well as what their top requested functionalities are for how they want their communication technology to work [16]. This paper presents the results of this analysis, examining problems and requested functionalities to highlight the unique needs of the first responders interviewed across disciplines. Ultimately, results from this paper will provide insights and guidance for developers and designers to create and improve communication technology tailored to the needs of first responders.

2   Methods

As previously mentioned, a multi-phase mixed methods study was conducted to examine human factors issues for first responders with their communication technology. In Phase 1, qualitative interviews were conducted [8, 15]. Findings from Phase 1 then informed the design of the survey used in Phase 2 [14, 17].

This paper focuses on the qualitative data obtained as part of Phase 1. Conducting a qualitative study had many advantages. First, a qualitative approach allowed for an in-depth and contextualized understanding of first responders and their perspectives on their work, environment, and communication technology. Second, using semi-structured interviews allowed for interviews to be dynamic, exploring the topics and needs that were top of mind for first responders. Third, this approach allowed for inclusion of first responders in the research process, aligning with user-centered design principles [9, 10].

2.1 Data Collection

Recruitment. To ensure the study represented the breadth of first responders, purposive sampling was used to recruit a sample that varied across first responder disciplines in urban, suburban, and rural areas of the U.S. First responders across four disciplines were represented in the interviews: COMMS, EMS, FF, and LE. First responders of different ages and genders as well as various levels of experience also participated. This resulted in a sample of 193 first responders from across the U.S.

Procedure. Interviews with first responders occurred at their place of work in a private room or area. A primary goal of the research design was to reduce the burden as much as possible on first responders; therefore, the interview session was designed to last approximately 45 min. Moreover, to increase efficiency, some interviews were conducted with multiple first responders at a time. This resulted in 158 interviews with 193 first responders. With permission, the research team recorded interviews so that they could be transcribed later for use in the data analysis process. In five interviews, participants opted out of recording; in these instances, the interviewer's notes served as interview data. Prior to the interview, participants completed a short demographic form.

All participants were informed that their participation was voluntary and that they could leave the interview at any time. The NIST Research Protections Office reviewed the protocol for this project and determined it met the criteria for "exempt human subjects research" as defined in 15 CFR 27, the Common Rule for the Protection of Human Subjects.

2.2 Measures

Interview Methodology. A semi-structured interview protocol was developed for interviews based on the project's research questions and a review of prior literature. The instrument also was reviewed by subject matter experts and piloted by first responders. This helped ensure the final instrument's content sufficiently addressed the research questions. It also served as a check that the content and language were appropriate for first responders. These reviews determined that two interview protocols were needed: one for EMS, FF, and LE who respond to incidents on-scene, and one for COMMS who coordinate incident response off-scene in communications centers.

The instrument included questions about first responders' context of work and communication technology. The context of work questions focused on the first responders' roles, daily tasks and routines, interactions with other people, and specific work environments. Questions about first responders' perceptions of and experiences with communication technology focused on what kinds of technology and information they use and what problems they encounter with communication technology. The instrument also included questions that asked them to describe their top requested functionalities: if they could have anything, what communication technology they would want? This paper focuses on responses to queries about communication technology problems and their requested functionalities.

Demographics Questionnaire. The demographics questionnaire asked for participants' genders, ages, years of service, and technology experience and adoption. These questions were also assessed by subject matter experts and piloted by first responders.

2.3 Demographics

All four first responder disciplines were represented in the data, with most participation from first responders in FF (n = 71; 36.8%) and LE (n = 72; 37.3%) disciplines and fewer from COMMS (n = 25; 13.0%) and EMS (n = 25; 13.0%). Figure 1 displays the percentage of participants in each discipline by area.

First responders from across urban (39.90%), suburban (27.46%), and rural (32.64%) areas were interviewed in eight of the ten U.S. Federal Emergency Management Agency (FEMA) regions [18]. A majority (86%) of the sample was male, which is consistent with the rates found nationwide for FF [19] and LE [20] first responder populations. Figure 2 displays the participants' ages and years of service (note that two participants did not answer these demographic questions). A majority of participants were between 26 and 55 years old, and experience in public safety ranged from one year to over 30 years of experience.

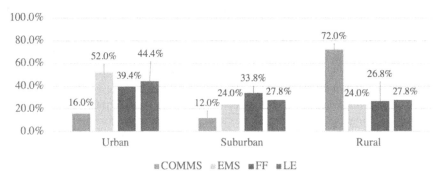

Fig. 1. Participants' disciplines by area

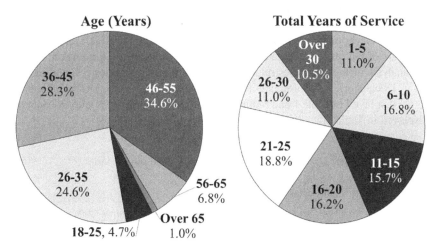

Fig. 2. Demographic characteristics

2.4 Data Analysis

To analyze the interview data as part of the larger project, transcripts were coded. In qualitative research, coding is the process of labeling or categorizing participant responses so that they can be extracted to identify themes in the data. For this project, the coding process first started by generating an *a priori* list of coding categories based on the research questions and literature review. The research team then used the coding categories to code all responses in five transcripts. The researchers met to discuss how each coding category was defined and applied to responses. This discussion resulted in the formation of a final coding list that was then applied in a consistent manner to the remaining transcripts. Once transcripts were coded, the coded responses were extracted together into a document where researchers identified themes across responses. Choong et al. [8] describes the coding process and resulting categories and themes in detail.

To provide a more in-depth look at first responders' problems and needs, additional analyses of the interview data were performed by further examining two of the initial coding categories: "Problems with Technology" and "Wish List". The coding category "Problems with Technology" captured responses in which problems with communication technology were discussed. The coding category "Wish List" captured responses in which first responders described their requested functionalities for how they wanted their communication technology to work. Responses for each coding category were separately extracted, meaning that data associated with each code were collected into separate documents. Once in these documents, responses were further categorized into more specific categories and subcategories to capture deeper nuances and insights.

Independent researchers examined problems and requested functionalities separately and developed the categories and subcategories. Category and subcategory lists included items that could be found in interviews across disciplines, but some were specific to certain disciplines. For instance, the problems category "9-1-1 calls" was only categorized in COMMS interviews. Additionally, because a single quote may relate to multiple categories and subcategories, there was overlap in the responses within and between categories. After an initial classification, the researchers discussed their categories and subcategories to generate a final list used to categorize all relevant responses. The analysis of the responses related to problems resulted in 1,729 quotes in 25 categories; analysis of the responses related to requested functionalities resulted in 1,143 quotes in 18 categories. Communication technology problems categories and subcategories are displayed in Table 1 and requested functionality categories and subcategories are displayed in Table 2.

Table 1. Technology problems categories and subcategories

Category	Subcategories
9-1-1 Calls	Next Generation 9-1-1 (NG 911), caller location, nuisance calls
Audio Clarity	Hard to hear, audio feedback

(continued)

Table 1. (*continued*)

Category	Subcategories
Body Camera	Functional issues, physical issues
Connectivity	Reception, bandwidth issue
Disruption of Operations	Continuity of Operations (COOP), mobile operations
Implementation/IT Infrastructure	Implementation/Installation issues, cost as a prohibitor, IT management, no user requirements collected/considered, public safety network reservations
Interoperability	External interoperability, internal interoperability
Microphone/Earpiece	Cord, earpiece, wireless microphones
Mobile Data Computer (MDC)/ Mobile Data Terminal (MDT)	Navigation/mapping, functionality
Overwhelmed	Sensory overload, situational awareness
Physical Ergonomics	Robustness, battery problems, bulky and heavy, too many devices, physical discomfort, display size, safety concerns
Radio	Dead zones, traffic, channel switching, usability
Reliability	Unreliable technology, redundancy, unreliable transmissions
Security Constraints	Authentication, access control
Technology Outdated	Outdated, incomparable to personal technology
Technology Overrated	Problems with new technology, doesn't solve communication problems
User Interfaces	Ineffective and inefficient, alerting, modality
Video	Data issues, surveillance videos

Table 2. Requested functionality categories and subcategories

Category	Subcategories
All-In-One	Cell phones and/or radios, tablets, software and apps, general multifunctional devices, cameras
Communications Center Technology	Improved dispatch interface, multimedia data package, access to caller cell camera, large multi-view display
Functionality	Reliability, better coverage, clearer communication, improved functionality, longer battery life, faster devices
Futuristic	Media/Science-fiction influenced, smart buildings, face and object recognition software, self-driving vehicles, augmented reality (AR), emergency traffic light system
Integrated Gear/ Wearables	Heads-up display (HUD), in-mask microphone/earpiece, responder vitals, personal protective equipment (PPE) technology

(*continued*)

Table 2. (*continued*)

Category	Subcategories
Interoperability	Software/hardware compatibility, interagency communication system, patient care reporting (PCR), body camera integration, interjurisdictional criminal data
Microphones/Earpieces	Wireless, specialized earpieces
Mobile Apps	Information references, discipline-specific apps
Physical Ergonomics	Smaller and lighter, fewer devices, robustness, larger devices
Radios	Channel switching, multiple talk groups, prevent accidental transmissions
Real-Time Technology	Live video and images - capture/live feed technology, traffic and navigation, drones, language translation, identification devices
Tracking	Responder location, caller location, search technology
Usable security	Single sign-on
User Interfaces	User friendly, hands free, non-verbal communication
Vehicles	Windshield HUD, built-in camera, automatic license plate reader, dashboard computer

3   Results

This section presents key themes found in the data for first responders' problems and needs for communication technology. Along with findings and themes, representative quotes from participants are presented. These quotes are meant to encapsulate themes from the data rather than depicting a single person's perspectives. All quotes are anonymous and cannot be tied back to participants. To provide context for the quote, each is presented with an identifier to show the discipline (COMMS, EMS, FF, LE), area (U = Urban; S = Suburban, R = Rural), and the interview number.

Cross-discipline findings are presented first, followed by discipline-specific sections to highlight problems and requested functionalities emphasized in interviews of participants from each discipline. Problems and requested functionalities are presented together as the first responders' requests were often to have their current problems addressed.

3.1   Across Discipline Results

The communication technology problems and requested functionality categories displayed in Fig. 3 and Fig. 4, respectively, are proportional to responses in the data. Although a variety of problems and requested functionalities were identified, four key areas for improvement for communication technology emerged in the data: reliability, usability (e.g., physical ergonomics, user interfaces), interoperability, and real-time technology. While problems with radios was the top problem category, this paper focuses more broadly on problems and needs that may impact multiple communication technologies.

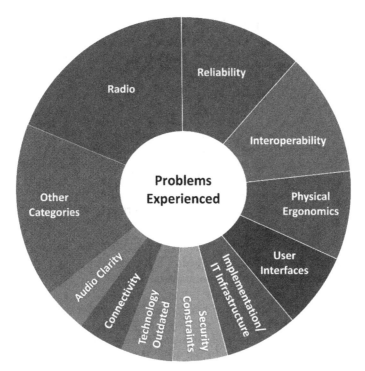

Fig. 3. Technology problems

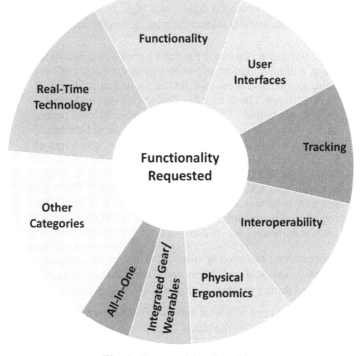

Fig. 4. Requested functionalities

Reliability. Many participants felt their communication technology was often unreliable, describing experiences in which their technology failed or did not work in the way intended. Often first responders expressed that they expected their communication technology to fail, causing them to devise back up plans and redundant systems to ensure they could still perform vital tasks during incident response.

> "In any type of critical incident, that is one of the first things that goes is the communications on cell phones... we try to have the redundant systems in place, probably more so in public safety than any other profession; we try to have those redundant systems but it still doesn't mean that, you know, some of them haven't been utilized in years and we are not sure that they are going to continue to work if we need them to do so." (LE-R-059)

Because of these failures, first responders often did not trust their communication technology. This lack of trust often resulted in first responders abandoning unreliable products altogether or opting for older solutions.

> "Everything we use...we don't have time to mess with it, or tweak it, or play with it. It has to work the first time, every time, or people will just to stop using it. They will just refuse to use it and go back to the old way." (EMS-U-003)

Often unreliability stemmed from challenges obtaining coverage and connectivity for communication technology. Many first responders mentioned that geographic dead zones (e.g., mountains) and structural dead zones (e.g., basements, tunnels) prevented their technology from successfully transmitting and receiving information.

> "The downside is when a firefighter goes down in a basement, and his radio doesn't see a repeater, he can't call for help, so the radio is useless. So the fix to that is to go to a direct channel. The downside of being on a direct channel is only people within a mile can hear the radio, so other people across the city or incoming to the fire don't get to hear what's going on before they get there until they get into range of the direct channel. So that's a conundrum. I guess there are some fixes. You can put a repeater on every chief's buggy that will also take that direct channel and put it into a repeater system that way everybody to hear it that way. That requires infrastructure, investment, and installation, and so forth, and money, so." (FF-U-016)

Improving connectivity and coverage was one of the top requested functionalities. By improving network access, first responders could continue to communicate and access information they need during incident response.

Usability. Participants expressed a wide variety of usability challenges with their communication technology. Many were related to physical problems they had with their communication technology, but they also experienced challenges with their devices' user interfaces.

Many participants indicated their communication technology was ill-suited to their environments and daily tasks. The combined weight and bulkiness of all the devices they carried impeded their ability to perform their jobs.

> "We have a lot of things that we carry. So there's so much on our belts… Just a little bit of weight off your belt is huge. So I have a hard time trying to fit everything on my belt as required in policy. Especially if you're some of the smaller officers, male or female just depending on your waist size, it's like you don't have enough real estate to fit all this stuff that's required. So a lot of people have dropped tasers or that kind of stuff…So I would hope that sometime the technology could help us remove some of all this hardware that we're carrying around all the time. That would be a big deal. I mean health wise for officers too." (LE-U-007)

As voiced by this LE participant, limited mobility was sometimes associated with putting first responders' health and safety at risk. For these reasons, many first responders were interested in having lightweight communication technology as well as technology that is better integrated, allowing them to carry fewer devices at a time. This could not only decrease the physical burden on first responders, but this could also allow them to have fewer distractions when responding to incidents.

Decreasing cognitive load was especially of interest to COMMS responders, who are often required to view multiple screens and use multiple devices simultaneously.

> "…with all the things that everybody wants to integrate. They want you to have apps, they want you to be able to bring in apps, they want you to be able to bring in photos and videos and texting and this and that. The more stuff we add-- the more computer screens, the more keyboards, the more mice. It just keeps adding, and it's the more burden." (COMMS-U-007)

In addition to physical usability challenges, first responders also described problems using user interfaces. Many described overly complicated user interfaces that did not function effectively and efficiently. Because first responders must often react quickly during incident response, they do not have time to interact with complex user interfaces.

> "When we need the technology, we need it to be simple. We don't need it to be complex because we don't have the time to work through complexities in anything technology because our decisions are instant…And so technology is great, but if it's complex, it kind of is counterproductive." (FF-U-025)

Lightweight devices that are easy to use and learn and that can be integrated into their current equipment and systems may address first responders' needs for more usable communication technology.

Interoperability. First responders emphasized that communication and coordination across disciplines, agencies, and jurisdictions was vital for successful incident response. Unfortunately, many first responders described challenges in effectively communicating due to poor interoperability of communication technology across different disciplines. These communication challenges often resulted in confusion and delays in incident response.

> "…communication is the key to either success or failure and you're only as good as your communication components and your knowledge of communication. So
>
> we're always lacking, in my opinion, when it comes to radio communication. There's always problems…getting on the right channel or being able to communicate with a different entity or different agency. You see that in, unfortunately, but you've got mass shootings and there's always a problem with cops being able to talk to firefighters. There are paramedics… And I don't know what the answer is… But I mean, there's always technology that's going to give you problems." (FF-U-021)

Improved interoperability was one of the primary requested functionality categories in the interviews, as addressing this problem could improve coordination for incident response as well as allow for sharing data and other information.

Real-Time Information. Although a theme in many interviews was first responders' desire for solutions to the problems they currently experience with their communication technology, participants also expressed interest in having new technology that could provide them with real-time information. Many participants discussed that having information from videos and images may save time and allow first responders to be better prepared when they arrive on the scene of an incident.

> "If you could text message a picture to 911, and they could send it to us, that would help as far as we could look and say, 'This car accident here and the people can't get out of their vehicle.' A lot of times, the engine is dispatched by themselves. We could see that picture and say, 'Hey, let's add on a truck,' and achieve to that so we can extricate. Let's get that ball rolling sooner. Images would be pretty fantastic…" (EMS-S-005)

Although pictures and videos were often discussed, participants expressed interest in a variety of real-time technology including GPS navigation for traffic, language translation in real-time, and drones.

3.2 Discipline-Specific Results

All disciplines desired improvement to their communication technology's reliability, usability, and interoperability, but first responders in each discipline also expressed problems and needs unique to their individual contexts.

COMMS. COMMS responders' problems with communication technology were related to their unique context of work taking 9-1-1 calls and dispatching first responders from call centers and public safety answer points (PSAPs). COMMS responders mentioned challenges in planning to maintain continuity in the event that the communication centers' operations are interrupted. COMMS responders also saw utility for new technology to improve user interfaces, allowing them to more effectively access critical information or more intuitively navigate monitors and information.

However, many also expressed some concerns with new communication technology. Some discussed concerns about text to 9–1-1 and Next Generation 9-1-1, a digital-based 9-1-1 system [21].

> "I'm not going to have a 30-minute conversation over text whenever I could hear your voice and…and I can really hear are you okay. I can't tell that over here…that's my fear with the Next Generation 911 is are we going to lose that important piece of our communications with technology…But I'm hoping that the texting feature and the apps that we're using on smartphones and other devices that they don't take away that human communications during an emergency because 90% of all communication is nonverbal in nature. And hearing that voice, hearing the background noise of a particular call gives us so much more information than just the words that that caller is saying." (COMMS-R-016)

As stated in the quote, many COMMS responders were concerned that these technologies may take away valuable information gained from voice calls.

COMMS responders also discussed situations in which their communication technology delayed their incident response. Some COMMS responders experienced delays in dispatching help to incidents when their equipment was not interoperable with the equipment of the disciplines with which they were working. Additionally, because of the abundance of cell phones in the general population, COMMS responders often have taken multiple bystanders' calls for a single incident, causing high call volumes and delays in dispatching first responders to other incidents. Receiving nuisance calls, pocket dials, and unintended calls from smart devices also prevented them from sooner taking emergency calls.

Although COMMS responders discussed many challenges and unintended negative consequences of communication technology, they were interested in new communication technology, especially technology that could automatically locate callers. They mentioned that callers are often unable to accurately provide their location, which inhibits COMMS responders' ability to dispatch first responders to the correct scene.

"So location information is very important…this is a pretty big wish but one day I would love to be able to see you know accurate you know x, y, z coordinates… If we get a 911 hang up from a cell phone… and it comes back to-- you know, we don't know where you are but you're calling and you're just screaming and then I have to go trace your phone and I trace your phone. And … even if they can give me an address, [if] it's an apartment complex, I don't know where you are. We can't have the officers go check every apartment. We just can't do it right? So knowing kind of an approximate would be really cool. That would be awesome. Anything where we can better direct people to where you are." (COMMS-U-006)

Communication technology that can quickly and accurately provide callers' exact locations to COMMS responders could help COMMS responders more quickly send other disciplines to the correct location to administer help.

EMS. EMS responders reported problems with efficiently and effectively sending important patient information to healthcare providers (e.g., hospitals) during incident response. Many discussed that these problems were often related to their communication technology's unreliability, radio dead zones, and connectivity issues.

"I know we have issues with WiFi every once in a while. If I'm on the WiFi of the computer and then I drive to the hospital and now I'm inside the hospital writing my report and I'm on the hospital's WiFi and I go to leave, there is a space in between where I'm on neither network until I get away from the hospital. And I've had reports just get lost." (EMS-S-015)

Although EMS responders were interested in improved reliability and coverage, they also requested improved interoperability of medical equipment with external systems and organizations

"Maybe something along the lines that patient tracking because that's a good tool. Doesn't get used a lot though. I think something that would be an automatic download to the Red Cross. If we had victims, multiple victims from an incident…once we had their name and information, if we could tap a drop-down menu and say Red Cross or whatever, then that information would go right to their databank. And they would know where that person is…" (EMS-U-009)

Ultimately an improved and streamlined information sharing process could allow EMS responders to improve patient outcomes and help more patients.

FF. FF responders described problems communicating during incident response because of audio clarity issues. When responding to incidents, loud sounds (e.g., alarms, burning and crackling from fires, chainsaws running) often prevented FF responders from hearing others. Some FF responders also mentioned that their equipment (e.g., self-contained breathing apparatuses (SCBAs)) also contributed to audio clarity issues, often muffling voices and audio reception.

> "And depending on what's going on inside with other noises and things, that can sometimes challenge it. But every once in a while you get a garbled communication coming from somebody wearing a mask just because of placement of the radio and where they're talking." (FF-S-038)

Improving audio clarity and making communication clearer could improve communication and coordination during incident response.

FF responders were also interested in technology that could integrate communication technology with their personal protective equipment (PPE) and SCBAs. Some were interested in new technology such as heads-up displays (HUDs) or technology that could integrate microphones and earpieces directly into PPE.

> "A heads-up display in our face piece. So I've got the thermal imager attached to my face piece, so where I look, I've got a little heads-up display right in front of me. So I can either look out through my face piece and just see what's in the environment or I can glance down at that HUD and look through the thermal imager if the smoke is too thick for me to be able to see through otherwise. A HUD for the radio would not be a bad thing either. To put a display that mirrors the display on my radio so I can see what my coverage is, I can see what talk group I'm on. I can see all the stuff." (FF-S-040)

As described by this FF participant, a HUD could improve FF responders' access to information that may otherwise be difficult to obtain in conditions with limited visibility. It could provide them with information about the physical environment as well as assist them with coordinating with other FF responders during incident response.

LE. As previously mentioned, LE participants reported usability issues in their devices' physical weight and bulkiness. Additionally, they discussed problems with body camera usability. Some mentioned body cameras were not well suited to their day-to-day incident response; because incidents often happen quickly, many described challenges in turning their body cameras on and off at the correct time. Relatedly, attaching body cameras and ensuring they stay attached was often difficult when incidents were physically challenging or in situations where equipment or clothing occluded recordings.

> "…The first week I had it…it was in my badge, because it was just where it was going to fit well for me on when I was wearing a jacket…The problem was, that would put it on my right side, which meant it was angling to the right, and suddenly I'm talking to people, and I tend to be [inaudible] up against them with my left side towards them, so it wasn't seeing anything, it was just pointing in the wrong direction, so I just had to learn how to move it around." (LE-U-056)

Some LE responders described spending significant time and effort ensuring their body cameras were securely attached, working properly, and uploading videos effectively. In some cases, features of the body camera such as flashing indicator lights put officers in danger, revealing their location in dangerous situations. Thus, these problems may have downstream effects on LE responders' efficiency, effectiveness, and safety.

In addition to improving body camera usability, some LE participants requested usable security. For example, some were interested in leveraging single sign-on (SSO) to improve authentication on devices.

> "[New technology is] over-complicated… just make it simple… When you would get in the car, you only needed like one password to get onto the computer. Now, you need like [five]. And they have to be all different, and it has to have a hashtag. It has to have this, a number. It has to have-- so me, I put them all on my phone, because I forget. I'm only almost 40, but I'm already forgetting things. But you have to know nine passwords to get on your technology." (LE-U-013)

Like FF, many LE participants were also interested in better integration of communication technology with their equipment. Specifically, some participants requested integrating communication technology into their vehicles through technology such as windshield HUDs.

> "…Everything is visual on the screen, transparent to you, in front of you while you're driving…So the officers in itself will be able to see everything on the screen. Touchscreen, everything that make it fast for time, have an earbud in there, so they can hear everything that's going on… Voice commands, 'Can you repeat the address that I'm going to?' And it'll show everything. Callback number, 'Can you call for me to make sure that the victim is there or I'm at the right address?'
>
> Or, 'I need an interpreter.' Stuff like that. So everything is hands free…I don't have to press my mic. I'm just going to voice activate and start talking, and the computer's going to dial the numbers for you. You can have it all on the screen on your windshield. Everything." (LE-U-012)

As described in the quote, LE responders were often interested in user interfaces that would allow them to more simply and intuitively receive and act upon information. Technology such as windshield HUDs could provide LE responders with accurate real-time information as well as allow them to more intuitively coordinate the resources they need for incident response.

4   Conclusion and Future Work

As development of the NPSBN and new communication technology continues, it will become increasingly important to create and refine user requirements for new communication technology designed for first responders. This study was an initial step in this process, examining first responders' problems with communication technology and their requested functionalities. Although first responders saw great potential for communication technology to assist them with incident response, ultimately they felt that their technology was often unreliable and did not include functionalities well-suited to the environments they work within and the tasks they perform. Results from this study suggest that developers and designers may improve communication technology by addressing first responders' current problems in three key areas.

First, first responders wanted their communication technology to be reliable. Addressing coverage and connectivity issues could help ensure first responders do not lose communication during incidents, making them safer and also allowing them to continue to send and receive information vital to incident response success. Second, developers and designers must carefully consider the usability needs of each first responder discipline. Lightweight communication technology that also integrates multiple devices or features into one device could improve the physical burden placed on first responders. Additionally, improving user interfaces to prioritize simplicity could optimize how quickly and effectively first responders react during incidents and send and receive mission critical information. Finally, first responders wanted improved interoperability with other disciplines, agencies, and jurisdictions. Many mentioned that communication was a critical component for incident response success, but many felt limited by their communication technology's ability to quickly connect them with other disciplines and information. Communication technology that can quickly and easily connect first responders may improve how effectively and efficiently they are able to prepare for and respond to emergencies. Taken together, new communication technology that takes into account first responders' needs for reliability, usability, and interoperability may result in more accurate, efficient and effective incident response. First responders can spend less time focused on their communication technology, and more time preparing for and responding to incidents.

Although many participants were most interested in improvements to current communication technology, they were open to new technology. As stated by an FF responder, "I think there's room for [new technology] as long as it's durable and it's user- friendly. That's huge." (FF-U-025) Many participants specifically discussed the utility of new devices that can capture and transmit real-time video or images. They also were interested in HUDs and user interfaces that can provide information accurately and quickly during incident response. This suggests opportunities exist for developers and designers to create new communication technology to help first responders. However, first responders in this study stressed that their most immediate need was for improvements to the communication technology they currently have. As stated by an FF responder, "Instead of introducing all this extra new stuff let's, one, make sure what we have actually works better. And then two, let's not rely on it so much." (FF-U-042) This quote underscores that first responders are less interested in new devices, and more interested instead in new solutions to their problems and challenges.

As the NPSBN continues to be built out, there is great opportunity for researchers and developers to design innovative new communication technology for and with first responders. To provide solutions to first responders' communication technology problems and needs, it will be critical for future work to use the findings from this study to inform technology development. As highlighted in this study, it will also be important to continue employing user-centered design principles in research and development efforts, seeking to first understand first responders' requirements and context of use before developing communication technology for them [9, 10]. Communication technology should be designed *for* as well as *with* first responders [8]. By including first responders in the product development process, new communication technology may address first responders' problems and ultimately provide them with technology addressing their needs. This may help ensure first responders will adopt and use new technology, and also may allow them to perform their duties with more effectiveness, efficiency, and satisfaction.

Acknowledgments. NIST would like to thank the many first responders, public safety personnel, and public safety organizations who graciously gave their time and input for this project.

References

1. Balachandran, K., Budka, K.C., Chu, T.P., Doumi, T.L., Kang, J.H.: Mobile responder communication networks for public safety. IEEE Commun. Mag. **44**(1), 56–64 (2006). https://doi.org/10.1109/MCOM.2006.1580933
2. Baldini, G., Karanasios, S., Allen, D., Vergari, F.: Survey of wireless communication technologies for public safety. IEEE Commun. Surv. Tut. **16**(2), 619 641 (2014). https://doi.org/10.1109/SURV.2013.082713.00034
3. Middle Class Tax Relief and Job Creation Act of 2012, Public Law 112–96, 126 Stat. 156. http://www.gpo.gov/fdsys/pkg/PLAW-112publ96/pdf/PLAW-112publ96.pdf
4. Grandi, J.G., Ogren, M., Kopper, R.: An approach to designing next generation user interfaces for public-safety organizations. In: 2019 IEEE Conference on Virtual Reality and 3D User Interfaces (VR), Osaka, Japan, pp. 944–945. IEEE (2019). https://doi.org/10.1109/VR.2019.8797895
5. Doumi, T., et al.: LTE for public safety networks. IEEE Commun. Mag. **51**(2), 106–112 (2013). https://doi.org/10.1109/MCOM.2013.6461193
6. Kumbhar, A., Güvenç, İ.: A comparative study of Land Mobile Radio and LTE-based public safety communications. In: SoutheastCon 2015, Fort Lauderdale, FL, pp. 1–8. IEEE (2015). https://doi.org/10.1109/SECON.2015.7132951
7. Park, E., Kim, J.H., Nam, H.S., Chang, H.-J.: Requirement analysis and implementation of smart emergency medical services. IEEE Access **6**, 42022–42029 (2018). https://doi.org/10.1109/ACCESS.2018.2861711

8. Choong, Y.-Y., Dawkins, S., Furman, S., Greene, K.K., Prettyman, S.S., Theofanos, M.F.: Voices of first responders – identifying public safety communication problems: findings from user-centered interviews, Phase 1, Volume 1. NIST Interagency or Internal Report (NISTIR) 8216, National Institute of Standards and Technology (2018). https://doi.org/10.6028/nist.Ir.8216

9. Hackos, J.T., Redish, J.: Chapter 2: Thinking about users. In: User and task analysis for interface design, pp. 23–50. Wiley, New York (1998)

10. International Organization for Standardization (ISO): Ergonomics of human-system interaction—Part 210: Human-centred design for interactive systems. ISO 9241–210:2019, (2019)

11. National Institute of Standards and Technology (NIST): Research Portfolios. https://www.nist.gov/ctl/pscr/research-portfolios

12. National Institute of Standards and Technology (NIST): User Interface/User Experience. https://www.nist.gov/ctl/pscr/research-portfolios/user-interfaceuser-experience

13. Theofanos, M.F., Choong, Y.-Y., Dawkins, S., Greene, K.K., Stanton, B., Winpigler, R.: Usability Handbook for Public Safety Communications: Ensuring Successful Systems for First Responders. NIST Handbook (HB) 161, National Institute of Standards and Technology (2017). https://doi.org/10.6028/NIST.HB.161

14. Greene, K.K., et al.: Voices of First Responders—Nationwide Public Safety Communication Survey Methodology: Development, Dissemination, and Demographics, Phase 2, Volume 1. NIST Interagency or Internal Report (NISTIR) 8288, National Institute of Standards and Technology (2020). https://doi.org/10.6028/NIST.IR.8288

15. Greene, K.K., et al.: Characterizing first responders' communication technology needs: towards a standardized usability evaluation methodology. In: Mattson, P.J., Marshall, J.L. (eds.) ASTM Symposium on Homeland Security and Public Safety: Research, Applications, and Standards. STP 1614, pp. 23–48. ASTM International, West Conshohocken, PA (2019). https://doi.org/10.1520/stp161420180048

16. Dawkins, S., et al.: Voices of First Responders – Examining Public Safety Communication Problems and Requested Functionality: Findings from User-Centered Interviews, Phase 1, Volume 2.1. NIST Interagency or Internal Report (NISTIR) 8245, National Institute of Standards and Technology (2019). https://doi.org/10.6028/nist.Ir.8245

17. Dawkins, S., Greene, K.K., Prettyman, S.S.: Voices of First Responders—Nationwide Public Safety Communication Survey Findings: Mobile Devices, Applications, and Futuristic Technology, Phase 2, Volume 2. NIST Interagency or Internal Report (NISTIR) 8314, National Institute of Standards and Technology (2020). https://doi.org/10.6028/NIST.IR.8314

18. Federal Emergency Management Agency (FEMA): Regions. https://www.fema.gov/about/organization/regions

19. Evarts, B., Stein, G.P.: NFPA's US Fire Department Profile 2018. Report, National Fire Protection Association (2020)

20. Crooke, C.: Women in Law Enforcement. Community Policing Dispatch 6(7), (2013). https://cops.usdoj.gov/html/dispatch/07-2013/women_in_law_enforcement.asp

21. National Highway Traffic Safety Administration's Office of Emergency Medical Services National 911 Program: Next Generation 911. https://www.911.gov/issue_nextgeneration911.html

Exploring the Antecedents of Verificator Adoption

Tihomir Orehovački[1]([⊠]) and Danijel Radošević[2]

[1] Faculty of Informatics, Juraj Dobrila University of Pula, Zagrebačka 30, 52100 Pula, Croatia
tihomir.orehovacki@unipu.hr
[2] Faculty of Organization and Informatics, University of Zagreb, Pavlinska 2, 42000 Varaždin, Croatia
danijel.radosevic@foi.hr

Abstract. This paper aims to identify the determinants of students' behavioral intentions related to the use of Verificator, an educational tool designed for acquiring good programming habits. Based on the literature review, a research framework that represents an interplay of twelve adoption constructs was proposed. Data was collected by means of the post-use questionnaire. The sample of study participants was composed of novice programmers who were using Verificator at least one semester for the purpose of solving assignments during lab-based exercises. The psychometric features of the framework were examined by means of the partial least square structural equation modelling technique. Reported findings can be used as a foundation for future advances in the field with respect to the adoption of tools designed for learning programming concepts.

Keywords: Verificator · Educational tool · Learning programming · Adoption · PLS-SEM · Post-use questionnaire

1 Introduction

Programming is a fundamental course in every computer science and information and communication science curriculum. Its aim is to teach students how to employ logical thinking and knowledge on programming concepts to develop skills in creating algorithms and solving problem assignments. Course is commonly composed of lectures delivered by teachers and lab-based exercises during which students must solve a problem by writing a source code in one of the integrated development environments. Topics which constitute lectures usually include data types, program constructs (sequence, selections, iterations, and jump statements), arrays and strings, structures and unions, functions, recursions, searching and sorting algorithms, and files. Although a wide variety of teaching materials is available to students on learning management system, they commonly perceive it as difficult and thus struggle to pass it. Some of the possible causes are lack of previous knowledge and fear of programming, and syntax of programming language [39]. Instead of accepting the challenge and become eager to advance, students are becoming discouraged and prone to developing bad habits such as cheating

© Springer Nature Switzerland AG 2021
M. Kurosu (Ed.): HCII 2021, LNCS 12764, pp. 400–417, 2021.
https://doi.org/10.1007/978-3-030-78468-3_27

on exams. With an aim to help students to overcome the set forth obstacles and acquire programming skills with more passion, various tools have been proposed. They can be, based on their features, classified into several groups.

The first ones are visualization tools which are guiding students through a series of animated techniques thus enabling them to create a mental model of program execution. Visualization tools can be further decomposed into mini languages, flowcharts, virtual worlds, and simulation tools. Mini languages like Guido van Robot [17] provide instant visual feedback to students thus facilitating the understanding of programming concepts. The player's objective is to write a code that would guide a robot Guido through the world made od walls and beepers which can be set or collected. Flowcharts such as Rapid Algorithmic Prototyping Tool for Ordered Reasoning (RAPTOR) [6] allow students to develop algorithms by combining basic graphical symbols thus preventing them to make logical errors. Virtual worlds like Alice [3], currently in its third installment, are puzzle-based coding environments that enable students to design games, build interactive narrations, and make animations. Their playful design encourages students to acquire programming skills through creative exploration. Simulation tools such as ViSA [43] are displaying and elaborating every step in the execution of the most common sorting algorithms which simplifies their understanding and allows their analysis. The second ones are games designed for learning programming. Considering that games are stimulating students' imagination and curiosity and can hold their attention for a long period of time, they have proved to be useful for gaining programming skills. For instance, in a CodeCombat [9], students need to write a code in a Python, JavaScript, or HTML to solve puzzles or make their avatars to move, avoid, or attack opponents.

Although all these tools are beneficial in teaching programming, they are mostly focused on fundamental programming concepts and are paying too less attention to the syntax of the programming language being taught. With an aim to address the set forth, a Verificator was developed.

1.1 Verificator

Verificator is an educational tool designed for teaching and learning concepts of the C++ programming language [40]. It is an interface that enables students to write the code, debug, and run their programs. The underlying objective of Verificator is to motivate students to implement solutions to problem assignments in the form of logical blocks rather than sequentially from the first to the last line of code. The aforementioned is achieved by means of the traffic light, the graphical indicator which warns students that open units of their solution, such as program blocks, functions, and classes, need to be closed in order for source code to be compiled and checked for errors. Such a source code implementation approach prevents the accumulation of errors and stimulates students to acquire skills of logical program structuring.

Before one can use Verificator's interface functionalities, he or she needs to personalize his or her session by entering data such a student ID, student's first and last name, and title and description of the program. Verificator can be operated in two timing-wise modes. In the first one, there is no time limit to complete a solution and is usually applied when students are using Verificator at home practicing and preparing themselves for the examination. The second one is commonly used during the lab-based exercises when students need to complete solution to the assignments on their own within a limited period of time, mostly 90 min.

When using Verificator, students cannot import or copy a source code but write it from the scratch. Checksum that is integrated into Verificator guarantees that a source code is not written outside the tool. However, internal copy/paste is enabled to improve students' efficiency in completing the solution to the assignment. In that respect, Verificator prevents acquiring bad programming habits which students, programing novices, are inclined to. The set forth includes plagiarism, copying snippets of code from their peers, learning the code by heart i.e., memorizing the whole solution without understanding anything of it, etc.

As soon as a student starts writing first line of the source code, traffic light will appear on the left side of the interface indicating by number and color how many lines student still has before (s)he would need to compile the program. The number within curly brackets reflects the number of blocks the program is composed of. When program consist of between 0 and 4 lines, the traffic light will be green while when program has between 5 and 10 lines, the traffic lights will be yellow. If program is composed of 11 or more lines, there will be red on the traffic light thus indicating that source code can no longer be compiled. In that case, a student needs to delete some parts of code (it should be noted that deleting empty lines would not be of any help) or convert some parts of the code into comments in order to obtain at least yellow traffic light. When traffic light is green or yellow, students can compile the source code. If source code does not contain any errors, traffic light will turn green with the line counter set to zero which means that student will be able to extend his/her program with additional up to ten new lines of code. However, if the compiler determines errors in the current version of the solution, traffic light will not turn nor line counter initialized to zero until the errors are corrected. In order to facilitate the process of finding and correcting errors in the source code, Verificator has implemented feature that paints in red all lines in which errors have been detected.

Analysis of program is a feature that helps students in finding syntax and logical errors in their source code, mainly associated with program structure and use of curly brackets and parentheses. More specifically, this feature provides an overview of all structures (e.g., selections, iterations, jump statements, functions, classes, data structures and unions, etc.) in the program and their hierarchy and counts the number of open and closed brackets. In case when any of the structures is not referenced anywhere in the program, the corresponding message is displayed to the student.

Interruptions are also one of the Verificator's features that is used for finding and correcting logical errors, that is, debugging. It is most commonly employed in the form of breakpoints that stop the program in the predefined parts of the code and print current values stored in variables.

The Tutor, presented in Fig. 1, is a feature that helps students with C++ syntax in a more intuitive way than compiler/linker errors and warnings do. Verificator amends a common set of compiler/linker related error messages and warnings with tutor messages that are designed to explain the cause of errors. It should be noted that all tutor messages are optional, i.e., the student needs to decide whether to accept them or not. Tutor appears in a window with compiler/linker output in form of a button with a bulb icon. In order to get clarification on the origin of particular error, the student needs to click on the bulb.

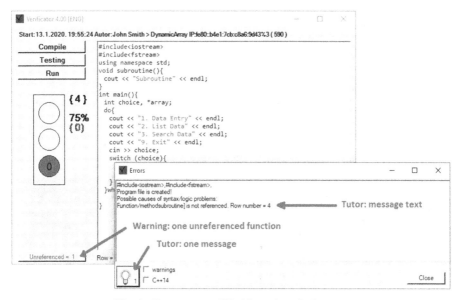

Fig. 1. Tutor as one of Verificator's main features

Testing mode illustrated in Fig. 2 enables counting program blocks (part of code in {}) during program execution. A student aims to reach all blocks his or her program is made of. For this reason, the program must not have any unreachable blocks such as e.g., orphan functions. Inability to reach some program blocks indicates that there are logical errors in the program. There are also some additional testing functions like tracking files opened by a program and memory usage. Testing should be done for each testing interval, depending on the program size expressed in the number of program blocks (first testing interval 3–7 blocks, second 8–12, etc.), not only for the final version of program.

Students are themselves highly involved in the development of Verificator, especially in its testing and identification of program bugs, which is honored by extra points.

Current studies related to this educational tool were dealing with the analysis of novice programmers' compilation behavior [41] as well as examination of Verificator's acceptance by students [36] and its quality [37]. As a follow up, research presented in this paper draws on the findings of these studies with an objective to determine which constituents of the most common adoption theories and models contribute to the behavioral intentions related to the Verificator.

The remainder of the paper is structured as follows. Details on employed research methodology are explained in the second section. Findings of an empirical study are reported in the third section. Conclusions are drawn in the last section.

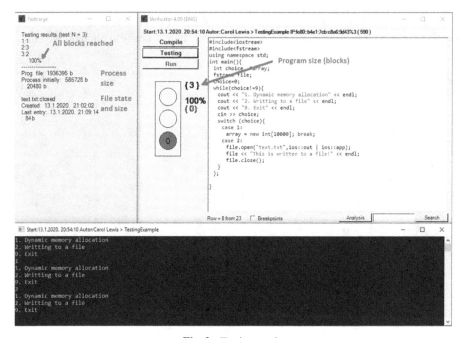

Fig. 2. Testing mode

2 Methodology

2.1 Procedure

During the winter semester, as an integral part of the Programming course curriculum, the study participants had to employ Verificator to solve fifteen different assignments, one per week. Every assignment was based on the lecture that was delivered to students a week before the examination. Students also had the opportunity to use Verificator at home to prepare themselves for the inspection that was conducted during lab-based exercises. At the end of the semester, students were asked to complete the post-use questionnaire.

2.2 Framework

The research framework in the form of a model represents an interplay of twelve constructs related to the adoption of the educational tool Verificator.

Programming anxiety (ANX) refers to a psychological state caused by negative experiences or expectations to lose self-esteem when confronting a situation in which students have to solve problem assignments by means of particular programming language. Venkatesh [50] postulated computer anxiety as a factor that negatively affects the perceived ease of use of a new system. As a follow up, a lot of studies confirmed the aforementioned in the context of educational ecosystem in particular (e.g., [8, 8, 27, 35]) and technology use in general (e.g., [18, 45]). When programming anxiety is considered,

Idemudia et al. [26] found that it has negative influence on behavioral intention while Orehovački et al. [36] discovered that it positively contributes to the attitude towards using an educational tool. In that respect, we propose following hypothesis:

H1. Programming anxiety will have a negative effect on perceived ease of use of educational tool Verificator.

Confirmation (CNF) denotes the extent to which the use of an educational tool Verificator for the purpose of solving problem assignments has met students' expectations. According to Bhattacherjee [4], confirmation positively contributes to the satisfaction with information system because it reflects the manifestation of expected benefits of information system employment. Recent studies [30, 47] carried out in the educational settings have confirmed that confirmation of students' expectations is positively related to their satisfaction. The same holds when users' expectations were examined in the context of web portals [31] and internet shopping [7]. Therefore, the following hypothesis is proposed:

H2. Confirmation of students' expectations related to the use of educational tool Verificator will have a positive effect on their satisfaction in the same respect.

Perceived ease of use (EOU) refers to the degree to which the interaction with an educational tool Verificator does not take much effort. This construct was established as an essential predecessor of the perceived usefulness in all versions of the technology acceptance model [11, 50, 51]. Literature offers an abundance of studies in which strong and positive influence of perceived ease of use on perceived usefulness have been confirmed (e.g., [2, 8, 30, 32, 36]). In that respect, we propose the following hypothesis:

H3. Perceived ease of use with respect to educational tool Verificator will have a positive effect on students' perceived usefulness related to the same tool.

Habit (HBT) denotes the extent to which students tend to subconsciously employ the educational tool Verificator when solving problem assignments. In the recent version of the unified theory of acceptance and use of technology [54], habit was postulated as a significant predictor of behavioral intention. Findings on the connection between these constructs in the educational environment are quite mixed. While some studies confirmed it (e.g., [28, 35]), in others habit failed to have significant impact on behavioral intention (e.g., [1, 42]). Taking the set forth into account, we propose the following hypothesis:

H4. Habit will have a positive effect on behavioral intention related to the educational tool Verificator.

Hedonic motivation (HEM) refers to the degree to which the interaction with educational tool Verificator is perceived by students as interesting, pleasant, and fun. Current studies on technology adoption in educational ecosystem have supported significant impact of hedonic motivation on behavioral intention (e.g., [28, 35, 42]). On the other hand, the influence of hedonic motivation on satisfaction is mainly validated in the context of continued engagement intention with technology in general (e.g., [23, 29]). Therefore, we propose the following hypothesis:

H5. Hedonic motivation will have a positive effect on satisfaction with the educational tool Verificator.

Job relevance (JOR) denotes the extent to which students believe that the educational tool Verificator is suitable for acquiring good programming habits. This construct is postulated as a predictor of perceived usefulness in the second [52] and the third [51] version of the technology acceptance model. The relationship between these two constructs was empirically validated inside [24] and outside educational settings [21]. In that respect, we propose following hypothesis:

H6. Job relevance will have a positive effect on students' perceived usefulness related to the educational tool Verificator.

Playfulness (PLY) refers to the degree to which interaction with the educational tool Verificator holds students' attention and stimulates their imagination in solving problem assignments. Although Moon and Kim [32] established perceived ease of use as a predictor of playfulness, extant body of knowledge provides evidence in confirming inverse relationship between these two constructs (e.g., [18, 38, 50]). Therefore, we propose following hypothesis:

H7. Playfulness will have a positive effect on students' perceived ease of use related to the educational tool Verificator.

Self-efficacy (SEF) denotes the level to which students are self-confident in their abilities to use the educational tool Verificator. In the technology acceptance model [50, 51], self-efficacy was identified to have significant positive influence on perceived ease of use which was later empirically confirmed in many empirical studies (e.g., [5, 8, 24, 27, 36, 49]). Considering the set forth, we propose following hypothesis:

H8. Self-efficacy will have a positive effect on students' perceived ease of use related to the educational tool Verificator.

Social influence (SIN) represents the degree to which a student perceives that most people who are important to him/her think (s)he should use the educational tool Verificator for the purpose of solving problem-based assignments. This factor originates from technology acceptance model [51, 52] where it was entitled as 'subjective norm' as well as from unified theory of acceptance and use of technology [53, 54] from which the name of the construct was adopted in the first place. In both models, social influence was postulated to have impact on behavioral intention which was empirically validated in a variety of studies (e.g., [1, 28, 30, 42]). Therefore, we propose following hypothesis:

H9. Social influence will have a positive effect on students' behavioral intention related to the use of educational tool Verificator.

Satisfaction (STF) refers to a positive emotional state resulting from the use of educational tool Verificator. This factor plays an important role in an expectation-confirmation theory where it is defined as direct predecessor of behavioral intention [4, 33]. It appeared that satisfaction significantly contributes to behavioral intention when use of web portals [31], electronic textbooks [47], mobile social applications [23], self-service technologies [55], and Internet shopping [7], among others, is considered.. In that respect, we propose following hypothesis:

H10. Satisfaction will have a positive effect on students' behavioral intention related to the use of educational tool Verificator.

Perceived usefulness (UFL) signifies the extent to which using an educational tool Verificator enhances students' performance in solving problem-based assignments. In all versions of the technology acceptance model [11, 50-52], perceived usefulness was declared to have significant influence on behavioral intention which was consequently empirically confirmed in a lot of studies (e.g., [2, 5, 7, 8, 23, 24, 30, 31, 36, 47]). However, it must be noted that behavioral intention is not always affected by perceived usefulness (e.g., [49]). Therefore, we propose following hypothesis:

H11. Perceived usefulness will have a positive effect on students' behavioral intention related to the use of educational tool Verificator.

Behavioral intention (BIT) reflects the degree to which students are willing to recommend Verificator to their peers and novice programmers as well as use it during other programming-related courses. This construct is a common endogenous latent variable in all models and theories related to the adoption, including technology acceptance model [11, 50-52], expectation-confirmation theory [4, 33], and unified theory of acceptance and use of technology [53, 54].

2.3 Apparatus

Data were collected with the use of the post-use questionnaire that was administrated online by means of the Google Forms questionnaire builder. The questionnaire comprised 7 items related to participants' demography and 59 items meant for exploring the 12 facets of adoption: programming anxiety (7 items), behavioral intention (7 items), confirmation (3 items), perceived ease of use (6 items), habit (3 items), hedonic motivation (3 items), job relevance (4 items), playfulness (6 items), self-efficacy (3 items), social influence (3 items), satisfaction (4 items), and perceived usefulness (10 items).

Items assigned to constructs were adopted from existing models and tailored to the context of the research. Confirmation of expectations and satisfaction were measured by items adopted from [4], job relevance was assessed with items adopted from [51], perceived usefulness and perceived ease of use were examined by items adopted from [11] and [53], behavioral intention was explored by items adopted from [4] and [11], self-efficacy and programming anxiety were evaluated by items adopted from [51] and [53], social influence, habit and hedonic motivation were assessed by items adopted from [54], and playfulness was measured by items adopted from [32] and [51]. It should be noted that initial pool of items that was adopted from the literature was enhanced by the authors of this paper for every construct that constitute the research framework. Responses to the questionnaire items were modulated on a five-point Likert scale (1-strongly agree, 5-strongly disagree).

The validity and reliability of the proposed research framework and associated hypotheses were examined by means of the partial least squares structural equation modelling (PLS-SEM) technique. PLS-SEM maximizes the explained variance of the endogenous latent variables by estimating partial model relationships in an iterative sequence of ordinary least squares (OLS) regressions [20]. An essential feature of PLS-SEM is that it estimates latent variable scores as exact linear combinations of their associated manifest variables [20] thus threating them as a perfect substitution for the manifest variables. The remaining reasons why we have chosen PLS path analysis (PLS-SEM) over its covariance-based counterpart (CB-SEM) are as follows: (1) PLS-SEM does not require sound theoretical foundations and is therefore employable in exploratory studies [22]; (2) when the sample size is relatively small, PLS-SEM achieves higher level of statistical power than CB-SEM does [48]; (3) if data significantly deviate from normal distribution, PLS-SEM algorithm transforms them in accordance with the central limit theorem which makes parameter estimates highly robust [19]. The minimum sample size for the sound PLS-SEM path analysis should be at least equal to the greater of the next two values [14]: (i) 10 times larger than the number of items for the most complex construct, or (ii) 10 times the largest number of independent constructs impacting a dependent construct. In the proposed research model, the most complex construct (perceived usefulness) is measured with ten items while the largest number of independent constructs affecting the dependent construct is four (for behavioral intention). Accordingly, the minimum required sample size is 100, which suggests that sample size of 121 is deemed adequate. The software tool SmartPLS 3.3.3 [44] was used to assess the measurement and the structural model.

3   Results

3.1   Participants

A total of 121 subjects (83.47% male and 16.53% female) participated in the study. All the respondents were second-year undergraduate students enrolled in the Information and Communication Science program. The age of study participants ranged from 19 to 28 years (M = 20.89, SD = 1.315). Majority of study participants (56.20%) had good knowledge of C++ programming language syntax while 43.80% of them perceived their programming skills as good. When the frequency of using the Verificator was examined, 83.47% of students reported they are using it between once and twice a week while 63.64% of them are employing this educational tool between one and three hours per week. Finally, most participants (84.30%) had up to four years of programming experience.

3.2   Findings

PLS-SEM path analysis draws on the algorithm that during its first step iteratively approximates the parameters of the measurement model while in its second step estimates standardized partial regression coefficients in the structural model [12]. In that respect, the assessment of the psychometric characteristics of the research framework was conducted in two stages. The quality of the measurement model was examined by evaluating the reliability of manifest variables (items), reliability of latent variables (constructs), convergent validity, and discriminant validity.

Reliability of manifest variables was explored by assessing the standardized loadings of manifest variables with their respective latent variable. The purification guidelines proposed by Hulland [25] suggest that manifest variables should be retained in measurement model only if their standardized loadings are greater than 0.707. Results of the confirmatory factor analysis (CFA) presented in Table 1 indicate that standardized loadings of all manifest variables were over the recommended acceptable cut-off level. More specifically, standardized loadings of manifest variables that constitute the measurement model were in the range from 0.7316 to 0.9409 which means that latent variables accounted for between 53.52% and 88.53% of their manifest variables' variance.

Table 1. Standardized factor loadings and cross loadings of manifest variables (MVs)

MVs	ANX	BIT	CNF	EOU	HBT	HEM	JOR	PLY	SEF	SIN	STF	UFL
ANX1	**0.7316**	0.0076	−0.1116	−0.1967	0.1012	0.0676	−0.0912	−0.0355	−0.2782	0.1140	−0.1558	0.0116
ANX2	**0.8565**	−0.0916	−0.1909	−0.2151	−0.0417	−0.0295	−0.1276	−0.0869	−0.2084	0.0554	−0.1378	−0.0721
ANX3	**0.8447**	−0.1467	−0.1920	−0.2722	−0.0210	−0.0397	−0.1434	−0.1269	−0.1886	0.0738	−0.1414	−0.0903
ANX4	**0.8959**	−0.0991	−0.1757	−0.2497	−0.0037	0.0424	−0.0853	−0.0701	−0.1997	0.1058	−0.0985	−0.0555
ANX5	**0.8554**	−0.1545	−0.1326	−0.2975	−0.0177	−0.0949	−0.0918	−0.0721	−0.0979	0.0268	−0.1527	−0.0418
ANX6	**0.9120**	−0.1882	−0.2398	−0.3480	−0.0701	−0.1205	−0.1287	−0.1283	0.1887	0.0253	−0.1970	−0.1148
ANX7	**0.7565**	−0.1429	−0.2889	−0.2408	−0.0353	−0.0389	−0.1660	−0.1230	−0.1376	−0.0636	−0.1906	−0.0561
BIT1	−0.1245	**0.8854**	0.7019	0.5370	0.5942	0.7385	0.6506	0.7304	0.0782	0.6039	0.8109	0.7990
BIT2	−0.1699	**0.7849**	0.5740	0.4426	0.4306	0.6317	0.6318	0.6460	0.1445	0.4790	0.6931	0.6807
BIT3	−0.0859	**0.8585**	0.5760	0.4097	0.5446	0.6319	0.5466	0.6080	−0.0273	0.5342	0.6259	0.7055
BIT4	−0.0584	**0.8816**	0.5656	0.4191	0.6172	0.6588	0.5798	0.6269	−0.0660	0.5787	0.6162	0.7270
BIT5	−0.0292	**0.8508**	0.6206	0.4084	0.6466	0.6114	0.5634	0.5831	−0.0394	0.6356	0.6093	0.6441
BIT7	−0.1586	**0.8462**	0.6698	0.3995	0.5119	0.6446	0.5905	0.6936	0.0145	0.5955	0.6788	0.7307
BIT8	−0.2501	**0.8248**	0.6738	0.4772	0.5771	0.6881	0.6608	0.6871	0.0982	0.5320	0.7591	0.7352
CNF1	−0.2366	0.7484	**0.9094**	0.5336	0.6445	0.6647	0.6157	0.7037	0.2454	0.5343	0.8026	0.6637
CNF2	−0.1355	0.3462	**0.7369**	0.1672	0.2441	0.2693	0.3746	0.3196	0.1720	0.1770	0.4527	0.2986
CNF3	−0.1861	0.6715	**0.8913**	0.4626	0.5257	0.6312	0.6461	0.6806	0.2601	0.4844	0.7984	0.6631
EOU1	−0.2852	0.3438	0.4277	**0.8374**	0.2669	0.3410	0.3953	0.4150	0.4573	0.1992	0.4617	0.3326
EOU2	−0.3026	0.4412	0.3823	**0.8108**	0.2129	0.3690	0.3031	0.3753	0.2901	0.1317	0.4326	0.3699
EOU3	−0.2386	0.4529	0.3816	**0.8534**	0.2968	0.4407	0.3713	0.4388	0.3385	0.2643	0.4354	0.3808
EOU4	−0.2317	0.4707	0.3443	**0.7942**	0.3035	0.4838	0.3127	0.4524	0.2200	0.2619	0.4756	0.3608
EOU5	−0.2518	0.4587	0.4372	**0.8631**	0.2888	0.3846	0.4334	0.5009	0.3046	0.2980	0.5093	0.4194
EOU6	−0.2950	0.4733	0.5322	**0.8763**	0.3126	0.4760	0.4274	0.4438	0.3234	0.2919	0.5424	0.4393
HBT1	−0.0734	0.4532	0.5055	0.2865	**0.7427**	0.4894	0.5374	0.4761	0.1117	0.3719	0.5134	0.4373
HBT2	0.0514	0.5906	0.4190	0.2075	**0.8374**	0.4821	0.4044	0.4297	−0.0991	0.5813	0.4398	0.4375
HBT3	−0.0460	0.5966	0.5833	0.3476	**0.9111**	0.4910	0.4802	0.6068	0.1114	0.5310	0.5249	0.4826
HEM1	−0.0609	0.7144	0.6052	0.4668	0.5114	**0.9311**	0.5926	0.6887	−0.0352	0.5711	0.7161	0.6792

(*continued*)

Table 1. (*continued*)

MVs	ANX	BIT	CNF	EOU	HBT	HEM	JOR	PLY	SEF	SIN	STF	UFL
HEM2	−0.0363	0.7527	0.6386	0.4909	0.5646	**0.9397**	0.6068	0.6436	−0.0472	0.6202	0.7641	0.6999
HEM3	−0.0363	0.7111	0.6148	0.4265	0.5513	**0.9304**	0.5783	0.6958	−0.0133	0.6035	0.7417	0.6615
JOR1	−0.1248	0.6817	0.6277	0.4015	0.4661	0.6106	**0.8644**	0.5883	0.0963	0.4671	0.6501	0.7373
JOR2	−0.1008	0.5817	0.5975	0.3199	0.4993	0.4864	**0.8735**	0.5825	0.1952	0.4670	0.6132	0.6894
JOR3	−0.1243	0.6045	0.5561	0.4525	0.4878	0.5638	**0.8520**	0.5892	0.1757	0.4786	0.6073	0.6597
JOR4	−0.1475	0.6351	0.5914	0.4045	0.5150	0.5688	**0.9258**	0.6430	0.2105	0.4633	0.6153	0.7351
PLY1	−0.0061	0.5887	0.6609	0.3924	0.5066	0.6796	0.5620	**0.7620**	0.0949	0.5116	0.6958	0.6118
PLY2	−0.0695	0.7243	0.6502	0.4790	0.5155	0.5771	0.5802	**0.8346**	0.1707	0.4688	0.6680	0.7036
PLY3	−0.0929	0.6022	0.5276	0.3895	0.4566	0.5599	0.5639	**0.8394**	0.1021	0.4001	0.5643	0.6209
PLY4	−0.1493	0.6507	0.5478	0.4277	0.5186	0.5683	0.5651	**0.8538**	0.0949	0.4925	0.5746	0.5807
PLY5	−0.1674	0.5997	0.5238	0.3743	0.4808	0.5459	0.5519	**0.8283**	0.1184	0.4836	0.5483	0.5513
PLY6	−0.0734	0.5939	0.5810	0.4661	0.4729	0.6036	0.5179	**0.7691**	0.1905	0.4316	0.6394	0.5641
SEF1	−0.0212	0.0515	0.2556	0.3035	0.0767	0.0282	0.2432	0.2163	**0.8067**	−0.0387	0.2314	0.1640
SEF2	−0.3376	−0.0114	0.2669	0.3134	−0.0380	−0.0594	0.1348	0.1138	**0.8254**	−0.0567	0.1327	0.0614
SEF3	−0.1645	0.0464	0.1632	0.3318	0.0657	−0.0503	0.1009	0.0740	**0.8319**	−0.0894	0.0852	0.0625
SIN1	0.0139	0.6389	0.4909	0.2705	0.5389	0.6164	0.4531	0.5574	−0.0997	**0.9144**	0.5682	0.5256
SIN2	0.0456	0.6039	0.4759	0.2484	0.5767	0.5926	0.5040	0.5314	−0.0754	**0.9409**	0.5136	0.5017
SIN3	0.0907	0.5758	0.4293	0.2704	0.5284	0.5363	0.4992	0.4615	−0.0284	**0.8707**	0.4941	0.5038
STF1	−0.1738	0.7361	0.8086	0.5207	0.4908	0.6793	0.6288	0.6736	0.2301	0.5391	**0.9058**	0.7214
STF2	−0.1116	0.7163	0.7646	0.4531	0.5359	0.7121	0.6528	0.6762	0.1123	0.4616	**0.8832**	0.6578
STF3	−0.1901	0.6620	0.6853	0.5089	0.4210	0.6414	0.5771	0.6150	0.2013	0.5075	**0.8339**	0.6383
STF4	−0.1667	0.6929	0.6841	0.4887	0.5802	0.7166	0.5882	0.6609	0.0782	0.4995	**0.8395**	0.6078
UFL1	−0.0345	0.7216	0.6056	0.4121	0.4864	0.6389	0.7403	0.6487	0.1451	0.4757	0.6998	**0.8522**
UFL2	−0.0569	0.7890	0.6003	0.3818	0.4846	0.6732	0.7030	0.7140	0.0830	0.5426	0.6459	**0.9027**
UFL3	−0.1517	0.6649	0.6100	0.4018	0.4527	0.5487	0.7021	0.6085	0.2466	0.4040	0.6261	**0.8374**
UFL4	−0.0046	0.6927	0.5811	0.4033	0.4979	0.5526	0.6421	0.5625	0.0509	0.4516	0.6533	**0.8064**
UFL5	−0.0609	0.6663	0.5848	0.4337	0.4604	0.5388	0.7127	0.5537	0.1202	0.4821	0.6244	**0.8150**
UFL6	−0.0657	0.7358	0.6354	0.3932	0.4443	0.6807	0.7359	0.6635	0.1309	0.4960	0.7163	**0.8778**
UFL7	−0.0242	0.7270	0.5245	0.3556	0.4339	0.6380	0.6614	0.6549	0.0489	0.4093	0.6173	**0.8933**
UFL8	−0.0768	0.7663	0.5587	0.3992	0.4612	0.6717	0.6542	0.6749	0.0195	0.5121	0.6418	**0.8764**
UFL9	−0.0928	0.7872	0.5975	0.4208	0.4638	0.7043	0.6763	0.6827	0.0175	0.5642	0.6918	**0.8748**
UFL10	−0.0907	0.7572	0.6128	0.3525	0.4866	0.6233	0.6994	0.6603	0.1342	0.4957	0.6234	**0.8844**

Reliability of latent variables was tested using two indices: the composite reliability (CR), and Cronbach's alpha (α). Based on the assumption of equal weightings of items, Cronbach's α represents a lower bound estimate of construct reliability. On the other hand, the CR includes the actual item loadings and therefore offers better estimate of internal consistency. As shown in Table 2, estimated values were above the recommended thresholds of 0.707 [19] for both CR and Cronbach's α.

Convergent validity was evaluated by means of the average variance extracted (AVE). An AVE value of 0.50 and higher means that the shared variance between a latent variable and its manifest variables is larger than the variance of the measurement error and is therefore considered acceptable [13]. Study results reported in Table 2 are confirming that all latent variables have met this criterion.

Table 2. Convergent validity and internal consistency of latent variables (LVs)

Latent Variables (LVs)	AVE	Composite Reliability (CR)	Cronbach's Alpha (α)
Behavioral intention (BIT)	0.7192	0.9471	0.9347
Confirmation (CNF)	0.6918	0.8688	0.7772
Habit (HBT)	0.6943	0.8713	0.7778
Hedonic motivation (HEM)	0.8719	0.9533	0.9265
Job relevance (JOR)	0.7733	0.9317	0.9019
Perceived ease of use (EOU)	0.7051	0.9348	0.9161
Perceived usefulness (UFL)	0.7441	0.9667	0.9616
Playfulness (PLY)	0.6648	0.9223	0.8988
Programming anxiety (ANX)	0.7030	0.9428	0.9289
Self-efficacy (SEF)	0.6747	0.8615	0.7591
Social influence (SIN)	0.8265	0.9346	0.8946
Satisfaction (STF)	0.7502	0.9231	0.8886

Discriminant validity refers to the degree of dissimilarity among latent variables in a measurement model. It was examined with two measures: the cross loadings and the Fornell-Larcker criterion. The first measure postulates that manifest variables should load higher on their respective latent variable than on the other latent variables in the model. Data provided in Table 1 illustrate that loadings of all manifest variables with their associated latent variables are higher than their loadings with all remaining latent variables which suggests that the model has met the first measure of discriminant validity. According to the Fornell-Larcker criterion [13], the square root of the AVE of each latent variable should be greater than its highest correlation with any other latent variable in the model. As presented in Table 3, each latent variable shares more variance with its assigned manifest variables than with other latent variables in the model which implies that requirements of the second measure of discriminant validity with respect to the measurement model are met. All the set forth confirms the sound reliability and validity of the measurement model.

After having identified the adequacy of the measurement model, the quality of structural model was examined with endogenous latent variables' determination coefficient, path coefficients' significance level, exogenous latent variables' effect size, and exogenous latent variables' predictive relevance.

The determination coefficient (R^2) reflects the proportion of endogenous latent variables' variance explained by the set of predictors. Acceptable values of R^2 depend on the specific research discipline as well as on the particularities of specific study [16]. As an outcome of the four models estimation, Orehovački [34] proposed that R^2 values of 0.15, 0.34, and 0.46 can be, as a rule of thumb in empirical studies related to the evaluation of quality and adoption of various pieces of software, interpreted as weak, moderate, and substantial, respectively. Study findings indicate that 40.75% of variance in perceived ease of use was explained by programming anxiety, playfulness, and

Table 3. Discriminant validity of latent variables (LVs)

LVs	ANX	BIT	CNF	EOU	HBT	HEM	JOR	PLY	SEF	SIN	STF	UFL
ANX	**0.8385**											
BIT	−0.1489	**0.8481**										
CNF	−0.2290	0.7406	**0.8317**									
EOU	−0.3184	0.5235	0.5000	**0.8397**								
HBT	−0.0220	0.6620	0.5998	0.3344	**0.8332**							
HEM	−0.0474	0.7780	0.6638	0.4944	0.5815	**0.9338**						
JOR	−0.1418	0.7128	0.6754	0.4482	0.5593	0.6347	**0.8794**					
PLY	−0.1130	0.7730	0.7174	0.5222	0.6049	0.7234	0.6836	**0.8154**				
SEF	−0.2140	0.0352	0.2763	0.3854	0.0426	−0.0343	0.1918	0.1614	**0.8214**			
SIN	0.0536	0.6678	0.5128	0.2894	0.6027	0.6413	0.5329	0.5701	−0.0759	**0.9091**		
STF	−0.1844	0.8110	0.8511	0.5683	0.5860	0.7936	0.7070	0.7584	0.1797	0.5791	**0.8661**	
UFL	−0.0765	0.8484	0.6856	0.4581	0.5416	0.7286	0.8035	0.7461	0.1152	0.5617	0.7587	**0.8626**

self-efficacy, 81.79% of variance in satisfaction was accounted for by confirmation and hedonic motivation, 65.76% of variance in perceived usefulness was explained by perceived ease of use and job relevance, while 82.61% of variance was accounted for by habit, social influence, satisfaction, and perceived usefulness. Taking the set forth into consideration, predictors of behavioral intention, satisfaction, and perceived usefulness have substantial explanatory power whereas predictors of perceived ease of use have moderate explanatory power.

With an aim to test the hypothesized interplay among latent variables in the research framework, the evaluation of the path coefficients' goodness was carried out. The significance of path coefficients was tested with asymptotic two-tailed t-statistics derived from a bootstrapping resampling procedure. The number of bootstrap samples was 5.000 while the number of cases was equal to the sample size. Results of hypotheses testing are presented in the first five columns of Table 4. It was discovered that perceived anxiety ($\beta = -0.2098$, $p < 0.01$), playfulness ($\beta = 0.4554$, $p < 0.00001$), and self-efficacy ($\beta = 0.2670$, $p < 0.01$) significantly contribute to the perceived ease thus providing support for H1, H7, and H8, respectively. Data analysis also uncovered that confirmation ($\beta = 0.5798$, $p < 0.00001$) and hedonic motivation ($\beta = 0.4088$, $p < 0.0001$) significantly affect satisfaction thereby supporting hypotheses H2 and H5. Furthermore, perceived ease of use ($\beta = 0.1227$, $p < 0.05$) and job relevance ($\beta = 0.7485$, $p < 0.00001$) were found to have significant impact on perceived usefulness thus demonstrating support for H3 and H6. Finally, study findings indicate that habit ($\beta = 0.1548$, $p < 0.01$), social influence ($\beta = 0.1502$, $p < 0.01$), satisfaction ($\beta = 0.2763$, $p < 0.001$), and perceived usefulness ($\beta = 0.4705$, $p < 0.00001$) significantly contribute to the behavioral intention related to the Verificator which provides support for H4, H9, H10, and H11, respectively.

The effect size (f^2) denotes the change in the endogenous latent variable's determination coefficient. Values for f^2 of 0.02, 0.15, or 0.35 suggest that exogenous latent variable has small, medium, or large influence on endogenous latent variable, respectively [10]. Considering the values presented in the sixth column of Table 4, both confirmation (f^2 = 1.03) and hedonic motivation ($f^2 = 0.51$) have large impact on satisfaction. Perceived usefulness is, on the other hand, strongly affected by job relevance ($f^2 = 1.31$) and modestly by perceived ease of use ($f^2 = 0.04$). While playfulness has moderate influence ($f^2 = 0.20$) on perceived ease of use, the same construct is affected by self-efficacy ($f^2 = 0.11$) and programming anxiety ($f^2 = 0.07$) to the somehow smaller extent. Finally, it appeared that perceived usefulness and satisfaction are strong ($f^2 = 0.50$) and medium ($f^2 = 0.17$) predecessors of behavioral intention, respectively, while both habit and social influence have the same ($f^2 = 0.07$) small impact on this construct.

The predictive validity of exogenous latent variables was examined with the nonparametric Stone's [46] and Geisser's [15] cross-validated redundancy measure Q^2 that based on the blindfolding reuse technique predicts the endogenous latent variable's indicators. Changes in Q^2 indicate the exogenous latent variables' relevance (q^2) in predicting the observed measures of an endogenous latent variable. According to [22], q^2 values of 0.02, 0.15, or 0.35 signify weak, moderate, or substantial predictive relevance of a particular exogenous latent variable, respectively. Study results provided in the last column of Table 4 suggest that job relevance ($q^2 = 0.65$) and confirmation ($q^2 = 0.40$) have substantial relevance in predicting usefulness and satisfaction, respectively. It was also found that hedonic motivation ($q^2 = 0.22$), playfulness ($q^2 = 0.19$), and usefulness ($q^2 = 0.19$) are moderate predictors of satisfaction, perceived ease of use, and behavioral intention, respectively. Remaining exogenous latent variables appeared to have small relevance in predicting corresponding endogenous latent variable.

Table 4. Results of testing the hypotheses, effect size, and predictive validity

Hypotheses	β	T Statistics	p-value	Supported?	f^2	q^2
H1. ANX -> EOU	−0.2098	3.2402	.001546	Yes	0.07	0.04
H2. CNF -> STF	0.5798	10.7307	<.00001	Yes	1.03	0.40
H3. EOU -> UFL	0.1227	2.187	.030682	Yes	0.04	0.02
H4. HBT -> BIT	0.1548	2.731	.007267	Yes	0.07	0.06
H5. HEM -> STF	0.4088	7.3882	<.00001	Yes	0.51	0.22
H6. JOR -> UFL	0.7485	14.2785	<.00001	Yes	1.31	0.65
H7. PLY -> EOU	0.4554	6.4542	<.00001	Yes	0.20	0.19
H8. SEF -> EOU	0.2670	2.8555	.005065	Yes	0.11	0.07
H9. SIN -> BIT	0.1502	2.9074	.004342	Yes	0.07	0.04
H10. STF -> BIT	0.2763	3.5949	.000472	Yes	0.17	0.08
H11. UFL -> BIT	0.4705	6.1959	<.00001	Yes	0.50	0.19

4   Conclusion

The aim of this paper was to determine which factors that originate from common adoption theories and models affect behavioral intention with respect to the Verificator, educational tool designed for learning programming concepts and acquiring good programming habits. In that respect, an empirical study was conducted during which data was collected from students as a representative sample of Verificator users. Drawing on the theoretical foundation that included expectation-confirmation theory and all versions of the technology acceptance model and unified theory of acceptance and use of technology, a research framework in the form of a model composed of twelve constructs was proposed. The psychometric features of the research framework were examined by means of partial least squares structural equation modelling.

Findings of the study indicate that students who are feeling anxious when programming is considered will have to invest substantial amount of effort to become skillful in interaction with an educational tool such as Verificator. It was also discovered that if students believe that Verificator has met their expectations, they will experience a positive emotional state when using it. The analysis of the model revealed that if students find interaction with Verificator clear and understandable, they will perceive it as a beneficial tool for acquiring programming skills. It was also found that if students tend to subconsciously employ the educational tool Verificator when solving problem assignments, they will gladly recommend it to anyone who wants to acquire good programming habits. Furthermore, study results are implying that if students find interaction with Verificator interesting and pleasant, their overall impression with this educational tool will be highly positive. It also appeared that students who believe that Verificator is an appropriate tool for implementing solutions to problem-based assignments will find it useful for acquiring good programming habits. Study results suggest that if Verificator can hold students' attention and stimulate their imagination in solving problem assignments, they will find it easy to use. It was also confirmed that students who are self-confident in their abilities to employ Verificator will not have difficulties in interaction with this educational tool. Findings of the study uncovered that if people who are important to students think they should employ Verificator for the purpose of solving problem-based assignments, they will surely do it and even recommend the same to their peers. It was also found that if interaction with the Verification left a good impression on students, they would recommend it to programming novices. Finally, study findings revealed that if using an educational tool Verificator enhances students' performance in solving problem-based assignments they would continue to use it.

When the effect size is considered, it appeared that confirmation and hedonic motivation have strong impact on satisfaction, job relevance strongly contributes to the perceived usefulness which in turn strongly affects behavioral intention. On the other hand, perceived ease of use is moderately affected by playfulness while satisfaction has moderate influence on behavioral intention. All remaining relationships hypothesized in the model (perceived ease of use on perceived usefulness, self-efficacy, and programming anxiety on perceived ease of use, and habit and social influence on behavioral intention) were found to be small in size.

The reported findings can be useful for researchers who can employ them as a foundation for conducting future studies as well as for practitioners who can take them into consideration when developing environments for learning programming concepts.

As all other empirical studies, this one also has its limitations which should be acknowledged. The first one is related to the homogeneity of participants. Although students in our study served as a representative sample of Verificator users, they were from only one university. Given that a more heterogeneous sample of study participants could provide entirely different answers to post-use questionnaire items, the reported findings should be interpreted carefully.

The second limitation concerns the number of tools that were included in the study. More specifically, this paper was focused on determining the predictors of Verificator and therefore reported findings cannot be generalized to other tools meant for learning programming. Keeping that in mind, further studies are required to examine the robustness of reported findings.

References

1. Ain, N., Kaur, K., Waheed, M.: The influence of learning value on learning management system use: an extension of UTAUT2. Inf. Dev. **32**(5), 1–16 (2015)
2. Alenezi, A.R., Abdul Karim, A.M., Veloo, A.: An empirical investigation into the role of enjoyment, computer anxiety, computer self-efficacy and internet experience in influencing the students' intention to use e-learning: a case study from saudi arabian governmental universities. Turkish Online J. Educ. Technol. **9**(4), 22–34 (2010)
3. Alice (2020). http://www.alice.org
4. Bhattacherjee, A.: Understanding information systems continuance: an expectation confirmation model. MIS Q. **25**(3), 351–370 (2001)
5. Brown, I.T.J.: Individual and technological factors affecting perceived ease of use of web-based learning technologies in a developing country. Electron. J. Inf. Syst. Dev. Countr. **9**(5), 1–15 (2002)
6. Carlisle, M., Wilson, T., Humphries, J., Hadfield, M.: RAPTOR: introducing programming to non-majors with flowcharts. J. Comput. Sci. Colleg. **19**(4), 52–60 (2004)
7. Chen, Y.-Y., Huang, H.-L., Hsu, Y.-C., Tseng, H.-C., Lee, Y.-C.: Confirmation of expectations and satisfaction with the internet shopping: the role of internet self-efficacy. Comput. Inf. Sci. **3**(3), 14–22 (2010)
8. Chuo, Y.-H., Tsai, C.-H., Lan, Y.-L., Tsai, C.-S.: The effect of organizational support, self efficacy, and computer anxiety on the usage intention of e-learning system in hospital. Afr. J. Bus. Manage. **5**(14), 5518–5523 (2011)
9. CodeCombat (2013). https://codecombat.com
10. Cohen, J.: Statistical Power Analysis for the Behavioral Sciences. Lawrence Erlbaum Associates, Hillsdale (1988)
11. Davis, F.D.: Perceived usefulness, perceived ease of use, and user acceptance of information technology. MIS Q. **13**(3), 319–340 (1989)
12. Esposito Vinzi, V., Trinchera, L., Amato, S.: PLS path modeling: from foundations to recent developments and open issues for model assessment and improvement. In: Esposito Vinzi, V., Chin, W.W., Henseler, J., Wang, H. (eds.) Handbook of Partial Least Squares, pp. 47–82. Springer, Heidelberg (2010). https://doi.org/10.1007/978-3-540-32827-8_3
13. Fornell, C.G., Larcker, D.F.: Structural equation models with unobservable variables and measurement error: Algebra and statistics. J. Mark. Res. **18**(3), 328–388 (1981)
14. Gefen, D., Straub, D., Boudreau, M.C.: Structural equation modeling and regression: guidelines for research practice. Commun. Assoc. Inf. Syst. **4**(7), 2–77 (2000)
15. Geisser, S.: The predictive sample reuse method with applications. J. Am. Stat. Assoc. **70**(350), 320–328 (1975)

16. Götz, O., Liehr-Gobbers, K., Krafft, M.: Evaluation of structural equation models using the Partial Least Squares (PLS) approach. In: Esposito Vinzi, V., Chin, W.W., Henseler, J., Wang, H. (eds.) Handbook of Partial Least Squares, pp. 691–711. Springer, Heidelberg (2010). https://doi.org/10.1007/978-3-540-32827-8_30

17. Guido van Robot (2009). http://gvr.sourceforge.net

18. Hackbarth, G., Grover, V., Yi, M.Y.: Computer playfulness and anxiety: positive and negative mediators of the system experience effect on perceived ease of use. Inf. Manage. **40**(3), 221–232 (2003)

19. Hair, J.F., Ringle, C.M., Sarstedt, M.: PLS-SEM: indeed a silver bullet. J. Market. Theory Pract. **19**(2), 139–151 (2011)

20. Hair, J.F., Sarstedt, M., Ringle, C.M., Mena, J.A.: An assessment of the use of partial least squares structural equation modeling in marketing research. J. Acad. Mark. Sci. **40**(3), 414–433 (2012)

21. Hart, M., Porter, G.: The impact of cognitive and other factors on the perceived usefulness of OLAP. J. Comput. Inf. Syst. **45**(1), 47–56 (2004)

22. Henseler, J., Ringle, C.M., Sinkovics, R.R.: The use of partial least squares path modeling in international marketing. Adv. Int. Mark. **20**, 277–319 (2009)

23. Hsiao, C.-H., Chang, J.-J., Tang, K.-Y.: Exploring the influential factors in continuance usage of mobile social Apps: satisfaction, habit, and customer value perspectives. Telematics Inform. **33**(2), 342–355 (2016)

24. Hu, P.J.H., Clark, T.H.K., Ma, W.W.K.: Examining technology acceptance by school teachers: a longitudinal study. Inf. Manage. **41**(2), 227–241 (2003)

25. Hulland, J.: Use of partial least squares (PLS) in strategic management research: a review of four recent studies. Strateg. Manag. J. **20**(2), 195–204 (1999)

26. Idemudia, E.C., Dasuki, S.I., Ogedebe, P.: Factors that influence students' programming skills: a case study from a Nigerian university. Int. J. Quant. Res. Educ. **3**(4), 277–291 (2016)

27. Jashapara, A., Tai, W.-C.: Knowledge mobilization through e-learning systems: understanding the mediating roles of self-efficacy and anxiety on perceptions of ease of use. Inf. Syst. Manage. **28**(1), 71–83 (2011)

28. Kang, M., Liew, B.Y.T., Lim, H., Jang, J., Lee, S.: Investigating the determinants of mobile learning acceptance in Korea using UTAUT2. In: Chen, G., Kumar, V., Kinshuk, Huang, R., Kong, S.C. (eds.) Emerging Issues in Smart Learning. LNET, pp. 209–216. Springer, Heidelberg (2015). https://doi.org/10.1007/978-3-662-44188-6_29

29. Kim, Y.H., Kim, D.J., Wachter, K.: A study of mobile user engagement (MoEN): engagement motivations, perceived value, satisfaction, and continued engagement intention. Decis. Support Syst. **56**, 361–370 (2013)

30. Lee, M.-C.: Explaining and predicting users' continuance intention toward e-learning: an extension of the expectation-confirmation model. Comput. Educ. **54**(2), 506–516 (2010)

31. Lin, C.S., Wu, S., Tsai, R.J.: Integrating perceived playfulness into expectation-confirmation model for web portal context. Inf. Manage. **42**(5), 683–693 (2005)

32. Moon, J.W., Kim, Y.G.: Extending the TAM for a world-wide-web context. Inf. Manage. **38**(4), 217–230 (2001)

33. Oliver, R.L.: A cognitive model for the antecedents and consequences of satisfaction. J. Mark. Res. **17**, 460–469 (1980)

34. Orehovački, T.: Methodology for evaluating the quality in use of web 2.0 applications (In Croatian: Metodologija vrjednovanja kvalitete u korištenju aplikacijama Web 2.0), Ph.D. thesis. University of Zagreb, Faculty of Organization and Informatics, Varaždin (2013)

35. Orehovački, T., Etinger, D., Babić, S.: Modelling an interplay of adoption determinants with respect to social Web applications used in massive online open courses. Univ. Access Inf. Soc. **18**(3), 469–487 (2019). https://doi.org/10.1007/s10209-019-00673-y

36. Orehovački, T., Radošević, D., Konecki, M.: Acceptance of verificator by information science students. Proceedings of the 34th International Conference on Information Technology Interfaces, Cavtat, pp. 223–230. IEEE (2012)
37. Orehovački, T., Radošević, D., Konecki, M.: Perceived quality of verificator in teaching programming. In: Proceedings of the 37th International Convention on Information and Communication Technology, Electronics and Microelectronics, Opatija, pp. 643–648. IEEE (2014)
38. Padilla-Meléndez, A., del Aguila-Obra, A.R., Garrido-Moreno, A.: Perceived playfulness, gender differences and technology acceptance model in a blended learning scenario. Comput. Educ. **63**, 306–317 (2013)
39. Radošević, D., Orehovački, T., Lovrenčić, A.: New approaches and tools in teaching programming. In: Proceedings of the 20th Central European Conference on Information and Intelligent Systems, pp. 49–57. University of Zagreb, Faculty of Organization and Informatics (2009)
40. Radošević, D., Orehovački, T., Lovrenčić, A.: Verificator: educational tool for learning programming. Informatics in Education **8**(2), 261–280 (2009)
41. Radošević, D., Orehovački, T.: An analysis of novice compilation behavior using verificator. In: Proceedings of the 33rd International Conference on Information Technology Interfaces, Cavtat, pp. 325–330. IEEE (2011)
42. Raman, A., Don, Y.: Preservice teachers' acceptance of learning management software: an application of the UTAUT2 model. Int. Educ. Stud. **6**(7), 157–164 (2013)
43. Reif, I., Orehovački, T.: ViSA: visualization of sorting algorithms. In: Proceedings of the 35th International Convention on Information and Communication Technology, Electronics and Microelectronics, Opatija, pp. 1146–1151. IEEE (2012)
44. Ringle, C.M., Wende, S., Becker, J.-M.: SmartPLS 3.3.3, SmartPLS GmbH, Boenningstedt (2021). http://www.smartpls.com
45. Saadé, R.G., Kira, D.: Mediating the impact of technology usage on perceived ease of use by anxiety. Comput. Educ. **49**(4), 1189–1204 (2007)
46. Stone, M.: Cross-validatory choice and assessment of statistical predictions. J. Roy. Stat. Soc. B **36**(2), 111–147 (1974)
47. Stone, R.W., Baker-Eveleth, L.: Students' expectation, confirmation, and continuance intention to use electronic textbooks. Comput. Hum. Behav. **29**(3), 984–990 (2013)
48. Tenenhaus, M., Esposito Vinzi, V., Chatelin, Y.-M., Lauro, C.: PLS path modeling. Comput. Stat. Data Anal. **48**(1), 159–205 (2005)
49. Terzis, V., Economides, A.A.: The acceptance and use of computer based assessment. Comput. Educ. **56**(4), 1032–1044 (2011)
50. Venkatesh, V.: Determinants of perceived ease of use: integrating control, intrinsic motivation, and emotion into the technology acceptance model. Inf. Syst. Res. **11**(4), 342–365 (2000)
51. Venkatesh, V., Bala, H.: Technology acceptance model 3 and a research agenda on interventions. Dec. Sci. **39**(2), 273–315 (2008)
52. Venkatesh, V., Davis, F.D.: A theoretical extension of the technology acceptance model: four longitudinal field studies. Manage. Sci. **46**(2), 186–204 (2000)
53. Venkatesh, V., Morris, M.G., Davis, G.B., Davis, F.D.: User acceptance of information technology: toward a unified view. MIS Q. **27**(3), 425–478 (2003)
54. Venkatesh, V., Thong, J.Y.L., Xu, X.: Consumer acceptance and use of information technology: extend-ing the unified theory of acceptance and use of technology. MIS Q. **36**(1), 157–178 (2012)
55. Zhao, X., Mattila, A.S., Tao, L.-S.E.: The role of post-training self-efficacy in customers' use of self service technologies. Int. J. Serv. Ind. Manage. **19**(4), 492–505 (2008)

Are Professional Kitchens Ready for Dummies? A Comparative Usability Evaluation Between Expert and Non-expert Users

Valeria Orso[1]([✉]), Daniele Verì[2], Riccardo Minato[1], Alessandro Sperduti[1,3], and Luciano Gamberini[1,2]

[1] Human Inspired Technology Research Centre, University of Padova, Padua, Italy
valeria.orso@unipd.it
[2] Department of General Psychology, University of Padova, Padua, Italy
[3] Department of Mathematics, University of Padova, Padua, Italy

Abstract. Professional kitchens are hectic and complex environments, due to the high working pace and the plethora of skills required to operators. Such complexity has become even more severe by the increasing number of unspecialized operators employed in the foodservice. Advanced machines hold the potential to help keeping high quality standards of the final product. However, such machines have never been systematically evaluated before. In the present study, we compared the performance of expert and non-expert users in interacting with three professional machines, namely a blast chiller, an oven and a sous-vis machine, all embedded with a touch-screen interface. Results indicate that all users can accomplish the required tasks effectively, regardless of their expertise level. Still machines cannot level out the differences in the competence between the groups.

Keywords: Usability · User experience · Professional kitchens · Touch-screen interfaces

1 Introduction

Traditionally, professional kitchens have been a complex environment, where spaces and tasks were rigidly shared by several professionals. Nowadays, this scenario has changed, and an increasing number of workers in professional kitchens are unspecialized [1]. The machinery used in kitchens have also changed, as they are typically capable to execute pre-saved programs and recipes and they are equipped with touch-screen interfaces, thereby facilitating the usage. Research on this topic is still very limited, but a general sentiment of skepticism toward the simplification introduced by new kitchen machinery has been reported [2, 3]. However, to the best of writer's knowledge, no study has been run yet to explore whether innovative kitchen machines can facilitate the work of unspecialized operators.

The aim of the present study was to investigate the usability of the touch-screen interfaces embedded in three professional machines, an oven, a blast chiller and a sous-vis machine. To this end, a laboratory-based experiment has been set up and two groups

© Springer Nature Switzerland AG 2021
M. Kurosu (Ed.): HCII 2021, LNCS 12764, pp. 418–428, 2021.
https://doi.org/10.1007/978-3-030-78468-3_28

of users have been involved, one consisting of kitchen professionals and one consisting of novices. Data including systematic behavioral observations and self-reported metrics have been collected and analyzed.

2 Background

The professional kitchen is a workplace that is well-known for being stressful and tiring, where the environment is hectic and the work pace is intense [1, 4]. Indeed, employees in this sector often struggle to cope with these conditions, which can ultimately result into physical strain. [5] and colleagues reported that more than the 70% of the operators employed in school lunch services suffered from low back pain, which was found to be also related to the kitchen environment and the very physical features of the kitchen machinery (i.e., height).

Nevertheless, there is an ongoing debate regarding the competences that kitchen professionals should have to thrive in this environment. The chef is typically considered as the one who holds the skills to manage and lead the brigade, select the best ingredients, and manipulate them into novel combinations [1]. Yet, not all the operators in a professional kitchen need to master both technical and managerial competences. Still, they are expected to operate proficiently the machinery and to keep their competences updated [2]. It should be noticed that in the foodservice the turnover rate is extremely high [6], and there is a reported increasing trend of unspecialized operators [1]. These conditions challenge the competences of the brigade as a whole, and also threaten the quality of the final product. Advanced machines can help, by facilitating the access and the usage of cooking and preservation functions, and by enabling the chef to save pre-set recipes, thus reducing the amount of skilled work required to the operator.

3 The Experiment

In the following, the experimental design and the equipment employed are presented, together with the task lists that have been created and the questionnaires that have been devised. The description of the experimental procedure and the sample follow.

3.1 Experimental Design and Equipment

The experiment followed a between-subject design, with the expertise being the independent variable. Therefore, two groups of participants were compared, being expert and non-expert users. The experiment was run in a laboratory that was equipped with a professional oven, a blast chiller and a sous-vis machine. All machines were embedded with a touch-screen interface (Fig. 1) allowing the user to control both basic programs (e.g., temperature, time) and advanced functions (e.g., recipe input). To record participants' interactions a head-mounted camera was used (resolution 1280×720 pixel, 60 Hz).

Fig. 1. The professional machines employed for the experiment, from the left: the professional oven, the blast chiller and the sous-vis machine.

3.2 Task Lists

For each machine, a task list has been devised. The tasks selected did not resemble a realistic interaction with the machine in a professional kitchen, rather they were meant to make the user explore the various functions of the machines. Additionally, the tasks were grouped based on their level of complexity[1] into easy tasks, medium tasks, and complex tasks. More specifically, for the blast chiller a total of six tasks were selected: four were easy (i.e., setting up and launching the pizza defrost program, changing the drying program, changing the time, setting up and launching a manual program), one was moderately complex (i.e., moving the label of a program on top of the list), and one was complex (i.e., creating a new program for reducing the fish temperature). For the oven, a total of eight tasks were selected, four being easy (i.e., switching on the light, changing the cooking function, setting up the timer, selecting the pizza recipe from the gallery), three were categorized as moderately complex (i.e., modifying a recipe, modifying the phases of a recipe, recipe history), and one was complex (i.e., creating a new recipe). Finally, for the sous-vis machine, a total of six tasks were identified, four of them were easy (i.e., selecting and launching a pre-set degas cycle, changing the settings of a sous-vis program and save it, finding and launching a pre-set program, changing the settings of a program for the 'vasocottura' and save it), one was moderately complex (i.e., making a copy of a sous-vis program and rename it), and finally one was complex (i.e., finding the firmware version).

The task lists selected for each machine did not have the same length, because the three machines supported a different number of functions.

4 Materials

Two questionnaires were devised. One collected participants' background information and their professional experience (Background Questionnaire). The other one (23 items) investigated the experience of use with each of the three interfaces (Post-experience

---

[1] The level of complexity reflected the number of actions needed to accomplish a given task, so that easier tasks required a smaller number of actions to be accomplished.

Questionnaire). More specifically, the following dimensions were explored: intuitiveness (3 items, adapted from [7]), clarity (2 items, adapted from [8]), errors (2 items, adapted from [9]), learnability (2 items, adapted from [8]), ease of use (2 items, [10]), readability (2 items, adapted from [11]), feedback (2 items, [9]), satisfaction (2 items, ISO/IEC 9126-4, 2004 [12]), and acceptance (6 items, adapted from [10]). Participants answered on a 7-point Likert scale. The wording of the items was rephrased to refer specifically to each machine, resulting in three versions of the Post-experience questionnaire.

5   Procedure

On the day of the test, participants were welcomed in the laboratory and were debriefed on the aim and the overall procedure. Then they signed the informed consent form, and they completed the background questionnaire. Next, they were trained to use one of the three machines, and they were left some time to familiarize with it. When they felt ready to start, the experimenter read aloud each of the task to complete. When all the tasks were fulfilled, they were asked to answer to the Post-experience questionnaire. The procedure was then repeated for the other two machines. Participants were presented with tasks of increasing complexity. The order of presentation of the machines was counterbalanced across participants.

6   Participants

The sample included 24 participants, half of them were expert and the other half were non-expert users. The experts (3 women) included individuals employed in professional kitchens, while the non-experts were composed of individuals with a different employment (6 women). The experts had an average age of 39 years (SD = 25.1) and a professional experience of 17 years on average (SD = 13.2). The average age of the non-expert group was 25 years old (SD = 2.7). None of the experts had ever used the machines presented before.

7   Analysis

Participants' performance was assessed by systematically analyzing the videos using Behavioral Observation Research Interactive Software (B.O.R.I.S.) [13]. The time to complete the task, and the task outcome were coded. More specifically, the task outcome could be coded as:

- full success, indicating that the participant could successfully fulfill the task;
- partial success, meaning that the participant could complete only a part of the task assigned;
- success with help, indicating that the participant could accomplish the task only with the experimenter's help;
- failure, meaning that the task was failed.

Participants' errors were also coded, dividing them into critical and non-critical ones. Errors were critical when their occurrence would abort the task, while they were non-critical in all the other cases.

Additionally, the number of taps was coded. The taps were split into effective taps, being those directed to an active area of the interface, and ineffective ones, being those addressed to an inactive area of the interface.

Performance metrics were then compared between groups using a series of Mann-Whitney tests.

Regarding the questionnaires, an average score was computed for each of the dimensions assessed. The scores were compared between the two groups with a series of Mann-Whitney test.

8 Results

Below are reported the results of the participants' performance with each of the machine under evaluation. Next are reported the results pertaining to the post-experience questionnaire.

8.1 Performance

<u>Blast Chiller.</u> All of the tasks were completed successfully by the majority of participants in both groups (Fig. 2). It is worthy to notice that the 41.7% of the novice users was not able to complete one of the more complex tasks (i.e., moving the label of a program on top of the list). Interestingly, the 8.3% of the experts failed the easiest task (namely, activating the pizza defrost program) because s/he withdraw the task. No other critical error was made. A total of 42 non-critical errors were recorded, 22 made by experts and 20 by novice. The main reasons for those errors was the lack of visibility of the multiple functions linked to several buttons on the interface, i.e., to save changes a prolonged tapped is needed, but the interface shows no hint about that.

A series of Mann Whitney tests was run to compare the number of effective and ineffective taps made by the two groups. The only significant difference emerged pertained to the task requiring to change the time ($U = 100, p < .001$), for which non-expert users made less taps ($Mdn = 5$), as compared to experts ($Mdn = 8$). Nevertheless, in both groups at least the 80% of the taps made were effective (no significant difference between groups), suggesting that the interface shows clearly which areas are selectable and which aren't.

Finally, the time to complete the tasks were compared between groups. The only difference emerged regarded the most difficult task ($U = 0, p < .001$), in which experts were faster ($Mdn = 10$) than novice users ($Mdn = 21.39$).

<u>Oven.</u> In the interaction with the oven, the task outcomes were more mixed (Fig. 3). Only the easiest task, switching on the light, was accomplished successfully by the 100% of users in both groups. The task requiring to select the pizza recipe from gallery was failed by the 54.55% of the experts and accomplished partially by the 33.33% of the non-experts (the remaining 45.45% of the expert and 66.67% of non-expert users completed the task successfully). Users failed because they accessed and interacted with the wrong menu.

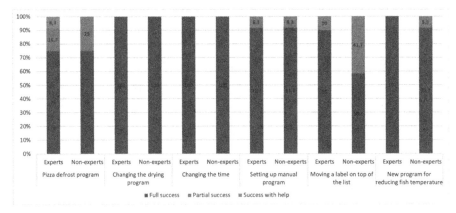

Fig. 2. The success rate of expert and non-expert participants interacting with the blast chiller

Interestingly, all non-expert users accomplished successfully the task requiring to change the cooking function, while only the 54.55% of the experts succeeded. The 36.36% of the experts set up different parameters than those requested by the experimenter, or did not tap on the button to start the cooking process. Only two participants in the expert and non-expert user groups needed help to complete the task requiring to set up the timer (success rate: 90.91% of expert and 91.67% of non-expert users). More specifically, they change the cooking time from the "Cooking menu" instead of changing the setting in the "Timer menu". Both the tasks requiring to modify a recipe and to modify the phases of a recipe were problematic for some users in both groups. In the former, the 70% of the experts (the remaining 30% scored a partial success) and the 91.67% of the non-experts succeeded (the remaining 8.33% scored a partial success). Likewise, the 77.78% of the experts and the 88.33% of the non-experts completed the modification of the phases of a recipe (the 22.22% of the experts and the 16.67% of the non-experts accomplished partially). For both tasks, participants struggled to identify the "Modify button" on the interface, thereby failing to change the parameters. Regarding the task requiring to access the recipe history, the 88.89% of the experts and the 91.67% of the non-experts succeeded (the remaining 8.33% of the non-experts completed the task partially). The 11.11% of the experts failed the task, because of a sudden reboot of the oven. Interestingly, the most difficult task, i.e., creating a new recipe, was accomplished successfully by the 100% of the experts and only the 66.67% of the nonexperts. The remaining 33.33% of non-expert users saved the recipe in the wrong category.

The average number of effective and ineffective taps were compared between the groups. The only difference emerged according to a Mann-Whitney test showed that for the task requiring to add a new recipe ($U = 30.5, p < .001$), experts ($Mdn = 0$) made less ineffective taps than non-experts ($Mdn = 6$).

Also for the oven, participants of the expert groups were faster in accomplishing two tasks, the one requiring to switch on the light ($U = 4.5, p < .001$; experts $Mdn = 5.71$, non-experts $Mdn = 16.25$) and the one requiring to access the recipe history ($U = 11$, $p < .002$; experts $Mdn = 10.48$, non-experts $Mdn = 19.25$).

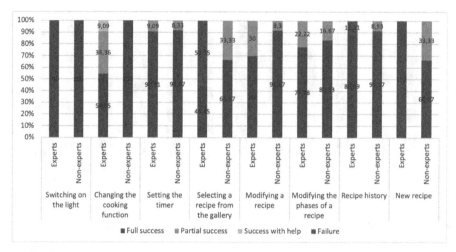

Fig. 3. The success rate of expert and non-expert participants interacting with the oven

Sous-vis Machine. When interacting with the sous-vis machine, all participants in both groups accomplished with no help three tasks, namely selecting and launching a pre-set degas cycle, selecting and launching a pre-set cycle, and finding the firmware version (Fig. 4). The task requiring to copy and rename a program was scored a partial success for all the participants in both groups, because of a technical problem. The task requiring to change the settings of a sous-vis program and save it was accomplished by the 58.33% of the expert and the 83.33% of the non-expert users (the remaining 41.67% of the experts and the 16.67% of the non-expert users scored a partial success). Finally, in the task requiring to change the settings of a program for the "vasocottura" and save it the 83.33% of the expert users and the 91.67% of the non-expert users succeeded (the 16.67% of the experts and the 8.3% of the non-experts succeeded partially). In both tasks, participants correctly changed the settings, but failed to save the changes.

The average number of effective and ineffective taps was compared between the groups using Mann-Whitney tests. The analysis comparing the number of effective taps showed that in the task requiring to select and launch a pre-set degas cycle ($U = 72.5, p = .039$), experts made more taps ($Mdn = 2,5$) than non-experts ($Mdn = 1,5$). Likewise, for the task requiring to change the settings of a pre-set cycle ($U = 104, p = .021$), experts ($Mdn = 50$) tapped more than non-experts ($Mdn = 24$). Finally, the task requiring to change the settings of the "vasocottura" cycle ($U = 77.5, p = .024$) again experts ($Mdn = 12,5$) made more taps than non-experts (Mdn $= 6,5$). Regarding the number of ineffective taps, a significant difference emerged only for the task requiring to copy a program ($U = 28, p = .010$), with experts ($Mdn = 1$) making far less ineffective taps than non-experts ($Mdn = 6$).

The time to complete the tasks was also compared between groups and also for the sous-vis machine, the expert users were faster than their non-expert counterparts. More specifically, experts were faster at copying program ($U = 11, p = .001$; expert Mdn $= 52,74$ non-expert $Mdn = 85.07$) and at changing and saving the settings of a program ($U = 5, p < .001$; expert Mdn $= 14.9$ non-expert $Mdn = 23$).

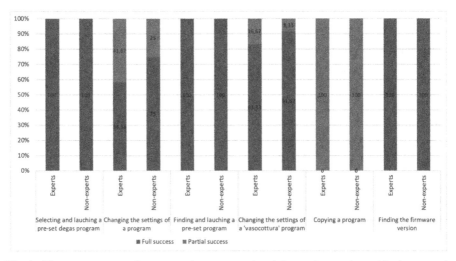

Fig. 4. The success rate of expert and non-expert participants interacting with the sous-vis machine

8.2 Questionnaires

<u>Blast Chiller.</u> The blast chiller was well-received by participants in both groups. No significant difference emerged between groups for any of the dimensions explored.

<u>Oven.</u> Participants assigned high scores also to the oven. According to a Mann-Whitney test ($U = 35.5$, $p = .018$), non-expert users ($Mdn = 6$) gave a higher rating to the learnability of the oven as compared to the expert users ($Mdn = 4.5$).

<u>Sous-vis Machine.</u> Also the *sous-vis* machine was well-evaluated by both groups, and no differences emerged between groups (Table 1).

Table 1. Reports the medians of the scores gained by each dimension of the post-experience questionnaire for each machine. It also shows the values of the Mann-Whitey tests comparing the scores between groups. *$p < .05$.

Dimension	Blast chiller		Oven		Sous-vis machine	
	Experts	Non experts	Experts	Non experts	Experts	Non experts
	Mdn	*Mdn*	*Mdn*	*Mdn*	*Mdn*	*Mdn*
Intuitiveness	6	6.17	6	5.67	4.67	5.33
	U = 53		U = 66.5		U = 68.5	
Clarity	4.75	4.76	5	5.25	4	5.25
	U = 69		U = 67.5		U = 47	

(continued)

Table 1. (*continued*)

Dimension	Blast chiller		Oven		Sous-vis machine	
	Experts	Non experts	Experts	Non experts	Experts	Non experts
	Mdn	*Mdn*	*Mdn*	*Mdn*	*Mdn*	*Mdn*
Errors	4.5	5.75	5	5.55	5.25	4
	U = 60.5		U = 53.5		U = 50.5	
Learnability	5.5	6.5	4.5	6	4.75	5.5
	U = 36		U = 35.5*		U = 51	
Ease of use	5	6	4.75	5.5	4.25	5.5
	U = 56.5		U = 64		U = 42	
Readability	6	6.25	5.75	6	4.25	5.5
	U = 68		U = 71		U = 71	
Feedback	4.75	4	5.77	6	4	3.5
	U = 67		U = 43.5		U = 51.5	
Satisfaction	6	6.25	5.25	5.5	5	5.5
	U = 56.5		U = 72		U = 66.5	
Acceptance	6	5.67	5.75	5.75	4.75	5.92
	U = 62		U = 66.5		U = 70	

9   Discussion and Conclusions

In the present study we involved a group of users with professional experience in the foodservice sector and a group of users with no expertise in the sector, with the purpose to evaluate whether professional kitchen machinery with embedded touch-screen interfaces can be usable also by operators with little or no experience. To this end, a laboratory-based experiment was set up, in which users were asked to execute a selection of tasks with three machines, namely a blast chiller, an oven and a sous-vis machine.

Referring to participants' effectiveness, no dramatic differences emerged between the groups. In other words, all participants were able to accomplish the assigned tasks with all the three machines. A difference yet emerged regarding the execution times, especially for the more complex tasks, in which the experts were faster than non-experts. This occurred especially with the oven, which is the machine with the more numerous and complex functions to manage.

Additionally, all the machines were well-received by all the participants in both groups, as shown by the scores at the post-experience questionnaire. The only exception was the oven, which was considered easier to learn by non-experts than by experts.

Taken together, our findings suggest that modern kitchen equipment can be effectively employed even by individuals with no formal expertise in professional kitchens. Such machinery seems thus to well respond to the current trends in the foodservice sector, which sees an increasing percentage of unspecialized personnel [1]. At the same time, it should be underlined that advanced machines cannot level out the differences in expertise, which emerged in terms of higher efficiency by the expert user group, even in a lab-based context.

Still, it should be acknowledged that in many tasks, the experts were not more successful than non-experts. This probably happened because professional machinery with embedded touch-screen interface are not very popular yet in professional kitchens, and were they are installed, the advanced functions are not exploited much [3]. Additionally, experts may have been influenced by their consolidated practice of using different pieces of machinery. Participants in the non-expert user group were younger on average, and this may also have influenced their familiarity with touch-screen interfaces.

The experiment was purposefully run in the lab, to better control the possible confounding variables, and the tasks were selected to favor the exploration of various functions of the machines. The experimental setting was thus very different from that of an actual kitchen, and also the tasks were proposed out of a realistic context, thereby limiting the generizability of the results. Future research will evaluate the extent to which non-expert operators can manage the professional machinery in a more ecologic context, as compared to experienced operators.

In sum, the findings from the present study support the view that advanced professional machinery can be profitably employed also by operators with little or no professional experience, thereby being a valuable tool for professional kitchens, especially in large production scenarios, e.g., catering, industrial kitchen. It should also be highlighted that advanced machinery cannot compensate for the lack of knowledge and expertise, therefore it cannot be considered as a replacement for the human competences. However, advanced machinery can significantly contribute to ensure standard levels of quality of the final product, thereby representing a valuable ally in such a stressful working context.

References

1. Suhairom, N., Musta'amal, A.H., Amin, N.F.M., Kamin, Y., Wahid, N.H.A.: Quality culinary workforce competencies for sustainable career development among culinary professionals. Int. J. Hospit. Manage. **81**, 205–220 (2019)
2. Fraser, S., Lyon, P.: Chef perceptions of modernist equipment and techniques in the kitchen. J. Culinary Sci. Technol. **16**(1), 88–105 (2018)
3. Orso, V., Sperduti, A., Gamberini, L.: The automatization of professional kitchen: exploring chefs' opinions. In: Proceedings of the 13th Biannual Conference of the Italian SIGCHI Chapter: Designing the Next Interaction (2019)
4. Marinakou, E., Giousmpasoglou, C.: Chefs' competencies: a stakeholder's perspective. J. Hosp. Tourism Insights (2020)
5. Nagasu, M., et al.: Prevalence and risk factors for low back pain among professional cooks working in school lunch services. BMC Public Health **7**(1), 1–10 (2007)
6. Robinson, R.N., Beesley, L.G.: Linkages between creativity and intention to quit: an occupational study of chefs. Tourism Manage. **31**(6), 765–776 (2010)
7. Blackler, A., Popovic, V., Mahar, D.: Intuitive use of products. In: Durling, D., Shackleton, J. (eds.) Proceedings of the Common Ground Design Research Society International Conference, London, UK (2002)

8. Tullis, T.: Measuring the User Experience (Interactive Technologies): Collecting, Analyzing, and Presenting Usability Metrics (2013)
9. Rusu, V., et al.: A Methodology to establish Usability Heuristics. ISBN: 978-1-61208-117-5 (2011)
10. Chuttur, M.: Overview of the Technology Acceptance Model: Origins, Developments and Future Directions. Sprouts: Working Papers on Information Systems. 9 (2009)
11. Gilmore, J.: "Design principle for online information: readability, usability, and accessibility". In: SAS Global Forum Proceedings, Washougal, WA (2004)
12. ISO/IEC, ISO/IEC TR 9126-4: Software Engineering - Product Quality - Part 4: Quality in Use Metrics, International Organization for Standardization, Geneva, Switzerland (2004)
13. Friard, O., Gamba, M.: BORIS: a free, versatile open-source event-logging software for video/audio coding and live observations. Methods Ecol. Evol. **7**(11), 1325–1330 (2016)

Verification of the Appropriate Number of Communications Between Drivers of Bicycles and Vehicles

Yuki Oshiro[✉], Takayoshi Kitamura, and Tomoko Izumi

Graduate School of Information Science and Engineering, Ritsumeikan University,
Kusatsu, Shiga 525-8557, Japan
{is0399ef,ktmr,izumi-t}@fc.ritsumei.ac.jp

Abstract. Because vehicles and bicycles run on the same roads at different speeds, there are many cases in which vehicles overtake bicycles. In such cases, communication between drivers and bicyclists is crucial for sharing intentions and facilitating cooperative behaviors. However, the main existing communication method is one-way communication from bicyclists and vehicle drivers are unable to communicate.

This study aims to clarify the appropriate number of communications between vehicle drivers and bicyclists. We considered four communication patterns between a vehicle driver and bicyclist: two-way communication, two patterns of one-way communication, and no communication. We analyzes the effects of these communication patterns on the impressions of drivers and driving behaviors. In an experiment, participants were asked to perform the actions of communication while viewing a recorded video of a scene in which a bicycle was overtaken by a vehicle approaching from behind. We then asked the participants to complete a questionnaire on their impressions of driving and communication.

We concluded that from a vehicle's perspective, two-way communication (sending and receiving messages) is the safest and most comfortable communication method. However, from a bicycle's perspective, it is sufficient to send a one-way message to the other party for comfortable driving.

Keywords: Driving support system · Bicycles and vehicles · Communication · Sharing of intentions

1 Introduction

1.1 Background and Motivation

Bicycles are an important means of transportation around the world. Many people use bicycles because they are cheap and do not require a driver's license. Additionally, bicycle transportation does not produce carbon dioxide. The use of bicycles is also expected to promote the health of users and reduce traffic congestion. Therefore, bicycles are being promoted for use in various scenarios, including tourism, and are becoming an increasingly popular means of transportation.

© Springer Nature Switzerland AG 2021
M. Kurosu (Ed.): HCII 2021, LNCS 12764, pp. 429–441, 2021.
https://doi.org/10.1007/978-3-030-78468-3_29

However, bicycle-related traffic accidents have become a major concern. Bicycle accidents have increased since 2016 according to the Metropolitan Police Department's traffic accident report [1]. The rate of accidents involving bicycles among total traffic accidents is also increasing. Although the number of people dying in bicycle accidents has been decreasing, more than 400 people still die every year [2]. Based on the fact that approximately 75% of the fatal accidents involve motorized vehicles, we can conclude that accidents between bicycles and vehicles tend to cause more damage.

Because bicycles run on the sides of roadways, bicycles and vehicles often pass each other at different speeds. Bicycles are slow and unstable, so vehicle drivers must overtake them carefully. In some cases, this can be very difficult. Additionally, bicyclists may feel a sense of danger when being overtaken by a vehicle depending on the distance to and speed of the vehicle. Therefore, both bicycle and vehicle drivers often feel a sense of danger related to each other, leading to negative relationships between these two types of drivers.

Hand signals are one solution to this problem. These are signals that bicyclists use to express their intentions to others by performing arm and hand gestures when turning right or left, or when stopping. In other words, hand signals are a communication tool between bicyclists and their surroundings. However, hand signals are a type of one-way communication, meaning it is not possible for a vehicle driver to communicate back to a bicyclist. Additionally, it is difficult for a bicyclist to know if their intentions are understood. Insufficient communication between drivers and bicyclists can lead to unexpected behaviors, which can result in negative emotions such as "road rage" [3]. However, frequent communication while driving is difficult. Therefore, it is necessary to develop a means of understanding the situations of other drivers and understanding their intentions through appropriate communication.

1.2 Our Contributions

This study aims to clarify the appropriate number of communications between vehicle drivers and bicyclists. In [4], a jacket presenting a sign from bicyclists to vehicles behind them was proposed. However, this method has the same problem as hand signals in that it only provides one-way communication. Other possible methods of communication are for a vehicle driver to presents a sign to a bicyclist or for one driver to receive a sign and then reply to the other driver.

In this study, we consider four communication patterns between a vehicle driver and bicyclist: two-way communication, two patterns of one-way communication, and no communication. We analyze the effects of these communication patterns on the impressions of drivers and driving behavior. Because each of the four communication patterns have perspectives from a vehicle driver and bicyclist, a total of eight patterns were examined. For our experiment, videos of a scene in which a bicycle is overtaken by a vehicle approaching from behind (from both the bicycle's and vehicle's perspectives) were captured in advance. Participants were asked to perform the actions of communication while viewing the recorded videos. We then asked them to complete a questionnaire on their impressions of driving and communication.

This remainder of this paper is organized as follows: Sect. 2 introduces related research. The communication patterns considered in this study are described in Sect. 3.

In Sect. 4, we describe our experiment. The results of the experiment are presented in Sect. 5 and we conclude this paper in Sect. 6.

2 Related Works

Studies on driving support typically consider scenarios in which a bicycle and vehicle run on the same road. Target systems may detect an approaching vehicle based on sound data [5] or use a device to inform bicyclists regarding detected information [6]. Such devices are typically designed to fit a handlebar, which is naturally positioned in the bicyclist's view. Similar to our study, there was a study by Omoda et al. that focused on the scenario of a vehicle overtaking a bicycle [7]. They investigated the impact of differences in driving skills on driving behaviors in terms of risk avoidance when overtaking a bicycle. They determined that in order to reduce the risk of collision, it is important to pass at a suitable distance from bicycles. However, previous studies have largely focused on either a bicyclist's or vehicle driver's perspective and only supported notification of vehicle conditions.

Some studies have focused on communication support in scenarios where vehicle drivers, bicyclists, or pedestrians are approaching each other. Kin et al. investigated the differences in consciousness between bicyclists and pedestrians when bicyclists overtook pedestrians [8]. They determined that there is a difference in levels of consciousness and that overtaken pedestrians feel the need to communicate more than bicyclists. Additional studies on communication between drivers and pedestrians were conducted by Taniguchi et al. [9] and Yano et al. [10]. Taniguchi et al. investigated relationships based on communication via eye contact and cooperative behaviors [9]. In their study, behaviors before and after the occurrence of cooperative behaviors were called pre-communication and post-communication behaviors, respectively. Their results demonstrated that when vehicles move at low speeds, more pre-communication occurs. When there is increased pre-communication, more cooperative behaviors occur. Yano et al. investigated communications and concessions between pedestrians and drivers at pedestrian crossings without traffic lights [10]. They found that signals from drivers to pedestrians before crossing are important for allowing pedestrians to cross safely and that signals from pedestrians to drivers often represented gratitude for concessions. Additionally, driver signals increased the number of signals of appreciation from pedestrians. Although previous studies have highlighted the meaning and impact of communication, they have not examined the differences between two-way and one-way communication between drivers and bicyclists.

In this study, we considered a scenario in which a bicycle was overtaken by a vehicle and analyzed the differences between one-way and two-way communication between drivers and bicyclists from each perspective. Based on this analysis, we discuss communications that allow both bicyclists and drivers to drive comfortably.

3 Communication Patterns

In this section, we describe the communication patterns considered in this study. We consider the scenario illustrated in Fig. 1, where a bicyclist is traveling on a straight road and a vehicle is driving behind the bicyclist. The bicycle is then overtaken by the vehicle. Four communication patterns were analyzed in our experiments. A user can be either a driver or bicyclist. Figure 2 presents the communication patterns in the case where the user is a bicyclist.

Fig. 1. The scene considered in this study.

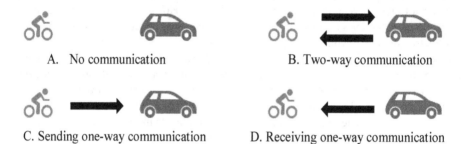

A. No communication   B. Two-way communication

C. Sending one-way communication   D. Receiving one-way communication

Fig. 2. Communication patterns when a user is a cyclist.

- No communication: Neither the driver nor the bicyclist sends any messages (Fig. 2-A).
- Two-way communication: One user sends a message and the other user replies (Fig. 2-B).
- Sending one-way communication: One user side sends a message, but no reply is received from the other user (Fig. 2-C).
- Receiving one-way communication: One user side receives a message from the other user, but does not send any return message (Fig. 2-D).

In this study, we used pictograms (i.e., emojis) to represent these communications. Emojis makes it easy to understand another person's intentions visually. Saito et al. implemented an application for smartphones that notifies drivers and pedestrians using emojis and examined how the transmission of emotions affects driving behaviors [11]. They determined that the awareness of driver and pedestrian emotions provided by emojis encourages drivers to drive more safely. In this study, we also used emojis to express the emotions or intentions of drivers and bicyclists. Two emojis were used in our study. The first is an emoji showing the eyes (i.e., 👀), which is used by drivers to express the message of "I am aware of you." The second is an emoji showing the thumbs up (i.e., 👍), which is used by bicyclists to express the message of "I am aware of you and it is okay to overtake."

We explain how these emojis can be used for two-way and one-way communications in our target scenario below.

- In the case where the user is a bicyclist (Fig. 3 illustrates communication in this case):

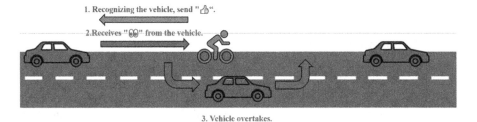

Fig. 3. Communication when the user is a bicyclist.

- Two-way communication: A user sends 👍 when he/she recognizes a vehicle approaching from behind. The user then receives 👀 from the vehicle, and the vehicle overtakes the user. All of the actions shown in Fig. 3 are performed in this communication.
- Sending one-way communication: A user sends 👍 when he/she recognizes a vehicle approaching from behind. The vehicle then overtakes the user without replying. This process is represented by actions 1 and 3 in Fig. 3.
- Receiving one-way communication: A user receives 👀 from a vehicle approaching from behind. The user does not reply and the vehicle overtakes the user. This process is represented by actions 2 and 3 in Fig. 3.

- In the case where the user is a driver (Fig. 4 illustrates communication in this case):

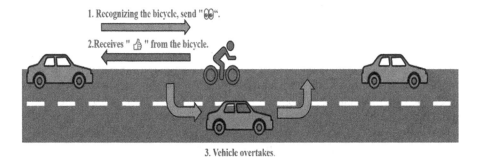

Fig. 4. Communication when the user is a driver.

- Two-way communication: A user sends 👀 when he/she recognizes a bicycle running ahead. The user then receives 👍 from the bicycle, and the user overtakes the bicycle. All of the actions shown in Fig. 4 are performed in this communication.

- Sending one-way communication: A user sends 👣 when he/she recognizes a bicycle running ahead. The bicycle does not respond and the user overtakes the bicycle. This process is represented by actions 1 and 3 in Fig. 4.
- Receiving one-way communication: A user receives 👍 from a bicycle running ahead. The user does not reply, and then overtakes the bicycle. This process is represented by actions 2 and 3 in Fig. 4.

4   Verification Experiment

4.1   Experimental Setup

In our experiments, we considered a scenario in which a vehicle and bicycle are running on the same road and they communicate with each other when the vehicle overtakes the bicycle. The goal of this experiment was to analyze the differences between the four patterns of communication and determine the appropriate number of communications to allow drivers and bicyclists to travel comfortably. We also wished to gather impressions of driving behaviors and communication.

An ideal experiment would be conducted using real vehicles or a driving simulator, but in this study, we adopted an experimental method that could be conducted online in consideration of COVID-19 restrictions. For this experiment, we captured videos showing a vehicle approaching a bicycle and overtaking it from the perspectives of both the vehicle and bicycle in advance. Participants were asked to communicate from the perspective of a bicyclist or driver while watching a video. They were then required to complete a questionnaire on their impressions of driving behaviors and communication. Based on the results of the questionnaire, we analyze the appropriate number of communications required to allow drivers and cyclists to travel comfortably.

4.2   Experimental Video

The experimental videos were captured on the road bordering our university campus. This road is mostly straight with a slight bend to the left and good visibility. The distance covered in the experimental videos is approximately 200 m. Approximately 100 m from the starting point, a vehicle overtakes a bicycle running in front of it. For safety reasons, the vehicle drove at a maximum speed of 20 km/h. However, the video from the driver's perspective does not include the speedometer, so the participants could not see the exact speed. The experimental video from the driver's perspective lasts approximately 50 s and that from the bicyclist's perspective lasts approximately 40 s.

We describe the details of the videos from the driver and bicyclist perspectives below. In the video from the driver's perspective, the driver is driving on a one-lane road and sees a bicycle running on the left side of the road. To determine when to overtake the bicycle, the driver follows behind the bicycle for a short period. The bicycle then moves farther to the left side of the road and the driver overtakes the bicycle. In the video from the bicyclist's perspective, the bicyclist is driving on the left edge of a one-lane road and hears a vehicle approaching from behind. The bicyclist then observes the vehicle visually. The bicyclist moves farther to the left side of the road and is then overtaken by the vehicle, which maintains a safe distance.

4.3 Experimental Environment

For our experiments, Zoom was used to communicate and share information with participants. The videos were displayed on the left side of the screen and an experimental communication tool on a smartphone was displayed on the right side of the screen. Figures 5 and 6 present example screens from the driver and bicyclist perspectives, respectively. We shared these screens with the participants through Zoom. Video playback was controlled by an experimenter and a participant only had to press the send button on the communication tool.

Fig. 5. Example experimental screen for the driver's perspective

Fig. 6. Example experimental screen for the bicyclist's perspective.

A simulated system of communication between drivers and bicyclists was adopted in our experiments. Examples of the system screen are presented on the right sides of Figs. 5 and 6. The system uses a chat-like interface. Messages sent by a user are displayed on the right side and messages received from the other party are displayed on the left side. To make it easy to understand who is sending a message, the vehicle symbol is shown if the other party is a driver and the bicycle symbol is shown if the other party is a bicyclist. The emoji to be sent by a user is displayed on the button at the bottom. When a participant wishes to send the emoji, they can press any key on the keyboard and then the emoji will be sent to the system. In the case where the participant receives a reply (i.e., two-way communication), the reply comes immediately after the message is sent.

4.4 Experimental Procedure

The flow of our experiments is summarized below. First, we obtained informed consent from all participants. We then explained the overall flow of the experiment and simulated experimental system. Next, we described the scenarios displayed in the experiment and the emojis used in the system with their corresponding definitions. After answering any questions from participants regarding the experiment, the participants were asked to complete a questionnaire about their personal attributes. Each participant watched a video and completed another questionnaire four times. Two of the videos were from the driver's perspective and the other two were from the bicyclist's perspective. After watching the two videos from each perspective, participants were required to complete a final questionnaire.

In this study, we considered four communication patterns for each perspective, meaning we considered eight patterns in total. The participants would be overloaded if they were subjected to all patterns. Additionally, the four patterns include communications in which the other party behaves differently. Therefore, the four patterns were divided into two groups for our experiments. The first group consisted of no communication and sending one-way communication, where no emoji was received from the other party. The other group consisting of receiving one-way communication and two-way communication, where emojis were received from the other party. Table 1 summarizes these groups. Each participant was assigned to one of the two groups and completed experiments from both the driver and bicyclist perspectives. Therefore, each participant completed four experiments. The order of the experiments on communication patterns was fixed, as shown in Table 1, but we conducted experiments in the different order of driver and bicyclist perspectives for each participant. For example, one of the participants in Group 1 performed the experiment with no communication from the driver's perspective and then performed the experiment of sending one-way communication from the same perspective. Next, they performed the experiments from the bicyclist's perspective in the same order.

Table 1. Experimental group

	Group 1 (No emoji receiving)	Group 2 (Emoji receiving)
First experiment	No communication	Receiving one-way communication
Second experiment	Sending one-way communication	Two-way communication

Table 2. Questionnaire regarding the appropriateness of communications

No.	Questions
Q1	Were your emotions conveyed properly in this run?
Q2	Did you express your emotions properly in this run?
Q3	Was the emoji appropriate as a communication sign to convey your intentions?
Q4	Was the number of communications appropriate for comfortable driving?
Q5	Was the number of communications appropriate for safe driving?
Q6	Was the number of communications appropriate for exchanging intentions?

4.5 Questionnaire

After watching each video, the participants answered questions regarding the appropriateness of communications. Table 2 lists the questionnaire items regarding the appropriateness of communications. For each question, participants answered on a scale of one (insufficient) to five (sufficient).

5 Experimental Results

Our experiments were completed by 20 participants with driver's licenses and experience driving.

5.1 Regarding the Appropriateness of Communication

The results of a questionnaire on the appropriateness of communications are presented in this paper. A t-test was performed on the questionnaire results for pairs of two communication patterns with a 5% threshold. Patterns were paired to analyze differences between the presence or absence of emoji transmissions from participants and the presence or absence of replies from the other party.

First, we will discuss the results of the experiment from the vehicle perspective. Table 3 compares no communication and sending one-way communication, and receiving one-way communication and two-way communication, which differ only in the transmission of messages from participants. In the experiments from a vehicle perspective, two-way communication received the highest score among all questionnaire items. In the comparison between no communication and sending one-way communication, sending one-way communication was more highly evaluated for all items and there were significant differences between questions 1, 2, 5, and 6. Similarly, in the comparison between receiving one-way communication and two-way communication, two-way communication was more highly evaluated and there were significant differences between questions 1, 2, 4, and 5. Table 4 compares the cases of receiving and not receiving replies from another party from the vehicle perspective. All comparisons between no communication and receiving one-way communication rated the latter higher with significant differences for questions 4 and 5. All comparisons between sending one-way communication and two-way communication also rated the latter higher with significant differences between questions 4 and 5.

Table 3. Comparison of average answer values with/without sending a message in the experiments from the vehicle perspective

No	No communication	Sending one-way	Receiving one-way	Two-way
Q1	2.5	4.1**	3.1	4.3**
Q2	2.6	4.0**	3.1	4.2**
Q3	2.9	3.9*	3.0	4.3*
Q4	2.8	3.4	3.9	4.4**
Q5	2.6	3.4**	4.0	4.4**
Q6	2.4	3.7**	3.4	4.1

*: $p < 0.1$, **: $p < 0.05$

Table 4. Comparison of average answer values with/without receiving a reply in the experiments from the vehicle perspective

No	No communication	Receiving one way	Sending one-way	Two-way
Q1	2.5	3.1	4.1	4.3
Q2	2.6	3.1	4.0	4.2
Q3	2.9	3.0	3.9	4.3
Q4	2.8	3.9**	3.4	4.4**
Q5	2.6	4.0**	3.4	4.4**
Q6	2.4	3.4	3.7	4.1

*: $p < 0.1$, **: $p < 0.05$

Tables 5 and 6 lists the results of the experiments from the bicycle viewpoint. In the experiments from the bicycle perspective, two-way communication is not always the most highly valued option, unlike in the case of the vehicle perspective. Sending one-way communication was the most highly rated answer for several questionnaire items. Table 5 compares the average answer values with and without sending a message in the experiments from the bicycle perspective. In the comparison between no communication and sending one-way communication, sending one-way communication was highly evaluated on all items and there were significant differences between questions 1, 2, 3, 4, and 6. Similarly, two-way communication was more highly evaluated on all items compared to receiving one-way communication and there were significant differences on questions 1, 2, 4, 5, and 6. These results show the same trend as the results from the vehicle perspective. However, Table 9, which compares communications with and without replies from the other party from the bicycle perspective, reveals a different trend. Receiving one-way communication is evaluated higher on all items than no communication, but there are no significant differences. Furthermore, in the comparison between sending one-way communication and two-way communication, sending one-way communication was more highly evaluated on questions 1, 2 and 3, while two-way communication was more highly evaluated on the other items.

Table 5. Comparison of average answer values with/without sending a message in the experiments from the bicycle perspective

No	No communication	Sending one-way	Receiving one-way	Two-way
Q1	2.9	4.7**	3.6	4.4*
Q2	2.5	4.4**	3.2	4.3*
Q3	3.3	4.7**	3.3	4.2
Q4	2.9	4.0**	3.2	4.3*
Q5	2.8	3.6	3.4	4.3*
Q6	2.6	4.1**	3.2	4.1*

*: $p < 0.1$, **: $p < 0.05$

Table 6. Comparison of average answer values with/without receiving a reply in the experiments from the bicycle perspective

No	No communication	Receiving one way	Sending one-way	Two-way
Q1	2.9	3.6	4.7	4.4
Q2	2.5	3.2	4.4	4.3
Q3	3.3	3.3	4.7	4.2
Q4	2.9	3.2	4.0	4.3
Q5	2.8	3.4	3.6	4.3
Q6	2.6	3.2	4.1	4.1

*: $p < 0.1$, **: $p < 0.05$

5.2 Discussion

There are differences in the evaluation results between the vehicle and bicycle perspectives. From the vehicle perspective, two-way communication, which has the largest number of communications, has the highest evaluation value for all questions. In contrast, from the bicycle perspective, sending one-way communication is rated more highly than two-way communication on some items. Therefore, we hypothesize that the optimal number and style of communication differ between the vehicle and bicycle perspectives.

Table 3 compares the results with/without sending a message in the experiments from the vehicle perspective. The communications in which participants sent messages had higher scores for all questions. Additionally, there were significant differences or significant trends for almost all questions. This indicates that from the vehicle perspective, it is always better to send a message, regardless of the behavior of the other party. Table 4 compares the results for whether or not a message is received. The cases in which a reply message was received were rated higher on all questions. Additionally, there were significant differences on question 4 ("Was the number of communications appropriate for comfortable driving?") and question 5 ("Was the number of communications appropriate for safe driving?"). This indicates that from the vehicle perspective, it is beneficial to receive a reply message, regardless of the user's behavior. Based on these findings, it can be concluded that two-way communication, where messages are sent and received, is the safest and most comfortable communication type from the vehicle perspective.

Tables 5 and 6 present the results of the experiments from the bicycle perspective. Table 5 focuses on the differences between sending and not sending messages from a user. The communications in which users sent a message were rated higher on all questions. Additionally, there were significant differences and significant trends for almost all questions. This indicates that from the bicycle perspective, it is always desirable to send a message, regardless of the behavior of the other party. Table 6 compares the results with and without a reply message from the other party. In the comparison between sending one-way communication and two-way communication, sending one-way communication had a higher score on questions 1, 2, and 3. However, there were no significant differences between these communication modes. Therefore, it can be concluded that it is sufficient to send a message to the other party for comfortable driving from the bicycle perspective. A bicycle has a weak position on the road. Therefore, a vehicle driver wishes to convey their intentions to bicyclists and confirm their intentions. In contrast, from the bicycle perspective, it is sufficient to express intentions for comfortable operation, but no further communication is necessary.

6 Conclusions

In this study, we analyzed the types of communication that allow the drivers of vehicles and bicycles to drive comfortably. Experiments were conducted using a simple communication system. Based on the results, from the vehicle perspective, it can be concluded that two-way communication, which sends and receives messages, is the safest and most comfortable type of communication. In contrast, from the bicycle perspective, it is sufficient to send a message to vehicles for comfortable operation.

In our experiments, communication was performed only once for one transmission and one reception. From the vehicle perspective, two-way communication was evaluated highly. In the future, we will consider additional cases with more communication. Additionally, because our experiments were conducted by watching videos, our evaluations are not necessarily representative of a real driving environment. Therefore, verification in a real environment should also be considered in the future.

...   ...

Property GP-TM-24(c1,login:=toto) is false: Property GP-TM-38(login:=toto) is false:
counterexample: counterexample:
-q0 -> q1   -q0 -> q1
 !Req(from:=c1,to:=c2,login:=toto;   !Req(from:=c1,to:=c2,login:=toto;
password:=1234),   password:=1234),
  Request,   Request,
  output,   output,
  loginAttempt(c2),   loginAttempt(c2),
  begin,   begin,
  sensitive(login:=toto),   sensitive(login:=toto),
  sensitive(password:=1234),   sensitive(password:=1234),
  credential(login:=toto),   credential(login:=toto),
  credential(password:=1234)   credential(password:=1234)
  from(c1),   from(c1),
  to(c2)   to(c2)
-q1 -> q2   -q1 -> q2
...   ...

Property GP-TM-42(c3) is false:
counterexample: Property GP-TM-42(c1) is true
-q0 -> q1
...   Property GP-TM-53 is true
-q4 -> q5
 !Req(from:=c2,to:=c3,switch:=On),   ...
  request,
  output,
  from(c2),
  to(c3)

Fig. 8. Example of results obtained with the verification of five ENISA measures on the LTS $\mathscr{L}(c2)$. The counterexamples shows the LTS paths that do not satisfy the property instances.

4 The Model Learning Checking Approach

This section details the MLCA's steps 2 to 5. More details of the model learning step are available in [29,30]. Before describing these steps, we provide some definitions and notations to be used throughout the remainder of the paper.

4.1 Preliminary Definitions

As in many works dealing with the modelling of atomic components, e.g., [4,13], we express the behaviours of components with the well established Labelled Transition System (LTS) model. An LTS is defined in terms of states and transitions labelled by actions, themselves taken from a general action set $\mathcal{L}$.

Definition 1 (LTS). *A Labelled Transition System (LTS) is a 4-tuple $\langle Q, q0, \Sigma, \rightarrow \rangle$ where:*

- *Q is a finite set of states;*
- *$q0$ is the initial state;*
- *$\Sigma \subseteq \mathcal{L}$ is a finite set of labels,*
- *$\rightarrow \subseteq Q \times (\mathscr{P}(\Sigma) \setminus \{\emptyset\}) \times Q$ is a finite set of transitions (where $\mathscr{P}(\Sigma)$ denotes the powerset of Σ). A transition (q, L, q') is also denoted $q \xrightarrow{L} q'$.*

An execution trace is a finite sequence of labels in $\mathcal{L}^*$. ε denotes the empty sequence. The concatenation of two traces σ_1, σ_2 is denoted $\sigma_1.\sigma_2$.

Furthermore, we express security properties with LTL formulas, which concisely formalise them with the help of a small number of special logical operators and temporal operators [16]. Given a set of atomic propositions AP and $p \in AP$, LTL formulas are constructed by using the following grammar $\phi ::= p \mid (\phi) \mid \neg\phi \mid \phi_1 \vee \phi_2 \mid \mathbf{X}\phi \mid \phi_1 \mathbf{U}\phi_2$. Additionally, a LTL formula can be constructed with the following operators, each of which is defined in terms of the previous ones:

$$\top \overset{def}{=} p \vee \neg p, \; \bot \overset{def}{=} \neg\top, \; \phi_1 \wedge \phi_2 \overset{def}{=} \neg(\neg\phi_1 \vee \neg\phi_2), \; \phi_1 \to \phi_2 \overset{def}{=} \neg\phi_1 \vee \phi_2, \; \mathbf{F}\phi \overset{def}{=} \top\mathbf{U}\phi,$$
$$\mathbf{G}\phi \overset{def}{=} \neg\mathbf{F}(\neg\phi).$$

$SF(\phi)$ denotes the set of sub-formulas of ϕ. This set is is defined inductively as follows: $SF(p) \overset{def}{=} \{p\}; SF(\neg\phi) \overset{def}{=} \{\neg\phi\} \cup SF(\phi); SF(\phi_1 \vee \phi_2) \overset{def}{=} \{\phi_1 \vee \phi_2\} \cup SF(\phi_1) \cup SF(\phi_2); SF(\mathbf{X}\phi) \overset{def}{=} \{\mathbf{X}\phi\} \cup SF(\phi); SF(\mathbf{U}\phi) \overset{def}{=} \{\mathbf{U}\phi\} \cup SF(\phi)$. When the other operators are used, their definitions allow to inductively recover the set of sub-formulas as well.

4.2 Property Type

We use property types to express general features, which are independent of the type of system under audit. A property type is a specialised LTL formula whose atomic propositions are predicates, a predicate being either an expression of one or more variables defined on some specific domains, or a nullary predicate, which corresponds to an atomic proposition.

Definition 2 (Property Type).

- *Pred denotes a set of predicates of the form P (nullary predicate) or $P(x_1,\ldots,x_k)$ with $x_1,\ldots,x_k$ some variables that belong to the set denoted X;*
- *The domain of a predicate variable $x \in X$ is written $Dom(x)$;*
- *A property type Φ is a LTL formula built up from predicates in Pred. $\mathscr{P}$ denotes the set of property types.*

Property types cannot be evaluated by model-checkers as they are composed of predicates. They require to be instantiated before, i.e. predicate variables have to assigned to values. The instantiation of a property type is called a property instance. It has the same LTL structure as its property type, but the instantiated predicates now form propositions.

Definition 3 (Property Instance). *A property instance ϕ of the property type Φ is a LTL formula resulting from the instantiation of the predicates of Φ.*

The function that instantiates a property type to one property instance, i.e. which associates each variable of the predicates to a value, is called a binding:

Definition 4 (Property Binding). *Let X' be a finite set of variables $\{x_1,\ldots,x_k\} \subseteq X$. A binding is a function $b : X' \to Dom(X')$, with $Dom(X') = Dom(x_1) \times \cdots \times Dom(x_k)$.*

References

1. Metropolitan Police Department Homepage. https://www.keishicho.metro.tokyo.jp/about_mpd/jokyo_tokei/tokei_jokyo/bicycle.html. Accessed 23 Dec 2020. (in Japanese)
2. Official Statistics of Japan. https://www.e-stat.go.jp/en/stat-search/files?page=1&layout=datalist&toukei=00130002&tstat=000001027458&cycle=7&year=20190&month=0&tclass1val=0. Accessed 23 Dec 2020
3. Joint, M.: Road Rage. Automobile Association, London (1995)
4. Ford: Emoji Jacket helps people to share the road. https://media.ford.com/content/fordmedia/feu/en/news/2020/02/06/emoji-jacket-helps-people-to-share-the-road.html. Accessed 23 Dec 2020
5. Kawanaka, S., Kashimoto, Y., Firouzian, A., Arakawa, Y., Pulli, P., Yasumoto, K.: Approaching vehicle detection method with acoustic analysis using smartphone for elderly bicycle driver. In: 10th International Conference on Mobile Computing and Ubiquitous Network, pp. 1–6 (2016)
6. Kaihara, S., Akaike, H.: A proposal and prototyping of the smart handle. In: Human Interface Symposium (2018)
7. Omoda, Y., Iwaki, R., Abe, G., Fukushima, M.: Analysis of vehicle driver's behaviors while overtaking a bicycle focusing on differences in driving skill. Trans. Soc. Automot. Eng. Jpn. **50**(2), 455–460 (2019). (in Japanese)
8. Kin, T.: Basic study on the traffic consciousness gap and the traffic communication between bicycle and pedestrian. J. City Plann. Inst. Jpn. **51**(3), 661–666 (2016). (in Japanese)
9. Taniguchi, A., Yoshimura, T., Ishida, H.: A study on cooperative behavior arised by communication between vehicle and pedestrian and bicycle rider. J. Jpn. Soc. Civ. Eng. **68**(5), 1115–1122 (2012). (in Japanese)
10. Yano, N., Mori, K.: Pedestrian-driver communication at crosswalks without signals: driver yielding gesture effects on pedestrian decisions for road crossing. Jpn. J. Traffic Psychol. **33**(1), 13–27 (2017). (in Japanese)
11. Saito, Y., Nakano, Y., Suzuki, K., Nishida, D., Murayama, Y., Takahashi, Y.: A study of emotion awareness for human-friendly automobile society. IPSJ SIG Technical report, vol. 2014-DPS-158, no. 25, pp. 1–6 (2014). (in Japanese)

User Assessment of Webpage Usefulness

Ning Sa[1]([✉]) and Xiaojun Yuan[2]

[1] Rensselaer Polytechnic Institute, Troy, NY 12180, USA
[2] University at Albany, State University of New York, Albany, NY 12222, USA
xyuan@albany.edu

Abstract. During a web search, the search engines provide relevant pages while the users decide the usefulness of them. The usefulness assessment has been found to be related to various factors. In this study, the effects of task domain and task type on webpage usefulness assessment were investigated. The two task domains involved were health and travel and the two task types were fact finding and decision making. In an experimental environment, 24 participants were asked to do internet search on 4 pre-defined tasks. In the interview after each search task, the users were asked to evaluate the usefulness of each web page they had clicked and talked about why the page was evaluated as such. According to the results of the experiment, we found that the task domain, task type, and various other factors had impacts on the usefulness assessment during web search.

Keywords: Interactive information search · Usefulness assessment · Task domain · Task type

1 Introduction

A typical online web search session consists of (1) users' multiple query inputs, which were then used by the information retrieval system to evaluate the relevance of the documents in the databases of the system; (2) users' evaluation of the results returned by the system; and (3) users' refinement of their search queries. The system evaluation, which is the matching process between the query and the documents, has been investigated for decades. Ideally, the documents marked as relevant could be useful to users. However, it is not always the case. Many relevant documents are not useful to users. Contextual factors, including user preference, search context, task characteristics are important to be considered in the search process [9, 11]. For example, [9] reported that user preference plays an important role in "making retrieval evaluation faster, cheaper, and more user centered" (p. 43). Task type and task domain are found to affect the user's search behavior, strategies used, and search results [7, 8, 15].

In this paper, we are interested in the research question:

RQ: How the task type and task domain affect the user assessment of webpage usefulness?

Specifically, we aimed to investigate the criteria used by users in travel domain tasks and health domain tasks and whether the task domain has any impact on the user

© Springer Nature Switzerland AG 2021
M. Kurosu (Ed.): HCII 2021, LNCS 12764, pp. 442–457, 2021.
https://doi.org/10.1007/978-3-030-78468-3_30

assessment. For each of the domain, we further developed two types of tasks, fact-finding task and decision-making task. By performing a user-centered experiment with 24 participants, this study examined the document assessment criteria used by the users in these tasks and how the task characteristics affected user search behavior. In this paper, we report the results on webpage usefulness assessment.

2 Previous Work

Researchers have identified a variety of criteria in webpage usefulness assessment and grouped them into different categories. Barry [1] listed 21 criteria used in text document assessment and classified them into seven groups: the information content of documents, the user's previous experience and background, the user's beliefs and preferences, other information and sources within the information environment, the sources of documents, the document as a physical entity, and the user's situation. Tombros, Ruthven, and Jose [14] examined the assessment of web pages and identified 24 criteria in five major categories: *text, structure, quality, non-textual items, and physical properties*. Xie and co-workers investigated the multidimensionality of user evaluation [16]. Eighteen criteria were identified and classified into four categories: *content coverage, quality, design, and access*.

The importance of various criteria has been investigated. Tombros et al. [14] found that text was the most important category in terms of the number of mentions, followed by structure. Xu and Chen [17] applied human communication theory and defined five core factors: *topicality, novelty, reliability, understandability, and scope*. Among the five factors, topicality and novelty were found to be essential in the assessment. Understandability and reliability are also significant factors but less influential while scope is not significant. Chu's study [3] identified eleven important factors, among which specificity/amount of information was ranked the highest followed by ease of use, while order of presentation was ranked the lowest. Freund and Berzowska [6] identified six main criteria in assessment: *topic, situation, purpose, presentation, quantity, and quality*. According to the frequency of mention, topic remained as the most important criteria while situation and purpose were more important than they had been reported in other studies.

Most of the studies mentioned above focused on the identification of assessment criteria. There are also studies focusing on the various factors that influence the user's document assessment. Taylor [13] investigated the assessment criteria in different stages of the information seeking process. The study indicated that certain criteria, such as novelty, source quality, accuracy, structure, and time, were mentioned more frequently in later search stages. Also, the importance of different criteria varied in different stages of search. Scholer and colleagues [12] found that the users' relevance threshold was affected by the overall relevance level of the documents presented. In the same study, they also examined the effects of need for cognition and found that users with higher need for cognition had higher level of agreement with experts. Tombros et al. [14] and Freund and Berzowska [6] examined how people assess the document usefulness on different types of tasks. [6] reported that different task types were associated with different criteria and [14] reported "a considerable dependence of feature mentions on task characteristics" (p. 339). According to Freund's study [5], not only task type, but also the document genre significantly affects the user's usefulness assessment.

Some research has investigated the impact of task domain on usefulness assessment. Freund's study [5] involved two domains, that is, software engineering and E-government, but the domains were not their research focus. In health domain, many previous studies focused on information credibility. Crystal and Greenberg [4] examined how users evaluated health information during web search but the results were not compared with the results from other domains. [18] analyzed the factors affecting the trustworthiness of websites about menopause. [19] investigated the age difference in credibility assessment of health webpages. In the travel domain, [20] proposed a theory that users' satisfaction was affected by a complex configuration of information needs, information sources, information barriers, and personal characteristics when they search for travel-related information online.

In this study, we focus on how the factors of task domain and task type can affect users' usefulness assessment.

3 Methodology

A within-subject experiment was performed in a human computer interaction lab in University at Albany. In this experiment, each participant searched on four pre-defined tasks. For each task, the search process was recorded and played back to the participant. The participant then explained his/her selection from the result list and his/her evaluation of each webpage opened. Consequently, the experiment was composed of four sessions. Each session was in turn composed of several steps, which will be explained in detail later. Twenty-four graduate students from University at Albany participated in the experiment. At the end of the experiment, each participant received a $20 Amazon Gift Card as compensation of completing the experiment.

3.1 Tasks and Topics

We chose two task types from the three different task types in [21], that is: fact-finding, which is close-ended, and decision-making, which is open-ended. The two task domains selected in this study were travel domain and health domain. Generally speaking, users search for health-related tasks more seriously and the level of difficulty of such tasks could be high. Users search for travel-related tasks mostly for fun, and the level of task difficulty could be low. As a result, four tasks were generated in this study, as displayed in Table 1.

Table 1. Task domain and type design

	Fact Finding (FF)	Decision Making (DM)
Health	Task 1 (T1): Find out if it is safe for a pregnant woman to take amoxicillin	Task 3 (T3): Decide if one should change from ordinary food to organic food
Travel	Task 2 (T2): Find redwood tree parks in two different states	Task 4 (T4): Decide whether to visit the Everglades national park or key west during the weekend

The design of the tasks followed the principle of Situated Work Task Situation [2]. Some example tasks are listed as below.

T2 (Travel, Fact Finding)
Topic: Your nephew Tom, who is 10 years old, is very interested in redwoods. He asked you to take him to a park where he can see redwoods. You heard that redwoods are very rare and can be seen only in a few states.

Task: Please find national or state parks in at least two different states where there are redwoods.

T3 (Health, Decision Making)
You usually buy ordinary food from supermarkets without paying special attention to organic food. Recently, several of your friends have warned you that most of the food you bought are genetically modified and has long term side-effects to your health. You would like to do some search about the ordinary food you buy, including meat, fruits, and vegetables. You want to figure out whether they are genetically modified, the harmful effects of genetically modified food on people's health, and if it would be helpful to change to organic food.

Task: Please find enough information to support your decision about whether or not you should change or partially change your diet.

3.2 Experimental Design and Procedure

A within-subjects experiment was carried out with each participant performing four tasks. Task order was changed among the participants so that possible learning effects could be avoided.

At the beginning of the experiment, the participants filled out an entry questionnaire, which collected demographic information and the information related to their web search experience. Then the participants performed four search tasks. For each task, each participant completed the pre-task questionnaire, web search, post-task questionnaire, and then an interview at the end.

Pre-task Questionnaire. After the participants read the task description, a pre-task questionnaire was used to collect their perceptions about the task, including familiarity, interests, and confidence in finding relevant information, which could affect user's relevance judgment [10]. The predicted difficulty of the task was also collected in the pre-task questionnaire.

Web Search. After the pre-task questionnaire, the participants started web search by using Google search engine. They were told to search as usual and stop when they want to. There was no time limit on each task. All desktop activities including keyboard operations, mouse clicks, and web page changes, were logged by Morae V3.1 usability software (http://www.techsmith.com/morae.html). The participants were encouraged to think aloud in their searching processes. They were also informed that the search process is recorded (Fig. 1).

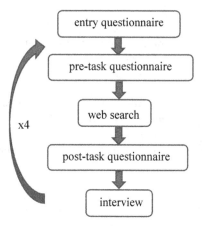

Fig. 1. Experiment procedure

Post-task Questionnaire. When the participants finished searching a task, a post-task questionnaire asked about their perceptions about the search, including the perceived difficulty of the task and their satisfaction about the search.

Interview. Following the post-task questionnaire, a semi-structured interview was conducted. Along with the replay of the recorded screen videos during web search, questions related to the search process were asked. The questions included:

- What results did you expect when issuing the query?
- Why did you decide to click this link?
- What is the usefulness of this page? Why?

The usefulness of a web page was evaluated by using a 5-point Likert scale. The interview was audio-recorded, and the participants were informed about the recording.

3.3   Content Analysis

A qualitative content analysis was performed to analyze the interviews, focusing on why the participants opened a URL and why the participants found a result page useful or not useful. After thorough walk through of the interview transcripts of the participants, a set of coding schemas was generated (see Table 2, 3, and 4).

Table 2. Coding schema on why a URL was opened

	Code	Description
Topic	KWTT	Notice some words in url or title
	DSCT	Notice the content in the description
	TPC	URL and/or title is relevant to the topic
	TTIC	The title does not show full information
Source	FML	Familiar with the website (source)
	TST	Trust the source, content is reliable
	TGTS	The website is the target of the search
	DMN	Simple domain
Source type	GOV	.gov site
	OFC	Official site
	ORG	.org site
	EDU	.edu site
	UGC	User generated content (QA, blog, wiki, forum …)
	SCL	Scholarly articles, peer-reviewed journal/book
Rank	TPLT	URL on top of the result list
	RDM	Random pick
Link	LNK	Link from the previous page
	SCCR	The source of the previous page
Confirm	CFM	To confirm the content of the previous pages

Table 3. Coding schema on why a webpage was found useful

	Code	Description
General useful	USF	The webpage is 'useful'
	KNL	Webpage contributes to personal knowledge
Content	ANS	The webpage answers the query

(continued)

Table 3. (*continued*)

	Code	Description
	SPC	Webpage gives specific information
	LNK	Webpage gives useful links or hints
	CMPT	The webpage has complete information
	DEC	Webpage helps decision making
	NEW	Webpage has something new
	PLS	Webpage has additional and valuable info
Confirm	CFM	The information found is confirmed
Credibility	TST	Participant trusts the source
	OBJ	The content is objective, not biased
Content type	IMG	Webpage contains images
	SCIT	Webpage has scientific information, like numbers
	REF	Webpage has references
	UGC	Webpage contains user comments/reviews
	NAD	Webpage has no ads
Info presentation	LGC	The info on the page is logically presented
	LOT	Webpage layout/organization is good

Table 4. Coding schema on why a webpage was found *not* useful

	Code	Description
Amount of the information on the page	NUSF	It's not the information the user is looking for
	NMIN	Not much info
	MSDI	Some specific info the user looks for was missing
	NCMP	Info not complete
	NANS	Not give the answer
	OTPC	Off topic
Not credible	NTST	Not trust the content
	BSD	Biased information
	UGC	User generated content
	NFML	Not familiar with the site

(continued)

Table 4. (*continued*)

	Code	Description
	NTWB	Not trust internet
	NCVN	Content not convincing
Quality of the information	UCLR	Info not clear
	NHDM	Not help decision making
	NGEN	Overall, the webpage not good enough
	CFLC	There exists conflicting content
Information presentation	UDPT	Too simple or too hard
	NLOT	Layout/organization not good
	OLD	Not up to date
	LNG	Too long
	ADS	Contained ads
Repeated info	REPT	Repeated info which is presented in previously opened pages

Using the same coding schemas, one coder performed independent and complete coding of the 24 interview transcripts twice with an interval of three months. The codes and snippets of supporting text were collected in an Excel spreadsheet. The average percent agreement between the two coding was 79%.

4   Results

Twenty-four graduate students from University at Albany participated in the experiment. There were 11 females and 13 males. Twenty participants were in their twenties and four in their thirties. On average, the participants had performed online searching for 10.54 years. Using a 7-point Likert scale, the mean self-rated search engine experience was 6.5. Almost all the participants reported that their last search happened on the same day of the experiment or the previous night. The topic distribution of the participants' last search was listed in Table 5.

Table 5. Topic distribution of the participants' last search

Topic	Count	Example
Course/Research	13	Master project in privacy and security
Direction	4	Address of xx downtown campus
Music	3	The chords to a few songs
Shopping	2	JCPenney online shopping
Other	2	Best credit cards/Art market

More than half of the participants (54.17%) had searched for topics related to their courses and research; four (16.67%) searched for addresses and directions; three (12.5%) searched for music and songs; and two (8.33%) searched for shopping.

4.1 Usefulness Assessment of the Webpages

It was assumed that by opening a webpage, the user expects that the webpage will be useful for the task and that s/he can get some valuable information from the page. As a result, in the interview, participants were asked to explain why they opened a specific webpage.

Table 6 shows the codes mentioned in each task, ranked by the number of participants mentioning the code. The top reason why a webpage was opened in all the four tasks was that the participants have noticed some specific words in the URL or the title of the webpage (KWTT). Additionally, at least ten participants claimed that they were familiar (FML) with the information source, the website the page belonged to. Another popular reason was that the webpage was at the top of the list on the search engine result page (TPLT). For the T1 (H-FF), eleven participants mentioned that they opened some webpages because they trusted the information source (TST). The TST reason was mentioned by six participants in each of the two DM tasks and by four participants in T2 (T-FF). Ten participants opened webpages to confirm what they had already found in the previous webpages (CFM) when searching for T1 while CFM was mentioned by no more than 3 participants in the other tasks. When working on T2 (T-FF), twelve participants opened a webpage by clicking on a link in the previous page (LNK), not from the search result list. In other tasks, LNK was not among the top reason why a webpage was opened. Eleven participants in T3 (H-DM) opened webpages because they were interested in the description of some specific search results (DSCT). Nine participants opened official websites (OFC) in T4 (T-DM).

Table 6. The reasons why the participants clicked a URL. Codes are presented in the form of 'code# participants'

T1 (H - FF)		T2 (T - FF)		T3 (H - DM)		T4 (T - DM)	
KWTT	13	KWTT	17	KWTT	20	KWTT	14
TST	11	LNK	12	FML	12	FML	12
FML	10	FML	10	DSCT	11	TPLT	10
CFM	10	TPLT	9	TPLT	10	OFC	9
TPLT	8	TGTS	5	TGTS	6	TGTS	7
DSCT	6	GOV	5	TST	6	LNK	6
TPC	4	TST	4	RDM	4	TST	6
GOV	4	DSCT	4	LNK	3	DSCT	4

(continued)

Table 6. (*continued*)

T1 (H - FF)		T2 (T - FF)		T3 (H - DM)		T4 (T - DM)	
LNK	4	TTIC	3	GOV	3	RDM	2
TGTS	3	CFM	3	EDU	2	GOV	2
ORG	2	TPC	2	DMN	2		
SCL	2	RDM	2	SCCR	2		
DMN	1	ORG	2	SCL	2		
OFC	1	UGC	1	TPC	2		
UGC	1	OFC	1	CFM	1		
RDM	1						

The reasons why a webpage was considered useful were described in Table 7, where the codes were ranked by the number of participants mentioning the code. The participants would generally evaluate a webpage as useful (USF) or talk about some specific piece of information on the page (SPC) to indicate the page was useful. Both USF and SPC were among the top three codes of usefulness in all the four tasks. In the two fact-finding tasks, more than half of the participants said that some webpages were useful because they responded to the queries or answered the tasks (ANS), while less than one third of the participants mentioning about ANS in the two decision-making (DM) tasks. On the other hand, more participants considered the webpages as useful in providing complete information in decision-making tasks, especially in the travel domain, than in fact-finding tasks. Whether the participants trusted the information source (TST) was among the top useful reasons in health domain tasks while it was not frequently mentioned in the travel domain tasks. Scientific contents (SCIT) were also considered important by more participants in health domain than in travel domain. More participants in fact-finding tasks than in decision-making tasks assessed a webpage as useful because the page confirmed previously found information (CFM). Good webpage layout and information organization (LOT) was more important in usefulness assessment in decision-making tasks than in fact-finding tasks. Similar results were found in image contents (IMG), especially for the decision-making tasks in travel domain.

Table 7. The reasons why the participants found a result useful. Codes are presented in the form of 'code# participants'

T1 (H - FF)		T2 (T - FF)		T3 (H - DM)		T4 (T - DM)	
ANS	14	SPC	17	USF	20	USF	16
SPC	10	ANS	14	SPC	14	SPC	13
USF	10	USF	9	TST	9	CMPT	13

(continued)

Table 7. (*continued*)

T1 (H - FF)		T2 (T - FF)		T3 (H - DM)		T4 (T - DM)	
TST	9	CFM	7	ANS	8	IMG	9
CFM	8	LNK	5	SCIT	8	ANS	7
SCIT	6	CMPT	3	LOT	7	DEC	5
CMPT	3	IMG	2	REF	7	LOT	4
LNK	3	TST	2	NEW	5	TST	2
KNL	3	KNL	2	CMPT	5	UGC	2
LOT	2	LOT	1	DEC	4	PLS	2
LGC	1	NEW	1	IMG	4	KNL	2
PLS	1			CFM	3	LNK	1
DEC	1			LNK	3	NEW	1
IMG	1			NAD	3		
UGC	1			OBJ	2		
NEW	1			LGC	2		
				KNL	1		
				UGC	1		

The participants were also asked to explain why a webpage was not useful and the corresponding results were presented in Table 8. Generally, the most common reason why a webpage was not useful was that the information on the webpage was not what the participant was looking for (NUSF). When some specific information was not presented in the webpage (MSDI), the participants also considered the page as not useful despite the task type and task domain. That the participants did not trust the information source (NTST) was brought up by almost half participants in the two health domain tasks, but it was not very important in the travel domain tasks. When a webpage contained less amount of information (NMIN and NCMP), it was more likely to be not useful in the two decision-making tasks as well as in T2 (T-FF), where the participants were asked to search for two different states which had redwood parks. For T2, the top reason was that its content was already presented in the previously opened webpages (REPT). When performing the two decision-making tasks, if the webpage layout and the information organization was not well presented, the participants were more likely to evaluate the page as not useful.

Table 8. The reasons why the participants found a result not useful. Codes are presented in the form of 'code# participants'

T1 (H - FF)		T2 (T - FF)		T3 (H - DM)		T4 (T - DM)	
NTST	12	REPT	15	NUSF	11	NUSF	11
MSDI	10	NUSF	9	NLOT	10	MSDI	10
NUSF	7	MSDI	7	NTST	10	NCMP	7
ADS	6	NMIN	7	NMIN	9	NLOT	6
REPT	4	UCLR	7	REPT	8	NTST	5
NFML	3	OTPC	5	UDPT	7	NMIN	5
NLOT	3	NCMP	5	MSDI	6	ADS	4
UCLR	4	NTST	4	BSD	5	LNG	3
NANS	3	NANS	3	NHDM	5	NHDM	3
NMIN	2	NLOT	3	LNG	4	UGC	2
NTWB	2	LNG	2	OTPC	4	NANS	2
UGC	2	ADS	1	ADS	4	UCLR	2
OLD	2			NCMP	3	NGEN	2
NCVN	2			UCLR	3	OTPC	1
OTPC	1			CFLC	2	OLD	1
NCMP	1			NANS	2	REPT	1
				NTWB	1	CFLC	1
				NCVN	1		
				OLD	1		

5 Discussion

As shown in the results, topic relevance was found to be important for all the four tasks in selecting a URL to open. As shown in Table 6, at least half of the participants mentioned about opening a webpage because they noticed some terms in the URL or the title of the webpage (KWTT). As P15 mentioned *"the non-GMO project caught my eye"* when asked about why a webpage from www.nongmoproject.org was opened. Though the participants might not be familiar with the specific task *per se*, they might have some experiences searching for other topics in the same domain. As a result, the participants tended to open webpages from familiar sites in all the four tasks (FML). When searching on T4 (T-DM), P9 said that *"So I've used TripAdvisor for other places, so I know that they have a lot of information"*. Examples of familiar websites are www.WebMD.com and www.fda.gov in the health domain, and www.TripAdvisor.com in the travel domain. Meanwhile, www.wikipedia.com was found to be a familiar website in all the four tasks and some participants searched for it in the query. However, in addition to FML, the participants used multiple criteria in the same search task. It is also possible that a URL was clicked because *"the page is on top of the result list (P6)"* (TPLT). This could be explained by the "trust bias", which referred to the observation that that users tent to click on the top result even though it might not be relevant [22].

In addition to the criteria mentioned above which were commonly used in all the four tasks, some factors were used by more participants in one task than in the other tasks, such as TST and CFM in T1, LNK in T2, DSCT in T3, and OFC in T4. Though it could be deduced that the trustable websites are usually the familiar websites, much less participants mentioned about 'trust' than those talked about 'familiar' in all tasks except for T1 (H-FF). That being said, when searching for health-related facts, the participants would like to visit familiar and credible information sources. Additionally, after the participants found some information from a trustable website, they tended to confirm the information by checking different sources. P9 explained that "*I decided to check a couple of the other websites, just in case to make (sure) things are consistent across the board*".

For the fact-finding task in travel domain (T2), twelve participants (50%) opened webpages by clicking links from previous pages (LNK). T2 was a relatively difficult fact-finding task and most of the participants issued more queries than they did in other tasks. The results indicated that in order to find the answers of the task, the participants not only tried the search engine results, but also clicked the internal links on the webpages. The fact is that quite a few participants found the answers by following internal links.

The reason why more participants decided which result to click by looking into the description of the search results (DSCT) in T3 was not very clear to us. It might be partially because the topic had a scientific nature and the participants were looking for webpages related to research studies. The titles of the results might not display much information, so the participants needed to read the descriptions to figure out whether the content was about scientific studies. P5 said that "*... and this one is like 'study finds' so I want to see what does it find*" and P20 said "*it says 'recent studies about ...' so I think there might be updated.*" Two participants opened scholarly articles (SCL) and another two participants selected '.edu' websites. T4 asked the participants to decide which place to visit during the weekend, the Everglades national park or key west. As a result, it is understandable that the more participants visited the official site of the national park in T4 than in other tasks.

In all the four tasks, when a webpage was evaluated as useful, the participants would often say "it is useful" in general or mentioned some specific information (SPC) provided on the webpage. The results also showed that a webpage was useful in responding to the query or answering the task (ANS) was mentioned more in the two fact-finding tasks than in the two decision-making tasks. On the other hand, providing complete information (CMPT) was mentioned by more participants in decision-making tasks than in fact-finding tasks. Considering the task type, it is not difficult to understand the result. Fact-finding tasks are close-ended and request the users to find specific answers. Decision-making tasks are open-ended, and the users need to read information in different aspects. Consequently, in decision-making tasks, the participants might want a webpage that provide all the information needed for the task. Alternatively, they would have to visit multiple websites before making a decision. This finding agreed with Chu's study [3] that specificity and the amount of information was important in webpage usefulness assessment. It is worth noting that the factors of SPC, ANS, and CMPT are all content factors which are the most important criteria in [6, 16, 17]. Accordingly, the amount of information for the users to read on one webpage in decision-making tasks tended to be larger than that in fact-finding tasks where the participants mostly skimmed the content and focused on specific piece of information. As a result, the layout and the organization of the webpage (LOT) in decision-making tasks played more important roles than that in fact-finding tasks.

Trusting the information source (TST) was among the top reasons why a webpage was useful in health domain tasks but was not equally important in travel domain tasks. This indicates that in health domain, the credibility of the information source not only affects if the user would open the webpage but also affects the webpage's usefulness assessment. In comparison to travel domain, more participants considered a webpage as useful because the webpage had scientific content (SCIT) when searching on health domain tasks.

Given that TST was one of the top reasons why a webpage in health domain was considered useful, it is not difficult to understand that NTST was among the top reasons why a webpage was assessed as not useful in the health domain tasks. Other factors related to webpage credibility, such as BSD, NCVN, NTWB, and UGC, were also mentioned by more participants in health tasks than in travel tasks. It is worth noting that though same number of participants (two) took UGC as a not-useful factor in both T1 (H-FF) and T4 (T-DM), much more participants opened webpages with user-generated contents in T4, e.g., www.tripadvisor.com, than in T1, e.g., www.babycenter.com. TripAdvisor was some participants' familiar, even targeted, website. Similarly, in decision-making tasks, corresponding to LOT being related to useful webpages, NLOT was usually related to not-useful webpages.

Novelty was found to be used more frequently in later search stages [23]. Our results showed that in later search stages, the usefulness of one webpage was often accessed by combining the webpage itself and the other webpages opened in the same search. Fifteen participants in T2 evaluated some webpages as not very useful because the information contained in the webpages was already found in the previously opened webpages (REPT). As P5 considered a webpage in T2 not useful by saying "*not because it's not useful. It's just because it came in late*". A webpage in T4 was scored 4 (with 5 as most useful) by P19 and the explanation to the assessment was "*this gave me the idea. It solves the problem for me but it wasn't the same caliber as the other one (which was scored 5)*".

6 Conclusion

A user experiment was performed to investigate the impact of task type and task domain on the user assessment of webpage usefulness. The results indicated that both task type and task domain could affect the user's usefulness assessment. Additionally, as shown in Tables 2, 3, and 4, the various criteria were put into more general categories, such as topic, source, and source type in Table 2, and content, content type, and info presentation in Table 3. In deciding which webpage to open and assessing the webpage usefulness, the participants used multiple criteria from multiple categories, even in the same task. Results indicate that webpage usefulness assessment is a dynamic process and depends on multiple factors, such as the task, user, and search stage. This study has limitations in that only two task types and two task domains were investigated. We plan to compare user search behavior across multiple task types and domains in the future.

Acknowledgements. This experiment was supported by the research grant awarded by the university's Graduate Student Association. We also thank all the participants.

References

1. Barry, C.L.: User-defined relevance criteria: an exploratory study. J. Am. Soc. Inform. Sci. **45**(3), 149–159 (1994). https://doi.org/10.1002/(SICI)1097-4571(199404)45:3%3c149:AID-ASI5%3e3.0.CO;2-J
2. Borlund, P.: The IIR evaluation model: a framework for evaluation of interactive information retrieval systems. Inform. Res. **8**(3), 152 (2003). http://informationr.net/ir/8-3/paper152.html
3. Chu, H.: Factors affecting relevance judgment: a report from TREC Legal track. J. Documentation **67**(2), 264–278 (2011). https://doi.org/10.1108/00220411111109467
4. Crystal, A., Greenberg, J.: Relevance criteria identified by health information users during web searches. J. Am. Soc. Inform. Sci. Technol. **57**(10), 1368–1382 (2006). https://doi.org/10.1002/asi.20436
5. Freund, L.: A cross-domain analysis of task and genre effects on perceptions of usefulness. Inf. Process. Manage. **49**(5), 1108–1121 (2013). https://doi.org/10.1016/j.ipm.2012.08.007
6. Freund, L., Berzowska, J.: The goldilocks effect: task-centred assessments of e-government information. Proc. Am. Soc. Inform. Sci. Technol. **47**(1), 1–10 (2010). https://doi.org/10.1002/meet.14504701261
7. Kinley, K., Tjondronegoro, D., Partridge, H., Edwards, S.: Relationship between the nature of the search task types and query reformulation behaviour. In: Proceedings of the Seventeenth Australasian Document Computing Symposium, pp. 39–46. ACM, New York, NY, USA (2012). https://doi.org/10.1145/2407085.2407091
8. Kim, J.: Task as a context of information seeking: an investigation of daily life tasks on the web. Libri, vol. 58, no. 3 (2008). https://doi.org/10.1515/libr.2008.018
9. Radlinski, F., Kurup, M., Joachims, T.: How does clickthrough data reflect retrieval quality? In: Proceedings of the 17th ACM Conference on Information and Knowledge Management, pp. 43–52. ACM, New York, NY, USA (2008). https://doi.org/10.1145/1458082.1458092
10. Ruthven, I., Baillie, M., Elsweiler, D.: The relative effects of knowledge, interest and confidence in assessing relevance. J. Documentation **63**(4), 482–504 (2007). https://doi.org/10.1108/00220410710758986
11. Saracevic, T.: The stratified model of information retrieval interaction: extension and applications. Proc. ASIS Ann. Meet. **34**, 313–27 (1997)
12. Scholer, F., Kelly, D., Wu, W.-C., Lee, H.S., Webber, W.: The effect of threshold priming and need for cognition on relevance calibration and assessment. In: Proceedings of the 36th International ACM SIGIR Conference on Research and Development in Information Retrieval, pp. 623–632 (2013)
13. Taylor, A.: User relevance criteria choices and the information search process. Inf. Process. Manage. **48**(1), 136–153 (2012). https://doi.org/10.1016/j.ipm.2011.04.005
14. Tombros, A., Ruthven, I., Jose, J.M.: How users assess web pages for information seeking. J. Am. Soc. Inform. Sci. Technol. **56**(4), 327–344 (2005). https://doi.org/10.1002/asi.20106

15. Toms, E.G., Freund, L., Kopak, R., Bartlett, J.C.: The effect of task domain on search. In: Proceedings of the 2003 Conference of the Centre for Advanced Studies on Collaborative Research, pp. 303–312. IBM Press, Toronto, Ontario, Canada (2003). http://dl.acm.org/cit ation.cfm?id=961322.961370
16. Xie, I., Benoit III, E., Zhang, H.: How do users evaluate individual documents? an analysis of dimensions of evaluation activities. Inform. Res. **15**(4), 723 (2010). http://InformationR. net/ir/15-4/colis723.html]
17. Xu, Y., Chen, Z.: Relevance judgment: what do information users consider beyond topicality? J. Am. Soc. Inform. Sci. Technol. **57**(7), 961–973 (2006). https://doi.org/10.1002/asi.20361
18. Sillence, E., Briggs, P., Fishwick, L., Harris, P.: Trust and mistrust of online health sites. In: Proceedings of the SIGCHI Conference on Human Factors in Computing Systems, pp. 663–670 (2004)
19. Liao, Q.V., Fu, W.T.: Age differences in credibility judgments of online health information. ACM Trans. Comput.-Hum. Interact. **21**(1), 1–23 (2014)
20. Kourouthanassis, P.E., Mikalef, P., Pappas, I.O., Kostagiolas, P.: Explaining travellers online information satisfaction: a complexity theory approach on information needs, barriers, sources and personal characteristics. Inf. Manag. **54**(6), 814–824 (2017)
21. Toms, E.G., et al.: Task effects on interactive search: the query factor. In: Fuhr, N., Kamps, J., Lalmas, M., Trotman, A. (eds.) INEX 2007. LNCS, vol. 4862, pp. 359–372. Springer, Heidelberg (2008). https://doi.org/10.1007/978-3-540-85902-4_31
22. Agichtein, E., Zheng, Z.: Identifying "best bet" web search results by mining past user behavior. In: Proceedings of the 12th ACM SIGKDD International Conference on Knowledge Discovery and Data Mining, pp. 902–908. ACM, New York, NY, USA (2006). https://doi.org/10.1145/1150402.1150526
23. Vakkari, P., Hakala, N.: Changes in relevance criteria and problem stages in task performance. J. Documentation **56**(5), 540–562 (2000)

How Workarounds Occur in Relation to Automatic Speech Recognition at Danish Hospitals

Silja Vase[(✉)]

University of Copenhagen, Karen Blixens Plads 8, 2300 København S, Denmark
siljavase@hum.ku.dk

Abstract. This paper attempts to show how healthcare professionals navigate in relation to Automatic Speech Recognition (ASR) by examining workarounds. The use of ASR in entering information into electronic health records (EHRs) is an important topic to study as hospitals increasingly adapt to the technology. This paper is based on ethnographic multi-sited fieldwork. It gathers information about the use of ASR in workflows, its limitations, how physicians perceive it, and what workarounds they employ when it does not work as expected. The study analyses a Danish hospital that underwent an ASR implementation almost two decades ago, yet they still experience frequent system modifications. Once the physicians experience these changes, they promptly criticize the technology for failing to live up to proclaimed expectations. The paper demonstrates how a simplistic understanding and a following of a predetermined plan of complex technology, such as ASR, contributes to workflow-related challenges and workarounds. As a result, the research proclaims a concern towards information recording, saving, and retrieval related to differences in how information is entered into an EHR by using ASR. Further, studies of workarounds proclaim these to be a way for physicians to achieve the desired goal of patient safety, where this study finds some workarounds as contradictory actions based on revolt practices towards managerial decisions.

Keywords: Electronic Health Records · Automatic Speech Recognition · Human-Computer Interaction · Workarounds

1 Introduction and Motivation

The fundamental objective of implementing healthcare technologies, such as Automatic Speech Recognition (ASR), is to enable improvement of efficiency through documentation time and accuracy and further to allow patients to access their Electronic Health Records (EHR) the same day as their medical consultations [1, 2]. Healthcare technologies are often associated with unintended impacts or workflow blocks caused by predefined work processes and underlying intentions of systematic procedures, which can be perceived as deviating from healthcare professionals' normal workflow. The deviation can lead professionals to comprehend these technological implementations as relatively inefficient and inconvenient [3]. As such technologies do not always reflect

M. Kurosu (Ed.): HCII 2021, LNCS 12764, pp. 458–472, 2021.
https://doi.org/10.1007/978-3-030-78468-3_31

on the current workflows or even dissuade professionals from performing these, health-care professionals circumvent the technology by creating alternative processes. The performing of "workarounds" creates hesitations about whether the intended work tasks are performed, as these actions cannot necessarily be traced.

Further, workarounds could postpone the expected quality and safety of the intended medical work. A study of workarounds in a specific context can detect areas where the intended workflow encoded in the implemented technology creates challenges or complicates professional actions [4]. This paper illustrates an ongoing study that emerges from previous fieldwork of the ASR algorithm and sees an opportunity to examine how workflows vary in relationship to ASR as it is adapted in practice by studying related workarounds.

While ASR plays a central role for a growing number of healthcare professionals, research remains scarce in the area [5] and has a statistical angle. This paper analyses challenges which should not be addressed in solitary throughput statistical substances, why the following pages endorse a social perspective by participating workarounds. As workarounds are commonly known in healthcare settings [6], little empirical research has been done in the area [4].

2 Related Work

The development and implementation of new technologies and information systems in healthcare is a well-researched issue and will continue to be so as medical work and medical information systems are highly intertwined. Technologies certainly improve information retrieving, processing, and shorten work processes, yet studies point out several obstacles when measuring these expected improvements. Some of the difficult to spot measurements are estimated prevented working hours, which often relate to unforeseen or undisclosed workflows that are not applicable to predetermined strategies implementing new technologies. Since many organizations seem to comply with planned implementations of technologies over the actual workflow [7], they entail a darkening of these workflows is created. These invisible workflows amplify new technologies to occur opaque when considering the accountability. Information systems in healthcare often touch upon several professions, software, and hardware, which does not smooth out the possibility of locating the actual or hidden practices, which may seem out of place from an organizational planning perspective.

This study draws attention to a speech recognition algorithm. Various studies related to Human-Computer Interaction (HCI) have critically inspected algorithms and how they are configured in practice by drawing on ethnographic research [8–11]. In general, they question how algorithms can be located. They point out an obstacle when algorithms are purely researched as mere code or by isolating it from examining the everyday encounter with explicit and implicit organizational dimensions, since "the limits of the term algorithm are determined by social engagements rather than by technological or material constraints" [10]. Thus, algorithms are comprehended by social engagements connected to the technology and could be connected to users, developers, and technology producers. The perception of and use of algorithms thus touches upon various backgrounds with possible limited connection and communication.

2.1   Automatic Speech Recognition

Physicians use ASR to produce EHRs, which documents ward rounds, operations, and clinical results in general. ASR is based on an algorithm that offers an alternative input medium. It claims to be faster for physicians than the use of a keyboard; however, compared to the former use of dictation, the digital transformation of practices concerning ASR is often associated with increased documentation time for physicians and outsourcing or even exclusion of other healthcare professionals [5, 12]. ASR has matured over the last few years [2], while it has evolved to 'smaller' languages such as Danish [12], which nearly 6 million people speak. Since introducing the technology to Danish healthcare, hospitals implement ASR to enable faster completion of EHRs and upload them in real-time [5]. ASR offers a replacement to the 'standard' way of entering records where physicians dictate medical records, which clerks subsequently transcribe. Clerks' role has now changed by automating the specific activity producing medical records and taking over other responsibilities such as setting up physicians' ASR profiles.

The ASR algorithm has been in the searchlight of medical researchers for quite some time [e.g., [13–15]]. Ramaswamy et al. [16] as the technology has matured and become more widespread in healthcare [12, 17]. Investigations concerning ASR have been surveying vocabularies as they enable the recognition rate of words spoken. However, many other factors play a role when it comes to recognition rates, such as clarity of pronunciation [18], external noise [19], and conflicts considering special features of the Danish language such as pressure, vocal extension and 'stød' [17]. Studies have thus emphasized the more technical aspects. Considering how social engagements determine algorithmic limits, these external artifacts interfere with how physicians perceive the technology. Alapetite et al. [12] covered physicians' attitudes towards ASR, which depended on external artifacts, and further how physicians considered American healthcare procedures related to EHR. The normative effect on how physicians in the study perceived the technology illustrates how a survey of ASR should consider the technical aspects as the use may reflect the technology's preconceptions.

2.2   Workarounds as a Way to Achieve Goals

Social engagements with healthcare technology often outline a meeting between users and complex technology and often puts healthcare professionals on the spot as they need to provide care while conforming to technologies' systematization [20, 21]. Implementing new technologies can lead to challenges that force users to develop alternative workflows from what is predicted when applying technology in an already accustomed work routine.

This article examines how users meet the ASR algorithm, which is a subtype of algorithms in general and is designed to take over a specific task that clerks performed. ASR is designed to replace a humanly performed task rather than compliment it without adding any workloads to physicians, as they exchange dictation with ASR.

Previous research by Dupret and Friborg [22] on technological infrastructures in Danish hospitals contributes to understanding how healthcare work is increasingly based on streamlined processes caused by technology. The study establishes a need for diverse professional viewpoints when understanding how technology facilitates or does not facilitate workflows. Dupret and Friborg [22] emphasize that employees do not work against a managerial decision or in contradiction to a given technological implementation, but rather have other work 'goals' than expected or planned by management. These other goals can create workarounds that bypass the planned use and challenge the possibility of transforming the use into a unit of measurement or even locating it as the use does not match managerial expectations.

Kobayashi et al. [4] define workarounds as "informal temporary practices for handling exceptions to normal workflow". However, a 'normal' workflow is normative to the user who carries out actions that do not follow explicit or implicit protocols [23], unlike particularly non-deep learning algorithms that follow encoded rules to conduct action or not. The concept workaround requisites an obstacle in achieving a normal workflow that must be circumvented by overriding what has been coded and allows users to tolerate a systems' presence while avoiding possible impracticable demands. Workarounds are therefore intentional. However, Halbsleben [3] address that little is known about actors' perceiving of obstacles to normal workflow, why there is a need for an in-depth study of workaround practitioners and their impediments in practice.

Workarounds are at risk of undermining patient safety in urgent situations [24, 25] and are therefore of important nature when the use of technology in connection with healthcare is investigated. To understand the 'normal' use of ASR, one should thus focus on actions while carried out in practice. To acquire such an understanding, this paper considers the process of entering and retrieving information when using speech recognition. This facilitation is crucial for how ASR works in the specific context of producing EHR, as it applies as the main existence of the technology and depends on its ability to be a medium between physicians and the EHR.

Although the term workaround is no stranger to healthcare professionals' ethnographic studies, many papers identify workarounds as negative activities [4] and rarely have a distinct approach defining the phenomenon [3, 20]. Further, more research is needed on unveiled potential risks and benefits associated with workarounds emerging from technology implementation in healthcare [21].

2.3 Locating Workarounds in Practice

To locate workarounds is to locate actions that intentionally disrupt prescribed work processes and creates work patterns. These actions are carried out by individuals or a group of individuals [3]. Using ASR to compose EHR is rarely an isolated task due to hospitals' hectic environment, which entails sudden tasks, disruptions, simultaneous intersecting collaborations, and several interdependent technological elements. The latter has values inscribed in them and, these need to be made visible as they may not reflect upon healthcare professionals' normativity. This paper does not wish to declare challenges related to the use of ASR as 'good' or 'bad', as research within healthcare practices [26, 27] considers such judgment inapplicable due to the many levels of everyday practices that technology touches upon. Continuing practice theoretical thinking, this study will concentrate on actions performed individually or by groups of individuals and will focus on these healthcare professionals and their daily work, which are crucial to this study of human-computer interaction and the unintended or hidden consequences of such practices.

More recent accounts of practice theory stage the actual practices, actions, expressions, and materiality's roles should be central when analyzing the social [28] aligning practice theory with socio-technical approaches. In his study of organizational phenomena, Nicolini [29] develops a site ontology that draws from these recent accounts. This approach or 'practice turn' [30] sees all social phenomena as rooted in practices. The perspective allows the researcher to materialize actions such as workarounds as practices are found by various interests and are thus "subject to multiple interpretations, and open to contradictions and tensions" [29]. Consequently, this study perceives practices as continuously evolving through the use of artifacts such as technology and can comprehend the social practices themselves and the technological mechanisms that engage with or support a practice. Additionally, the author expects the approach to lead to an analysis that considers practices in an orthopedic department and leads through several other sites since ASR could touch upon numerous workflows before it is in the end-user's hands. Thus, healthcare professionals will be investigated to locate workarounds in recognized practices that do not relate to the inscribed values or codes in ASR.

3   Research Methods

To do fieldwork in healthcare is doing fieldwork in hectic environments, yet, organizational practices and how they evolve with technologies should be studied in real-life settings. This study's empirical material is thus collected during ethnographic fieldwork, which is divided into two parts. The first part extends over three months and consists of qualitative interviews [31], focus group interviews [32], and field notes recording observations of workflows [33] in various environments (two IT departments and remote departments such as doctors' and clerks' offices) and in the orthopedic ward department at a Danish hospital. The second part occurs at the same hospital and consists of shadowing [34] physicians at the ward and outpatient clinics. Shadowing compromises the researcher to observe practices in real-time by following a specific actor closely for a period of time. The technique is thus well fitted for organizational research, as it allows for follow-up questions and short interviews during an in-depth observation [34]. Additionally, the ASR suppliers are interviewed several times to grasp how the technology is set up and reflects an intentional workflow.

Nicolini [29] suggests a re-presenting of practices to grasp different aspects of these to materialize them and perceive how the phenomenon addressed is located in time and touches upon multiple interpretations. Context is thus found through an individual practice that is historically situated and determined. He proposes an approach that illuminates the connection between the local accomplishment of practices and practices elsewhere to 'trail' how these are associated with mapping out daily organizational life [29].

Inspired by Nicolini's changeable approach, the first part of the fieldwork is completed by alternately approaching the use of ASR from an emic perspective and then looking at the technology from a technological point of view. Drawing on these aspects, this study attends and code the retrieved data based on an open approach. This examination will find and frame the somewhat setting continuously during the fieldwork to meet the field with an overall setting and allow for it to change as the fieldwork develops. The initial fieldwork prompted the analysis to focus on the local real-time practices and further trail how these are connected elsewhere. The second part is built on these findings to create a more in-depth understanding of ASR workflows and how the technology is adapted in practice.

3.1 Physicians' Workflow

The following illustrates physicians' workflow regarding ASR to delimit the study, as the boundaries of where ASR affect workflows are somewhat fluid and can interfere with several individuals and groups. To use the technology, physicians speak into a microphone connected to a computer, where their speech is then translated into written text. The text appears on their screen within seconds after the physicians have spoken into the microphone. Physicians either speak in whole sentences, divide them as they wait for the system to write the spoken words, or speak in singular terms. They can subsequently edit the text using a keyboard or by repeating terms to train the algorithm for a better translation in the future. Physicians use ASR as part of their workflow at several Danish hospitals. Their chores start with a joint meeting at ward rounds, where nurses, heads of departments, and physicians review the hospitalized patients. Then the individual physician visits the assigned patients. At each visit, the patient is examined, and an EHR must then be filled in with information about the person's situation and future actions. In an outpatient clinic, physicians work individually in a clinical office to call a patient from a waiting room. During the examination, physicians can ask for assistance from other healthcare professionals such as nurses or physiotherapists. Once the patient is examined, the physician completes an EHR using ASR. Participating actors are anonymized to maintain their discretion and opportunity to participate in future surveys.

4   Analysis

The overview below in Table 1 describes workarounds found during an inductive data collection, where no emphasis was placed on the workarounds themselves, but rather how they work with and around ASR to map out the impact on workflows concerning the technology. The collected data material has been deductively coded based on the definition of workarounds as "informal temporary practices for handling exceptions to normal workflow" [4] where workflows deviate from what the employees consider as normal in individual situations are taken into account. The identified workarounds led to a subsequent shadowing of physicians performing these. As illustrated below, actions can lead to multiple workarounds where the analysis traces how ASR touches upon different areas, departments, and distinctive professions emerging from physicians' profiles.

Table 1. List of identified workarounds (WA)

Label	Description	Obstacle
WA1	Approve insufficient trained profile	Technical literacy
WA2	Produce EHR in hallway	Usability, personal appearance
WA3	Produce EHR using PC	Usability, personal appearance
WA4	Produce EHR using keyboard	Usability, technical literacy
WA5	Do not report errors	Lack of time
WA6	Produce EHR at the end of shift	Technical issues
WA7	Do not use ASR at night	Technical issues, technical literacy
WA8	Produce records on a piece of paper	Technical issues
WA9	Produce EHR insufficiently	Technical issues, Managerial contradiction
WA10	Avoids ASR	Technical issues, Managerial contradiction
WA11	Trains profile deliberately incorrect	Managerial contradiction

4.1 Setting Up an ASR Profile

Physicians must set up an ASR profile to record EHRs that occurs with enrollment. They read a text out loud by which the acoustic model detects their speech while clerks review the process and approve the setup. Dialects or accents can challenge the model and can lead clerks to enforce a profile approval due to time delay. Clerks refer to the system as "teasing", which courses the workaround. Approval of an insufficient setup profile challenges the acoustic model in recognizing the user's speech and leaves the physician obligated to train the algorithm to a greater extent. The establishment of how ASR performs is vital as physicians consider using the technology as "mandatory" or "highly expected" by management. Even profiles set up without miscalculations can translate poorly. Translation errors may have implications for the clarity of texts, where some sentences can appear incomprehensible and even humorous. However, there are agonizing incidents where diagnoses or other vital information are unintentionally modified due to a challenged recognition. Physicians often overlook such incidents as they feel "blind" when they read the text seconds after speaking aloud.

4.2 ASR at Wards

At ward rounds, physicians are expected to use a portable Computer on Wheels (COW). Every orthopedical department has three COWs available for the two physicians doing ward rounds, leaving one to spare if a COW is broken or used for other tasks. COWs allow immediate entry of information at patients' bedside. The physician can turn to the patient and relatives who can attend and ask questions regarding the EHR produced using ASR. Paradoxically interruptions challenge the speech flow initiating the technology to recognize poorly, and physicians thus appear unprofessional:

I am not fond of the quality today. It is embarrassing if it works poorly or if the system freezes when you are in front of the patient. It would seem like we do not know what we are doing (Martin, physician).

The poor recognition causes physicians to leave patients' bedsides, produce EHRs in hallways, or avoid COWs and use a PC in a shared office. Other factors such as uncomfortable odors or discomfort of patients in pain or need to sleep also entail working around the expected use of COWs. In both examples, physicians are visible to a broader population scope and are further interrupted when producing EHR. Only a few PCs have microphones installed enabling ASR, and these are often unavailable as physicians share the ward office with nurses and management. In some cases, physicians choose to produce EHR for the entire shift after all patients have been examined, which can result in a lack of information on the patients.

COWs must be reported if physicians experience challenges concerning ASR. However, such reports are time-consuming or challenging to specify, which leaves physicians to dismiss the reports and leave COWs in office corners with a post-it that writes "out of order". Technical errors are often corrected automatically during updates, yet the COWs remain unused due to the post-its. The orthopedic surgery department sent less than 25 error messages to the IT department in 2019 concerning ASR. The errors included that the system "freezes", malfunctioning hardware, that ASR fails to register new words, and requests resetting profiles. According to the IT department, this reflects a system that works well because of the low number of errors reported. In 2020, there were so few errors reported that they were not considered. Conversely, this study may note that all of the errors mentioned above happen several times a week, without being report

The widespread use of ASR related to orthopedical wards leads to several workarounds arising from a lack of usability where users do not possess the required technological literacy to locate accountability or defects. Due to lack of time and risk of appearing ignorant or unprofessional, employees circumvent the technology's expected use. In some cases, these actions result in possible data loss, which may have consequences for the patient and other staff who depend on an error message or a correctly performed EHR for a specific period of time.

4.3 ASR at Outpatient Clinics

In outpatient clinics, examinations occur in a single, enclosed room. It is up to the individual physician to use ASR after an examination, where the patient can attend the EHR production or leave. Some Physicians combine reduced recognition with types of shifts and avoid ASR during the night:

I experience a delay during the afternoons and especially during nighttime. Perhaps my voice changes, but I think the system is rebooted or something. It is always slower during the nighttime (Jørgen, Physician).

Others point out the reduced recognition as continuous and try to improve it by refreshing the system or restarting the computer. Despite time pressure and patients waiting, physicians keep using ASR to produce EHR due to their responsibility to train the algorithm for better recognition, which is anticipated by management:

When you work here, you can feel how you are expected to use it [ASR]. If you do not, they [management] will speak in capital letters. (Lars, physician)

Despite managerial expectations, several physicians have chosen to avoid ASR to protest against executive decision-making. Furthermore, some have tried to sabotage their profile by intentionally training it incorrectly or filling in the EHR insufficiently, hoping to expose the technology as unsatisfactory or to dodge the expected use of ASR. Consequently, these workarounds have led to great frustration among physicians who examine the patients with insufficient EHRs as they cannot use the files.

4.4   ASR Illustrated as Data

The ASR supplier measures each profile's use by the number of EHR recorded and the average percentage of corrections made when producing these each month. It should be mentioned here that the supplier does not further specify these calculations and thus opaque to indicate when it is a complete EHR, a sentence, a correction, or if corrections made later in the same health record is considered. The IT department and clerks use these data to assess physicians' use of ASR. However, the individual physician's use is challenging to spot as the data illustrate a systematic use of ASR in the orthopedic department. For example, one month represents 56 physicians' profiles used ASR to produce an average of 103.64 medical records. Several profiles used ASR once during this month, which could be a fault activation of the technology, while the highest amount of use was 285 times. The percentage of edited characters is calculated by each text, where 'edited characters' or 'text' are not specified further. The IT department or even the supplier cannot access these values since the calculation is hidden by the algorithmic providers. At the orthopedic department, one profile corrected 30% of the EHR produced by the physician. A 30% correction is displayed as a recognition rate of 70% presented as a bar chart when entering the ASR data as a supplier, IT employee or a medical clerk. In defiance, physicians who do not correct EHRs will have a correction rate of 0%, thus recognizing 100%. Thus, the average use includes profiles that do not correct EHR or do not use ASR at all, and the technology thus appears to be error-free. The data further illustrate an average of EHR corrections below 10% for the orthopedic department, and consequently, a recognition rate over 90. This is interesting as the supplier assures a 90–95% recognition rate for profiles that have used the technology for about a year. Why the recognition rate on average lives up to the expected level.

Like many other HCI studies, this is a study of organizationally assessed information based on systematic and standardized data collection. This approach is certainly not foreign to studies of, e.g., big data [10, 11]. However, the departmental dataset of 56 licenses is not 'big' data and could illustrate an individual use. It is noteworthy that the actual use is not attributed more attention, as the individual doctor's difference in corrections is significant, leading to certain doctors being overlooked, as the focus is only on the average use.

This analysis clarifies that the technology is perceived differently based on the disparate accesses and interfaces the various disciplines have. This distinction is not expressed in the data collection of recognition rates and data visualizations, but it is also not visible to the individual professionals. The model below illustrates how technology captures actions that are expected and therefore systematic. The filled arrows and bold text illustrate the visible actions, and the dashed arrows the actions that the system cannot see and are overlooked by the IT department, which prevents them from improving the conditions.

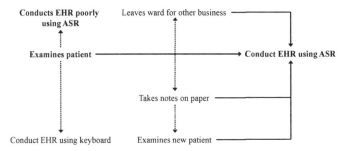

Fig. 1. Process model of workarounds at wards and outpatient clinics

5   Discussion

This study set out to assess workflow in connection to ASR and has led to a discussion of how the use of the technology leads healthcare professionals to perform workarounds. This study indicates that workarounds intersect with many other activities at numerous departmental layers and consequently various professions. This finding is consistent with that of Kobayashi [4], who recognizes workarounds as having a cascading effect that can lead to another layer of workarounds, leading to potential shortages. Beerepoot and Van de Weerd [35] also mentions possible shortages when conducting workarounds as healthcare professionals depend on each other to stay in line with the systematic everyday life at a hospital. If not, deviations of responsibilities can appear down the line [35]. This study infers that a single workaround activates a somewhat snowball effect; however, where the above studies indicate consequences of workarounds to accomplish collective tasks, this study assesses that workarounds carried out in one place also affect actions far away from the place in question.

The current article supports evidence from previous health care literature observations [e.g., [4, 25]] of the validity of workarounds and workaround behavior. These can appear as both solving and problematic in practice. Staying within healthcare, some papers [e.g., [35, 36]] on workarounds focus on possible solutions and recommendations for future handling of such actions. The current research goes deeper by following up on the foundation for workarounds related to ASR and further understanding actors' perceiving of impediments to normal workflow. Workarounds can be seen in the light of both positive and negative perspectives depending on the point of interest.

Nonetheless, what is noteworthy is why practitioners carry out actions despite these perspectives, as they are aware of these actions challenge predetermined workflows. Figure 1 in the previous chapter shows the scheduled disposition (filled arrows) of how physicians produce EHR after examinations appear straightforward. Physicians are aware of this expected workflow and state the same goals whether they work at wards or outpatient clinics. However, physicians only need to deviate from this plan once in order for their actions to become invisible to the system, IT department, clerks, and subsequent management. Further, when physicians create workarounds on top of workarounds, this workflow can lead to additional hiding, which continues a distortion concerning the expected workflow that the system is programmed for and can support. The actual actions carried out by physicians. Such a distortion can cause other system errors and continue unsustainable situations that create frustrations among physicians who depart entirely from the expected workflow.

The use of ASR at wards reflects more complex actions than in outpatient centers, which seems to be due to greater flexibility. Doctors stay in their referred rooms in outpatient centers because only one computer is available. However, several physicians choose to produce EHR while the patient is present, so they use ASR in the hallway of wards. Workarounds are embedded in spaces where the interaction between users and the technology is determined based on its influence.

5.1 Measuring Workarounds

It is interesting to note that several workarounds found in this study show how obstacles were moved around instead of being solved. Physicians who produce EHR in corridors or at a shared office continuously try to avoid interruptions, although they move the problem to destinations where other more frequent interruptions occur. Although these solutions appear to hinder physicians from improving their ASR profiles' recognition rate, they see these actions as promoting. In addition, it is crucial whether they appear professional to the patient, where this consideration does not apply to their colleagues. The personal appearance thus surpasses reliability and the training of ASR insolent. Therefore, users' perceptions of impediments to normal workflow depend primarily on whether they are challenged on their professional appearance.

These considerations fall into the discussion of how workarounds can be analyzed and measured, as Halbsleben [3] points out a concern considering how to capture workarounds. They propose a measurement of workarounds that encompasses both qualitative and quantitative methods. The topic has led this study to re-consider the technical elements of how ASR is measured systematically. However, the discussion of how to capture the personal perceiving of professional appearance is less tangible, which can seem challenging to capture. Nevertheless, these workarounds still affect data treatment since the recognition rate is affected by interruptions.

Beerepoot and Van de Weerd [35] have experimented with workaround 'snapshots' which "contains the essential information about the social and technical aspects of the deviation and forces the creator to keep the information concise, so that it allows for quick analysis" [35]. However, such captures depend on participants' contribution and explanatory ability, where invisible workflows can remain invisible. Why a more in-depth understanding of, e.g., the use of a specific technology in practice is necessary. Snapshots could delimitate possible contexts for further mapping of workarounds. This study has done so by framing a specific technology used by orthopedical physicians to capture repetitive actions due to a distortion of liability that lies outside physicians' profession. Physicians are expected to use ASR but are responsible for the technology to work themselves by training their profile. Thus, the responsibility is relinquished from digitally trained employees and further the management leaving physicians with a technology that requires a digital literacy they do not possess. Following this, insufficient setup ASR profiles require increased training, which exposes these users to time pressure in an already time-constrained workplace.

5.2 Common Goals?

Studies show that workarounds occur with a desire for the patient's well-being [3, 4, 24, 25], represent a common goal for health care professionals. Contrary to expectations, this study found several workarounds to avoid or even counteract a normal workflow. By training their ASR profile deliberately wrong or producing EHRs insufficiently to oppose the top-down managerial decision to use ASR when producing EHRs, physicians comprehend themselves as set aside and their professionalism as challenged. Such workarounds challenge time-constrained workflows and result in fewer patients examined. Managerial decisions can thus lead to resistance, causing physicians to perform almost childish actions, which have consequences for future examinations. Studies considering workarounds in a Danish context [22] state that employee's express dissatisfaction with employees and management's overall relationship. A top-down culture is pervasive, yet workarounds do not lead to one-sided 'resistance to change' [22]. This study has been unable to demonstrate that workarounds do not reflect upon a resistance to change since the mentioned workarounds illustrate an intentional counterproductive action possible by the technology. Further, these workarounds put patients at risk and do not represent aspirations for patient's well-being.

These workarounds, which can be overridden by confrontation with decisions that physicians do not accept, lead to a discussion about Technical affordances, as physicians' technical ability vis-à-vis ASR is not compatible with and relevant to their workflow in a healthcare environment. Physicians' use of ASR exemplifies a possible false affordance and leads to inconsistent actions with the expected actions that the system expects and coded for. Future HCI studies considering workarounds in a healthcare environment may advantageously consider the concept of affordances and the configuration of properties.

5.3 Normal Workflow

This article examines workarounds as informal temporary practices for handling exceptions to normal workflow. However, the definition seems inadequate concerning well-established workarounds that have shifted from an expected workflow to a new normal workflow. Even though some of these new normal workflows have been part of physicians' ward rounds for more than a decade, these do not represent the systematically expected workflow. Since these actions do not reproduce or follow a predetermined organizational decision regarding the use of ASR, the new normal remain invisible to management and subsequently the technology.

This study does not bring forward an apparent for such permanent progress. However, it points towards a possible hierarchical division as digital decision-making in Danish healthcare is based on top-down direction [22], where technology implementations root on efficiency. Future studies should further examine the area, as the organizational foundation and communication flow seem crucial to the overall perception and use of ASR.

Time pressure prevents users from investigating ASR and consequently comprehending why exceptions happen. Thus, the technology becomes noticeable when it creates omissions to the expected use, motivating users to understand the technical operations. Users' encounter with technological challenges creates an incentive to comprehend the technology, which time pressure suspends. The neglected incentive causes frustrations for both clerks and physicians, who thus invents technical undertakings or give up the use, leading to workarounds based on technical literacy. Based on how workarounds are an act of exceptions of workflows, several workarounds created from exceptions of ASR workflows can be seen as a hope for problem-solving. These results match those observed in earlier studies [3, 6], which concern a lack of understanding and addressing the underlying problems. The lack of immersion and understanding of the technology leads to a deliberate alienation of ASR. The technology appears to users as incomprehensible, and therefore the underlying seems to be invisible or, in several examples, a personal illusion. Such an approach is well known in Science and Technology Studies (STS), where technology division is referred to as black boxing [37]. Very little was found in the literature on how employees prevent technological challenges by exploring them. However, it could be a way to examine these illusions or technical imaginaries that lead physicians and clerks to specific workarounds.

6 Conclusion

The purpose of the current study was to determine healthcare professionals' navigation concerning ASR by examining workarounds at a Danish hospital based on ethnographic multi-sited fieldwork. Workarounds were considered as informal temporary practices for handling exceptions to the normal workflow [4]. The most prominent finding to emerge from this study is that physicians normatively perceive actions, categorized as workarounds, as solving obstacles. However, these workarounds regarding ASR do not solve problems, as they merely postpone obstacles by taking them elsewhere. This research's findings provide insights into healthcare technologies' shortcomings in locating such deviating workflows compared to the expected systematic workflows, even though these workarounds have been carried out in a decade. This study has raised important questions about the nature of physicians' self-perception of the use of ASR and the subsequent managerial decision-making that has led to the implementation of the technology. Physicians invent imaginary designs for the invisible parts of the complex technology since ASR encounters their technical literacy. This study's empirical findings provide a new consideration regarding the locating of workarounds as they challenge professional appearance and should be ethnographically examined. The scope of this study was limited in terms of the managerial perspective. Despite its exploratory nature, this study offers some insight into the workarounds concerning ASR. This work's natural progression is to consider the concept of affordances and the configuration of properties when analyzing workarounds in healthcare.

References

1. Møller, J.E., Vosegaard, H.: Experiences with electronic health records. IT Prof. **10**(2), 19–23 (2008)
2. Derman, Y.D., Arenovich, T., Strauss, J.: Speech recognition software and electronic psychiatric progress notes: physicians' ratings and preferences. BMC Med. Inform. Decis. Mak. **10**(1), 1–7 (2010)
3. Halbesleben, J.R., Wakefield, D.S., Wakefield, B.J.: Work-arounds in health care settings: literature review and research agenda. Health Care Manage. Rev. **33**(1), 2–12 (2008)
4. Kobayashi, M., Fussell, S.R., Xiao, Y., Seagull, F.J.: Work coordination, workflow, and workarounds in a medical context. In: CHI 2005 Extended Abstracts on Human Factors in Computing Systems, pp. 1561–1564 (2005)
5. Hodgson, T., Magrabi, F., Coiera, E.: Efficiency and safety of speech recognition for documentation in the electronic health record. J. Am. Med. Inform. Assoc. **24**(6), 1127–1133 (2017)
6. Tucker, A.L., Edmondson, A.C.: Managing routine exceptions: a model of nurse problem solving behavior. In: Advances in Health Care Management. Emerald Group Publishing Limited (2002)
7. Pasquale, F.: New Laws of Robotics: Defending Human Expertise in the Age of AI. Belknap Press, Cambridge (2020)
8. Burke, A.: Occluded algorithms. Big Data Soc. **6**(2), 2053951719858743 (2019)
9. Thomas, S.L., Nafus, D., Sherman, J.: Algorithms as fetish: faith and possibility in algorithmic work. Big Data Soc. **5**(1), 2053951717751552 (2018)
10. Dourish, P.: Algorithms and their others: algorithmic culture in context. Big Data Soc. **3**(2), 2053951716665128 (2016)
11. Seaver, N.: Algorithms as culture: some tactics for the ethnography of algorithmic systems. Big Data Soc. **4**(2), 2053951717738104 (2017)
12. Alapetite, A., Andersen, H.B., Hertzum, M.: Acceptance of speech recognition by physicians: a survey of expectations, experiences, and social influence. Int. J. Hum. Comput. Stud. **67**(1), 36–49 (2009)
13. White, K.S.: Speech recognition implementation in radiology. Pediatr. Radiol. **35**(9), 841–846 (2005)
14. Hayt, D.B., Alexander, S.: The pros and cons of implementing PACS and speech recognition systems. J. Digit. Imaging **14**(3), 149–157 (2001)
15. Alapetite, A.: Impact of noise and other factors on speech recognition in anaesthesia. Int. J. Med. Inform. **77**(1), 68–77 (2008)
16. Ramaswamy, M.R., Chaljub, G., Esch, O., Fanning, D.D., VanSonnenberg, E.: Continuous speech recognition in MR imaging reporting: advantages, disadvantages, and impact. Am. J. Roentgenol. **174**(3), 617–622 (2000)
17. Kirkedal, A.S.: Danish Stød and Automatic Speech Recognition. Ph.D. dissertation, Copenhagen Business School, Frederiksberg (2016)
18. Lai, J., Karat, C., Yankelovich, N.: Conversational speech interfaces and technologies. In: The Human-Computer Interaction Handbook. CRC Press, Boca Raton, pp. 407–418 (2007)
19. Debnath, S., Roy, P.: Study of speech enabled healthcare technology. Int. J. Med. Eng. Inform. **11**(1), 71–85 (2019)
20. Dupret, K.: Working around technologies—invisible professionalism? N. Technol. Work Employ. **32**(2), 174–187 (2017)
21. Debono, D.S., et al.: Nurses' workarounds in acute healthcare settings: a scoping review. BMC Health Serv. Res. **13**(1), 175 (2013)

22. Dupret, K., Friborg, B.: Workarounds in the danish health sector–from tacit to explicit innovation. Nordic Journal of Working Life Studies, vol. 8 (2018)
23. Koppel, R., Wetterneck, T., Telles, J.L., Karsh, B.T.: Workarounds to barcode medication administration systems: their occurrences, causes, and threats to patient safety. J. Am. Med. Inform. Assoc. 15(4), 408–423 (2008)
24. Ash, J.S., Berg, M., Coiera, E.: Some unintended consequences of information technology in health care: the nature of patient care information system-related errors. J. Am. Med. Inform. Assoc. 11(2), 104–112 (2004)
25. Blijleven, V., Koelemeijer, K., Wetzels, M., Jaspers, M.: Workarounds emerging from electronic health record system usage: consequences for patient safety, effectiveness of care, and efficiency of care. JMIR Hum. Factors 4(4), (2017)
26. Nicolini, D.: Practice Theory, Work, And Organization: An Introduction. OUP Oxford, Oxford (2012)
27. Gherardi, S., Nicolini, D.: The organizational learning of safety in communities of practice. J. Manag. Inq. 9(1), 7–18 (2000)
28. Knorr-Cetina, K., Savigny, E., Schatzki, T.R. (eds) The Practice Turn in Contemporary Theory. Routledge, Milton Park (2001)
29. Nicolini, D.: Zooming in and out: studying practices by switching theoretical lenses and trailing connections. Organ. Stud. 30(12), 1391–1418 (2009)
30. Schatzki, T.: The Site of the Social: A Philosophical Exploration of the Constitution of Social Life and Change. University Park, PA, Pennsylvania State University Press, Pennsylvania (2002)
31. Kjeldsen, L., Ingemann, J.H., Rasmussen, S., Nørup, I.: Kvalitative Undersøgelser i Praksis: Viden om Mennesker og Samfund. Samfundslitteratur, Frederiksberg (2018)
32. Halkier, B.: Fokusgrupper (3. udg. ed.). Samfundslitteratur, Frederiksberg (2016)
33. Fabian, J.: On recognizing things. the "ethnic artefact" and the "ethnographic object". L'Homme. Rev. Fr. D'Anthropol. 170, 47–60 (2004)
34. McDonald, S.: Studying actions in context: a qualitative shadowing method for organizational research. Qual. Res. 5(4), 455–473 (2005)
35. Beerepoot, I., Van De Weerd, I.: Prevent, redesign, adopt or ignore: Improving healthcare using knowledge of workarounds (2018)
36. de Vargas Pinto, A., Maçada, A.C.G., Mallmann, G.L.: Workaround behaviour in information systems research. Revista de Gestão (2018)
37. Latour, B.: Opening pandoras black box. Technol. Organ. Innov. Theor. Concepts Paradigms 2, 679 (2000)

Secondary Task Behavioral Analysis Based on Depth Image During Driving

Hao Wen[ORCID], Zhen Wang[✉], and Shan Fu

School of Electronic Information and Electrical Engineering, Shanghai Jiao Tong University,
Shanghai, People's Republic of China
b2wz@sjtu.edu.cn

Abstract. In order to reduce the probability of human error when driving and provide support for the design of control method of in-vehicle information system, hand motion analysis is important to evaluate driver performance. This paper introduces a depth-based method using hand motion analysis to evaluate the performance of the secondary task when driving. The secondary task is designed to use the central control panel in the car to adjust the temperature of the air conditioner. 3D spatial hand coordinates are determined by background subtraction on depth images. After obtaining the 3D spatial hand coordinate of each frame, the velocity, the operation time and the hand movement trajectory length of the secondary task can be determined. The angle of velocity between consecutive frames (AOV) is calculated to analyze the consistency of hand motion. Besides, sample entropy (SampEn) is used to measure the regularity of change in speed and direction of hand movement velocity. The experimental data show that the participant completes the secondary task with shorter operation time and trajectory length, fewer times of retrace, higher consistency ratio and smaller SampEn of AOV and speed when the primary task is less difficult. The results indicate that when the primary task is less difficult, the performance of the secondary task is better. Our method proposed in this paper can effectively evaluate the performance of the secondary task when driving.

Keywords: Secondary task when driving · Performance evaluation · Hand motion analysis

1 Introduction

With development of automobile manufacturing, in-vehicle information system (IVIS) is used to provide integrated and personalized information services for drivers. Although the use of IVIS provides drivers with more comfortable driving environment, it diverts drivers' attention to the secondary tasks of information processing and operation, such as using a central control panel, pushing buttons and so on. When one hand is off the steering wheel, drivers are usually slow to adjust the driving direction and react to obstacles on the road. Therefore, performing secondary tasks have brought the potential threat to driving safety. To ensure safe driving, it is necessary to analyze the hand motion and evaluate the performance of the secondary tasks during driving, which can not only

© Springer Nature Switzerland AG 2021
M. Kurosu (Ed.): HCII 2021, LNCS 12764, pp. 473–485, 2021.
https://doi.org/10.1007/978-3-030-78468-3_32

reduce the probability of human error but also provide support for the design of control method of IVIS.

The operational activities in cars are recognized as to a complex human-computer interaction (HCI) task, involving driver's physical and mental states. Generally, driving performance evaluation methods can be divided into subjective evaluation and objective evaluation. The subjective methods are easy to implement by self-rated item. But they depend too much on scorers' feelings, leading to low validity. Therefore, many scholars have analyzed the physiological characteristics using objective methods like EEG signal [1], EMG signal [2], pupillometry [3], etc. However, due to frequent interactions between the driver and the car during driving, hand motion analysis is essential for performance evaluation but is not monitored efficiently by above physiological signals. To analyze the hand motion, hand segmentation and hand motion feature extraction are needed.

In order to determine the position of the hands, it is necessary to identify the hand regions from image. The most direct way is to use color (RGB, HSV, YCbCr) as hand features for segmentation [4, 5]. Although the color-based segmentation is simple and fast, it often fails when the light changes and the image contains other objects with similar skin color [6]. Li and Kitani focus on local appearance-based strategy combining color features to improve the effect of detection compared to only using color features [7]. With the emergence of deep learning, some scholars have achieved good hand segmentation results in egocentric videos [8–10]. However, this kind of approach needs a great deal of marked data and relies on GPU. As the accuracy of depth cameras is improving, scholars start using depth camera to study hand segmentation [11–14]. In addition, another reason to use depth camera is that it is not affected by light and can be used at night.

After detecting the hand, the hand motion feature can be extracted. Hand motion analysis (HMA) is widely used in assessing surgical procedures [15–18]. HMA usually uses features like the operation time, the trajectory length, the number of movements, the velocity and the trajectory. Dosis et al. [15] apply these features to assess surgical procedures and confirm the effectiveness of HMA. And Zago et al. [16] use the working volume, the number of movements and other similar features mentioned in [15] to evaluate technical proficiency. However, researches on analyzing the consistency of hand motion are rare. The consistency is manifested in changes in the direction and speed of hand movement. Changes in the speed of hand movement can be measured with high accuracy using the approximate entropy and cross-approximate entropy features in surgical procedures [17]. Although these methods are good for HMA, the equipment used is too complicated, leading to high operation difficulty and experiment costs. For example, an electromagnetic filed generator and 2 sensors are used in [15], 9 infrared sensors are used in [16] and a camera and an acceleration transducer are used in [17]. HMA is rarely used in secondary task behavioral analysis during driving, but it works because performing secondary tasks has similarities with surgical procedures.

In this paper, a new approach is proposed to analyze the operation process of the secondary task while driving. For the hand segmentation, we use a depth-method which is not affected by light changes and does not require a large number of marked data. Using depth camera, 3D spatial hand positioning method based on background subtraction is applied to locate the left and right hands. For the hand motion feature extraction, we use common features such as the operation time, the trajectory length and the velocity. Besides, we use sample entropy (SampEn) [19] and the angle of velocity between consecutive frames (AOV) to measure changes in the direction and speed of hand movement.

The remainder of the paper is organized as follows. Section 2 demonstrates the depth-based method. In Sect. 3, we introduce the task and procedure of the experiment and give a brief description of the apparatus. Results and discussions are in Sect. 4 and Sect. 5. In the final section, the conclusion and future work are presented.

2 Method

2.1 Hand Detection

The hand segmentation with skin color is often used, but is easily affected by light changes and other objects with similar color to the skin. Therefore, we choose depth-based segmentation method to cope with the various light conditions during driving. Considering that the depth camera is fixed in the car, we use the background subtraction to extract the areas of hands and arms.

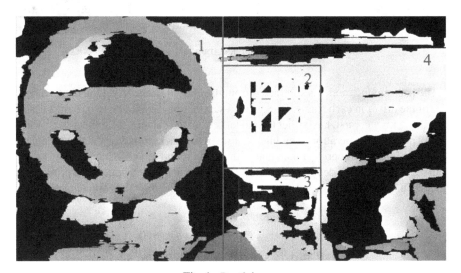

Fig. 1. Depth image

The depth image is divided into 4 areas, including the steering wheel area (part 1 in Fig. 1), the central control panel area (part 2 in Fig. 1), the gear shift area (part 3 in Fig. 1), and ignorable area (part 4 in Fig. 1). The modeling methods for areas above are slightly different. For parts 1–3, the background is modeled by the mean value of each pixel in 30 frames of driving scene without hands on the steering wheel. For part 4, ignorable area is modeled by zero depth value to reduce the interference of recognition and the amount of calculation for image processing. However, the background subtraction result is affected by the rotating steering wheel spokes in part 1. Therefore, we use a disc to model the steering wheel. By marking on the first frame of the depth image, the center coordinate and radius of the disc are successfully determined. The result of background modeling is shown in Fig. 2.

Fig. 2. Result of background modeling

The background model is subtracted from the current frame to get the hand and arm areas of the driver in each frame. Background subtraction is based on two characteristics of the depth image. First, the farther the object is from the camera, the greater depth value it has. The driver's operation is an intervention in the background so the depth value of the current frame is not greater than that of the background image. Second, many invalid depth regions with zero depth value are caused by the depth data generation principle of camera. Therefore, background subtraction result is defined by the following equation:

$$result_{x,y} = \begin{cases} \left| cur_{x,y} - bg_{x,y} \right| & if \ cur_{x,y} \le bg_{x,y} \\ cur_{x,y} & if \ bg_{x,y} = 0 \\ 0 & if \ cur_{x,y} = 0 \end{cases} \tag{1}$$

where, $result_{x,y}$, $cur_{x,y}$ and $bg_{x,y}$ denote the depth value of the background subtraction result, the current frame and background modeling result at coordinates (x, y) respectively. If $cur_{x,y} \le bg_{x,y}$, the objects are closer to the camera, considered as the hands and arms of the driver. If $bg_{x,y} = 0$, invalid value occurs in the background and the value of the current frame should be kept. Finally, we let $result_{x,y} = 0$ when the value of current frame is invalid.

After background subtraction, the foreground image is shown in Fig. 3. Then, hand areas are obtained from binary processing on the background subtraction result. With morphological processing and limitation of connected domain area, the noises in the binary image are removed and the result is shown in Fig. 4.

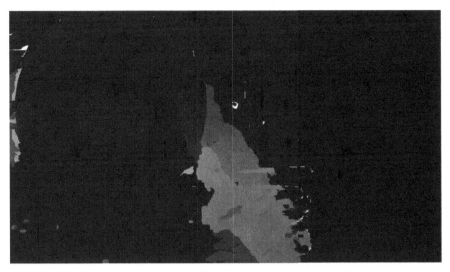

Fig. 3. Background subtraction result

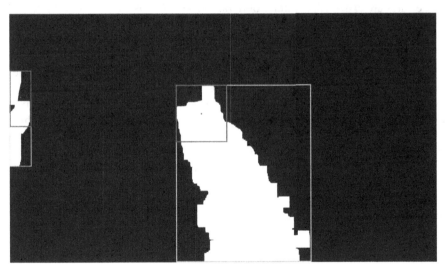

Fig. 4. Hand binary image. The smallest bounding box of connected domain is yellow. The preset size box is red. The red point is regarded as the hand plane coordinate. (Color figure online)

Finally, left and right hands are distinguished from the hand binary image by the bottom right points of the connected domains. If the point falls near the driver's right shoulder, the connected domain is regarded as the driver's right hand and arm area because the position of the camera is fixed above the driver's right shoulder. If not, the connected domain represents driver's left hand and arm area. Then, the smallest bounding box of each connected domain is determined. The right hand is located in the upper left corner of the smallest bounding box and the left hand is located in the upper right corner of the smallest bounding box. To indicate the location of the hand, a preset size box is applied and the center point of the box is regarded as the hand plane coordinate. Above all, combining the plane coordinate, depth value and camera intrinsic parameter, the 3D spatial hand coordinate is obtained.

2.2 Hand Motion Analysis

After obtaining the 3D spatial hand coordinate of each frame, the velocity could be calculated by the coordinate and the timestamp. In addition, the total operation time and hand movement trajectory length of the secondary task can also be determined.

To measure the consistency of hand motion, Zhao et al. [20] design a variable using the cosine of the key points' velocities between consecutive frames. In this paper, a similar feature using the angle of hand velocity between consecutive frames (AOV) is used. According to the definition, the value of AOV ranges from 0 to 180° and the smaller the AOV is, the smaller the change in the direction of movement is. Based on the AOV, two features are extracted, the times of retrace and the consistency ratio. If the AOV is greater than 120°, the hand movement is defined as retrace. When the AOV is less than 45°, the movement is considered to be consistent. And the number of AOVs less than 45° is divided by the total number of AOVs to get consistency ratio.

Because the speed of hand movement and the AOV are changing with time series, sample entropy (SampEn) is raised to measure the regularity of change. SampEn, proposed by Richman and Moorman [19], is the negative natural logarithm of an estimate of the conditional probability that patterns of length e that match point-wise within a tolerance r also match at the next point. It is like Approximate Entropy (ApEn), but SampEn is independent of record length and displays relative consistencies under circumstances where ApEn does not, meaning that the changes in the parameters e and r have the same effect on the SampEn. The larger value of SampEn indicates that the data are more irregular and vice versa. In our experiment, e is taken as 2 and r is taken as 0.1 times the sample standard deviation.

3 Experiment

3.1 Task

The participant was asked to drive at a constant speed on different road scenarios, while using the central control panel to adjust the temperature of the air conditioner. We analyzed the performance of the secondary tasks while driving and studied whether it varied due to the difference in the primary tasks. The experiment was carried out under the premise of safety.

In the primary task, the participant was asked to maintain a constant speed on the straight or curve roads and the speed during driving was recorded by GPS for the primary task evaluation. The driving route record by GPS is shown in Fig. 5.

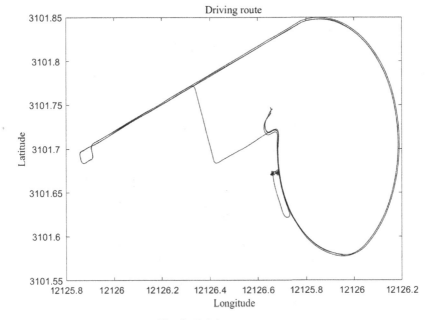

Fig. 5. Driving route map

In the secondary task, the participant was asked to adjust the left and right air conditioners by operating touch screen. Because the processes of adjusting the left and right air conditioner are similar, we believed that the difficulty of these two operations is the same.

3.2 Procedure

At the beginning of the experiment, the participant was asked to drive on the curve road at a speed of 20 km per hour and followed instructions. During driving, participant was first asked to adjust the temperature of the left air conditioner from 16 to 24° and then asked to adjust the temperature of the right air conditioner from 16 to 24°.

After driving on the curve road, the participant was asked to drive on the straight road at the same speed as driving on the curve road and also followed instructions. The participant was first asked to adjust the temperature of the left air conditioner from 24 to 16°, and then asked to adjust the temperature of the right air conditioner from 24 to 16°.

3.3 Apparatus

Intel RealSense Camera D435 is fixed on the upper right of the main driver's seat to record the movement information of hands with a first-person perspective as shown in Fig. 6. Besides, we adjust the position of the camera to keep the depth of the target acquisition areas within 0.3–1.0 m to ensure the accuracy and reliability of the depth information. The vision data are saved in *rosbag* format, which contains RGB images, depth images and timestamps. The resolution of the recorded images is 1280 * 720 and the sampling rate is 30 Hz. Subsequent data analysis is done on a PC with a 3.6 GHz Ryzen 7 processor and 16 GB RAM.

Fig. 6. Fixed position of Intel RealSense Camera

4 Result

4.1 Hand Detection Result

In order to display the hand detection results in the depth map more intuitively, we project the results into the color map as shown in Fig. 7.

Fig. 7. Depth-based hand detection results return to color image. The right hand is surrounded with red box and the left hand is surrounded with green box. (Color figure online)

4.2 Secondary Task Behavior Analysis

The movement characteristics of the right hand when performing secondary tasks are the key to the performance evaluation of secondary tasks. We extract the movement information of the right hand leaving the steering wheel, clicking the central control panel and returning to the steering wheel. This information is composed of hand coordinates in space, with a 33 ms time interval between every two points. The sampling time interval is determined by the camera sampling rate.

According to these coordinates and time intervals, both the space trajectory of the right-hand execution of the secondary task and the speed change with time can be obtained. The following diagrams show the trajectory and speed change of the driver adjusting the left air conditioner when driving on straight and curved roads. Adjusting the right air conditioner has a similar situation.

It can be seen from Fig. 8 that, in different road scenarios, trajectories of the secondary task are different, which is manifested in curvature and motion consistency. And in Fig. 9, both the operation time and the change of hand speed to perform the secondary task differ under different road conditions. Besides, the change of hand speed complies Fitts's law. In either road scenario, the participant hand first approaches the central control panel at a high speed, then make precise adjustments at a slow speed when operating central control panel and finally return to the steering wheel at a high speed.

Based on the above results, we can draw the conclusion that the result of hand detection is in line with expectations and performance of the secondary task varies in different scenarios. This method can be used to further analyze the performance of secondary tasks.

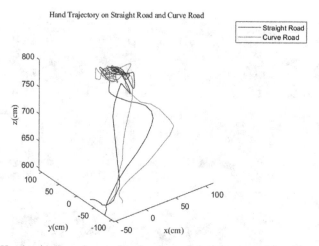

Fig. 8. Hand trajectory when performing secondary tasks on straight and curve road

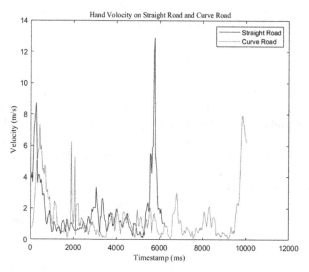

Fig. 9. Hand velocity when performing secondary task on straight road and curve road

5 Discussion

To a certain extent, the completion time of the same operation can reflect the performance of the participant. For the same task, generally speaking, the shorter operation time indicates that the participant is more proficient in this task. In addition, the hand trajectory can also help evaluate performance, as hand stagnation and sway can be caused by hesitation as well as target change. Therefore, when the trajectory is shorter, the participant should have a stronger purpose and fewer redundant actions.

The consistency of hand motion is signaled by the regularity of velocity changes. When AOV is greater than 120°, it is manifested as a sudden change in the direction of hand movement, which is probably caused by the operator's ambiguity of the target. When the operator has a clear goal and consistent operation, the degree of AOV will remain within 45°. Therefore, the higher the consistency ratio is, the more consistent the participant's hand movement is. In addition, SampEns of AOV and speed measure the regularities of direction change and speed change respectively. The smaller SampEn indicates the better operation consistency of participant.

Table 1. Hand motion features

Road condition	Operation time (s)	Trajectory length (cm)	Times of retrace	Consistency ratio	SampEn of AOV	SampEn of speed
Straight	5.78	102.78	2	88.50%	1.0552	0.6935
Curve	8.90	132.78	4	83.57%	1.2228	0.8603

According to the result given in Table 1, when the participant drives on the straight road, he completes the secondary task with shorter operation time and trajectory length, fewer times of retrace, higher consistency ratio and smaller SampEns of AOV and speed. This indicates that the performance on the secondary task when driving on straight roads is better.

Table 2. Main task speed maintenance

Road scenarios	Average speed (km/h)	Standard deviation
Straight	14.18	0.6628
Curve	15.71	0.5130

The primary task is to maintain the vehicle speed at 20 km/h. The average and standard deviation of vehicle speed under different road conditions are calculated as shown in Table 2. In the process of performing the secondary task on the curve road, the average speed is closer to the target speed and the standard deviation is smaller.

In the experiment, although it is more difficult to drive on the curve road, the participant performs the primary task better, indicating more attention put on the primary task. In the case where more attention is allocated to the primary task and attention on the secondary task is limited, the hand motion is more complicated and the performance is worse. The results of the secondary task performance evaluation based on HMA are consistent with the attention distribution theory.

6   Conclusion

In this paper, we propose a method to analyze the driver's operation process and evaluate the performance of the secondary task when driving. The 3D spatial hand coordinates are obtained by background subtraction using depth images. We use the operation time, the trajectory length, the times of retrace, the consistency ratio and SampEns of AOV and speed to evaluate the performance of the secondary task. Besides, we evaluate the primary task performance with average and standard deviation of vehicle speed.

From the results, the secondary task behavior varies under different road scenarios in the same task. For one thing, various possible operating scenarios should be considered comprehensively when evaluating human-machine interface. For another, when performing difficult primary tasks, a simple operation will become inefficient and bring uncertainty to driving safety. Therefore, a more efficient interactive mode is required for complex primary tasks.

However, our method also has some shortcomings that need to be improved in the future. First of all, we cannot distinguish the left and right hand when they overlap. Secondly, we do not study the details of finger movements during operation. Finally, we do not use the color information collected by the camera in the hand detection algorithm.

We believe that the depth-based hand operation behavior analysis method has broad application in the future. Not only can it evaluate the performance of the driver in secondary tasks, but also provide support for the design of control method of IVIS.

References

1. Yang, L., Ma, R., Zhang, H.M., Guan, W., Jiang, S.: Driving behavior recognition using EEG data from a simulated car-following experiment. Accid. Anal. Prev. **116**, 30–40 (2018)
2. Lee, B.G., Chong, T.W., Lee, B.L., Park, H.J., Kim, Y.N., Kim, B.: Wearable mobile-based emotional response-monitoring system for drivers. IEEE Trans. Hum.-Mach. Syst. **47**(5), 636–649 (2017)
3. Maccora, J., Manousakis, J.E., Anderson, C.: Pupillary instability as an accurate, objective marker of alertness failure and performance impairment. J. Sleep Res. **28**(2), e12739 (2019)
4. Shaik, K.B., Ganesan, P., Kalist, V., Sathish, B.S., Jenitha, J.M.M.: Comparative study of skin color detection and segmentation in HSV and YCbCr color space. Procedia Comput. Sci. **57**, 41–48 (2015)
5. Kolkur, S., Kalbande, D., Shimpi, P., Bapat, C., Jatakia, J.: Human skin detection using RGB, HSV and YCbCr color models. arXiv preprint arXiv:1708.02694 (2017)
6. Bandini, A., Zariffa, J.: Analysis of the hands in egocentric vision: a survey. IEEE Trans. Pattern Anal. Mach. Intell. (2020)
7. Li, C., Kitani, K.M.: Pixel-level hand detection in ego-centric videos. In: Conference on Computer Vision and Pattern Recognition, pp. 3570–3577. IEEE (2013)
8. Urooj, A., Borji, A.: Analysis of hand segmentation in the wild. In: IEEE Conference on Computer Vision and Pattern Recognition, pp. 4710–4719 (2018)
9. Cai, M., Lu, F., Sato, Y.: Generalizing hand segmentation in egocentric videos with uncertainty-guided model adaptation. In: Conference on Computer Vision and Pattern Recognition, pp. 14392–14401. IEEE/CVF (2020)
10. Bambach, S., Lee, S., Crandall, D.J., Yu, C.: Lending a hand: detecting hands and recognizing activities in complex egocentric interactions. In: International Conference on Computer Vision, pp. 1949–1957. IEEE (2015)
11. Ren, Z., Yuan, J., Zhang, Z.: Robust hand gesture recognition based on finger-earth mover's distance with a commodity depth camera. In: 19th International Conference on Multimedia, pp. 1093–1096. ACM (2011)

12. Rogez, G., Supancic, J.S., Ramanan, D.: Understanding everyday hands in action from RGB-D images. In: International Conference on Computer Vision, pp. 3889–3897. IEEE (2015)
13. Sridhar, S., Mueller, F., Zollhöfer, M., Casas, D., Oulasvirta, A., Theobalt, C.: Real-time joint tracking of a hand manipulating an object from RGB-D input. In: Leibe, B., Matas, J., Sebe, N., Welling, M. (eds.) ECCV 2016. LNCS, vol. 9906, pp. 294–310. Springer, Cham (2016). https://doi.org/10.1007/978-3-319-46475-6_19
14. Kang, B., Tan, K.H., Jiang, N., Tai, H.S., Tretter, D., Nguyen, T.: Hand segmentation for hand-object interaction from depth map. In: Global Conference on Signal and Information Processing (GlobalSIP), pp. 259–263. IEEE (2017)
15. Dosis, A., et al.: Synchronized video and motion analysis for the assessment of procedures in the operating theater. Arch. Surg. **140**(3), 293–299 (2005)
16. Zago, M., et al.: Educational impact of hand motion analysis in the evaluation of fast examination skills. Eur. J. Trauma Emerg. Surg. **46**(6), 1421–1428 (2020)
17. Zia, A., Sharma, Y., Bettadapura, V., Sarin, E.L., Essa, I.: Video and accelerometer-based motion analysis for automated surgical skills assessment. Int. J. Comput. Assist. Radiol. Surg. **13**(3), 443–455 (2018). https://doi.org/10.1007/s11548-018-1704-z
18. Sharma, Y., et al.: Video based assessment of OSATS using sequential motion textures. Georgia Institute of Technology (2014)
19. Richman, J.S., Moorman, J.R.: Physiological time-series analysis using approximate entropy and sample entropy. Am. J. Physiol.-Heart Circ. Physiol. **278**, H2039 (2000)
20. Zhao, Y., Wang, Z., Lu, Y., Fu, S.: A visual-based approach for manual operation evaluation. In: Harris, D., Li, W.-C. (eds.) HCII 2020. LNCS (LNAI), vol. 12186, pp. 281–292. Springer, Cham (2020). https://doi.org/10.1007/978-3-030-49044-7_23

Research on the Relationship Between the Partition Position of the Central Control Display Interface and the Interaction Efficiency

JiHong Zhang[✉], Haowei Wang, and Zehua Li

Nanjing University of Science and Technology, Nanjing 210094, China

Abstract. To carry out information classification and information division on the vehicle central control display interface, and explore the influence of different division positions on the driver's interaction efficiency. According to the driving relevance of the displayed information and the frequency of use, it is divided into levels. According to the location of the area, the eye movement experiment is designed and the user's visual fixation time and task operation completion time are analyzed. When the shortcut menu function partition is located on the left side of the display interface, the user can be the first to notice and complete the specified operation task in the shortest time. The design of automobile central control display interface should consider the division of user operation functional areas. The main functional area should be placed on the left side of the display interface to facilitate user observation and operation.

Keywords: Automobile human-computer interaction · Central control display interface · Eye movement experiment · Visual priority · Interaction efficiency

1 Partition of Car Central Control Display Interface

1.1 Research Background

At present, automobile human-computer interaction has entered the era of intelligence, and the main functions of the automobile are showing a trend of integration. Digital control systems and electrical systems are gradually replacing traditional mechanized systems. The human-computer interaction mode of the car's central control screen replaces the physical buttons and becomes the mainstream operation mode. The most typical example is Tesla's Model S and Model X models. Most of its operations are done on the central control screen. Compared with the traditional physical button-type physical operator, the virtual central control screen. The operating cognitive load is low, the recognition area is clear, but the amount of information is too concentrated and overlapping. The completion of a specific operation task requires the cooperation of hands and eyes, the overall operation response is slow, and the line of sight leaves the road environment for a long time, which is likely to cause safety hazards. Safety is the primary consideration in the design of automobile human-computer interaction. In the current complex human-computer interaction situation, a reasonable layout of the central control display

M. Kurosu (Ed.): HCII 2021, LNCS 12764, pp. 486–497, 2021.
https://doi.org/10.1007/978-3-030-78468-3_33

interface can provide the driver with a good display and control interface, reducing the driver. Therefore, this article starts from the information arrangement of the central control display interface, and explores the influence of the arrangement of different types of information on the driver's interaction efficiency.

1.2 Current Status of Central Control Display

The traditional human-computer interaction methods of automobiles mainly include knobs and buttons. The human-computer interaction methods of smart automobiles mainly include touch screen interaction, voice interaction, gesture interaction and system active interaction. The automotive central control display interface mainly refers to the touch screen interactive interface. As a typical natural interactive interface, the touch screen interactive interface has made a major breakthrough in the application of handheld devices. However, in the automotive information system, the central control display interface has become the interactive entertainment interface for information inside and outside the car, including listening to radio music, in-car entertainment, telephone, GPS navigation, and online sending and receiving of information and mail, etc., its operability is much lower than that of handheld devices due to driving scenarios. The accumulation of information facilitates the operation of the driver, and at the same time increases the visual pressure of the driver [6]. The reasonable arrangement of information resources on the central control display interface can effectively reduce the visual attention burden of drivers under driving conditions and improve the efficiency of human-vehicle interaction.

1.3 Display Information Classification

The automobile central control display interface cannot present all the information to the driver at one time, so the priority of the information display is very important. The main basis for displaying information classification is driving correlation and frequency of use, but for safe driving considerations, driving correlation index is higher than the frequency of use index. The central control display interface information can generally be divided into three levels: the first level information is vehicle information, including vehicle status, driving information, road information, etc.; the second level information is driving assistance function information, including navigation, car air conditioning, Seat adjustment, music playback, address book, etc.; the third-level information is switchable information, which is a detailed expansion of the second-level information, including navigation maps, reversing images, address book information, audio and video playback, etc.

1.4 Display Interface Partition

According to the classification of the displayed information, the vehicle central control display interface is divided: the first level information is divided into the vehicle live area, the second level information is divided into the function catalog area, and the third level information is divided into the content presentation area. Among them, the vehicle live area is the often displayed information area, and its location should be most conducive to the driver's observation and operation; the function directory area is the driver's touch operation area, which is the driver's main operating area on the central control display interface and also serves as the main The location of the information transfer station has a serious impact on the driver's information recognition and touch operation. It is the most likely to cause the driver's sight shift and distraction in the entire central control display interface; the content presentation area is the function directory The secondary interface of the area occupies the largest area on the central control display screen, and is responsible for presenting the detailed content of the function catalog area. The touch operation frequency is lower than that of the function catalog area.

2   Study on Design of Eye Movement Experiment in Simulated Driving Environment

2.1   Experimental Purpose

Existing car brands in the market, such as Tesla, Roewe, Weilai, etc., all use a full-touch central control display, and their function menu areas are located at the bottom of the central control display screen. According to the principle of visual priority, the human visual priority is upper left > upper right > lower left > lower right. When the arrangement position of the function menu area is at the upper left of the central control display interface, the interaction efficiency between the driver and the car central control reaches highest. To this end, simulating the driving environment of the vehicle to study the arrangement of the function menu partitions on the central control display, using eye movement experiment technology to track the driver's eye movements when using the central control display, and analyzing the driver's Task operation time, gaze point distribution map and path map and other data, explore the relationship between the arrangement position of the function menu area on the central control display screen and the driver's interaction efficiency.

2.2   Experimental Design

In the design of the existing car's central control display interface, Tesla has realized a complete touch operation. Therefore, in order to eliminate the influence of physical buttons in the following experiments and to facilitate the experiment, this article chooses to use Tesla. The central control display interface of model 3 was used as the experimental object. The style of the Tesla central control display interface was extracted, and the information arrangement was re-planned while retaining the displayed information. Compare the completion of the subjects in different arrangements of the same information. The same operation task time and visual recognition time are used to explore the relationship between the arrangement position of the function menu area in the car central control interface and the driver's operating efficiency.

First, the display information is classified according to the extracted information presented by the Tesla central control display interface style. The first-level information is driving information, including vehicle status, road conditions, driving speed, and power status; the second-level information is virtual buttons Columns include windshield defogging, left and right seat adjustment, left and right air conditioning adjustment, air conditioning wind speed adjustment, mobile device information, music playback, etc.; the third-level information is vehicle driving map, music playback interface, etc. Secondly, the Tesla central control display interface is partitioned according to the three levels of information that have been divided, as shown in Fig. 1, area A is the vehicle live area with first-level information, and area B is the function of second-level information Directory area, C area is the content presentation area of the third level information. As the functional catalog area, the B area has the most concentrated information. The driver needs to cooperate with his hands and eyes at the same time when operating, which can easily cause the driver to be distracted and cause accidents. Therefore, in this experiment, the focus is on the arrangement of the B area. The position and size of area A and C remain basically unchanged, and at the same time, considering that areas A and C may affect the information recognition of subjects in the experiment, they are block-based processing, using less saturated The color block replaces the two areas A and C, and its size remains basically unchanged.

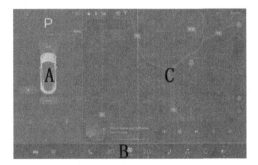

Fig. 1. Display interface partition map.

In this experiment, the location of area B was used as the experimental independent variable, and four groups of experiments were set up, as shown in Fig. 2. Experimental group one (B1) is the control group experiment. The location of area B is the current layout of the Tesla Model 3 central control display, which is located at the bottom of the central control screen. Experimental group two (B2) according to the driver's usage habits and the location of the main driver, place B area on the left side of the central control display screen close to the main driver's position. Experimental group three (B3) is placed on the right side away from the main driver, in contrast to experimental group two. Experimental group four (B4) is placed on the upper part of the central control display screen according to the principle of visual priority.

Each group of experiments contains three tasks, as shown in Table 1 below, which are task a, task b, and task c. The completion areas of the three tasks are respectively distributed on the two sides and the middle part of the B area to ensure the completeness of the subjects' observation and operation of the B area in the experiment. In the data statistics, the subjects are in each group. The mean value of the experimental data for completing the three tasks in the experiment is to ensure the accuracy of each group of

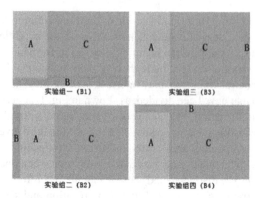

Fig. 2. The layout of the B area of the experimental group.

experimental results. In addition, design a set of simulation experiments to be placed before the start of the experiment, and the experiment materials are randomly selected from the experimental group, so that users can familiarize themselves with the specific operation task flow in the experiment in advance, and avoid unfamiliar operations that may occur in the first group of experiments. The experimental results are too different, the simulation group data is not included in the final statistical analysis. During the whole experiment, the subjects were only allowed to use their right hand to complete the task to simulate the state of the driver's one-handed operation touch interface under driving conditions. Secondly, to ensure the unity of all subjects in the experiment operation process to avoid differences. The influence of the subjects' use of hands or different hands on the results of the experiment.

Table 1. Task details table.

Task	Operating
Task a	Click the "Defogging" icon as prompted
Task b	Click on the "air conditioner" icon as prompted
Task c	Click the "mobile device" icon as prompted

2.3 Experimental Materials

Select the central control display interface style of the Tesla model 3 model car, use Photoshop and other software to process its interface, and block the display information according to the information level. Among them, the A and C areas are with lower saturation Instead of yellow and blue blocks, neutral colors are used in area B in the task operation materials to avoid color interference with subjects' perception. The test materials of the four groups of experiments are divided into three categories according to their functions. The first category is cognitive learning materials, which contains four pictures, one for each group of experiments, for the subjects to be familiar with the layout of the B area interface in the experiment, Eliminate the interference of novice users and occasional user conditions (as shown in Fig. 3). In this material, area B is marked with a low-saturation red color block, and the arrangement of the virtual button bar in area B can be observed; The second type is jump and task reminder materials, which contain twelve pictures, three of which are for each experiment group, which are used to remind the test task that the subjects need to complete (as shown in Fig. 4), and the B area is saturation. The lower red color block coverage allows the subjects to know the location of area B before the operation; the third category is task operation materials, which contains four pictures, one for each group of experiments, which is the specific task of the subject. Operating material diagram (Fig. 5), the B area restores the virtual button layout of the central control interface under real conditions, and the color selection is black and white neutral colors.

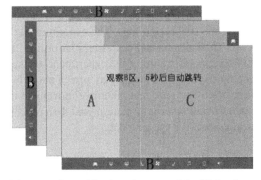

Fig. 3. Diagram of cognitive learning materials. (Color figure online)

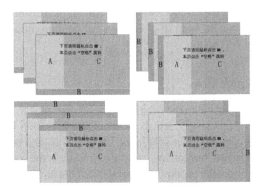

Fig. 4. Jump and task prompt material diagram. (Color figure online)

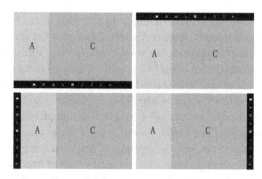

Fig. 5. Task operation material diagram.

2.4 Experimental Equipment

This experiment was carried out in the laboratory of the School of Design, Art and Media, Nanjing University of Science and Technology. The experimental equipment used was a Tobii T120 eye tracker. The analysis and reporting platform of the experiment were all supporting Tobii Studio software. During the experiment, the subject sat in front of the display screen, keeping the eyes and the display screen about 60–70 cm, the device calculated the eyeball position and gaze and other eye movement information through the corneal reflection pattern and other information, and then processed the software to obtain the relevant information. Eye tracking data.

2.5 Subjects

This experiment invited 8 graduate students from Nanjing University of Science and Technology with a C1 driving license as the subjects, and all the subjects had more than three years of driving experience. Among them, there are 5 boys and 3 girls, aged between 21–29. The subjects were in good physical condition during the experiment and had normal visual perception.

2.6 Experimental Procedure

Before the start of the experiment, the subjects were numbered, 1 to 6 respectively. Then take the subjects to the laboratory, tell them about the operation items and operation methods of the experiment, conduct simulation experiments, and become familiar with the experimental equipment. Participants only need to stare at the screen after the experiment starts, and then follow the prompts to operate with the mouse. After the experiment started, only the researchers and the subjects who were participating in the experiment were left in the laboratory, and the other personnel withdrew from the laboratory to avoid affecting the experiment.

At the beginning of the experiment, the subjects corrected their binocular vision according to the prompts; after the correction was completed, they began to enter the formal experiment. The first is the B1 picture of cognitive learning materials. Participants start to observe the picture of cognitive learning materials; after five seconds, the picture will automatically jump to the B1-a task prompt picture. After the participant has cleared the B1-a task, click the keyboard space with his right hand Key to jump; then jump to the B1-a operation diagram, use the right hand to operate the mouse to complete the task; after the B1-a task is completed, jump to the B1-b task prompt diagram, and complete the operation task according to the prompt; after the B1-c task is completed, The picture jumps to the B2 cognitive learning material picture, and then follow the B1 group experiment process to complete the B2 group experiment, and repeat the above process in turn; each experiment lasts 2 min until the B4 group experiment is completed. The next subject repeats the previous steps until the end of the experiment. (Fig. 6).

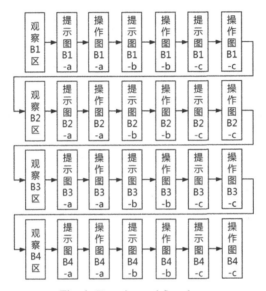

Fig. 6. Experimental flowchart.

2.7 Data and Analysis of Experimental Results

Before statistical analysis of the experimental data, the validity of the sample data was first screened. By analyzing the mouse clicks and the gaze trajectory diagram of the subjects in the task area, it was found that all subjects successfully completed the operation tasks and their sight lines. The trajectories are all in the experimental picture area (Fig. 7). Therefore, the number of invalid samples is 0, and 8 valid eye movement observation results are obtained. Extract fixation count statistics Fixation Count, Visit Duration, Time from First Fixation to Next Mouse Click as sample data for statistical analysis. In order to avoid the influence of the difference of the operating area in the same group of experiments on the experimental results, the experimental data of the three tasks in the same experiment are used as the main reference data in the experimental data statistics.

(1) Analyze from the statistics of the Fixation Count: in the gaze trajectory of the human eye, the area where the gaze saccade trajectory stays for a period of time is

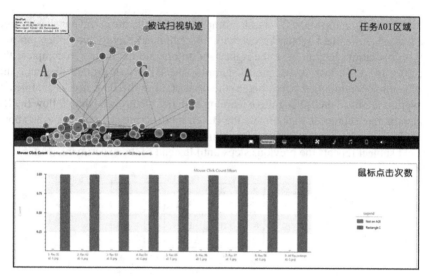

Fig. 7. Sample data screening process diagram taking B1-a as an example.

the fixation point, which means that the subject has a long-term fixation on the area during the observation process behavior, which can reflect the subjects' attention to the gaze area. The number of fixation points indicates the distraction of subjects in the observed area. In the context of the experimental task, a large number of fixation points means that the subjects are more distracted in the observation area and have more visual attention information; on the contrary, it means that the attention is more concentrated and the recognition information is faster. Statistics of the experimental data obtained by the subjects are shown in Table 2. The data showed that the average number of fixation points in group B2 was significantly lower than that of the other three groups, indicating that the subjects had higher visual attention in group B2 and recognized information faster.

Table 2. Statistics of the number of the fixation count.

	Task a	Task b	Task c	Mean
B1	3.38	3.57	4.68	3.88
B2	3.13	2.12	3.00	2.75
B3	3.62	3.25	3.34	3.40
B4	4.21	4.17	4.38	4.25

(2) Analyze from the Visit Duration: the Visit Duration represents the length of time that the human eye is watching and scanning the AOI area. In this experiment, given

that the subjects have all completed the operation tasks, the longer the scanning time indicates the subjects' For zone B, the recognition speed is slower, and the recognition efficiency is faster. Statistics of the experimental data obtained by the subjects are shown in Table 3. The B2 and B3 areas have shorter visit times, and the B1 and B4 areas have longer visit times. It means that the gaze and stay time of the subjects in the B2 and B3 areas is short, and the task identification can be completed in a short time.

Table 3. The visit duration statistics table (unit: second).

	Task a	Task b	Task c	Mean
B1	1.34	1.29	1.50	4.13
B2	1.02	1.08	1.16	3.26
B3	1.18	1.30	1.28	3.76
B4	1.42	1.21	1.45	4.08

(3) Analyze the Time from First Fixaton to Next Mouse Click: This data is the total time it takes for the subject to look at the test area to the completion of the test. It indicates the total time required for the subject to understand and operate a certain test item. Processing time. In this experiment, the subjects were required to use their right-handed operation throughout the entire process to restore the driver's one-handed operating conditions in the driving state, and process the experimental data obtained by the subjects, as shown in Table 4. From the point of view of the total time, the shortest time for the subjects to complete the operation in the B2 experiment group was 1.54 s. The B1 experiment used the existing car central control interface arrangement method, and the operation took 2.07 s to complete, and the B3 experiment took the most time long, 2.29 s.

Table 4. Statistical table of the time from first fixation to next mouse click.

	Task a	Task b	Task c	Mean
B1	1.77	2.11	2.14	2.01
B2	1.57	1.53	1.52	1.54
B3	2.37	2.13	2.36	2.29
B4	1.68	2.03	2.27	1.99

3 Results Discussion

By extracting the Tesla central control display interface as the main material of the experiment, the relationship between the information arrangement of the vehicle central control display interface and the driver's interaction efficiency is studied. After partitioning the information displayed on the central control interface, the location of the function directory area was used as the independent variable of the experiment, and four sets of experiments were designed according to the principle of visual priority. The experimental results are as follows:

(1) According to the statistical analysis results of the number of gaze points, when the function catalog area in the car central control display interface is located on the left and right sides of the display screen, that is, when the function catalog is arranged vertically, the gaze points are less scattered and the subjects are concentrated, The possibility of distraction while driving is low.
(2) According to the statistical analysis results of the access time, when the function catalog area is arranged on the left side of the display screen, the subjects have the lowest visual access time under the premise of completing the experimental task, that is, under driving conditions, the driver can reach the left area More efficient information recognition than other experimental areas.
(3) According to the statistical analysis results from the first gaze point to the next mouse click time, the layout of the car central control display interface also needs to consider the driver's operating state and the placement of the central control screen in the cab. The result of simulating the right-hand operation of the central control display screen in the driving state of the driver is displayed. The function directory area, that is, the secondary information area, takes the shortest time to complete the operation when it is placed on the left side of the screen adjacent to the driver. When it is located on the right side of the display screen, it takes the longest time to operate because it is far from the main driving position. The experimental results do not completely conform to the principle of visual priority in the experimental design. The reason is speculated to be affected by the maneuverable distance of the subjects.

4 Conclusion

This paper studies the relationship between the partition position of the central control display interface and the interaction efficiency. According to the principle of visual priority, an eye movement experiment is designed. The analysis shows that when the secondary information area is arranged longitudinally on the left side of the central control display interface, the driver's Attention is more concentrated, and the efficiency of information recognition operation is relatively high. When designing the central control display interface, it is necessary to fully consider the driver's visual effective scanning path, reduce unnecessary distraction time during driving, improve the driver's operating efficiency on the central control interface, and ensure a safe driving environment.

References

1. Wang, L., Yu, S., Chu, J.: Design of display position of car interior information based on eye movement analysis. J. Zhejiang Univ. (Eng. Sci. Ed.), **54**(04), 671–677+693 (2020)
2. Ren, H., Tan, Y.: Analysis of gaze behavior of vehicle touch screen based on eye movement experiment. Packag. Eng. **41**(20), 97–101 (2020)
3. Gao, H., Huang, W.: Layout optimization design of automobile human-computer interaction information interface based on visual cognition theory. West. Leather, **41**(21), 87+89 (2019)
4. Sun, B., Yang, J., Sun, Y.: Research on hierarchical design of automobile human-computer interaction interface. Mech. Des. **36**(02), 121–125 (2019)
5. Wang, R., Dong, S., Xiao, J.: Research on human-computer natural interaction in smart car interface design. Mech. Des. **36**(02), 132–136 (2019)
6. Sun, B., Yang, J., Sun, Y., Yan, H., Li, S.: Research on the color design of vehicle man-machine interface based on eye movement experiment. Packag. Eng. **40**(02), 23–30 (2019)
7. Zong, W., Chen, L., Ling, J.: Research on the classification and display of human-machine interaction information of vehicle-mounted intelligent information terminals. Sci. Technol. Bull. **33**(12), 221–224 (2017)
8. Tan, H., Zhao, D., Zhao, J.: Research on the design of automobile man-machine interface for complex interactive situations. Packag. Eng. **33**(18), 26–30 (2012)
9. Tan, H., Zhao, J., Wang, W.: Research on the design of automobile human-computer interaction interface. J. Autom. Eng. **2**(05), 315–321 (2012)

HCI, Social Distancing, Information, Communication and Work

Attention-Based Design and Selective Exposure Amid COVID-19 Misinformation Sharing

Zaid Amin[1,2], Nazlena Mohamad Ali[1(✉)], and Alan F. Smeaton[3]

[1] Institute of IR4.0 (IIR4.0), Universiti Kebangsaan Malaysia, Bangi, Malaysia
nazlena.ali@ukm.edu.my
[2] Faculty of Informatics Engineering, Universitas Bina Darma, Palembang, Indonesia
zaidamin@binadarma.ac.id
[3] INSIGHT: Centre for Data Analytics, Dublin City University, Dublin 9, Ireland
alan.smeaton@dcu.ie

Abstract. One of the significant limitations in human behaviour when receiving online information is our lack of visual cognitive abilities, the ability to pay greater attention in a short time. The question arises about how we handle online messages, which contain and send people with the same associated interests as ourselves, regarding social influences and individual beliefs. This study aims to provide some insight into misinformation sharing. The availability of enormous amounts of COVID-19 information makes the selectivity of messages likely limited by the distortion of perceptions in the communicating environment. It is also in line with the fact that human attention is essentially limited and depends on the conditions and tasks at hand. To understand this phenomenon, we proposed a Tuning Attention Model (TAM). The model proposes tuning and intervene in a user's attention behaviour by incorporating an attention-based design when users decide to share COVID-19 misinformation. In pilot study results, we found that attention behaviour negatively correlated with misinformation sharing behaviour. The results justify that when attention behaviour increased, misinformation sharing behaviour will decrease. We suggest an attention-based design approached on social media application's that could intervene in user attention and avoid selective exposure caused by the spread of COVID-19 misinformation. The study expected to produce continuous knowledge leading to non-coercive handling of sharing COVID-19 misinformation behaviour and laying the basis for overcoming misinformation issues.

Keywords: Attention · Design · Selective exposure · COVID-19 · Misinformation sharing · User interfaces

1 Introduction

Since the advent of online messages, our internal and external environments have been flooded with rising amounts of information. According to Cisco (2018), "Global IP traffic is expected to reach 396 Exabyte per month by 2022, up from 122 Exabyte per month in 2017. There will be 4.8 billion internet users by 2022. That's up from 3.4 billion

© Springer Nature Switzerland AG 2021
M. Kurosu (Ed.): HCII 2021, LNCS 12764, pp. 501–510, 2021.
https://doi.org/10.1007/978-3-030-78468-3_34

in 2017 or 45% of the world's population". Being aware of the incredible explosion of information today in online media makes us realize that it is significantly inversely comparable to our ability to access it. It is merely because our attention remains very limited. As humans, we have limited cognitive skills in processing and understanding information obtained from the surrounding environment. Therefore, in the early stages of every task-oriented, it is essential for those focusing on designing Human-Computer Interaction (HCI) to examine characteristics of attention and their interactive association with action planning (Salihan et al. 2017).

Understanding the value or quality of information is also vital to how users should consume information for constructive purposes or have a detrimental impact on individuals or social structures. Amid the increasing burden of the COVID-19 pandemic, there are parallel emergencies that need to be tackled simultaneously—the rise of counterfeit drugs, fake news, and misinformation on treatment around COVID-19. Credible sources of information from health experts are also the key to justifying health professionals' suggestions with the skills and training necessary to fight this emergency. Essentially, they can be a source of accurate and reliable information relevant to the public or other associate health professionals, thereby reducing the spread of misinformation on the treatment of COVID-19. Ideal conditions can achieve by presenting accurate and reliable information based on relevant health authorities and professional associations recommendations to ensure that the public is not affected by other exposure factors.

COVID-19 is not only a global pandemic and has a multidimensional effect. According to the WHO, it is also an "infodemic", highlighting the immediate social problems arising from a large amount of misinformation and fake news circulating about COVID-19 (Laato et al. 2020). Numerous issues of COVID-19 misinformation are relatively found in social media, which plays an essential role in the spread of misinformation (Allcott and Gentzkow 2017). It also raises questions regarding what platforms can prevent fake news spread (Figueira and Oliveira 2017). During the COVID-19 pandemic, clear communication about the severity of the situation and suggested medical standards are needed to ensure people take the right action and do not suffer unnecessary anxiety (Farooq et al. 2020). The abundance of unclear, ambiguous, and incorrect information during COVID-19 leads to information overload and accelerated health anxiety (Laato et al. 2020). Although sufficient research has shown that people exhibit confirmation bias related to selective exposure on social media, the lack of research trying to untangle the several effects of selective exposure and sharing in the context of COVID-19 is still urgently needed.

This study aims to produce a model that can describe the selective phenomenon amid COVID-19 misinformation and proposed attention-based design, which is expected to intervene in the attention of user interactions in the behaviour of sharing misinformation. As well as modelling the psychological dimensions occurs with attention-based design approach solutions.

The paper is structured as follows. The first part contains an introduction that briefly describes the phenomenon of selective exposure in COVID-19 misinformation. The second part includes a background on the existing literature on attention-based design, selective exposure, and its relationship to the spread of misinformation about COVID-19. The third section contains the material and method applied. The fourth section contains the result's main findings, and the fifth part includes a discussion of the implications and the sustainability of future research.

2   Background

2.1   Attention-Based Design

Designing a system that can intervene in user attention is a significant challenge for research in HCI and cognitive techniques. Attention interface is one crucial part of the human and machine (computer) interaction process, which explicitly focuses on human attention as an essential input for computers. One of the most dominant modalities is to increase user attention with interface application design through a visual approach. Visual is the dominant modality for information transfer in HCI (Spence et al. 2000). One example is the concept of selective visual attention, which is closely related to increasing attention behaviour and can increase the certainty of choice in human decision making and goal-directed behaviour in facing an efficient task when viewed from time consumption (Zizlsperger et al. 2012; Chelazzi 2013). Gaining insight into the user's visual attention is very important to obtain information about the influence of brand or product sales in consumer decision making (Pieters and Warlop 1999).

Because humans have limited cognitive resources and capacities, we struggle with information overload in today's information-rich society (Edmunds and Morris 2000). Deciding which material to access or attend is a challenge for individuals (Dukas 2002), but at the same time, offers an exploratory topic of interest to researchers. Such information overload has also manifested itself in academia and other fields, which has developed into a "*battle of attention*" (Torgler and Piatti 2013). Readers face the tradeoffs of what to read and, therefore, allocate their attention to neglecting other stimuli. In general, attention is explored in various fields, such as cognitive science, neuroscience, sociology, or primatology (Lanham 2006). It has been defined (collectively) as "psychological and neural mechanisms that mediate perceptual selectivity" (Yantis 2000).

Previous research suggests that designers should view attention as a dynamic process when designing attention management views, particularly regarding handling COVID-19 misinformation sharing behaviour. Visual display events that temporarily precede the contextual content of a current message may need to be considered for further investigation. A developer can make several technical approaches. First, to use a zoom-lens metaphor, previous views may have affected the user's current attention 'zoom setting'. Second, the last state view may have resulted in the user shaping his current area of concern to a specific object shape. Third, there may be a negative priming effect of previous stimuli that the user is actively trying to ignore. Lee and Choo (2013) reviewed how attention works using appropriate metaphors. According to the spotlight metaphor, attention can be characterized as an internal radiance illuminating the location where an object is placed and clearly enhances the user's focus (Posner et al. 1980). Hodas and Lerman (2012), mention the attentiveness factor is inherently the property of individual users and is limited for each task and situation. Social media designers would influence users through the user interface's design choices. Interface design can manipulate user visibility to maximize user attention when consuming COVID-19 information on social media applications.

2.2 Selective Exposure

Attention to COVID-19 continues to grow on Twitter and possibly other platforms as well. People tend to care about the news that exposures them personally (shares their own beliefs), making sense that relevant conversations will develop as the pandemic continues to involve more people on a personal level. Likewise, attention is focused on the countries hardest hit by the disease, demonstrating that attention, discussion, and information sharing have the most significant impact on those most affected (Singh et al. 2020).

However, at the end of February 2020, the comparative flu myth and the misinformation of home remedies for COVID-19 appeared almost as frequently in the data collected by Singh et al. (2020), although there is some evidence to suggest that the comparative flu myth may have declined by the end of their data collection. In mid-March, the myths about heat kill COVID-19 and vaccine development also emerged from time to time. Users' selective exposure maintained their relative position compared to other myths and tended to reflect only topic's conversations. It is also important to note that tweets that counter or debunk certain COVID-19 myths are also likely to be part of an identified tweets pool. Almost everyone agrees that "prevention is better to care for". However, the critical prevention process is not only the responsibility of stakeholders (government, health agencies, and experts). Furthermore, the fundamental prevention of the infodemic problem is how to reduce the exposure that occurs continuously to someone's knowledge and belief. If it is not mediated, it will quickly "*crystallize*" in behaviour and create new social problems in addressing COVID-19 treatment.

Besides, as seen in the prevention of COVID-19, according to Singh et al. (2020), recipients and stakeholders can lose patience with prevention because evaluations that are not obtained immediately provide results. Although other evaluation types (e.g., formative) are useful, stakeholders (e.g., leaders, political figures) may intervene to fix problems quickly. However, as evidenced by the rushed attention to developing a vaccine for COVID-19, infectious disease scientists remind us that development will take a long time, require collaboration across the scientific community, and incur considerable costs before it becomes robust and secure (Corey et al. 2020).

A significant impact that continues to occur is that selective exposure can lead to an echo chamber's emergence on social media. A group of like-minded people working together to frame and reinforce a shared narrative, thus facilitating fake news and the general flow of COVID-19 misinformation. In both cases, the main driver of selective exposure is interested in a topic, where people prefer information that matches their interests while avoiding off-topic information. The understanding of interest as a driver of attention is also at the root of selective exposure theory. Based on cognitive dissonance theory, selective exposure is defined as "preference information consistent with previously held beliefs along with avoidance of information contrary to such beliefs" (Graf and Aday 2008).

3 Material and Methods

The method used in this study is carried out, starting with the determination of sampling and questionnaire design. The data collection technique in this study used nonprobability sampling with a purposive sampling method approach. The instrument used was an online questionnaire that provides questions to determine the user's answers (n = 112) about the relationship of attention behaviour in sharing misinformation on social media.

The questions consist of demographic information, gender, profession, age, education, and frequently used social media platforms. Respondents were asked to choose the most appropriate item (5 Likert scales). One example of questionnaire materials is shown in Fig. 1. This question is related to whether they would share information if there were information about the application of the rubella vaccine in children, and the narrative of this application can cause an adverse effect. This question also investigates whether a selective exposure factor occurs when the user decides to share or not share the question given.

4 Results

The pilot study findings in a questionnaire show selective exposure happened when users asked to share or not share information circulating on social media. These findings are very relevant to the issue of medical knowledge in dealing with sharing COVID-19 misinformation. The following are some of the results that we highlight concerning the pilot studies we have conducted.

4.1 Questionnaire Results

We collected data from 112 respondents from October 1, 2018, to November 30, 2018 (8 weeks). Demographic data collected consists of numerous sections, namely gender, age group, recent education, occupation, and cyberspace most regularly used (see Table 1). The results show that the sample contains slightly more women (55.4%). The origin of the largest participating country is Indonesia at 92.9%. The most widely used social media platform is WhatsApp at 86.6%, and the age range of most participants is 30–39 years at 39.3%.

The questionnaire results also show that 34% of 112 respondents agree that users easily share misinformation without reading the content first (especially when dealing with their exposures, including beliefs and social influences). Approximately 75% of respondents agree that sharing misinformation with attentive behaviour is essential. Previous research has confirmed that quality is not a mandatory requirement for online virality (Weng 2012). The results we obtained in examining selective exposure factors clearly show that the top element is an epistemic belief within one's internal self. This epistemic belief factor becomes affected when social influences factors predominate. These results are consistent with justification from Chua et al. (2017), who mentions that epistemic belief significantly affected users' decisions to share online health rumours. The question about belief factors in sharing misinformation shows that 78% of respondents

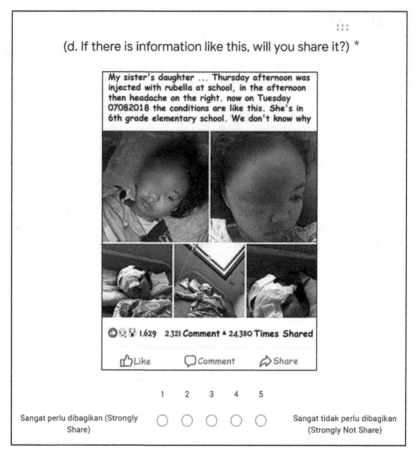

(d. If there is information like this, will you share it?) *

My sister's daughter ... Thursday afternoon was injected with rubella at school, in the afternoon then headache on the right. now on Tuesday 07082018 the conditions are like this. She's in 6th grade elementary school. We don't know why

1.629   2.321 Comment ▲ 24.380 Times Shared

Like   Comment   Share

         1   2   3   4   5

Sangat perlu dibagikan (Strongly Share)   Sangat tidak perlu dibagikan (Strongly Not Share)

Fig. 1. An example of the questionnaire materials regarding the harmful effects of applying the rubella vaccine to children

share information because they want to share their beliefs with others. The majority of respondents share information on social media because they want to help and share the knowledge they believe in others. It is also stated by Garrett and Weeks (2017), which is that individuals are inclined to think misperceptions, and this exposure/bias rises with opportunity (e.g., time to think) and with the ability (e.g., cognitive resources). Furthermore, we find that selective exposure to social influences factors emerge in second place. Still, these two states are also influenced by how long it takes the user to pay more attention to the information obtained.

One of the material's contexts was medical information containing rumours spread on social media about vaccinating children's harmful impacts. This question shows that 112 participants dominantly answered doubtful (neutral), particularly 28.6%. These results show that the participants experienced a dissonance phase, which tends to be influenced by the exposure (bias) from within them, precisely with the belief and social influence factor. These cognitive dissonance phases emerge where the user has doubts in deciding

Table 1. Respondent's demographics.

Demographic data		Number	Demographic data		Number
		Percentage			Percentage
Gender	Male	44.6%	Country of origin	Indonesia	92.9%
	Female	55.4%		Malaysia	7.1%
Age	<17 years	12.5%	The most used cyberspace	Twitter	11.6%
	18–20 years	2.7%		WhatsApp	86.6%
	21–29 years	33%		Facebook	50%
	30–39 years	39.3%		Instagram	55.4%
	40–49 years	8%		YouTube	24.1%
	50–69 years	4.5%			
	60> years	2.7%			
Highest education	Less than high school degree	12.5%			
	High school degree	15.2%			
	Diploma degree	3.6%			
	Bachelor degree	40.2%			
	Master degree	28.6%			
	Postgraduate degree	12.5%			

whether to share the information or not. This critical phase will "boil down" depending on how much pressure the epistemic belief and social influence factors face. This finding is consistent with McLeod's (2008) results, stating that cognitive impairment involves conflicting attitudes, beliefs, or behaviours.

4.2 Proposed Tuning Attention Model (TAM)

In the context of the development of a model, we construct the findings from the questionnaire results and understand related theories into an initial model that will clearly explain this phenomenon, including proposed assigning the role of attention-based design. We built an initial concept called the Tuning Attention Model (TAM) based on the questionnaire results. This TAM model suggests the phenomena that occur, including psychological dominance and intervention tools through COVID-19 misinformation sharing by the attention-based design approach (see Fig. 2).

In the initial model (Fig. 2), thick red lines indicate ideal conditions (target behaviour), where the user is at the expected level of attention. The user is exposed to higher social influence factors than the epistemic belief factor (as shown in the blue

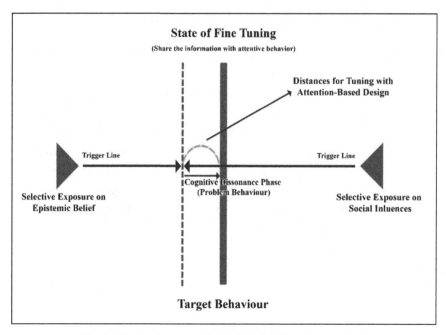

Fig. 2. Tuning Attention Model (TAM) (Color figure online)

arrow as a trigger). The user tends not to have attention, and this exposure triggers user behaviour to share misinformation. This is shown in the lacking of dashed red lines.

The behavioural conditions that need to be tuned and measured are as shown in the dotted yellow line. The attention-based solution or approach used in this model is the tuning treatment (reversing the target behaviour condition). The attention-based design implies that misinformation containment policies should also emphasize behavioural interventions, like labelling and incentives to dissuade the spread of misinformation, particularly on COVID-19 misinformation. These intervention tools based on psychological understanding is significantly more essential rather than focusing exclusively on bots. These findings suggest that concerted cognitive psychological efforts are needed to be embedded on design social media applications and encourage users to flag and constructively refute misinformation (Chen et al. 2015).

5   Discussion

This study's significance is a comprehensive investigation that integrates psychological aspects, which mainly become one of the HCI field's core domains. Unfortunately, very little research emphasizes the integrated approach of human cognitive psychological factors in dealing with COVID-19 misinformation sharing behaviour and in line with research by (Vosoughi et al. 2018; Bakshy et al. 2009; Cook et al. 2017), encouraging investigation on human judgment factors. These justifications imply that misinformation containment policies should also emphasize behavioural interventions, like labelling and incentives to dissuade the spread of misinformation, rather than focusing exclusively on bots.

The significants of increasing attention behaviour to influence selective exposure has been identified in this study. This study's finding indicated that attention-based design is needed to further application to COVID-19 misinformation sharing behaviour phenomena. The attention-based design also implied that a particular strategy would suggest intervening selective exposure amid COVID-19 misinformation. Research into attention-based design and how those designs would affect selective exposure on a user in sharing COVID-19 misinformation is required. Research is also needed to share useful COVID-19 information with attentive behaviour based on health sources credibility. Research that focuses on detecting COVID-19 misinformation with machine learning approaches or robotic applications is expected to be complementary when a user fails to detect COVID-19 misinformation. Research using a hybrid approach to seeing COVID-19 misinformation with a unifying machine and human collaboration will be necessary. As social beings, devices have limitations in terms of individual and social interactions.

The studies reveal that selective exposure occurs when users encounter medical information such as vaccine use in children. The selective exposure could influence user attention in handling sharing COVID-19 misinformation. By taking a practical approach to future research through attention-based design, it is expected to produce user interfaces that prioritize solving the COVID 19 misinformation phenomenon in a non-coercive manner, particularly prioritizing a humanist approach.

Acknowledgement. We thank all participants in the study. The work was supported by the university research grant UKM GPK-4IR-2020-019.

References

Allcott, H., Gentzkow, M.: Social media and fake news in the 2016 election. J. Econ. Perspect. **31**(2), 211–236 (2017)

Bakshy, E., Karrer, B., Adamic, L.A.: Social influence and the diffusion of user-created content. In: Proceedings of the 10th ACM Conference on Electronic Commerce, pp. 325–334 (July 2009)

Corey, L., Mascola, J.R., Fauci, A.S., Collins, F.S.: A strategic approach to COVID-19 vaccine R&D. Science **368**(6494), 948–950 (2020)

Cisco: Cisco Predicts More IP Traffic in the Next Five Years Than in the History of the Internet (2018). https://newsroom.cisco.com/press-release-content?type=webcontent&articleId=1955935. Accessed 6 Feb 2021

Chelazzi, L., Perlato, A., Santandrea, E., Della Libera, C.: Rewards teach visual selective attention. Vis. Res. **85**, 58–72 (2013)

Chua, A.Y., Banerjee, S.: To share or not to share: the role of epistemic belief in online health rumors. Int. J. Med. Inform. **108**, 36–41 (2017)

Cook, J., Lewandowsky, S., Ecker, U.K.: Neutralizing misinformation through inoculation: exposing misleading argumentation techniques reduces their influence. PloS one **12**(5), e0175799 (2017)

Chen, X., Sin, S.C.J., Theng, Y.L., Lee, C.S.: Why do social media users share misinformation?. In Proceedings of the 15th ACM/IEEE-CS Joint Conference on Digital Libraries, pp. 111–114 (June 2015)

Dukas, R.: Behavioural and ecological consequences of limited attention. Philos. Trans. R. Soc. Lond. Ser. B: Biol. Sci. **357**(1427), 1539–1547 (2002)

Edmunds, A., Morris, A.: The problem of information overload in business organisations: a review of the literature. Int. J. Inf. Manag. **20**(1), 17–28 (2000)

Figueira, Á., Oliveira, L.: The current state of fake news: challenges and opportunities. Procedia Comput. Sci. **121**, 817–825 (2017)

Farooq, A., Laato, S., Islam, A.N.: Impact of online information on self-isolation intention during the COVID-19 pandemic: cross-sectional study. J. Med. Internet Res. **22**(5), e19128 (2020)

Graf, J., Aday, S.: Selective attention to online political information. J. Broadcast. Electron. Media **52**(1), 86–100 (2008)

Garrett, R.K., Weeks, B.E.: Epistemic beliefs' role in promoting misperceptions and conspiracist ideation. PloS one **12**(9), e0184733 (2017)

Hodas, N.O., Lerman, K.: How visibility and divided attention constrain social contagion. In: 2012 International Conference on Privacy, Security, Risk and Trust and 2012 International Conference on Social Computing, pp. 249–257. IEEE (September 2012)

Johnston, D.W., Piatti, M., Torgler, B.: Citation success over time: theory or empirics? Scientometrics **95**(3), 1023–1029 (2013)

Lee, K., Choo, H.: A critical review of selective attention: an interdisciplinary perspective. Artif. Intell. Rev. **40**(1), 27–50 (2013)

Laato, S., Islam, A.N., Islam, M.N., Whelan, E.: What drives unverified information sharing and cyberchondria during the COVID-19 pandemic? Eur. J. Inf. Syst. **29**(3), 288–305 (2020)

Lanham, R.A.: The Economics of Attention: Style and Substance in the Age of Information. University of Chicago Press, Chicago (2006)

Ab Rahman, M.S., Ali, N.M., Mohd, M.: Comelgetz prototype in learning prayers among children. Asia-Pac. J. Inf. Technol. Multimedia **6**(1), 115–125 (2017)

McLeod, S.: Cognitive dissonance. Simply Psychol. **31**(1), 2–7 (2008)

Pieters, R., Warlop, L.: Visual attention during brand choice: the impact of time pressure and task motivation. Int. J. Res. Mark. **16**(1), 1–16 (1999)

Posner, M.I., Snyder, C.R., Davidson, B.J.: Attention and the detection of signals. J. Exp. Psychol. Gen. **109**(2), 160 (1980)

Spence, C., Lloyd, D., McGlone, F., Nicholls, M.E., Driver, J.: Inhibition of return is supramodal: a demonstration between all possible pairings of vision, touch, and audition. Exp. Brain Res. **134**(1), 42–48 (2000)

Singh, L., et al.: A first look at COVID-19 information and misinformation sharing on Twitter. arXiv preprint arXiv:2003.13907 (2020)

Vosoughi, S., Roy, D., Aral, S.: The spread of true and false news online. Science **359**(6380), 1146–1151 (2018)

Weng, L., Flammini, A., Vespignani, A., Menczer, F.: Competition among memes in a world with limited attention. Sci. Rep. **2**(1), 1–9 (2012)

Yantis, S.: Goal-directed and stimulus-driven determinants of attentional control. Attent. Perform. **18**, 73–103 (2000)

Zizlsperger, L., Sauvigny, T., Haarmeier, T.: Selective attention increases choice certainty in human decision making. PLoS One **7**(7), e41136 (2012)

Digital Communication to Compensate for Social Distancing

Results of a Survey on the Local Communication App DorfFunk

Matthias Berg(✉) ⓘ, Anne Hess ⓘ, and Matthias Koch ⓘ

Fraunhofer IESE, 67663 Kaiserslautern, Germany
{matthias.berg,anne.hess,matthias.koch}@iese.fraunhofer.de

Abstract. This paper aims to determine the potentials as well as the limitations of digital communication to compensate for the massive decrease in direct social interaction due to the Covid-19 pandemic. The availability of "DorfFunk" – a smartphone app for communication in local rural communities – was expanded in three German federal states during the spring of 2020 to counteract some of the negative consequences of measures taken to contain the spread of the virus (curfews, quarantines, social distancing). Here, we present the results of a survey on the experiences, needs, and perceived benefits/limitations of DorfFunk users in times of the pandemic. The results indicate that DorfFunk can contribute to coping with such a situation, especially in the local sphere. Local information and the connection to the community turned out to be of importance, while functionalities for the interaction with other individuals were regarded as secondary. The benefits of DorfFunk were valued more positively in regions where the service had been established already before the pandemic.

Keywords: Digital media communication · Corona virus · Physical/social distancing

1 Introduction

Digital media are becoming ever more important for everyday life. While the influence of digitalization on social life in general is discussed critically by some authors [1, 2], others point out that together with direct interaction and other forms of media use, digital media have become fundamental to our relationships, community building, and sense of belonging [3]. Currently, however, we find ourselves in a situation where common practices of sociality are massively affected by a global health crisis. Measures such as (partial) shutdowns, curfews, and quarantines are being taken to reduce the spread of Covid-19. Such measures have a massive influence on how we interact socially. Physical (or social) distancing reduces direct interaction on the level of personal relationships, social groups, as well as larger communities. Personal encounters with other individuals, gatherings for shared leisure activities or community events are either totally impossible or strongly restricted. At the same time, various forms of mediated communication, including countless messengers, video conferences, social media, but also the telephone

© Springer Nature Switzerland AG 2021
M. Kurosu (Ed.): HCII 2021, LNCS 12764, pp. 511–526, 2021.
https://doi.org/10.1007/978-3-030-78468-3_35

are becoming ever more important for us to connect to single individuals, groups of people, and even larger communities.

Recent pieces of empirical work unsurprisingly state that media and online use in general have intensified on a global level during the Covid-19 pandemic. A representative survey in 17 countries carried out by the market research company GlobalWebIndex [4] indicates, among other things, that the use of streaming services (52%), online videos (52%), messaging services (45%), and social media (44%) at home has intensified [4, p. 96]. This increase is also reflected in the time spent using digital devices: 71% of the respondents confirmed that they are spending more time on their smartphone, laptop (45%), and desktop PC (32%) [4, p. 102].

A more detailed view on the influence of the Covid-19 pandemic on digital communication with friends and family is presented by Nguyen et al. [5]. Of the 1,374 US adults they surveyed, 43% reported an increase of text messages, followed by voice calls (36%), social media use (35%), and video calls (30%), in order to stay in touch with remote social contacts [5, p. 2]. Furthermore, they show that factors such as living situation, worries concerning one's Internet access, as well as Internet skills influence not only the increase but also the decrease of digital communication during the Covid-19 pandemic [5, pp. 2–3]. Overall, the authors conclude that the process of digitalization has been accelerated by the pandemic.

This also applies to rural areas in Germany. One example is the mobile application "DorfFunk" (*VillageRadio*). It was developed and released with the aim to facilitate local communication among citizens in rural communities already before the Covid-19 pandemic. During the first lockdown period in Germany in the spring of 2020, the application spread geographically and gained a large number of registered users. This motivated us to conduct a survey in order to analyze DorfFunk with respect to its benefits and limitations during the Covid-19 pandemic from its users' point of view. The survey investigated typical usage patterns, motivations for using the app, as well as the perceived effects on the individual level and on the level of social life in rural communities.

The following section outlines the background of the project "Digital Villages" as the context in which the DorfFunk app was developed, tested, and distributed. As part of the research methodology in Sect. 3, we will introduce the research questions that guided the study and describe the parameters of our online survey. Section 4 contains the central results of the study, followed by their interpretation in the discussion in Sect. 5. Section 6 concludes the article with a short résumé and proposes some more general implications.

2 Background

The project "Digitale Dörfer" (*Digital Villages*) started in 2015 with the intention to create digital services for rural areas in order to make the potentials of digitalization tangible and improve the quality of life. A consortium including partners from government, research, and municipalities in the German federal state of Rhineland-Palatinate aimed at developing a digital ecosystem for rural areas comprising several digital solutions and services interconnected through a central platform. The project followed a co-creation approach, with living labs established in three model municipalities playing a pivotal role [6]. Participation in this co-creation process involved mainly citizens of the municipalities. The fields of action covered by the "Digital Villages Platform" and its services include local supplies, volunteer work, municipal administration, and local communication in general.

Belonging to the latter category, DorfFunk is one of the solutions that were developed and evaluated during the project's second phase (2017–2019). The app enables digital communication in rural communities and intends to foster local interaction and participation. It aims to support typical aspects of rural life such as neighborly help and mutual exchange. Through communication as well as information, DorfFunk offers identification with the region and a local sense of belonging.

Fig. 1. DorfFunk screenshot

DorfFunk is a smartphone app that runs on Android and iOS smartphones and is provided by the Fraunhofer Institute for Experimental Software Engineering IESE. It is free of charge for its users, but needs to be activated by the municipal administration. After completing the registration process, users can select their home village and define the extent to which they want to interact with surrounding communities. The mobile application holds up to seven channels (see Fig. 1), which offer various forms of interaction within the defined local area: The channel "Gossip" contains plain everyday talk with public text messages and pictures regarding local issues, incidents, or questions. "Seek" and "Offer" are intended for the non-commercial exchange of goods as well as services. The channel "Groups" facilitates public as well as private spaces of communication on special topics such as leisure activities or clubs. "Tell us" connects citizens to the local administration so that they can indicate deficiencies or make suggestions – and receive feedback on their requests from the responsible authorities. Additionally, the two channels "News" and "Events" are connected to DorfNews, a website featuring regional news, official announcements, and events. Every registered user can create posts in these channels and comment on these issues publicly. Additionally, fellow citizens can be contacted via private messages.

The field trial of the app under real-life conditions started in March 2018 in three model municipalities. By the end of 2019, DorfFunk had more than 14,000 registered users, predominantly in Rhineland-Palatinate. Different evaluation activities were carried out during the field trial in 2019. Their results can be summarized as follows: The age distribution of DorfFunk users covers a range from 16 up 80 years, but is dominated by middle-aged persons between 31 and 60 years of age. As the backend data indicate, roughly one third of the registered users is active in the sense that they create posts or comment on posts by others [7, p. 48]. The major motivation for using the app is to participate in community affairs, followed by staying in touch with the community and fellow citizens, respectively. Out of 253 participants of an online survey conducted in 2019, 228 (90%) individuals reported that they feel informed when they use DorfFunk and 94 (37%) confirmed a feeling of connectedness. A survey based on the system usability scale (SUS) carried out with a small sample of 20 participants showed a very positive user experience [7, p. 81].

With the beginning of the Covid-19 pandemic in Germany and the subsequent lockdown in March and April of 2020, DorfFunk was made available to all municipalities in the three federal states of Bavaria, Rhineland-Palatinate, and Schleswig-Holstein free of charge. The intention was to allow a larger part of the population to benefit from the communication possibilities offered by DorfFunk. As a consequence, the number of registered users tripled within three months, from approx. 15,500 at the end of February to more than 49,000 at the end of May. By the end of the year, DorfFunk reached a total of more than 67,600 registered users. Given this massive resonance, we conducted a study in order to shed light on the users' use of DorfFunk and their perception of its benefits as well as limitations in times of massively reduced direct social interaction.

3 Research Methodology

This section introduces the research methodology, respectively the design, of our study. We conducted the study in the form of an online survey. According to the Goal Questions Metrics paradigm, the overall research goal (RG) of this survey was stated as follows:

RG: Identification of the potentials and limitations of the mobile application DorfFunk for social life in rural areas during the Covid-19 pandemic

In a second step, we refined this research goal (RG) into a set of research questions (RQ) and corresponding metrics, which ultimately served as a baseline for the definition of the survey questions. These research questions are given below:

- *RQ₁: What are typical usage patterns of DorfFunk?* With this RQ, we investigated metrics like (1) typical user activities with DorfFunk, (2) typical locations of usage, as well as (3) favored communication channels. The results of our study with regard to this RQ will be discussed in Sect. 4.2

- *RQ₂: Did the Covid-19 pandemic affect the usage patterns of DorfFunk?* With this RQ, we investigated any changes in the frequency of usage, respectively the general atmosphere in DorfFunk, during the pandemic compared to the time before the pandemic. The results of our study with regard to this RQ will be discussed in Sect. 4.3
- *RQ₃: What are factors that motivate users to use DorfFunk?* With this RQ, we investigated metrics such as factors that supported the decision to install and use DorfFunk (purpose and motivation) as well as users' expectations towards DorfFunk. The results of our study with regard to this RQ will be discussed in Sect. 4.4
- *RQ₄: What are the perceived effects of DorfFunk both in terms of benefits and limitations?* With this RQ, we investigated metrics such as emotions as well as positive/negative effects on different aspects such as being informed and solidarity during the Covid-19 pandemic. The results of our study with regard to this RQ will be discussed in Sect. 4.5

To investigate these RQs, we prepared and implemented a questionnaire using the LimeSurvey application. The questionnaire comprised 21 predominantly closed-ended questions categorized into ten different sections. In addition, the respondents were asked to elaborate on a small set of open-ended questions. The link to the online survey was spread via the general DorfFunk chat channel "Gossip", which reached all DorfFunk users. The online survey started on 21 April 2020 and closed on 2 September 2020. At the time the survey started, DorfFunk had approx. 45,000 registered users (45,157 on 30 April). Towards the end of the survey, almost 57,000 users were registered (56,940 on 31 August). That is, the population of our study comprised both people who had used DorfFunk already before the Covid-19 pandemic and users who started using DorfFunk during the pandemic after its rollout in Rhineland-Palatinate, Bavaria, and Schleswig-Holstein in March and April 2020. More detailed demographic data of the users who participated in the online survey is summarized in Sect. 4.1.

4 Results

We received responses from a total of 1,059 participants. Out of these participants, a total of 860 people completed the questionnaire. The data of these 860 participants[1] was subjected to our statistical data analysis activities, which particularly focused on descriptive statistics and their interpretation with regard to the research questions (RQ) introduced in Sect. 3.

4.1 Demographic Data

In the last part of the questionnaire, the participants were asked to provide demographic data on a voluntary basis. Out of the 860 participants, 478 were male (57%) and 359

---

[1] Access to the primary data can be requested via https://www.iese.fraunhofer.de/de/mediathek/primaerdaten.html using the PDI 53037.

female (43%). One participant selected the gender option "diverse" and 22 participants selected the option "no answer".

The participants indicated their age by assigning themselves to an age range. As illustrated in Fig. 2, all age groups (with the exception of those older than 80 years) were represented in our group of participants. The majority was between 51 and 60 years old (241; 28%), 23% (201 persons) were 41 to 50 years old, and 21% (181 persons) were 31 to 40 years of age. A total of 118 participants (14%) assigned themselves to the age group 61 to 70 years old, 64 participants (7%) assigned themselves to the age group 20 to 30 years old, and 24 participants (3%) assigned themselves to the age group between 71 and 80 years. Fifteen participants (2%) were younger than 20 years old.

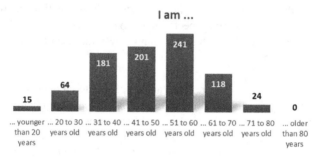

Fig. 2. Age distribution of users (n = 844)

About two thirds of the survey participants (562 persons; 65%) indicated that they had not used DorfFunk before the Covid-19 pandemic (respectively the associated lockdown situation), whereas the remaining third (298 persons; 35%) indicated that they had used DorfFunk already before (see Fig. 3).

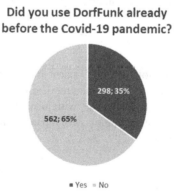

Fig. 3. Usage before the Covid-19 pandemic (n = 860)

4.2 Usage Patterns (RQ$_1$)

In the following, we will share typical usage patterns of DorfFunk (RQ$_1$). To investigate **typical communication activities**, we asked the participants which activities they typically do when using DorfFunk (reflected by the question "How do you use DorfFunk?"). To answer this question, we allowed them to select one or more of four options: "I read posts and comments", "I create and comment on posts", "I chat privately", and "I am active in groups".

As illustrated in Fig. 4, the vast majority (804, 93%) of the participants indicated that they read posts and comments in the various DorfFunk channels. Half of the participants (425, 49%) actively created and commented posts, whereas the other half of the participants (435, 51%) used DorfFunk rather passively (only reading and consuming the information). The functionality "Private Chats" was used by 12% (101) of the participants. Similarly, the functionality of creating content and communicating in groups was rarely used by the participants (78, 9%).

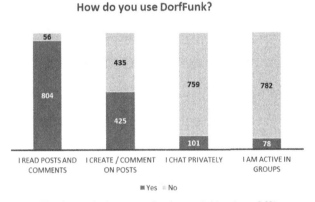

Fig. 4. Typical communication activities (n = 860)

Among the various options we provided to indicate **typical locations** of DorfFunk usage ("Where do you use DorfFunk?"), the data analysis revealed that the vast majority of the participants (97%; 830) used DorfFunk "at home" (see Fig. 5). The option "when out and about" (e.g., while shopping, while going for a walk) was selected by 23% of the participants (198). 17% of the participants (144) used DorfFunk "at school/at work".

To investigate **favorite DorfFunk channels**, the participants could rate their interest in the various channels with the help of a 5-point Likert scale ("very interesting", "rather interesting", "neither/nor", "rather uninteresting", "very uninteresting"). Figure 6 illustrates the data analysis results for each of the four channels "Events", "Offers", "Search", "News", and "Gossip".

Consolidating the options "very interesting" and "rather interesting", we identified the channel "News" as the channel with the most interesting posts from the viewpoint of the participants (68%, 530; n = 778), immediately followed by the posts in the channel "Events" (66%; 418; n = 630). However, the other channels ("Offers", "Search", and "Plausch") were also quite popular, with only minor differences in the ratings.

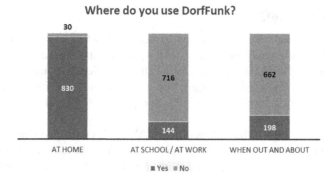

Fig. 5. Typical locations (n = 860)

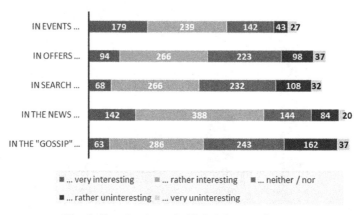

Fig. 6. Favorite channels ("I find the posts in ...")

4.3 Changes in Usage Patterns Due to Covid-19 (RQ₂)

In the following, we will share our results with regard to changes in usage patterns that occurred during the Covid-19 pandemic (RQ₂). The respondents were split into those who had used DorfFunk already before the outbreak of the pandemic and those who started using it after the release of DorfFunk all over Rhineland-Palatinate, Bavaria, and Schleswig-Holstein.

One of the survey questions aimed to collect data about any **changes in the frequency of DorfFunk usage** compared to the time before the outbreak of the pandemic. This question was answered by 271 respondents in total. As illustrated in Fig. 7, the data analysis revealed no significant change in the frequency with which the users used DorfFunk. That is, 195 respondents (72%) indicated that they had been using DorfFunk "the same as before", whereas 66 respondents (24%) used DorfFunk "rather more", respectively "a lot more". Only a minority of the respondents used DorfFunk "rather less", respectively "a lot less" (4%, 10 participants).

Since the Covid-19 pandemic,
I have been using DorfFunk …

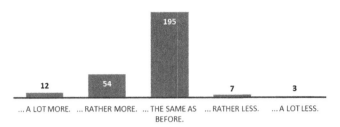

Fig. 7. Changes in frequency of usage (n = 271)

Another question investigated **any changes in the overall atmosphere** in DorfFunk. This question was answered by 247 participants (see Fig. 8). Compared to the time before Covid-19, a large majority of 70% (173) of the respondents perceived the atmosphere in DorfFunk to be the same as before. While 17% of the respondents saw an improved atmosphere (41 participants), 14% reported that the atmosphere was rather, respectively much, worse than before.

Compared to the time before Corona, the
atmosphere in DorfFunk is …

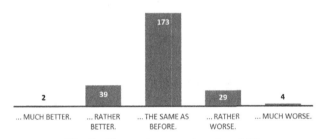

Fig. 8. Changes in atmosphere (n = 247)

4.4 Expectations and Motivations (RQ₃)

This section investigates the factors that influence the motivation of the respondents to use DorfFunk (RQ$_3$).

The main **purpose** of the usage of DorfFunk (n = 860) was for exactly three quarters of the respondents the possibility to take part in what is happening in the village (see Fig. 9). Less than half of the respondents used DorfFunk for being in contact with the community and with fellow citizens (49% and 42%, respectively). The opportunity to get to know new people did not play a role for most respondents, since only 9% selected this option in the multiple-choice question. In the open response section, a total of 156 participants provided miscellaneous answers, where they mainly stated more precisely their need to take part in their village's life with respect to sharing and receiving local and regional information and communicating with fellow citizens. However, another frequently mentioned reason for using DorfFunk was purely curiosity and eagerness to try out something new.

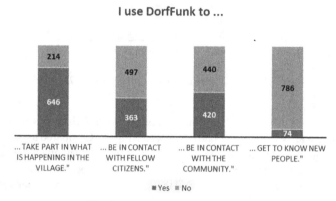

Fig. 9. Purpose of usage (n = 860)

There are two main **motivations** why the respondents decided to use DorfFunk (see Fig. 10): curiosity and connection to their place of residence (65% each). The advertisement of the app by public authorities had influenced the decision of 39% of the respondents, while 26% had decided to use DorfFunk because it appeared more trustworthy than Facebook, Twitter, and Co. A minority of 7% of the respondents were motivated to use DorfFunk because friends, acquaintances, or family were already using it. In total, 29 respondents added their own motivation as miscellaneous answers to the multiple-choice question. Ten respondents made the decision based on the trustworthiness of DorfFunk and its regional character opposed to globally active social networks. Another motivation mentioned by three respondents was the fact that the application had been available for free in their region since the outbreak of the pandemic.

Most of the respondents expressed the **expectation** (Fig. 11) of getting informed through DorfFunk (81%). Further expectations referred to bonding with fellow citizens in the region (64%), strengthening of neighborhood assistance (54%), or strengthening of solidarity in general (41%). Bridging of the imposed contact restrictions ("social distancing") was expected by only 15% of the respondents. 13% of the respondents did not have any expectations towards DorfFunk. To this multiple-choice question, 21 participants provided miscellaneous answers. Eleven of them emphasized the expectation of sharing information, communicating, and collaborating through digital means. Three respondents expected these to be an alternative to well-known global social networks.

Why did you decide to use DorfFunk?

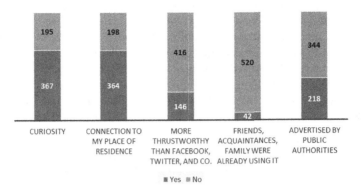

Fig. 10. Motivation to use DorfFunk (n = 562)

What are your expectations regarding DorfFunk?

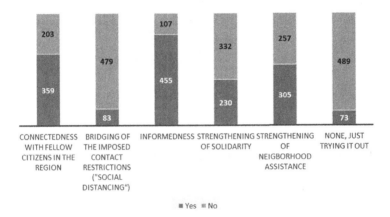

Fig. 11. Expectations (n = 562)

4.5 General Experiences (RQ4)

With respect to the **aspects potentially affected by DorfFunk during the Covid-19 pandemic**, the *respondents who had used DorfFunk already before* experienced a positive development in almost all aspects (see Fig. 12). The strongest positive aspects were being informed through DorfFunk (67%, n = 278) and the strengthening of neighborhood assistance (62%, n = 274). About half of the respondents reported a positive influence on connectedness with fellow citizens in the region (52%, n = 270) and solidarity (51%, n = 272). 39% of the respondents perceived a bridging of the imposed contact restrictions (n = 260). Negative developments are negligible, ranging from 3% to 6% for all aspects.

The results from the group of *respondents who joined DorfFunk after the outbreak of the pandemic* show a slightly different picture (see Fig. 13). The aspect in which these respondents saw a predominantly positive development was the aspect of being informed (54%, n = 500). Strengthening of neighborhood assistance (45%, n = 483), connectedness with fellow citizens in the region (43%, n = 491), and solidarity (39%, n = 483) were perceived as positive by less than half of the respondents. Positive developments with respect to the bridging of the imposed contact restrictions were perceived by 33% of the respondents (n = 481). Similar to the established DorfFunk users, negative developments for all the aspects were only seen by 2% to 5% of the respondents.

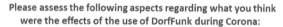

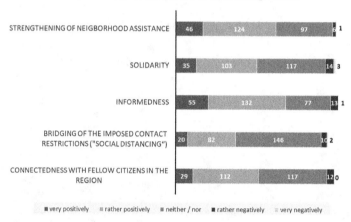

Fig. 12. Factors affected by DorfFunk in times of the Covid-19 pandemic (established users)

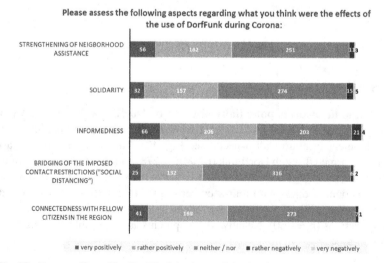

Fig. 13. Factors affected by DorfFunk in times of the Covid-19 pandemic (new users)

Besides the quantitative data, the respondents provided replies to open-ended questions with respect to positive and negative experiences as well as further aspects they liked to share. In total, 1,163 answers were given in these three categories.

The positive experiences ranged from rather generic ones such as the availability of information, mutual support in the community, and discussions or digital get-togethers of companions to private successes such as a particularly nice conversation, a shared photo, or the opportunity to sell a used mobile phone. Negative experiences mainly focused on the following topics: *Quality of the posts:* The respondents perceived the contributions of other users as irrelevant or observed poor behavior when communicating with each other. *Number of participants:* In various regions, the respondents reported on too few active users, and thus little interaction between them. *Technical issues:* The respondents mentioned issues with loading times and battery consumption of the app. Further aspects stated by the respondents cover a broad range of topics. One cluster of feedback focuses on the level of awareness for DorfFunk among the citizens, which was perceived as too low in various regions. Thus, the respondents wanted more advertisement for DorfFunk to increase its popularity and associated activities. Since DorfFunk is not (yet) available everywhere, the non-availability of DorfFunk in certain regions was another frequently mentioned topic. Furthermore, the respondents expressed their wishes for various additional features of DorfFunk, such as an overview of all active users in a region, the possibility to write posts in the name of a club or local organization, or the possibility to search for specific content.

5   Discussion

5.1   Interpretation

When looking at the results, the survey shows lots of parallels with the evaluations carried out before the Covid-19 pandemic. The age distribution with an emphasis on middle-aged users, for example, confirms previous findings. Concerning the **usage patterns of DorfFunk in general (RQ$_1$)**, the outcomes of the survey do not substantially differ from previous evaluations, either: DorfFunk is predominantly appreciated for providing information on local issues and events, but also for bartering and informal exchange. This is also echoed in the fact that information channels are rated as more interesting than those focusing on personal interaction or exchange in groups. People use DorfFunk mainly at home, which of course intensified during the lockdown period. With 49% of the users creating posts as well as making comments, the level of active participation is rather high compared to other social media such as Facebook or Instagram [8, p. 475]. This might be a result of the massive boost in the number of registrations during the period of data collection and the novelty of the service to the new users, which led to them actively testing the app's features.

Furthermore, once established, the **patterns of usage (RQ$_2$)** seem to remain fairly stable. This is suggested by the fact that the majority of respondents who had been using the app already before the Covid-19 pandemic reported neither a substantial increase nor a decrease in their frequency of use. However, approx. a quarter of the respondents used the service more often, which supports the general increase in digital media usage during the lockdown period.

As concerns the **motivations as well as expectations (RQ₃)**, the results show that people's main purpose is to participate in community affairs and to stay connected to the community in general as well as to other citizens. Very similarly, and following plain curiosity, a communicative connection to one's place of residence is one of the driving motivations for registering for DorfFunk. The expectations of new DorfFunk users include being informed, being connected to their fellow citizens, as well as neighborhood assistance. These replies overall indicate a need that is related to the region and the local community, respectively. With DorfFunk, people seek to get connected to their immediate living environment. In the context of the Covid-19 pandemic, this might imply that people are eager to receive information on the consequences this global crisis has on the very concrete local level. This explains why being informed in combination with being connected ranks high in the expectations, while the potential to bridge physical distancing is only sparsely referred to (15% of the respondents).

When looking at the **effects and general experiences (RQ₄)**, however, 33% (new users) and 39% (established users) of the respondents assessed DorfFunk positively in terms of bridging contact restrictions. This means that the actual perceived effect of the app's usage exceeded the initial expectations. The way this manifests itself is through information, mutual support, and connectedness: The perceived benefits of DorfFunk during the Covid-19 pandemic included especially the supply of information, but also neighborly help, the connection to other locals, as well as a feeling of solidarity. While the ranking of these characteristics is consistent throughout the sample, it is significant that they were evaluated more positively by persons who had been using the app already before the lockdown. This suggests that the formation of local communities on DorfFunk is a process along which positive effects increase over time.

5.2 Threats to Validity

In this section, we will shortly reflect threats to validity with regard to our survey based classifications [9]. To reduce the risk of *inadequate preoperational explication of constructs*, we defined our measurement instrument (i.e., the questionnaire) carefully. That is, we systematically refined our research goal of identifying the potentials and limitations of DorfFunk for social life in rural areas during the Covid-19 pandemic into clear questions and metrics. Moreover, the questionnaire was reviewed by an independent reviewer in order to assure the understandability of the questions. Social threats to construct validity such as *evaluation apprehension* were reduced because we did not evaluate the performance of the subjects. Rather, we collected subjective opinions regarding the investigated metrics from the user's point of view. Also, participation was voluntary.

To reduce the risk of selection bias, we selected and shared the link to the online survey with participants that perfectly matched our target group, i.e., real users of DorfFunk. This fact also positively affects the external validity of our study. Finally, to mitigate the risk of violated assumptions, we applied suitable statistical data analysis methods to the questionnaire data, thereby only considering data sets of the 860 participants who finished the questionnaire. The latter two measurements ultimately increase the conclusion validty of our study.

6   Conclusion

With this study, we aimed at revealing the potentials as well as the limitations of the local communication app DorfFunk on social life in rural areas during the Covid-19 pandemic from the viewpoint of its users. The results show that a need for local information is the primary driver for people to use DorfFunk. While the app was intended as a tool for communication among citizens, these functionalities seem to be only of secondary relevance to its users. But even with a focus on information rather than mutual interaction, feelings of connectedness, solidarity, and belonging to one's local community emerge.

In this way, DorfFunk helps to digitally compensate for physical distancing. Its benefits especially refer to opportunities to connect to the local community or the region. At the same time, the service seems to be rather limited in terms of bridging gaps on the level of personal relationships. On the level of the individual user, DorfFunk is only one component of a person's "media repertoire" [10, p. 28]. This means that people rely on various technologies, tools, and services to stay in touch with each other. Especially for close relationships, other media obviously seem to be more relevant than DorfFunk. On the level of rural communities, however, this application can be an important part of the local "media ensemble" [10, p. 28].

In addition to being interpreted at the local and micro level, our results also need to be interpreted against the background of the wider public discourse dealing with the current exceptional situation. Quite often, the Covid-19 pandemic is framed as a driver of digitalization, forcing various institutions to engage with digital processes. Examples include enterprises reducing office capacities due to the positive experience made with remote work [11], or economic potentials for certain industries [12]. In this line of argumentation, the Covid-19 pandemic also has positive side effects for the process of digitalization. To some degree, this also applies to rural areas. However, at the same time our survey shows that positive effects were especially reported by those who had been using the app already before the Covid-19 pandemic. On the community level, the integration of such an application into local social life is a process that includes a multitude of aspects. As our experience shows, many of them involve offline and non-digital activities (e.g., marketing campaigns in local newspapers, release events, townhall meetings, workshops). If these forms of interaction are suspended, the dynamics of the digital transformation seem to be limited. This should be considered at a time when the Covid-19 pandemic is being discussed as a catalyst of digitalization. Communication tools such as DorfFunk bear potential, but their effects on digitalization in general need to be observed much more carefully than it is happening right now.

Acknowledgements. The project "Digitale Dörfer" is funded by the Ministry of the Interior and for Sports, Rhineland-Palatinate.

References

1. Wittel, A.: Towards a network sociality. In: Hepp, A., Krotz, F., Moores, S., Winter, C. (eds.) Connectivity, Networks and Flows: Conceptualizing Contemporary Communications. The Hampton Press Communication Series. Communication, Globalization and Cultural Identity. Hampton Press, Cresskill (2008)

2. Turkle, S.: Alone Together: Why We Expect More from Technology and Less from Each Other. Basic Books, New York (2011)
3. Hepp, A., Berg, M., Roitsch, C.: Mediengeneration als Prozess: Zur Mediatisierung der Vergemeinschaftungshorizonte von jüngeren, mittelalten und älteren Menschen. In: Krotz, F., Despotović, C., Kruse, M.-M. (eds.) Mediatisierung als Metaprozess. MKK, pp. 81–111. Springer, Wiesbaden (2017). https://doi.org/10.1007/978-3-658-16084-5_5
4. GlobalWebIndex: Coronavirus research April 2020: Multimarket research wave 3. https://www.globalwebindex.com/hubfs/1.%20Coronavirus%20Research%20PDFs/GWI%20coronavirus%20findings%20April%202020%20-%20Multi-market%20research%20(Release%209).pdf. Accessed 21 Jan 2021
5. Nguyen, M.H., Gruber, J., Fuchs, J., Marler, W., Hunsaker, A., Hargittai, E.: Changes in digital communication during the COVID-19 global pandemic: implications for digital inequality and future research. Soc. Media Soc. 6(3) (2020). https://doi.org/10.1177/2056305120948255
6. Hess, A., Magin, D.P., Koch, M.: Co-Creation in den Dörfern: Ein Living Lab für ländliche Regionen. In: Hess, S., Fischer, H. (eds.) Mensch und Computer 2017 – Usability Professionals, GI e.V., Regensburg. https://doi.org/10.18420/MUC2017-UP-0221
7. Berg, M., Heß, A., Hess, S., Koch, M.: Abschlussbericht zum Projekt "Digitale Dörfer 2.0": 2017–2019. https://www.digitale-doerfer.de/wp-content/uploads/2020/09/Abschlussbericht-DigitaleDoerfer-2.0.pdf. Accessed 22 Jan 2021
8. Beisch, N., Schäfer, C.: Internetnutzung mit großer Dynamik: Medien Kommunikation, Social Media. Media Perspektiven 9, 462–481 (2020)
9. Wholin, C., Runeson, P., Höst, M., Ohlsson, M.C., Regnell, B., Wesslén, A.: Experimentation in Software Engineering. An Introduction. Springer, Boston. https://doi.org/10.1007/978-1-4615-4625-2
10. Hepp, A., Hasebrink, U.: Researching transforming communications in times of deep mediatization: a figurational approach. In: Hepp, A., Breiter, A., Hasebrink, U. (eds.) Communicative Figurations. TCSCR, pp. 15–48. Springer, Cham (2018). https://doi.org/10.1007/978-3-319-65584-0_2
11. Groll, T.: Corona und Digitalisierung: Viele Unternehmen wollen Büroflächen reduzieren. In: Die Zeit, August 2020. https://www.zeit.de/wirtschaft/2020-08/corona-digitalisierung-umfrage-kpmg-unternehmen-homeoffice-arbeitsplatz. Accessed 21 Jan 2021
12. John, A.: Digitalisierung bietet Firmen neue Chancen in der Krise. https://www.tagesschau.de/wirtschaft/digitalisierung-zulieferer-101.html. Accessed 21 Jan 2021

An Evaluation of Remote Workers' Preferences for the Design of a Mobile App on Workspace Search

Cátia Carvalho[1], Edirlei Soares de Lima[1,2(✉)], and Hande Ayanoğlu[1,2]

[1] IADE, Universidade Europeia, Av. D. Carlos I, 4, 1200-649 Lisbon, Portugal
{edirlei.lima,hande.ayanoglu}@universidadeeuropeia.pt
[2] UNIDCOM/IADE, Av. D. Carlos I, 4, 1200-649 Lisbon, Portugal

Abstract. New ways of communication and the growth of mobile technologies allows a high degree of interaction between people, places, and even things, making it possible to work anywhere, anytime. This has led to the creation of new working models, where an increased number of independent workers fight the blurred line between working and personal life. The rise of the coworking spaces and their popularity came to fight that line and, also, help remote workers dealing with loneliness, promoting a collaborative and dynamic working environment. However, little is found in the literature about the specific preferences of the users of these types of spaces. This paper aims to identify and evaluate remote workers' preferences of working spaces characteristics, in the capital area of Portugal, to design a real time system that can help user's efficiency when looking for a space to work in. The paper presents the results of the study and the Heuristic Evaluation (Nielsen's 10 Heuristics) of the proposed system. Results show that working from home or in a Coworking spaces are the most common options among remote workers and their main motivations to work in those spaces were looking for a space that brings them comfort, allows an affordable accommodation and social interaction with other workers. WIFI quality, location and a quiet environment are the most important characteristics when choosing a specific working space. The results of the proposed system' evaluation showed that 6 usability problems were found, and 2 out of 10 heuristics were violated. However, the overall SUS score evaluation showed a score of 91 points, considered as "acceptable". These results can guide designers designing or developing working spaces related applications, or even owners creating those spaces.

Keywords: Remote work · Working spaces · Think aloud · User testing · User preferences

1 Introduction

The evolution in new ways of communication have led to changes in society. The advances of the internet have provided people with information from different places with fewer barriers. Today, people, goods, and information are moving quickly and easily to all parts of the globe [1]. The tendency is the daily use of communication devices,

© Springer Nature Switzerland AG 2021
M. Kurosu (Ed.): HCII 2021, LNCS 12764, pp. 527–541, 2021.
https://doi.org/10.1007/978-3-030-78468-3_36

such as smartphones and mobile internet, along with the growing need for information while on the go. The continued advancement of digital technology and the rise of the gig economy led to the growth of new working models [2], increasing need for flexibility [3], increasing number of self-employed workers [4], and increasing use for public spaces as workplaces [5]. All these, along with the growth in the use of new technologies, decreased and changed the need for office space [5]. These changes blurred the distinction between where a person lives (i.e., first place or home), where a person works (i.e., second place or office), and where a person spends time in between (i.e., third place). Oldenburg [6] defined this third place as a "generic designation for a great variety of public places that host the regular, voluntary, informal, and happily anticipated gatherings of individuals" and listed public places like cafés, coffee shops, community centers, general stores, and bars as exemplary third places [6]. However, as mentioned, different changes blurred this distinction, as nowadays, cafés and coffee shops are synonymous with workspaces, as flexible workers often choose to work at such third places that are neither their homes nor offices [7].

Independent consultants, short-term contractors, and freelancers creating portfolios of work in lieu of full-time jobs, are transforming the way we work, by disconnecting work from the office [8]. According to Eurostat, 5,4% of employees, in the European Union (EU), aged between 15–64, are working from home. Additionally, 9% work remotely somedays [9]. In Portugal, the number of Portuguese citizens working remotely have grown between 2015 and 2019. Recent numbers have pointed to approximately 6,5% of Portuguese population working remotely, standing out from countries like Italy (3,6%), Spain (4,8%) and Germany (5,2%) [9]. With new working models and the increased number of independent workers, it is possible to witness the rise of new types of workplaces (emerging as third places) to work in the digital age. Those, known as coworking spaces or shared office environments, for independent professionals, have been increasing rapidly [10], and gain popularity over the past years [11–13]. In 2020, a study published by Coworking Resources [14], titled "Global Coworking Growth Study 2020", registered approximately 2 million people working in over 20 million co-working spaces worldwide, crossing over 40 million by 2040. Portugal has been distinguished as one of the 20 largest markets by number of coworking spaces and the corresponding share over all spaces worldwide (280 spaces), followed by Hong Kong (255 spaces) and Vietnam (251 spaces). Coworking spaces can be considered as the optimum third places to work as they combine the best of both first and second places (i.e., working at home and traditional office) by offering "control, autonomy, and scheduling flexibility of remote work combined with optional access to the structure and community of an office if and when the worker wants it" [8]. Their popularity can result from the increasingly looking for a workspace, by self-employees and other remote workers, outside their home, due to feelings of loneliness, when working from home, and the need for a better balance between their work and personal life [11, 15], increasing their efficiency and performance [16].

There are some studies focusing on specific subjects of coworking, such as, their knowledge dynamics contribution of coworking to the creativity of the city [13], economic growth and sustaining productivity and innovation [12, 17], and promoting entrepreneurship by coworking spaces [18]. However, not much can be found in the literature about remote workers preferences for working spaces characteristics. Currently, a large number of existing mobile applications are focused on providing users with information about existent working spaces [19], and allowing them to make reservations [20, 21]; though, most of the existing systems have not been developed or adapted in Portugal and do not provide users with real time information related to occupation, noise levels, or internet speed. Also, the existing solutions only show outdated information about spaces which does not reflect the current situation in the country. Therefore, the aim of this paper is to identify and evaluate remote worker's preferences of working spaces characteristics in the capital area of Portugal, to design a real time system that can improve user's efficiency when looking for a space to work in. For this study, remote workers were defined as employees who work in a physically separate location as their teammates. This paper presents the user evaluation stage from an on-going project aiming to develop a mobile application for workspace search. The ongoing project will propose a system design that explores working spaces' characteristics and features, aiming for comfort of remote workers when looking for a space. The system is based on real-time sensors (occupation, noise levels, and internet speed) that monitor the activities in the space and send the information to the mobile application.

2 Methods

The study was divided into three stages: (i) Pre-study, (ii) Pilot Study, and (iii) Main Study.

(i) *Pre-study.* A survey was carried out, which was tested in the form of an online questionnaire, through *Google Forms*. Data was collected between April and October 2020. Inclusion criteria were working remotely/telecommuting or desire to work remotely for a day. The questionnaire remained open until the 100 answers were reached. The questions concerned remote workers' daily life choices, frustrations, preferences and challenges when looking for a working space. The results of this stage were used to build the low-fidelity prototype for the pilot study.

(ii) *Pilot study.* In the pilot study, a low-fidelity prototype was tested with the help of the Think Aloud protocol. Think-aloud protocol method refers to a type of research data used in empirical research processes. Data gathered is known as "thinking aloud", meaning that participants in the test are asked to verbalize their thoughts, while performing a task [22]. This stage was performed to ensure that the proposed method was viable. Figure 1 shows three of the main screens of the low-fidelity prototype, used for the pilot study.

(iii) *Main study.* The same prototype had been further developed, and an internal moderated Think Aloud test was conducted. Additionally, participants were given tasks to perform.

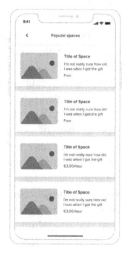

Fig. 1. Low fidelity prototype interface.

2.1 Pre-study

Sample. Table 1 shows the user characteristics of the sample. As can be seen, the sample consists of a close number of male (53%) and female (47%) co-workers. Deskmag [23], an online magazine about co-working worldwide, showed that female members in coworking spaces have been rising steadily, compared to early years, so, it is possible to note that the number of females working remotely is rising. The age of the remote workers is in the Y generation (30–45 years) (M = 32,7, SD = 6,99). Most respondents

Table 1. Participants' demographic data.

	Total (N=100) n (%)	EW (N=43) n (%)	SE (N=16) n (%)	F (N=33) n (%)	S (N=5) n (%)	OFW (N=3) n (%)
Gender						
Female	47(47)	20(47)	5(31)	17(52)	2(40)	3(100)
Male	53(53)	23(53)	11(69)	16(48)	3(60)	0(0)
Age						
18-29	35(35)	17(40)	4(25)	6(18)	5(100)	3(100)
30-45	62(62)	24(56)	12(75)	26(79)	0(0)	0(0)
>45	3(3)	2(4)	0(0)	1(3)	0(0)	0(0)
Nacionality						
Portuguese	87(87)	39(90)	13(81)	30(91)	5(100)	0(0)
European	4(4)	2(5)	1(6)	0(0)	0(0)	1(33)
American	6(6)	2(5)	2(13)	2(6)	0(0)	1(33)
African	3(3)	0(0)	0(0)	1(3)	0(0)	1(33)
Education						
High school graduate	12(12)	6(14)	4(25)	1(3)	0(0)	0(0)
Bachelor's degree	56(56)	25(58)	5(31)	18(55)	5(100)	3(100)
Posgraduate degree	11(11)	3(7)	3(19)	5(15)	0(0)	0(0)
Master's degree	19(19)	8(19)	2(13)	9(27)	0(0)	0(0)
Doctorate degree	3(3)	1(2)	2(12)	0(0)	0(0)	0(0)

EW = Employed for Wages; SE = Self-Employed; F = Freelancer; S = Student; OFW = Out of work.

are highly educated (89%), which means they have completed at least a higher vocational education. It is possible to divide the respondents into 5 different categories: Employers (43%), Self-Employers (16%), Freelancers (33%), Students (5%) and Out of work (3%).

Procedure. The questionnaire was published mostly on social media boards, related to digital nomadism and remote work, and in communities. To increase the response rate, the questionnaire was also sent individually. Participants were invited to fill in a 5–10-min online questionnaire with a total of 25 questions. The questionnaire was divided into 5 different sections: demographic data (age, gender, nationality, education and occupation), company's stance on remote work (in order to filter who can work/works remotely), individual's preferences on working spaces, struggles and frustrations when looking for working spaces and opinions related to mobile applications and its information.

Results and Discussion. Users preferences were measured with open- and multiple-choice questions. Respondents were asked about socio-demographic characteristics including gender, age, nationality, and education level. Furthermore, they were asked about work-related characteristics, such as their company stance on remote work.

Participants were also asked about the primarily and second most common location where they work from. The choice options were Coffee shop and cafes, Coworking spaces, Home, Libraries, Park or Other (Table 2).

Table 2. Participants' preferences when choosing a location to work.

	Total (N = 80)	EW (N = 30)	SE (N = 16)	F (N = 32)	S (N = 2)
	n (%)	n (%)	n (%)	n (%)	n (%)
What location do you primarily work from? (N = 80)					
Coffee shop and cafes	4(5)	1(3)	1(27)	2(13)	0(0)
Coworking spaces	5(6)	1(3)	3(0)	1(8)	0(0)
Home	67(85)	26(87)	11(63)	29(73)	1(50)
Libraries	1(1)	0(0)	0(0)	0(0)	1(50)
Park	1(1)	0(0)	1(0)	0(0)	0(0)
Other (somewhere with a 4g internet)	1(1)	0(0)	0(0)	0(0)	0(0)
Other (Personal office / Shared office)	1(1)	2(7)	0(0)	0(0)	0(0)
What is the second most common location that you work from? (N = 80)					
Coffee shop and cafes	21(26)	7(23)	6(38)	8(25)	0(0)
Coworking spaces	23(28)	7(23)	5(31)	11(34)	0(0)
Home	15(20)	6(20)	2(12)	6(19)	1(50)
Libraries	12(15)	4(13)	3(19)	4(13)	1(50)
Park	7(9)	5(17)	0(0)	2(6)	0(0)
Other (somewhere with a 4g internet)	1(1)	0(0)	0(0)	1(3)	0(0)
Other (Personal office/ Shared office)	1(1)	1(4)	0(0)	0(0)	0(0)

EW = Employed for Wages; SE = Self-Employed; F = Freelancer; S = Student; OFW = Out of work.

Next, respondents were asked about their main motives to choose the mentioned places to work in. Figure 2 shows the eleven motives mentioned by respondents. Most participants mentioned "Comfort" (24%) as their main motive. This can be associated with the previous questions about the primarily and second most common location where they work from, in which people mentioned "Home" as their preferred location. "Affordable/Free accommodation" (13%) and "Social interaction with co-workers" (13%) were found to be the most important second motive. Respondents were also asked what working spaces attributes they considered the most important. Figure 3 shows the most rated attributes for the participants. Respondents attach more importance to "WIFI quality" (25,1%), "Location" (22%) and "Silence" (17,5%). The least important workspaces amenities/attributes are "Supporting Equipment" (13,5), "Price" (11,2%) "Plenty of space" (5,8%) and "Environment" (4,5%).

Furthermore, respondents were asked about their biggest struggles when working remotely. As Fig. 4 shows, most participants mentioned "Distractions/Interruptions" (38%) as the most common struggle. The second most common struggle is "Feelings of loneliness/Lack of interaction with others" (28%), followed by "Other" (13%) which includes "Knowing when to stop working" and "Family duties".

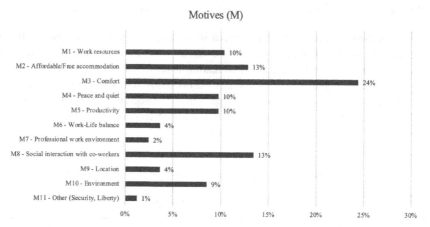

Fig. 2. Remote workers main Motives (M) when choosing places to work.

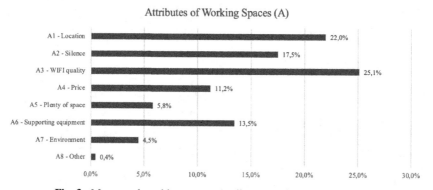

Fig. 3. Most rated working spaces Attributes (A) by remote workers.

2.2 Pilot Study

Sample. Five participants, between 18 and 27 years of age (M = 23.8, SD = 4.08) volunteered in this experiment. Inclusion criteria were working remotely/telecommuting

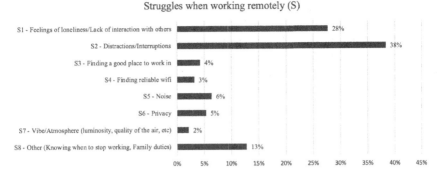

Fig. 4. Struggles (S) that the majority of remote workers face when working remotely.

or desire to work remotely for a day. 1 participant was a student, 1 was a freelancer, and 3 participants were employed for wages. Five users were considered enough for the emergence of a consistent pattern [24].

Procedure. The sessions were scheduled individually and had a maximum duration of 15 min. Tests were conducted using a mobile device provided by the researcher. All the sessions were video recorded to be transcribed later for producing verbal data.

The procedure was done in 2 stages:

(i) *Briefing.* The participants were informed about the general objectives of this study and signed an informed consent form to be recorded. A pre-questionnaire was applied to obtain participant's data regarding demographics, work experience, and experience/contact with mobile applications related to working spaces. Additionally, a cover story was given to the participants so that they could get familiar with the objective and purpose of the study. Cover Story: Imagine you are working remotely for a company. You have a home office; however, you get too distracted and there is too much noise so you cannot focus on your work. There are a few working spaces from your knowledge, but you do not want to waste your time going there and turning back if they do not meet your expectations. Luckily, you know a mobile app that can help. Having this scenario in mind, you are invited to operate with the mobile application and verbalize your feedback and critics and describe what you are looking and/or trying to do.

(ii) *Think-aloud protocol.* The users performed think-aloud protocol to find usability problems they face within each interface of each given task.

Results and Discussion. Although the pilot study consisted in a small sample of participants, it was possible to find a consistent pattern related to interface, iconography, and terminology. The 5 participants were familiar with remote work and mentioned past experiences with mobile applications related to working spaces. Overall, the participants were able to navigate through the application without major problems and it was possible to notice that some interface options were already familiar (e.g., back buttons, filter options, search bar). Participants showed satisfaction and interest related to the real-time information showed on screen. Some of the iconography presented in the prototype raised some questions and the size was considered small (see Fig. 5). Only one out of the five participants were familiar with the term "amenities" used in the prototype. The researcher highlighted and described each usability problem while participants were interacting with the system. The problems found were sorted into 4 categories: labelling, visual consistency, terminology, and interaction (see Fig. 6) and, later, resolved in further development.

Fig. 5. Prototype iconography: lack of labeling, small iconography, and poor visual representation.

Usability problem	Caterogy
Selecting only one filter option at the beginning prevines user from moving further in the process	Interaction
Overall small touch targets	Interaction
Lack of iconography labelling	Labelling
Iconography too small	Visual consistency
Wrong use of iconography for representation of a map	Visual consistency
User's weren't familiar with the terminology "Amenities"	Terminology

Fig. 6. Usability problems categorized.

2.3 Main Study

Sample. Ten remote workers, between 19 and 32 years of age (M – 25.7, SD = 4.79), participate voluntarily in this study. 3 participants were between the ages of 18 to 24 years of age and the 7 remaining participants were aged between 25–34 years. 1 participant was a student, 1 was a freelancer and 8 participants were employed for wages.

Procedure. The same procedure was applied as in the Pilot Study. Due to different circumstances, related with the COVID-19 pandemic, the main study was performed as online remote sessions through the application Zoom, where participants shared their computer screen while performing the given tasks. The tasks are as following:

(i)   "You need to work in a quiet space and also make video calls. Find a coworking space with individual desks and meeting rooms" (Fig. 7).

(ii) "You don't take public or private transportation but walk to the workplace. Choose a place that is closest to you" (Fig. 8).

(iii) "You want to use your car to go to the workplace due to the rain and also you need individual desks to spread your paperwork. Find a coworking space with individual desks and free parking lots" (Fig. 9).

(iv) "Locate the perfect place to work. See the location of the place called "Outside Lisbon" (Fig. 10).

(v) "You want to work in a cafe today while eating and drinking along the day. Find the most popular cafe to work" (Fig. 11).

Additionally, after each session, users evaluated the prototype according to the System Usability Scale (SUS) to quantify the users experience on product satisfaction. The SUS, developed by John Brooke in 1996 [25], is a 10 items questionnaire using a 5-point Likert scale numbered from 5 (as "Strongly agree") to 1 (as "Strongly disagree") and, if any item gets no answer, it should be assigned as a 3 (the center of the rating scale) [25].

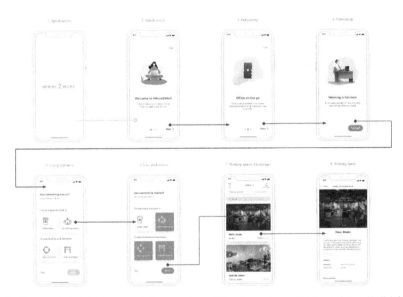

Fig. 7. Flow task I. A higher resolution version of the figure is available at: https://edirlei.com/papers/HCI2021/FlowTask_I.jpg

Results and Discussion. A task analysis was performed to identify usability problems. During the evaluation, usability problems were described, categorized, and analyzed according to Nielsen's heuristics [26].

Analysis and Heuristic Evaluation. In total, 6 usability problems were found and 2 out of 10 heuristics were violated. The heuristics violated were "Visibility of the system" (H1) and "Match between system and the real world" (H2). The missing heurists had no violations identified. The problems were sorted into 3 categories: visual consistency, terminology and interaction. The usability problems found in the task analysis are reported in Table 3. At the screen related to the user preferences, the visual of the header was

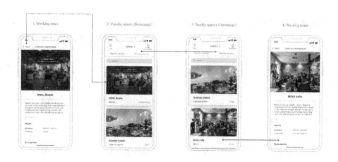

Fig. 8. Flow task II. A higher resolution version of the figure is available at: https://edirlei.com/papers/HCI2021/FlowTask_II.jpg

Fig. 9. Flow task III. A higher resolution version of the figure is available at: https://edirlei.com/papers/HCI2021/FlowTask_III.jpg

Fig. 10. Flow task IV. A higher resolution version of the figure is available at: https://edirlei.com/papers/HCI2021/FlowTask_IV.jpg

Fig. 11. Flow task V. A higher resolution version of the figure is available at: https://edirlei.com/papers/HCI2021/FlowTask_V.jpg

considered affordable, even though it is not. This problem can confuse and frustrate the user. Another problem, related to visual consistency, was identified in the homepage screen where the menu buttons were considered disabled due to their color and contrast. At the filters screen, the terminology "sockets" was not recognized, leading to the problem of missing representation icons in this screen. Having icons representing the labels can help users recognize terms faster [26]. The last 2 problems were identified in the working space screen. The wrong use of the term "full" when the place was not at its full capacity confused the user. Another problem found was the lack of comparison between everyday sounds and the decibel scale that was presented to the user. Being the user unfamiliar with the decibel scale, it is important that he understands the meaning of the scale without having to look up for a possible comparison outside the application [26].

Table 3. Common usability problems identified.

Place of occurrence	Problem category	Problem description	Heuristics violated
Screen 6 User preferences	Visual consistency	Header visual looks like it is affordable	H1
Screen 22 Popular spaces (homepage)	Visual consistency	Buttons (filters, map of spaces) look disabled	H1
Screen 30 Filters	Visual consistency	Missing representation icons	H2
Screen 30 Filters	Terminology	Term is not recognized: "Abundance of sockets"	H2
Screen 36 Working space	Terminology	Wrong use of word "full" when place is not at full capacity	H1
Screen 36 Working space	Interaction	No comparison between everyday sounds and decibel scale (dB)	H2

Note. "Visibility of the system" (H1), "Match between system and the real world" (H2)

SUS Results. After receiving the SUS results, to calculate each item's score contribution the range would scale from 0 to 4 [25]. All participants (P) scored over 80 points. 4 participants scored over 90 points while 2 scored the maximum of 100 points. 4 participants had lower scores between 80 and 87.5 (Fig. 12). Although, on the final SUS score the total average score was 91. According to Bangor et al. [27], the score 91 can be considered as "acceptable" on acceptability ranges, which represents an A score, as it is shown on Fig. 13.

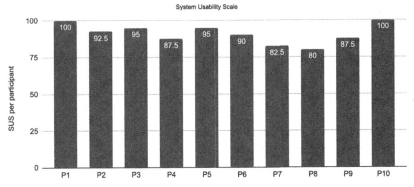

Fig. 12. SUS individual results.

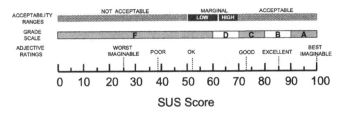

Fig. 13. SUS acceptability range by Bangor et al. [27].

3 Conclusion and Future Work

This paper presents the user evaluation stage from an on-going project aiming to develop a mobile application for workspace search. The ongoing project proposes a system design that explores working spaces' characteristics and features, aiming for comfort of remote workers when looking for a space. The objective of the paper is to report findings of a think aloud protocol method and a heuristic evaluation that identified potentially usability problems which could be faced by the users while interacting with the system. This study offered insights into the preferences for working spaces' characteristics that remote workers display when choosing where to work, which can be used when designing or developing a related mobile application or even a coworking space. The results showed that the majority of remote worker's chose to work at home as their first option, however, when working outside their home, remote workers' go for coworking spaces and cafes. The main motives of most remote workers when choosing a workplace outside their home are comfort, affordable accommodation, and the opportunity for social interactions with other remote workers. Remote workers' preferred workspaces amenities/attributes are the WIFI quality, the space location, and a silent environment. Through the usability tests the researcher identified potential usability problems that could impact users' overall experience. The SUS study revealed a score of 91 that can be considered as "acceptable" on acceptability ranges, representing an A. This study showed that applying a Think Aloud methodology can provide relevance and knowledge to improve a system's usability and experience. As a future work, the design review of the system and the implementation of real time sensors will be prioritized, followed by individual usability tests in order to obtain more feedback. The same methodology will be applied to the same target users. Therefore, it is interesting for future research to analyze which (other) preferred aspect of working spaces can be applied into this system.

References

1. Frand, J.L.: The information-age mindset: changes in students and implications for higher education. EDUCAUSE Rev. **35**(5), 15–24 (2000)
2. Hannam, K., Butler, G., Paris, C.: Developments and key issues in tourism mobilities. Ann. Tour. Res. **44**, 171–185 (2013)
3. Gibson, V.A., Lizieri, C.M.: The role of serviced office space in office markets and corporate property portfolios. University of Reading, Reading (1999)
4. Smeaton, D.: Self-employed workers: calling the shots or hesitant independents? A consideration of the trends. Work Employ Soc. **17**(2), 379–391 (2003)
5. Weijs-Perrée, M., van de Koevering, J., Appel-Meulenbroek, R., Arentze, T.: Analysing user preferences for co-working space characteristics. Build. Res. Inf. **47**(5), 534–548 (2019)
6. Oldenburg, R.: The Great Good Place: Café, Coffee Shops, Community Centers, Beauty Parlors, General Stores, Bars, Hangouts, and How They Get You Through the Day. Paragon House Publishers, New York (1989)
7. Lee, S.S.: Third places to work in the digital age: implications from coworking space users' motivations and preferred environmental features (2018)
8. Mulcahy, D.: Will the gig economy make the office obsolete? Harv. Bus. Rev. **3**, 2–4 (2017). http://hbr.org/2017/03/will-the-gig-economy-make-the-office-obsolete
9. Ec.europa.eu.: How usual is it to work from home? (2020) https://ec.europa.eu/eurostat/web/products-eurostat-news/-/DDN-20200424-1. Accessed 14 July 2020
10. Spinuzzi, C.: Working alone together: coworking as emergent collaborative activity. J. Bus. Tech. Commun. **26**(4), 399–441 (2012)
11. Huwart, J.Y., Dichter, G., Vanrie, P.: Coworking collaborative spaces for micro entrepreneurs. EBN Technical Notes, no. 1 (2012)
12. Moriset, B.: Building new places of the creative economy, the rise of coworking spaces. In: Proceedings of the 2nd geography of innovation international conference 2013. Utrecht University (2013)
13. Parrino, L.: Coworking: assessing the role of proximity knowledge exchange. Knowl. Manag. Res. Pract. **13**, 261–271 (2015)
14. Coworking Resources: Global coworking growth study 2020 (2019). https://news.malt.com/wp-content/uploads/2018/10/EFS-2018-Infographics.pdf. Accessed 29 Dec 2020
15. Fuzi, A., Clifton, N., Loudon, G.: New in-house organizational spaces that support creativity and innovation: The co-working space. Paper presented at R&D management conference, Stuttgart, Germany (2014)
16. Bouncken, R.B., Reuschl, A.J.: Coworking-spaces: how a phenomenon of the sharing economy builds a novel trend for the workplace and for entrepreneurship. Rev. Manag. Sci. **12**(1), 317–334 (2016). https://doi.org/10.1007/s11846-016-0215-y
17. Deijl, C.M.: Two heads are better than one, a case study of the co-working community in the Netherlands. Master's thesis. Erasmus University Rotterdam, Rotterdam (2011)
18. Fuzi, A.: Coworking spaces for promoting entrepreneurship in sparse regions: the case of South Wales. Reg. Stud. Reg. Sci. **2**(1), 462–469 (2015)
19. Workfrom (2021). https://workfrom.co/. Accessed 15 Jan 2021

20. LiquidSpace: rent flexible office from coworking, serviced offices, sublets & owner spec suites (2021). https://liquidspace.com/. Accessed 15 Jan 2021

21. Croissant: Enjoy coworking anywhere in NYC, Brooklyn, LA, SF, London & more (2021). https://www.getcroissant.com/. Accessed 15 Jan 2021

22. Nielsen, J.: Thinking aloud: the #1 usability tool (2012). https://www.nngroup.com/articles/thinking-aloud-the-1-usability-tool/. Accessed 11 Jan 2021

23. Deskmag.com: 2019 State of coworking: over 2 million coworking space members expected | deskmag | coworking (2019). http://www.deskmag.com/en/2019-state-of-coworking-spaces-2-million-members-growth-crisis-market-report-survey-study. Accessed 2 July 2020

24. Nielsen, J.: Why you only need to test with 5 users (2000). https://www.nngroup.com/articles/why-you-only-need-to-test-with-5-users/. Accessed 11 Jan 2021

25. Brooke, J.: SUS - a retrospective. J. Usability Stud. **8**(2), 29–40 (2013)

26. Nielsen, J.: Ten usability heuristics (2005)

27. Bangor, A., Staff, T., Kortum, P., Miller, J., Staff, T.: Determining what individual SUS scores mean: adding an adjective rating scale. J. Usability Stud. **4**(3), 114–123 (2009)

Feasibility of Estimating Concentration Level for not Disturbing Remote Office Workers Based on Kana-Kanji Conversion Confirmation Time

Kinya Fujita[✉] and Tomoyuki Suzuki

Tokyo University of Agriculture and Technology, Koganei 184-8588, Japan
kfujita@cc.tuat.ac.jp

Abstract. Aiming at reducing distractions of remote office workers while they are concentrating on their work, this study discusses the feasibility of estimating the concentration level of PC users. In particular, it focuses on the kana-kanji conversion confirmation time. Kana-kanji conversion, which is popular input method for Japanese, requires users to confirm that the converted kanji characters are correct. Since distributed cognition is known to increase reaction time, the confirmation time is expected to be affected by the cognitive resource allocated to the text-input task, i.e. the level of concentration on the task at hand. We conducted a set of experiments with six participants. We instructed them to copy kana text by typing and concurrently convert the given kana text into kanji. We set three conditions; Concentration, Dual-task, and Distraction. In the Dual-task condition, we gave an instruction to the participants to listen to the news and count the names of places mentioned in it while performing the main typing task. The Distraction condition was used in the final experiments that were conducted after lunch and light physical exercise for inducing fatigue and drowsiness. The results suggested that the kana-kanji conversion confirmation time statistically increases when a user is less concentrated on a task because of a subtask or some other distraction.

Keywords: Concentration level · Kana-kanji conversion · Cognitive resource

1 Introduction

COVID-19 has been forcing massive numbers of office workers to work at home. One serious issue regarding working-at-home is distractions that interrupt concentration. Various interruptions, e.g. pop-ups for e-mails, chat systems, and video meetings, distract workers from their tasks. When such interruptions occur, workers need to "store" their working memory, which is used for the task they are engaged in, in order to handle the interruption. Then, after finishing the interruption task, they need to recall the stored memory [1]. Thus, interruptions reduce the productivity of a worker by not only interrupting their tasks but also by requiring additional cognitive processes, i.e. storing and recall of working memory. Here, there have been studies that have tried to estimate of the level of interruptibility of workers on the basis of task boundaries [2, 3] and on automatic mediation of interruptions [4].

M. Kurosu (Ed.): HCII 2021, LNCS 12764, pp. 542–553, 2021.
https://doi.org/10.1007/978-3-030-78468-3_37

Although task-boundaries are opportune moments for interruptions, we should take note of the concentration level of the worker as well. Workers lose their concentration through a decrease in motivation, fatigue, and other reasons. Such times are also chances for interruption. In addition to interruption management, an automatic means of estimating a worker's concentration level might enable systems to feedback to workers their concentration level and consequently improve their productivity. This paper discusses the feasibility of such an automatic estimation of the concentration levels of office workers using PCs.

Only few studies have tried to assess or estimate the concentration level of office workers. Miyagi et al. proposed CTR [5], which is defined as the aberration rate from the log-normal distribution of the completion times of simple tasks. Although CTR enables a quantitative assessment of the concentration level of a worker, it is not applicable to a real office work scenario because CTR principally relies on the homogeneity of the tasks, and real tasks are complex, not homogeneous.

On the other hand, the cognitive resource of a person is basically constant [1]. This allows us to redefine the concentration level as the amount of cognitive resource allocated to the main task. In addition, in studies on distributed cognition, it is widely known that a dual-task scenario increases response time [6, 7]. Thus, we expect that concentration level can be estimated on the basis of the increase in the time for a cognitive process.

The main issue is the requirement for homogeneity of the tasks. Tasks need to be homogeneous rather than complex in order to discuss the increase/decrease in time for each task. However, real tasks are obviously not so homogeneous. Therefore, we need to find a homogeneous cognitive process that repeatedly appears in real office-work scenarios. The existence of such a cognitive process would allow us to estimate the concentration level of a worker engaged in actual office work.

Here, we focused on the kana-kanji conversion confirmation time (KKCCT), which is supposedly a homogeneous, indispensable, and frequently performed cognitive process in Japanese text input. This study reports the feasibility of using the increase in KKCCT under dual task and fatigue conditions, which was observed in a kana to kanji conversion text input task.

2   Related Work

2.1   Cognitive Resource and Multitasking

Working memory is a cognitive system that holds temporarily and manipulates information, whereas short-term memory only refers to temporal storage [8]. The capacity of working memory is known to have individual differences [9].

Reaction time increases in a multitasking scenario, in which a person performs two or more tasks at a time [10]. This phenomenon is explained as a decrease in the available cognitive resource, i.e. working memory, due to interference from the subtask [7]. The decrease in task-performance measures such as reaction time is attributed to the overhead for temporarily storing and recalling the working memory for the main task [1].

These findings suggest that an unintentional decrease in the cognitive resource allocated to the task the worker is engaged in, i.e. loss of concentration, increases the time of the cognitive process in the task. That is to say, we can estimate the concentration level of a PC user from the change in the time of the cognitive process, i.e. KKCCT in this study.

2.2 Mental Status and Keystrokes

Keystroke dynamics, which represents individual variations in keystroke-related indices such as durations of keystrokes and intervals between keystrokes, has been studied as a biometric authentication technique [11, 12]. In recent years, keystroke dynamics has been reported to reflect the user's mental status. Emotional states have been estimated by using keystroke features [13] and by combining keystroke and mouse features [14]. Mental stress has been demonstrated to induce noticeable differences in bigram and trigram features [15]. Detection of boredom and engagement has also been tried [16].

As these studies suggest, keystrokes are supposed to reflect the mental status of users. Therefore, the cognitive resource allocated to the main task may also be reflected on the keystroke dynamics in some form.

3 Cognitive Process of Japanese Text Input with Kana-Kanji Conversion

As mentioned above, Japanese text input requires users to devote a cognitive process for confirming that the converted kanji characters on the PC screen are the expected ones. Figure 1 illustrates the process of kana-kanji conversion.

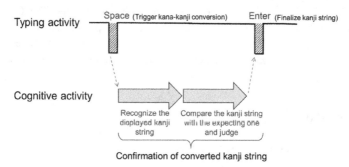

Fig. 1. Sequence of kana-kanji conversion and its confirmation in Japanese text input.

Users basically perform the following sequence:

1. (Type kana characters composing a string.)
2. (Collaterally confirm that the characters have been correctly typed.)
3. Trigger kana-kanji conversion by pressing the spacebar.
4. Recognize the displayed kanji string.
5. Compare the recognized kanji string with the expected one.

6. Judge whether the displayed string is correct.
7. If correct, finalize the kanji characters by pressing the Enter (in most cases) key.

As shown in the figure, the time from pressing the spacebar to pressing Enter or some other key is supposed to be spent confirming the converted kanji characters. Thus, this study experimentally discusses the feasibility of KKCCT being affected by the concentration level of the user.

4   Method

4.1   Design of Experiment

The preferable task for the experiment is text input similar to what occurs in actual office-work scenarios. However, free text writing requires composition, and devising content could affect KKCCT. On the other hand, just copying text by typing appears to be too simple compared with the actual tasks in office-work scenarios. Thus, we chose a task involving copy by typing, but with kana-text to kanji-text conversion. We instructed the participants to read a fairy tale written in kana and type it in kanji.

In addition, we presumed two situations of losing concentration. One is a situation in which a worker has something on his/her mind other than the task at hand, e.g. the schedule of activities on the coming weekend. The other is one in which a worker has nothing unnecessary in his/her mind but becomes distracted by fatigue, poor health, or drowsiness. Thus, we set three conditions: Concentration, Dual-task, and Distraction. The details of each condition are described in Subsect. 4.4.

4.2   Participants

We recruited eight university students who had been using computers on a daily basis. Two out of the eight participants had a habit of finalizing the converted kanji string before they confirmed it; i.e., they corrected the errors after finalizing the converted kanji string. Thus, we excluded their data from the analysis target because typing-based features will not adequately reflect their cognitive process for confirming the converted kanji string.

The experiment was conducted after an ethical review by a committee at the university. All participants agreed to take part in the experiment by signing an informed consent form.

4.3   Copy by Typing Task

The text to be copied was a fairy tale that was written in kana characters [17]. As shown in Fig. 2, the original text was displayed on the left half of an LCD display with 1920 × 1080 resolution, while the right half displayed a word processor window for typing the converted kanji text.

To avoid any influence from the computer input system, we turned off the autocomplete and predictive kanji conversion functions. We did not instruct the participants about whether each word had to be converted into kanji or to be left in kana; we let them judge by themselves.

Original kana text  Typed kanji text

Fig. 2. Example of the display during performance of the task. The left window displays the original kana text, and the right window is for typing the kanji text.

4.4 Procedure and Conditions

Figure 3 represents the time course of the experiment.

Practice	10 min
Break	5 min
Concentration condition	30 min
Subjective scoring and break	15 min
Dual-task condition	30 min
Subjective scoring	-
Physical exercise	15 min
Lunch and break	60 min
Break inducing drowsiness	15 min
Distraction condition	30 min
Subjective scoring	-
Dummy task	10 min

Fig. 3. Time course of the experiment.

We repeatedly conducted a 30-min copy-by-typing session for each condition. We logged the typing timings by using our own recording program, which worked on Microsoft Windows 10. We also required the participants to score their subjective concentration level after each session. The order of the Concentration and Dual-task conditions was switched for some participants to counter-balance learning effects. The last of the sessions (conducted in the afternoon) were conducted under the Distraction condition in order to include the influence of lunch and fatigue. We conducted an additional 10-min dummy task to avoid the ending effect, i.e. an increase in motivation due to the expectation of ending work, on the Distraction condition.

We instructed the participants to perform 30-min and 2.5-h exercises two days before and a day before the experiment for acclimating them to the task and the system, especially to the keyboard. The details of the experiment conditions are as follows.

Concentration Condition. To let participants concentrate without imposing mental stress, we instructed them to perform the task as they would usually engage in their own tasks. We also requested them to wake up at least three hours before the experiment. The room temperature was kept at 19 °C.

Dual-Task Condition. For simulating a situation in which a worker has something on his/her mind other than the task to be performed, we imposed a subtask in addition to the main copy-by-typing task. Furthermore, we wanted to examine a situation where competition occurs in cognitive resource requirements between the main and sub- tasks. Thus, we chose a linguistic cognitive subtask, since the main task required linguistic cognition. We instructed the participants to wear headphones, listen to a news show while performing the main task, count the numbers of place names mentioned in the show, and report the total number they counted after finishing the 30-min session.

Distraction Condition. To distract the participants, we had them perform 15 min worth of physical exercise (walking) before lunch and the afternoon session as a means of inducing light fatigue. Then, we allowed the participants to take lunch and take rest for 15 min in a room kept at 26 °C with the expectation that it would cause drowsiness. After these protocols, we started the 30-min task session.

4.5 Analysis

First, we analyzed the subjective concentration levels, the number of input characters, and the accuracies for validating the control of the concentration levels. The accuracy of the input characters Acc was calculated by using Eq. 1. The variables N, Cw, Cm, and Cu, represent the number of kana-kanji conversions, incorrect characters, missed characters, and unconverted (supposedly by mistake and unconsciously) kana characters in the session. The unconverted kana characters were determined by three evaluators after the experiment.

$$Acc = \{N - (Cw + Cm + Cu)\}/N \tag{1}$$

Next, we analyzed the tendency of the KKCCT based on the histograms. However, KKCCT was widely distributed and several percent of the samples exceeded 1 s. We also examined the relationship between the length of the original kana character string and the KKCCT and found a weak but positive correlation. Thus, we only targeted the data for the kana strings shorter than 7 characters in order to reduce the effect of the string length.

We excluded the data on which the participant converted the kana string multiple times, i.e. the cases that a suitable kanji character was not suggested at the first conversion, to ensure that the analysis would not be influenced by factors other than the cognitive process for kanji confirmation. We also excluded cases in which an error occurred while typing a kana string to be converted because the recognition of the error and the process for preparing for correction appeared to affect the cognitive process for confirming the converted kanji string. KKCCT data longer than 1 s were also removed.

5 Results

Table 1 summarizes the subjective concentration levels, numbers of input characters, and accuracies. The subjective concentration levels of all the participants were lower in the Dual-task and Distraction conditions than in the Concentration condition ($p < 0.001$, 0.001, paired t-test). The decrease in concentration level was less in the Distraction condition than in the Dual-task condition in 5 out of 6 participants.

Table 1. Summary of subjective concentration levels, number of input characters, and accuracies. Co, Du, and Di represent the Concentration, Dual-task, and Distraction conditions, respectively. ** and * on the bottom line represent the results of a student t-test with the Concentration condition (**: $p < 0.01$, *: $p < 0.05$)

Participant	Subjective concentration level (%)			Number of input characters			Accuracy		
	Co	Du	Di	Co	Du	Di	Co	Du	Di
P1	90	50	70	2434	1919	2221	0.977	0.978	0.983
P2	90	50	70	2207	1784	1976	0.990	0.972	0.982
P3	80	60	60	1985	1780	1916	0.993	0.986	0.982
P4	90	50	75	2273	2028	2562	0.963	0.951	0.961
P5	85	50	60	1401	1140	1486	0.980	0.948	0.952
P6	80	60	75	1649	1352	1610	0.972	0.968	0.947
		**	**		**	n.s.		*	*

The numbers of input characters showed a similar tendency to the subjective concentration levels. The decrease in the number of input characters was observed in the Dual-task and Distraction conditions in all the participants except for the Distraction condition in P4 and P5. The decrease was significant in the Dual-task condition, but not significant in the Distraction condition ($p = 0.001$, 0.36, paired t-test).

The accuracies again showed a similar decrease in the Dual-task and Distraction conditions, except for P1 ($p = 0.027$, 0.044, paired t-test).

In summary, it appeared that the concentration levels of the participants were successfully controlled in terms of subjective awareness and task performance. The results also suggest that the effect of control was weaker in the Distraction condition than in the Dual-task condition.

Figure 4 represents examples of the fluctuation of KKCCT in the Concentration condition for P1 and P6. In these graphs, we did not exclude the KKCCTs for the strings longer than 6 characters, but excluded the data longer than 1 s and cases with typing errors or multiple conversions. As can be seen, the KKCCTs for P6 had a greater deviation than those for P1. Even after excluding the data for the strings longer than 6 characters, this apparently random fluctuation remained in P6 (not shown). In contrast, the KKCCTs ranged mainly between 200 to 400 ms in P1 with some exceptionally longer samples.

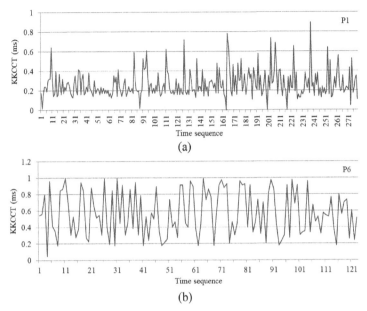

(a)

(b)

Fig. 4. Time-sequence diagrams of KKCCT in Concentration condition for (a) P1 and (b) P6 after exclusion of KKCCTs longer than 1 s and cases with typing errors or multiple conversions.

The histograms of KKCCT for each participant are listed in Fig. 5. Single-peaked patterns appear in the results of five participants, except P6. Although we assumed that kana-kanji conversion would be a homogeneous cognitive task, the actual KKCCTs were widely distributed from 100 ms to more than 1000 ms. The reason for this distribution is discussed in Subsect. 6.2.

In the Dual-task condition, the peaks shifted to the right, i.e. KKCCT increased, in P1, P2, P3, and P4 (p = 0.041, 0.006, 0.02, 0.065, t-test). Consequently, the average KKCCT values also increased. No clear difference was observed in P5. In P6, whose pattern was exceptional, the peak appeared to shift to the left, against our expectation.

In the Distraction condition, the peaks again appeared to shift to the right in P1, P2, and P3. (p = 0.001, 0.045, 0.131, t-test). No clear difference from the Concentration condition was observed in P5 and P6. The peak appeared to shift to the left in P4.

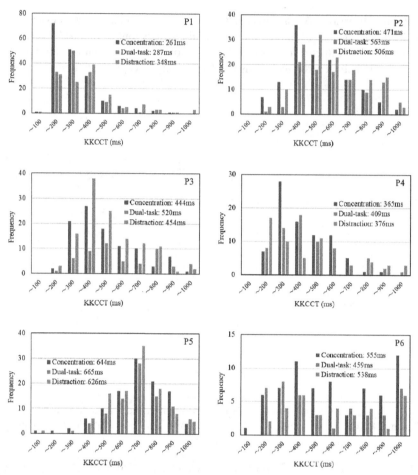

Fig. 5. Histograms of KKCCT for each participant. The left (blue), center (orange), and right (gray) bars represent the results in the Concentration, Dual-task, and Distraction conditions, respectively. The values at the right of the graph legends are the average KKCCTs for each condition. (Color figure online)

6 Discussion

6.1 Validity of KKCCT as a Cognitive Index

The measured KKCCTs were widely distributed from 100 ms to over 1000 ms even after limiting the converted character strings to be shorter than 7 characters. A previous study suggested that the reaction time of humans to light or sound is around 200 ms and that the reaction time increases to around 300 ms in the case of unknown stimuli [18].

Here, as Fig. 4(a) shows, KKCCTs ranged mainly between 200 and 400 ms in P1 with some occasionally longer samples. The distributions of P2, P3, and P4 were similar, as shown in Fig. 5. These results suggest that KKCCT reflects the duration of the cognitive process for confirming the converted kanji string, but that it is also influenced by some other factors.

In addition, P5 and P6 had more KKCCTs longer than 500 ms, as shown in Fig. 4(b). Since the results shown in Fig. 5 are only for the kana strings shorter than 7 characters, the complexity of the converted strings is not the cause of this longer KKCCT. The details of the user behaviors remain to be analyzed.

In total, although KKCCT might include some cases not covered by our hypothesis, KKCCT appeared to reflect the cognitive processing time for confirming the converted kanji string in a statistical sense. To use KKCCT as a cognitive index, we will need to apply statistical processing because KKCCT seemingly has random fluctuations, as can be seen in Fig. 4. One possible method is to average KKCCT for several minutes. However, since the simple average is seriously affected by outliers, we need to examine other indices as well.

6.2 Effect of Concentration Level on KKCCT

This study hypothesized that loss of concentration decreases the cognitive resource allocated to the main task and consequently KKCCT increases. In the experiment, the KKCCTs increased in the Dual-task condition in P1, P2, P3, and P4 and in the Distraction condition in P1, P2, and P3. The change in concentration level of these participants appeared to increase KKCCT.

On the other hand, in P5, whose KKCCT ranged over 500 ms, and P6, whose histogram showed an exceptional pattern, we did not observe a clear increase in KKCCT.

In summary, we observed two types of user. One type of user has KKCCTs mainly distributed around 300 ms; their KKCCTs seem to be longer when they concentrate less on the task. This group supported our hypothesis. The other type of user has longer KKCCTs and appears not to be influenced by the concentration level. The apparent absence of the effect of concentration level in this group could be attributed to the anomalous distribution patterns of KKCCTs. We will need to explore other types of indices for these users.

In addition, because the decrease in task performance was smaller in the Distraction condition, we also need to review and improve our experiment design in terms of control of concentration level, especially for the Distraction condition. Aside from the need for further improvement, KKCCT appeared to reflect the concentration level in some types of PC user, i.e. users with shorter KKCCTs, in a statistical sense.

6.3 Limitations

The analysis based on KKCCT is obviously not applicable to users who finalize the converted kanji string before finishing confirmation. In addition, the copy-by-typing task used in this study is rather formulaic compared with tasks appearing in real office-work scenarios. Further experiments with improved design are needed. Finally, since kana-kanji conversion is a process specific to Japanese text input, we need to explore similar homogeneous cognitive processes underlying other languages in order to apply our idea to them.

7 Conclusion

Aiming at estimating the concentration levels of office workers, this study analyzed KKCCT, which is supposed to be a homogeneous cognitive process that is influenced by the distribution of the cognitive resource. The results of a kana-to-kanji copy-by-typing task performed by six participants suggested that KKCCT statistically increases while a user is disturbed by a subtask or is otherwise distracted. In other words, KKCCT appears to reflect the concentration level of an office worker using a PC.

On the other hand, some participants' KKCCTs showed an exceptional distribution pattern. Further study is needed, in particular, to improve the method for controlling the concentration level.

Acknowledgments. The authors would like to thank Professor Hiroshi Shimoda at Kyoto University who provided useful suggestions on the experiment design. This work was partly supported by funds from the Japan Society for the Promotion of Science (KAKENHI).

References

1. Salvucci, D.D., Taatgen, N.A.: Threaded cognition: an integrated theory of concurrent multitasking. Psychol. Rev. **115**(1), 101–130 (2008)
2. Iqbal, S.T., Bailey, B.P.: Leveraging characteristics of task structure to predict the cost of interruption. In: Proceedings of the SIGCHI Conference on Human Factors in Computing Systems, pp. 741–750 (2006)
3. Tanaka, T., Fujita, K.: Study of user interruptibility estimation based on focused application switching. In: Proceedings of the ACM 2011 Conference on Computer Supported Cooperative Work, pp. 721–724 (2011)
4. Kobayashi, Y., Fujimoto, Y., Fujita, K.: Development of e-mail delivery mediation system based on interruptibility. IEEE Access **7**, 94084–94096 (2019)
5. Miyagi, K., Kawano, S., Ishii, H., Shimoda, H.: Improvement and evaluation of intellectual productivity model based on work state transition, In: Proceeding of the 2012 IEEE International Conference on Systems, Man, and Cybernetics, pp. 1491–1496 (2012)
6. Pashler, H.: Dual-task interference in simple tasks: data and theory. Psychol. Bull. **116**(2), 220–244 (1994)
7. Schmitter-Edgecombe, M.: The effects of divided attention on implicit and explicit memory performance. J. Int. Neuropsychol. Soc. **2**(2), 111–125 (1996)
8. Baddeley, A.D., Hitch, G.: Working memory. Psychol. Learn. Motiv. **8**, 47–89 (1974)
9. Daneman, M., Carpenter, P.A.: Individual differences in working memory and reading. J. Verbal Learn. Verbal Behav. **19**(4), 450–466 (1980)
10. Davis, R.: The human operator as a single channel information system. Q. J. Exp. Psychol. **9**(3), 119–129 (1957)
11. Obaidat, M.S., Sadoun, B.: Verification of computer users using keystroke dynamics. IEEE Trans. Syst. Man Cybern. Part B **27**(2), 261–269 (1997)
12. Bergadano, F., Gunetti, D., Picardi, C.: User authentication through keystroke dynamics. ACM Trans. Inf. Syst. Secur. **5**(4), 367–397 (2002)
13. Epp, C., Lippold, M., Mandryk, R.L.: Identifying emotional states using keystroke dynamics, In: Proceedings of the SIGCHI Conference on Human Factors in Computing Systems, pp. 715–724 (2011)

14. Shikder, R., Rahaman, S., Afroze, F., Al Islam, A.A.: Keystroke/mouse usage based emotion detection and user identification. In: 2017 International Conference on Networking, Systems and Security (NSysS), pp. 96–104 (2017)
15. Kolakowska, A.: Towards detecting programmers' stress on the basis of keystroke dynamics. In: 2016 Federated Conference on Computer Science and Information Systems (FedCSIS), pp. 1621–1626 (2016)
16. Bixler, R., D'Mello, S.: Detecting boredom and engagement during writing with keystroke analysis, task appraisals, and stable traits. In: Proceedings of the 2013 International Conference on Intelligent User Interfaces, pp. 225–234 (2013)
17. http://hukumusume.com/douwa/. Accessed 24 Dec 2020
18. Donders, F.C.: On the speed of mental processes. Acta Physiol. (Oxf) **30**, 412–431 (1969)

A Smart City Stakeholder Online Meeting Interface

Julia C. Lee[✉] and Lawrence J. Henschen

Northwestern University, Evanston, IL 60208, USA
j-leeh@Northwestern.edu, henschen@eecs.northwestern.edu

Abstract. We propose an online meeting interface aimed for smart city projects and which can be extended/modified for other types of online meetings. The interface will be connected to the central data storage for the smart city project, and there will be processing software tools behind the interface to analyze/format the data collected from the interface.

Keywords: Smart city · Stakeholder · Online meeting · Interface · Database

1 Introduction

1.1 Smart City

Smart City projects are booming around the world. Smart City projects are aimed to provide quality of life, economic competitiveness, and sustainability [1]. Smart city projects are being pushed forward by the development of the science/technology of different fields, especially Information and Communication Technology (ICT); smart city projects also host the development of these fields. Over 250 Smart City projects around the world were reported in 2017 [2]. Smart City projects are ranked by research firms and media based on whether "the cities that have been able to combine technologies, leadership and a strong culture of 'living and acting together' should be able to better withstand the most damaging effects of such crises," [3].

Smart city projects integrate information and communication technology (ICT) and various physical devices connected to the IoT network to optimize the efficiency of city operations and create a people centric urban society environment. [8] People-centric projects are designed by the people, built by the people, and aimed for the people. One of the important means to achieve the "people-centric" goal is communication among all stakeholders during the design and development of the project.

1.2 Stakeholders

A project is normally initiated and supported by its stakeholders. Stakeholders are the "people of Smart city projects". A large project like a smart city project has a large number of stakeholders from different areas. Researchers have been trying to identify the stakeholders that might be involved in a smart city project [6]. For example, Jayasena et al.

© Springer Nature Switzerland AG 2021
M. Kurosu (Ed.): HCII 2021, LNCS 12764, pp. 554–565, 2021.
https://doi.org/10.1007/978-3-030-78468-3_38

postulated that stakeholders of a smart city project can come from 13 areas: academia and research institutions, local and regional administrations, financial suppliers/investors, energy suppliers, citizens, government, property developers, non-profit organizations, planners, policy makers, experts and scientists, political institutions, and media [4]. Stakeholders contribute to and support the smart city project, but stakeholders also are beneficiaries of the project. The involvement of stakeholders from different areas is the key to the success of a smart city project [5].

A critical early activity in a project is for stakeholders to present their requirements and contribute ideas on how the project should be handled. Stakeholders need to be involved throughout the entire development process. Of course, specific issues may involve different specific stakeholders, and common issues may involve all the stakeholders. The communication among stakeholders can be and should be very frequent and dynamic [5].

1.3 Communication Among Stakeholders

Meetings among stakeholders are an important and efficient way to accomplish dynamic communication. In a conventional meeting, participates are seated together to talk; there will be a predefined agenda; a moderator assures the progress of the meeting; discussion among and activities by the participants may be recorded. Due to the world-wide COVID-19 pandemic, meetings are more and more going online. We propose an online meeting interface for smart city projects that allows for virtual (and therefore medically safe) meetings but also has some interesting advantages over face-to-face meeting formats. Although we present and illustrate the idea using smart city projects as the example, the concepts are easily extended/modified for other types of online meetings.

Online meetings may not be as "intimate" as in-person meetings, but this form of meeting has advantages besides avoiding in-person disease transmission, advantages that could be useful in normal – non-pandemic – times. Some obvious advantages are no need for travel or to find a venue – saving time, effort, and budget. Because of traffic reduction, there can be environmental benefit, too. One important advantage of online meetings is that the ideas produced from the meeting and the interactions among the participants can be more easily and much more accurately recorded.

Existing platforms, such as zoom, are inadequate for the kinds of interaction among participants that are necessary for efficient and productive project planning/design/implementation meetings. Zoom, for example, allows users to make comments, but these are displayed outside the scope of the main window. It is hard for any participant other than the main speaker to present his/her information beside raising his/her hand and then being unmuted. More ways to allow interaction and encourage participation are needed. For example, a participant should be able to search the project history and previous stakeholder meetings to make prompt comments on the issues being discussed. The meeting manager/moderator should be able to summarize the discussion not just verbally but also in text. This summarized text should be stored in the project database for future reference.

The meeting interface and system structure that we propose will allow interactions among the meeting participants (in a controlled way to avoid collision, of course), allow automatic and accurate recording of all the meeting data, and allow reference to and searching for related information during the meeting. The recording process includes not only voice recording; the voice recognition system will convert the voice into text, so both voice recording and text recording will be saved in the project database for future reference.

2 An Efficient Online Meeting System for Smart City Projects

We will present our online meeting system structure in the following subsections. In Sect. 2.1 we present the interface of the meeting system. In Sect. 2.2 we present the system structure. In Sect. 2.3, we use an example meeting scenario to illustration the usage of the proposed online meeting system.

For simplicity of reference, we abbreviate our meeting system as OMS4SC.

2.1 Interface Windows

The interface of the OMS4SC includes 3 different types of windows and groups of common widgets. The common utility widgets are similar to the ones provided by many of the existing general purpose online meeting software applications such as zoom [7]. The widgets include the participant video views, the join/leave button, the mute/unmute buttons for video and speaker, etc.

One of the key differences between the general purpose online meeting applications and our OMS4SC is to allow more dynamic interactions during the meeting. The participants are not just webinar listeners and question providers; they are the stakeholders of the smart city project and active contributors to the meeting.

Participant's Input Window. The participant window in OMS4SC includes more options than just typing a message to the meeting manager or asking a question. The participant's input window is shown in Fig. 1.

- An input field to type in the full name (first, last, middle initial) of the participant.
- A dropdown menu to allow the participant to choose which area he/she is from. The dropdown menu will include all the stakeholder areas for this particular project.
- A dropdown menu to allow the participant to choose an institute that he/she belongs to. The menu will display all the institutes involved based on the area he/she chose in the first dropdown menu. A choice of "Other" will be provided if the meeting invites new institute representatives.
- A search field to allow the participant to type keywords for searching. The search field is provided 3 buttons: "project", "city", and "web". After the participant types in the search criteria, he/she presses one of the buttons to direct the searching to the corresponding domain. Note that the participant can copy and paste the search result to the input field below to send to the manager or the shared window depending on what button he/she presses below the input field.
- A multi-purpose Input field for input messages serving different purposes.

  - When the "attention" button is pressed, the message in the input field will be sent to the meeting manager. The meeting manager can decide what he/she would like to do.

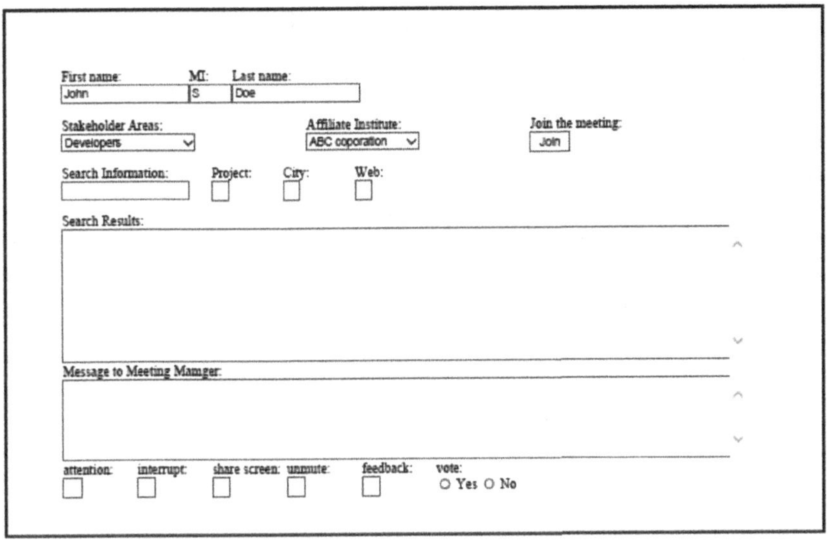

Fig. 1. Participant's input window

- When the "interrupt" button is pressed, the message in the input field is also sent to the meeting manager with higher priority. This requests the meeting manager's immediate attention, who may then possibly change the current meeting process, e.g. allowing the participant to speak or changing the shared window content. See the following two dashed items.
- When the "interrupt" button is pressed, the message in the input field is also sent to the meeting manager with higher priority. This requests the meeting manager's immediate attention, who may then possibly change the current meeting process, e.g. allowing the participant to speak or changing the shared window content. See the following two dashed items.
- When the "share screen" button" is pressed, the content of the input field will be displayed on the shared window after the request is granted by the meeting manager.
- When the "unmute" button is pressed, the participant is asking to speak, and his/her speaker will be unmuted after the meeting manager grants the request.
- When the "feedback" button is pressed, the content of the input field will be sent to the meeting manager as feedback when a "feedback" request is initiated by the meeting manager.

- A yes/no button for voting on a specific issue.

Meeting Manager's Windows. Besides the window/tool used by the meeting initiator in a general-purpose online meeting system, the meeting manager in OMS4SC will have 4 additional windows with more functions to control the meeting progress interactively and efficiently. Two of them will be the same as all the other participants have, i.e. the participant input window and the shared display window. In addition, the meeting manager will have two windows used to manage/control the meeting progress. We will illustrate the two control windows in the following.

Global Control Window. One of the meeting manager's windows is used for global control of the meeting. Figure 2 shows the possible functions provided by the global control window.

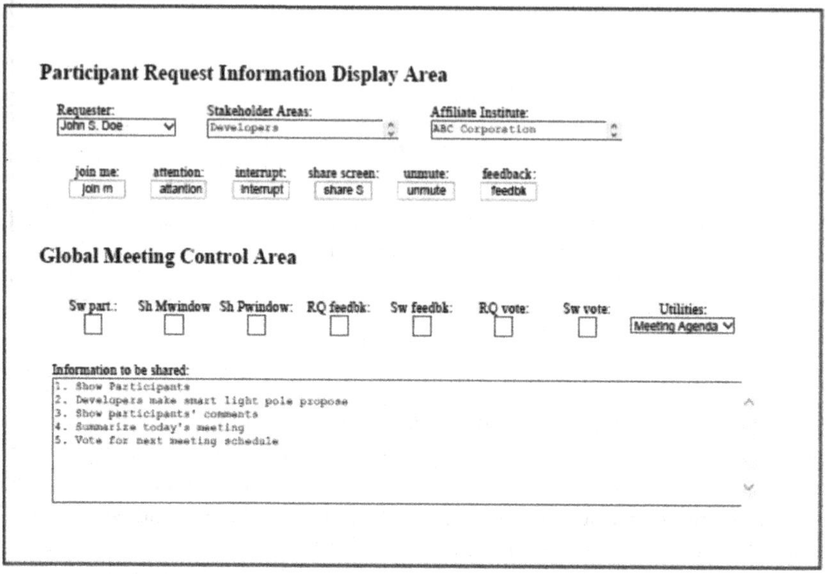

Fig. 2. Meeting manager's global control window

This window is divided into two areas: the "Participant Request Information Display Area" and the "Global Meeting Control Area".

The "Participant Request Information Display Area" provides fields that allow the meeting manager to monitor the requests from the participants. A highlighted button indicates that some participant(s) is (are) making requests. The participants who are making a request are listed in the left most dropdown menu on the top. The corresponding area and institute associated with the listed participant is shown in the next two fields on the top. When the meeting manager clicks on the name, a pop-up "Individual Control Window" will be opened to allow the meeting manager to respond to each individual request separately. The "Individual Control Window" will be described in the next subsection.

In the "Global Meeting Control Area" of the window, there are functionality buttons to allow the meeting manager to perform different meeting control functions such as:

- Show participants. The list of participants along with their stakeholder areas and institutes will be displayed on the shared meeting widow.

- Switch shared meeting window. This button switches the contents of the current shared meeting window with the contents chosen by the meeting manager, which normally will be the contents of the input information from an individual participant.
- Switch shared meeting window with a computer window (not part of the OMS4SC). This button allows the manager to switch to a window containing a tool not built into OMS4SC, such as MS Office or a browser or another application.
- Request for feedback. The meeting manager can send a request to all participants for feedback on the presentation/issue currently in progress.
- Request for vote. The meeting manager can send a request for a vote to all participants on the current issue.
- Show vote result. The meeting manager can show the vote result, so that all the participants will know the status of the vote on the issue.
- A dropdown menu can be used to provide more options/tools to the meeting manager such as:

  – Show meeting agenda.
  – Show collected feedback.
  – Show history of an issue.
  – Show previous meeting data.
  – Show statistics and/or charts relating to an issue.

Individual Control Window. As indicated above, the meeting manager can reply to an individual participant's request separately in the "Individual Control Window". Figure 3 Shows the possible functions provided by the Individual Control Window.

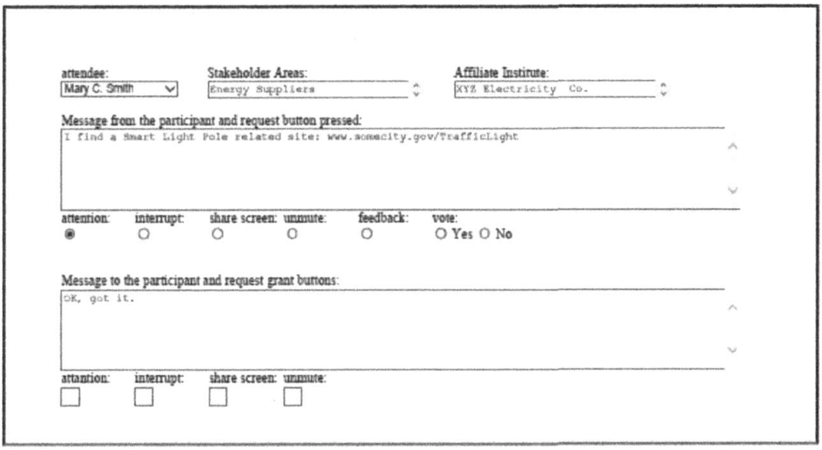

Fig. 3. Individual control window for meeting manager

The Individual Control Window has the following fields/information:

- At the top of the window, the name, representation area, and associated institute of the participant is displayed.

- There is a text area containing the message sent to the meeting manager or some information the participant would like to share with other participants.
- The next row contains the indicators that indicate what the request submitted to the meeting manager is, for example:

  - Attention: request attention from the meeting manager.
  - Attention: request attention from the meeting manager.
  - Interrupt: request an interrupt to the current meeting process, for example, a presentation. This could be a request to share some important information related to the issues being presented or a request to be unmuted so that he/she can speak.
  - Share screen: see "interrupt" above. The participant requests to share his/her screen to show some important or closely related information he/she found. If this indicator is on, the interrupt must also be on.
  - Unmute: the participant is asking to be unmuted so that he/she can speak to the other participants. If this indicator is on, the interrupt must be also on.
  - Feedback: this indicates that the participant is responding to the request by the meeting manager for feedback on an issue.
  - The vote indicator: this indicates the voting choice by the participant when the meeting manager requests a vote on an issue.

- The next two rows are used by the meeting manager to respond to the participant's request:

  - The text area allows the meeting manager to type in some message to the requesting participant.
  - The next row of buttons allows the meeting manager to take corresponding action, e.g. allow the participant to share screen or to speak. If the meeting manager pressed the "attention" button, the message in the text area is sent to the requesting participant. In this case, no unmute and screen switch is performed because the meeting manager deems that the request is not urgent enough to interrupt the main course of the meeting.

Shared Display Window. The shared display window in OMS4SC can be used to display the presentation of the main speaker; it can also display the information participants request to be displayed when the request is granted by the meeting manager. The display can have different looks if the owner of the displayed content uses different presentation tools, e.g. power point or just the window format of the meeting tool. The shared window is display-only. No widgets for performing other functions are on this window, and this window is available to all the participants. Of course, one can minimize it when necessary.

However, if the shared window is displaying a computer native window (not part of the OMS4SC), then that window inherits the computer "native" windows functionality. Of course, only the owner of the window can perform whatever the functions are, others can still just view the contents, for example a MS power point window.

The following two figures show examples of possible shared window displays (Figs. 4 and 5).

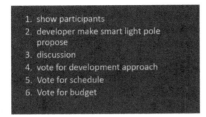

Fig. 4. Shared window in meeting   **Fig. 5.** Shared computer "native" window

2.2 Supporting System Structure

In this section we will describe the system structure that supports the OMS4SC as shown in Fig. 6 below.

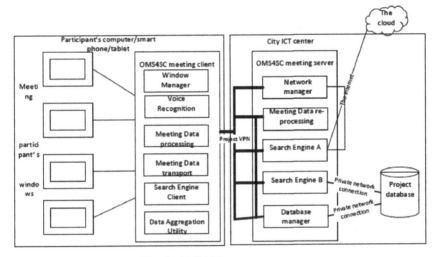

Fig. 6. OMS4SC system structure

The system utilizes a client-server structure. The server part will be inside the information technology center of the city that hosts the Smart City project. The client-side software will be on the computers, smart phones, or tablets of the participants. For security purposes, the communication between the clients and the server should be via a VPN that is dedicated to the Smart City project.

On the client side of the system, there are the following elements.

- Window Manager is responsible to manage the windows opened for the participant. Besides the general window managing functions such as open/close, minimize/maximize, etc., the window manager is also responsible to collect data from each window and send the data to other client-side software. For example, send raw data to the meeting data processing software.

- The Voice Recognition software records the speech of the participants and converts it into text. The speech text will also be sent to the meeting data processing software for further processing before being sent to the server.
- Meeting Data Processing software is responsible to group, categorize, and format the data collected from the participants' meeting activities. For example, group data by individual participant; group data by subject, etc. [9].
- The meeting Data Transport element sends data to the server. It may do some further data processing before transferring, for example encrypting the data for security purposes.
- The Search Engine Client allows the participants to search the project database.
- The Data Aggregation Utility provides tools for computation such as statistics, summations, averaging, comparison, etc.

Note that a client-side data cache is needed on the client side. This data cache is appropriate to be located on the meeting manager's computer. All data collected as described above are sent to the client-side cache before being processed.

On the server side, there are the following system components.

- The Network Manager Component manages network traffic. The system allows access to private data storage, the cloud, and the public Internet. The Network Manager Component plays an important role to ensure the efficiency and security of the system [10].
- The Meeting Data Processing component processes the data sent from the client. This processing can be done during the meeting duration; it can also be done after the meeting is closed. Processing during the meeting allows storing the real-time process of the meeting. Processing after the close of the meeting allows analysis of the data from the entire meeting and further aggregation [9].
- Search Engine A directs the search by the client side to the designated clouds and public internet.
- Search Engine B directs the search by the client side to the private project database.
- The Database Manager Component performs tasks essentially the same as a general-purpose database manager [11].

2.3 A Sample Meeting Scenario

In this subsection, we will walk through a sample meeting scenario to illustrate some of the functionality of our proposed OMS4SC system.

Assume the initial house-keeping process is the same as a general-purpose meeting system. The meeting notice is either posted on the project website or sent to potential participants through email. When a participant registers for the meeting, a link will be sent to the participant to join the meeting when the meeting starts.

When the meeting is started by the meeting manager, participants will click the link to join the meeting. Before a participant actually joins the meeting, the participant's input window will pop-up asking the participant to type in his/her name and to choose the associated area and institute, after which he/she clicks the "Join" button. He/she is in the meeting. His/her name will be sent to the client-side data cache. The participant's small video window will show up on the screen.

While waiting for participants to show up, the meeting manager displays the meeting agenda on the shared screen by using the meeting manager's Global Control screen.

When all the anticipated participants show up, the meeting manager displays the list of participants with their associated areas and institutes in the shared window by using the Global Control screen. When there is a new participant attending the meeting, the meeting manager may give an oral introduction of the new participant.

The meeting manager then orally introduces the main speaker, say a person named John Doe representing the system development area from ABC Corporation.

The meeting manager switches the shared display window to the main speaker's power point presentation window on the speaker's native computer, again, by using the Global Control screen. Note that the Window Manager component on the client-side system should be able to make the switch. The Window Manager software also needs to make sure that once a participant's native window is switched to the shared window in the system, the native window's contents can be accessed by the client-side software, e.g. Meeting Data Processing, etc.

The main speaker starts to do his/her presentation about an issue in the smart city project. The "Smart Light Pole" initiative is aimed to dynamically control the street lighting in order to provide ample illumination to the street traffic, to conserve energy, to be friendly to the environment, and to communicate traffic data with the Smart City Data Center in real time [12].

Suppose that during the presentation, one of the participants does some web search while listening to the presentation and finds some reference information and would like to send it to the meeting manager for reference. He/she copies from the search results text area of his input window, pastes the information in the message area of his input window, and clicks the "attention" button to send the information. In the meeting manager's Global Control window, the "Attention" indicator blinks. The meeting manager clicks the indicator/button, the Requestor drop down menu will list the name of the participant(s) who made an "attention" request. When the meeting manager clicks the name on the list the "Individual Control Window" pops up. The related information is in the text area below the requestor's name. The meeting manager can decide what to do with this request and information. If he/she decides to put the information into the summary of all the responses, he/she can simply type in an acknowledgement to the requestor and click the attention button.

Assuming that while the main presentation is progressing, there is another request from a participant. The meeting manager's Global Control window shows two flashed indicators – the "interrupt" indicator and the "unmute" indicator. The meeting manager clicks the requestor's name, and an Individual Control Window pops up. From the individual control window, the meeting manager sees a request from a local government representative asking for an interruption. The message from the participant text area shows "schedule conflict!". The meeting manager recognizes that this is going to be a short interrupt and quick correction, so he/she decides to allow the interrupt by clicking both the "interrupt" and "unmute" buttons, allowing the participant to speak about the schedule conflict. Meanwhile, the main presentation makes a note/correction on the schedule.

After the main speaker finishes the presentation, the meeting manager displays a summary including all the comments made from the participants by using a utility tool in the drop-down menu and clicks "Sh Mwindow". The shared display window will show the comments made by all the participants. Of course, the summarized information will be further processed and sent to the project database.

The meeting manager types the date for continuing the meeting in to the "information to be shared" text area of the Global Control Window and clicks both "Sh Mwindow" and "RQ vote" buttons. The meeting manager can speak to all participants asking for a vote on the next meeting schedule. Participants can use "Participant's Input Window" to commit the vote. The meeting manager can click the "Sw Vote" button to display the voting result in the shared display window.

The meeting manager can use the tool provided in the Global Control window to generate a quick summary for this meeting. The summary will include (but not be limited to): Date/time of the meeting, participants and associated representing areas and institutes, planned agenda, main speaker and topic, number of comments from the participants, issues voted, voting results, etc. If needed, the meeting manager can do a comparison with previous meetings. If there are numerical issues involved, statistical or other computational comparisons can also be included in the summary.

The meeting manager announces the commit to the next meeting and ends of this meeting.

Note that the client-side system software components will continue working until all the collected data have been processed and sent to the server.

3   Summary and Discussion

We have presented an online meeting system that can serve Smart City projects efficiently and intelligently. We illustrated the interface for the OMS4SC system and its system structure.

The system provides real time interaction among the meeting participants and allows them to search the project database, clouds, and/or internet to present related information and comments promptly. The system records all the information from the meeting automatically and stores the information into the project database for future reference. The system utilizes more advance technology such as voice recognition and text analysis. Smart City projects will be benefit from these characteristics of the system.

The system can be easily modified for special purpose on line meetings of other projects/businesses. The modification could be as easy as changing the database and network interface of the system to adopt to different environments.

AI powered analysis can be adopted to the system to further increase the efficiency and intelligence of the system [13, 14].

References

1. Deloitte. https://www2.deloitte.com/us/en/pages/consulting/solutions/smart-cities-of-the-fut ure.html. Accessed 19 Dec 2020
2. GuidehouseInsights. https://guidehouseinsights.com/news-and-views/more-than-250-smart-city-projects-exist-in-178-cities-worldwide. Accessed 19 Dec 2020
3. U.S.News. https://www.usnews.com/news/cities/articles/2020-09-18/singapore-ranks-as-the-top-smart-city-for-2020. Accessed 19 Dec 2020
4. Jayasena, N., Mallawarachchi, H., Waidyasekara, A.: Stakeholder Analysis for Smart City Development Project: An Extensive Literature Review. https://www.researchgate.net/public ation/331225610_Stakeholder_Analysis_For_Smart_City_Development_Project_An_Ext ensive_Literature_Review. Accessed 26 May 2020
5. Karin, A., Malin, G.: Stakeholders' stake and relation to smartness in smart city development: insights from a Swedish city planning project. Gov. Inf. Q. **35**, 693–702 (2018)
6. Marrone, M., Hammerle, M.: Smart cities: a review and analysis of stakeholders' literature. Bus. Inf. Syst. Eng. **60**, 197–213 (2018). https://doi.org/10.1007/s12599-018-0535-3
7. Zoom Help Center. https://support.zoom.us/hc/en-us/articles/206175806. Accessed 21 Dec 2020
8. Smart city – Wikipedia. https://en.wikipedia.org/wiki/Smart_city. Accessed 02 Jan 2021
9. Marcu, D., Popescu, A.-M.: Towards developing probabilistic generative models for reasoning with natural language representations. In: Gelbukh, A. (ed.) CICLing 2005. LNCS, vol. 3406, pp. 88–99. Springer, Heidelberg (2005). https://doi.org/10.1007/978-3-540-30586-6_8
10. James, K., Keith, R.: Computer Networking: A Top-Down Approach, 7th edn. Pearson Publishing Company, London (2016)
11. Hoffer, J., Ramesh, V., Topi, H.: Modern Database Management, 13th edn. Pearson Publishing Company, London (2019)
12. Lee, J.C., Henschen, L.J.: Design interface and modeling technique. In: Kurosu, M. (ed.) HCII 2020. LNCS, vol. 12181, pp. 97–111. Springer, Cham (2020). https://doi.org/10.1007/ 978-3-030-49059-1_7
13. Microsoft Azure – Text Analytics. https://azure.microsoft.com/en-us/services/cognitive-ser vices/text-analytics/. Accessed 13 Jan 2021
14. Young, T., Hazarika, D., Poria, S., Cambria. E.: Recent trends in deep learning based natural language processing. In: Computational Intelligence Magazine, pp. 55–75. IEEE (2018)

Fostering Empathy and Privacy: The Effect of Using Expressive Avatars for Remote Communication

Jieun Lee[1], Jeongyun Heo[1(✉)], Hayeong Kim[1], and Sanghoon Jeong[2]

[1] Kookmin University, Seoul, South Korea
{jel4046,yuniheo,hayeongkim}@kookmin.ac.kr
[2] Mookwon University, Daejeon, South Korea
diasoul@mokwon.ac.kr

Abstract. The importance of effective remote communication is currently being emphasized as education moves from offline to online due to acceleration of the Untact Era (a contact-free society). In this study, we analyze the hindrances to effective distance learning, observe the effect on users of communicating through Expressive Avatar (EA), and suggest effective ways to use EA. First, through a questionnaire, 84% of the respondents quantitatively demonstrated experiencing a psychological burden due to exposure of their faces, in addition to low concentration during remote classes. Second, through in-depth interviews, they were found to prefer to replace their images with two- and/or three-dimensional avatars and believed that the avatars' unique characteristics were important. Content using EA is expected to contribute to improved quality in distance learning by reducing psychological burden and promoting transmission of emotions.

Keywords: Expressive avatar delivering empathy · Gesture interaction · Eye-gaze interaction · Emotion design

1 Introduction

As social distancing becomes vital due to the COVID-19 pandemic situation and the mode of non face-to-face work has changed, remote communication using videoconferences has become important [1]. The Ministry of Education announced the opening of online school from March 31, 2020, along with social distancing regulations to prevent the spread of the COVID-19 virus [2]. UNESCO provides distance-learning materials and educational policy measures during the COVID-19 crisis, highlighting the importance of distance-learning, to ensure that the education of students who have become distant in an educational environment with a large number of people (For example school, workplace, public institution) is not interrupted. The problem that occurred with the start of non-face-to-face distance-learning classes through online school opening was the dissemination of technology and content.

However, as the problem of dissemination was gradually resolved, issues faced by users in distance education turned into limitations of communication. Many people predict that distance lessons will be more flexible compared to face-to-face lessons, but

© Springer Nature Switzerland AG 2021
M. Kurosu (Ed.): HCII 2021, LNCS 12764, pp. 566–583, 2021.
https://doi.org/10.1007/978-3-030-78468-3_39

researchers predicted that the autonomy (space limitation due to the range of camera angle) between teachers and students may be lower than before due to the space constraints caused by the video camera being on during distance lessons. In the previous experiment which observed the recognition process through the video camera during the remote class, researchers found that users feel burdened (anxiety about privacy invasion of exposure to cameras) when they are exposed through video camera. As a result of this behavior, the user felt a psychological pressure to stay within the scope of the camera during class and during distance education, it caused the phenomenon of watching the self in the screen. Afterwards, researchers recognized that the user felt bored of distance lessons due to the limited camera angle and interactive area. This leads to a decline in the user's concentration, which can predict a decline in the quality of education as a result of the inability to concentrate on the class [3].

To facilitate distance-learning classes, non-verbal communication should be improved. The process of conveying non-verbal communication smoothly presupposes a video connection between students and teachers. However, most of the students are reluctant to turn on their video cameras for non-face-to-face (remote) lessons.

Marist Circle media from Dr. Peterson, according to a survey conducted by Peterson, 29.6% of the 18 students who do not use a camera daily during video classes ranked the most important reason as self-consciousness. Many students choose to "turn off my videos" while taking a virtual class. Most students generally agreed that turning on videos in online classes is helpful for learning, but suggest that they would turn them off for comfort and privacy reasons. Dr. Peterson argues that these learners' attitudes may have traditionally been challenged by unfamiliar situations, situations with mental, and emotional discomfort. However, researchers suggested that the situation in which a large number of learners turn off their video cameras for a long period may cause a decrease in their motivation for learning during class, and it may hinder expressing active opinions and the formation of a positive class atmosphere [4]. The student's behavior of placing visual restrictions [5] (video-off, no eye contact) on access to distance-learning classes makes giving educational feedback to students difficult for teachers. This is because the teacher's ability to "see" students is limited.

Teachers' role is central to measuring and teaching students' understanding by catching non-verbal behavior during learning, and the context of the entire class is completed through immediate feedback. This process makes it possible to see that the solution to problem situations during distance-learning classes lies in smooth communication between teachers and students. Teachers must not only emphasize the importance of transmitting knowledge and information but also communicate and exchange emotions with students who currently need to be physically distanced from school. This is because for the teacher and student to have a successful class, the possibility of recognizing the other's emotions more completely increases when it is possible to grasp the other's non-verbal behaviors, including the behavior of displaying the other's emotional cues, eye contact, and body language. However, since the use of video cameras during class is currently recommended, the possibility exists that the degree of satisfaction of the teacher's visual information may not be sufficient, which may degrade the student's educational experience [6, 7].

According to the results of a one-off survey on video cameras conducted by Castell, 41% of users said they were reluctant to turn on videos because of their complexes about their appearance. Teachers' opinions on this proposed to provide a new alternative to expose students' faces less. This study is a new communication method using the EA to address the communication problem that is disconnected through video-off and the psychological factor that induces the "video-off" mode of users among the problems of remote class prolonged due to the COVID-19 pandemic situation. We wanted to observe the impact on users. By using Expressive Avatar (EA) in remote classes, the psychological burden that users feel can be reduced, and emotional expression can be used to facilitate communication between students and teachers. This it expected to ultimately contribute to enhancing the quality of learning.

2 Consideration of Existing Research to Overcome the Limitations of Distance-Learning

2.1 Emoticon and Emoji

Emoticon is a method mainly used in text-based communication and is mainly used in Internet chat and remote communication situations through smartphones. Developed from the form of early pictorial words, it was labeled emoticon as a combination of "emotion" and "icon" meaning "symbol." Currently, it is visualized in the emoticon 2D method, which was made with the existing symbols in social networking services such as kakao talk, line, and telegram messenger, and it is used to prompt users' communication more smoothly and induce interest [8]. During remote communication, vague expression of emotion through text often elicits "expression" of emotion through emoticons, which illustrate the emotions of subjects who use mainly graphic icons. Emoticons were introduced with e-mail, and their ultimate purpose is to convey emotions using simple symbols express writers' mood to readers.

However, with the advent of social networking services, mobile communication has transformed. As the number of e-mail users decreases and the number of social networking service users increases with the spread of smartphones, gif-shaped icons are more vivid and used. According to the analysis of the results of facial recognition enhancement experiments using animation by Gonzalez-Franco of the Institute of Electrical and Electronics Engineers (IEEE), researchers concluded that participants could exhibit a stronger bond with animation avatars with voice and motion. It was said that the increased interest by the children demonstrated a positive effect of improving familiarity [9]. As new communication spaces expand to users, they want content that allows them to share emotions and communicate with others. As such, emoji was created as an element that helps to build intimacy in communication in cyberspace. Similar to an emoticon, it is an emotional mediator given to users as the communication path of smartphones expands [10, 11]. However, due to the incongruity of face recognition and difficulty in distinguishing from others due to similar characters, emoji had a difficult condition to become a medium for long-term emotion transmission [12]. As the new space of remote communication expands, a new emotional communication medium is needed for students and teachers who engage in long-term distance lessons.

2.2 Expressive Avatar (EA) Purpose of Use

Communication with the public using avatars is becoming increasingly common. On November 17, 2020, SM Entertainment in Korea proposed a character that exists in the real and virtual worlds. Aespa members and avatars, a group that exist in real life, coexist in the virtual and real worlds at the same time and communicate through a sync connection signal of Navis, an artificial intelligence system. The avatar that exists in the virtual world acts like an existing member's alter ego, accepts real-time member information posted on social networks, and applies it to the avatar.

Expressive Avatar (EA) is a 3D expression method that devises an extended range from Emoji's communication, which is transmitted in 2D format with text. This is a virtual video filter applied through the user's face recognition and was created for expressing the user's personality and mood. In November 2020, the Korea Institute of Electronics and Telecommunications (ETRI) and EQ4 all conducted research and development on the Sign Language Avatar, hosted by the Korea Deaf People's Association to expand the right to access information for the deaf. Sign Language Avatar provides information on the COVID-19 personal quarantine guidelines, step-by-step standards for social distancing, and current actions to users by investigating the information needed by the deaf. It was conducted to secure the right to know of people with hearing loss by providing disaster information in sign language to overcome the limitation of accessibility of the digitally underprivileged in essential communication [2].

Table 1. Transformation program used for remote classes

Transformation program	Voice dubbing program
Snap camera	Naver clova
Samsung AR Emoji	Typecast

Table 1 shows the programs currently used by users when conducting remote classes. These are face modification and voice dubbing programs currently used in remote classes due to the issue of the portrait rights of teachers and the psychological stability of users. It can be seen that through these new needs of users, they are more focused on distance-learning classes and are seeking ways to communicate emotionally with the person who conducts the conversation [13]. S. Lee and his colleagues, who have researched important elements for expressing emotions, proposed a Lifelike Responsive Avatar Framework (LRAF) that can convey emotional expression through realistic avatars during face-to-face communication. Experiments using LRAF-created avatars showed that happiness and sadness can be conveyed accurately (i.e., happiness and sadness were correctly identified) [14]. MarGonzalez-Franco and colleagues, who researched recognition through avatars, proved experimentally that avatar self-identification can be enhanced through changes in facial expressions during conversation and not just through general visual resemblance [9]. The progressed EA study applied to EA information caught from the gaze and behavior that humans unconsciously process during communication. Thus, experimental results are presented to measure the user's sensation through an avatar that provides autonomous communication motion after presenting the user with text information through a free and extensive remote situation. A study by M.D. Hanus and Fox found that communication using avatars in a virtual environment increased persuasive power. In particular, when the user can customize the avatar's shape, the reliability of the avatar's message increases [15] (see Table 2). Having researched Intelligent Virtual Agents (IVA) over the past 15 years, Norouzi and his colleagues suggest that human–agent collaboration and learning or user perception of virtual agents in social collaboration is an important research topic [16].

Table 2. Overseas case of content creation using visual humans

Author name (Year)	Journal name	Main findings
Lee et al. (2010) [14]	International Conference on Intelligent Virtual Agents	Suggesting Lifelike Responsive Avatar Framework, which expresses emotion states through realistic avatars
Gonzalez-Franco et al. (2020) [10]	IEEE transactions on visualization and computer graphics	Self-identification about avatars increases through the facial change in conversation
Hanus et al. (2015) [15]	International Journal of Human–Computer	Increase communication persuasion by customizing message expressions delivered through customized avatars
Norouzi et al. (2018) [16]	The 18th international conference on intelligent virtual agents	Providing systematic review on Intelligent Virtual Agents and suggesting the importance of human perception on virtual intelligence

These examples show that EA is a relatively novel, unique, and attractive element of communication. This study was conducted to discover whether EA can provide a form of expression attractive to users in a space where two-way communication is difficult psychologically. If a situation in which a user's body is directly exposed through a combination of EA and user video is limited, the burden learners' experience when turning on their video is expected to decrease. Therefore, by switching on their video camera, the number of active participants in class increases. In all likelihood, the class atmosphere will improve, students will respond more proactively, and they will participate voluntarily in various ways. In this study, surveys and interviews were conducted to analyze user experiences and to demonstrate specifically the effects of using EA in remote classes.

3 Experiment

3.1 Survey

Purpose of the Survey. The survey proposed to identify students' psychological situation in remote classes and discover the factors that affect the class. We tried to determine what shape(s) and expression(s) students preferred when they used Expressive Avatar (EA) instead of appearing themselves.

Participants and Procedure of the Survey
As shown in the Table 3 above, the survey was conducted on 25 people who have conducted distance-learning classes more than ten times over 30 days. In particular, 17 student's position and 8 teachers in the class leader's positions participated the survey. Before the experiment, the experiment situation of a videoconference using an EA was provided to the user in the Wizard of Oz Prototyping method. The survey was conducted online, and a 7-point evaluation scale and multiple-choice questions were designed to allow a wide selection of user opinions. It took about 5 min on average to proceed each survey.

Table 3. Criteria for participants of survey

Content	
Standard	Those who have conducted distance-learning classes more than 10 times over 30 days
Experiment type	survey
Experiment time	5-min
Number of respondents	25 people (10 males, 15 females)
Position	17 Students (average age: 25.8…), 8 Teachers(average age: 31.75)

Survey Scale
Facial expressions were created by expanding the Paul Ekman's Macro-Expression, which expresses a clear emotional form, through micro-expressions, including happiness, displeasure, anger, fear, surprise, and sadness. Among 24 expressions proposed by Paul Ekman's in the study of emotion classification six were proposed by combining [17] micro-expressions and excluding macro-expression emotion such as happiness, displeasure, anger, fear, surprise, and sadness that are unlikely to be expressed in remote classes. 'Amusement' fine expression A, 'satisfaction' fine expression B, 'concern' and 'sternness' combination C, 'disdain' and 'sternness' combination D, 'alertness' and 'dejection' combination. The six expressions of F that combine E, 'wonder' and 'concern' were applied to Expressive Avatar (EA) (see Fig. 1).

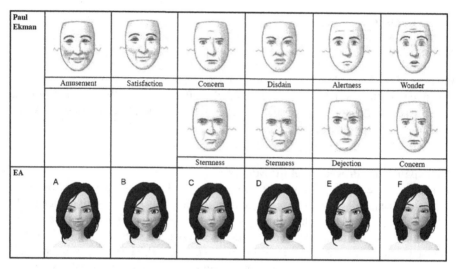

Fig. 1. EA Expression 01. [17]

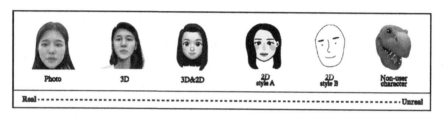

Fig. 2. EA Expression 02

We proposed 6 EA types, from real to unreal, to find out what kind of form the subjects prefer to see to others in online classes and what EA image they want to see when they see other users [10]. The most basic person photo was used as the reference point for real, and in turn, the most similar 3D avatars, 2D&3D combined avatars, flat 2D avatars, very simple avatars, and character avatars were placed in order. The most basic portrait photo is the reference point for real, and the 3D avatar that resembles the picture most, the 2D&3D combination type avatar, the 2D avatar in the flat form, the avatar with only eyes, nose and mouth, and the avatar of the character are not human. In addition, by providing real and unreal Expressive Avatar (EA), we tried to understand the allowable level of exposure of user's personal information and visual elements that can be distinguished when looking at others [18, 19] (see Fig. 2).

Survey Results and Implications

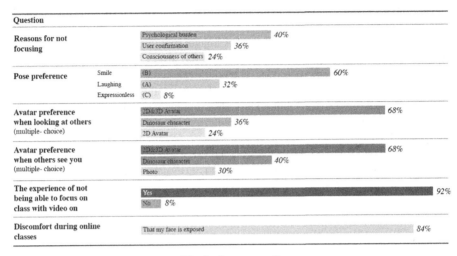

Question		
Reasons for not focusing	Psychological burden	40%
	User confirmation	36%
	Consciousness of others	24%
Pose preference	Smile	(B) 60%
	Laughing	(A) 32%
	Expressionless	(C) 8%
Avatar preference when looking at others (multiple-choice)	2D&3D Avatar	68%
	Dinosaur character	36%
	2D Avatar	24%
Avatar preference when others see you (multiple-choice)	2D&3D Avatar	68%
	Dinosaur character	40%
	Photo	30%
The experience of not being able to focus on class with video on	Yes	92%
	No	8%
Discomfort during online classes	That my face is exposed	84%

Fig. 3. Survey results

a) Concentration of the class according to the face exposure

Of the users, 92% answered yes to the question of whether they had any experience in being unable to concentrate on learning because of their appearance on the screen during class. For this reason, 40.00% mentioned the psychological burden of showing one's face, 36.00% answering that they could not concentrate for checking their face and 24% of them could not concentrate for checking the face that others see. Through the content derived, it was confirmed that the concentration of the class was reduced due to the psychological burden of exposing their faces or privacy on the screen during the remote class (Fig. 3).

b) Reasons for turning off the video cameras

84.00% of the participants were confirmed to be burdened with the situation of turning on their video cameras during remote classes. Through the content derived, proving quantitatively that users who conduct remote classes in the same context as the existing user survey do not turn on the video cameras, because they feel burdened by the situation in which their faces or privacy are exposed, was possible.

c) Preferred EA Appearance and Visual Expression

As for the expression students wanted to see onscreen or what expression they preferred during remote classes, 60% preferred B (smile), which is a facial expression derived from "satisfaction" in Paul Ekman's human facial expression analysis; 32% chose A (laughing) derived from "enjoyment"; and 8% preferred C (expressionless) derived by combining "worried" and "hardening."

In the questionnaire conducted about provision of EA, a marked difference was found in the preferences of questions about the EA image that expresses themself and what they want others to see. In the case of the EA images that are intended to be displayed to other users, the EA image that represents itself has a very high preference for Non-Avatar in human appearance (68.00%). The preference for EA, which shows a human appearance (68.00%), was equally high as that of EA they wanted to show. Next, dinosaur characters scored 40% (double choice) and 36% (double choice), respectively. Survey results show that in remote classes, users preferred EA for delivering images rather than photos that expose faces. The second highest preference for fully unreal images—dinosaur characters—can be attributed to some users preferring not to be exposed in remote classes. The highest preference for 2D and 3D avatars supports existing research results that require each person's characteristics to represent them- or themself or to recognize others during remote classes.

3.2   In-Depth Interview

Purpose of In-Depth Interview. The in-depth interview provides more specific, deeper content than that gathered through the survey.

Table 4. In-depth interview target

Content	
Standard	Those who have conducted distance-learning classes more than 10 times over 30 days
Experiment type	In-depth interview
Experiment time	30 min
Number of respondents	5 of the survey participants (2 males and 3 females)
Position	3 students, 2 teachers

There were five in-depth interviewees: Three students participating in the survey and two teachers were randomly selected (see Table 4, Fig. 4).

In-depth interviews were conducted on a one-to-one basis but through Zoom due to COVID-19. This prevented opinions from being contaminated by responses from other interviewees. Interviews were conducted three days after the survey, and the interview duration per person did not exceed 30 min. The procedure and common questions shown in Table 6 were used, and additional questions were asked according to the interviewee's responses, allowing in-depth analysis of EA's effect in remote classes.

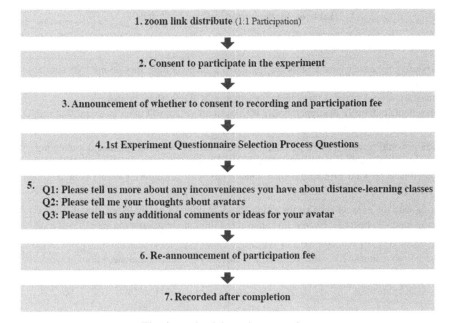

Fig. 4. In-depth interview procedure

In-Depth Interview Results Analysis

Table 5. In-depth interview results (student)

Interview result 01 (student)
I pay more attention to the screen of my face than to see other people's video screens If you apply the avatar filter, I expect that I will be able to focus a little more on the class because I am less concerned about my face
The feeling of someone looking into me during a distance class, but if I apply an avatar, I think it will ease the burden because I'm seeing a substitute, not my body
Sometimes I have to turn off the video screen, but I wonder if someone is watching me. I think that if this part is replaced with an avatar, the autonomy of body movements will increase, and the burden will be reduced
I want to show my face as a character, and I want other people to be human faces. Others want me to be easy to recognize and I want to show my face
I use Zoom correction because of the part that is visible to others, but I think that if it is replaced with an avatar, the burden will be reduced and the class will be able to focus
Sometimes I feel as if I'm talking to the wall, I feel as if I'm lacking communication. I think using an avatar is a good way to draw the whole interest of the class

Table 6. In-depth interview results (teacher)

Interview result 02 (teacher)
Considering the case where avatars are applied to students, I hope they do not look similar to each other Elementary school students think that concentration will help them improve High school students in the upper grades often turn off video, so I think an avatar that supports facial recognition will be very helpful in finding out whether they are focusing on learning
I think it would be nice if there were a lot of avatar actions, whether I read and imitate my facial expressions, or press the action I want to apply, and if there are such things, I think it will be possible to respond without having to chat or talk with voice during class (without stopping the class)
Among with the expressions that the avatar shows to other users, the expression that is too smiling seems to be tense. Even if it is an avatar, I think it is important to show a soft look without tension
If there is no response from the students, feel that they are teaching alone. I think it would be nice if there were actions such as cheers or applause through avatars

a) Expressive Avatar (EA) to relieve psychological burden

Analysis of interview responses, especially those of students, confirmed that problems arising from consciousness of others' gaze during distance learning and its psychological burden were highly felt. On the other hand, if EA was used in distance learning, psychological burden was reduced, making it possible to focus better in class. Although not clearly shown in the survey, an unusual finding was that one person wanted to be shown as an avatar or character, not as an actual person and another wanted to be shown in his or her real photograph for clarity (see Table 5).

b) How to use Expressive Avatar (EA) classes

The results of analyzing the contents of the interview conducted with the teacher are as follows. When conducting distance classes, lower grades have difficulty concentrating on the class, and higher grades turn off videos and a large number of students take classes. Using EA helps higher grade students improve their concentration by inducing video on. In addition, it was expected that students in the lower grades would be able to proceed with interest-oriented learning. In addition, there was an opinion that students could be distinguished only by creating a unique avatar for each student by adding each individual's personality to the avatar's motion and appearance. He added that if contents such as applause and action using avatars are produced, it will be able to help a lot in forming the atmosphere of the class. Through such interview results, it was verified that it would be possible to provide personal identity and convey emotion expression using EA in distance classes (see Table 6).

4 Conclusion and Future Work

The Untact Era is accelerating due to uncertain circumstances, especially the COVID-19 pandemic. As social distancing became important and labor moved to remote workplaces, communication through video conferencing rapidly gained importance. The same happened in education, where distance learning is actively being conducted. Among distance education's problems, prolonged due to COVID-19, this study identified the communication problem of users voluntarily turning off their video cameras. To counteract the psychological factor that induces users to do so, we observed the effect of communicating through Expressive Avatar (EA). In addition, a survey and in-depth interviews were conducted to analyze user experiences and to detail the effects of using EA in distance education. Through existing research, we found that users are aware of EA, and we attempted to understand the extent of EA's influence on them. That happiness and sadness can be clearly communicated in expressing emotions through avatars was confirmed (Lee, S.). Furthermore, results of another study confirmed that not only external similarity to an individual but also similarity of the user's facial expressions during a conversation can increase self-identification (Mar-Gonzaleza-Franco). Thus, the avatar was expected to be a medium that could affect the user's emotions, including trust in the remote class. In demonstration of this, the experiment was conducted by recruiting subjects taking remote classes.

The study's findings are summarized as follows. First, students turned off video due to the psychological burden (invasion of privacy) of exposing one's face onscreen, in turn leading to their decreased concentration on class content. Second, results confirmed that they preferred EA, which can deliver their images to some extent, rather than use of their actual photos, also felt to invade their privacy. Third, as for EA's form, the preference for unreal characters was quite high, but the most preferred form was 2D and 3D avatars, in which individual characteristics expressed individual students' images and shapes. This suggests the importance of creating an avatar that reflects each student's unique identity, personality, and appearance, even through characteristic movement and gestures. Fourth, if EA is used for distance classes, the psychological burden revealed here will decrease, so students will be able to focus on class. Fifth, the study verified that if avatars use actions, for example, applause, a positive class atmosphere can be achieved. In sum, EA's use in remote classes reduces students' psychological burden and enables emotional communication, thereby facilitating communication among students, between students and teachers, and ultimately, facilitating learning.

We look forward to contributing to improving the quality of distance learning. However, concluding with this study's results alone the matters related to communication between students and teachers is limited, including content of actual user usability and that related to educational quality improvement. This study indicates that using EA can reduce students' psychological burden during distance learning and that emotional expressions (between students and teachers, and between students and students) can be communicated, thereby facilitating smoother communication. Survey and in-depth interview results have been verified, but more in-depth user verification through additional EA prototype design is needed. Moreover, further studying visual elements that can affect users' remote communication purposes (in meetings, classes, and group work) and applying EA to them is necessary. Therefore, as a future research project, I will designate time, place, and occasion (TPO) in EA, in order to discover whether that communication is possible through Expressive Avatar (EA) according to the situation and place and to its impact on users.

Acknowledgements. This research was partially supported by SKT.

Appendix

Questionnaire
The Measurements centered on the experience of remote training users.

Q1. Have you ever had an experience in class where you couldn't focus on learning because of what you see on the screen?

Q2. If you couldn't concentrate on the class, why couldn't you concentrate?

1) I want to check my face that others see
2) Because I feel the burden or awkward to show my face
3) I want to check what my state is like in my view

Q3. What are the inconveniences you face in online classes?

1) Lack of bonding with classmates through limited online encounters
2) show my face
3) It is difficult to determine if the student is focusing. (Teaching student or nearby classmates)

Q4. Was it easy for you to identify the instructor or student through the video screen during the online class?

Q5. Was it easy for you to grasp the teacher's or student's facial expressions through the video screen during the online class?

Q6. What poses do you prefer to be illuminated during online classes? (See Fig. 5)

Q7. Is it easy for you to understand the intentions of the instructor or student's behavior through videos during online classes?

Q8. What is your or your preferred expression that you would like to see on the video screen during online class? (See Fig. 6)

Q9. This is an avatar image designed by providing subtitle expressions to users who want to ask questions. Please select the one you think is the most convenient among the images provided to you. (See Fig. 7)

Q10. Look at the top image and check the usefulness, delivery efficiency, and friendliness for image delivery. (See Fig. 8)

Q11. Please select the image you like the most when viewing other users who are valuable in the online class through the photo above presented. (See Fig. 9)

Q12. Please select the image you like the most about what kind of visual form you prefer to appear to other users in the online class through the photo above presented.

Q13. Do you think that conducting online classes using avatars will be of great help in forming bonds with classmates who have not formed intimacy?

Q14. What percentage of the other person's poses during online classes do you prefer? (See Fig. 10)

Q15. What aspect ratio do you prefer for the other person during online classes? (See Fig. 11)

Q16. What kind of gaze do you prefer during online class? (See Fig. 12)

Figures Related Questionnaire

Fig. 5 Options for question 6

Fig. 6 Options for question 8

Fig. 7 Options for question 9

Fig. 8 Options for question 10

Photo   3D   3D&2D   2D
style A   2D
style B   Non-User
Character

Fig. 9 Options for question 11

Fig. 10 Options for question 14

Fig. 11 Options for question 15

Fig. 12 Options for question 16

References

1. Allen, J., Rowan, L., Singh, P.: Teaching and teacher education in the time of COVID-19. Asia-Pac. J. Teach. Educ. **48**, 233–236 (2020). https://doi.org/10.1080/1359866X.2020.175 2051
2. Ministry of Education. https://www.moe.go.kr/Incs. Accessed 5 Aug 2020
3. Kim, S., Lee, G., Sakata, N., Billinghurst, M.: Improving co-presence with augmented visual communication cues for sharing experience through video conference. In: 2014 IEEE International Symposium on Mixed and Augmented Reality (ISMAR), pp. 83–92. IEEE, Munich (2014). https://doi.org/10.1109/ISMAR.2014.6948412
4. Maristcircle. https://www.maristcircle.com/Incs. Accessed 27 Oct 2020
5. Savitsky, B., Findling, Y., Ereli, A., Hendel, T.: Anxiety and coping strategies among nursing students during the covid-19 pandemic. Nurse Educ. Pract. **46**, 102809 (2020). https://doi.org/10.1016/j.nepr.2020.102809
6. Cheshin, A., Rafaeli, A., Bos, N.: Anger and happiness in virtual teams: emotional influences of text and behavior on others' affect in the absence of non-verbal cues. Organ. Behav. Hum. Decis. Process. **116**, 2–16 (2011). https://doi.org/10.1016/j.obhdp.2011.06.002
7. Petrova, T.E., Riekhakaynen, E.I.: Processing of verbal and non-verbal patterns: an eye-tracking study of Russian. In: Yang, X.-S., Sherratt, S., Dey, N., Joshi, A. (eds.) Third International Congress on Information and Communication Technology. AISC, vol. 797, pp. 269–276. Springer, Singapore (2019). https://doi.org/10.1007/978-981-13-1165-9_24
8. Tossell, C.C., Kortum, P., Shepard, C., Barg-Walkow, L.H., Rahmati, A., Zhong, L.: A longitudinal study of emoticon use in text messaging from smartphones. Comput. Hum. Behav. **28**, 659–663 (2012). https://doi.org/10.1016/j.chb.2011.11.012
9. Gonzalez-Franco, M., Steed, A., Hoogendyk, S., Ofek, E.: Using facial animation to increase the enfacement illusion and avatar self-identification. IEEE Trans. Visual. Comput. Graphics **26**, 2023–2029 (2020). https://doi.org/10.1109/TVCG.2020.2973075

10. Teyssier, M., Bailly, G., Pelachaud, C., Lecolinet, E.: Conveying emotions through device-initiated touch. IEEE Trans. Affect. Comput. 1 (2020). https://doi.org/10.1109/TAFFC.2020.3008693.

11. Di Fiore, F., Quax, P., Vanaken, C., Lamotte, W., Van Reeth, F.: Conveying emotions through facially animated avatars in networked virtual environments. In: Egges, A., Kamphuis, A., Overmars, M. (eds.) Motion in Games. LNCS, vol. 5277, pp. 222–233. Springer, Heidelberg (2008)

12. Marengo, D., Giannotta, F., Settanni, M.: Assessing personality using emoji: an exploratory study. Personality Individ. Differ. **112**, 74–78 (2017). https://doi.org/10.1016/j.paid.2017.02.037

13. JiSun, S.: Online classes that teachers are really curious about. Sch. Libr. J., p. 234 (2020). ISBN: 9788969150813

14. Lee, S., Carlson, G., Jones, S., Johnson, A., Leigh, J., Renambot, L.: Designing an expressive avatar of a real person. In: Allbeck, J., Badler, N., Bickmore, T., Pelachaud, C., Safonova, A. (eds.) IVA 2010. LNCS, pp. 64–76. Springer, Heidelberg (2010). https://doi.org/10.1007/978-3-642-15892-6_8

15. Hanus, M.D., Fox, J.: Persuasive avatars: The effects of customizing a virtual salesperson's appearance on brand liking and purchase intentions. Int. J. Hum. Comput. Stud. **84**, 33–40 (2015). https://doi.org/10.1016/j.ijhcs.2015.07.004

16. Norouzi, N., et al.: A systematic survey of 15 years of user studies published in the intelligent virtual agents conference. In: Proceedings of the 18th International Conference on Intelligent Virtual Agents, pp. 17–22. ACM, Sydney (2018). https://doi.org/10.1145/3267851.3267901

17. Paul, E., Friesen, W.V.: Unmasking the Face: A Guide to Recognizing Emotions from Facial Expressions. Malor Books (2015)

18. Fu, Y., Li, R., Huang, T.S., Danielsen, M.: Real-time multimodal human–avatar interaction. IEEE Trans. Circuits Syst. Video Technol. **18**, 467–477 (2008). https://doi.org/10.1109/TCSVT.2008.918441

19. Gomez Jauregui, D.A., Argelaguet, F., Olivier, A.-H., Marchal, M., Multon, F., Lecuyer, A.: Toward "pseudo-haptic avatars": modifying the visual animation of self-avatar can simulate the perception of weight lifting. IEEE Trans. Visual. Comput. Graphics **20**, 654–661 (2014). https://doi.org/10.1109/TVCG.2014.45

20. Candarli, D., Yuksel, H.G.: Students' perceptions of video-conferencing in the classrooms in higher education. Procedia Soc. Behav. Sci. **47**, 357–361 (2012). https://doi.org/10.1016/j.sbspro.2012.06.663

21. Correia, A.-P., Liu, C., Xu, F.: Evaluating videoconferencing systems for the quality of the educational experience. Distance Educ. **41**, 429–452 (2020). https://doi.org/10.1080/01587919.2020.1821607

22. Cassell, J., Vilhja, H.: Fully embodied conversational avatars: making communicative behaviors autonomous 20

23. Lee, K., Choi, J., Marakas, G.M., Singh, S.N.: Two distinct routes for inducing emotions in HCI design. Int. J. Hum.-Comput. Stud. **124**, 67–80 (2019). https://doi.org/10.1016/j.ijhcs.2018.11.012

24. Dodds, T.J., Mohler, B.J., Bülthoff, H.H.: Talk to the virtual hands: self-animated avatars improve communication in head-mounted display virtual environments. PLoS One **6**, e25759 (2011). https://doi.org/10.1371/journal.pone.0025759

25. Garau, M., Slater, M., Vinayagamoorthy, V., Brogni, A., Steed, A., Sasse, M.A.: The impact of avatar realism and eye gaze control on perceived quality of communication in a shared immersive virtual environment. New Horiz. 8 (2003)

26. SuJin, L.: How to design Ontact: highly interactive online classes. VIVI2 (2020)

27. Parent, R.: Modeling and animating human figures. In: Computer Animation. pp. 283–315. Elsevier (2012). https://doi.org/10.1016/B978-0-12-415842-9.00009-5
28. Tang, H., Hu, Y., Fu, Y., Hasegawa-Johnson, M., Huang, T.S.: Real-time conversion from a single 2D face image to a 3D text-driven emotive audio-visual avatar. In: 2008 IEEE International Conference on Multimedia and Expo, pp. 1205–1208. IEEE, Hannover (2008). https://doi.org/10.1109/ICME.2008.4607657
29. Lugrin, J.-L., Wiedemann, M., Bieberstein, D., Latoschik, M.E.: Influence of avatar realism on stressful situation in VR. In: 2015 IEEE Virtual Reality (VR), pp. 227–228. IEEE, Arles (2015). https://doi.org/10.1109/VR.2015.7223378

PerformEyebrow: Design and Implementation of an Artificial Eyebrow Device Enabling Augmented Facial Expression

Motoyasu Masui[1], Yoshinari Takegawa[1(✉)], Nonoka Nitta[1], Yutaka Tokuda[2], Yuta Sugiura[3], Katsutoshi Masai[3], and Keiji Hirata[1]

[1] Future University Hakodate, Hakodate, Japan
{g2120045,yoshi,b1017177,hirata}@fun.ac.jp
[2] City University of Hong Kong, Hong Kong, China
[3] Keio University, Tokyo, Japan
{sugiura,masai}@imlac.ics.keio.com

Abstract. In communication, it is important to clearly convey one's own emotions to others and to accurately read the emotions intended by others. There are two ways to communicate emotions: nonverbal information and verbal information. The psychologist Merhrabian argues that non-verbal information is more important than verbal information, and that visual information such as facial expressions and gestures play a major role in inferring emotions. However, there are times when our own emotions are not understood by others, leading to misunderstandings. In this study, we propose an artificial eyebrow shape control device, PerformEyebrow, which extends the wearer's facial expression by presenting various eyebrow shapes. The eyebrows are drawn with thermochromic ink so that their shape can be changed dynamically. It takes about 9 s for the eyebrows of PerformEyebrow to change shape. In order to confirm the usefulness of the device as an expression enhancing device, we conducted an experiment to evaluate the impression made by eyebrow shape when the eyebrow shape was changed by wearing PerformEyebrow.

Keywords: Human extension · Communication · Cognitive psychology

1 Problem

It is important to communicate one's emotions to others and to read accurately the emotions that others intend. Nonverbal and verbal information can be used to communicate emotions. Psychologist Merhrabian [8] argues that nonverbal information is more important than verbal information and that, among nonverbal information, visual information such as facial expressions and gestures

---

This work was supported by JSPS KAKENHI Grant Number JP19H04157.

M. Kurosu (Ed.): HCII 2021, LNCS 12764, pp. 584–597, 2021.
https://doi.org/10.1007/978-3-030-78468-3_40

Fig. 1. Shape changeable eyebrows

play a major role in emotion inference [9,10]. It has also been shown that facial expressions can be used to judge the emotions of joy, sadness, anger, disgust, fear, and surprise [2]. These results indicate that facial expressions are an effective means of communicating one's emotions. In some cases, however, an interlocutor may infer an emotion different to that of the other person's facial expression. For example, the interlocutor may think that the other person is angry even though the other person shows no particular facial expression, or that the other person, despite displaying a happy expression, may not actually feel happy, because the change in facial expression is only slight.

The mouth, eyes, and eyebrows are considered to be the parts of the face that form facial expressions. The mouth is used for speech and the eyes are used for purposes other than expressing facial expressions. On the other hand, though the eyebrows are located between the forehead and the eyes and thus have the function of preventing sweat and debris from entering the eyes, the main function of the eyebrows is said to be the formation of facial expressions [3].

This paper proposes PerformEyebrow, an artificial eyebrow shape control device that can extend facial expressions by presenting a variety of eyebrow shapes. The color of the thermochromic ink applied to the artificial eyebrows is changed by placing an electric wire printed with conductive ink directly underneath the artificial eyebrows. For example, we can extend facial expression by changing the shape of the eyebrows with thermochromic ink, as shown in Fig. 1.

2 Related Research

Related studies have proposed systems and devices that can change the entire face or parts of the face.

As media art, there are works that propose the use of a tablet PC attached to the face, such as Taro Yamada Project [1] and TABLETMAN[2], in which a tablet PC is attached to the face. Taro Yamada Project is a temporary and anonymous performance in which a performer photographs the faces of people on the street using an iPad and then projects the images onto his own face; TABLETMAN is a character created by Toshiba Corporation for advertising purposes, comprising a man wearing a special effects hero-like suit with illuminated lines and a number of tablet PCs attached to the head, arms and abdomen.

Examples of telepresence systems include video call software such as Skype, and ChameleonMask [11], which displays the faces of remote users. In ChameleonMask, a proxy wears a display showing the face of a remote user, to clarify the remote user and to give a sense of physical presence in telepresence. Therefore, a proxy can stand in for a remote user, which has the effect of bringing a sense of closeness and realism to conversation between the remote user and an interlocutor.

There have been previous studies on the virtual change of the whole or part of the face of an interlocutor or oneself for use in face-to-face communication. Akaike et al.'s face-to-face conversation support system [1] uses augmented reality technology and an HMD to display a static avatar on the face of the interlocutor. This reduces the influence of appearance, which is a factor that inhibits face-to-face communication at a first meeting.

Osawa's Agencyglass [12] is in the shape of a pair of sunglasses, with a liquid crystal display of the same size as the eyes embedded as a lens. The movements of the wearer's eyes, which have been captured beforehand, are projected on the LCD. For example, in the customer service industry, clerks have to control their own emotions and serve customers with a smile even when they are depressed. In order to reduce the burden of such emotional labor, The LCD of AgencyGlass shows the eye movements of the clerk when he or she is smiling. Our study aims to expand the eyebrows, making it different from AgencyGlass, which replaces the face itself and the eyes with a display.

ChromoSkin [4,5] proposes an application to change the color of eye shadow using thermochromic powder, as an augmented cosmetic. In this study, however, we aimed at enhancing facial expressions by changing the shape of eyebrows, and the target and purpose were different.

As research that changes the shape of the eyebrows, there is FacialMarionette by Maruyama et al. [6]. The position and movement of the eyebrows can be controlled by using a motor to pull strings attached to the eyebrows. Our study differs from FacialMarionette, which uses a motor to directly change the actual eyebrows, because we use artificial eyebrows.

---

[1] https://vimeo.com/82250584.

[2] https://www.greatworks.jp/works/tablet-man.html.

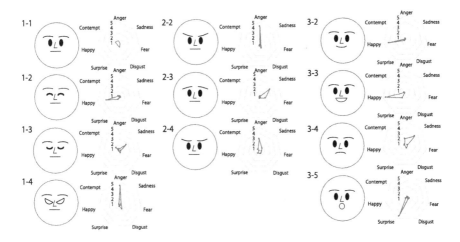

Fig. 2. Pictographs used and experimental results

3   Preliminary Experiment of Eyebrow Shape Change

In this study, we focus on eyebrow shape change as a means of expression expansion. In addition to the eyebrows, the mouth and eyes are used to express emotions. The mouth is an important part of speech, breathing, and eating, and the eyes are important in the overall act of seeing. It is difficult to place an augmentation device directly above or around the mouth and eyes without interfering with these activities. We selected the eyebrows as a facial expression expansion site because eyebrows do not have the functions of input and output of materials and information that the mouth and eyes have. However, it is not clear whether the eyebrows have significant ability to express emotions when compared to the mouth and eyes, hence we conducted preliminary experiments to verify this point.

3.1   Experimental Methods

As shown in Fig. 2, we prepared pictograms with different shapes for eyes only, eyebrows only, and mouth only. For each pictogram presented in random order, the participants were asked to indicate their impressions of the Ekman [2] universal facial expressions of happiness, disgust, anger, surprise, fear, and sadness on a 5-point Likert scale (1: not felt to 5: felt).

3.2   Experimental System

As shown in Fig. 3, we constructed an experimental system that displays pictograms and allows users to input emotions using a slider bar. The system consists of a set of pictograms and a slider bar. Scrolling the screen brings up the

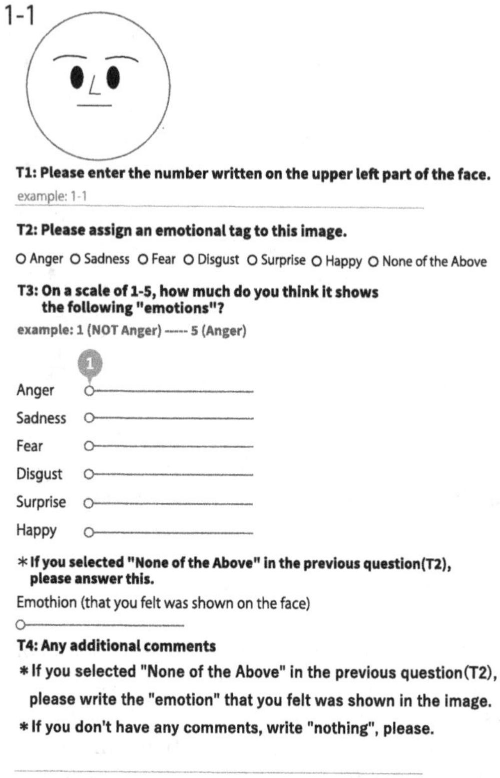

1-1

T1: Please enter the number written on the upper left part of the face.
example: 1-1

T2: Please assign an emotional tag to this image.
○ Anger ○ Sadness ○ Fear ○ Disgust ○ Surprise ○ Happy ○ None of the Above

T3: On a scale of 1-5, how much do you think it shows the following "emotions"?
example: 1 (NOT Anger) ----- 5 (Anger)

1

Anger   ○——————————
Sadness ○——————————
Fear   ○——————————
Disgust ○——————————
Surprise ○——————————
Happy   ○——————————

✳ **If you selected "None of the Above" in the previous question(T2), please answer this.**
Emothion (that you felt was shown on the face)
○——————————

T4: Any additional comments
✳ **If you selected "None of the Above" in the previous question(T2), please write the "emotion" that you felt was shown in the image.**
✳ **If you don't have any comments, write "nothing", please.**

Fig. 3. Screen snapshot of the experimental system

next pictogram and the slider bar corresponding to that pictogram. The order in which the 11 pictograms appear is random. This experimental system was implemented on Amazon Mechanical Turk.

3.3 Subjects

We asked 100 subjects to respond using Amazon Mechanical Turk, and paid them $11 per person in honorarium.

The results of the experiment are shown in Fig. 2. 1-1 is the neutral pictogram, and the characteristic emotions were expressed for the pictograms with different eyes, eyebrows, and mouth. For anger, pictogram 2-2 was the strongest, and a Mann-Whitney U test showed a significant difference between 1-1 (M = 1.64, SD = 0.95) and 2-2 (M = 4.31, SD = 0.75) (U = 81, p<0.01). The Mann-Whitney U test was also applied to the 2–3 pictogram for sadness, and a significant difference was observed between the 1-1 (M = 1.38, SD = 0.82) and 2-3 (M = 3.18, SD = 1.46) pictograms (U = 320, p<0.01). We verified that eyebrows are highly capable of expressing emotions with regard to the two emotions of anger and sadness.

4 Design

4.1 Usage Scenario

PerformEyebrow can be divided into two main types of usage scenario: amplifying the wearer's emotions and concealing them. These are explained in detail below.

Emotional Amplification. One usage scenario is to amplify the wearer's emotions.

For example, there is the performance of playing a musical instrument. In instrumental performances, the performers express their feelings through music and facial expressions. By using PerformEyebrow, we can change the shape of the performer's eyebrows to create an emotional performance for the audience.

There is also support for beginners in theater. In theater, one of the most effective ways for the audience to become emotionally involved and immersed in the story is for the performers to convey their emotions. For example, by using PerformEyebrow to exaggerate eyebrows, the performer can express the emotion of sadness more strongly.

Furthermore, there is communication when wearing a medical mask. The PerformEyebrow can change the shape of the eyebrows and thus assist in communicating emotions when wearing a mask.

Emotional Replacement. There is a scenario in which the wearer's true emotions are masked and replaced with other emotions.

For example, there is the substitution of emotional labor. Emotional labor is work that requires workers to repress their emotions. Emotional labor has become essential in a variety of occupations such as flight attendant, nurse, caregiver, and teacher. Workers in these occupations must behave cheerfully toward customers, even when they are feeling depressed. By wearing the PerformEyebrow, workers can hide their emotions.

There are also presentations. Even if a presenter is nervous, he or she is required to make a dignified presentation without showing facial expressions. Even if the presenter does not have a lot of experience in giving presentations, he or she can give an emotional presentation like a TED talk by wearing the PerformEyebrow.

In addition, there are face-to-face psychological warfare games such as mahjong and werewolf games. In such games there are situations where you must deceive your opponent by hiding or faking your emotions. By wearing the PerformEyebrow, even those who are not good at hiding their emotions can engage in heated psychological battles.

4.2 Requirement

The requirements that satisfy the usage scenarios described above are listed below.

1. Small size and light weight: The system must be light-weight and small-sized, as it is designed to be worn on the face.
2. Diversity of design: It must be possible to design various shapes of eyebrows, with differing length, shape and thickness.
3. Eyebrow shape change: The shape of the eyebrows must be able to be changed dynamically.

4.3   Examination of Shape-Changing Materials

There are two types of approach to controlling facial expressions: chromic materials and displays. There are two types of chromic material: thermochromic, which reacts to temperature changes, and photochromic, which reacts to infrared or ultraviolet radiation. We will examine whether these materials meet the above requirements.

Thermochromic. A thermochromic is a material that changes color at a certain temperature. There are several temperatures at which thermochromic materials change color. For example, SFXC's thermochromic ink[3] has four temperature settings: 15 °C, 21 °C, 31 °C, and 47 °C. In addition, Recording Materials Research Institute, Inc.[4] sells thermochromic inks with different discoloration temperatures in 5 °C increments from −20 °C to 60 °C. Using the property of thermochromic ink to change color with temperature, the shape of eyebrows drawn with thermochromic ink can be dynamically changed by heating or cooling the ink.

There are two types of thermochromic ink: powder type and solution type. Solution-type thermochromic inks are as easy to handle as paints. It is necessary to allow time for the ink to dry, but this only takes a few minutes Furthermore, they can be applied to various materials such as paper and cloth. For example, it is possible to apply thermochromic ink to false eyebrows. Due to its nature as an ink, thermochromic ink is small and lightweight. It is also possible to create eyebrows of various shapes.

Photochromic. Photochromic is a material that changes color when irradiated with non-visible light such as infrared or ultraviolet light. Eyebrows drawn using photochromic materials can be partially irradiated with infrared or ultraviolet light to dynamically change the eyebrow shape. The eyebrows can be applied to materials such as paper and cloth in a similar way to paints. However, there are only a few color variations. In order to change the color of the eyebrows, lights with different frequencies are needed, and infrared or ultraviolet LEDs laid in a tile-like pattern are required, making miniaturization difficult. Also, a mechanism to block sunlight is required.

---

[3] https://www.sfxc.co.uk.
[4] https://www.kirokusozai.com/.

Display. Liquid crystal displays and organic electroluminescent displays are difficult to process, making it difficult to create displays that fit the shape of the face. It is also difficult to make them smaller and lighter. However, they have the advantage of being able to change the shape of eyebrows in a variety of ways and express a variety of colors.

Based on the above analysis, it can be said that thermochromic ink is the most suitable material that satisfies the requirements described in Sect. 4.2.

4.4   Examination of Heat-Generating Materials

Electric heating wire, a Peltier device, and a pump for liquid are considered as possible materials or devices to change the color of thermochromic ink. As in the previous section, we will analyze the advantages and disadvantages of each heat-generating material based on the requirements (1) small size and light weight, (2) diversity of design, and (3) change in eyebrow shape, and consider the heat-generating material to be used. The PerformEyebrow system divides the eyebrows into blocks as shown in Fig. 4, and changes the shape of the eyebrows by switching the heat generation for each block.

Electrically-Heated Wire. Using silver nano-ink, it is possible to create precise electric heating circuits using a commercial printer, and to produce lightweight, bendable, and variously shaped electric heating wires. At the same time, multiple connectors can be easily installed, and each block of electric heating circuit can be controlled independently. The disadvantage of electric heating wire is that it needs to be cooled naturally.

Liquid Pump. The coloration and fading of the thermochromic ink can be controlled by stretching tubes around the back of the eyebrows coated with thermochromic ink and running coolant or hot water through them. However, in order to control each block of eyebrows independently, many tubes are required, making miniaturization difficult.

Peltier Device. The Peltier device is a device that can realize both cooling and heat generation in the same way as a liquid pump. In general, Peltier devices are produced only in rectangular shape, and it is difficult to make a shape that fits eyebrows. It is also difficult to make them bend to fit the face.

From the above analysis, each material has its own advantages and disadvantages. Considering the requirements (1) to (3), we use the heat generated by an electric heating wire to change the color of Performeyebrow's thermochromic ink.

4.5   System Configuration

As shown in Fig. 5, PerformEyebrow consists of two layers: an electro-thermal circuit layer and a thermochromic ink layer. Each layer is described in detail below.

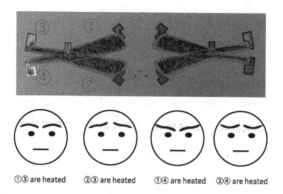

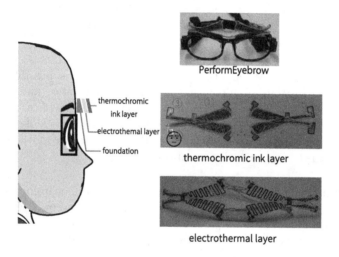

Fig. 4. Eyebrows divided into four blocks.

Fig. 5. System configuration

Electric Heating Circuit Layer. The electric heating circuit layer consists of twisted circuits, as shown in Fig. 5-(a). The electric heating circuit generates heat by passing current through this circuit.

Thermochromic Ink Layer. On the aforementioned electric heating circuit, skin-colored acrylic paint is applied and eyebrows are drawn with thermochromic ink as shown in Fig. 5-(b).

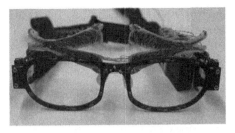

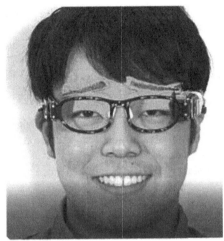

Fig. 6. Prototype

5   Implementation

The prototype of PerformEyebrow is shown in Fig. 6. We show the details of the implementation of the electro-thermal circuit layer and thermochromic ink layer in Fig. 5 below.

5.1   Electric Heating Circuit Layer

We explain, using the implementation of the X-shaped eyebrows shown in Fig. 6 as an example. Whether or not the electric heating circuit of each block is heated can be independently controlled. The electric heating circuit was printed out using silver nanoparticle ink (NBSIJ-FD02) and special media (NB-TP-3GU100) from Mitsubishi Paper Mills Co.

5.2   Thermochromic Ink Layer

The thermochromic ink layer consists of two layers. The entire sheet of the electric heating circuit layer is painted with skin color (acrylic ink). This prevents the electric heating circuit from being visible even when the thermochromic ink disappears. In addition, we used thermochromic ink (water-based screen ink) from the Recording Material Research Institute, Inc. that changes color from black to transparent at a temperature of 35 °C. In order to reproduce realistic eyebrows, a 5/0 size brush from golden maple was used.

5.3   Performance Evaluation of Operating Speed

Using PerformEyebrow, we measured the time required for eyebrow shape change and evaluated the performance. The electric heating circuit of PerformEyebrow was printed twice in layers to reduce the resistance value. The resistance values of ① to ④ in Fig. 4 were measured using a tester. The values of ① and ② were 6 to 7 Ω, and the values of ③ and ④ were 17 to 18 Ω.

In addition, for each of the electric heating circuits in Fig. 4, the duty ratios were PWM controlled so that ①:②:③:④=96:96:255:255. A voltage of 5 V was applied to PerformEyebrow.

It takes 9 s for the eyebrows to completely change their shape from the initial state. It is possible to increase the speed of operation by applying a higher voltage, but the electric heating circuit will melt, so it is necessary to investigate the optimal voltage and shape of the electric heating circuit.

6   An Experiment to Evaluate the Impression Given by Changes in Eyebrow Shape

We conducted an evaluation experiment using PerformEyebrow to assess the change in impressions caused by changing the shape of the eyebrows. The emotions used in the evaluation were the six universal facial expressions proposed by Ekman et al. (happiness, disgust, anger, surprise, fear, and sadness) [2] and the expression claimed to be universal by Matsumoto (contempt) [7].

6.1   Experimental Method

We used PerformEyebrow to change the shape of the eyebrows, and asked the participants to evaluate the seven facial expressions shown in Fig. 7 using a questionnaire. In the questionnaire, the participants were asked to rate their impression of each expression based on to what extent they felt each of the seven emotions of anger, sadness, fear, disgust, surprise, happiness and contempt on a 5-point Likert scale (1: not felt - 5: felt). The order in which each expression was presented was randomized.

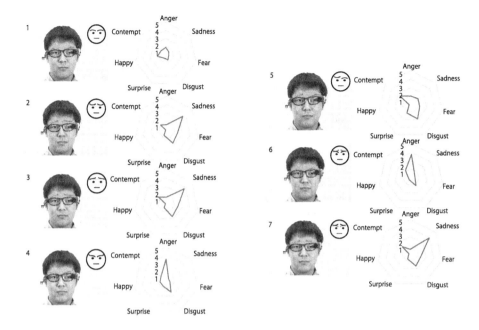

Fig. 7. Facial images used and experimental results

6.2 Subject

This experiment was conducted on 86 university students.

6.3 Result

The results of the experiment are shown in Fig. 7. The average values of the emotions felt for each expression are summarized in a radar chart. In contrast to the neutral expression 1, each expression with a different eyebrow shape showed different characteristics. The lowered eyebrows in expressions 2, 3, and 7 showed more sadness. When the Mann-Whitney U test was applied to sadness, a significant difference was observed between expression 1 ($M = 1.48$, $SD = 0.76$) and expression 2 ($M = 3.35$, $SD = 1.26$) ($U = 1412$, $p<0.01$). A significant difference was also observed between expression 1 and expression 3 ($M = 3.62$, $SD = 1.33$) ($U = 1213$, $p<0.01$). Furthermore, a significant difference was observed between expression 1 and expression 7 ($M = 3.78$, $SD = 1.25$) ($U = 1007$, $p<0.01$). Therefore, we can say that the lowered eyebrows form a sad expression compared to expression 1.

Next, the eyebrows with a raised shape, such as expressions 4 and 6, showed particularly strong anger. Similarly, when the Mann-Whitney U test was applied, a significant difference was observed between expression 1 ($M = 1.81$, $SD = 1.08$) and expression 4 ($M = 3.38$, $SD = 1.46$) ($U = 1611$, $p<0.01$). We also observed a significant difference between expression 1 and expression 6 (M = 3.31, SD = 1.47) (U = 1669, p<0.01). Therefore, we can say that the eyebrows with a raised shape form an angry expression compared to expression 1.

Furthermore, in the case of expression 5, where one eyebrow was lowered in the same way as the eyebrow in expression 2, sadness did not appear as strongly as in the expression where both eyebrows were lowered. When a chi-square test was applied to expression 5 and expressions 2, 3, and 7, a significant difference was observed ($x^2(3) = 31.791$, p < 0.01), and residual analysis revealed that expression 5 had significantly less sadness (pSPSVERBc10.05) and significantly more disgust (p < .05). Therefore, we can say that, compared to the lowered eyebrows, expression 5 is an expression in which only disgust is felt.

The shape of the eyebrows showed a coherent division of features, and we were able to verify that changes in the shape of the eyebrows resulted in different impressions.

7 Conclusion

In this study, we constructed an artificial eyebrow shape control device, PerformEyebrow, which can extend facial expressions. The proposed device dynamically changes the shape of eyebrows based on the identified facial expressions of the wearer. We implemented a prototype of PerformEyebrow and conducted an evaluation experiment to evaluate the impressions made by the eyebrow shape change when wearing PerformEyebrow.

Future work includes conducting impression evaluation experiments using different eyebrow shapes and improving the speed of PerformEyebrow.

References

1. Akaike, Y., Komeda, J., Kume, Y., Kanamaru, S., Arakawa, Y.: AR Go-Kon: a system for facilitating a smooth communication in the first meeting. In: 2014 IEEE 11th International Conference on Ubiquitous Intelligence and Computing and 2014 IEEE 11th International Conference on Autonomic and Trusted Computing and 2014 IEEE 14th International Conference on Scalable Computing and Communications and Its Associated Workshops, pp. 120–126 (2014)
2. Ekman, P.: Facial expressions of emotion: new findings, new questions (1992)
3. Godinho, R.M., Spikins, P., O'Higgins, P.: Supraorbital morphology and social dynamics in human evolution. Nat. Ecol. Evol. (2018). http://www.nature.com/articles/s41559-018-0528-0
4. Kao, C.H.L., Nguyen, B., Roseway, A., Dickey, M.: EarthTones: chemical sensing powders to detect and display environmental hazards through color variation. In: Proceedings of the 2017 CHI Conference Extended Abstracts on Human Factors in Computing Systems, CHI EA 2017. Association for Computing Machinery, New York (2017). https://doi.org/10.1145/3027063.3052754
5. Kao, H.L.C., Mohan, M., Schmandt, C., Paradiso, J.A., Vega, K.: ChromoSkin: towards interactive cosmetics using thermochromic pigments. In: Proceedings of the 2016 CHI Conference Extended Abstracts on Human Factors in Computing Systems, CHI EA 2016, pp. 3703–3706. Association for Computing Machinery, New York (2016). https://doi.org/10.1145/2851581.2890270

6. Maruyama, E., Kakehi, Y.: FacialMarionette: an on-skin interface for controlling facial expressions and its applications. In: Proceedings of the CHI 2017 Workshop on Amplification and Augmentation of Human Perception (2017)

7. Matsumoto, D.: More evidence for the universality of a contempt expression. Motiv. Emot. **16**(4), 363–368 (1992)

8. Mehrabian, A.: Nonverbal betrayal of feeling. J. Exp. Res. Pers. (1971)

9. Mehrabian, A.: Nonverbal Communication. Transaction Publishers (1972)

10. Mehrabian, A., Ferris, S.R.: Inference of attitudes from nonverbal communication in two channels. J. Consult. Psychol. **31**(3), 248 (1967)

11. Misawa, K., Rekimoto, J.: ChameleonMask: embodied physical and social telepresence using human surrogates. In: Proceedings of the 33rd Annual ACM Conference Extended Abstracts on Human Factors in Computing Systems, CHI EA 2015, pp. 401–411. Association for Computing Machinery, New York (2015). https://doi.org/10.1145/2702613.2732506

12. Osawa, H.: Emotional cyborg: complementing emotional labor with human-agent interaction technology. In: Proceedings of the Second International Conference on Human-Agent Interaction, HAI 2014, pp. 51–57. Association for Computing Machinery, New York (2014). https://doi.org/10.1145/2658861.2658880

Improving Satisfaction in Group Dialogue: A Comparative Study of Face-to-Face and Online Meetings

Momoko Nakatani$^{(\boxtimes)}$, Yoko Ishii, Ai Nakane, Chihiro Takayama, and Fumiya Akasaka

NTT Service Evolution Laboratories, 1–1 Hikarinooka Yokosuka-shi, Kanagawa 239–0847, Japan

Abstract. Our objective is to clarify how to increase the satisfaction of participants in a service design group dialogue. As a basic study, experiments were conducted, and two dialogue corpora were constructed: one face-to-face and the other online. The face-to-face dialogue corpus consisted of 17 groups of four people, and the online corpus consisted of ten groups of four people. Each dialogue lasted 40 min, and various video, voice, data, and 3D point cloud data were acquired. We also administered multiple questionnaires to investigate the participants' satisfaction. We introduce the contents of the corpora and describe our initial analysis comparing face-to-face and online communication.

Keywords: Group dialogue · Service design · Satisfaction

1 Introduction

Group dialogues take place in various aspects of daily life, such as at meetings and during discussions. For example, new products and services are typically developed through discussions at companies. As many of these dialogues have moved online due to COVID-19, it is crucial to examine the effect of going online in detail.

In the field of service design, living labs [1, 2], where users, companies, and governments co-create services over a long period of time, have been attracting attention in recent years. However, even in living labs, where diverse stakeholders meet face to face for co-creation activities, many activities have been forced to switch to online.

In such group dialogues aimed at "designing new services," services and products are not created in a single meeting. Rather, it is necessary for stakeholders to engage in repeated dialogues through which needs are gradually concretized, multiple seeds of ideas are generated, and the final plan is formulated by selecting and expanding on the ideas. With such dialogues, it is not enough to design a meeting only for efficiency and productivity; it is also necessary to raise the participants' level of satisfaction. Put simply, if we want to encourage users to continue to participate, they need to feel as though it was a good experience. However, involving users in a longitudinal design process is

© Springer Nature Switzerland AG 2021
M. Kurosu (Ed.): HCII 2021, LNCS 12764, pp. 598–610, 2021.
https://doi.org/10.1007/978-3-030-78468-3_41

not easy [1, 3]. Moreover, it is not clear whether the same level of satisfaction can be achieved in online meetings as in face-to-face meetings.

Against the backdrop of the worldwide COVID-19 pandemic, our focus is to clarify whether there are differences in satisfaction and other related subjective factors between face-to-face and online meetings. We conducted laboratory experiments comparing these two types of meeting as a preliminary study. Three dialogues were conducted individually for groups consisting of four members who had not met before, which is an increasingly common scenario with the prevalence of COVID-19.

In Sect. 2 of this paper, we discuss related research, and in Sect. 3, we describe how we constructed the dialogue corpora. Section 4 reports the results of our comparison between the face-to-face and online meetings, which we discuss in further detail in Sect. 5. We conclude in Sect. 6 with a brief summary and mention of future work.

2 Related Work

2.1 Group Dialogue Corpus

A number of corpora containing group dialogues have been constructed in previous studies. One of the most popular is the AMI corpus [4], which contains 100 h of meeting data from the Augmented Multi-Party Interaction (AMI) consortium and is annotated for language and behavior. There are also corpora collected by the MIT Media Lab [5] and a Japanese corpus constructed by Hayashi et al. [6].

Dialogue corpora are usually designed in accordance with the purpose of the research. For example, in a study that investigated the relationship between communication skills and personality traits, dialogue participants were asked to complete a questionnaire that measured personality traits, and communication skills were evaluated by an external expert [6, 7]. In recent years, with the development of sensing devices, there has been extensive research on group dialogues to automatically estimate the state and characteristics of people by sensing non-verbal information during the dialogue, and many corpora are often used for such purposes. For example, studies on the automatic detection of which participants show leadership [8] and which participants are dominant [9, 10]. In particular, one report has shown that the automatic estimation of dominance can reach a correct answer rate of 75% based on objectively obtainable data such as participants' speaking time and the number of speaking turns [9]. In a dialogue corpus for automatic detection, external evaluators who are not involved in the speaking typically annotate the video after the dialogue. The annotated data are then used as correct answers for training the detection model.

In our study, in an alternative approach, we collect data on the participants' subjective evaluation values. This is because we are focusing on "satisfaction," which is difficult to observe externally. While the AMI corpus contains items for measuring "satisfaction" that are answered by the participants [4, 11], the word "satisfaction" can be interpreted in various ways. Very few studies have focused on participant satisfaction in group dialogues, and so the mechanism underlying these findings remains unclear. Therefore, we collect subjective data on several items that may be related to satisfaction.

2.2 Comparison of Face-To-Face and Online Dialogue

The overall effectiveness of computer-mediated communication (CMC) groups is known to be lower than that of face-to-face teams, especially for tasks that require higher levels of coordination [13, 14]. For example, CMC groups require more time than face-to-face groups to come to an agreement [15–17]. Studies that have looked more closely at interactions during dialogue have shown that face-to-face conversations result in more speaker exchanges (turns) [18], shorter lengths of turns [19], and more interruptions [20] than video-mediated dialogues.

Research is also underway on how to dispel these differences [12]. Studies have shown that online meetings can be enhanced upon formation when the team members have a shared history [21], when teams have the ability to build personal relationships in the mediated environment [22], when the media enables the team to adapt its behavior to match the nature of the task (and other constraints), and when the team has a shared understanding of effective communication [23].

On the other hand, there have been relatively few studies that compare face-to-face and online meetings in terms of satisfaction. Now that online meetings are becoming a regular practice, it is crucial to understand in detail which aspects of online and face-to-face meetings make a difference in the way people feel. In order to compare the level of satisfaction between online and offline meetings, we collected dialogue data and built two corpora, one for online and one for offline, as detailed in the next section.

3   Dialogue Corpora

3.1   Data Collection Procedure

Data were collected through experiments in a seated format with four participants, following many other dialogue corpora [4, 5]. The participants were women who had never met before because they do not necessarily know each other when designing a new service with users in the living lab. In the face-to-face experiment, participants interacted around a round table. In the online experiment, participants were divided into four private rooms and interacted via Zoom. Figure 1 shows scenes from both experiments.

The dialogue topic was "Creating a travel service plan for women," and the four participants were instructed to work together to make the best proposal possible. The dialogue consisted of three sessions, and the topics to be discussed in each session were as follows.

(1) Experience session (Session 1): Talk about your travel experiences. Tell about as many as possible in as much detail as possible (10 min).
(2) Ideation session (Session 2): Generate as many ideas as possible. (10 min)
(3) Proposal session (Session 3): Write a proposal to a travel agency and fill in forms that consisted of four columns: "Concept," "Idea number referred to (see below)," "Detailed explanation," and "Attractive points." In the face-to-face experiment, these forms were filled in on paper by hand, and in the online experiment, they were typed onto Google Slides. (20 min)

The experiments began with an ice-breaker, followed by an explanation of the dialogue theme and cautions (e.g., do not contradict the others, do talk about anything positive). During the experience and ideation sessions, the experimenter took notes on the experiences and ideas, and the written notes were presented to the participants in the next session. The experiences and ideas were summarized in short sentences such as "Singapore was very friendly and relaxing" and "I saw the Northern Lights in Finland". In the face-to-face experiment, each experience/idea was written on a card, which was placed on the table and referred to as needed in the following dialogue session. In the online experiment, the list of memos from the experience session was shared on the screen in the next session, and the memos from the ideation session were printed out and distributed to all participants. Each memo was given an ID number, and participants were instructed to indicate this number in the "Idea number referred to" column of the proposal during the proposal session.

The face-to-face experiment was conducted in a laboratory room with a one-way mirror. The experimenter waited outside the room during the experiment, observed through the mirror, and recorded using a video camera placed in the room. In the online experiment, the experimenter gave instructions over Zoom and then turned off the video and the microphone during the experiment.

Fig. 1. Scene from face-to-face experiment (left) and online experiment (right).

3.2 Number of Participants

A total of 17 groups of 68 people participated in the face-to-face experiment, and ten groups of 40 people participated in the online experiment. The participants were all women aged from 22–55. The participants in the online experiment were recruited from those who used video conference at least one day a month and had a certain level of PC literacy, such as using office software. Due to equipment difficulties, the first group in the online experiment completed only the first two of the three sessions.

In the second and third sessions of the online experiment, some participants were sent individual messages that complimented their personal behavior during the dialogue, because we also had a different purpose than comparing face-to-face to online meetings. The participants who received these messages were excluded from the analysis because the conditions were different from those of the face-to-face experiment, so here we only include the data of 12 participants from the online experiment.

3.3 Collected Data

(1) Visual, Auditory, and Other Sensor Data

In the face-to-face experiment, seven video cameras were used to acquire video data, and pin microphones were attached to each participant for individual voice recording (1 ch, 44.1 kHz, 16 bit). In the online experiment, video data were acquired by video cameras placed in front of the participants, and audio and video data from the built-in camera of each participant's laptop and headphones were recorded using Zoom. 3D point cloud data were collected using Kinect in both experiments. We also measured eye movement by using a gaze tracker in the online experiment, but since the data were not the subject of this study, no analysis was performed. Further, pulse waves were recorded using a Fitbit Ionic in the face-to-face experiment, and facial surface temperatures were recorded using a thermal camera in the online experiment, and while these were included in the corpus, we did not analyze them.

(2) Overall Satisfaction

To understand the overall satisfaction of each session, participants indicated their level of satisfaction on a 9-point Likert scale, where 9 was very positive and 1 was very negative. In addition, after all the dialogues had been completed, we asked three questions to clarify the overall satisfaction.

- (a) How satisfied are you with the dialogues (experiences, ideas, and plans) so far? (9-point scale)
- (b) Imagine you have been newly invited to participate in a dialogue where you talk about your own experiences and come up with new ideas. How would you feel at that moment? (9-point Likert scale; 1: very negative, 9: very positive)
- (c) Would you be likely to recommend the following initiatives to a friend or colleague? [Initiatives = various people getting together to talk about their own experiences and think of new ideas, while working together with companies to create new services] (12-point Likert scale, later normalized to 9 as the maximum value for the analysis)

Item (a) is the most basic and important question in that it asks about the overall level of satisfaction throughout the entire dialogue. Item (b) is also an important item, as it is an indicator that leads to continued participation if the dialogue is held multiple times. Item (c) is an indicator for attracting new participants to the dialogue.

(3) Items Related to Overall Satisfaction

Since there are various reasons/aspects for the level of overall satisfaction with the dialogue, more detailed subjective ratings were obtained after each dialogue on several items related to overall satisfaction. In particular, responses were collected for several items that were expected to differ between face-to-face and online meetings.

We had predicted that whether or not the discussion was enjoyable would have the greatest impact on satisfaction, and we were interested in seeing what differences there would be between face-to-face and online discussions. Therefore, we asked about the feelings of enjoyment which was consisted of two questions — "Was the dialogue fun?"

and "Was it interesting to make experiences/ideas/decide on a plan?"—and used the average of these answers in our analysis.

We also assumed that online participants who were joining from different locations might experience difficulties with the dialogue or have a negative impression about the overall atmosphere, so we asked two questions to clarify this: "Was it difficult to come up with experiences/ideas/proposal)?" and "Was the overall atmosphere of the dialogue good?".

Considering that online is more inefficient and takes more time to reach an agreement [15–17], online participants are more likely to feel that they are not talking enough, which may affect their satisfaction level. Therefore, we also asked about the time aspect of the dialogue after each session: "Did you talk enough in the allotted dialogue time?".

We also asked about satisfaction with the output, which was a travel proposal (as shown later). It was measured by the mean of two questions — "Are you satisfied with the plan you made?" and "Was the plan you made was convincing to you?".

We also obtained other subjective evaluation items, but as they are not the subject of this analysis, we do not describe them here.

(4) Dialogue Output

Examples of the proposals created in the meetings are shown in Fig. 2. Proposals were written by hand in the face-to-face experiment and electronically via Google Slides in the online experiment. The items to be filled in both conditions are equal, differing only in whether they were handwritten or electronically entered.

To acquire an objective evaluation, the number of ideas was counted after the second session from the notes taken by the experimenter. The number of characters in the proposals was also counted and used as a reference for measuring the output.

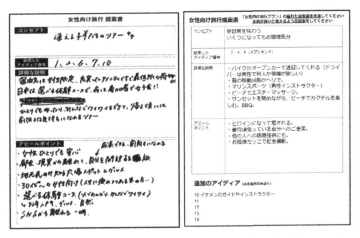

Fig. 2. Example of proposal from face-to-face experiment (left) and online experiment (right).

4   Results

4.1   Overall Satisfaction

Figure 3 shows the results of the overall satisfaction in the two meetings. There were no significant differences between the two in (a) Satisfaction (t(78) = 1.26, p > 0.1), (b) Next participation (t(78) = 0.41, p > 0.1), or (c) Recommendation to friends (t(78) = 0.15, p > 0.1) as a result of t-test. All the average scores tended to be high, as shown in Table 1.

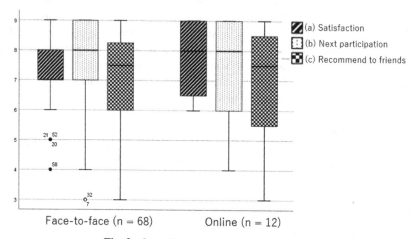

Fig. 3. Overall satisfaction in both meetings.

Table 1. Means (standard deviation) of overall satisfaction in both meetings.

	Face-to-face	Online
(a) Satisfaction	7.29 (1.13)	7.75 (1.29)
(b) Next participation	7.70 (1.52)	7.50 (1.83)
(c) Recommendation to friends	7.08 (1.62)	7.00 (1.91)

Figure 4 shows the satisfaction for each session in the two meetings. The results of a two-factor mixed-design analysis of variance (ANOVA) showed that the main effect of each session was significant (F(1.72,134.24) = 4.72, p < 0.05). The results of Bonferroni's multiple comparisons showed significant differences between Sessions 2 and 3 (p < 0.01) and between Sessions 1 and 3 (p < 0.1). In other words, Session 3 tended to be more satisfactory than Sessions 1 and 2. There were no significant differences between face-to-face and online.

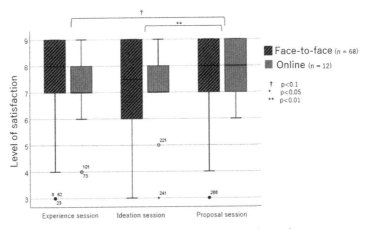

Fig. 4. Satisfaction for each session in both meetings.

4.2 Factors Related to Overall Satisfaction

1) Feeling of Enjoyment

Figure 5 shows the results of feelings of enjoyment for each session in both meetings. A two-factor mixed-design ANOVA showed that the main effect of each session was significant ($F(1.74, 135.75) = 5.05$, $p < 0.05$). The results of Bonferroni's multiple comparisons showed significant differences between Session 1 and 2 ($p < 0.05$), and between Session 2 and 3 ($p < 0.1$). In other words, participants did not find the ideation session as enjoyable as the other sessions. There was no significant difference between face-to-face and online.

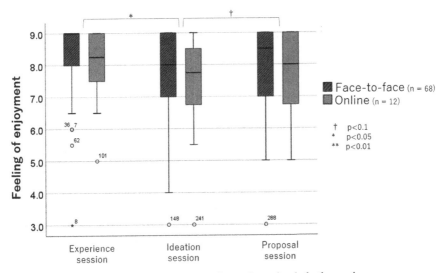

Fig. 5. Feelings of enjoyment for each session in both meetings.

2) Difficulty in Carrying Out the Task

Figure 6 shows the difficulty in carrying out the task for each session in both meetings. A two-factor mixed-design ANOVA revealed a marginally significant interaction effect between the types of the sessions and online/offline ($F(1.46, 113.99) = 3.185, p < 0.1$), and the statistically significant difference was between face-to-face ($M = 6.49, SE = 0.23$) and online ($M = 7.58, SE = 0.55$) in the ideation session ($F(1, 78) = 3.38$). In other words, participants tended to find it more difficult to create ideas in the online meeting than in the face-to-face one. There were also significant differences between Session 1 and 2 ($p < 0.01$), Session 2 and 3 ($p < 0.01$), and Session 1 and 3 ($p < 0.01$) in both face-to-face and online meetings. In other words, participants felt that the Ideation session was the most difficult compared to the other sessions and felt the difficulty even more strongly in the online meeting.

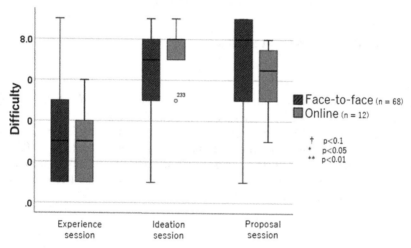

Fig. 6. Difficulty in carrying out the task for each session in both meetings.

3) Atmosphere of Members

There were no significant differences in the members' atmosphere by types of the dialogue or by face-to-face/online.

4) Talked Enough

Figure 7 shows the result of the degree of feelings of not having talked enough in the allotted dialogue time. The results of two-factor mixed-design ANOVA showed that the main effect of the face-to-face/online was significant ($F(1, 5.13) = 14.68, p < 0.01$) in having talked enough; Compared to the online dialogues, the face-to-face dialogues were perceived to be more time deficient. There were no significant differences between the sessions ($F(1.84, 143.6) = 0.09, n.s.$).

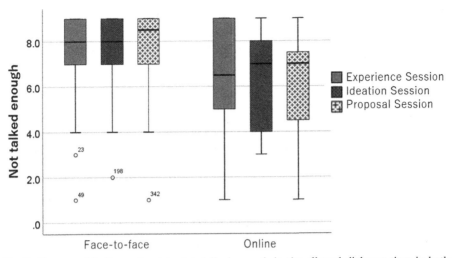

Fig. 7. Degree of feelings of not having talked enough in the allotted dialogue time in both meetings.

5) Satisfaction with the Output

The results of t-tests showed there was a significant difference between face-to-face (M = 7.22, SD = 1.51) and online responses (M = 8.04, SD = 0.92) in the output satisfaction (t(23.20) = 2.56, p < 0.05), which means that they were more satisfied and convinced about the final proposal when they were interacting online than face-to-face.

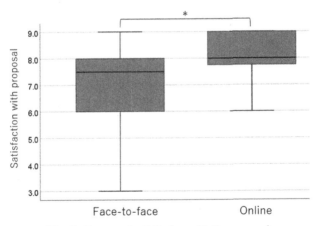

Fig. 8. Degree of satisfaction with the proposal.

4.3 Objective Values

The number of ideas, which was the output of Session 2 (ideation session), was lower in the online session (M = 8.00, SD = 2.12) than in the face-to-face session (M = 12.47,

SD = 5.15) (t(23.15) = 3.115, p < 0.01). As for the output of Session 3 (the proposal), more characters were written in the online session (M = 267.22, SD = 64.65) than in the face-to-face session (M = 173.65, SD = 59.65) (t(24) = 3.70, p < 0.01).

5 Discussion

5.1 Different Degrees of Feeling that Speech Was Inadequate

In all sessions, the participants felt they did not talk enough in the face-to-face meeting compared to in the online meeting. This result is surprising given that many prior studies have shown that it takes longer to reach an agreement via computer than face-to-face [15–17]. We feel there are two possible reasons people felt that they did not talk enough in the face-to-face condition in our experiment. First, more speech was exchanged at a faster pace in the face-to-face session, which may have created a desire to talk more. Another possibility is that, in online meetings where the tempo is slower and there are fewer speech alternations, only the minimum necessary statements are made to reach a conclusion, and as a result, the conclusion may be reached faster. Analyzing which of the two reasons (or both) are responsible will be the focus of our future work.

5.2 Difficulty in Coming up with Ideas and Satisfaction with the Proposal

Participants were more satisfied and convinced with the proposal they made in the online sessions than in the face-to-face ones. This result is consistent with the fact that face-to-face participants felt they had less time: the more time they felt they had, the more satisfying and convincing their proposals would have been in the online meeting.

We also found that the online participants had greater difficulty coming up with ideas than the face-to-face participants. This difference only occurred in the ideation session, which suggests that ideation was the most difficult part of the online dialogue. This is also supported by the fact that the number of ideas was significantly lower in the online meetings than in the face-to-face ones. Further analysis is required to understand the reason, but one possibility may be that turn-taking tends to be less prevalent in online meetings [18, 19]. Here, the participants might have thought their ideas over before expressing them in the online experiment, which made them feel there was a difficulty. This suggests that it is more important to speak up without hesitation in an online meeting, even if an idea is trivial.

On the other hand, it is interesting to note that even though the participants felt it was difficult to come up with ideas, their satisfaction increased at the stage of finalizing the plan in the third session, and their satisfaction with the final plan was higher online than in face-to-face. Further analysis of the reasons for this is necessary, but there are a few possibilities. First, as an objective result, given that the number of words in the proposal was higher online, we can expect that the quality of the output was actually higher in the online meeting. This could be for the simple reason that typing on a computer is easier than writing by hand. Also, given the small number of ideas generated in Session 2, it is possible that the satisfaction level of the participants was higher because they only had to compile ideas from a small number of options when putting together their plans, and there were fewer ideas to dismiss. We could also explain this from the perspective of cognitive dissonance theory: namely, participants might have felt the need to convince themselves that they had produced a good proposal because it was the result of a difficult ideation session. In any case, it is necessary to clarify whether good proposals were actually being produced or whether the participants were simply highly satisfied with them.

5.3 Limitations

The participants in this experiment were all Japanese women who had never met before. Since national character and gender are likely to have an influence on the results, further research is needed before generalizing the findings to other countries.

6 Conclusion

In this work, we conducted dialogue experiments as a basic study for improving the satisfaction of participants in group dialogues aimed at creating services. We constructed dialogue corpora of 17 face-to-face groups and ten online groups, each lasting 40 min, for a total of more than ten hours, and recorded a variety of data including video, voice, heartbeat, and 3D point cloud data. As an initial analysis, we compared the face-to-face and online discussions and found that, while there was no significant difference in terms of overall satisfaction, there were some differences in individual sessions. The participants tended to feel they did not talk enough in the face-to-face sessions compared to in the online ones, and conversely, in the online dialogue, they found the ideation more challenging and were more satisfied with the final proposal. Our future work will involve further analysis of the dialogue corpora to clarify the reasons underlying these results.

References

1. Hossain, M., Leminen, S., Westerlund, M.: A systematic review of living lab literature. Int. J. Cleaner Product. **213**, 976–988 (2019)
2. Folstad, A.: Living labs for innovation and development of information and communication technology: a literature review. J. Virtual Organ. Netw. **10**, 99–131 (2008)
3. Stahlbrost, A., Bertoni, M., Folstad, A., Ebbesson, E., Lund, J.: Social Media for User Innovation in Living Labs: A Framework to Support User Recruitment and Commitment. In: Proc. XXIV ISPIM Conference, pp. 16–19 (2013)
4. Carletta, J.: Unleashing the killer corpus: experiences in creating the multi-everything AMI meeting corpus. Lang Res. Eval. **41**, 181–190 (2007)
5. Dong, W., Lepri, B., et. al: Using the influence model to recognize functional roles in meetings. In: Proceedings of International Conference Multimodal Interfaces(ICMI07), pp. 271–278 (2007)
6. Hayashi, Y., Nihei, F., Nakano, Y., Huang, H.-H.: Development of group discussion interaction corpus and analysis of the relationship with personality traits. IPSJ J. **56**(4), 1217–1227 (2015). in Japanese
7. Okada, S., Matsugi, Y., Nakano, Y., Hayashi, Y., Huang, H.-H., Nitta, K.: Estimating communication skills based on multimodal information in group discussions. Trans. Jpn. Soc. Artif. Intell. **31**(6), 1–12 (2016)

8. Sanchez-Cortes, D., Aran, O., Mast, M.S., Gatica-Perez, D.: A nonverbal behavior approach to identify emergent leaders in small groups. IEEE Trans. Multimedia **14**(3), 816–832 (2012)
9. Rienks, R., Zhang, D., Gatica-Perez, D., Post, W.: Detection and application of influence rankings in small group meetings. In: Proceedings of 8th International Conference on Multimodal interfaces (ICMI), pp. 257–264 (2006)
10. Hung, H., et al.: Using audio and video features to classify the most dominant person in a group meeting. In: Proceedings of the 15th ACM international conference on Multimedia (ICMI), pp. 835–838 (2007)
11. Lai, C., Murray, G.: Predicting group satisfaction in meeting discussions. In: Proceedings of the Workshop on Modeling Cognitive Processes from Multimodal Data, **1**, pp. 1–8 (2018)
12. Guo, Z., D'ambra, J., Turner, T., Zhang, H.: Improving the effectiveness of virtual teams: a comparison of video-conferencing and face-to-face communication in China. IEEE Trans. Prof. Commun. **52**(1), 1–16 (2009)
13. Straus, S.G., McGrath, J.E.: Does the medium matter? The interaction of task type and technology on group performance and member reactions. J. Appl. Psychol. **79**(1), 87–97 (1994)
14. Sniezek, J.A., Crede, M.: Group judgment processes and outcomes in video-conferencing vs. face-to-face groups. In: Proceedings of 35th Annual Hawaii International Conference on System Sciences, pp. 495–504. IEEE (2002)
15. Dennis, A.R., Kinney, A.R., Hung, S.T., Caisy, Y.: Gender differences in the effects of media richness. Small Group Res. **30**, 405–437 (1999)
16. Valacich, J.S., Schwenk, C.: Devil's advocate and dialectical inquiry effects on face -to-face and computer-mediated group decision-making. Organ. Behav. Hum. Decis. Process. **63**, 158–173 (1995)
17. Kiesler, S., Sproull, L.: Group decision making and communication technology. Organ. Behav. Hum. Decis. Process. **52**, 96–123 (1992)
18. Cook, M., Lalljee, M.: Verbal substitutes for visual signals in interaction. Semiotica **3**, 212–221 (1972)
19. Rutter, D., Stephenson, G.: The role of visual communication in synchronizing conversation. Euro. J. Soc. Psychol. **2**, 29–37 (1977)
20. O'Conaill, B., Whittaker, S., Wilbur, S.: Conversations over video conferences: an evaluation of the spoken aspects of video-mediated communication. Hum.- Comput. Interact. **8**(4), 389–428 (1993)
21. Alge, B.J., Wiethoff, C., Klein, H.J.: When does the medium matter? knowledge-building experiences and opportunities in decision-making teams. Organ. Behav. Hum. Decis. Process. **91**(1), 26–37 (2003)
22. Pauleen, D., Yoong, P.: Facilitating virtual team relationships via internet and conventional communication channels. Internet Res.: Electron. Netw. Appl. and Policy **11**(3), 190–202 (2001)
23. Tan, B.C., Wei, K.K., Huang, W.W., Ng, G.N.: A dialogue technique to enhance electronic communication in virtual teams. IEEE Trans. Prof. Commun. **43**(2), 153–165 (2000)

EmojiCam: Emoji-Assisted Video Communication System Leveraging Facial Expressions

Kosaku Namikawa$^{(\boxtimes)}$, Ippei Suzuki, Ryo Iijima, Sayan Sarcar,
and Yoichi Ochiai

University of Tsukuba, Tsukuba, Ibaraki, Japan
namikawa@digitalnature.slis.tsukuba.ac.jp

Abstract. This study proposes the design of a communication technique that uses graphical icons, including emojis, as an alternative to facial expressions in video calls. Using graphical icons instead of complex and hard-to-read video expressions simplifies and reduces the amount of information in a video conference. The aim was to facilitate communication by preventing quick and incorrect emotional delivery. In this study, we developed EmojiCam, a system that encodes the emotions of the sender with facial expression recognition or user input and presents graphical icons of the encoded emotions to the receiver. User studies and existing emoji cultures were applied to examine the communication flow and discuss the possibility of using emoji in video calls. Finally, we discuss the new value that this model will bring and how it will change the style of video calling.

Keywords: HCI theories and methods · Emoji

1 Introduction

In recent years, with the spread of smartphones and instant messaging applications, visual expressions, such as emoji, emoticon, and sticker have been increasingly used in text communication. These visual expressions are called Graphicons (Graphical+Icon) [7] or visual communication markers (VCMs) [10]. VCMs mainly mimic facial expressions and other symbolic objects, and they can be used in different ways and for different purposes. One of the most typical purposes is to supplement nonverbal information by substituting nonverbal cues. Emoji and emoticon, in particular, often express facial expressions, and play the role of supplementing nonverbal information such as emotions, which are transmitted through facial expressions in face-to-face (F2F), in text communication [2,3,19]. In addition, we can effectively and more emphatically express our emotions in text-based communications by adding emojis to text. Emoji has the following features:

- Emojis are used as a substitute for nonverbal cues [16].
- A uniform interpretation has been defined in the process of standardization by Unicode and ISO [9].

© Springer Nature Switzerland AG 2021
M. Kurosu (Ed.): HCII 2021, LNCS 12764, pp. 611–625, 2021.
https://doi.org/10.1007/978-3-030-78468-3_42

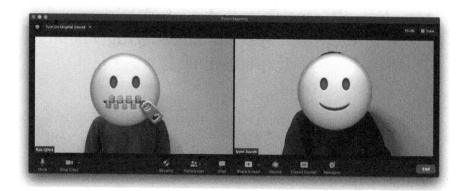

Fig. 1. People using EmojiCam system in a zoom meeting.

- In the text message conversations, emoji works as a shortcut to quickly convey content to the recipient [19].
- Emoji emphasizes the emotions of the sender and other information, making it easier for the recipient to understand [3].

These features of emojis can be useful not only in text-based communication but also in communication using media other than text. Video-based communication such as video calls or video conferencing is an example of visual communication other than text. As an existing utilization of emojis in video-based communication, there is a function of nonverbal feedback and reactions. For example, Zoom, a video conferencing tool, displays specific emojis in the upper left of the participant's video as a reaction [1]. This function is used for attendance confirmation, questionnaires, and raises one's hand to express one's desire to speak. However, these functions are an extension of the use of emojis in text-based communication, and they cannot take advantage of the amount of information in video communication.

Unlike text-based communication, video communication allows users to interact with each other while also conveying nonverbal information through facial expressions and gestures. However, low-bandwidth networks reduce the video resolution and cause latency. This makes it difficult for users to recognize nonverbal information from nonverbal cues such as facial expressions and gestures. Based on these problems, the use of emojis in video communication as well as text communication was proposed in this study, to complement the lack of nonverbal information and to facilitate nonverbal communication by simplifying and emphasizing it. The design of a communication technique that uses emoji was introduced as an alternative to facial expressions in video communication. The flow of nonverbal communication was defined using emojis in video conferencing (Fig. 2). This flow intended to convey nonverbal communication performed by facial expressions using emojis in video-based communication. To achieve this flow, the EmojiCam system (Fig. 1) was developed to support communication through emojis. EmojiCam encodes the emotions of the sender with automated facial expression recognition or manual keyboard input and presents the corresponding emoji to the receiver. By using this system, the user can hide their faces with emojis and express their emotions effectively, which were otherwise expressed only with their faces.

This study makes the following contributions:

1. Design of the EmojiCam system to address the problems of nonverbal communication in video communications.
2. Implementation of a proof-of-concept of the EmojiCam to evaluate the feasibility of the design.
3. Experimental evaluation of the effect of nonverbal communication by Emojis in video communication.

2   Related Work

2.1   Sending Nonverbal Information in Computer Mediated Communication

With the development of various input devices, such as cameras, and systems that process inputs, such as machine learning, there is increasing interest in recognizing and transmitting nonverbal information, such as emotions in computer mediated communication (CMC). There are studies that map user facial expressions to avatars and illustrations [5,18], and research on instant messaging applications that use a tactile interface [12,13,15]. However, most of these studies focus on text-based, lower-bandwidth communication, and few studies focus on higher-bandwidth communications.

Koh et al. proposed a emoji input system using gesture recognition and its use in video calls as an application [10]. However, the effect of actual application by the user has not been investigated. In other words, regarding the recognition and transmission of nonverbal communication in higher-bandwidth communication, new systems have been created owing to the evolution of input devices and systems. There has been no study examining whether the nonverbal communication performed there can accurately convey information, nor has there been any comparison with F2F nonverbal communication. Therefore, the purpose of this study is to evaluate nonverbal communication extended by CMC by conducting discussions using actual user studies and interviews.

2.2   Sync/Async and Higher-Bandwidth/Lower-Bandwidth

In the field of CMC, communication is often discussed through a computer in two categories. One is synchronous communication performed on rich media, such as video and audio, and the other is asynchronous communication performed on poor media, such as text chat and email [16]. As a similar classification, CMC can be divided into higher-bandwidth/lower-bandwidth [10]. Higher-bandwidth communication has expressiveness and intimacy, whereas lower-bandwidth communication is convenient and cautious. In general, these two types of communication have a trade-off between expressiveness and convenience. Walther et al.

has revealed that VCM has the ability to supplement the lack of nonverbal cues in low-bandwidth CMC, arguing that VCM has brought the benefits of higher-bandwidth to lower-bandwidth communication [17].

Focusing on emoji in VCM, as mentioned above, emoji has a unique culture. Some of them are not in synchronous/higher-bandwidth communication. For example, emoji accelerates communication and emphasizes emotions. We focus on this feature and use the culture of emojis, which has developed uniquely in asynchronous/lower-bandwidth communication. Therefore, a method is proposed to solve the problem of the lack of nonverbal communication in higher-bandwidth/synchronous against F2F.

3   Implementation

3.1   Communication Flow

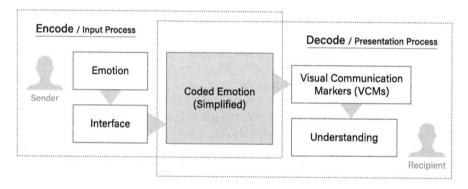

Fig. 2. The communication flow when using EmojiCam system.

Figure 2 shows the communication flow wherein a sender conveys nonverbal information to a receiver using VCMs. First, the system classifies the emotions of the sender in several predefined types of emotions, either through facial expression recognition or through a manual keyboard input. The coded emotions were defined based on Ekman's seven basic emotions [4]. The system then presents VCMs corresponding to the coded emotions of the sender to the receiver. The receiver interprets the VCMs, considering the context and the relationship with the sender. The proposed system simplifies the emotion of the sender into a coded emotion, making it easier for the receiver to interpret. In addition, the emotion-emphasizing property of emoji makes nonverbal communication simpler and more efficient.

3.2 System Overview

video: ☑   canvas: ☑   background image: ☐   blur video: ☐   [statics] [exportLog]   [help]
camera device: [device 1 ▾]   emoji size: ●▬▬▬▬   manual: ☐   background color : [   ]
background image: [Choose File] No file chosen

neutral: [☺]   angry: [☻]   disgusted: [☺]   fearful: [☻]   happy: [☺]   sad: [☺]   surprised: [☺]

Fig. 3. The user interface of EmojiCam.

To achieve the aforementioned communication flow, a system that converts the emotions of the sender into encoded emotions and displays emoji is developed.

The system has been implemented on the Web (Fig. 3), primarily because it is accessible to many people and can be used easily. In addition, because the video input and output are provided as a browser API, the implementation is relatively simple.

Users can stream the video output from EmojiCam to video conferencing platforms (e.g., Zoom, Google Hangout, etc.) using a virtual camera application (e.g., CamTwist, OBS, and ManyCam).

3.3 Emotion Encoding Method

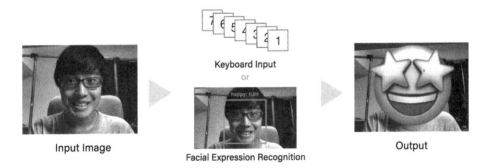

Input Image   Keyboard Input   Output
or
Facial Expression Recognition

Fig. 4. Input methods of EmojiCam. Users can manually select emoji using keyboard input or automatically using facial expression recognition.

We have implemented two methods for senders to input coded emotion: manual keyboard input and facial expression recognition (Fig. 4). Users can switch the input method by clicking on the checkbox or by typing the shortcut key. In the manual keyboard input, each coded emotion is assigned a key, and the user inputs the emotion by pressing the desired key. For the facial expression recognition, we used the face-api.js[1] for facial expression recognition. There are many libraries for facial expression recognition available on the web, such as clmtrackr.js[2] and pico.js[3], however we chose face-api.js because it is relatively lightweight and easy to change the machine learning model and to configure the number of people recognized. For the models, we used SSDMobilenetv1 [8] for face detection and faceExpressionNet for facial expression recognition.

3.4 Emotion Decoding Method

The system provides users with two ways to visually express their coded emotions visually. One is a normal video, and the other is a text that includes letters, emoticons, and emojis. Users can switch between showing and hiding the video and text respectively using check boxes and shortcut keys, respectively. Users can display the video as they are captured by their web camera, or they can apply a blurring effect to the video. Users can register a VCM for each coded emotion by entering a character, emoticon, or emojis in a text box next to the name of each coded emotion. The user can enter the desired emoji using the emoji picker provided by OS. The system tracks the face and displays the VCM over the face. Users can control the size of the VCMs using a slider.

4   Experiments

Using the EmojiCam system, two user studies were conducted to investigate how nonverbal communication transfer through facial expressions affects video calls. All of these studies were conducted remotely using video calling applications and online forms on the web. This study is approved by the Institutional Review Board at the University of Tsukuba.

4.1   User Study 1

As an example of nonverbal communication in EmojiCam, it was investigated whether the receiver could correctly interpret the emotions of the sender when communicating with EmojiCam. In this user study, emotions were conveyed as nonverbal information to be communicated.

Participants. We recruited 11 participants as a sender: nine males and two females; ages 20 to 24 (M: 21.82; SD: 1.54). We recruited 21 participants as a receiver: 10 males, 10 females, and one non-binary; ages 18 to 55 (M: 37.24; SD: 13.71) using snowball sampling [6].

---

[1] https://justadudewhohacks.github.io/face-api.js/docs/index.html   (last   accessed Feb. 12, 2021.).

[2] https://github.com/auduno/clmtrackr (last accessed Feb. 12, 2021.).

[3] https://github.com/nenadmarkus/picojs (last accessed Feb. 12, 2021.).

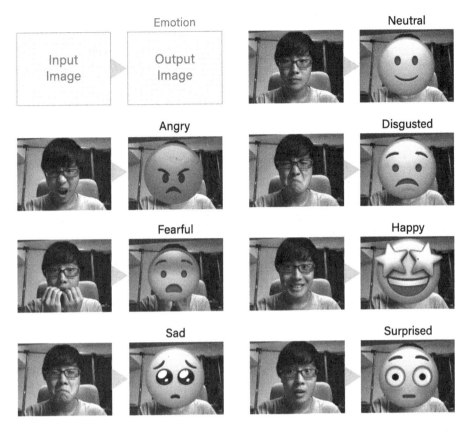

Fig. 5. Example Videos for User Study 1. In this example, sender was given examples of emotion recognition patterns.

Procedure. First, the 11 participants from the laboratory (senders) were asked to record a 5 s video for seven emotions (angry, disgusted, fearful, happy, neutral, sad, and surprised). The laboratory students were divided into two groups: one group was given examples of emotion recognition patterns, and the other was asked to make the facial expression they associate with a given emotion. EmojiCam was used to create a video with each video's facial expression converted into an emoji (Fig. 5). In other words, there are three factors; exemplification/ non-exemplification, Seven emotions (angry/disgusted/fearful/happy/neutral/ sad/surprised) and EmojiCam/video.

Second, 21 participants (as a receiver) were asked to guess the emotion from the seven emotions in the video. Each participant was asked to watch 56 videos (exemplification/non-exemplification, seven emotions, EmojiCam/video, two senders). The videos were randomly sampled from the same set of factors.

Table 1. Number of correct answers and expectation of User Study 1.

	EmojiCam		Video		EmojiCam		Video	
	Count	Expected	Count	Expected	Count	Expected	Count	Expected
Fearful	21	18.5	16	18.5	0	4.5	9	4.5
Sad	30	22	14	22	13	17	21	17
Surprised	15	11	7	11	21	24	27	24
Happy	37	37.5	38	37.5	14	11	8	11
Angry	34	31	28	31	2	8.5	15	8.5
Neutral	29	32.5	36	32.5	13	11	9	11
Disgusted	11	18	25	18	0	8.5	17	8.5

Table 2. The results of chi-square test for each emotion, exemplification and non-exemplification in User Study 1.

	Exemplification	Non-Exemplification
Fearful	$p > .05$	$p < .05$
Sad	$p < .05$	$p > .05$
Surprised	$p < .05$	$p > .05$
Happy	$p > .05$	$p > .05$
Angry	$p > .05$	$p < .05$
Neutral	$p > .05$	$p > .05$
Disgusted	$p < .05$	$p < .05$

Results. The number of correct responses for each emotion is illustrated in Table 1. The columns correspond to emotions, and the rows correspond to exemplification and non-exemplification, EmojiCam and video; for each field, the number of correct answers and expectations in 42 trials (21 participants and two senders) are described. Based on these aggregate data, a chi-square test was conducted. The results are listed in Table 2. When there was a statistically significant ($p < 0.05$) difference in the number of correct answers, the cases with more correct answers using EmojiCam are shown in red, and the cases with more correct answers using normal video calls are shown in blue. In the group with examples of facial expression recognition, the number of correct responses was significantly higher for EmojiCam in sad and surprised expressions. On the contrary, in the disgusted group, normal videos had more correct responses than EmojiCam. In the group where no examples of facial expression recognition were provided, the number of correct responses was significantly higher for video than for EmojiCam in fearful ($p < 0.05$), angry ($p < 0.05$), and disgusted ($p < 0.05$) expressions. Happy and neutral expressions did not show statistically significant differences with or without examples of grading recognition. The number of correct responses for disgusted expressions was significantly higher for the video calls with and without the example of rating recognition.

Fig. 6. Examples of User Study 2 experiments; on the left is a screenshot of a Room using EmojiCam, and on the right is a screenshot of a Room using video.

4.2   User Study 2

An experiment was conducted in which participants were asked to have a light conversation with each other using EmojiCam and a standard video calling application, and a questionnaire survey was conducted on usage and communication (Fig. 6). The emotional distribution of the recorded data were then analyzed and user interviews on usability and user experience were conducted.

Participants. We recruited 18 participants: 16 males and two females, aged between 19 and 33 (M: 23.33; SD: 3.12). A total of ten participants used EmojiCam and eight participants did not use EmojiCam. All participants belonged to the same laboratory, and were acquainted with each other. Participants who participated in recording the video in User Study 1 were included.

Procedure. The subjects were divided into two groups: one group (10 participants) was given the condition to use EmojiCam, and the other group (eight participants) was given the condition to use standard video conferencing applications (Zoom, Skype, etc.). Each group created a room with four people and asked them to have a light conversation for 15 min without setting a topic. In the EmojiCam group, two participants took part in the experiment twice to adjust the number of people in the room to four. Each participant's emotion per frame was recorded and the distribution of emotions was measured over 15 min. Finally, user interviews were conducted using the following items:

- Q1: What did you feel was different between a normal video call and EmojiCam?
- Q2: What features would you like to see in EmojiCam?

Results. We conducted Mann-Whitney's U-test on the distribution of emotions during 15 min in the EmojiCam group and in the video group. There was no significant difference between the EmojiCam group and the video group ($p > 0.05$).

The user interviews provided a variety of useful insights into EmojiCam. Both positive and negative comments were received from Q1. Some participants were enjoying new ways to communicate using EmojiCam. P1 stated that, "It was fun to change the Emoji according to what I was saying.", and P2 stated that, "It was fun to talk while choosing my facial expressions (to input emoji with facial expression recognition).". Feedback was received that people started to watch their own videos more than normal video calls. P9 stated that, "I paid more attention to how I looked than I usually do.", and P3 stated that, "Because I usually turn off the camera, I was more conscious of the movement of my face than usual." In addition, P2 noted the following, "It was easy to convey my emotions to the other person because small micro expressions were emphasized as pictograms." Some participants noted the anxiety and inconvenience of not being able to see the other person's or their own facial expressions. P5 stated that, "There are times when not being able to see the other person's face is a problem (such as in conversations with people with whom you don't have a good relationship)." Some negative comments were received regarding EmojiCam distracting the user and making it difficult to concentrate. P4 stated that, "I could not figure out where to look at and what to say", and P6 said that, "I felt like EmojiCam was stealing my attention."

In Q2, there were mainly requests for gesture and facial expression recognition. Many participants wanted to convey their agreement by recognizing nods. P1 said that, "I want EmojiCam to recognize the nod that means yes", and P3 said that, "I want an emoji that shows that I am nodding." P10 wanted the function to recognize gestures, such as hands. Feedback was also received for wanting to adjust the facial expression recognition. P9 stated that, "I am usually laughing, therefore I would appreciate if I could adjust my criteria for being happy to be neutral."

5   Discussion and Limitation

5.1   Accuracy of Facial Expression Recognition

The results of User Study 1 showed that in the sender with exemplification, the number of correct answers for a video was higher or unchanged for all emotions. The user interviews in User Study 2 also showed that the users wanted to fix the facial expression recognition, suggesting that the accuracy of EmojiCam in conveying emotions strongly depends on the accuracy of facial expression recognition. As facial expression recognition technology becomes more low-latency and highly accurate, user input will become easier and smoother communication will be realized. Currently, facial expression recognition is performed using publicly available datasets, however the accuracy of facial expression recognition can be improved by having senders create datasets in their own environments and use facial expression recognition optimized for themselves.

In addition, as users become more familiar with video calls using EmojiCam, further accuracy can be improved by using the keyboard in combination with manual input if an accurate input is desired. Another possible method is for users to create facial expressions based on their facial expression recognition. The group of the senders with exemplification in User Study 1 had emotions that were significantly higher in EmojiCam with a significantly higher number of correct responses, however the group of the senders without exemplification did not have significantly more correct or a difference in the number of correct responses in the video. If facial expression recognition technology is still in its infancy and users are not familiar with EmojiCam and cannot use the manual input functions, it is better to provide exemplification of facial expression recognition.

5.2   Characteristics and Differences for Each Emotion

The number of correct answers was higher for "happy" in User Study 1, regardless of whether it is EmojiCam or video. This can be assumed to be because of the fact that "happy" expressions, which are frequently used and have important meanings, are easy for facial expression recognition and for people to recognize, and that the emoji chosen by users do not vary much in interpretation. On the contrary, "disgusted" and "fearful" are difficult for facial expressions recognition and for people to recognize. In addition, the number of correct answers was significantly higher for video because there was variation in the emoji chosen by users, a factor that reduced the number of correct answers for both encoding and decoding in the figure. On the contrary, for "sad" expression the number of correct responses was significantly higher for EmojiCam for senders with examples of facial expression recognition, suggesting that the number of correct answers may have increased because of the use of tears in the emoji to emphasize the expression of sad, which is difficult to read in the video.

5.3   Missing Information Due to Encoding and Decoding Process

In this study, the emotions to be conveyed were limited to basic ones. However, facial expressions can express complex emotions that cannot be defined by basic emotions alone. Because complex facial expressions are difficult for the receiver to decipher and often have a negative effect on smooth communication, they are outside the scope of this study's objectives. However, it should be noted that complex facial expressions do not generally stagnate communication, and EmojiCam is not capable of expressing such complex emotions. In addition, with EmojiCam, only emotions can be conveyed through facial expression recognition. Facial gestures such as nodding and eye contact cannot be expressed. In fact, in the user interviews for User Study 2, we received comments such as the desire for nodding and gesture recognition functions. Future challenges include the creation of applications and integrated video conferencing environments for video conferencing that supports not only facial expressions but also other forms of nonverbal communication.

5.4   Limitations Because of Japanese Cultural Characteristics

This experiment was conducted entirely in Japan. This is expected because the results of the experiment include many characteristics unique to Japanese people.

For example, Japanese people have fewer facial expressions than Westerners, and Japanese people focus on the eyes in their expressions, while Westerners focus on the mouth [11]. In addition, many of the facial expression recognition technologies and the seven emotions by Ekman are made with reference to Western facial expressions, and there is a discussion on whether these standards are adaptable to Japanese people [14]. There is a need to incorporate such discussions into our selection of possible input emotions and analysis of the results in more detail and in the light of various cultures.

6   Future Work

6.1   User Interface

In our experiments, we did not investigate how the user interface of EmojiCam affects the usability of the system. Therefore, improving the UI is a topic for future work. In particular, the location of Emoji remains to be investigated. In the current system, emoji is placed over the faces. Another possibility is to display emoji at the bottom of the screen so that it can be viewed along with a normal video. We will improve the user interface to make it easier for senders to input their emotions, so that they can accurately convey information through EmojiCam. Currently, users run the system locally. However, if we embed this system in a video conferencing application, users will be able to apply EmojiCam to the other person's video. We hope that this will lead to a more comfortable communication.

6.2   Display Method of Emoji

Instead of continuously displaying emoji, it would be better to use facial expressions and emoji as appropriate. In the user interview, we received comments such as, "I sometimes have trouble seeing my mouth when I am talking." By using voice recognition to hide the sender's emoji when the sender is speaking, or by switching between various display methods, such as converting gestures into VCMs, depending on the conversation scene, it is believed thought that communication support can be tailored to the situation.

6.3   Facial Expression Translation

The mapping of facial expressions to emotions varies from region to region, and even further, there are individual differences. As a representative example, in the Western cultures, emotions are often expressed by the shape of the mouth, whereas Asian cultures, emotions are often expressed by the shape of the eyes [11]. Discrepancies in the mapping between facial expressions and emotions lead to communication discrepancies and are a major barrier to communication between different cultures. In the history of its standardization, pictograms were born from the agreement between Asian cultures, especially Japan, and Western cultures. Therefore, the mapping between pictograms and emotions is uniquely defined by referring to standards such as Unicode, which is believed to facilitate accurate communication of intent.

6.4 Audience Reaction Summary

Emotional data can be collected statistically in a group video chat. By introducing statistical data on emotions into video conferencing, it is possible to visualize the mood within a group chat and the overall reaction. For example, by displaying in real time the number of students with troubled or angry faces in a school class, the teacher can easily ascertain whether all the children are understanding, etc.

6.5 Extension to Visual Communication Marker

EmojiCam can output emoticons and Chinese characters (kanji) in addition to emojis. Future work should consider how to use VCMs other than emoji in video conferencing, as is done in text-based communications. In Japan and China, Chinese characters, which are ideographic and hieroglyphic characters, are also used. EmojiCam can use Chinese characters to create a unique culture.

7   Conclusion

In this paper, user studies were conducted and discussed with the aim of solving problems such as the lack of nonverbal communication that video conferencing has by using emoji, which serves to compensate for the lack of nonverbal communication in text communication.

First, we summarized the problems that video conferencing faces, such as the lack of nonverbal communication, and how VCM, including emoji, is used in text communication, showing related research.

Second, we summarized the communication flow in video conferencing using emoji instead of facial expressions and developed the EmojiCam system to realize the flow.

Third, two user studies were conducted to verify the effectiveness of the EmojiCam system. The user study compared normal video with the use of EmojiCam and investigated whether the sender's emotions were accurately conveyed to the receiver through the subject experiment. The results showed that EmojiCam significantly conveyed more emotion in "sad" and "surprised" when the sender was given an example of facial expression recognition. In the other user study, when we asked participants to actually perform the task of light conversation using EmojiCam, there was no significant difference in the distribution of emotions during the call, however there was a change in behavior during the video call and impressions of the video call from user interview. On the contrary, many issues were found, such as the accuracy of facial expression recognition and dealing with the characteristics of each emotion.

Finally, we summarized the future potential of the EmojiCam system and items that need further investigation based on the findings of the communication flow design and subject experiments.

References

1. Non-verbal feedback and reactions - zoom help center. https://support.zoom.us/hc/en-us/articles/115001286183-Non-verbal-feedback-and-reactions-. Accessed 02 Aug 2021
2. Amaghlobeli, N.: Linguistic features of typographic emoticons in SMS discourse. Theor. Pract. Lang. Stud. **2** (2012). https://doi.org/10.4304/tpls.2.2.348-354
3. Derks, D., Fischer, A.H., Bos, A.E.: The role of emotion in computer-mediated communication: a review. Comput. Hum. Behav. **24**(3), 766–785 (2008)
4. Ekman, P.: Basic Emotions, pp. 45–60. Wiley (1999). https://doi.org/10.1002/0470013494.ch3
5. El Kaliouby, R., Robinson, P.: FAIM: integrating automated facial affect analysis in instant messaging. In: Proceedings of the 9th International Conference on Intelligent User Interfaces, IUI 2004, pp. 244–246. Association for Computing Machinery, New York (2004). https://doi.org/10.1145/964442.964493
6. Goodman, L.A.: Snowball sampling. Ann. Math. Stat. **32**(1), 148–170 (1961). http://www.jstor.org/stable/2237615
7. Herring, S., Dainas, A.: "nice picture comment!" graphicons in Facebook comment threads. In: Proceedings of the 50th Hawaii International Conference on System Sciences (2017)
8. Huang, J., et al.: Speed/Accuracy trade-offs for modern convolutional object detectors (2017)
9. Universal Multiple-Octet Coded Character Set (UCS). Standard, International Organization for Standardization, Geneva, CH, December 2003
10. Koh, J.I., Cherian, J., Taele, P., Hammond, T.: Developing a hand gesture recognition system for mapping symbolic hand gestures to analogous emojis in computer-mediated communication. ACM Trans. Interact. Intell. Syst. **9**(1) (2019). https://doi.org/10.1145/3297277
11. Park, J., Barash, V., Fink, C., Cha, M.: Emoticon style: interpreting differences in emoticons across cultures. In: Seventh International AAAI Conference on Weblogs and Social Media (2013)
12. Pırzadeh, A., Wu, H.W., Bharali, R., Kim, B.M., Wada, T., Pfaff, M.S.: Designing multi-touch gestures to support emotional expression in IM, CHI EA 2014, pp. 2515–2520. Association for Computing Machinery, New York (2014). https://doi.org/10.1145/2559206.2581347
13. Rovers, A., van Essen, H.: HIM: a framework for haptic instant messaging. In: CHI 2004 Extended Abstracts on Human Factors in Computing Systems, CHI EA 2004, pp. 1313–1316. Association for Computing Machinery, New York (2004). https://doi.org/10.1145/985921.986052
14. Sato, W., Hyniewska, S., Minemoto, K., Yoshikawa, S.: Facial expressions of basic emotions in Japanese laypeople. Front. Psychol. **10**, 259 (2019). https://doi.org/10.3389/fpsyg.2019.00259
15. Shin, H., Lee, J., Park, J., Kim, Y., Oh, H., Lee, T.: A tactile emotional interface for instant messenger chat. In: Smith, M.J., Salvendy, G. (eds.) Human Interface 2007. LNCS, vol. 4558, pp. 166–175. Springer, Heidelberg (2007). https://doi.org/10.1007/978-3-540-73354-6_19

16. Tang, Y., Hew, K.F.: Emoticon, emoji, and sticker use in computer-mediated communication: a review of theories and research findings. Int. J. Commun. **13**, 27 (2019)

17. Walther, J.B., D'addario, K.P.: The impacts of emoticons on message interpretation in computer-mediated communication. Soc. Sci. Comput. Rev. **19**(3), 324–347 (2001)

18. Wang, H.C., Lai, C.T.: Kinect-taped communication: using motion sensing to study gesture use and similarity in face-to-face and computer-mediated brainstorming. In: Proceedings of the SIGCHI Conference on Human Factors in Computing Systems, CHI 2014, pp. 3205–3214. Association for Computing Machinery, New York (2014). https://doi.org/10.1145/2556288.2557060

19. Zhou, R., Hentschel, J., Kumar, N.: Goodbye text, hello emoji: mobile communication on wechat in China. In: Proceedings of the 2017 CHI Conference on Human Factors in Computing Systems, pp. 748–759 (2017)

Pokerepo Join: Construction of a Virtual Companion Experience System

Minami Nishimura[1], Yoshinari Takegawa[1(✉)], Kohei Matsumura[2], and Keiji Hirata[1]

[1] Future University Hakodate, Hakodate, Japan
{g2119033,yoshi,hirata}@fun.ac.jp
[2] Ritsumeikan University College of Information Science and Engineering, Kyoto, Japan
matsumur@acm.org

Abstract. The purpose of this study is the Construction and implementation of a Virtual Companion Experience System, "Pokerepo Join", that considers user relationships. Virtual Companion Experience refers to the experience when a client in a remote location is assisted by a reporter at a certain site, in such a way that the client feels as though they are actually out with the reporter. The client is able to act and experience based on his or her own will. In particular, in this study, we consider that the information required for the realization of the Virtual Companion Experience differs depending on the human relationship between the client and the reporter, and propose an interface that considers the relationship between users. In addition, the proposed system has a mechanism that allows two or more people to communicate, in consideration of the intervention of a third party who is on-site. Requirements for constructing the system were defined through two experiments. After that, we constructed and actually operated the proposed system.

1 Introduction

There are various events in the world, such as exhibitions, school festivals and athletics meets, that involve participants going to a viewing site. However, not everyone who wants to watch can necessarily go to the desired exhibition etc. Many people abandon the exhibition for a variety of reasons, such as because they are far away from the venue, in hospital, or recuperating at home.

On the other hand, with the spread of video communication tools such as Skype, Hangout, and Zoom, anyone can share their interests and events occurring around them with others, through video and audio. By using video communication tools, a virtual companion experience could be provided in which people who cannot act and experience by themselves (hereinafter referred to as clients) receive assistance and feel as if they are going out with people who are

This work was supported by JSPS KAKENHI Grant Number JP19H04157.

M. Kurosu (Ed.): HCII 2021, LNCS 12764, pp. 626–642, 2021.
https://doi.org/10.1007/978-3-030-78468-3_43

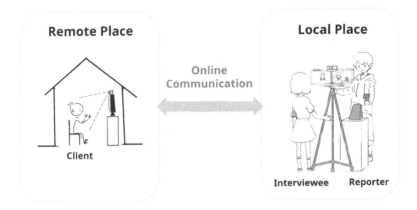

Fig. 1. Construction of virtual companion experience

on-site (hereinafter referred to as reporters). However, most of the video contents distributed by individuals mainly use a monocular camera mounted on a smartphone or the like, with which the reporter captures the subject (such as an object or a person the reporter wants to film). For this reason, there were limits to the virtual companion experience, such as the fact that it was not possible for users to enjoy viewing while looking between each other's facial expressions and exhibits, and that there was no intervention from a third party, such as a clerk or a museum curator talking to the client (Fig. 1).

The purpose of this study is to build Pokerepo Join, which solves these problems. Through preliminary experiments of a virtual accompaniment experience using a video communication tool on a tablet, we clarify the problems of the existing methods and define the requirements of Pokerepo Join. Based on the requirement definition, we construct the proposed Pokerepo Join. Pokerepo Join has a function that can provide face-to-face conversation and multiple video images. This allows the reporter to respond to the client's verbal viewing requests and allow a third party on site to naturally participate in the conversation between the reporter and the client.

In Pokerepo Join, the reporter mainly performs camera operation and video editing to deliver to the client. A client in a remote location only needs to convey viewing requests verbally to the reporter, based on the delivered video. In this study, we assumed a client with a physical disability or who was not accustomed to operating digital devices, such as an elderly person. Therefore, we adopted such a reporting style.

2   Related Research

This section describes studies that are closely related to our study.

2.1   Appreciation Support

TEROOS [5] is a wearable avatar that is worn on the shoulder of a person on location, and is operated by a remote operator. TEROOS has the function of outputting the utterance of the remote operator from the speaker mounted on it, and expressing the operator's feeling at that time by using the open/close eyes mechanism and swing mechanism with which it is equipped. However, in this system a third party on-site only talks to a remote operator through the robot called TEROOS, so it is difficult for the third party to understand what kind of person the operator is. Also, it is difficult for third parties to voluntarily talk to TEROOS (the operator).

In our research, we aim to transfer non-verbal information and promote the intervention of third parties in the field by installing a mechanism that provides the facial expressions of the remote operator (client), instead of using a robot. In addition, it is assumed that the remote operator is accustomed to operating a digital device and operates a camera spontaneously. However, in this study, the reporter also generates images to be provided to remote people.

2.2   Mobile Devices

Engström [2] proposes a support system that focuses on the function of recommending suitable camera positions in a live music shooting environment. The purpose of this system is to create a Video Jockey video collaboratively by mixing the video taken by photographers at the live music venue.

Schofield and colleagues have proposed Bootlegger [9], a project that supports interactive video shooting and editing. In this project, the opportunity for Bootlegging, i.e. the (sometimes illegal) production of video works, such as live music performances filmed by fans, is offered as one motivation to participate in a live performance. The purpose of Bootlegger is to produce, so participants work together to provide high-quality Bootlegs. The system provides templates and timings for shooting, enabling photographers who are not familiar with shooting techniques to cooperate with each other to support high-quality video production.

These studies are particularly aimed at editing footage shot by multiple people, such as in live performance venues. On the other hand, in our research, we propose a system to support multi-tasking work that simultaneously combines shooting and editing, focusing on live reports by one person.

Additionally, our research group has developed Pokerepo GO [7], which supports live broadcast reports by one person. We have also developed Pokerepo Go++ [10], which allows remote commentators to participate in live broadcasts. In Pokerepo Go++, the reporter wears a digital mask that displays the reporter's face and the commentator's face, so that a single reporter is able to play two roles. Pokerepo Go++ is an approach close to the concept of our research, but presupposes a conversation between a commentator and an interviewer, and a reporter and an interviewer. Unlike Pokerepo Join, Pokerepo Go++ does not consider support for conversation with a third party.

2.3   Robot

There are attempts to shoot videos with robots such as wearable robots and UAVs. Matsumoto et al. have proposed a system called Journalist Robot [6], in which a robot equipped with a camera, speakers and a moving mechanism automatically collects and stores the news events around it. This is a proposal for zero journalism, but there are still many issues that need to be resolved in order to realize it fully.

A more practical example is the attempt at robotic photography [1] by Byers et al. In this method, the robot automatically takes an appropriate photograph based on a preset composition. Attempts to turn a composition into a template and take photographs based on that template have been adopted in Bootlegger [9], and are more realistic in terms of robotic assistance.

Higuchi et al. have proposed a system for capturing free-viewpoint video content using UAVs called Flying Eyes [4]. This system has a UI for autonomous photography and camera work instructions.

Applying the robot reporting and the technology proposed for automatic photography, as described above, can be considered as one possibility to support live reporting, such as through automation of camera work. On the other hand, in automatic filming by a robot, it can be imagined that the robot conveys the experience as a reporter and that it is difficult to interact with the presenter, who is the target of the report. In our study, we focus on design to support reporting by one person.

3   Preliminary Experiment

In order to clarify the definition of requirements for Pokerepo Join, two types of preliminary experiment were performed. One type of preliminary experiment assumes local viewing and the other assumes remote viewing. In remote viewing, we used a video communication tool on a tablet, which is a typical example of existing methods. The problems of the existing method are clarified by comparing the local appreciation preliminary experiment and remote appreciation preliminary experiment.

3.1   Local Viewing

Method
The subjects are two college students who are friends. Without prior knowledge of the contents of the exhibition, they freely appreciated the Mucha exhibition held at the Hakodate Museum of Art. The viewing time was about 40 min. Based

on the nature observation method, which is one of the behavior observation methods [3], we observed and analyzed the subjects' appreciation methods. A semi-structured interview was conducted with the subjects after the experiment.

Result

The subjects tried to communicate with each other through verbal communication. During the appreciation, the subjects checked each other's expressions and reactions, and they looked at exhibits while discussing their opinions. When one subject made a comment such as "This is good", behaviour was observed in which, immediately after confirming the speaker's facial expression, the other subject also directed his gaze to the indicated exhibition. In response to this behavior, the subject states that "If you appreciate while watching each other's reactions and facial expressions, the conversation will be lively."

When third-party intervention occurred, through the subjects' conversation and pointing, the third-party understood what the subjects were talking about. This resulted in smooth joint attention and face-to-face conversation.

In addition, the subjects gave directions by using directives such as "that" and "it" for the exhibits, and pointing at them. The subjects were also seen leaning in to see the exhibits more closely. Regarding this behavior, one subject said, "I thought that if the person actually looking at an exhibits reacts to it by starting a conversation with 'This is...', I would be saying 'Eh? What?', so I'd like to be able to see the exhibit from close by."

3.2   Remote Viewing

Subject

Ten university students and one working woman participated as subjects. The subjects participated in the experiment as clients. The role of reporter was assigned to one experimenter, so that the quality of the presented video did not differ.

Procedure

The experimenter explained the purpose of the experiment to the clients who were the subjects. As a client, a subject sends a viewing request from a remote location (Japan) to a reporter in the local location (UK) via a live streaming service (Skype). The reporter operates the tablet and transmits the video to the client based on the client's viewing request. The client views the delivered video and feeds back further viewing requests to the reporter. The viewing time was about one hour, and the established viewing scenario was a visit to facilities at Sussex University.

The subjects were asked in advance to look at a map showing the facilities at Sussex University, which is what the subjects would be viewing, and to consider what facilities they would like to visit and in what order. After the appreciation, in an interview we asked the clients to talk freely about what they noticed about their appreciation behavior through the tablet. The interview is a semi-structured interview of about twenty minutes. There are three interview questions.

- How did you communicate with the reporter?
- How did you communicate with third parties?
- What is needed for better remote viewing?

Result
In order to analyze the remote appreciation, we conducted an interview analysis using thematic analysis and investigated the relationship between the frequency of use of each camera and the subject being shot. The latter is omitted due to space limitations. In this experiment, no third party participated during the reporter and client's appreciation.

Interview Result
Thematic analysis of the interview results was performed by four analysts. We explain the method of thematic analysis. First, the interview contents are transcribed. After that, the contents of the interview are coded by multiple people called coders (analysts). Coding is the process of labeling the transcribed content. Next, the obtained codes are grouped, the characteristics are described in one phrase and high-order codes are created. Main themes are created from themes that emerge from these high-order codes.

After having performed thematic analysis on the interview results, we broadly classified them as follows.

Communication Method
The client communicated the viewing request to the reporter by speaking simple instructions and explaining the features of the item that they wanted to see. This is because the reporter and client were able to mutually understand what kind of video the reporter delivered to the client, and what kind of video the reporter wanted to show. It can be considered that joint attention has been established through simple exchanges.

Request for Better Remote Viewing
There were requests to see the exhibits more closely and to view them from various camera angles. However, due to the problem that a tablet can only provide a single image, there is limited ability to respond to requests to view various angles and multiple videos. In addition, there was a request to experience appreciation while listening to the expression and reaction of the reporter on-site.

Tablets can only provide a single image. For this reason, there was a problem that an image of the exhibits could not be provided at the same time as an image of the reporter, thus there was a limit to simultaneous viewing. Furthermore, there was a demand for simultaneous viewing of multiple video images. However, as a tablet can only provide a single video image, response to this request is limited.

Requirement Definition
In this section, the following two requirements are set for Pokerepo Join based on the results obtained in local viewing and remote viewing.

(a) Response to Client Viewing Requests
In the remote-viewing interview, there were requests to see the exhibits more closely, view them at various camera angles, and see the reporter's expression. On the other hand, in the case of local viewing, there was appreciation while confirming each other's reactions and expressions, and viewing while approaching the exhibits. These requirements correspond to the observation results of local appreciation. Also, in response to a request to view multiple videos at the same time, in local viewing, after confirming the expression of the speaker, there was behavior of immediately shifting the line of sight to the indicated exhibition, which also agrees.

In this way, it became clear that clients in remote areas had various demands such as sharing of facial expressions, appropriate camera angles and zooming for exhibits and landscapes, and simultaneous viewing of multiple images.

(b) Participation by a Third Party (Interviewee)
In remote viewing, there was no situation in which a third party who was spotted in the local viewing participated in the conversation. Sasaki [8] proposes a five-dimensional system of appreciation behavior. Among the dimensions is the strengthening of human relations, such as becoming acquainted with new people, and the promotion of knowledge to deepen understanding of the society and people's lifestyle in the place one is visiting, and it is an important experience for clients to actively engage with local third parties. In remote viewing, the reporter was talking with the client while holding the tablet, and it was not clear what kind of client he was talking to. Accordingly, it is considered that this formed an atmosphere that made it difficult for a third party to talk to the reporter. Therefore, it is necessary to provide a mechanism that allows third parties to participate naturally.

4   Design and Implementation

Based on the requirements and knowledge of the virtual companion experience derived in the preliminary experiment in Chap. 3, we propose Pokerepo Join.

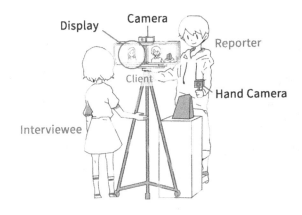

Fig. 2. Proposed system "Pokerepo Join"

Fig. 3. System flow

Using Fig. 2 and Fig. 3, we explain the basic workflow of Pokerepo Join. The reporter selectively uses three cameras to shoot video of a location. The captured video is transferred to the client through a video communication service (such as Skype). The client views the transmitted video through a home display. In addition, a camera for photographing the client's facial expression is installed in the client's home. The client's viewing requests and reactions are fed back to the reporter through the client's facial expression video and audio. It is also assumed that a third party such as a curator or an accompanying friend (hereinafter referred to as an interviewee) happens to intervene at the site. In addition, the operator of Pokerepo Join is assumed to be a single reporter carrying out one-man operation. Therefore, it is necessary to consider an interface design that enables the user to perform multitasking while responding to viewing requests from the client in a situation that changes from moment to moment, so that three parties can communicate smoothly.

4.1 Camera

Pokerepo Join has three types of camera for different purposes. Hereafter, each camera is described in detail (Fig. 4).

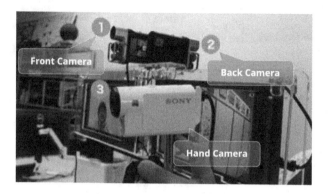

Fig. 4. On-board camera

Front Camera and Back Camera

The front camera is a camera that shoots the direction in which the reporter is proceeding. It is used to shoot images that appear in the reporter's field of vision and facial expressions of the interviewee. In this study, the video taken by this camera is called the front-camera image. The back camera is a camera that captures the reporter's facial expressions and is referred to in this study as the back-camera image. These cameras can capture facial expressions and gestures of the reporter and interviewee and convey nonverbal information that cannot be conveyed by voice alone.

Hand Camera

The hand camera is a close-up camera with which the reporter films the exhibits and posters etc. Since the reporter holds the camera itself, he can freely and intuitively control zooming and camera angles. **Contributing to the fulfillment of requirement (a) by providing appropriate zoom and camera angles for exhibits**. In this study, the video captured by this camera is called the hand-camera image.

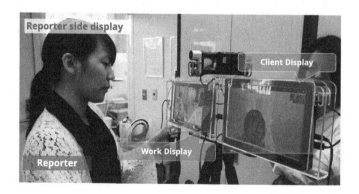

Fig. 5. Reporter-side display

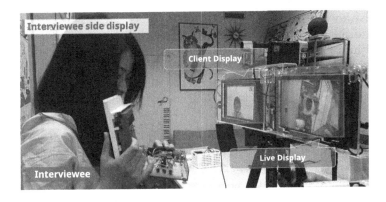

Fig. 6. Interviewee-side display

4.2 Display

As shown in Fig. 5 and Fig. 6, Pokerepo Join has three types of display for different purposes. The following describes each display (Fig. 7).

Client Display

The client display presents the facial expressions of the remote client. One client display is installed on both the reporter's side and the interviewee's side. This allows the reporter and the interviewee to talk face-to-face while each checking the facial expressions of the client presented on the display. Not only does this promote communication between the reporter and the client and between the client and the interviewee, but also the client's facial expression is displayed largely, allowing the third party to understand that the client is remote. For this reason, **is expected to promote the intervention of third parties. This contributes to the fulfillment of requirement (b).**

Fig. 7. Work display

Work Display

The work display is a display mounted to face the reporter. The work display is divided into four parts, and the images taken by the reporter are displayed in real-time in each divided area. This allows the reporter to check the multiple camera images being captured. While checking the video on the work display, the reporter selects the final video to be presented to the client and the interviewee.

Live Display

The live display displays the final video that the reporter is delivering to the client. Through this, the reporter, the interviewee, and the client always view the common video. The reporter does not watch the final video itself, but can easily imagine the final video, because he selects the camera image to be distributed to the client from the video on the work display. By sharing the distributed video, it becomes easy for the three parties to build joint attention, such as what they are watching and what they are paying attention to.

4.3   Screen Layout of Final Video

In order to satisfy the requirement (a) for simultaneous viewing, three types of final video are provided, as shown in Fig. 8. 'Main' displays an image selected from the three camera images (Front-camera image, Back-camera image, Hand-camera image). In addition, 'H&H' can be used for face-to-face conversations, and the interviewee video and the reporter video can be watched simultaneously. Also, 'PinP' uses the hand-camera image as the main image and displays the back-camera image (image of the reporter) as a sub-image. Other options could be considered but the types of video were determined based on the frequency of camera use in remote viewing in the preliminary experiments. These screen layouts are operated by a hand-held controller.

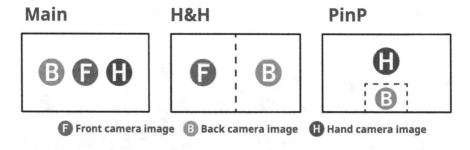

Fig. 8. Types of screen layout

5   Evaluative Experiment

An evaluative experiment was conducted to investigate whether each function of the proposed system, constructed based on the established requirements, was useful in the virtual companion experience.

Regarding requirement (a) 'Provision of video that meets the client's viewing requests', because we implement the system based on the conditions that were clarified in the preliminary experiment, it can be said that the system already functionally meets this requirement. For that reason, in this evaluative experiment we investigate the usefulness of the function introduced to promote third-party participation (requirement (b)), i.e., the function that enables viewing of the exchange between reporter and client. The usefulness of the function is verified by investigating to what extent it influences the occurrence of 'Interjection (= third-party participation)'.

5.1 Method

Subjects and Procedure

A survey was carried out among a total of 49 adult subjects, of which 35 were male and 14 were female. None of the subjects had any prior knowledge of Pokerepo Join. The subjects took on the role of interviewee and we compared the case of using the proposed method (Pokerepo Join) with the case of using a comparative method (a tablet PC). As shown in Fig. 9, we set four methods from A to D. Methods A and B are the proposed method which presents multiple images (Pokerepo Join), while methods C and D are the comparative method that presents a single image (tablet). Additionally, the methods were divided into those using the screen seen by the reporter (A, C) and those using the screen seen by the interviewee (B, D), and we investigated which method produced the most interjection.

In this experiment, we had subjects look at an illustration showing the state of both the proposed method and comparative method being used, and asked the subjects to answer a questionnaire. We also considered a method in which subjects would answer the questionnaire after having attended the site at which the prototype system was actually being used, but it was considered that, because regulating the conversational content and behaviour of the reporter and client is difficult, the subjects' answers would be affected. For this reason, we adopted the method of having subjects look at illustrations. Also, we did consider using photographs instead of illustrations, but decided on illustrations to prevent the questionnaire results being influenced by the physical appearance of the reporter and client.

The illustrations used in the experiment show the reporter and client talking to each other, but the content of their conversation is not specified. Whether or not a subject would interject is influenced by the content of the conversation between the reporter and client. In this experiment we wanted to investigate whether, independent of conversational content, being able visually to observe the exchange between reporter and client affects interjection. Therefore, we did not clarify the content of the conversation. In order to eliminate dispersion caused by the relationships between system users (client/reporter/interviewee), we informed subjects of the precondition that all the system users had the relationship of being friends, before subjects answered the questionnaire.

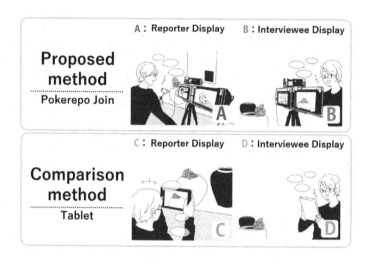

Fig. 9. Proposed method and comparison method

Table 1. Questions

Number	Question content
Question1	Would you speak to the system users, or not?
Question2	What information would be necessary to make an interjection?
Question3	Is being able to observe the state of the reporter and client important
	When an interviewee participates in conversation, or not?

Questions

The questionnaire comprises the 3 questions shown in Table 1, each of which was set to investigate to what extent the function enabling observation has influence as a condition of the occurrence of 'Interjection (= third-party participation)'. Question 1 was set to evaluate the significant difference between the proposed method and comparative method according to 'presence or absence of interjection'. In question 2, we investigate the information necessary to make an interjection. This question was set with the aim of establishing what kind of information would motivate someone to join in conversation, by comparing the question results with the results of question 1. Question 3 was set to investigate to what extent 'being able to observe the state of the reporter and client', which is the special feature of the proposed system, is seen as important when an interviewee participates in conversation. Question 1 was answered with one of two options (I would speak to them/ I would not speak to them). Question 2 could be answered freely. Question 3 had two answer options (It is important/ It is not important) and subjects were asked to write a comment giving the reason for their answer.

5.2   Results

Question 1:
Would you Speak to the Reporter, or not?
Regarding the proposed method, 43% of subjects answered that they would speak to the reporter, while only 26% answered in the same way for the comparative method. Also, we used a chi-squared test to analyze in which, out of the proposed method and comparative method, an interviewee was most likely to speak or not speak to the reporter. The null hypothesis is that 'there is no connection between the difference in the proposed method and comparative method and the motive to interject', and the alternative hypothesis is that 'there is a connection between the difference in the proposed method and comparative method and the motive to interject'. As a result, the P value was 0.0007 and, this being a result of $p < .05$, a significant difference was observed. Accordingly, the alternative hypothesis was adopted and it was found that there is a connection between the difference in the proposed method and comparative method and the occurrence of interjection.

Question 2:
What Information Would be Necessary to Make an Interjection?
The results of question 2 are shown in Fig. 10. Regarding motivation to interject, the information considered most important was 'conversational content' (35.0%), followed by 'the appearance of the other people' (31.7%). Other answers are summarized from the responses given by subjects in the comment section, in which there were fewer than two comments. As specific examples of 'the appearance of the other people', subjects mentioned the client and reporter's facial expressions, gestures and the circumstances they were in.

Question 3:
Is Being Able to Observe the State of the Reporter and Client
Important When an Interviewee Participates in Conversation, or not?
In this question, we judge the appropriateness of the design policy of 'the function enabling observation', created in response to requirement (b). We had subjects answer whether or not 'the function enabling observation' was important, along

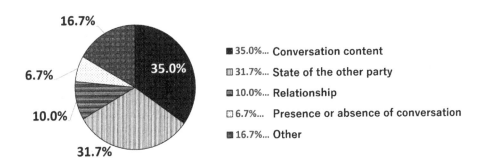

Fig. 10. Proposed method and Comparison method

with the reason for their answers. As a result, 77% of subjects answered that observing the exchange between the client and reporter is important for grasping the situation. As a reason this was seen as important, subjects gave the opinion that understanding the situation is essential for deciding when is an appropriate time to interject. As reasons the observation function was not seen as important, subjects gave the opinions that it was unnecessary, as they would not be inclined to interject in the first place, and that the situation could be grasped from audio alone.

5.3   Consideration

In question 1, we obtained a result showing that in the proposed method, which enables 'observation' of the situation which the client and reporter are in, it is easier to interject than in the comparative method. In question 2, 'conversational content' (35.0%) was given as the information regarded as most important. However, the proposed system does not have a function to recognize or propose the content of the system users' conversation. In contrast, regarding the second-most important information, 'the appearance of the other people' (31.7%), the proposed system is equipped with a function for grasping the state of the other people. Specifically, the system has a facial expression camera that constantly captures the expressions of the system users and an interviewee-side display that presents the state of the exchange between the client and reporter to the interviewee. These are considered to be the reasons that the proposed method, which has a function enabling observation of the circumstances of the client and reporter, made interjection easier than the comparative method.

However, under half of the subjects still answered that they would not participate in conversation. In future, it is necessary to improve the system in terms of a function to further promote participation in conversation, based on the information seen as important for participation, which we obtained in question 2. At present, regarding the appearance of the other people, in the proposed system is it possible to confirm facial expression, gestures, and so on. Nevertheless, it is difficult to understand what kind of situation the client and reporter are in. It is considered that, in future, participation in conversation can be promoted by making it easier for an interviewee to grasp the situation of the other people, that is, the situation of the client and reporter. For example, we plan to present icons or phrases on the interviewee-side display that express the situation of the client and reporter, such as 'currently busy' or 'participation recommended'. From question 3, it can be considered that the function enabling observation of the system users is useful for third-party participation. From this, we were able to reconfirm the importance of the proposed system's design policy that 'it is possible to observe the facial expressions and appearances of system users'.

6   Conclusion

In this research, we constructed Pokerepo Join, which supports a virtual companion experience. Based on preliminary experiments of remote appreciation and on-site appreciation, it was clarified that the requirements of Pokerepo Join were to meet the client's viewing requests and to enable third parties (interviewees) to join the conversation. We proposed Pokerepo Join, which satisfies these requirements, and developed a prototype system. We conducted a feasibility study on whether each function of Pokerepo Join was used as expected. Each of the functions proposed in Pokerepo Join was used, although the frequency of use was biased.

In the future, we plan to solve the problems that were clarified by the evaluative experiments, by improving the system by constructing an interface that takes into account operability by the reporter, and conducting additional experiments.

References

1. Byers, Z., Dixion, M., Smart, W.D., Grimm, C.M.: Say cheese! experiences with a robot photographer **25**, 37–46 (2004)
2. Engstrom, A., Esbjornsson, M., Juhlin, O.: Mobile collaborative live video mixing. In: Proceedings of the 10th International Conference on Human Computer Interaction with Mobile Devices and Services, MobileHCI 2008, pp. 2001–2004. Association for Computing Machinery, New York (2008). https://doi.org/10.1145/1409240.1409258
3. Haynes, S.N., O'Brien, W.H.: Principles and Strategies of Behavioral Observation, pp. 225–263. Springer, Boston (2000). https://doi.org/10.1007/978-0-306-47469-9_12
4. Higuchi, K., Ishiguro, Y., Rekimoto, J.: Flying eyes: free-space content creation using autonomous aerial vehicles. In: Extended Abstracts on Human Factors in Computing Systems, CHI 2011, pp. 561–570. Association for Computing Machinery, New York (2011). https://doi.org/10.1145/1979742.1979627
5. Kashiwabara, T., Osawa, H., Shinozawa, K., Imai, M.: TEROOS: a wearable avatar to enhance joint activities. In: Proceedings of the SIGCHI Conference on Human Factors in Computing Systems, CHI 2012. Association for Computing Machinery, New York (2012). https://doi.org/10.1145/2207676.2208345
6. Matsumoto, R., Nakayama, H., Harada, T., Kuniyoshi, Y.: Journalist robot: robot system making news articles from real world, pp. 1234–1241 (2007). https://doi.org/10.1109/IROS.2007.4399598
7. Matsumura, K., Takegawa, Y.: Reporting solo: a design of supporting system for solo live reporting. In: Proceedings of the 13th International Conference on Advances in Computer Entertainment Technology, ACE 2016. Association for Computing Machinery, New York (2016). https://doi.org/10.1145/3001773.3001792
8. Nakayachi, K.: Toshiji sasaki (author), psychology of traveler behavior, 2000, Kansai University Press. Soc. Psychol. Res. **16**(1), 64–65 (2000). DOIurl10.14966/jssp.KJ00003724836. https://ci.nii.ac.jp/naid/110002785354/

9. Schofield, G., Bartindale, T., Wright, P.: Bootlegger: turning fans into film crew. In: Inkpen, K., Woo, W. (eds.) CHI 2015 - Proceedings of the 33rd Annual CHI Conference on Human Factors in Computing Systems, pp. 767–776. Association for Computing Machinery (ACM) (2015). https://doi.org/10.1145/2702123.2702229

10. Takegawa, Y., Matsumura, K., Manabe, H.: PokeRepo Go++: one-man live reporting system with a commentator function. In: Proceedings of the 2019 ACM International Conference on Interactive Experiences for TV and Online Video, TVX 2019, pp. 230–238. Association for Computing Machinery, New York (2019). https://doi.org/10.1145/3317697.3325126

Visual Information in Computer-Mediated Interaction Matters: Investigating the Association Between the Availability of Gesture and Turn Transition Timing in Conversation

James P. Trujillo[1,2(✉)], Stephen C. Levinson[2], and Judith Holler[1,2]

[1] Donders Institute for Brain, Cognition and Behaviour, Radboud University Nijmegen, Nijmegen, The Netherlands
j.trujillo@donders.ru.nl

[2] Max Planck Institute for Psycholinguistics, Wundtlaan 1, 6525XD Nijmegen, The Netherlands

Abstract. Natural human interaction involves the fast-paced exchange of speaker turns. Crucially, if a next speaker waited with planning their turn until the current speaker was finished, language production models would predict much longer turn transition times than what we observe. Next speakers must therefore prepare their turn in parallel to listening. Visual signals likely play a role in this process, for example by helping the next speaker to process the ongoing utterance and thus prepare an appropriately-timed response.

To understand how visual signals contribute to the timing of turn-taking, and to move beyond the mostly qualitative studies of gesture in conversation, we examined unconstrained, computer-mediated conversations between 20 pairs of participants while systematically manipulating speaker visibility. Using motion tracking and manual gesture annotation, we assessed 1) how visibility affected the timing of turn transitions, and 2) whether use of co-speech gestures and 3) the communicative kinematic features of these gestures were associated with changes in turn transition timing.

We found that 1) decreased visibility was associated with less tightly timed turn transitions, and 2) the presence of gestures was associated with more tightly timed turn transitions across visibility conditions. Finally, 3) structural and salient kinematics contributed to gesture's facilitatory effect on turn transition times.

Our findings suggest that speaker visibility--and especially the presence and kinematic form of gestures--during conversation contributes to the temporal coordination of conversational turns in computer-mediated settings. Furthermore, our study demonstrates that it is possible to use naturalistic conversation and still obtain controlled results.

Keywords: Multimodality · Kinematics · Adaptation

1 Introduction

Natural human interaction involves the fast-paced exchange of speaker turns. Remarkably, the gap between when one person stops speaking and the other begins speaking

© Springer Nature Switzerland AG 2021
M. Kurosu (Ed.): HCII 2021, LNCS 12764, pp. 643–657, 2021.
https://doi.org/10.1007/978-3-030-78468-3_44

is quite small, on the order of 200 ms (Stivers et al. 2009). This has posed an interesting challenge to models of language production and comprehension because if a next speaker were to wait with planning their turn until the end of the current speaker's turn, production models would predict inter-speaker gaps to be on the order of 500–600 ms, minimally, even for very short responses (Levinson 2016; Levinson and Torreira 2015). In order for this tight temporal coordination to be possible, next speakers must therefore prepare their turn in parallel to listening (Heldner and Edlund 2010; Levinson and Torreira 2015). Sensitivity to turn-final cues allows next speakers to then launch their pre-planned turn on time.

Human interaction is not, however, limited only to speech. In face-to-face interaction, the natural environment of language use, visual signals such as hand gestures are tightly integrated with speech ('co-speech gestures'), forming a multimodal communicative system (Bavelas and Chovil 2000; Holler and Levinson 2019; Kendon 2004; McNeill 1992). This multimodality also plays a role in the timing of speaker turn transitions it appears, as evidenced by the finding of questions receiving faster responses (i.e., shorter turn transition times) when they were uttered with gestures compared with responses to questions without a gestural component (Holler et al. 2018; ter Bekke 2020). These results therefore suggest that visual signals play an important role in efficient turn-taking behavior. However, the process by which this happens it not well understood.

The relation between gesture and inter-speaker turn transitions can be further elucidated by looking at how turn transition times are affected by the visibility of co-speech gestures, as well as how they are related to the communicative kinematic features of gestures. Mostly in gesture studies we have to be content with correlational accounts, but if it is possible to control precisely what an interlocutor sees, then it may be possible to give a stronger account of what features of gesture contribute to turn-taking efficiency. For example, using a computer-mediated channel it is possible to explore more precisely how gestures may contribute to fast turn transitions, by successively downgrading the visibility of visual signals. If very small, subtle finger movements and handshapes are most critical, then a beneficial effect of gestures on turn timing should mainly be observed during very low blur grades since this information disappears with more degrees of blur. However, if slightly more coarse-grained gestural features, such as larger handshapes and arm movements are most beneficial, then the effect of the presence of gestures may be most pronounced during medium blur grades. Here, the gestural information may also stand out more since other, non-gestural signals that can facilitate turn-taking (such as eye gaze) are not available anymore. However, if very coarse-grained gestural movements are most beneficial, then the effect of gesture on turn-transition should still be evident during stronger blur grades. Here, it may also be that the termination of gestures (e.g., the onset of the retraction) may stand out more than other information. This issue of granularity may be particularly relevant for the domain of human-computer-interaction, as the granularity of motion-tracking or motion recognition algorithms should reflect the way visual signals are used and understood in natural interaction.

Beyond the facilitatory presence of gestures, it is currently unclear how exactly gestures contribute to turn-taking timing. According to the seminal turn-taking model by Sacks et al. (1974), speakers try to minimize the turn-transition time or in other words, aim to reduce both gaps and overlaps as much as possible (Levinson and Torreira 2015).

Two questions arise. First, is it possible to replicate the finding from Holler et al. (2018) that showed a correlation between gestures and faster response times, and to do so in a computer-mediated setting which allows more systematic investigation? Second, is it possible to show that gestures not only speed responses but also – through indicating forthcoming speaker termination – lower the amount of overlap?

While manipulating visibility can be informative about the granularity of visual information that is contributing to turn-taking timing, investigating how different gesture types contribute to turn-taking can be informative on a more functional level. Specifically, while some types of gestures contribute largely to semantic meaning (e.g., iconics, metaphorics, McNeill 1992), others contribute more to the temporal structural and emphasis of an utterance (e.g., beats; McNeill 1992), and yet others more to the dialogic process between the interlocutors (e.g., interactive gestures, Bavelas et al. 1995). Note that these 'type categories' should not be considered as mutually exclusive, but rather as dimensions, with the foregrounded dimension serving to class a given gesture as one or the other type for the purpose of analysis. However, one such type of gesture may contribute more than others to turn-taking timing, shedding light on how gestures facilitate turn-transition times.

Further, examining the specific kinematic features of a gesture can provide insights into whether the form of the gesture, beyond how visible it is, also influences its effect on turn timing. This is relevant because kinematic features of gestures (such as their size, location in gesture space, etc.) have previously been linked to semantic and pragmatic functions (e.g., Campisi and Özyürek 2013; Gerwing and Bavelas 2004; Holler and Wilkin 2011; Trujillo et al. 2019, 2020). For example, subtle differences in kinematics such as the position of the gesture in space can signal communicative intention (Trujillo et al. 2018), while temporal features, such as how clearly segmented the gesture is into smaller constituent movements aids in the processing of the gesture's meaning (Trujillo et al. 2019). If, as discussed in Holler et al. (2018), utterances with co-occurring gestures lead to faster responses due to a facilitation of processing, then kinematically salient and clear gestures (e.g., those that are larger, more centrally located, or with clearly segmented structures) should be associated with even shorter turn-transition times when compared to gestures with less salient kinematics. Therefore, understanding which kinematic features relate to the duration of turn transitions, and how this interacts with the visibility of gestures, can provide further insights into how gestures may be influencing turn-taking behavior.

In order to assess how gesture contributes to the timing of turn-taking, we quantified the kinematics of co-speech gestures performed during unscripted, naturalistic, casual conversation. In order to manipulate the visual availability of the gestural signal, we employed a special computer-mediated set-up: Participants in each dyad were located in separate rooms and saw each other via a live feed, displayed on a large screen directly in front of them. The size of the screen ensured that the displayed image was close to life-sized. This set-up provides a crucial advantage to our study, as most studies of gesture use in conversation are mostly qualitative or correlational in nature. Utilizing computer-mediated interaction of this type allows an extra degree of experimental control, allowing us to more systematically examine the relationship between visual signals and turn-taking behavior.

Critically, the visual quality changed in ten separate steps (blur grades), with each step occurring after four minutes. This was performed in order to test whether the visibility of gestures, as well as any kinematic changes in their production (e.g., larger versus smaller movements) would affect turn transitions. Because gestures have been shown to be associated with a decrease in overall turn-transition time in face-to-face interaction, we suspected their gradual disappearance as a consequence of the increase in blur grade to also affect turn transition times in the present computer-mediated setting (i.e., to result in an increase of turn transition time). As visibility was systematically reduced over ten blur grades, we were also able to investigate the general shape of gesture's contribution to turn-transition times. We expected gestures to facilitate turn-transition timing the most during moderate visibility conditions, as turn-taking timing may be negatively affected by the decreased general visibility of the speaker, but gestures are expected to be visible enough to still facilitate. As visibility becomes more severely degraded, the gestural benefit will likely decrease again. Similarly, in low blur grades (i.e., high visibility), additional, potentially more spatially fine-grained cues to turn-taking, such as eye-gaze (Kendon 1967), are still visible. Gestures are therefore expected to stand out most in moderate compared to low blur grades.

To summarise, we first tested whether (RQ1) visibility of the speaker, and thus the visibility of visual signals, affected turn transition time. We expected turn-transition times to become less tight, with more gaps and overlaps. Next, we tested whether we could replicate the finding of (RQ2) gestures relating to faster responses, and whether this facilitation is specifically related to overall faster responses (i.e., shorter gaps, longer overlaps) or to more tightly coordinated turn-transitions (i.e., shorter gaps, shorter overlaps). As a secondary test, we also assess whether certain gesture types influence turn-transition times more than other types. Finally, we tested whether (RQ3) communicatively relevant gesture kinematics are associated with turn transition time. We expected increased kinematic salience to be associated with a decrease in gap and overlap duration.

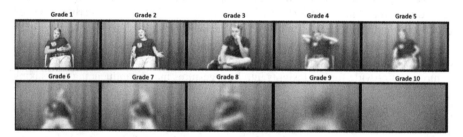

Fig. 1. Visual depiction of the actual blur grades used in this study

2 Methods

2.1 Participants

Data were initially collected from 38 dyads (74 participants), recruited from the participant database of the Max Planck Institute for Psycholinguistics. Dyads were excluded if there were technical errors in the audio or visual recordings of either participant (often caused by problems with the script implementing the blur grades), leaving 20 dyads (40 participants total; 31 females, mean age: 24.23 years) for analysis. Participants were all native speakers of Dutch and were familiar with the respective other person in the dyad.

2.2 Task

Dyads engaged in a natural, unscripted conversation, mediated by an audio-video based telecommunication interface, for 40 min each. Participants in each dyad were located in separate rooms and saw each other via a live feed, displayed on a large screen (27″, 16:9, 1920 × 1080 px, full HD) directly in front of them. The size of the screen ensured that the displayed image was close to life-sized. Visual quality changed in ten separate steps, with each step occurring after four minutes (see Fig. 1). The direction of quality change (clear to full blur or full blur to clear) was randomized across participants. Ten dyads went from blurry to clear, and ten dyads went from clear to blurry. Conversations were not constrained, and participants were instructed to simply talk as they would if they met at home or in a café for the duration of the experiment.

2.3 Audio Segmentation and Turn Transition Time

We performed automatic segmentation of the audio stream of each participant into speech and silence, and further segmented speech into discrete utterances following the methodology of Heldner and Edlund (2010) and Roberts et al. (2015). These analyses were performed using custom Python (version 3.7) scripts.

In order to segment the audio stream into speech and silence, we first calculated the amplitude of the audio file of each separate participant using the Python package Parselmouth (Jadoul et al. 2018) which allows direct interfacing of Python with PRAAT (Boersma and Weenink 2007) functions. Next, we used a threshold of 35 dB below the maximum value to separate the file into speech and silence. In order to exclude backchannels, we removed any speech segment of less than 700 ms, as up to 75% of speech segments less than 700 ms are likely to be backchannels (Roberts et al. 2015). We then merged any speech segments that were separated by less than 180 ms in order to reduce the risk of stop closures being mistaken for pauses between utterances (Heldner and Edlund 2010).

Based on the resulting speech annotations we calculated turn transition time. This was done by taking the offset (i.e., end time) of each speech utterance and finding the nearest speech onset time. For the calculation of nearest utterance, we used a window of 2 s, following the methodology of Heldner and Edlund (2010), who similarly used data from Dutch speakers (Heldner and Edlund 2010). The nearest onset could be either a successive speech utterance by the same speaker, or a new speech utterance by the other speaker. In the case of the nearest onset being produced by the other speaker, the time difference between the offset of the first utterance (speaker A) and onset of the second utterance (speaker B) was taken as the turn transition time. Therefore, negative values indicate an overlap, where speaker B started their utterance before speaker A stopped speaking, while positive values indicate gaps. Analyses were carried out on the total turn-transition time, consisting of both negative and positive values, as well as separately on gaps and overlaps (described below).

2.4 Gesture Annotation and Selection

For gesture, we utilized the SPUDNIG application (Ripperda et al. 2020) to detect all movements produced by each participant. These movements were then manually checked and non-gesture movements were removed. A second coder blind to the hypotheses manually identified gestures in 10% of the data (four minutes per participant). This subset of the data contained 12.7% of all gestures. Agreement reached 81% (Cohen's kappa could not be calculated as annotation categories were not included in this stage of the reliability testing). After removal of non-gesture movements we annotated each gesture as being representational (Alibali et al. 2001; e.g., iconics, metaphorics), pragmatic ((Kendon 2004); e.g., beats, emphatics, mood and stance modifiers), emblem (Ekman and Friesen 1969; e.g., "thumbs-up", "ok sign"), or interactive (Bavelas et al. 1995, e.g., palm-up open-hand gesture handing over the turn, addressee-directed deictics). In total we annotated 3,587 unique gestures (Representational: 980, Pragmatic: 627, Interactive: 1,897, Emblem: 83). Single gesture annotations could include multiple "beats" or movements, but were split when a continuous series of movements changed in either form or function. Annotations included only the preparation and main (stroke) phase of the gesture (Kita et al. 1998), but not the retraction. This was to ensure any abrupt retraction movements did not influence the speech-gesture alignment analyses. Reliability for gesture categorization was again performed on (a different set of) 10% of the data, which contained 18.5% of all gestures. Gestures identified by the primary coder were given to the second coder, without labels, and this second coder categorized each gesture. We observed a modified Cohen's kappa of 0.74, indicating substantial agreement (Landis and Koch 1977).

For each turn from speaker A with a corresponding next turn from speaker B (i.e., those for which turn transition times were calculated), we extracted any gestures that occurred during Speaker A's utterance. For these gestures, we calculated kinematic features, as described below.

2.5 Kinematic Feature Calculation

We calculated kinematic features that are related to visual salience and thus the communicative import of gestures. These features were the *peak velocity*, defined as the maximum velocity value during a gesture, number of *submovements*, defined as the number of individual ballistic movements (e.g., strokes, preparatory movements), *hold-time*, defined as the amount of time during gesture execution where the hands are still but depicting gestural information (i.e. excluding rest before initial movement and after final movement), *volume*, which is defined as the maximum geometric space utilized, *max distance,* which defines the maximum extension of the gesturing hand(s), and *McNeillian space*, which is based on McNeill's (1992) delineation of gesture space into center-center, center, periphery, and extra-periphery. Our McNeillian Space calculation is operationalized as the space category that is used most (i.e., the mode) during gesture production.

2.6 Analysis

All statistical tests were performed in R (R Core Team 2019) using the lme4 package (Bates et al. 2015), implementing mixed effects regression models. Models described below are performed separately for overlap data and gap data.

For all mixed models, we compared our model of interest, described below for each research question, against a null model that only contained the dependent variable, utterance duration as a covariate, and any random terms. Utterance duration was included as it has been demonstrated to affect subsequent turn-transition time (Roberts et al. 2015). This was done using chi-square tests of model of comparison.

To assess whether speaker visibility affected gap duration (RQ1), we tested a linear mixed model with transition time as dependent variable, and blur grade (i.e., visibility), together with utterance duration as independent variable. Dyad and participant were modeled as a nested random effect, with random slopes included when this did not lead to singular model fits. To assess whether the presence of gestures led to shorter turn transition times (RQ2), we first tested a model containing turn transition time as dependent variable, and gesture presence (together with utterance duration and blur grade) as independent variables. We additionally included an interaction term between blur grade and gesture presence, as well as a nested random effect of dyad and participant. As we were interested in how gesture visibility interacts with turn timing, we additionally tested whether a second-order polynomial (i.e., quadratic) model was a better fit than the linear model. As a final step, if gesture presence was a significant predictor of turn transition time, we tested this model against a 'gesture type model', in which switched out gesture presence as a predictor for gesture type as a predictor. Gesture type included the five types described above, as well as 'None', for the case of no gesture present. If this model was a better fit to the data, then this would indicate that turn transition time is differentially affected by different gesture types. To assess whether gesture kinematics influenced turn transition times (RQ3), we started with a maximal model including all kinematic features and their interaction with blur grade. Using chi-square tests, we systematically removed model terms until we found the best fit model of interest. This model was then compared against the null model. Due to differences in scale between kinematic features, all features were normalized (i.e., converted to a 0-1 scale) to facilitate model fitting.

3 Results

3.1 Effect of Visibility on Turn Transition Time

For total turn-transition time, we found a significant effect of reduced visibility leading to longer turn-transition time, $\chi 2(6) = 6.433$, $p = 0.011$. Splitting the data into gaps and overlaps, we found that decreasing visibility was associated with significantly higher inter-speaker overlaps, $\chi 2(3) = 120.58$, $p < 0.001$. However, visibility was not associated with any differences in inter-speaker turn gaps, $\chi 2(1) = 0.7663$, $p = 0.381$.

3.2   Effect of Gesture Presence on Turn Transition Time

For total turn-transition time, the best fit model included utterance duration, a quadratic effect of visibility, and gesture presence (χ^2 (2) = 23.157, p < 0.001; gesture type did not lead to a better model fit, $\chi^2(4)$ = 2.676, p = 0.614). Figure 2A shows that, when including the non-linear effect of visibility, utterances with gestures seem to have more overlaps (i.e., faster responses; see Fig. 2A). However, the highly overlapping confidence intervals make it difficult to draw firm conclusions. Splitting the data into gaps and overlaps provides more insights into what is happening. When utterances were accompanied by co-speech gestures, we observed a reduction in subsequent inter-speaker overlaps, $\chi^2(1)$ = 4.608, p = 0.032, as well as a reduction in inter-speaker turn gaps, χ^2 (7) = 57.446, p < 0.001 (see Fig. 2B and C). In other words, in the split analysis we see turn transition times moving towards zero when utterances are accompanied by a gesture. We additionally found that the quadratic model was a better fit than the linear model, χ^2 (2) = 46.539, p < 0.001, with gesture presence being associated with a reduction in overlaps during the first five grades of visibility, but falling off as visibility was reduced. We found a similar quadratic effect for gaps, $\chi^2(2)$ = 11.555, p = 0.003, with gestures reducing gap duration primarily during the first 5 blur grades. See Fig. 2

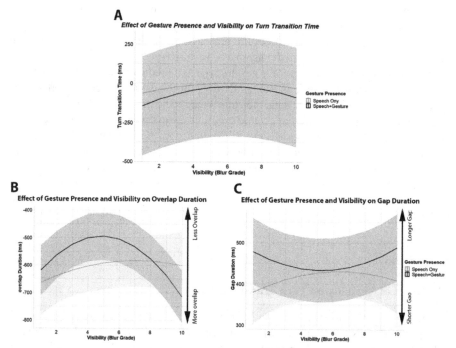

Fig. 2. Effects of gesture presence on turn transition times. Panel **A** depicts total turn transition time, panel **B** depicts overlaps, and panel **C** depicts gaps. Blur grade (i.e., visibility) is given on the x-axis. The y-axis gives overlap and gap duration. Speech only utterances are depicted by the red line, while speech-gesture utterances are depicted by the blue line. The shaded areas give the confidence interval. (Color figure online)

for an overview of the quadratic results. Similar to the total turn-transition time analysis, adding gesture type did not lead to a better model fit for overlaps, $\chi^2(4) = 3.772, p = 0.438$, or for gaps, $\chi^2(4) = 9.077, p = 0.059$.

3.3 Effect of Gesture Kinematics on Turn Transition Time

As the results of the gesture presence analysis indicated that the direction of association between gesture and turn transition time was dependent on whether we are considering gaps or overlaps, we focus our kinematic analyses on the split data. For utterances accompanied by gestures, we observed a significant association between the kinematic features of these gestures and both inter-speaker overlaps, $\chi^2(8) = 19.809, p = 0.011$, as well as inter-speaker gaps, $\chi^2 (8) = 24.215, p = 0.002$. While the individual kinematic parameters were somewhat non-homogenous in their effects, we see at least several consistent findings. Gesture size, measured by maximum distance, as well as segmentation, measured by holdtime, both led to longer turn transition times. Peak velocity and submovements, on the other hand, led to shorter turn transition times.

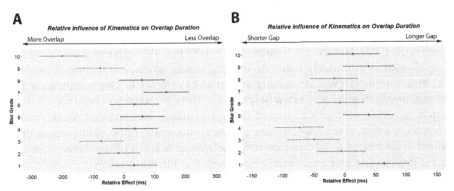

Fig. 3. Relative effects of gesture kinematics on turn transition times, over and beyond the main effects of visibility and gesture presence. The panel on the left depicts overlaps, while the panel on the right depicts gaps. Blur grade (i.e., visibility) is given on the y-axis. The x-axis gives net effect of all kinematic features relative to the intercept. In other words, positive values (given in blue) indicate longer turn transition times, while negative values (given in red) indicate shorter turn transition times. Mean effect, correcting for random effects and utterance duration, are indicated by circles, while the standard deviation is depicted as the lines behind the circles. Effect estimates are given for each of the blur grades. (Color figure online)

Overall, as can be seen in Fig. 3, the combination of these positive and negative effects is still able to explain a significant portion of the variation associated with reduced gaps and overlaps for utterances that are paired with gestures. Specifically, Fig. 3 shows how kinematics, as one synergistic set of features, can shift the extent of overlaps and gaps beyond the main effects of visibility and gesture presence. These main effects are thus the zero-point on the graphs, with the effect of increased kinematic salience or communicative import represented by the plotted values. Specific model terms can be seen in Appendix 1, and the effects on turn transition times across the visibility conditions can be seen in Fig. 3.

4 Discussion

We found that (1) turn transition time was significantly related to speaker visibility overall, 2) as well as to the presence of co-speech gestures (when they were visible) and 3) their kinematic properties. Examining the turn transition times across the spectrum of both gaps and overlaps, it seemed that decreased speaker visibility led to overall longer turn transition times. Looking at the presence of gestures and splitting the data into overlaps and gaps, we observed that the use of co-speech gestures was associated with a reduction in subsequent overlaps, but also in inter-speaker gaps. Furthermore, more kinematic salience and complexity correlated with a reduction in overlaps and gaps. This suggests that the way a gesture is performed may mediate a gesture's influence on upcoming turn transitions.

The finding of turn transition times being influenced by speaker visibility is at least partially in line with our hypotheses for RQ1. Specifically, that visual signals likely play a role in the timing of speaker turn transitions. Interestingly, decreased visibility was mostly associated with an increase in overlaps. This suggests that participants erred towards faster responses, at the risk of overlapping with the current speaker, rather than delaying their own speech onset. The increase in overlaps is in line with a previous report of increased overlaps in telephone conversations compared to face-to-face (ten Bosch et al. 2005). However, it is interesting to note that although turn transition times were affected in moderately reduced visibility, timing returned to the initial baseline (i.e., clear visibility) levels as visibility was removed completely. One possibility is that this difference arises because in ten Bosch et al. (2005), backchannels were not removed from the analysis, whereas we removed all short utterances from analysis. An alternative explanation is that, at least in computer-mediated interaction, full visibility versus fully blurred is not treated as face-to-face versus telephone in terms of turn-taking strategy. To put this another way, participants may employ a different strategy to coordinating turn-taking behavior when engaging in computer-mediated interaction. Gaining more insight into this issue will require future research.

When investigating the effect of co-speech gestures on the pooled turn-transition times, we found that utterances with gestures seemed to be followed by faster turn transitions. When splitting these analyses into gaps and overlaps, we specifically found more overlap in utterances without gestures. This finding would be in line with the findings of Holler et al. (2018) who found that questions accompanied by gestures get faster responses than those without a co-occurring gesture (Holler et al. 2018). However, splitting the data into gaps and overlaps shows a more nuanced picture: the presence of gestures is actually associated with a reduction in both overlaps and gaps. The reason for the pooled analysis showing a slightly different picture is likely because the effect of gesture on overlaps and gaps go in opposite directions, with the reduction in overlap being slightly stronger. This can be seen in the extent of the curves in Fig. 2, and could lead to a net effect, in the pooled data, of an overall increase in turn transition time. This finding provides more evidence for the idea that speakers may use a different strategy to coordinate turn-taking behavior during computer-mediated interaction. Rather than using the potential processing advantages of multimodal utterances to respond faster while overlapping with the other speaker (as they appeared to be doing in Holler et al. 2018), speakers in computer-mediated interaction seem to strive to minimize both gaps and overlaps. As we observe in these data, the presence of gestures seems to facilitate this coordination strategy.

The non-linear effect of gesture presence on turn transition times across visibility conditions suggests that these effects are most pronounced in moderate visibility reductions. We interpret this as meaning that moderately coarse-grained visual information is playing a prominent role in turn timing. In other words, rather than fine-grained information in finger configurations or subtle movements, the larger movements and configurations of the hands likely influence the turn-transition times. At the same time, the fact that the gestural contribution to turn timing begins to decrease before visibility is completely removed suggests that this is not just a low-level effect of seeing any visual motion. Another important advancement from this study is that the interaction between visibility and gesture presence strongly suggests that the mechanism by which gestures support tighter turn-taking is indeed through the visual channel. In other words, if the turn-taking effect was mainly driven by prosodic changes induced by the biomechanical forces of gesture production (Pouw et al. 2020), then gesture presence should have led to tighter turn-taking, regardless of visibility.

The finding of gesture playing the strongest role in moderately affected visibility conditions is also in line with a study by Drijvers and colleagues who found that, when assessing the contribution of co-speech gestures to understanding degraded speech, gestures provide the greatest enhancement to perception when presented in moderately degraded speech compared to severely degraded or clear speech (Drijvers and Özyürek 2017). While highly speculative to suggest any similarity between these findings, it is interesting to note that co-speech gestures seem to be most beneficial in moderately disrupted communicative settings. Future studies will be needed to corroborate this idea. However, the current findings offer support for the notion that gestures facilitate the tight temporal coordination of turns, while showing that this is through an overall smoother transition, affecting both overlaps and gaps.

We additionally found that enhancement of gesture kinematics was associated with both overlap and gap durations, across visibility conditions. Importantly, the increase in some kinematic features may have contributed to temporally more coordinated turn transitions, while the reduction in others may have had the same effect. In other words, it is not a simple case of larger, more complex, or faster movements facilitating turn coordination. Instead, there seems to be a complex relationship between gesture kinematics and turn transition times. As subtle differences in gesture kinematics can signal communicative intent (Trujillo et al. 2018, 2020) and make the meaning of silent gestures easier to recognize (Trujillo et al. 2019), it may be that certain kinematic features make the overall content of the utterance easier to predict. This could contribute to the turn-end being easier to predict, leading to temporally more tightly coordinated transitions between speakers (Levinson 2016), or it may facilitate turn content prediction (Holler and Levinson 2019). Together with the interaction effect between visibility and gesture presence (discussed above), these results suggest that gestures support tight turn-timing through the spatio-temporal characteristics of the more coarse-grained movements of the arms and hands.

4.1 Relevance

The current findings provide new insights into the role of visibility, and more specifically, manual gestures, in how individuals coordinate turn-taking during computer-mediated interaction. Manual co-speech gestures may provide a way for an addressee, whether human or machine, to more easily process the meaning and intention behind an utterance, thus allowing this addressee to time their turn in a more coordinated manner. In terms of kinematic features, it may be that particular combinations of kinematic qualities lead to gestures that are easiest to process. We speculate, based on previous kinematic studies on gesture production and comprehension, that gestures should have an optimal balance of communicative salience and clear structure, without being so large, fast, or overly complex so as to slow down processing. Importantly, as gestures were associated with the greatest reduction in gaps and overlaps during moderate visibility conditions, it seems that fine-grained information, such as relating to subtle movements and configuration of the individual fingers, may be less necessary for maintaining the general coordination-facilitatory effect of gestures when compared to the larger, more coarse-grained information in the movements and configurations of the arms and hands. Overall, these results show that speakers may be partly employing a different strategy for turn-taking (especially relating to overlap) during computer-mediated interaction when compared to face-to-face or telephone conversations, but further investigations are needed in this domain.

4.2 Strengths and Limitations

This study utilized an experimental manipulation of speaker visibility, while also allowing unconstrained, naturalistic conversation. This design contributes to the ecological validity of our findings. However, the unconstrained nature of the experiment also provided many degrees of freedom for participant behavior. Our processing and modeling choices for the data were aimed at controlling for as much of this variability as was feasible. Without directly manipulating more task parameters, however, we cannot draw strong conclusions about the causal relations between variables. Instead, these findings should serve as ecologically valid observations about the associations between communicative signals, visual availability, and turn-taking performance. Future studies should use experimental manipulation to verify these findings and tease apart the complex web of associations that characterizes multimodal conversational behaviour.

4.3 Conclusions

Overall, our findings provide new insights into the role of gestures in rapid turn-taking in computer-mediated human interaction, particularly related to visibility. These findings suggest that both the presence and form of manual gestures contribute to the temporal coordination of speaker turn-transitions. More generally, our study demonstrates that computer-mediated interaction may in part elicit different turn-taking behavior compared to face-to-face or telephone-based interactions. At the same time, our findings highlight the resilience and flexibility of human communication in response to different, potentially difficult communicative contexts, as well as the core contributions of the visual modality.

Appendix 1

Parameter overview of kinematic analyses

Model parameter	Parameter estimate*	Standard deviation	t-value
Overlaps			
Formula: turn_transition_time ~ utterance_duration + maxdist + peakvel*grade + MN_mode + submovements*grade + holdtime + volume + (1 I participant + (1 I utterance)			
(Intercept)	−442.20	3318.00	−0.13
utterance duration	0.00	0.00	−1.25
blur grade	898.10	331.60	2.71
maximum distance	184.80	126.70	1.46
peak velocity	−20.71	227.50	−0.09
McNeillian mode	49.83	40.27	1.24
submovements	−366.10	295.20	−1.24
holdtime	136.80	235.60	0.58
volume	−176.70	91.83	−1.92
peak velocity * grade	−60.62	22.12	−2.74
submovements * grade	88.97	39.00	2.28
Gaps			
Formula: turn_transition_time ~ utterance_duration + maxdist + peakvel + MN_mode * grade + submovements + holdtime* grade + volume + (1 I dyad/participant) + (1 I utterance)			
(Intercept)	1454.00	2044.00	0.71
utterance duration	0.00	0.00	−6.55
blur grade	−40.13	11.99	−3.35
maximum distance	79.07	81.79	0.97
peak velocity	−53.15	127.30	−0.42
McNeillian mode	−123.30	50.80	−2.43
Submovements	−58.75	120.50	−0.49
holdtime	224.10	220.20	1.02
volume	106.60	56.58	1.88
MCcNeillian Mode * grade	28.78	8.08	3.56
holdtime * grade	−34.44	31.19	−1.10

*Note that because kinematic values were normalized, parameter estimates cannot be directly interpreted in terms of effect on turn transition time, but rather should be interpreted in terms of effects relative to other kinematic features

References

Alibali, M.W., Heath, D.C., Myers, H.J.: Effects of visibility between speaker and listener on gesture production: some gestures are meant to be seen. J. Mem. Lang. **44**, 169–188 (2001)

Bates, D., Maechler, M., Bolker, B., Walker, S.: Fitting linear mixed-effects models using lme4. J. Stat. Softw. **67**(1), 1–48 (2015). https://doi.org/10.18637/jss.v067.i01

Bavelas, J.B., Chovil, N., Coates, L., Roe, L.: Gestures specialized for dialogue: Pers. Soc. Psychol. Bull. (1995). https://doi.org/10.1177/0146167295214010

Bavelas, J.B., Chovil, N.: Visible acts of meaning: an integrated message model of language in face-to-face dialogue. J. Lang. Soc. Psychol. **19**(2), 163–194 (2000). https://doi.org/10.1177/0261927X00019002001

ter Bekke, M., Drijvers, L., Holler, J.: The predictive potential of hand gestures during conversation: an investigation of the timing of gestures in relation to speech. (2020). https://doi.org/10.31234/osf.io/b5zq7

Boersma, P., Weenink, D.: Praat (Version 4.5. 25) (2007)

ten Bosch, L., Oostdijk, N., Boves, L.: On temporal aspects of turn taking in conversational dialogues. Speech Commun. **47**(1), 80–86 (2005). https://doi.org/10.1016/j.specom.2005.05.009

Campisi, E., Özyürek, A.: Iconicity as a communicative strategy: recipient design in multimodal demonstrations for adults and children. J. Pragmat. **47**(1), 14–27 (2013). https://doi.org/10.1016/j.pragma.2012.12.007

Drijvers, L., Özyürek, A.: Visual context enhanced: the joint contribution of iconic gestures and visible speech to degraded speech comprehension. J. Speech Lang. Hearing Res. **60**(1), 212–222 (2017). https://doi.org/10.1044/2016_JSLHR-H-16-0101

Gerwing, J., Bavelas, J.: Linguistic influences on gesture's form. Gesture **4**, 157–195 (2004)

Heldner, M., Edlund, J.: Pauses, gaps and overlaps in conversations. J. Phon. **38**(4), 555–568 (2010). https://doi.org/10.1016/j.wocn.2010.08.002

Holler, J., Kendrick, K.H., Levinson, S.C.: Processing language in face-to-face conversation: questions with gestures get faster responses. Psychon. Bull. Rev. **25**(5), 1900–1908 (2018). https://doi.org/10.3758/s13423-017-1363-z

Holler, J., Levinson, S.C.: Multimodal language processing in human communication. Trends Cogn. Sci. **23**(8), 639–652 (2019). https://doi.org/10.1016/j.tics.2019.05.006

Holler, J., Wilkin, K.: An experimental investigation of how addressee feedback affects co-speech gestures accompanying speakers' responses. J. Pragmat. **43**(14), 3522–3536 (2011). https://doi.org/10.1016/j.pragma.2011.08.002

Jadoul, Y., Thompson, B., de Boer, B.: Introducing parselmouth: a python interface to praat. J. Phon. **71**, 1–15 (2018). https://doi.org/10.1016/j.wocn.2018.07.001

Kendon, A.: Some functions of gaze-direction in social interaction. Acta Psychologica **26**, 22–63 (1967). https://doi.org/10.1016/0001-6918(67)90005-4

Kendon, A.: Gesture: Visible Action as Utterance. Cambridge University Press, Cambridge (2004)

Kita, S., van Gijn, I., van der Hulst, H.: Movement phases in signs and co-speech gestures, and their transcription by human coders. In: Wachsmuth, I., Fröhlich, M. (eds) Gesture and Sign Language in Human-Computer Interaction. GW 1997. Lecture Notes in Computer Science, vol. 1371, pp. 23–35. Springer, Berlin, Heidelberg (1998). https://doi.org/10.1007/BFb0052986

Landis, J.R., Koch, G.G.: The measurement of observer agreement for categorical data. Biometrics **33**, 159–174 (1977)

Levinson, S.C.: Turn-taking in human communication—origins and implications for language processing. Trends Cogn. Sci. **20**(1), 6–14 (2016). https://doi.org/10.1016/j.tics.2015.10.010

Levinson, S.C., Torreira, F.: Timing in turn-taking and its implications for processing models of language. Front. Psychol. **6**, 731 (2015). https://doi.org/10.3389/fpsyg.2015.00731

McNeill, D.: Hand and Mind: What Gestures Reveal about Thought. University of Chicago Press, Chicago (1992)

Pouw, W., Harrison, S.J., Dixon, J.A.: Gesture–speech physics: the biomechanical basis for the emergence of gesture–speech synchrony. J. Exp. Psychol. Gen. **149**(2), 391–404 (2020). https://doi.org/10.1037/xge0000646

R Core Team: R: A language and environment for statistical computing. R Foundation for Statistical Computing (2019). https://www.R-project.org/

Ripperda, J., Drijvers, L. Holler, J.: Speeding up the detection of non-iconic and iconic gestures (SPUDNIG): A toolkit for the automatic detection of hand movements and gestures in video data. Behav. Res. **52**, 1783–1794 (2020). https://doi.org/10.3758/s13428-020-01350-2

Roberts, S.G., Torreira, F., Levinson, S.C.: The effects of processing and sequence organization on the timing of turn taking: a corpus study, 509th edn, vol. 5. Frontiers in Psychology (2015). https://doi.org/10.3389/978-2-88919-825-2

Sacks, H., Schegloff, E. A., Jefferson, G.: A simplest systematics for the organization of turn-taking for conversation. **50**(40) (1974)

Stivers, T. et al.: Universals and cultural variation in turn-taking in conversation. PNAS. **106**, 10587–10592 (2009)

Trujillo, J.P., Simanova, I., Bekkering, H., Özyürek, A.: Communicative intent modulates production and comprehension of actions and gestures: a Kinect study. Cognition **180**, 38–51 (2018). https://doi.org/10.1016/j.cognition.2018.04.003

Trujillo, J.P., Simanova, I., Bekkering, H., Özyürek, A.: The communicative advantage: how kinematic signaling supports semantic comprehension. Psychol. Res. **84**(7), 1897–1911 (2019). https://doi.org/10.1007/s00426-019-01198-y

Trujillo, J.P., Simanova, I., Özyürek, A., Bekkering, H.: Seeing the unexpected: how brains read communicative intent through kinematics. Cereb. Cortex **30**(3), 1056–1067 (2020). https://doi.org/10.1093/cercor/bhz148

Author Index

Printed in the United States
by Baker & Taylor Publisher Services